Transitions Before the Transition

INTERDISCIPLINARY CONTRIBUTIONS TO ARCHAEOLOGY

Series Editor: *Michael Jochim, University of California, Santa Barbara, California*
Founding Editor: *Roy S. Dickens, Jr. Late of University of North Carolina, Chapel Hill, North Carolina*

THE ARCHEAOLOGIST'S LABORATORY
The Analysis of Archaeological Data
E.B. Banning

AURIGNACIAN LITHIC ECONOMY
Ecological Perspectives from Southwestern France
Brooke S. Blades

DARWINIAN ARCHAEOLOGIES
Edited by Herbert Donald Graham Maschner

EARLIEST ITALY
An Overview of the Italian Paleolithic and Mesolithic
Margherita Mussi

EMPIRE AND DOMESTIC ECONOMY
Terence N. D'Altroy and Christine A. Hastorf

EUROPEAN PREHISTORY: A SURVEY
Edited by Saurunas Miliasuskas

THE EVOLUTION OF COMPLEX HUNTER-GATHERS
Archaeological Evidence from the North Pacific
Ben Fitzhugh

FAUNAL EXTINCTION IN AN ISLAND SOCIETY
Pygmy Hippotamus Hunters of Cyprus
Alan H. Simmons

GATHERING HOPEWELL
Society, Ritual, and Ritual Interaction
Christopher Carr and D. Troy Case

A HUNTER-GATHERER LANDSCAPE
Southwest Germany in the Late Paleolithic and Neolithic
Michael A. Jochim

HUNTERS BETWEEN EAST AND WEST
The Paleolithic of Moravia
Jiri Svoboda, Vojen Lozek, and Emanual Vlcek

TRANSITIONS BEFORE THE TRANSITION
Evolution and Stability in the Middle Paleolithic and Middle Stone Age
Erella Hovers and Steven L. Kuhn

A Continuation Order Plan is available for this series. A continuation order will bring delivery of each new volume immediately upon publication. Volumes are billed only upon actual shipment. For further information please contact the publisher.

Transitions Before the Transition

Evolution and Stability in the Middle Paleolithic and Middle Stone Age

Edited by

Erella Hovers
The Hebrew University of Jerusalem
Jerusalem, Israel

and

Steven L. Kuhn
University of Arizona
Tucson, Arizona

 Springer

Erella Hovers
Institute of Archaeology
Hebrew University of Jerusalem
Jerusalem 91905
Israel
hovers@mscc.huji.ac.il

Steven L. Kuhn
Department of Anthropology
University of Arizona
Tucson, AZ 85721
USA
skuhn@u.arizona.edu

Series Editor:
Michael Jochim
University of California
Santa Barbara, CA
USA
jochim@anth.ucsb.edu

Cover image by Mary Stiner.

Library of Congress Control Number: 2005933037

ISBN-10: 0-387-24658-4   e-ISBN 0-387-24661-4
ISBN-13: 978-0387-24658-1

Printed on acid-free paper.

Printed in the United States of America.   (TB/IBT)

9 8 7 6 5 4 3 2 1

springeronline.com

Contributors

Ofer Bar-Yosef
  Harvard University, Cambridge, Massachusetts 02138

Anna Belfer-Cohen
  The Hebrew University of Jerusalem, Jerusalem, Israel 91905

Alison S. Brooks
  George Washington University, Washington DC 20052

Victor Chabai
  Institute of Archaeology, Crimean Branch, Simferopol, Crimea Ukraine 95007

Geoffrey A. Clark
  Arizona State University, Tempe, Arizona 85287–2402

Anne Delagnes
  Institut de Préhistoire et de Geologie du Quaternaire, Université Bordeaux 1, France

Sabine Gaudzinski
  Römisch-Germanisches Zentralmuseam Mainz, Forschungsbereich Altsteinzeit, Schloss Monrepos, 56567 Neuwied, Germany

Gideon Hartman
  Harvard University, Cambridge, Massachusetts 02138

Erella Hovers
  The Hebrew University of Jerusalem, Jerusalem, Israel 91905

M.R. Kleindienst
  University of Toronto at Mississauga, Mississauga, Ontario, Canada L5L 1C6

Steven L. Kuhn
    University of Arizona, Tucson, Arizona 85721–0030

Sally McBrearty
    University of Connecticut Storrs, Connecticut 06269

Anthony E. Marks
    Southern Methodist University, Dallas, Texas 75275–0116

Liliane Meignen
    C.N.R.S/CEPAM, Sophia Antipolis, 06560 Valbonne, France

Gilliane Monnier
    University of Minnesota, Minneapolis, Minnesota 55455

Lisa Nevell
    George Washington University, Washington DC 20052

Julien Riel-Salvatore
    Arizona State University, Tempe, Arizona 85287–2402

John J. Shea
    State University of New York, Stony Brook, New York 11794–4364

John D. Speth
    Museum of Anthropology, University of Michigan, Ann Arbor, Michigan 48109–
    1079

Mary C. Stiner
    University of Arizona, Tucson, Arizona 85721–0030

Christian Tryon
    Smithsonian Institution, Washington, DC 20560

Lyn Wadley
    University of the Witwatersrand, WITS, 2050 South Africa

John E. Yellen
    National Science Foundation, Arlington, Virginia 22230

Foreword

Challenges and Approaches in the Study of Middle Paleolithic Behavioral Change

Paul Mellars

Department of Archaeology, Cambridge University
Cambridge CB2 3DZ, UK

The present volume, and the symposia which gave rise to it, focus on what is rapidly emerging as one of the most important issues in human development - namely, the pattern of changes in human behavior and associated cognition which immediately preceded the emergence of fully "modern" communities in different areas of the world. Exactly how we define "modern" communities is of course an interesting issue in its own right, but I imagine that most of the contributors to the volume would take this to mean the communities that were established over most areas of the Old World by at least 30,000 BP, and whose behavior as reflected in the archaeological records shows generally close resemblances to that reflected in the material culture of recent hunting and gathering populations. The range of issues addressed by the different contributors has been spelled out clearly in the Introduction to the volume by Steven L. Kuhn and Erella Hovers. My aim here is simply to give my own perspective on what I see as some of the most interesting current issues posed by studies of modern human behavioral origins, and to highlight some of the key challenges to future research in this field.

At the outset we should have no doubts about the importance and the scale of the phenomenon we are attempting to investigate. However much one may castigate an overemphasis on the evidence from Europe and western Asia, the supreme advantage of this database is that it does demonstrate in a particularly graphic, fine-grained, and fully documented form at least one dimension of the eventual effects of the so-called "Human Revolution"—which in these regions was evidently connected closely if not precisely with the demographic replacement of "archaic" by anatomically and genetically modern populations. As discussed further below, there remain major issues to be resolved as to precisely how the archaeological evidence from western Eurasia should be interpreted in specific social, demographic, and cognitive terms, and there is certainly no implication that the patterns documented in this area can be extrapolated uncritically to other regions. But as one reflection of the overall *scale* of the behavioral changes which accompanied the emergence and dispersal of fully modern populations, the Eurasian archaeological record must still form a central element in the way in which we phrase questions about the nature and ultimate origins of this fundamental behavioral transition.

A second and equally self-evident feature of the current database is that any attempt to explain behavioral changes over the period of the "Human Revolution" itself must take due account not only of the massively accumulating genetic and skeletal evidence for the ultimate origins of the modern human genotype in Africa, but also of the equally clear evidence for the subsequent dispersal of these genetically and anatomically modern populations over the rest of the occupied world (Ingman *et al.* 2000; Krings *et al.* 2000; Richards and Macaulay 2000; Relethford 2001; Underhill *et al.* 2001; Stringer 2002; Wells 2002; White *et al.* 2003; Forster 2004; Serre *et al.* 2004). The precise mechanisms and timing of this demographic dispersal (or dispersals), and the extent to which it may have incorporated some elements of interbreeding with preceding archaic populations, are currently the topic of lively debate (*e.g.*, Eswaran 2002; Stringer 2002; Templeton 2002; Serre *et al.* 2004). But all of the most recent genetic data derived from both mitochondrial (mtDNA) and Y-chromosome DNA studies leave no doubt as to the reality of this "Out of Africa" dispersal and (ultimately) replacement event, for which most of the current evidence seems to focus on a date of around 50 to 60,000 BP (Richards and Macaulay 2000; Semino *et al.* 2000; Ingman *et al.* 2000; Underhill *et al.* 2001; Stringer 2002; Wells 2002; Caramelli *et al.* 2003; Forster 2004; Serre *et al.* 2004).

All of this may sound like common knowledge, and it is not of course the primary focus of the present volume. The point of emphasizing it here is that it does define the essential behavioral and demographic frameworks within which we have to work. The major aim of the present volume is to analyze, and hopefully explain, some of the critical developments in human behavioral and cognitive patterns which preceded this fundamental demographic dispersal and replacement event. Now that the basic patterns of the archaeological evidence in both Europe and, to a lesser extent, Africa are becoming increasingly clear, the most central challenge at present, as I see it, is to explain the patterns we see in the archaeological record. And here of course there are at least two separate dimensions to the challenge. One is to explain the developmental patterns we see in the continent which evidently gave rise to the evolution and dispersal of biologically modern humans, *i.e.*, Africa. The other, equally if not more daunting, is to document and explain the apparently very different trajectories of behavioral change which occurred in regions beyond Africa, particularly those in the well-documented region of Eurasia, among populations which, on the basis of both anatomical and direct mtDNA evidence, are of distinctively archaic, essentially Neandertal form (Krings *et al.* 1997, 2000; Stringer 2002; Caramelli *et al.* 2003; Serre *et al.* 2004).

If we accept that the main challenge facing current research is to explain the patterns we see in the archaeological records, then I take it as equally self-evident that the most appropriate framework within which to address these explanations is a primarily evolutionary, essentially Darwinian, perspective—*i.e.*, from a perspective that focuses explicitly on the kinds of adaptive and selective challenges which would have confronted human populations at different times and places in the past. This perspective puts the prime emphasis on the effects of specific behavioral innovations, which would have maximized the reproductive success of individuals and the survival of demographic units within the different environments (Tattersall 2002). This whole approach to analyzing human behavioral change within an essentially evolutionary framework has of course a long history in archaeology (*e.g.*, Dunnell 1980; Boyd and Richerson 1985), and has recently been comprehensively reviewed in the book by Stephen Shennan on "Genes, Memes and Human History" (Shennan 2002; see also Blackmore 1999). Without attempting to summarize more than a fraction of the relevant arguments here, it should be kept in mind that evolutionary explanations of this kind do not assume that more than a small proportion of individual evolutionary trajectories would have led to the long-term survival of the individuals and societies in question (*i.e.*, local population extinctions, as well as long-term survival patterns, are equally predictable in the evolutionary records). Similarly, evolutionary explanations make full allowance for the inevitability that processes of behavioral and cultural evolution involve much more complex information-sharing mechanisms than those inherent in biological descent systems. Nevertheless as a basic framework for analyzing and explaining the long-term behavioral patterns we see in the archaeological records of the Paleolithic (especially the Lower and Middle Paleolithic), I personally can see no viable or theoretically defensible alternative to adopting a primarily selective, evolutionary approach.

If we can accept all this as defining the broad parameters within which we have to work, then what are the more specific challenges posed by studying the archaeological records of the Middle Paleolithic? Excellent reviews of these questions have already been given in the Introduction to the present volume by the two editors, and in the final chapter by Ofer Bar-Yosef. At the risk of repeating some of the points made in their chapters, perhaps I can offer my own suggestions as to what I would regard as some of the most critical issues confronting present and future research.

First and most obviously we need much better control over how we turn our empirical observations on the archaeological record into meaningful *behavioral* interpretations. It would be easy to labor this point, but despite over 40 years of application of microwear and related studies, we are still remarkably ignorant as to the exact functions of many stone tools, including some of the most potentially interesting forms such as the early appearance of small geometrical forms in the South African Middle Stone Age industries, or the small retouched bladelet ("Dufour" and "Font-Yves") forms of the early Eurasian Upper Paleolithic. It would be even easier to lament our limited knowledge of wood, skin, fibre and other organic technologies (despite the spectacular discoveries from Schöningen and elsewhere), but at the end of the day we must never forget that stone tools, however prominent in the archaeological record, represent in one sense only the fingernails of total cultural and economic adaptations—perhaps not more than a few percent of the total artifact repertoires in use at any one time. Similar ambiguities bedevil studies of subsistence systems. Here our problem is not only the continuing scarcity of evidence for the use and relative importance of plant food supplies in different contexts, but continuing controversies over how we identify notions such as "specialization" or "selection" in the exploitation of animal resources—or indeed whether these notions have any real significance without a clear understanding of the specific behavioral *strategies* which lay behind the composition of the documented faunal assemblages (Mellars 1996a:196–201, 2004a; Gaudzinski 1999, this volume; Stiner, this volume). When we come to issues such as social organization, residential group sizes, population densities or kinship structures, our control over the archaeological record becomes, inevitably, even more tenuous. The purpose of this catalogue of archaeological headaches is not to cast readers into a form of academic depression about the limitations of the current database, but simply to recognize that one of the primary challenges in the present state of research must be to develop new approaches—and perhaps more importantly, explicit new models—as to how we can investigate these critical dimensions of "pre-modern" societies across the widest possible range.

    To strike a more positive note, one aspect which archaeologists are clearly in a much better position to exploit, is the close interrelationship between behavioral changes and the nature of contemporaneous climatic and environmental fluctuations. In one sense of course this has been a commonplace of Paleolithic research over at least the past 50 years. But the opportunities for this kind of fine-scale analysis are now far better than they were even one or two decades ago—especially as a result of the recent studies of ice-core records and some of the equally fine-grained records of climatic oscillations recovered from offshore ocean cores and the long pollen sequences now emerging from deep lake deposits in various parts of Europe and elsewhere (*e.g.*, Dansgaard *et al.* 1993; Huntley *et al.* 1999; Shackleton *et al.* 2000; Sánchez-Goñi *et al.* 2002; van Andel and Davies 2003). One classic illustration of this opportunity is provided by the recent surge of information on the patterns of climatic and ecological fluctuations over the period of oxygen-isotope stage 3 (OIS 3) between *ca.* 65,000 and 25,000 years BP—the period which is of course central to any understanding of the emergence and dispersal of fully modern populations (van Andel and Davies 2003). In a recent paper I have tried to examine the potential interrelationships between patterns of ecological oscillations and associated behavioral change over this period in Europe, focusing especially on the extraordinary rapidity and amplitude of the climatic oscillations (in some cases with temperature changes of 8–10°C within a space of a few decades) and attempting to analyze these relationships in terms of both short-term and longer-term evolutionary and selective pressures on the human populations (Mellars 2004b). To cut a long story short, I argued that the rapid climatic and ecological changes of OIS 3 would inevitably have promoted major shifts in both the distribution and overall densities of human populations in different areas of Europe, which in turn would have led to a sharp increase in the frequency of population interaction, and direct competition, between the adjacent groups for both space and resources. All of these competitive social pressures, combined with the scale of the environmental changes themselves, would have had equally inevitable impacts on the subsistence activities and associated technologies of the human groups, leading to inevitable, if not entirely predictable, patterns of technological change. A number of social adaptations (such as the formation of larger residential units, or perhaps increased separation of individual economic and social roles within the individual groups) could be seen as equally plausible adaptations to the combined environmental and demographic pressures.

The critical issue, of course, is whether this cycle of economic, social and technological "adaptations" to the rapidly oscillating climatic conditions of OIS 3 could potentially have led to an entirely indigenous, independent emergence of fully Upper Paleolithic culture among the final Neandertal populations of Europe (d'Errico *et al.* 1998; Zilhão 2001; d'Errico 2003; Mellars 2004b, 2004d). The obvious, and to my mind insuperable, objection to the latter scenario lies simply in the combination of the current archaeological, skeletal and mtDNA evidence, which demonstrates not only a very rapid transition to distinctively Upper Paleolithic culture in almost all areas of Europe between *ca.* 43,000–36,000 BP, but an apparently close if not precise correlation between this phenomenon and the simultaneous dispersal across Europe of anatomically and genetically modern populations— and the rapid extinction of the preceding Neandertals (Churchill and Smith 2000; Ingman *et al.* 2000; Krings *et al.* 2000; Richards and Macaulay 2000; Semino *et al.* 2000; Underhill *et al.* 2001; Stringer 2002; Wells 2002; Conard and Bolus 2003; Forster 2004; Mellars 2004c; Serre *et al.* 2004). This is in sharp contrast to the more gradual emergence of similar features in the archaeological records of Africa (Deacon 2000; McBrearty and Brooks 2000; Mellars 2002). To most workers, this coincidence between the records of effectively simultaneous cultural and demographic change still seems too close to be entirely accidental and fortuitous (*e.g.*, Ambrose 1998; Klein 2000; Davies 2001; Bar-Yosef 1998, 2000, 2002; Mellars 2004d). But exactly how we choose to answer this particular question is not the main issue here. I cite this example simply as an illustration of how I believe a close and sympathetic integration of the available archaeological and paleoclimatic data, viewed within an evolutionary framework, can be used to approach many of the critical issues involved in the study of the patterns of human behavioral evolution prior to the emergence of fully modern populations. The opportunities for this kind of close integration of the archaeological and paleoenvironmental data have never been better than they are at the present time. And yet, surprisingly perhaps, relatively few specific studies of this kind have been carried out (Finlayson 2004; Hopkinson 2004).

A third line of research which I believe will prove equally if not more fruitful is the nature and patterning of human demography over the critical archaic-to-modern human transition. As Kuhn and Hovers point out in their Introduction, there are at least two separate dimensions to these issues. Firstly, population density is increasingly recognized as one of the potentially prime factors in stimulating behavioral change (*e.g.*, Binford 2001; Shennan 2002; Read and LeBlanc 2003). As noted above, increasing population density can create increasing competition between adjacent communities for both space and resources, leading to various potential adaptations in both social and economic/technological spheres. Shennan (2001) and Hovers and Belfer-Cohen (this volume) have argued that critical population densities can influence both the frequency of occurrence of behavioral innovations in different contexts and the probability that these innovations will be diffused and maintained through later populations. One extreme view would be to see virtually the whole of the conventional "package" of typically Upper Paleolithic culture in Europe as an almost direct, and perhaps inevitable, reflection of increasing population densities associated with the replacement of Neandertals by more technologically complex anatomically modern populations (*cf.* Mellars 1996b). While this would almost certainly be a greatly oversimplified view of a much more complex situation, the potential role of increasing population densities in this transition should be kept clearly in mind.

The other important aspect of demographic studies lies in the precise spatial patterning of more or less discrete demographic units (in the sense of separate breeding communities, or in demographic terms "demes" or "connubia") over specific areas (Howell 1998; Tattersall 2002). These individual breeding units of course play a central role in human evolutionary patterns and, as Eswaran (2002) has recently demonstrated, would have played an equally critical role in any process of progressive dispersal of genetically and anatomically modern populations from Africa to Eurasia and elsewhere. Several of the papers in this volume reflect an increasing interest in these issues, and show that we can not only begin to identify these patterns reasonably closely in certain aspects of lithic technology, but that the overall patterns of technological change within particular regions can often only be convincingly interpreted by invoking major episodes of population movement, and associated population replacements, within the individual regional sequences (Mellars 1996a:343–348).

I have deliberately left the most daunting challenge to the end—that of adressing the perennial debates over the relative "intelligence" or "cognitive capacities" of archaic versus biologically modern populations. There has been so much written on this issue in recent years that it is hard to imagine what new there is to say (*e.g.*, Mithen 1996; Noble and Davidson 1996; Mellars and Gibson 1996; Lewis-Williams 2002; Henshilwood and Marean 2003). No one could seriously dispute what Colin Renfrew (1996) has termed the "Sapient paradox"—i.e., that one cannot make simple, one-to-one correlations between the patterns of *observed* behavior and the underlying mental and cognitive *capacities* for behavior. In earlier publications I have referred to the inescapable "asymmetry" of the archaeological evidence for behavioral potentials (Mellars 1991, 1996a: 366–8, 1998). Clearly, if an individual or human group is observed practicing a certain pattern of behavior (such as cave art, or the production of ivory ornaments) then the capacity for that behavior must, by definition, be present in the individuals and societies involved.

But if these particular behaviors are not being practiced, one can usually advance a whole range of potential explanations as to why such behavior might not have been appropriate, feasible, necessary or, of course, not yet "invented" in the societies in question (see Hovers and Belfer Cohen, this volume)—as the whole history of human behavioral and cultural development over the past 30–40,000 years clearly demonstrates.

In this situation, how can we seriously get to grips with the issues of changing mental *capacities*, in the sense of genetically determined shifts in cognitive abilities, over the course of human evolution (*e.g.*, Enard *et al.* 2002)? As regards the perennial issues of the cognitive capacities of the European Neandertals, I continue to be puzzled by why we seem to see so little evidence for major technological or other innovations within these societies over such a vast range of space and time—prior to their demonstrable contacts and interaction (and possibly interbreeding) with anatomically modern populations (Mellars 1996a, 1999, 2003, in press). Surely population densities, or the challenges posed by rapid climatic changes, would have been sufficient at certain specific times and places in the Neandertal universe to evoke some kind of cultural response analogous to that of anatomically modern populations. If one places a heavy emphasis on isolated "events" such as the hypothetical Berekhat Ram female "figurine," or the Tata ivory "plaque" then it remains puzzling why these artifacts are not only so morphologically ambiguous in most cases but, more significantly, why they remain so extraordinarily isolated and unique. There is a sharp contrast here with the two complex and closely similar geometrical engravings recently reported from the MSA levels (*ca.* 80,000 BP) in the Blombos Cave in South Africa (Henshilwood *et al.* 2002, 2004), and with the evidence for several distinct forms of symbolism (red ochre, perforated sea shells and unambiguous grave goods) associated with the multiple burials of anatomically modern humans in the 100,000-year-old levels in Qafzeh cave in Israel (Inizan and Gaillard 1978; Defleur 1993; Bar-Yosef 2000; Hovers *et al.* 2003). And I remain to be convinced that the capacity of the final Neandertals to replicate certain specific items of Upper Paleolithic technology, such as simple bone tools and perforated animal teeth, at one or two sites in Western Europe, implies that these items carried exactly the same cultural and symbolic *meanings* as those in the adjacent and contemporaneous anatomically modern populations—although they may have done (Mellars 1999, 2003; White 2001; Lewis-Williams 2002; Conard and Bolus 2003; Coolidge and Wynn 2004). Above all we should keep clearly in mind the increasing genetic evidence that the evolutionary trajectories of the European Neandertals and the emerging African "modern" populations are likely to have been separate over a period of at least 300–400,000 years (Krings *et al.* 1997, 2000), closer to 800,000 years in one recent estimate (Beerli and Edwards 2002). In other words, there was cumulatively almost a million years of potentially divergent evolution of the two lineages. Can we really assume that there were no significant divergences in specific cognitive or neurological capacities over this time span (Crow 2002; Bickerton 2002; Enard *et al.* 2002)?

Clearly, the critical question to ask in this context is not whether Neandertals' cognitive capacities were "inferior" to those of modern humans, but whether they could have been significantly different. No amount of special pleading or appeals to political correctness (*e.g.*, Zilhão 2001) can undermine the legitimacy of this particular question in the current state of research (Mithen 1996; Lewis-Williams 2002; Coolidge and Wynn 2004). I personally am happy to keep an open mind on this issue, and would prefer to regard it as a continuing focus for further research and investigation, than an *a priori* premise to be assumed for personal or quasi-political reasons (Mellars 2003). While the papers in this volume may not have resolved more than a fraction of the issues surrounding the emergence of fully modern behavior and cognition, they take us several important steps in that direction.

REFERENCES CITED

Ambrose S.H. 1998. Chronology of the Later Stone Age and food production in East Africa. *Journal of Archaeological Science* 25: 377–392.

Bar-Yosef O. 1998. On the nature of transitions: the Middle to Upper Palaeolithic transition and the Neolithic revolution. *Cambridge Archaeological Journal* 8: 141–163.

Bar-Yosef O. 2000. The Middle and Early Upper Paleolithic in Southwest Asia and neighbouring regions. In O. Bar-Yosef and D. Plibeam (Eds.), *The Geography of Neandertals and Modern Humans in Europe and the Greater Mediterranean*, pp. 107–156. Cambridge MA: Peabody Museum of Harvard University.

Bar-Yosef O. 2002. The Upper Palaeolithic revolution. *Annual Review of Anthropology* 31: 363–393.

Beerli P. and S.V. Edwards 2002. When did Neanderthals and modern humans diverge? *Evolutionary Anthropology* supplement 1: 60–63.

Bickerton D. 2002. From protolanguage to language. In T.J. Crow (Ed.), *The Speciation of Modern Homo Sapiens*, pp. 103–120. London: The British Academy, London.

Binford L.R. 2001. *Constructing Frames of Reference: An Analytical Method for Archeological Theory-Building using Hunter-gatherer and Environmental Data Sets*. Berkeley (CA): University of California Press.

Blackmore S. 1999. *The Meme Machine*. Oxford University Press, Oxford.

Boyd R. and P.J. Richerson 1985. *Culture and the Evolutionary Process*. Chicago: University of Chicago Press.

Caramelli, D., C. Lalueza-Fox, C. Vernesi, M. Lari, A. Casoli, F. Mallegni, B. Chiarelli, I. Dupanloup, J. Bertranpetit, G. Barbujani and G. Bertorelle 2003. Evidence for genetic discontinuity between Neandertals and 24,000-year-old anatomically modern Europeans. *Proceedings of the National Academy of Sciences USA* 100: 6593–6597.

Churchill S.E. and F.H. Smith 2000. Makers of the early Aurignacian of Europe. *Yearbook of Physical Anthropology* 43: 61–115.

Conard N.J. and M. Bolus 2003. Radiocarbon dating the appearance of modern humans and timing of cultural innovations in Europe: new results and new challenges. *Journal of Human Evolution* 44: 331–7

Coolidge F.L. and T. Wynn 2004. A cognitive and neuropsychological perspective on the Châtelperronian. *Journal of Anthropological Research* 60: 55–73.

Crow T.J. (Ed.) 2002. *The Speciation of Modern Homo Sapiens*. London: The British Academy.

Dansgaard, W., S.J. Johnsen, H.B. Clausen, D. Dahl-Jensen, N.S. Gundestrup, C.U. Hammer, C.S. Hvidberg, J.P. Steffensen, A.E. Sveinbjornsdottir, J. Jouzel and G. Bond 1993. Evidence for general instability of past climate from a 250-kyr ice record. *Nature* 364: 218–220.

Davies W. 2001. A very model of a modern human industry: new perspectives on the origins and spread of the Aurignacian in Europe. *Proceedings of the Prehistoric Society* 67: 195–217.

Defleur A. 1993. *Les Sépultures Moustériennes*. Paris: CNRS.

d'Errico F., J. Zilhão, M. Julien, D. Baffier and J. Pelegrin 1998. Neanderthal acculturation in western Europe? A critical review of the evidence and its interpretation. *Current Anthropology* 39 (supplement): S1–S44.

d'Errico F. 2003. The invisible frontier: a multiple species model for the origin of behavioral modernity. *Evolutionary Anthropology* 12: 188–202.

Dunnell R. 1980. Evolutionary theory and archaeology. In M.B. Schiffer (Ed.), *Advances in Archaeological Method and Theory*, Vol. 3, pp. 35–99. New York: Academic Press.

Enard W., M. Przeworski, S.E. Fisher, C.S.L. Lai, V. Wiebe 2002. Molecular evolution of FOXP$_2$, a gene involved in speech and language. *Nature* 418: 869–872.

Eswaran V. 2002. A diffusion wave out of Africa: the mechanism of the modern human revolution? *Current Anthropology* 43: 749–774.

Finlayson C. 2004. *Neanderthals and Modern Humans: an Ecological and Evolutionary Perspective.* Cambridge: Cambridge University Press.

Forster P. 2004. Ice ages and the mitochondrial DNA chronology of human dispersals: a review. *Philosophical Transactions of the Royal Society of London* B 359: 255–264.

Gaudzinski S. 1999. The faunal record of the Lower and Middle Palaeolithic of Europe: remarks on human interference. In W. Roebroeks and C. Gamble (Eds.), *The Middle Palaeolithic Occupation of Europe*, pp. 215–234. Leiden: University of Leiden.

Henshilwood C.S., F. d'Errico, R.Yates, Z. Jacobs, C. Tribolo, G.A.T. Duller, N. Mercier, J.C. Sealy, H.Valladas, I. Watts and A.G. Wintle 2002. Emergence of modern human behavior: Middle Stone Age engravings from South Africa. *Science* 295: 1278–1280.

Henshilwood C. and C. Marean 2003. The origin of modern human behavior. Critique of the models and their test implications. *Current Anthropology* 44: 627–651.

Henshilwood C., F. d'Errico, M. Vanhaeren, K. van Niekerk and Z. Jacobs 2004. Middle Stone Age shell beads from South Africa. *Science* 304: 404.

Hopkinson T. 2004. Leaf points, landscapes and environment change in the European late Middle Palaeolithic. In N.J. Conard (Ed.), *Settlement Patterns of the Middle Palaeolithic and Middle Stone Age*, vol. 2, pp. 227–258. Tübingen: Kerns Verlag.

Hovers E., S. Ilani, O. Bar-Yosef and B. Vandermeersch 2003. An early case of color symbolism: ochre use by early modern humans in Qafzeh Cave. *Current Anthropology* 44: 491–522.

Howell F.C. 1998. Evolutionary implications of altered perspectives on hominid demes and populations in the later Pleistocene of western Eurasia. In T. Akazawa, K. Aoki and O. Bar-Yosef (Eds.) *Neandertals and Modern Humans in Western Asia*, pp. 5–27. New York: Plenum Press.

Huntley B., W. Watts, J.R.M. Allen and B. Zolitschka 1999. Palaeoclimate, chronology and vegetation history of the Weichselian glacial: comparative analysis of data from three cores from Lago Grande di Monticchio (Italy): initial results. *Quaternary Science Reviews* 18: 945–960.

Ingman M., H. Kaessmann, S. Pääbo and U. Gyllensten 2000. Mitochondrial genome variation and the origin of modern humans. *Nature* 408: 708–713.

Inizan M.-L. and M.G. Gaillard 1978. Coquillages de Ksar-'Aqil: éléments de parure? *Paléorient* 4: 295–306.

Klein R.G. 2000. Archaeology and the evolution of human behavior. *Evolutionary Anthropology* 9: 17–36.

Krings M., A. Stone, R.W. Schmitz, H. Krainitzki, M. Stoneking and S. Pääbo 1997. Neandertal DNA sequences and the origin of modern humans. *Cell* 90: 19–30.

Krings M., C. Capelli, F. Tschentscher, H. Geisert, S. Meyer, A. von Haeseler, K. Grossschmidt, G. Possnert, M. Paunovic and S. Pääbo 2000. A view of Neanderthal genetic diversity. *Nature Genetics* 26: 144–146.

Lewis-Williams D. 2002. *The Mind in the Cave.* London: Thames & Hudson.

McBrearty S. and A.S. Brooks 2000. The revolution that wasn't: a new interpretation of the origin of modern human behavior. *Journal of Human Evolution* 39: 453–563.

Mellars P.A. 1991. Cognitive changes and the emergence of modern humans in Europe. *Cambridge Archaeological Journal* 1: 63–76.

Mellars P.A. 1996a. *The Neanderthal Legacy: An Archaeological Perspective from Western Europe.* Princeton: Princeton University Press.

Mellars P.A. 1996b. The emergence of biologically modern populations in Europe: a social and cognitive 'revolution'? In W.G. Runciman, J. Maynard-Smith and R.I.M. Dunbar (Eds.), *Evolution of Social Behavior Patterns in Primates and Man* (Proceedings of the British Academy vol. 88), pp. 179–202. London: The British Academy.

Mellars P.A. 1998. Neanderthals, modern humans and the archaeological evidence for language. In N.G. Jablonski and L.C. Aiello (Eds.), *The Origin and Diversification of Language*, pp. 89–115. San Francisco: The California Academy of Sciences.

Mellars P.A. 1999. The Neanderthal problem continued. *Current Anthropology* 40: 341–350.

Mellars P.A. 2002. Archaeology and the origins of modern humans: European and African perspectives. In T.J. Crow (Ed.), *The Speciation of Modern Homo Sapiens*,(Proceedings of the British Academy 106), pp. 31–48. London: The British Academy.

Mellars P.A. 2003. Symbolism, meaning and the Neanderthal mind. *Cambridge Archaeological Journal* 13: 273–275.

Mellars P. 2004a. Reindeer specialization in the early Upper Palaeolithic: the evidence from southwest France. *Journal of Archaeological Science* 31: 613–617.

Mellars P.A. 2004b. Stage 3 climate and the Upper Palaeolithic revolution in Europe: evolutionary perspectives. In J. Cherry, C. Scarre and S. Shennan (Eds.), *Explaining Social Change: Studies in Honour of Colin Renfrew*, pp. 27–43. Cambridge: McDonald Institute for Archaeological Research.

Mellars P.A. 2004c. Neanderthals and the modern human colonization of Europe. *Nature* (in press).

Mellars P.A. 2004d. The improbable coincidence: a single species model for the origins of modern human behaviour in Europe. *Evolutionary Anthropology* (in press).

Mellars P.A. and K. Gibson, K. (Eds), 1996. *Modelling the Early Human Mind*. Cambridge: McDonald Institute for Archaeological Research.

Mithen S. 1996. *The Prehistory of the Mind: A Search for the Origins of Art, Religion and Science*. London: Thames & Hudson.

Noble W. and I. Davidson 1996. *Human Evolution, Language and Mind: A Psychological and Archaeological Inquiry*. Cambridge: Cambridge University Press.

Read D.W. and S.A. LeBlanc 2003. Population growth, carrying capacity and conflict. *Current Anthropology* 44: 59–85.

Relethford J. 2001. *Genetics and the Search for Modern Human Origins*. New York: Wiley-Liss.

Renfrew C. 1996. The sapient behavior paradox: how to test for potential? In P.A. Mellars and K. Gibson (Eds.), *Modelling the Early Human Mind*, pp. 11–14. Cambridge: McDonald Institute for Archaeological Research.

Richards M. and V. Macaulay 2000. Genetic data and the colonization of Europe: genealogies and founders. In C. Renfrew and K. Boyle (Eds.), *Archaeogenetics and the Population Prehistory of Europe*, pp. 139–153. Cambridge: McDonald Institute Monographs.

Sánchez-Goñi, M.F., I. Cacho, J-L. Turon, J. Guiot, F.J. Sierro, J-P. Peypouquet, J.O. Grimalt, and N.J. Shackleton 2002. Synchroneity between marine and terrestrial responses to millennial-scale climatic variability during the last glacial period in the Mediterranean region. *Climate Dynamics* 19: 95–105.

Semino O., J. Passarino, P.J. Oefner, A.A. Lin, A. Arbuzova, L.E. Beckman, G. de Benedictis, P. Francalacci, A. Kouvatsi, S. Umborska, M. Marcikiae, A. Mika, B. Mika, D. Primorac, A.S. Santachiara-Benerecetti, L.L. Cavalli-Sforza and P.A. Underhill 2000. The genetic legacy of Paleolithic *Homo sapiens* in extant Europeans: a Y-chromosome perspective. *Science* 210: 1155–1159.

Serre D., A. Langaney, M. Chech, M. Teschler-Nicola, M. Paunovic, P. Mennecier, M. Hofreiter M., G. Possnert and S. Pääbo 2004. No evidence of Neandertal mtDNA contribution to early modern humans. *PLoS Biology* 2(3): 0313–0317.

Shackleton N.J., M.A. Hall and E. Vincent 2000. Phase relationships between millennial scale events 64,000–24,000 years ago. *Paleoceanography* 15: 565–569.

Shennan S.J. 2001. Demography and cultural innovation: a model and some implications for the emergence of modern human culture. *Cambridge Archaeological Journal* 11: 5–16.

Shennan S.J. 2002. *Genes, Memes and Human History: Darwinian Archaeology and Cultural Evolution*. London: Thames & Hudson.

Stringer C. 2002. Modern human origins: progress and prospects. *Philosophical Transactions of the Royal Society of London* B 357: 563–579.

Tattersall I. 2002. The case for saltational events in human evolution. In T.J. Crow (Ed.), *The Speciation of Modern Homo Sapiens*, pp. 49–60. London: The British Academy.

Templeton A.R. 2002. Out of Africa again and again. *Nature* 416: 45–51.

Underhill P., G. Passarino, A. Lin, P. Shen, M. Lahr, R. Foley, P. Oefner and L. Cavalli-Sforza 2001. The phylogeography of Y chromosome binary haplotypes and the origins of modern human populations. *Annals of Human Genetics* 65: 43–62.

van Andel T.H. and W. Davies (Eds.) 2003. *Neanderthals and Modern Humans in the European Land-scape during the Last Glaciation, 60,000 to 20,000 years ago.* Cambridge: McDonald Institute for Archaeological Research.

Wells S. 2002. *The Journey of Man: a Genetic Odyssey.* London: penguin.

White T.D., B. Asfaw, D. DeGusta, H. Gilbert, G.D. Richards, G. Suwa and F.C. Howell 2003. Pleistocene *Homo sapiens* from Middle Awash, Ethiopia. *Nature* 423: 742–747

White R. 2001. Personal ornaments from the Grotte du Renne at Arcy-sur-Cure. *Athena Review* 2: 41–46.

Zilhão J. 2001. *Anatomically Archaic, Behaviorally Modern: the Last Neanderthals and their Destiny.* 2001 Kroon Lecture in Archaeology, University of Amsterdam.

Preface

Each one of us had been working on Middle Paleolithic lithic technology for some time when we met in Jerusalem in 2001 with some time on our hands (always a dangerous thing) to talk about things Mousterian. Despite our different backgrounds, perspectives and approaches, we agreed that Middle Paleolithic research was not the way we had "grown up" expecting it should be. By that time it had become more or less axiomatic that the associations between archaeological cultures and specific hominin taxa, and the linkage of culture change with taxonomic replacement, were not straightforward issues. But it was the cultural evidence that we found most puzzling and intriguing. Despite what we had learned from textbooks, the Eurasian Middle Paleolithic was clearly not a straightforward and homogeneous entity. It was obvious that the nature of the Middle Paleolithic record varied a great deal from place to place, and that in some places Middle Paleolithic technology and even subsistence showed distinctive trends over time. Yet, in apparent contrast to the increasingly precocious Middle Stone Age record of South and East Africa, variability in the Middle Paleolithic of Eurasia was relatively uncoordinated, and change over time was slow and directionless. Or was it? It struck us that there was comparatively little talk about change over time within the Middle Paleolithic, perhaps because most of us expected that there would not be much to talk about.

We decided to open up the questions of dynamism and stability within the Middle Paleolithic and MSA to a larger forum of researchers, and we took the opportunity of the 2002 meetings of the Society for American Archaeology in Denver to organize two symposia: "The Middle Paleolithic: Climbing uphill slowly or going nowhere fast?" and "Stability and Change in the Middle Paleolithic and Middle Stone Age". We deliberately took a respite from the much publicized, never-ending debates about phylogenetic relationships and anatomical differences between hominin taxa of this period, and asked the participants to examine patterns in the MP/MSA and relate them to our questions about the tempo and mode of *cultural* evolution throughout the period, based on hard data and actual case studies.

In all, twenty-four papers were presented in these two symposia. They tackled issues of lithic technology, intra-site use of space, hunting practices, land-use and mobility and whole settlement systems. They expressed many different and contradictory answers to our questions, but they all had one thing in common: all were intriguing and stimulating. We were pleased with the impact of the symposia on participants and audience alike. Many of those who attended or participated in the symposia inquired about publication plans, and this volume came to be as a response to their interest and enthusiasm.

Of course the vagaries of life and professional obligations often intervene in projects like this. Several of the original presenters were unable to contribute a written paper to this volume: among these are Stanley Ambrose, Alicia Hawkins, Marcia Wiseman, Daniel Kaufman, Francesco d'Errico, Nick Conard, and João Zilhão. On the other hand, the eighteen contributions to this volume include a few from individuals, such as Paul Mellars and Lynn Wadley, who had not been able to participate in the SAA symposia.

We gratefully thank all the participants of the 2002 symposia, who shared the intellectual excitement and who contributed to our interest in seeing this project through. Even bigger thanks are due to the contributors to this volume, who responded kindly and (usually) promptly to our incessant messages, instructions and pleas, gracefully responded to critiques and comments, and in general stuck it out throughout the period of working on the book. Thanks are due also to Michael Jochim, editor of the series, who supported warmly the publication of this volume, to Teresa Krauss, Margaret McNicholas and Anne Meagher at Springer, who were there to answer our questions, ease our worries and guide us through the production process, and to two anonymous reviewers of the book for their comments and suggestions.

Each chapter in the volume presents its own conclusion to the specific local questions which it addresses. The volume as a whole does not speak in unison. We are pleased with this outcome. The main goal of this project was to open up questions about the cultural dynamics of the Middle Paleolithic/ Middle Stone Age to broader discussion. We look forward to new ideas and new research that will tackle the old questions as well as the new ones that emerge from the papers in this book.

Erella Hovers, Jerusalem
Steven L. Kuhn, Tucson
March, 2005

Contents

Transitions Before the Transition

Chapter *1*

General Introduction

Steven L. Kuhn

Department of Anthropology, University of Arizona, Tucson, AZ 85721-0030 USA

Erella Hovers

Institute of Archaeology The Hebrew University, Mount Scopus, Jerusalem 91905 ISRAEL

The origins of modern humans, and the fate of the Neandertals, are arguably the most compelling and contentious arenas in Paleoanthropological research today, and they have been at the forefront of the field for at least the past 20 years. The much-discussed split between advocates of a single, early emergence of anatomically modern humans in sub-Saharan Africa and supporters of various models of regional continuity represents only part of the picture. More interesting in our opinion are the relationships between anatomical and behavioral changes that occurred during the past 200,000 years. Although modern humans as a species may be defined in terms of their skeletal anatomy, it is their behavior, and the social and cognitive structures that support that behavior, which most clearly distinguish *Homo sapiens* from other animals and from earlier forms of humans. Moreover, it is the origin of our shared behavioral (rather than skeletal) characteristics that is of greatest interest to the rest of the social and behavioral sciences. Learning how humans, as a species, came to act the way they do is probably the greatest contribution that Paleoanthropology can make to understanding the human present.

Ideas about the paths of behavioral evolution have been, and in many cases continue to be, polarized along lines corresponding to the major positions on modern human origins (MHO). Many advocates of a replacement of archaic humans in Eurasia by expanding African populations support models of catastrophic behavioral change correlated with the origins (in Africa) or dispersal (into Eurasia) of anatomically modern groups. In Europe and western Asia, the Middle-to-Upper

Paleolithic transition has been taken to mark the end of anatomically and behaviorally archaic populations and the appearance of people modern in both body and mind. Not surprisingly, scholars that see a great deal more regional continuity in human biology favor models of behavioral gradualism, arguing that the roots of sophisticated behavior in the Upper Paleolithic were apparent much earlier and that the full range of Upper Paleolithic characteristics was actually slow to emerge, consolidating only in the later Upper Paleolithic.

Although they continue to drive the debate, especially in popular venues, extreme positions on MHO and accompanying behavioral change have become difficult to sustain as archaeological, paleontological and genetic data have accumulated. According to geneticists, a large number of extant genetic systems seem to have their roots in sub-Saharan Africa, but some genes appear to have older histories in other regions (Relethford 2001). Distributions of genetic systems once interpreted as evidence for rapid expansion of a small group of African moderns have been shown to be consistent with gradual diffusion of a small component of the human genome through existing human populations (Eswaran 2002). Similarly, it is now apparent that the earliest anatomically modern populations in both Africa and the Levant behaved in ways little different from their archaic forebears. Meanwhile, at least late Neandertals seem to have been capable of engaging in many of the technological and cultural pursuits once thought to distinguish behaviorally and anatomically modern Upper Paleolithic humans from all others (e.g., d'Errico et al. 1998).

Among archaeological specialists, new models and new findings have resulted in a reframing of the basic problems. For researchers working in Africa, there has never been a question of whether or not there was genetic and cultural continuity between some population of indigenous archaic *Homo* and early modern humans. The major issue is now how and when major changes in behavior occurred, and how these relate to changes in anatomy. Some researchers (Klein 2000, 2001; Ambrose 2001) argue that major developments in human behavior occurred long after the appearance of an essentially modern anatomical configuration, in association with the sudden emergence of the organic capacity for language and symbolic cognition. Others (McBrearty and Brooks 2000; Henshilwood et al. 2000, 2001) assert that the package of traits thought to indicate modern behavior emerged gradually over a very long period beginning about 200,000 years ago, more-or-less in parallel with the biological development of *Homo sapiens*. Meanwhile, in Europe, objects such as bone tools and ornaments have been recovered from Châtelperronian layers at La Grotte du Renne (White 2001). The realization that this early Upper Paleolithic industry may have been the product of Neandertals has forced researchers to re-evaluate ideas about the behavioral capacities of anatomically archaic and modern members of the genus *Homo*.

Despite the rapid expansion of knowledge, three questions remain central to the brave new world of 21st century inquiry into the origins of modern humans. First, how different and distinct was the behavior of anatomically modern, Upper Paleolithic/Late Stone Age humans from that of their predecessors? What was really new about so-called "modern human behavior"? Second, how "difficult" an evolutionary transition was this (Brantingham *et al.* 2004)? Did it involve a change in the fundamental behavioral capacities of hominins or simply a frequency shift in their behavioral tendencies? Finally of course, there is the historical trajectory of the transition in behavior. Did it occur quickly or gradually, and did different characteristics emerge in unison or piecemeal?

None of the questions outlined above is new. Researchers have been attempting to answer them, in whole or in part, for the past century. However, as debates over MHO and the significance of the transition from Middle to Upper Paleolithic have intensified over the past 30 years, some clear tendencies have emerged in how the questions are addressed. We believe that the framing of the questions in turn has important, if largely unintended consequences for the answers that people derive. The current volume, and the symposia that gave rise to it, were and are intended to provide fresh perspectives on these issues.

Researchers working in Eurasia tend to approach the question of MHO and the Middle-to-Upper Paleolithic transition in terms of general differences between the Middle and Upper Paleolithic, *sensu largo*. In some cases, they look more closely at the resemblance, or lack thereof, between the early Upper Paleolithic, the late Upper Paleolithic, and the Middle Paleolithic, again broadly defined. Lists of characteristics found in the two (or three) phases are compared, and the differences are interpreted in terms of the fundamental capacities or tendencies of the respective hominin populations. What is almost never addressed is what was going on earlier in the Middle Paleolithic, before modern humans and the Upper Paleolithic came on the scene. Researchers may consider what the terminal Middle Paleolithic was like, and whether there was evidence for disequilibrium just prior to the appearance of modern humans and/or the Upper Paleolithic. But the larger question of long-term evolutionary trends within the Middle Paleolithic seldom if ever arises. The Mousterian is treated as an essentially homogeneous unit, a set of variations on a narrowly defined theme, with little or no internal evolution.

In our view, there are three main reasons for this lack of attention to evolutionary change before the emergence of the Upper Paleolithic. One is the tendency to assume that there was nothing to pay attention to. The notion that the Middle Paleolithic (and quite possibly the Middle Stone Age) was essentially static and unchanging is a deeply entrenched one, repeated over and over in introductory texts and synthetic works. If the possibility of significant evolutionary dynamics is excluded *a priori* within the Middle Paleolithic, almost by definition truly important changes can only occur with its demise. As many of the contributors to this volume show, however, this account is too simplistic.

A second reason for the blindness with respect to Middle Paleolithic dynamics in Eurasia stems ultimately from fundamental ideas about the nature of human cultural evolution. A lasting legacy of early cultural evolutionist thought is the tendency to approach long-term trajectories of cultural change as accretive and progressive. Important intervals of change are marked by the addition of new cultural traits or forms of behavior to a relatively impoverished ancestral substrate. Because the appearance of novel characteristics is often used to define new stages or phases, change is recognized mainly as a transition from one state or taxonomic unit to another. Regardless of one's biases with regard to the historical facts of MHO, we think this myopia with respect to possible evolutionary dynamics within the Middle Paleolithic is a serious handicap in attempts to explain behavioral transitions. First, it constrains one to approach all change as a transformational (if not catastrophic) event rather than part of long-term evolutionary process (Dunnell 1980). Second, the notion that cultural evolution occurs mainly by the addition of new traits implies that earlier stages are less developed and less diverse than later ones. This again tends to discourage the investigation of evolutionary dynamics within earlier cultural phases. Finally, the notion of cultural evolution as an additive process leads many researchers to ignore what is distinctive about the Middle Paleolithic, greatly handicapping any attempt to test notions of cultural continuity over time.

A third factor limiting our ability to investigate important biological and behavioral transitions is geographic discontinuity in scientific knowledge. Not without reason, researchers have tended to argue from one or two areas in which the archaeological and fossil record of the transitions is best documented, and to base their arguments on one or two classes of data. For a variety of reasons, accounts of biological and cultural changes leading up to the appearance of anatomically and behaviorally modern humans have been dominated by the European and Levantine evidence. But because modern humans are a single species, studying their origins requires a global perspective. Certainly there is a longer history of research and a substantially greater density of sites in western Eurasia than in Africa or East Asia, but this situation is nonetheless unacceptable as a solid basis for a more profound understanding of the historical process or processes at play. Evolutionary dynamics within the late Middle Paleolithic of southern France or the Mediterranean Levant, while interesting, cannot be generalized to other parts of Eurasia. A more satisfying and scientifically useful account of biological and cultural changes during the Upper Pleistocene must be extensive in its geographic coverage. If the same story does not seem to pertain to different areas, all the better: diversity of process is as significant as is the nature of the process in any one area.

The African record is crucial, irrespective of one's position on the biological and cultural transitions. A number of characteristics which in Eurasia are confined to the Upper Paleolithic—carved and polished bone tools, decorative motifs—appear precociously in sub-Saharan Africa (*e.g.*, McBrearty and Brooks 2000; Henshilwood *et al.* 2001), and it is difficult to dismiss the possibility that these are somehow linked to a similarly early appearance of modern anatomical features. Even if one is skeptical about these early finds, sub-Saharan Africa is the one place *everyone* agrees there was biological, and therefore at least some measure of cultural continuity. The African record therefore shows us at least one version of how behavior evolved in the context of general biological continuity. Eventually, it may also reveal which features of behavior were causally associated with evolutionarily derived characteristics of anatomically modern *Homo sapiens*, and which are only associated by historical accident. Thus, even if the African record does not explain the Eurasian one, it nonetheless is useful in understanding it.

We will never arrive at a satisfying account of why the Mousterian disappeared, and why Upper Paleolithic technologies and lifeways became so widespread so rapidly after 45,000 years ago, without understanding why Middle Paleolithic adaptive patterns lasted so long. And we cannot hope to account for the durability of the Mousterian without understanding how, or if, they responded to changing conditions. The importance of the issue is not limited to advocates of a particular perspective on MHO. On one hand, if there is fundamental behavioral continuity between the Middle and Upper Paleolithic, it might best be seen as an extension of long-term trends. Otherwise, the existence of a period of unprecedented, explosive change at the end of the Middle Paleolithic, roughly coinciding with the appearance of modern humans in Eurasia, is too much of a coincidence to ignore. If, on the other hand, the spread of the Upper Paleolithic occurred as a result of a simple replacement, it behooves us to understand what was being replaced. Simple references to inherent superiority of modern-behaving, modern-looking humans are no longer adequate. What advantages did modern humans have over contemporary hominins and why did these result in rapid replacement in some places but much-delayed replacement in others? Understanding how earlier humans were, and were not, able to adjust their behavior is crucial to explaining what might have given modern *Homo sapiens* the upper hand. As for intermediate positions (sometimes known as "weak out-of-Africa" models), the timing of significant developments in behavior, or of deflections in the trajectories of change, is crucial.

The rationale for this volume, and for the symposia in which many of the papers were first presented during the 2002 SAA meetings in Denver, grows directly out of the problems just described. The book assembles researchers from Eurasia and Africa to discuss what was happening in the Middle Paleolithic and Middle Stone Age, prior to or during the appearance of anatomically modern humans. We asked the authors 1) to provide updates on the current state of knowledge about patterns of change over time in one or more categories of archaeological evidence within the MP and MSA and 2) to discuss the implications of such trends as could be identified for behavioral evolution later in the Pleistocene. The ultimate goal was to provide participants, and readers of the book, with the broadest and most current range of information available on the many transitions that might or might not have occurred before "The Transition."

In organizing the original symposia we attempted to involve researchers from throughout Europe, west Asia, and Africa. A number of other researchers were invited to participate in the book project in order to even out geographic representation. For a wide variety of reasons, not all of the invitees were able to participate and/or to produce written papers, and unfortunately, a number of those who could not participate were responsible for dealing with regions relatively poorly known to many Anglophone researchers, including southern Africa and central Europe. We still feel that this volume offers a comparatively broad geographic perspective. One region that is not covered at all, however, is East Asia. We do not wish to give the impression that the area is unimportant. However, researchers in that part of the world are currently dealing with a range of problems very different from their colleagues who are working in Africa and western Eurasia. Even the basic taxonomic units Lower, Middle and Upper Paleolithic have very different meanings in East Asia, and some scholars argue that they have little or no utility at all (Gao and Norton 2002). In light of the difficulties in comparing units and time periods, we felt that comparisons of trends and tendencies in the East and West would be best addressed in another context. Similarly, recent, hotly debated dates for early human arrival to Australia certainly have placed this continent in a time frame pertinent to the current discussion (O'Connell and Allen 1998; Stringer 1999; Bowler *et al.* 2003). We thought it appropriate to see the dust settle over this particular controversy before drawing the early archaeology of Australia into an already contentious discussion.

Several themes recur in the articles that make up this volume, as they did in the larger set of oral papers during the symposia. Not every author addressed all of these themes, but a synthetic reading of the papers reveals a number of common conclusions as well as problems for future study. We identify four principal topics: continental-scale difference in trajectories of change, the distinction between variability and directional evolutionary change, the potential consequences of demography, and the influence of terminology on research and thought.

One of the strongest patterns to emerge concerns differences in time-trends between the African and Eurasian records. Two of the contributors to this volume, McBrearty and Brooks, have already proposed that the African record shows a gradual and piecemeal development of various traits thought to indicate "behavioral modernity." This term itself is highly problematic and certainly deserves more careful scrutiny, but that's another volume. Not all African researchers see the data this way. The major proponent of a "catastrophic" model of behavioral change in the African Middle Stone Age, Richard Klein, was unable to contribute to this volume, though his view is well represented elsewhere (Klein 1995, 2000, 2002). The papers of McBrearty and Tyron and Brooks *et al.* here add more support for McBrearty and Brooks' earlier arguments. McBrearty and Tyron focus on the origins of the Middle Stone Age. Interestingly, for them the important transition occurs between the Acheulean and the Middle Stone Age, after which various manifestations of modern behavior occur throughout the Middle Stone Age. Similar to the later, more famous transition in Europe, the cultural changes are associated with *Homo sapiens*, in this case as a result of putative genetic events that led to the isolation of ancestral populations. Brooks *et al.* concentrate on the later Middle Stone Age. They argue that some of the most important developments concern projectile technology and the development of weaponry that can be used to kill at a distance. While this hypothesis requires further testing, it is provocative in that it identifies a behavioral/cultural characteristic, other than generic "modernity," that could have given *Homo sapiens* an advantage over contemporaneous hominins outside of Africa.

Virtually all of the contributors agree that the Eurasian Middle Paleolithic shows very different time trends compared with the African Middle Stone Age. That does not mean it is appropriate to describe the Mousterian as homogeneous and static: in fact, diversity and flexibility seem to be the operative themes here. Several of the papers (Delagnes and Meignen, Kuhn, Meignen *et al.*, Stiner, Marks and Chabai) document clear patterns of change over time in various local or regional

Middle Paleolithic sequences. What the papers also show, however, is that the trajectories of change in different regions were largely independent of one another, or at least that we are unable to identify the common themes. Moreover, trends within the Middle Paleolithic did not necessarily lead in the direction of the Upper Paleolithic. The Crimean evidence discussed by Marks and Chabai is a perfect illustration. In that area, Micoquian technology seems to have been remarkably stable whereas the Western Crimean Mousterian shows a distinct tendency towards the development of something like prismatic blade technology. And while prismatic blades are not essentially "modern" (Bar-Yosef and Kuhn 1999), they do represent the configuration lithic technological systems eventually took on in most places. The papers on France (Delagnes and Meignen) and the Levant, (Meignen *et al.*) also discuss distinctive patterns of evolutionary change within the Middle Paleolithic, neither of which shows a long-term trend towards Upper Paleolithic patterns, while the data from Italy (Kuhn) show different local trends, one seemingly "progressive" and the other not.

The contrasting trajectories of evolutionary change in the Middle Stone Age and Middle Paleolithic are not simply a matter of the Middle Stone Age being more dynamic or diverse. As McBrearty argues, it is not just change over time that marks the Middle Stone Age, but the accumulation of novel behavioral characteristics ("innovations"). In contrast, there is general agreement that the Eurasian Middle Paleolithic witnessed few if any novel behavioral developments. Much of what we know about Middle Paleolithic lithic technologies seems to represent refinements of very ancient techniques (Levallois, prismatic blade production, discoid core reduction).

Of course, not everyone agrees even that the Mousterian shows much in the way of time-transgressive tendencies. Monnier addresses the question of progressiveness in levels of artifact standardization during the Middle Paleolithic, and finds that expected "improvements" in tool-making cannot be documented, at least in France. Shea also emphasizes the relative constancy of later Levantine Mousterian technological and foraging patterns, although other researchers (Bar-Yosef, Meignen *et al.*) see much more robust chronological sequencing between what Shea treats as essentially contemporaneous patterns. Interestingly, faunal evidence from Eurasia (Gaudzinski, Stiner) shows few if any clear general trends, although there is considerable variation related to climate and local environmental characteristics. Middle Paleolithic hominins seem to have been successful large-game predators by 200,000 years ago, so effective at obtaining large hoofed animals in fact that they seldom resorted to intensive use of other animal resources. Somewhat less information is available concerning foraging patterns in the Middle Stone Age. Klein argues that Middle Stone Age foragers were able to take all but the largest and most dangerous animals (but see Milo 1998). Brooks points to the early appearance of fishing in southern Africa, 50,000 years before it became economically important in Eurasia. Evidence from site structure is even more equivocal. On the surface, the papers by Speth and Wadley suggest that Neandertals at Kebara 50,000 years ago organized their use of space in a more rigid manner than Middle Stone Age hominins (presumably *Homo sapiens*) only

30,000 years ago. However, both authors observe that evidence pertaining to the use of space is less easily interpreted than faunal or lithic evidence. First, there are simply too few cases to construct reliable time series. Second, expectations for how the use of space should be organized among behaviorally modern humans are not well defined, especially when different contexts, such as constrained and unconstrained spaces, must be taken into account.

In truth, the diversity of Middle Paleolithic behavior, and the apparent flexibility of Middle Paleolithic hominins, should come as no surprise. Mousterian hominins persisted for too long—upwards of 200,000 years—and in too wide a range of environments not to have been highly adaptable. Gaudzinski underlines an important problem with respect to interpreting this evidence: should the situational variability within the Middle Paleolithic be seen as evidence for sophisticated and highly responsive adaptive strategies, or should it be interpreted as simple expedience or opportunism? Answering the question hinges on the temporal scale of adaptive responses. It is necessary to understand how much of the diversity of Middle Paleolithic technological and foraging strategies was contained within the adaptive repertoire of a single population, as opposed to a series of rather more specialized solutions developed over millennia in response to specific local conditions. At present the temporal grain of most Paleolithic records simply does not permit us to answer this question, but it remains an important goal for future research.

A third major theme that cuts across data classes and regions is demography. Demography has a long and sometimes checkered history as an explanation for culture change, and some researchers may be dismayed to see it resurfacing here. On the other hand, Malthusian dynamics are central to the fundamental concept of evolution by natural selection, so it is entirely appropriate to consider population levels in addressing problems at evolutionary time scales. All of the authors who touch upon demographic issues agree that Middle Paleolithic hominins existed at very low population densities, lower in fact than any recently documented forager group (Hovers and Belfer-Cohen, Shea, Stiner; see also Gamble 1999; Kuhn and Stiner 2001). It is also widely held that localized population or lineage extinctions were common during the Middle Paleolithic. Due to the lesser densities of documented sites it is difficult to compare Africa and Eurasia directly. Geneticists do argue that sub-Saharan Africa has always had larger and more persistent populations than the temperate zones (Harpending *et al.* 1993; Relethford and Harpending 1995), although parts of the continent seem to have been abandoned during hyper-arid glacial intervals.

The possibility of major differences in population densities has important implications for phenomena ranging from prey choice (Stiner) to intergroup relationships and the propagation of cultural innovations (Hovers and Belfer-Cohen). If localized lineage extinction was as common as some authors argue (Hovers and Belfer-Cohen, Shea; see also Pennington 2001), then we also must consider the extent to which it structured the archaeological record. For example, how much of the appearance of diversity in the Middle Paleolithic is a result of cultural drift and eventual extinction of many small, isolated populations? It is also worth considering the extent to which differences in population sizes and persistence might be responsible for the contrast between sub-Saharan Africa and northern Eurasia. Many of the apparent "precocious" developments of the Middle Stone Age, from fishing and the use of grinding equipment to the development of systems of ornamentation, could be linked at least indirectly to the sizes of local human populations. As Hovers and Belfer-Cohen point out, the propagation and persistence of cultural innovations also require continuity in systems of information transmission across time. Hypothetically at least, the size and stability of African hominin populations compared with Eurasian ones could explain why certain novel behaviors became established in the former area and failed to thrive in more sparsely populated parts of temperate and sub-Arctic Eurasia.

The final theme, taken up explicitly by Kleindienst and Clark and Riel-Salvatore but addressed in passing in many other papers, is the influence of terminology and systematics on the structure of research. It is certainly nothing new to argue that what we call things has profound consequences for how we study them, but in truth the question has not been adequately addressed by paleoanthropologists. The cyclical reclassification of the Neandertals as a separate species or as a subspecies of *Homo sapiens* is an obvious case in point, as it seems to have more to do with prevailing models for MHO than with changes in the available anatomical evidence. Clark and Riel-Salvatore's paper addresses a wide range of generalizations about the Middle and Lower Paleolithic, arguing that these are often based on ambiguous, naive, and poorly-structured conventions of description, classification, and interpretation. Whether or not one agrees with Clark and Riel-Salvatore's particular interpretations, the necessity for continuing critical assessment of epistemology is undeniable. Kleindienst, reflecting on archaeological terminology in North Africa, points out that the most common terminology imposes the impression of a development sequence, and that there is an inherent circularity in developing chronostratigraphic frameworks based in such systems. Interestingly, a terminological system based more strictly on geological criteria and assemblage composition developed more than 30 years ago by the main authorities in the region was never adopted.

In our view, if there is a single, overriding lesson to be drawn from the papers in this volume, it is that the eventual evolutionary successes of modern humans and the Upper Paleolithic were ultimately contingent phenomena. There is nothing preordained about the Upper Paleolithic. Earlier hominins in Eurasia were successful at colonizing a wide range of environments, and in some of these environments they managed to resist the expansion of modern humans and the Upper Paleolithic for many millennia. To one extent or another, they succeeded in maintaining stable (if small) populations under changing conditions by adjusting their behavior in response to those conditions. Yet while Middle Paleolithic behavior did evolve over the course of the Upper Pleistocene, it did not necessarily evolve towards what eventually became the Upper Paleolithic (see also Hovers 1997, in press). A model of cultural evolution as the progressive ascent of a single adaptive peak, with ourselves (as tellers of the story) at the summit simply does not apply. Mousterian hunters or toolmakers were not simply ineffective, incomplete versions of later humans. Instead, the fitness landscapes (*sensu* Wright 1932; Palmer 1991) of the late Pleistocene were highly uneven or rugged, with many local peaks and valleys. The Neandertals and their contemporaries depended on successful strategies for coping with their circumstances. These strategies may have differed from those employed by later hominins, but they worked for a substantial period of time. The early appearance and subsequent disappearance of many "advanced" traits in sub-Saharan Africa may suggest that fitness landscapes in tropical Africa were similarly broken: sometimes generic Middle Stone Age technologies even had the advantage over the precocious Howiesons Poort (Ambrose and Lorenz 1990). It would benefit researchers to stop thinking about the appearance and spread of anatomically modern *Homo sapiens* and Upper Paleolithic technological adaptations as the final stage of a long, gradual climb towards modernity. Instead, we need to consider how these events altered the social and ecological arenas in which other contemporary hominins had been so successful, and in which the populations of modern humans themselves had to operate.

REFERENCES CITED

Ambrose S. and K. Lorenz 1990. Social and ecological models for the Middle Stone Age in southern Africa. In P. Mellars (Ed.), *The Emergence of Modern Humans: An Archaeological Perspective*, pp. 3–33. New York: Cornell University Press.

Ambrose S. 2001. Paleolithic technology and human evolution. *Science* 291: 1748–1753.

Bar-Yosef O. and S.L. Kuhn 1999. The big deal about blades: laminar technologies and human evolution. *American Anthropologist* 101: 322–338.

Bowler J.M., M. Johnston, J.M. Olley, J.R. Prescott, R.G. Roberts, W. Shawcross and N.A. Spooner 2003. New ages for human occupation and climatic change at Lake Mungo, Australia. *Nature* 421: 837–840.

Brantingham P.J., S.L. Kuhn and K.W. Kerry 2004. Introduction. In P.J. Brantingham, K.W. Kerry and S.L. Kuhn (Eds.), *Another World: The Early Upper Paleolithic East of the Danube*, pp. 1–13. Berkley: University of California Press.

d'Errico, F., J. Zilhão, M. Julien, D. Baffier and J. Pelegrin 1998. Neanderthal acculturation in Western Europe? a critical review of the evidence and its interpretation. *Current Anthropology* 39 (Supplement): S1–S44.

Dunnell R. 1980. Evolutionary theory and archaeology. In M.B. Schiffer (Ed.), *Advances in Archaeological Method and Theory*, Vol. 3, pp. 35–99. New York: Academic Press.

Eswaran V. 2002. A diffusion wave out of Africa: the mechanism of the modern human revolution? *Current Anthropology* 43: 749–774.

Gamble C. 1999. *The Paleolithic Societies of Europe*. Cambridge: Cambridge University Press.

Gao Xing and C. Norton 2002. A critique of the Chinese Middle Paleolithic. *Antiquity* 76: 397–412.

Harpending H., S. Sherry, A. Rogers and M. Stoneking 1993. The genetic structure of ancient human populations. *Current Anthropology* 34: 483–496.

Henshilwood C.S., F. d'Errico, C.W. Marean, R.G. Milo and R. Yates 2001. An early bone tool industry from the Middle Stone Age at Blombos Cave, South Africa: implications for the origins of modern human behaviour, symbolism and language. *Journal of Human Evolution* 41: 631–678.

Henshilwood, C.S., F. d'Errico, R. Yates, Z Jacobs, C. Tribolo, G.A.T. Duller, N. Mercier, J.C. Sealy, H.Valladas, I. Watts and A.G. Wintle 2002. Emergence of modern human behavior: Middle Stone Age engravings from South Africa. *Science* 295: 1278–1280.

Hovers E. 1997. *Variability of Lithic Assemblages and Settlement Patterns in the Levantine Middle Pale-olithic: Implications for the Development of Human Behavior.* Ph. D. dissertation, Hebrew University, Jerusalem.

Hovers E. in press. *The Organization of Lithic Technology in the Mousterian Layers of Qafzeh Cave, Israel.* Institute Of Archaeology (Qedem series). Institute of Archaeology, The Hebrew University, Jerusalem.

Klein R. 1995. Anatomy, behavior and modern human origins. *Journal of World Prehistory* 8: 167–198.

Klein R. 1999. *The Human Career: Human Biological and Cultural Origins.* 2nd edition. Chicago: University of Chicago Press.

Klein R.G. 2000. Archeology and the evolution of human behavior. *Evolutionary Anthropology* 9: 17–36.

Klein R. 2001. Southern Africa and modern human origins. *Journal of Anthropological Research* 57: 1–16.

Kuhn S.L. and M.C. Stiner 2001. The antiquity of hunter-gatherers. In C. Panter-Brick, R.H. Layton and P.A. Rowley-Conwy (Eds.), *Hunter-Gatherers, An Interdisciplinary Perspective*, pp. 99–142. Cambridge: Cambridge University Press.

McBrearty S. and A.S. Brooks 2000. The revolution that wasn't: a new interpretation of the origin of modern human behavior. *Journal of Human Evolution* 39: 453–563.

Milo R. 1998. Evidence for hominid predation at Klasies River Mouth, South Africa, and its implication for the behavior of early modern humans. *Journal of Archaeological Science* 25: 99–133.

O'Connell J. and J. Allen 1998. When did humans first arrive in Greater Australia, and why is it important to know? *Evolutionary Anthropology* 6: 132–146.

Palmer R. 1991. Optimization on rugged fitness landscapes. In E. Perelson and S. Kaufman (Eds.), *Molecular Evolution on Rugged Fitness Landscapes*, pp. 3–25. Redwood City: Addison.

Pennington R. 2001. Hunter-gatherer demography. In C. Panter-Brick, R.H. Layton and P.A. Rowley-Conwy (Eds.), *Hunter-Gatherers, an Interdisciplinary Perspective*, pp. 174–204. Cambridge: Cambridge University Press.

Relethford J. 2001. *Genetics and the Search for Modern Human Origins.* New York: Wiley-Liss.

Relethford J.H. and H. Harpending 1995. Ancient differences in population size can mimic a recent African origin of modern humans. *Current Anthropology* 36: 667–674.

Stringer C. 1999. Has Australia backdated the human revolution? *Antiquity* 73: 876–879.

White R. 2001. Personal ornaments from the Grotte du Renne at Arcy-sur Cure. *Athena Review* 2: 12–19.

Wright S. 1932. The roles of mutation, inbreeding, crossbreeding and selection in evolution. *Proceedings of the 6th International Congress on Genetics* 1: 356–366.

Chapter **2**

On Naming Things
Behavioral Changes in the Later Middle to Earlier Late Pleistocene, Viewed From the Eastern Sahara

M. R. Kleindienst

Department of Anthropology, University of Toronto at Mississauga, 3359 Mississauga Road North, Mississauga, Ontario, Canada L5L 1C6

ABSTRACT

Understanding of human behavioral changes during the later Middle to earlier Late Pleistocene, encoded in the rudimentary record of stone artifacts, is impeded by problems of communication among archaeologists. For example: continued use of broad-scale developmental stage terms, such as "Earlier" *vs.* "Middle Stone Age" impedes understanding because of the multiplicity of implied meanings; continued widespread application of the term "Acheulean" to almost any unit containing large, bifacially trimmed "tools" impedes the understanding of subtle design changes. Nomenclature devised for content units from Dakhleh and Kharga Oases, Western Desert, Egypt, is a modification of recommendations made in 1965, which were aimed at greater flexibility and precision in naming cultural stratigraphic units.

BACKGROUND

I was recently bemused by finding passionate arguments about whether or not something is "Middle Palaeolithic" or even "Acheulean" (*cf.* Ronen and Weinstein-Evron 2000). What such arguments denote is that archaeologists are not communicating (*cf.* Clark 2002:50):

It was, as such things go, "successful"—socially enjoyable, intellectually stimulating, and so forth. What struck me most about this conference, however, was what was **not** said. It became evident, just below a thin veneer of informed and sophisticated debate, that there were enormous differences in the biases, preconceptions, and assumptions that the participants brought to the resolution of problems thought to be held in common. At times, these differences were so great that there was literally no common basis for discussion [original emphasis].

Such arguments usually occur because the underlying assumptions and interpretations embodied "in a name" are not objectified. And in general they reflect common archaeological practice—to begin defining and naming things from the "top down," or the most general, rather than beginning with, and naming defined, basic analytic content units. That practice results in terms such as "Acheulean" becoming so over-extended, bearing so little precise meaning, that they are only the equivalent of the broad "developmental stage terms": the "Earlier", "Middle", and "Later Stone Age", or the "Lower", "Middle" and "Upper Palaeolithic" terms.

An example is the following exchange of views (in Ronen and Weinstein-Evron 2000:229):

> Romuald Schild: I agree. It [the Bockstein material] is Middle Palaeolithic. However, there are two sealed Late Acheulean sites at Dakhla, certainly before Stage 7, that contain classical Klausenischemesser and Prodniks together with unifacial side scrapers and hundreds of handaxes from amygdaloids through cordiforms, and Levallois technology. I think that they are three hundred thousand years old if not more. They also show the resharpening scars of Prondniks.
>
> Gerhard Bosinski: I agree, if you admit that this is Middle Palaeolithic.
>
> Romuald Schild: No. To me it is Late Acheulean. We published it as Late Acheulean. You can not change it.

NOMENCLATURE

If one cannot change the referent, how does one disagree with the original ascription and name? Must one always go through long discussions of who called what, by what term and when, in terms of field units and their ascriptions? Might it be advantageous to have some system of nomenclature that refers to content or evidential units without implying assignments to such broad-named entities as "Middle Palaeolithic", or "Late Acheulean"? It seems that whenever someone finds a large, bifacially worked lithic artifact in the Sahara they call it "Acheulean" (*e.g.*, Siiriäinen 1999; Hill 2001). In my opinion, many of these do not "fit" any precise definition of African Acheulean, including the material originally excavated at Dakhleh (*contra* Schild and Wendorf 1977; Wendorf and Schild 1980; Kleindienst 1985). In order to refer to that material, as originally described, and to similar aggregates found by members of the Dakhleh Oasis Project, I introduced the term

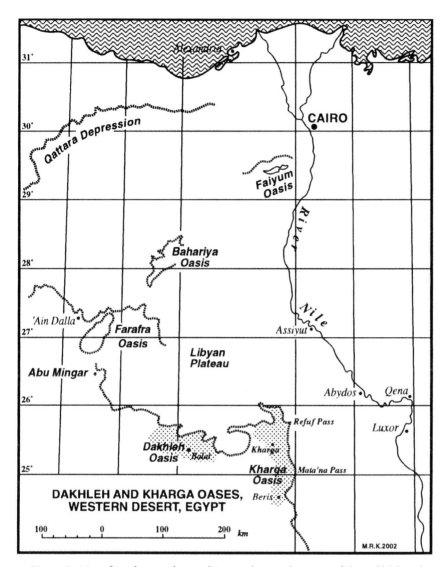

Figure 1. Map of northern and central Egypt, showing locations of the Dakhleh and Kharga Oasis depressions in the Western Desert.

"Balat Unit" (Kleindienst 1999:97–99), named for the nearest town in Dakhleh Oasis (Figure 1).

To justify that change in referent, I wish to hark back to a 1965 Burg Wartenstein symposium. Sadly, many participants are no longer with us. The person I most miss concerning the logic of classification and nomenclature is the late Glynn Isaac. The symposium participants made a number of recommendations regarding these fundamental archaeological procedures, which were published in *Background to Evolution in Africa* (Bishop and Clark 1967:892–895), and a brief explanatory paper, *Precision and Definition in African Archaeology* (Clark *et al.* 1966) (Figure 2). J. D. Clark and I applied the principles of the recommendations in publications on Kalambo Falls (*cf.* Clark and Kleindienst 1974), as did Isaac (1977; Isaac and Isaac 1997). In brief (Bishop and Clark 1967:893–894):

An *Industrial Complex* is that grouping of Industries . . . considered to represent parts of the same whole. . . .
    An *Industry* is represented by all the known objects that a group of prehistoric people manufactured in one area over some span of time. . . .
    An *Archaeological Horizon* (alternatively *Archaeological Occurrence*) is the minimal cultural-stratigraphic unit which can be defined at any place . . . it denotes the cultural material **in its context** [original emphases].

Ideally, all of these should be named using local geographical names when they are published. Arbitrary names may be used when no local terms are available (Figure 2).

CULTURAL STRATIGRAPHIC NOMENCLATURE

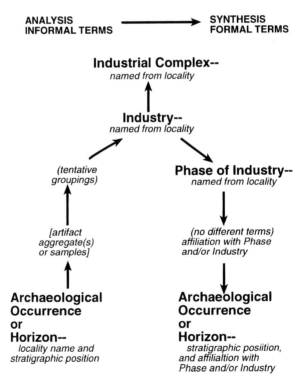

Figure 2. Nomenclature for cultural stratigraphic units as proposed in the 1965, Berg Wartenstein recommendations, after J. D. Clark *et al.* 1966:120. Note that the term(s) used for cultural materials extracted from Archaeological Occurrences or Horizons do not designate units.

Note that numerical or alphabetical designations are inherently inflexible, as are such designations as "early", "lower", "middle", "later" or "upper", especially those incorporating developmental stage terms. These produce confusion and miscommunication when one wishes to change the relative "positions" or time relationships among units named in that manner.

In the main, Berg Wartenstein recommendations have met with total disregard; although the term "cultural stratigraphic unit" has gained some currency (Kleindienst 1967), it is too often misused as "culture stratigraphic." However, the only real objections I have ever heard are:

1) *"What difference does it make what I call it?"* Surely those who have any training in linguistics know that nothing makes more difference than what one calls something; and

2) *"I can't remember all the names!"* Why would anyone want to do that? For instance, no geologist attempts to remember all the formation names in the world, and only uses the ones of immediate interest to the current research area. Nor does any palaeontologist attempt to remember all names for all biological species or genera, even in one area.

However, the Wartenstein recommendations were fatally flawed, because those in favor of such a system could not persuade their colleagues, particularly the European colleagues, to leave the "group of prehistoric people" out of the definition of the "Basic Unit," termed an "Industry". If one makes that assumption part of the definition, one is caught in a tautology when one actually wants to make interpretations of cultural content in terms of human behavior. In consequence, for use at Dakhleh and Kharga Oases in the Western Desert of Egypt, M. M. A. McDonald (dealing with Holocene prehistory) and I have modified the original definitions and call the Basic Unit just that: a cultural stratigraphic unit, or just (Cultural) "Unit" for short (Figures 3 and 4), which comprises only the cultural evidence. In using a structured, shorthand method of reference to facilitate scholarly communication, the intent is to divorce the nomenclature for evidential content units from *a priori* assumptions about the behaviors or relationships of the humans who may have produced that evidence. The principle is that one works using detailed comparisons from the "known" to the "unknown", rather than by "fitting" the unknown into some broad, imprecise, named unit or stage that is historically overburdened with multiple, often conflicting, meanings. In practice, when supported by evidence, it is always simpler to combine ("lump") lower-level units than it is to subdivide ("split") higher-level, broadly generalized units once they are embedded in the literature and in textbooks.

So far as I know, no one other than the Africanists has ever proposed a formal, named field unit that includes cultural evidence (not just "objects") in context (the Archaeological Occurrence or Horizon). Puzzling, for we all know that nothing is more important than context! And, in fact, most archaeological reports do subdivide the identified cultural evidence according to the recognized minimal contextual units, whatever they may be called. The cultural material extracted, then, can be called "aggregate", "sample" or "collection"—whatever *does not denote*

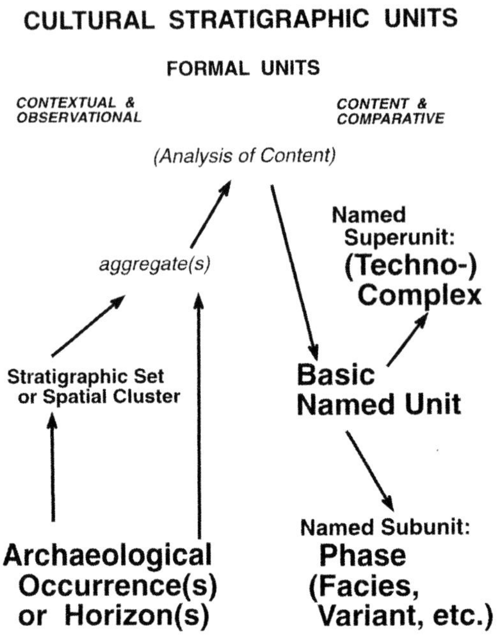

CULTURAL STRATIGRAPHIC UNITS

FORMAL UNITS

CONTEXTUAL &
OBSERVATIONAL

CONTENT &
COMPARATIVE

(Analysis of Content)

aggregate(s)

Named
Superunit:
**(Techno-)
Complex**

**Stratigraphic Set
or Spatial Cluster**

**Basic
Named Unit**

**Archaeological
Occurrence(s)
or Horizon(s)**

Named Subunit:
**Phase
(Facies,
Variant, etc.)**

Figure 3. Nomenclature used for designating cultural stratigraphic units recognized at Dakhleh and Kharga Oases, Western Desert, Egypt. Note that term(s) used for cultural materials extracted from Archaeological Occurrences or Horizons do not designate units.

any "group of people" assumed to be related in any social or biological sense. It only refers to content, or the material or observations of evidence interpreted to be humanly produced. Of course, that interpretation itself embodies a large body of theory, tested or untested hypotheses, and assumptions which should be objectified (*cf.* Kosso 2001:39-58).

Analyses of extracted evidence allow definition and formal naming of Basic Units. The named units *do not* designate or imply any "people" other than as individual producers of evidence; they *do not* indicate ethnicity or the physical form of the ancestors; they *do not* mean time placement, although they occur within past time ranges. They refer only to the cultural content as defined. Nothing more, nothing less. Definitions can subsequently be expanded, or altered, with cause, but the original name stands. Having done that, one can then speak about behavior of the "people" in any manner that one chooses to interpret the cultural evidence.

Obviously, definitions need to be published (see Hawkins [2001] for an example of definition of the Dakhleh Unit, assigned to the Aterian Complex). Note that there is a difference between "formal" and "informal" usage: one can say that something exists, without fully defining or naming it, or by using "unit" uncapitalized. (Try getting that past journal editors, however.) Too often, no clear definition is provided for named units. Changes in definitions also should be clearly stated and published.

CULTURAL STRATIGRAPHIC UNITS

Approximate Kyr ago	BASIC UNITS		COMPLEX
	DAKHLEH OASIS	KHARGA OASIS	
?			
	Sheikh Mabruk Unit	Khargan Unit	Khargan
40			
	Dakhleh Unit	Kharga Aterian Unit	Aterian
100			
	[(undefined unit(s)]	Mata'na Unit ("Upper Levalloisian")	? Refuf
200			
	Teneida unit		? Refuf
	Gifata Unit	Refuf Unit ("Lower Levalloisian")	
300			
	Balat Unit		? Balat
		Dharb el-Gaga unit KO10 unit	? Balat
400			
	[undefined unit(s)]	[undefined unit(s)]	"African Upper Acheulian, sensu stricto"

Figure 4. Pleistocene-aged cultural stratigraphic units recognized as of 2002 at Dakhleh and Kharga Oases, Western Desert, Egypt.

The named Basic Units can be subdivided after they are defined, but one must begin with local units based upon cultural evidence from Archaeological Horizons or Occurrences, *i.e.*, one starts at the lowest analytical level, not the highest. Burg Wartenstein (Bishop and Clark 1967:893) recommended using "Phase" for subdivisions, but such terms as "Facies" may be appropriate for sub-units that are not time differentiated. A Basic Unit might subsequently be subsumed as a Phase or Facies within another Basic Unit, or a subdivision might later be established as a Basic Unit in itself, but the original local name should not change. In some cases a new designator might be required to distinguish the new status if the original name causes confusion in referencing: for instance, if an inflexible designator was originally used.

The Basic Units can be combined into higher-order units: "Complexes", or "Techno-Complexes", although we find that the original definition of the latter term (Clarke 1968) is too restrictive. What level of similarity in cultural evidence is needed for inclusion within a Complex is debatable. However, complexes were intended to reflect a defined content. They were not intended to be overly generalized across time and space beyond the range of the included defined Basic Units (see below). Again, they are only content units.

Burg Wartenstein (Bishop and Clark 1967:896-897) also recommended that the developmental stage terms such as "Earlier Stone Age", or "Lower Palaeolithic" be discontinued. That has certainly not happened, possibly because they do continue to be useful when one does not wish to be precise. I use them also, but strictly as techno-typological developmental stage terms (see Kleindienst 1999), not related groups of people, not ethnicity, not time placement. If I use the words "Middle Stone Age" (MSA) I mean only that I have an archaeological occurrence, or possibly several similar, that I am not yet willing to define as a unit, but I can say that the culturally produced material bears the characteristics of the local MSA developmental stage. These terms are not part of the cultural stratigraphic system of nomenclature; they fall outside it.

DAKHLEH AND KHARGA OASES, WESTERN DESERT OF EGYPT

Figure 4 illustrates the use of archaeological nomenclature for prehistoric cultural stratigraphic units recognized to date at Dakhleh and Kharga Oases. We have found so little of what I, in desperation, have informally included within the African "Upper Acheulean Complex, *sensu stricto*" that I do not yet wish to give the material a unit name. We know that the material originally found at Kharga (Locus V, Refuf Pass, Caton-Thompson 1952) is beyond U-series dating range, *i.e.*, over 350,000–400,000 BP (Kleindienst *et al.* n.d.), as is "typical" African Upper Acheulean in southern Egypt (Schwarcz and Morawska 1993; Haynes *et al.* 1997).

We do have units, the Balat Unit in Dakhleh, and what I now informally designate as the KO10 unit and the Dharb el-Gaga unit in Kharga, which show design features in the production of bifaces that differ from the patterning usually seen in the African Upper Acheulean (Hawkins *et al.* 2001; Kleindienst *et al.* 2003). Caton-Thompson (1952) noted that in her original description of the material from locality KO10, as, in fact, did Schild at Dakhleh (Schild and Wendorf 1977). Although Kharga material is not identical to that from Dakhleh, many bifaces show working only of the point/bit, and of one or both laterals. This is related to, but not determined by, the selection of nodules or cobbles, mainly of cherts, rather than the production of large flakes for biface manufacture using mainly other raw materials. The forms produced are those noted by Schild (in Ronen and Weinstein-Evron 2000). In African typology, such forms are morphologically closer to "core axes" than to "handaxes" (Clark and Kleindienst 1974:95-98). However, at least some well-worked "handaxes" are included. The Dharb el-Gaga unit shows an interesting innovation in the selection of extremely thin chert nodules, which approximate "naturally-made" flakes, as the form of raw material used for manufacture of bifaces. Some are fully trimmed around the circumference; others are not. I have been unable to verify that extensive use of Levallois techniques occurred within these units at either Kharga or Dakhleh (Kleindienst 1999). Most occurrences are in geological context, which complicates matters: emplacement of the artifacts has been mainly or wholly by geological processes. Aggregates are found in gravels, in colluviums subjected to mass wasting and slope wash, in fossil artesian spring vents or on the surface of the desert veneer. They differ from the local MSA aggregates dominated by specialized reduction techniques, where large bifaces or heavy-duty tools occur, but are rare.

In calling Balat Unit-type bifaces "Late" or "Final Acheulean" (Schild and Wendorf 1977; Kleindienst 1985) in the Sahara, I think we have been overlooking traits which differentiate such units from "typical" African Upper Acheulean. The differences are seen especially in the different choices of raw materials, and different patterning in minimally working many or most of the larger pieces, although some pretty bifaces continued to be made. Similar change in patterning occurs in the shift to the Central and East African Sangoan Complex (Sheppard and Kleindienst 1996; Kleindienst 1999).

So far, we have found no technological "transition" between units that have little or no use of Levallois methods, and those that make extensive use of those and other more regulated techniques. What developmental stage the locally named units represent, then, remains a matter for discussion (e.g., Schild vs. Bosinski, above). Whether or not these units emphasizing large bifaces are regarded as terminal "Earlier Stone Age" does not change the local unit names. The important observation is that there were changes in what raw materials were selected, and in how those were treated after selection. Those are behavioral changes in preferences and design made by the ancestors. It is interesting that people may have hit upon similar designs in widely separated times and places, but calling those by the same name obscures that behavioral evidence. The relevant question is "why did that happen?"

In Kharga we know that predominant usage of Levallois and other specialized or more regulated techniques began at least 200,000 years ago, but we are still in the process of defining units and establishing time placements (Kleindienst et al. 1996, 2003; Churcher et al. 1999; Hawkins et al. 2001, 2002; Smith et al. 2004). Older, "larger-sized" generalized MSA units at Dakhleh (Kleindienst 1999) are now termed the Gifata Unit and the Teneida unit (Kleindienst 2003). I propose that Caton-Thompson's (1952) stratigraphically older, larger-sized "Lower Levalloisian" at Kharga be renamed the "Refuf Unit" (>220,000 ± 20,000 BP); her younger, medium-sized "Upper Levalloisian" might be renamed the "Mata'na Unit" (with associated dates of >125,000 ± 1,600 BP and >103,000 ± 15,000 BP). All of these could be grouped into the "Refuf Complex". I would choose the name "Refuf" because that was the key section for Caton-Thompson and Gardner in establishing their cultural stratigraphic units in the 1930s. Their work should have precedence in nomenclature, but some of their units need to be renamed using local geographic terms in order to simplify referencing and for inclusion of new occurrences.

Whether any other material from the Western Desert, or the Nile Valley, is sufficiently similar to be included within this local complex will require future investigation. The Combined Prehistoric Expedition has introduced potential confusion in reporting on southern Western Desert localities (Kleindienst 2001). They initially called all or much of the MSA there "Aterian", some "Mousterian", and then discarded "Aterian" except for surface occurrences, in favor of "Paléolithique moyen à denticulés et à pieces foliacées bifaciales" (Wendorf et al. 1990:389).

Then, they referred to "... three kinds of Middle Palaeolithic ... ": "Mousterian," "Aterian-related" and "Aterian" (Wendorf *et al.* 1993b:111). Finally, rather than defining "traditional" cultural units, "... we decided to emphasize those studies which would contribute to our understanding of Middle Palaeolithic behavior and its environmental context" (Wendorf *et al.* 1993a:4). Whether this is intended as informal usage of a developmental stage term is unclear.

Although the content definition of complexes is more problematic than that for Basic Units, complexes are not intended to extend over broad reaches of time and space for which evidence is lacking, or to be so generally defined as to include everything. For instance, researchers working in the Western Desert of Egypt (Schild 1998; Kleindienst 2000, 2003) and the Libyan Desert (Garcea 1998, 2001) have objected to the proposed "Nubian Complex" of Van Peer (1998; Van Peer and Vermeersch 2000). In 1998, Van Peer suggested that most North African material regarded as "Middle Stone Age" or "Middle Palaeolithic" or "Mousterian" should be designated as the "Nubian Complex", incorporating the long-accepted Aterian Complex. This term approximates "North African Middle Stone Age" in meaning, and ignores large areas for which evidence is lacking. This new complex was defined as having Levallois methods of specialized flake production, specifically the Nubian I and II methods for striking face preparation on cores (Vermeersch 2001). In 2000, the geographic extent for the "Nubian Complex" was apparently reduced to the southern portion of the Nile Valley in Egypt/northern Sudan and the surrounding Eastern Sahara, approximating "Middle Stone Age outside the central Nile Valley." Added to the definition were: bifacial foliates; retouched points, including "Mousterian" and "Nazlet Khater" types; truncated-facetted pieces; side scrapers; denticulates; and "... a good deal of Upper Palaeolithic types" (Van Peer and Vermeersch 2000:48-49). Schild noted the lack of Nubian methods in the southern Western Desert and Dakhleh. I have found little evidence for those methods in older generalized MSA units. Some usage occurs in the younger MSA units, and Nubian II is somewhat more common in Aterian Complex units at Kharga and Dakhleh, but Nubian cores are never the predominant method of Levallois flake production (Kleindienst 2003). Bifacial points are found in other African complexes (diagnostics in the Lupemban and the Stillbay), as are other retouched points. Truncated-facetting may be under-reported. Side scrapers and denticulated edges are ubiquitous. Why call any artifact class "Upper Palaeolithic" when it is found thousands of kilometers distant and tens of thousands of years earlier than a supposedly similar class in France?

A specific objection to subsuming the units of the Aterian Complex within a "Nubian Complex" is that the Aterian trait complex is not found in the central and northern Nile Valley in Egypt, nor in Nubia. Only one locality is known in a wadi draining into the main valley (Singleton and Close 1980; Kleindienst 2001). Aterian aggregates are sufficiently distinctive that one can recognize an occurrence before or without finding any diagnostic Aterian tangs (see Caton-Thompson 1946a). Further, there are still large areas of the flanking deserts, and even within the Nile Valley, for which we have no evidence. The term "Nubian Complex" masks variability rather than aiding communication about the clustering of typological and technological traits.

TRANSITIONS?

The interpretation of some unit contents as representing a "transition" is another problem: usually the word means a relatively rapid change in the condition or state of something. Given this book's title, the concept requires some note here. From an anthropological viewpoint, the underlying theme in the debate over relationships, and in the hindsight search for "transitions" between traditional developmental stages, seems still to be "us handsome clever moderns" vs. "them archaic, other, brutish" humans. The original view:

"In the whole racial history of western Europe there has never occurred so profound a change as that involving the disappearance of the Neaderthal race and the appearance of the Crô-Magnon race. It was the replacement of a race lower than any existing human type by one which ranks high among the existing types in capacity and intelligence. . . . the Upper Palaeolithic may almost be said to be the period of the Crô-Magnons . . . "(Osborn 1915:260).

The idea of looking for, or finding, supposed "transitions" embodies all the implications of all the assumptions about how change through time or space should, or could, occur as represented in cultural evidence. One implied assumption is that punctuated equilibrium characterizes changes in human behavior through time: *i.e.*, that the "Lower Palaeolithic" and the "Middle Palaeolithic" are relatively long-lived, static stages with a rapid "transition" in between. Such an assumption, however, ignores variability across time and space. The definitions of units, or of developmental stages, are our inventions. We draw the boundaries, so how can we expect there to have been "transitions"? Looking up the time scale rather than down, change is a continuum with no preordained direction. How change occurs differentially through time and space is the problem: studying that requires no system of nomenclature, but one for evidential units might aid comparative studies of their contents through reducing semantic confusions. Classifications are simplified, shorthand communication systems. Unless based upon demonstrably generic relationships between phenomena, classifications are inadequate as analytic tools.

The opposite assumption, that one should find continuity through time, previously characterized Pleistocene archaeology. For instance, at Kharga, Caton-Thompson and Gardner (Caton-Thompson 1946b, 1952), following Garrod at Tabun, thought they had found "transitions" between their "Acheulean" and "Levalloisian" units, termed "Acheulio-Levalloisian", and between their "Levalloisian" and "Khargan Industry" units, termed "Levalloiso-Khargan". Our geoarchaeological investigations indicate that in both cases, these "in between" units probably are multicomponent artifact aggregates created by geological redeposition (Hawkins *et al.* 2001; Kleindienst *et al.* n.d.).

To Africanists (*e.g.*, McBrearty and Brooks 2000), the search for the "Middle Paleolithic/Upper Paleolithic Transition" seems a search for evidential units that meet the assumptions for punctuated changes in developmental stages, whatever those stages are presumed to represent (Goring-Morris and Belfer-Cohen 2003). But, in terms of "human time" (minutes to days to years), if people rapidly change toolkits, or methods of manufacture, because something new has been invented or discovered that is viewed as "better" or "advantageous", what is a "transition"? What is it likely to look like? Why is it "transitional"? Do we see a "transition" between typewriters and computers? Although electronic communications may be transforming our lives for better or worse, in printing words, computers are just a new solution to an old problem. Typewriters were replaced and rapidly disappeared, although keyboard layout and the act of typing are retained. Is that in itself a major change in condition or state? Given our poor time control in the Pleistocene time ranges, could we expect to "see" any rapid transformations? Would evidence of intensified experimentation or increased variability be what we should look for when people are changing their minds about artifact production?

Moreover, what appears as "transition" in one area may be "continuity" in another. Copeland (2003:242-243) stated that:

I am assuming that the earliest dated manifestation of the Levantine Upper Palaeolithic [= developmental stage, or a "Super-Complex"?] is that of Boker Tachtit level 1 [= an Archaeological Occurrence] at *ca.* 46 thousand years ago . . . The Upper Palaeolithic start is defined as the magic moment when there was a sudden switch (or at least it appears to be sudden to us) to an Upper Palaeolithic toolkit made on blanks still produced by Mousterian techniques [= Complex]. . . . I will use the term Emiran [= a Basic Unit] when referring to the industry of this earliest Upper Palaeolithic phase [= subdivision of a developmental stage?].

Although Emiran is not defined only by the diagnostic Emireh point, this basally and ventrally thinned, small pointed flake was noted as different, and named in the Levant (Volkman and Kaufman 1983). This has then been taken as its locus of origin. At Sodmein Cave, in the Egyptian Eastern Desert:

Middle Palaeolithic level 1 (MP 1) [= Archaeological Occurrence]. Two Emireh points are present: one is complete and absolutely typical, the other is a distal fragment. Burins on blades occur as well. The cores that are present are all for blade production. A few Levallois endproducts are present. The presence of Emireh points in particular points to southwestern Asian contacts. Such points have never been found in African contexts up to now. Though the level is called Middle Palaeolithic here, it may in fact contain a transitional industry between the Middle and Upper Palaeolithic [= developmental stages], of the kind found at Boker Tachtit in the Negev (Van Peer *et al.* 1996:153).

Although not yet fully reported, the Sodmein cave sequence can as easily be interpreted to indicate that the shift from mainly Levallois-based lithic production in "Middle Palaeolithic level 5 (MP 5)" to blade production methods in "Upper Palaeolithic level 2 (UP 2)" covered a time span of some 90,000 years (Van Peer *et al.* 1996:153-154; Mercier *et al.* 1999). As Caton-Thompson noted long ago, in the Western Desert some blade production occurs throughout the MSA together with the other more specialized or regulated lithic production methods (Kleindienst 2003). As yet, we have no evidence for a mainly blade-based technology until the early Holocene.

In fact, the trait of basal thinning (unifacial on either flake face, or bifacial), worked on large or small pointed flakes, occurs in many African units and complexes dating from the late Middle to early Late Pleistocene. In the Western Desert, small retouched pointed flakes have been termed "Tabalbalat points" (Caton-Thompson 1946a), following Garrod and Bate (1937), who distinguished them from Emireh points (*cf.* discussion in Hawkins 2001:327–330). Of relevance here is that Caton-Thompson (1952) describes such points in her "Upper Levalloisian" (Mata'na Unit) at Kharga Oasis now dated by uranium series to ≥100,000 BP. This typo-technological trait, then, is older in the Eastern Sahara than in the Levant. It continues to occur in the succeeding Aterian Complex units at Dakhleh and Kharga, and across the Sahara (Hawkins and Kleindienst 2000) (note Aterian dating inserted by editors, not the authors [Hawkins 2001]). The Aterian Complex is now known to be beyond ^{14}C dating range in the Maghreb (Wrinn and Rink 2003), and probably dates at least 60,000 to 90,000 years BP in the Libyan Sahara (Cremaschi *et al.* 1998, 2000). As yet we have no chronometric dates for Aterian in the Western Desert (*contra* McBrearty and Brooks 2000), although it can be placed as younger than *ca.* 100,000 and older than *ca.* 40,000 years ago. Other traits such as variability in the Levallois core reduction patterns also indicate continuity of reduction methods in the Western Desert oases. In fact, there are units with Levallois methods of reduction that, based upon morphology, condition, and context, post-date the Aterian Complex (Wiseman 1999, 2001). The trait of ventral basal thinning has a long, continuous record in the Eastern Sahara. If this trait was transmitted to the Levant rather than independently invented there, possibly involving some useful innovation like a different method of hafting or just the idea of such, it came "out of Africa" (*cf.* Marks [2003] , who also proposes strictly technologically-defined Basic Units). How is that "transitional"?

CONCLUSION

The scheme of nomenclature outlined is precise in referring only to cultural content, and above all, it is flexible. Perhaps it is time that people take another look at it? A practice of formally describing (defining) cultural stratigraphic units tends to make one consider what one is doing more carefully. What is the minimal contextual unit? Why? What precisely is the evidence for similarity or dissimilarity that predicates inclusion of occurrences within the same Basic Unit, or in different units? What are the built-in assumptions? After definition, only many analytic approaches applied to the cultural contents can inform us about behavior of the "people", or challenge the original definitions. The issue is better communication between archaeologists regarding the observational and analytical evidence, which can then facilitate better behavioral interpretations. Nomenclature should facilitate communication, not impede it. Names do matter.

ACKNOWLEDGEMENTS

Long-term prehistoric research by members of the Dakhleh Oasis Project in Dakhleh and Kharga Oases, beginning in 1978 (and after 2000, also of the Kharga Oasis Prehistoric Project) was supported by: the Social Sciences and Humanities Research Council of Canada, the University of Toronto, the University of Calgary, and private donors; since 1991, by the National Geographic Society; and most recently by the Dakhleh Trust.

REFERENCES CITED

Bishop W.W. and J.D. Clark (Eds.) 1967. *Background to Evolution in Africa.* Chicago: University of Chicago Press.

Caton-Thompson G. 1946a. The Aterian Industry: its place and significance in the Palaeolithic world. *Journal of the Royal Anthropological Institute* LXXVI: 87–130.

Caton-Thompson G. 1946b. The Levalloisian Industries of Egypt. *Proceedings of the Prehistoric Society* n.s. XII: 57–120.

Caton-Thompson G. 1952. *Kharga Oasis in Prehistory.* London: Athlone Press.

Churcher C.S., M.R. Kleindienst and H.P. Schwarcz 1999. Faunal remains from a Middle Pleistocene lacustrine marl in Dakhleh Oasis, Egypt: palaeoenvironmental reconstructions. *Palaeogeoraphy, Palaeoclimatology, Palaeoecology* 154: 301–312.

Clark G.A. 2002. Neandertal archaeology–implications for our origins. *American Anthropologist* 104: 50–67.

Clark J.D., G.H. Cole, G.L. Isaac and M.R. Kleindienst 1966. Precision and definition in African archaeology. *South African Archaeological Bulletin* XXI: 114–121.

Clark J.D. and M.R. Kleindienst 1974. The Stone Age cultural sequence: terminology, typology and raw material. In J.D. Clark (Ed.), *Kalambo Falls Prehistoric Site,* pp. 71–106. Cambridge: Cambridge University Press.

Clarke D.L. 1968. *Analytical Archaeology.* London: Methuen & Company Ltd.

Copeland L. 2003. The Levantine Upper Palaeolithic: a commentary on contributions to the Philadelphia Symposium. In A.N. Goring-Morris and A. Belfer-Cohen (Eds.), *More than Meets the Eye: Studies on Upper Palaeolithic Diversity in the Near East,* pp. 242–248. Oxford: Oxbow Books.

Cremaschi M., S. Di Lernia and E.A.A. Garcea 1998. Some insights on the Aterian in the Libyan Sahara: chronology, environment and archaeology. *African Archaeological Review* 15: 261–286.

Cremaschi M., S. Di Lernia and E.A.A. Garcea 2000. First chronological indications on the Aterian in the Libyan Sahara. In L. Krzyzaniak, K. Kroeper and M. Kobusiewicz M. (Eds.), *Recent Research into the Stone Age of Northeastern Africa,* pp. 229–237. Poznan: Poznan Archaeological Museum.

Garcea E.A.A. 1998. Comment on Van Peer, The Nile Corridor and the Out-of-Africa model. *Current Anthropology* 39 (Supplement): S131–132.

Garcea E.A.A. 2001. A reconsideration of the Middle Palaeolithic/Middle Stone Age in northern Africa after the evidence from the Libyan Sahara. In E.A.A. Garcea (Ed.), *Uan Tabu in the Settlement History of the Libyan Sahara,* pp. 25–49. Firenze: All'Insignia del Giglio.

Garrod D.A.E. and D.M.A. Bate 1937. *The Stone Age of Mount Carmel: Excavations at the Wady el-Mughara vol. 1.* Oxford: Claredon Press.

Goring-Morris A.N. and A. Belfer-Cohen (Eds.) 2003. *More than Meets the Eye: Studies on Upper Palaeolithic Diversity in the Near East.* Oxford: Oxbow Books.

Hawkins A.L. 2001. *Getting a Handle on Tangs: The Aterian of the Western Desert of Egypt.* Ph.D. Dissertation, University of Toronto.

Hawkins A.L. and M.R. Kleindienst 2000. The Aterian. In P.N. Peregrine and M. Ember (Eds.), *Encyclopedia of Prehistory,* pp. 23–45. New York: Kluwer Academic/Plenum Publishers.

Hawkins A.L., J.R. Smith, R. Giegengack, M.M.A. McDonald, M.R. Kleindienst, H.P. Schwarcz, C.S. Churcher, M.F. Wiseman and K. Nicoll 2001. New research on the prehistory of the Escarpment in Kharga Oasis, Egypt. *Nyame Akuma* 55: 8–14.

Hawkins A.L., J.R. Smith, R. Giegengack, H.P. Schwarcz, M.R. Kleindienst and M.F. Wiseman (2002). Middle Stone Age adaptations and environments in Kharga Oasis, Western Desert Egypt. *Nyame Akuma* 57: 54–55.

Haynes C.V., T.A. Maxwell, A. El Hawary, K.A. Nicoll and S. Stokes 1997. An Acheulean site near Bir Kiseiba in the Darb el Arba'in Desert, Egypt. *Geoarchaeology* 12: 819–832.

Hill C.L. 2001. Geologic contexts of the Acheulean (Middle Pleistocene) in the Eastern Sahara. *Geoarchaeology* 15: 55–94.

Isaac G.L. 1977. *Olorgesailie*. Chicago: University of Chicago Press.

Isaac G.L. and B. Isaac (Eds.) 1997. *Koobi Fora Research Project*. Oxford: Clarendon Press.

Kleindienst M.R. 1967. Questions of terminology in regard to the study of Stone Age industries in eastern Africa: "Cultural stratigraphic units". In W.W. Bishop and J.D. Clark (Eds.), *Background to Evolution in Africa*, pp. 821–859. Chicago: University of Chicago Press.

Kleindienst M.R. 1985. Dakhleh Oasis Project. Pleistocene archaeology. Report on the 1986 season. *Journal of the Society for the Study of Egyptian Antiquities* XV: 136–137.

Kleindienst M.R. 1999. Pleistocene archaeology and geoarchaeology: a status report. In C.S. Churcher and A.J. Mills (Eds.), *Reports from the Survey of Dakhleh Oasis, Western Desert of Egypt, 1977–1987*, pp. 83–108. Oxford: Oxbow Books.

Kleindienst M.R. 2000. On the Nile Corridor and the Out-of-Africa model. *Current Anthropology* 41: 107–109.

Kleindienst M.R. 2001. What is the Aterian? The view from Dakhleh Oasis, and the Western Desert, Egypt. In C.A. Marlow and A.J. Mills (Eds.), *The Oasis Papers I: Proceedings of the First International Symposium of the Dakhleh Oasis Project*, pp. 1–14. Oxford: Oxbow Books.

Kleindienst M.R. 2003. Strategies for studying Pleistocene archaeology based upon surface evidence: first characterisation of an older Middle Stone Age unit, Dakhleh Oasis, Egypt. In G.E. Bowen (Ed.), *The Oasis Papers III: Proceedings of the Third International Conference of the Dakhleh Oasis Project*, pp. 1–42. Oxford: Oxbow Books.

Kleindienst M.R., M.M.A. McDonald and C.S. Churcher 2003. Kharga Oasis Prehistoric Project: 2002 field season. *Nyame Akuma* 59: 17–25.

Kleindienst M.R., H.P. Schwarcz, K. Nicoll, C.S. Churcher, J. Frizano, R.W. Giegengack and M.F. Wiseman 1996. Pleistocene geochronology and palaeoclimates at Dakhleh and Kharga Oases, Western Desert, Egypt, based upon uranium-thorium determinations from spring-laid tufas. Revised abstract. *Nyame Akuma* 46: 96.

Kleindienst M.R., H.P. Schwarcz, K. Nicoll, C.S. Churcher, J. Frizano, R.W. Giegengack and M.F. Wiseman n.d. Water in the desert: first report on uranium-series dating of Caton-Thompson's and Gardner's "classic" Pleistocene sequence at Refuf Pass, Kharga Oasis. In M.F. Wiseman (Ed.), *The Oasis Papers II: Proceedings of the Second International Symposium of the Dakhleh Oasis Project*, submitted. Oxford: Oxbow Books.

Kosso P. 2001. *Knowing the Past: Philosophical Issues of History and Archaeology*. Amherst, NY: Humanity Books.

Marks A.E. 2003. Reflections on Levantine Upper Palaeolithic studies: past and present. In A.N. Goring-Morris and A. Belfer-Cohen (Eds.), *More than Meets the Eye: Studies on Upper Palaeolithic Diversity in the Near East*, pp. 265–273. Oxford: Oxbow Books.

McBrearty S. and A.S. Brooks 2000. The revolution that wasn't: a new interpretation of the origin of modern human behaviour. *Journal of Human Evolution* 39: 453–563.

Mercier, N., H. Valladas, L. Froget, J.-L. Joron, P.M. Vermeersch, P. Van Peer and J. Moeyersons 1999. Thermoluminescence dating of a Middle Palaeolithic occupation at Sodmein Cave, Red Sea Mountains (Egypt). *Journal of Archaeological Science* 26: 1339–1345.

Osborn H.F. 1915. *Men of the Old Stone Age*. New York: Charles Scribner's Sons.

Ronen A. and M. Weinstein-Evron (Eds.) 2000. *Toward Modern Humans. The Yabrudian and Micoquian, 400–50 k Years Ago*. Oxford: Archaeopress.

Schild R. 1998. Comment on Van Peer, "The Nile Corridor and the Out-of-Africa model". *Current Anthropology* 39 (Supplement): S134–S135.

Schild R. and F. Wendorf 1977. *The Prehistory of the Dakhla Oasis and Adjacent Desert*. Warsaw: Polish Academy of Sciences.

Schwarcz H. and L. Morawska 1993. Uranium-series dating of carbonates from Bir Tarfawi and Bir Sahara East. In F. Wendorf, R. Schild, R. and A.E. Close (Eds.), *Egypt During the Last Interglacial. The Middle Paleolithic of Bir Tarfawi and Bir Sahara East*, pp. 205–217. New York: Plenum Press.

Sheppard P.J. and M.R. Kleindienst 1996. Technological change in the Earlier and Middle Stone Age of Kalambo Falls. *African Archaeological Review* 13: 171–196.

Siiriäinen A. 1999. Archaeological evidence for dating the sediment in a playa in Farafra, Western Desert of Egypt. In J. Donner (Ed.), *Studies of Playas in the Western Desert of Egypt,* pp. 113–146. Helsinki: Suomalainen Tiedeakatemia.

Singleton W.L. and A.E. Close 1980. Report on site E-78-11. In F. Wendorf and R. Schild (Eds.), *Loaves and Fishes: The Prehistory of Wadi Kubbaniya,* pp. 229–237. Dallas: SMU Press.

Smith, J., R. Giegengack, H.P. Schwarcz, M.M.A. McDonald, M.R. Kleindienst, A.L. Hawkins and C.S. Churcher 2004. Reconstructing Pleistocene pluvial environments and occupation through the stratigraphy and geochronology of fossil-spring tufas, Kharga Oasis, Egypt. *Geoarchaeology* 19: 407–439.

Van Peer P. 1998. The Nile Corridor and the Out-of-Africa model. An examination of the archaeological record. *Current Anthropology* 39 (Supplement): S115–S140.

Van Peer P. and P.M. Vermeersch 2000. The Nubian complex and the dispersal of modern humans in North Africa. In L. Krzyzaniak, K. Kroeper and M. Kobusiewicz (Eds.), *Recent Research into the Stone Age of Northeastern Africa,* pp. 47–60., Poznan: Poznan Archaeological Museum.

Van Peer, P., P.M. Vermeersch, J. Moeyersons and W. van Neer 1996. Palaeolithic sequence of Sodmein Cave, Red Sea Mountains, Egypt. In G. Pwiti and R. Soper (Eds.), *Aspects of African Archaeology. Papers from the 10th Congress of the Pan African Association for Prehistory and Related Studies,* pp. 149–156. Harare: University of Zimbabwe Publications.

Vermeersch P.M. 2001. "Out of Africa" from an Egyptian point of view. *Quaternary International* 75: 103–112.

Volkman P.W. and D. Kaufman 1983. A reassessment of the Emireh point as a possible type fossil for the technological shift from the Middle to the Upper Palaeolithic in the Levant. In E. Trinkaus (Ed.), *The Mousterian Legacy* (BAR International Series 164), pp. 35–52. Oxford: BAR.

Wendorf F., A.E. Close, R. Schild, A. Gautier, H.P. Schwarcz, G.H. Miller, K. Kowalski, H. Krolik, A. Bluszcz, D. Robins and R. Grün 1990. Le dernier interglaciaire dans le Sahara oriental. *L'Anthropologie* 94: 361–391.

Wendorf F. and R. Schild, (Eds.) (1980). *Prehistory of the Eastern Sahara.* Academic Press, New York.

Wendorf F., R. Schild and A.E. Close 1993a. Introduction. In F. Wendorf, R. Schild and A.E. Close (Eds.), *Egypt during the Last Interglacial. The Middle Paleolithic of Bir Tarfawi and Bir Sahara East,* pp. 1–7. New York: Plenum Press.

Wendorf F., R. Schild and A.E. Close 1993b. Middle Palaeolithic occupations at Bir Tarfawi and Bir Sahara East, Western Desert of Egypt. In L. Krzyzaniak, M. Kobusiewicz and J. Alexander (Eds.), *Environmental Change and Human Culture in the Nile Basin and Northern Africa until the Second Millenium BC,* pp. 103–111. Poznan: Poznan Archaeological Museum.

Wiseman M.F. 1999. Late Pleistocene prehistory in Dakhleh Oasis. In C.S. Churcher and A.J. Mills (Eds.), *Reports from the Survey of the Dakhleh Oasis, Western Desert of Egypt, 1977–1987,* pp. 109–115. Oxford: Oxbow Books.

Wiseman M.F. 2001. Problems in the prehistory of the late Upper Pleistocene of the Dakhleh Oasis. In C.A. Marlow and A.J. Mills (Eds.), *The Oasis Papers I: Proceedings of the First International Symposium of the Dakhleh Oasis Project,* pp. 15–25. Oxford: Oxbow Books.

Wrinn P.J. and W.J. Rink 2003. ESR dating of tooth enamel from Aterian levels at Mugharet el'Aliya (Tangier, Morocco). *Journal of Archaeological Science* 30: 123–133.

Chapter *3*

Observations on Systematics in Paleolithic Archaeology

Geoffrey A. Clark

Department of Anthropology, Arizona State University, Tempe AZ, 85287-2402; gaclark@asu.edu

Julien Riel-Salvatore

Department of Anthropology, Arizona State University, Tempe, AZ, 85287-2402; julienrs@asu.edu

ABSTRACT

The intellectual traditions that frame Paleolithic research in Europe and the United States are reviewed, and the European Middle Paleolithic archaeological record is examined for patterns that contradict the "textbook generalizations" embodied in Paul Mellars' "human revolution". The fact that different typologies are used to describe the Middle and Upper Paleolithic respectively emphasizes differences between them (especially if typology "trumps" any other systematic investigation of pattern), effectively precluding the perception of continuity in retouched stone tool form over the Middle-to-Upper Paleolithic transition. The proliferation of "transition industries" over the past 20 years has made the picture much more complicated than it was before *ca.* 1990, and the identification of *ca.* 20 Mousterian "facies" since 1985 strongly suggests that the west Eurasian Mousterian is more complex and variable than previously thought. We conclude that there is much under-acknowledged formal convergence in the kinds and frequencies of chipped stone artifacts, that patterns in lithic industries are mostly determined by raw material package size, quality and forager mobility, that changes in lithic technology are only "historical" at the macroscale (*i.e.*, over evolutionary time), and that formal convergence likely overrides any "cultural" component supposedly present in the form of retouched stone tools.

INTRODUCTION

Along with some others who approach the study of the Paleolithic from a broadly defined ecological perspective (*e.g.*, Hayden 1993; Stiner 1994; Kuhn 1995; Straus 2003; see Winterhalder and Smith 2002 for an overview), we believe there are major differences in the conceptual frameworks that guide this research, dependent, to a certain extent, on the intellectual traditions in which the archaeologists involved have received their formal training (*e.g.*, Bar-Yosef 1991; Clark 1993, 2002b; see papers in Straus 2002). These differences are thrown into sharp relief by different construals of the nature of the analytical units used in Eurasia to divide up the Paleolithic in time and space, and what those units are supposed to mean, or represent, in behavioral terms (*e.g.*, Neeley and Barton 1994; Goring-Morris 1996). Empirical generalizations about pattern within and across these units have been increasingly subjected to critical scrutiny in recent years, as more research is undertaken outside the historically important Franco-Cantabrian "heartland", where many of the units were first defined (*e.g.*, Marks and Chabai 1998; Chabai and Monigal 1999; Chabai *et al.* 2004; Brantingham *et al.* 2004).

Perhaps better than any other contentious modern human origins issue, debate about the nature of the Middle-to-Upper Paleolithic transition in Europe, as embodied in Paul Mellars' "human revolution" (*e.g.*, 1989, 1996), brings these different perspectives into sharp focus. Mellars thinks the Middle-to-Upper Paleolithic transition in Europe is an important divide in prehistory, that behavioral and anatomical modernity coincide there, and that blade and microlithic technologies, bone tools, range extension, hunting of prime-aged adult ungulates, the use of aquatic resources, long-distance exchange and procurement of raw materials, evidence for symbolic behavior manifest in beads, pigments and "art", retouched stone artifacts that exhibit "imposed form" and standardized shapes, and "well-organized" campsites all appear together as a "package" manifest archaeologically in the Aurignacian after 40,000 years BP. He believes the Aurignacian to be manufactured exclusively by anatomically modern humans (*H. sapiens,* or *H. sapiens sapiens*) originally derived from Africa, whereas local Neandertals (*H. heidelbergensis* or *H. neandertalensis*) made the preceding Mousterian and at least some of the transitional industries.

Africanists McBrearty and Brooks (2000) have taken issue with both the pattern implied by Mellars' views of the transition, and the eurocentric bias that permeates it. They suggest that the archaeological criteria invoked in support of behavioral modernity in Europe appear in Africa over a long interval during the Middle Stone Age (MSA), tens of thousands of years earlier than they do in Europe, and that these indicators of behavioral modernity do not occur together as a "package" (as they are often argued to do in Europe [*e.g.*, Tattersall 1998]), but rather as part of a continent-wide temporal and spatial mosaic that extends well back into the Middle Pleistocene. The authors contend that their pattern search best supports a gradual accumulation of the material indicators of behavioral modernity in Africa and their subsequent export to other regions of the Old World after *ca.* 60,000 years ago, probably through the Levantine corridor. The best evidence for *accelerated* change, however, coincides with the Middle-Later Stone Age boundary, after *ca.* 50,000 years ago. It is attributed to the combined effects of environmental deterioration, accelerated rates of population growth (in some areas), and the appearance of novel risk management strategies that would have tended to buffer subsistence uncertainty, improve nutrition, and reduce infant mortality, thus setting in motion a Flannery-like positive feedback system (*e.g.*, Flannery 1969) that had nothing whatever to do with the emergence of behavioral modernity *per se*. Still unexamined are (1) whether or not Mellars' criteria actually indicate "modern behavior", however defined (Clark 1999); (2) whether the "package" was exported *in toto* from Africa, or whether it developed to some extent autochthonously in Europe (Clark 1997, 2002a), and (3) what are the effects that the vastly different resolution in the archaeological records of the two areas might have had on perceptions of pattern (Henshilwood and Marean 2003).

We suggest that these two very different interpretations of pattern are bound up in different conceptions of the analytical units used by Mellars, on the one hand, and by McBrearty and Brooks, on the other, to assign meaning to differences and similarities among artifact assemblages. To Mellars, pattern in the Paleolithic is best (although certainly not exclusively) apprehended by artifact typology, and is interpreted as the tangible remains of technological and/or typological traditions held in common by identity-conscious groups of people and transmitted from one generation to the next through a process of social learning. The intellectual mandate for this approach is French, and ultimately comes from André Leroi-Gourhan's *Le Geste et la Parole* (1964–5), which sought to invest the study of lithic technology with social agency. Loosely based on Marcel Mauss' *Les Techniques du Corps* (1936), which established that technology was first and foremost a social process, Leroi-Gourhan proposed a unified approach to the study of the Paleolithic by uniting technology with social process, arguing that the long-term trajectory of social change can be examined by studying the evolution of technology, the latter accessible through the archaeological record.

To McBrearty and Brooks, pattern in the past is best apprehended by human behavioral ecology (HBE), a multifaceted approach perhaps best described as the marriage of cultural ecology based in ethnography (*e.g.*, Steward 1936) with "core" evolutionary principles like adaptation, selection and fitness. Often highly quantified, HBE uses ethnographic data to generate and test predictive models about human behavior and the environments in which they evolved by comparing observables against values generated by behavior optimizing theories, most of which have to do with subsistence (*e.g.*, linear programming, diet-breadth, patch-choice, or combinations thereof) (Winterhalder and Smith 2000). Underpinned by a neo-Darwinian conceptual framework, and expressed as formal mathematical models, patterns observed ethnographically or inferred archaeologically can be adjusted, so far as their test implications are concerned, by taking into account a small number of environmental constants (*e.g.*, effective temperature, precipitation) that change with latitude and elevation, and constants that appear to be universal among foragers (*e.g.*, mobility, technological portability). Two different approaches – two different perceptions of pattern – two different explanations for pattern.

In keeping with the aims of this volume, we first discuss differences between the Middle and Upper Paleolithic analytical units as they are defined by European typological systematics, the filter or lens through which many prehistorians perceive pattern. We submit that the typologies commonly used on either side of the transition are different, thus exaggerating differences that would appear clinal and/or mosaic if other monitors of human adaptation are taken into account (*i.e.*, if an ecological approach were adopted). We follow this with some brief observations on pattern similarities at two *Lower* Paleolithic sites, Gesher Benot Ya'aqov in northern Israel (Goren-Inbar *et al.* 2000), and an industry with large, bifacially worked cutting tools in south China's Bose Basin (Hou *et al.* 2000). The intent here is to underscore conceptual problems with the logic of inference implicit in typological systematics, and with historicity in the explanation of pattern. We conclude our essay with some observations on aspects of the Eurasian Middle Paleolithic archaeological record that appear to contradict the impression of stasis and uniformity often associated with that analytical unit. The pattern search shows that the Middle Paleolithic is, at best, a "fuzzy set" that overlaps extensively in time and space with the Lower Paleolithic and with the early Upper Paleolithic, and that it contains most of the "classic" Upper Paleolithic marker types and technologies, as well as evidence for symbolism, organic technologies and "well-organized" campsites. We suggest that the Middle Paleolithic can no longer be viewed as the changeless, monolithic entity described in many textbooks, and conclude that a mosaic of different human adaptations is as characteristic of the Middle Paleolithic as it is of the Upper Paleolithic.

TYPOLOGICAL SYSTEMATICS IN PALEOLITHIC ARCHAEOLOGY

It would not be inaccurate to assert that the European approach to Paleolithic archaeology is based to a very considerable extent upon a typological systematics that emphasizes retouched tools. Other factors are, of course, taken into account (especially technology), but typology remains the bedrock upon which inference rests (see discussion in Riel-Salvatore and Clark 2001). The cultural transition, therefore, is usually demarcated by changes in the retouched tool components of archaeological assemblages. Middle Paleolithic industries are made on flake blanks and are dominated by side-scrapers, notches and denticulates; Upper Paleolithic industries are blade- and bladelet-based and have substantial numbers of end-scrapers, burins, and a higher incidence of more formalized tools. The rationale and justification for doing this are seldom made explicit, but lurking just beneath the surface is the tacit assumption that the stone tools represent the remains of quasi-historical, stylistic microtraditions, transmitted from one generation to the next through the medium of culture. Since retouch modes, edge configurations and overall shape are equated with social learning, it is assumed that the time/space distributions of stone tools are, to a degree, "history-like"—congruent with the boundaries of identity-conscious social units of some kind. This kind of reasoning is then extended to modes in the overall forms and frequencies of the artifacts themselves. Problems with the enormous spatial extent and temporal persistence of such hypothetical social units have been largely ignored.

Views of the Middle-to-Upper Paleolithic Transition

Keeping in mind that the Paleolithic subdivisions themselves were created and defined by prehistorians, changes in the character of retouched stone tools over the European Middle-to-Upper Paleolithic transition have been interpreted in five contrastive ways. Some workers see the transition as an *in situ* phenomenon everywhere, with clear evidence for lithic continuity between late Middle and early Upper Paleolithic assemblages (*e.g.*, Clark 1997). Others argue that certain early Upper Paleolithic industries are "adaptive responses" by Neandertals to the arrival of modern humans producing Aurignacian industries (*e.g.*, Mellars 1996). While it is by no means clear what an "adaptive response" is, this implies that Neandertals modified existing Mousterian technologies *because* of contact with moderns to produce assemblages with mixed "Middle" and "Upper" Paleolithic characteristics. The Châtelperronian is the quintessential example. A third point of view is that no such intermediate industries exist and, when contemporaneous late Middle and early Upper Paleolithic assemblages are present in the same site or region, the early Upper Paleolithic (especially the Aurignacian) must therefore be intrusive (many authors, *e.g.*, Bietti 1997; Rigaud 1997). This scenario implies that the authorship of late Middle and early Upper Paleolithic industries is known with certainty and can be generalized, and that archaic and modern groups coexisted for millennia but did not interact with one another to any significant extent. Sometimes called "the indigenist model" (Harrold and Otte 2001), a fourth perspective is that typologically discrete Châtelperronian and Aurignacian industries are "hominin-specific," and that Neandertals making Châtelperronian artifacts underwent a separate and earlier Middle-to-Upper Paleolithic transition, independent of but fully equivalent to that involving moderns and the Aurignacian (*e.g.*, Zilhão and d'Errico 1999, but *cf.* Mellars 2000). Finally, some have remarked on the dozen or so "transitional" industries now known from eastern and central Europe (see papers in Zilhão and d'Errico 2003). Of mostly unknown authorship, these industries exhibit assemblage characteristics typical of neither the Middle nor the Upper Paleolithic as defined in the west. In some respects the opposite of the "indigenist" model, these scenarios tend to uncouple assemblage types from hominin types, except in respect of the Aurignacian (Kozlowski 2000), and interpose a separate "transition interval" between the Middle and Upper Paleolithic.

Increased Variation at the Macroscale

Leaving aside preconceptions about authorship which cannot fail to influence the meaning assigned to pattern, and restricting the discussion to the retouched tool components of European Middle and Upper Paleolithic industries, it has become evident in recent years that there is much more formal continuity across the transition than has generally been recognized. The proliferation of

Mousterian variants (Howell 1998, 1999) and transitional industries (Zilhão and d'Errico 2003), and the recognition that many Eurasian assemblages cannot be accommodated by models developed in the West (see papers in Brantingham *et al.* 2004; Chabai *et al.* 2004) offer compelling support for this assertion. These different perceptions of pattern are filtered by, and are inextricably bound up with the classifications used to compare Middle and Upper Paleolithic retouched stone tool inventories, and this is particularly true where typology "trumps" any other systematic investigation of pattern (*e.g.*, technology, raw material, archaeofaunal analysis, taphonomic studies). As has often been remarked, quite distinct and incompatible typological systems are used to characterize these assemblages (see Riel-Salvatore and Barton 2004). This affects perceptions of pattern and of what pattern might mean in behavioral terms. We focus on the Upper Paleolithic typology here (de Sonneville-Bordes and Perrot 1954, 1955, 1956). Although contested with some success by Mellars (1996: 95–140), there is a fairly broad consensus that the form of Middle Paleolithic retouched stone artifacts made on flakes (esp. sidescrapers, notches, denticulates, backed pieces) is determined largely by functional contingencies, including intended use, prehension or hafting, the initial form of the blank, and the degree to which the tool has been reworked (Bisson 2000), and that the 17 Bordesian scraper types are analytical constructs rather than the material consequences of templates held in the minds of long-dead Neandertals (Dibble 1987, 1995). To the best of our knowledge, however, this interpretation has never been applied to Middle Paleolithic bifacial tools (*i.e.*, *blattspitzen,* Mousterian of Acheulean Tradition handaxes, Micoquian bifaces) which appear to exhibit the formal constraints implied by mental templates. Also unexamined is whether or not these same contingencies might apply, and with equal cogency, to the Upper Paleolithic typology.

The Upper Paleolithic Typology

As anyone who has used it recognizes very quickly, Upper Paleolithic typological variation by no means consistently displays a high degree of formal standardization, nor do the types themselves segregate neatly and unambiguously (*e.g.*, Barton 1991; Marks *et al.* 2001). In fact, as Sackett (1988: 418) has pointed out, "the amount of intergradation between types is sometimes so great as to frustrate even the most experienced typologist." which suggests that the types (and perhaps even the type groups) might represent no more than modal points along a continuum of morphological variation, the modes being determined by recurrent combinations of raw material attributes and the situational variables noted above.

A second point is that there are good reasons to think that *all* Paleolithic stone tools were subjected to varying amounts of modification over the course of their use-lives by continual use, breakage, subsequent rejuvenation and/or intentional reworking (Riel-Salvatore and Barton 2004). This means that a continuum of formal transformation is likely the rule, rather than the exception. It implies that there might not be much design specificity in either the Middle or the Upper Paleolithic, and that Dibble's arguments about formal convergence in Mousterian side-scrapers could apply with equal cogency to most of the Upper Paleolithic tool types, including the *fossiles directeurs.*

Finally, most Upper Paleolithic sites contain relatively few of the 92 types recognized in a conventional type-list (de Sonneville-Bordes and Perrot 1954, 1955, 1956) suggesting that what are perceived by archaeologists to be discrete types more often than not simply represent successive stages in the modification of a single generalized tool and/or minor alterations in form primarily determined by variations in blank morphology (Sackett 1988, 1991, 1997). The implication is that many (perhaps most) Upper Paleolithic retouched tool inventories are not more complex than their Middle Paleolithic counterparts, nor do they conform to more rigorous design specifications, nor are they more functionally specific— considerations that all but erase the supposed cognitive differences between the hominins that produced them.

Rather than taking their adequacy for granted, we need to directly confront the possibility that the existing systematics might not be up to the task of answering many questions deemed important in Paleolithic research, indeed that they might constitute obstacles to their resolution (Freeman 1994; Clark 2002a). We suggest that we don't even know what the conventional archaeological analytical units are, or mean, or represent, in behavioral terms (and see Kleindeinst this volume). It is a facile assumption of those who have faith in the adequacy of the existing systematics that we are discovering, via retouched stone artifact typology, something very like the remains of identity-conscious social units analogous to the tribes, peoples, and nations of history. To many European workers, Paleolithic archaeology is essentially culture history projected back into the Pleistocene, and patterns are typically explained post-hoc by invoking processes analogous to those operating in recent historical contexts. The whole approach is predicated on (1) the existence of tool-making "traditions" manifest in artifact form that are detectable over hundreds of thousands (even millions) of square kilometers; (2) the idea that such "traditions" persisted unchanged and intact over tens (or, in the case of the Lower Paleolithic, hundreds) of millennia; and, (3) the conviction that they are detectable at points in space separated by thousands of kilometers and tens of thousands of years of time (*e.g.*, Hou *et al.* 2000, Goren-Inbar *et al.* 2000).

Conflicts between Culture History and Behavioral Ecology

Clark has argued at length (*e.g.*, 1993, 1997, 1999; 2002a, 2002b) that this culture historical paradigm, while internally consistent in respect of its logic of inference, cannot be reconciled with the ecological perspectives typical of many American workers, and (1) that most of the Paleolithic "index fossil" tool types are ubiquitous (or nearly so), at least in western Eurasia, and carry little temporal and probably no social information whatsoever; (2) that there is only a minimal and generalized learned behavioral component to chipped stone artifact form; (3) that there are no universal correlations between particular kinds of hominins and particular kinds of artifact assemblages; (4) that there is much formal convergence in the (few) processes by which humans chip stone; (5) that this formal convergence is conditioned by recurrent contextual factors—technology, raw material quality, size, distribution in the landscape, *etc.*—especially as affected by mobility; and (6) that it almost certainly overrides any hypothetical "cultural" component. In other words, it is possible to explain pattern similarities in Paleolithic archaeological assemblages without recourse to typology-based tool-making traditions, nor to the historicist preconceptions, biases and assumptions upon which they are based (see Clark 2002a for an extended discussion). To illustrate some of the implications of formal convergence, we examine proposed explanations for pattern similarities at two Middle Pleistocene open sites in Israel and China, both long pre-dating the Middle-to-Upper Paleolithic transition, both excavated according to "modern" standards.

FORMAL CONVERGENCE IN LOWER PALEOLITHIC TECHNOLOGIES

The Acheulean at Gesher Benot Ya'aqov, Israel

Goren-Inbar *et al.* (2000) have argued recently that the Acheulean site of Gesher Benot Ya'aqov (GBY) in Israel's Jordan Rift Valley exhibits strong technological (the "Kombewa" technique) and stylistic affinities with Acheulean industries from Olduvai Gorge, Olorgesailie, and other East African Acheulean sites. They explain these similarities by invoking a hominin migration at *ca.* 780,000 years ago, which records the earliest appearance of these patterns outside Africa, asserting that GBY constitutes evidence of a "distinct, culturally-different entity" (Goren-Inbar *et al.* 2000: 947) that later becomes evident in the west Eurasian archaeological record. We are thus asked to believe (1) that the formal properties of bifacial tools are largely or entirely a consequence of social learning, (2) that tool-making traditions manifest in technology and style are detectable over tens of millions of square kilometers, (3) that such "traditions" (ways of making stone tools transmitted in a social context from one generation to the next) persisted intact over tens of thousands of years, and (4) that they are detectable at two points in space (the Levant, East Africa) separated by *ca.* 4,500 kilometers. While the pattern similarities themselves are uncontested, what is supposedly causing them to occur (historical connectivity over vast geographical areas and time ranges) is, in our view, deeply problematic.

For one thing, the physics of lithic reduction have been well understood for decades, and document an enormous amount of formal convergence in the morphology of chipped stone artifacts (*e.g.,* Crabtree 1972; Speth 1972, 1975; Dibble and Whittaker 1981). A substantial literature identifies the processes that affect technological variables in Paleolithic contexts (*e.g.,* size, availability, quality and distance to raw materials; hominin mobility patterns at different scales and time intervals [determined by resource distributions, mate availability]; local group characteristics [age, sex, number of individuals]; duration of site occupation;

anticipated uses of stone; site function, and so on [Dibble 1991, 1995; Kuhn 1991, 1992a,1992b, 1994a,1994b]). Although under-acknowledged by many workers, it is highly likely that the widespread convergence of form in the Paleolithic is almost entirely due to constraints imposed on form by the interaction of contextual factors and rock mechanics, and that those constraints override any hypothetical cultural component manifest in a tool-making tradition. Thus formal convergence has little or nothing to do with history "writ small" in the form of retouched stone artifacts. It is a consequence of repeated combinations of these relatively few factors, except perhaps on the global scale of Grahame Clark's modes (*e.g.*, 1969). Even then it is arguable whether Clarks's modes are in fact adequate descriptors of lithic macroevolution as currently understood, whether innovation in lithic technology can be treated cladistically as a series of temporally ordered and diagnostic apomorphies, and whether those apomorphies are associated with the appearance of particular hominin taxa, as argued by Foley and Lahr (1997).

There are also serious conceptual problems with the notion of a cultural component in the form of Paleolithic artifacts. The time-space distributions of prehistorian-defined analytical units (*e.g.*, Acheulean) *exceed by orders of magnitude* the time-space distributions of any actual or imaginable social entity that might have produced and transmitted them. Unless one resorts to essentialism (*i.e.*, there is an ineffable "Acheuleaness" manifest in bifacial handaxes) or genetic determinism (*i.e.*, making bifacial handaxes is encoded genetically in particular hominin taxa), there is simply no behavioral or cultural mechanism by which a hypothetical tool-making tradition could be transmitted over hundreds of thousands of years and millions of square miles. So, whatever the Acheulean is, it is manifestly not a "culture" or a "tradition."

Then there is the question of resolution and its consequences for identifying a tradition "on the ground." No known Paleolithic site sequence, or series of site sequences, is anywhere near fine-grained enough to allow us to identify the remains of the hypothetical social units that would have been the bearers of these lithic "traditions" (*i.e.*, assemblage resolution, integrity are far too low). Moreover, the generally acknowledged fluidity of forager territorial boundaries would, in short order, have impossibly confounded stylistic patterns manifest in stone tool form in the archaeological context. So, even if there were a "cultural" component in the form of Paleolithic stone artifacts, we could not possibly detect it (Binford and Sabloff 1982; Clark 1989, 1993, 1994).

The "Large Cutting Tools" in the Bose Basin of South China

A second example concerns the Bose Basin "large cutting tool" (LCT) sites in south China, like GBY dated to *ca.* 800,000 years ago (Hou *et al.* 2000). China had not produced any instances of Acheulean or Acheulean-like bifacial technology before the discovery of these sites, far to the east of the "Movius Line" (Movius 1948). It would appear that a meteor hit the Bose Basin *ca.* 806,000 years ago, that it was a major impact that stripped off all the vegetation in the Basin, and that massive erosion ensued, exposing deeply buried conglomerate beds with large, ovate cobbles suitable for the manufacture of handaxes. Suddenly, briefly, and locally, hominins (probably *H. erectus*) began making bifacially-worked LCTs morphologically similar to Acheulean handaxes in the West. They apparently did this for as long as the cobble beds were exposed and thus available for exploitation, but ceased doing it when the conglomerates were buried by subsequent deposition. Like Goren-Inbar and her colleagues (2000), however, Hou *et al.* (2000) explain the appearance of LCTs not by contingent circumstances, but by invoking some kind of an historical connection – hominins making bifacial handaxes migrated or radiated to the area at some point prior to 800,000 years ago. Their artifacts were not found before because they were buried under meters of sediment accumulated over the past 800,000 years. The two explanations usually offered to explain the existence of the Movius Line are (1) hominin migration to East Asia before the Acheulean originated in Africa (Swisher *et al.* 1994), and (2) the loss of "cultural knowledge" of Acheulean bifacial technologies after the initial hominin colonization of East Asia (Toth and Schick 1993; Schick and Toth 1994). Both could certainly have occurred, but Hou *et al.* (2000) overlook a third, more plausible, explanation for the occurrence of large, bifacial tools in the Bose Basin and elsewhere.

Unless (1) hominins are "hard-wired" genetically to make bifacial artifacts (which is extremely unlikely (however, *cf.* Foley 1987, Clark 1989b); (2) there is a robust correlation between particular kinds of hominins and particular kinds of stone artifact assemblages (again, unlikely, but see Foley and Lahr 1997); and (3) unless the time-space distribution of "Acheulean" bifaces corresponds to that of a real or imaginable human, hominin, or hominoid social unit that could have transmitted knowledge of these technologies from one generation to the next, we suggest that they cannot possibly be the remains of stone tool-making traditions. The explanation for their extremely wide geographical distribution must lie in general contextual and situational factors that would have caused Old World hominins to make these common objects, which can occur in the thousands in Middle Pleistocene river terraces in Europe and elsewhere.

Following Toth's (1985, 1987) ideas about the behaviors associated with early stone technologies, and given that the overwhelming majority of handaxes do not exhibit symmetry on *any* axis (see Wynn [1979, 1981, 1985] on symmetry as a monitor of hominin cognitive evolution), we reconceptualized most handaxes as cores rather than tools. If such is the case, the formal convergence that is so much a part of lithic reduction everywhere would have produced them simply as an accidental consequence of centripetal flaking of large, relatively flat, oval cobbles and flakes. The objective would have been to produce unmodified flakes, which are far more efficient general-purpose cutting tools than any retouched or shaped stone artifact. Areas where bifaces are commonly found today (*e.g.*, Spain's Manzanares river valley, the valley of the Somme in northern France, the Thames estuary) were probably areas where raw material of a suitable size, shape, and quality was exposed and accessible repeatedly over geological time at different intervals. The fact that bifaces can occur locally in such large numbers implies a wasteful, or "expedient" use of stone probably related to compromises imposed on hominins by the mobility characteristic of all foragers, and the necessity for provisioning individuals with portable supplies of sharp stone. None of this precludes the use of handaxes as "large cutting tools" if circumstances required it.

Bifacial artifacts morphologically very similar to "Acheulean" handaxes show up all over the world throughout space and time (*e.g.*, Simpson 1978, 1982). As noted by many workers, the physics of rock knocking severely constrain the "learned" or "behavioral" component in chipped stone artifact technologies, resulting in a kind of equifinality in the form of stone artifacts incorporated, in this case, into ancient geological deposits. Thus the Acheulean cannot constitute the material remains of a "culture" or a "tradition" in stone tool manufacture. Although we acknowledge the existence of many unequivocal examples of intentionally shaped "large cutting tools" (*e.g.*, Boxgrove in England [Roberts 1986; Roberts *et al.* 1995], MTA sites in France, Micoquian sites in central Europe [Bordes 1968; Mellars 1996]), most Lower and Middle Pleistocene bifaces were quite possibly cores. Their morphological similarities over vast reaches of time and space likely resulted from the mechanical constraints imposed by centripetally flaking relatively large ovoid cobbles and flakes.

It is not enough to claim, as some have done (*e.g.*, Potts *et al.* pers. comm. 2000), that we cannot yet model "paleoculture" adequately. In fact, we can model it reasonably well using the powerful conceptual frameworks of behavioral ecology (*e.g.*, Stiner 1994; Kuhn 1995; Winterhalder and Smith 2000). By invoking migrants whose peregrinations are supposedly manifest in tool-making traditions, both Goren-Inbar *et al.* (2000) and Hou *et al.* (2000) treat process in the remote past as if it were analogous to process in recent historical contexts. Such an approach to the study of formal variation might be justified: justified or not, it is commonly used in more recent contexts where, for example, a fluid medium like design elements painted on prehistoric pottery is concerned. As the beneficiaries of an extremely "high-resolution" time-space grid, where change is measured in decades, and there is direct historical evidence for continuity between past and present, Southwestern archaeologists are the prototypical example. They study the distributions of attributes that plausibly can be argued to correspond directly to those of the identity-conscious social units known to us from ethnography or history. But stone artifact attributes are poor analogues to the design element *repertoires* painted on prehistoric pots; the latter are infinitely more free to vary than the former according to well-understood social and historical constraints.

What we think of as Paleolithic technology almost certainly constituted a range of options very broadly distributed in time and space, held in common by all contemporaneous hominins, and invoked differentially according to context. The challenge of future work is to determine what contextual factors constrained choice amongst these options. Such factors include the range and size of and distance to raw materials, forager mobility strategies (a consequence of resource distributions, mating networks, *etc.*), anticipated tasks, group size and composition (which change seasonally, annually, generationally, over the evolutionary long-term), structural pose of the occupants of a site in an annual round and, more generally, duration of site occupation. If there are technological and typological convergences between the Acheulean assemblages at GBY and some African sites, and between the Bose Basin LCT sites and Acheulean sites west of the Movius line, it is because of similarities in the constraints imposed on rock knocking by these contextual factors, and not because of any historical connection between the hominins involved.

MIDDLE PALEOLITHIC VARIABILITY IN EURASIA

Until the collapse of the Soviet Union (1990), and the resurgence of multinational collaboration that ensued from it, our picture of Middle Paleolithic variability was framed by the Bordes-Binford (or culture-function) debate of the 1960s and 1970s. While the work of Dibble (*e.g.*, 1984, 1987) raised important questions about the extent to which Mousterian side-scraper shapes were the tangible results of mental templates, the debate itself ended in stalemate in the late 1970s. In accordance with the biases underlying Continental research traditions, many European workers opted for the "cultural" position (or at least accorded it relatively greater importance) while many Americans tended to favor functional explanations over cultural ones. The past 15 years have witnessed an enormous proliferation of new fieldwork, re-excavation or reanalysis of "classic" sites, and publication (often in English) in the former Soviet Union and elsewhere, and the result has been a radically different and still emerging picture of the Middle Paleolithic that bears little resemblance to the entity described in the textbooks.

The eminent paleoanthropologist F. Clark Howell (1999) has recently summarized the ever-increasing number of spatially and temporally distinguishable variants (facies) of the Eurasian Middle Paleolithic (Table 1). Recognized primarily on technological and typological grounds, the 20 Mousterian facies shown in Table 1 represent a quantum increase in qualitative and quantitative variation over the half-dozen or so variants recognized as recently as the late 1980s. Ignoring the inevitable problem of sampling error, the facies appear to vary amongst themselves according to diverse aspects of raw material (availability, package size, quality), modal production sequences (*chaînes opératoires*), the extent of reduction and utilization of particular artifact categories (esp. side-scrapers), functional constraints related to forager behavior (especially mobility), and the nature, size, duration, integrity and intensity of use or occupation of the site context. Taken together, they document a complex mosaic of adaptations that, in aggregate, persists for *ca.* 200,000 years (*ca.* 230,000 to < 30,000 years BP), overlapping extensively with both the Lower and Upper Paleolithic over the entire geographical extent of western Eurasia. When combined with the many "transitional" industries now recognized in the same area, it is possible that Mousterian formal variation, site characteristics, and faunal inventories rival (perhaps even exceed) those of the early Upper Paleolithic. Below we discuss four aspects of Paleolithic archaeology (technology, typology, the Mousterian "facies", and raw material acquisition) where alleged Upper Paleolithic "diagnostics" or patterns appear in sites generally regarded as Middle Paleolithic.

Table 1. Currently recognized Eurasian Mousterian Facies (Howell 1998, 1999)

Facies	Geographical distribution
Charentian Mousterian	Pan-Europe
Ferrassie subtype	
Quina subtype	
Typical Mousterian	Pan-Europe
Levalloiso-Mousterian	
Levantine Mousterian	West Asian Levant
Tabun B	
Tabun C	
Tabun D	
Typical Mousterian/Crvena Stijena type	Balkans
Mousterian/Vasconian type	Northern Spain
Denticulate Mousterian	Pan-Europe
Mousterian of Acheulean Tradition	Franco-Cantabria
MTA – A	
MTA – B	
Mousterian/Châtelperronian type	Franco-Cantabria
Mousterian/Cambresian type	Northwestern Europe
Mousterian/Pontinian type	Greater Latium
Mousterian/Karstein type	Central Europe
Mousterian/Tata type	Bükk Mountains, Hungary
Mousterian/Starosele type	Crimea
Mousterian/Tsutskhvatskaya type	Crimea, Western Caucasus
Mousterian/Khostinskaya type	Western Caucasus
Mousterian/Kudaro type	Western Caucasus, Georgia
Zagros Mousterian	Greater Zagros Mountains, Iran, Iraq
European Micoquian	Central and Eastern Europe
Ak-Kayan	*Crimea*
Altmühlian	*Upper Danube*
Babonyian	*Bükk Mountains, Hungary*
Bocksteinian	*Central Europe*
Jankovician	*Trans/Lower Danube*
Kiik-Koban	*Crimea*
Acheuleo-Yabrudian	Levant
Levantine Mugharan Tradition	Levant

Technology

The Mousterian is sometimes identified historically with Levallois reduction strategies of various kinds (classic, lineal, recurrent with subdivisions, *etc.*) but the existence of many alternative technologies was recognized from the very beginning of Middle Paleolithic research, employed either alongside Levallois methods, or to their exclusion. Perhaps the best known example of the latter is the so-called "Quina subfacies" of the Charentian Mousterian, which appears to lack Levallois technique altogether. Blade technologies have also long been known in the eastern Mediterranean (*e.g.*, in the Lower Paleolithic "Pre-Aurignacian" at the Haua Fteah [Libya], which contains blades, burins, end-scrapers, and backed knives resembling those found in Upper Paleolithic industries like the Aurignacian). Other early Paleolithic examples are the Yabrudian (Syria), the Amudian (= the Pre-Aurignacian), the Acheuleo-Yabrudian or Mugharan (all in the central and southern Levant), and the Tabun D-type Mousterian (Israel, Jordan). Regionally, these "bladey" industries occur interstratified with those rich in flake side-scrapers, and with those containing small handaxes (by virtue of which they are considered Acheulean, as there is no MTA in the Levant). More recently, blade-dominated early Paleolithic assemblages have been reported in at least nine sites in France, Germany and Belgium (Seclin, Riencourt lès-Bapaume, Rheindahlen, Tönchesberg, St. Germain-des-Vaux, Vallée de la Vanne, St. Valery-sur-Somme, Coquelles) and at Crayford, in southeastern England (Ameloot-van der Heijden 1993). Both Levallois and non-Levallois methods are recognized by Boëda (e.g., 1988), with some examples from Seclin (Pas de Calais), dated by thermo-luminescence (TL) to ca. 90,000 years BP, constituting prismatic blade cores with detachments extending around most or all of the platform, and standardized blades indistinguishable from those of the Upper Paleolithic (Révillon 1989). Blade technologies with a distinctively "Upper Paleolithic" cast, and associated with the crested blades often found in Upper Paleolithic contexts, are also documented at St. Valery (Heinzelin and Haesaerts 1983) and at Riencourt (Tuffreau 1992).

In this brief review, it is impossible to do justice to the wide diversity and variety of primary reduction strategies exhibited by industries generally regarded as Middle Paleolithic (see Delagnes and Meignen this volume). About a half-dozen different kinds of Levallois technique recur over the >200,000 years allotted the European Middle Paleolithic; a similar number of non-Levallois techniques that are common in the Upper Paleolithic have also been extensively documented, along with the blade technologies just mentioned (see also Bar-Yosef and Kuhn 1999). The sheer complexity of some of the strategies described by Boëda (1988, 1993) and others for the Middle and even Lower Paleolithic (e.g., Maastricht-Belvédère in Holland, Grotte Vaufrey in France, Bilzingsleben in Germany) rival or exceed those inferred from reconstructions of Upper Paleolithic technologies. The recurrent Levallois technology at the 250,000-year-old site of Biache-Saint-Vaast (France), for example, involved at least six sequential operations to produce three kinds of primary blanks that were, in turn, used selectively to make equally specific (and evidently hafted) retouched tools (Beyries 1988). Because it implies mental processes that differ little, if at all, from our own, technological complexity like that seen at Biache raises serious questions about the allegedly different cognitive abilities of modern and pre-modern European hominins – at least so far as lithic technology is concerned.

Typology

A great deal has been written about Middle Paleolithic tool morphology, function and typology, much of it having to do with the implications of Dibble's side-scraper reduction model, and the extent to which it undermines the notion of shaped or standardized artifact form (e.g., Dibble and Rolland 1992). The major distinctions in Bordes' Lower and Middle Paleolithic typology (1961) are based on the position of the retouched edges in relation to the axis of detachment of the blank, and on the shape of the retouched portion itself, regardless of the overall shape of the piece. These criteria differ sharply from the shape-dependent, time-sensitive, stylistic marker types (*e.g.*, Dufour bladelets, Solutrean points, keeled scrapers) that supposedly identify the various European Upper Paleolithic subdivisions (de Sonneville-Bordes and Perrot 1954, 1955, 1956). The retouched tool types commonly found in European Middle Paleolithic sites (side-scrapers, points, notched and denticulated pieces, backed knives, bifacial foliates [leaf points] and handaxes) vary considerably among themselves in the extent to which one could argue that they were intentionally shaped, with a pretty good consensus that notches and denticulates, at least, were expediently produced on a wide range of blanks as needed to shape wood (more generally, plant material [Anderson-Gerfaud 1990]). While acknowledging the "overfine" shape distinctions evident in Bordes' 17 side-scraper types, and conceding the role played by formal convergence in overall morphology, Mellars (1996:95–140) amasses considerable evidence that the more common side-scraper forms and, especially, bifacial pieces almost certainly were conceptually distinct tool forms that existed as mental templates in the minds of their makers. Paradoxically, though, he also maintains that the "imposed form" (large-scale reduction of blanks affecting not only working edges but overall shape) clearly present in the extensively shaped bifacial points and handaxes is mostly absent in the Middle Paleolithic (albeit evident in the Châtelperronian and the Uluzzian, thought by many to have been made by Neandertals).

In addition to the common Middle Paleolithic retouched types, a very considerable variety of "typical" Upper Paleolithic tools show up in most of the Middle Paleolithic facies, including perforators, *becs, rabots* (planes), truncated pieces, end-scrapers and burins morphologically indistinguishable from their Upper Paleolithic counterparts (these often end up in Type 62 – various). Although present at low frequencies (<2%) in many European sites, they are quite common in some Levantine sites (*e.g.*, dihedral burins account for 10–20% of the retouched pieces at Rosh Ein Mor in Israel [Crew 1976]). The early last-glacial French site of Riencourt, in particular, has produced a spectacular array of single and multiple dihedral burins made on blade blanks. Like Bordes (1963), Mellars (1996:122–124) tends to dismiss them as the accidental products of taphonomic processes (*e.g.*, trampling, cryoturbation) and/or as unfinished pieces broken or discarded in manufacture.

Mousterian Facies—Are They Real?

As noted earlier, much of the formal variation captured by the Bordes' typology has been aggregated into a rapidly proliferating number of regional variants, or facies (Table 1). The facies concept was created by Bordes in 1950 to bring order to a bewildering array of essentially idiosyncratic and local terms and methods used to describe the retouched component of Middle Paleolithic artifact assemblages. Based on the relative frequencies of the major tool groups, Bordes thought the facies were largely non-overlapping and, with one exception, the Mousterian of Acheulean Tradition (MTA) B, essentially contemporaneous over tens of millennia, at least in the Franco-Cantabrian heartland where they were first defined (however, *cf.* Mellars 1989). In his view, they had little to do with adaptations to different environments, topographies, functional constraints, or raw material distributions, and were equated with tool-making traditions held in common by distinct, identity-conscious groups of Neandertals who expressed their uniqueness in terms of tool group proportions. However unlikely an explanation from an Americanist point of view, the notion of modal variation in the major Mousterian type groups persists to the present day (see Table 1), and along with it, the possibility that Bordes' explanation for pattern might be correct. If it could be shown that type group variation within the Mousterian is essentially continuous, that would demolish the "reality" of the facies as Bordes defined them, and with it, his proposed explanation.

There have been several statistical attempts to evaluate the compositional integrity of the facies (Doran and Hodson 1966; Mellars 1967; Callow and Webb 1981; Freeman 1994), and they have led to contradictory results: (1) strong support for modal facies variation in France; and (2) equally strong evidence for a continuous distribution in nearby Cantabrian Spain. Most of these efforts have focused on the Mousterian of southwestern France, where there is a high density of well-excavated and published sites, and abundant flint of high quality and large package size. Multivariate approaches applied to assemblages in the French "heartland" have consistently produced reasonably good facies separations. For example, Mellars (1967) analyzed 33 Mousterian assemblages from southwestern France using multidimensional scaling of the typological categories, and got good separations based mainly on the relative frequency of side-scrapers. Quina, Ferrassie, Typical and MTA-A assemblages tend to have lots of side-scrapers, whereas Denticulate and MTA-B assemblages do not. Both major groups were replicated in Mellars' analysis, as were the constituent facies of the former. Callow and Webb (1981) analyzed 96 French assemblages using canonical variates and discriminant functions to determine whether or not, and to what extent, *a priori* classifications of the material (*i.e.*, Bordes' facies, as identified by the excavators) are replicated by those implied by robust pattern in the statistical data (here both the types and Bordes' technological indices). Again, with the possible exception of the 27 Typical collections, excellent separation was achieved. They conclude that "not only are the typological and technological data multimodal . . . but it is possible to identify several discrete clusters of assemblages corresponding to [Bordes'] variants" (Callow and Webb 1981:137).

Unfortunately, exactly the opposite conclusion was reached in an analysis of 15 collections from flint-poor Cantabrian Spain, where Paleolithic industries are dominated by quartzite, and where flint is generally rare, of poor quality, and available only in the form of small nodules (Freeman 1994). Noting that the extreme zonal variation within a single Mousterian level (16) at Cueva Morín would have resulted in different facies assignments to adjacent squares, Freeman used a non-parametric Kolmogorov-Smirnov (K-S) *k*-sample test (Siegal 1956)

Mousterian Assemblage Intergradation

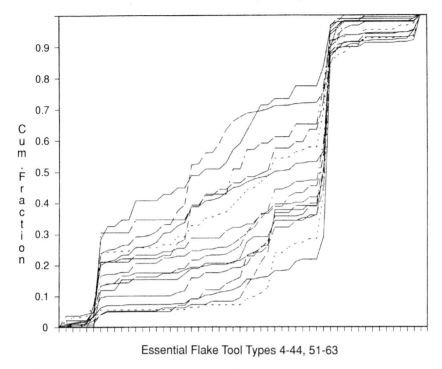

Essential Flake Tool Types 4-44, 51-63

Figure 1. Cumulative percentage graphs of 16 Cantabrian Mousterian collections showing facies intergradation (from Freeman 1994: 51, used with permission).

to compare 15 Mousterian collections from Morín, El Castillo, El Pendo and La Flecha that he himself had classified according to Bordes' typology. Unlike other non-parametric tests that evaluate differences in central tendency, the K-S tests are not only sensitive to differences in mean or median values, but also to the magnitude of differences in any part of the frequency distribution. More powerful than χ^2, they are also more efficient (Siegal 1956). Freeman's results showed unequivocally that the facies in Cantabria constituted a continuously distributed series, and that as mutually exclusive, well-differentiated modes of proportional representation, they are arbitrary constructs of the classifier (Figure 1). If they do not exist, he concluded, there is no point in searching for the causes or correlates of facies differences (Freeman 1994:51–52). Given the geographical proximity of the two regions, and the existence of the same facies on both sides of the border, it is difficult to escape the impression that raw material differences (flint *vs* quartzite) and differences in topography (hence resource distributions, mobility) play significant roles in the perception of modal variation in southern France and continuous variation in northern Spain. It is very likely true that both sets of conclusions are correct. As Table 1 shows, however, efforts to differentiate Mousterian assemblages using the relative frequencies of their major type groups continue unabated, despite the possibility that the facies – whatever might be causing them to occur – are not "real" (or are not "real" everywhere).

Raw Material Distributions

The procurement and distribution of raw materials in Paleolithic sites has been used over the past 20 years to monitor patterns of movement of human groups, possible relations amongst them, as a proxy measure for technological differences, and an indication of how lithic technologies were organized. Again, much of this work has been undertaken in France, and French scholars such as Geneste (1988, 1989a, 1989b) and Turq (1988, 1989, 1992) have played a leading role. Lithic provenience studies have been admirably summarized by Mellars (1996: 141–168) who points out that, although most Middle Paleolithic raw materials are derived from local sources (<5 km from a site), there is a very considerable presence of material derived from more distant sources (20–30 km away), and an occasional appearance in almost all sites of small quantities of high-quality material derived from much greater distances (80–100 km). When quantities of raw materials are plotted against the distances over which they were transported, the patterns usually correspond to a roughly exponential distance decline curve, recalling the fall-off curves exhibited by later sites, up to and including those of the Neolithic (e.g., Renfrew 1969). The patterns of raw material procurement in France during the Middle Paleolithic appear to be broadly similar to those of the Upper Paleolithic, raw materials are traveling along the same East-West trending river valleys (and up and down their North-South trending tributaries) in both periods, come from similar sized catchment areas, and exhibit the same kind of strong correlation between high-quality stone and complex tools (Mellars 1996: 165–168). The major differences have to do with the quantities of high-quality raw material transported over long distances (ca. 1–2% in most Middle Paleolithic sites, as high as 20–25% in a few Upper Paleolithic sites) and in the form in which the more distant materials were transported (finished pieces are more common in the Middle Paleolithic, prepared cores in the Upper). Unambiguous quarry, extraction, or "workshop" sites (ateliers de taille) were long thought to be confined to the Upper Paleolithic, although recent research has demonstrated their presence in the Middle Paleolithic of Italy, Egypt, and the Levant (Vermeersch et al. 1997; Barkai et al. 2002; Del Lucchese et al. 2000–2001).

Other Monitors of Adaptation

Although the aspects of lithic technology and typology just described are, in some sense, "primary," because most Middle Paleolithic sites do not preserve organic remains, much the same pattern of under-acknowledged variability within the Middle Paleolithic also appears to be documented for subsistence, site place-ment within the landscape and intra-site spatial organization (i.e., "well-organized campsites"). Although Middle Paleolithic foragers probably scavenged when the opportunity to do so presented itself (Stiner 1994), they could also be effective hunters of prime-age adult animals (Chase 1986, 1988, 1989), capable of highly selective predation on large bovids (*e.g.*, at Mauran, La Borde, Coudoulous, Le Roc [see summary in Mellars 1996:217-219, 231–236]). There is good evidence for game drives, with all of the complex cognitive and organizational abilities they entail (*e.g.*, at La Cotte de St. Brelade [Scott 1986, 1989], at La Quina [Chase 1989]), and for the intensive, seasonal exploitation of large, gregarious bovids (*e.g.*, aurochs at La Borde [Jaubert and Brugal 1990, *cf.* Slott-Möller 1990], bison at Mauran [David and Farizy 1994]), implying cooperative intercept hunting linked tightly to migration routes. Furthermore, Middle Paleolithic faunas contain evidence for the systematic transport of carcasses or parts thereof (*e.g.*, at Mauran, Champlost [Farizy and David 1992, David and Farizy 1994]), complex butchery practices, including filleting, marrow extraction, and other "modern" kinds of animal processing (Jaubert and Brugal 1990, Farizy *et al.* 1994).

Much the same can be said of the placement of Middle Paleolithic sites in the landscape, although the tendency to ignore or to minimize the importance of the numerous but usually untested and undated open sites introduces a source of bias, as does the tendency for European scholars to de-emphasize survey research (though in the Levant in particular, and in western Eurasia generally, survey research is more common, possibly because of the ancient, denuded, easily accessible landscapes, and the absence of a thick mantle of Holocene deposition [Schuldenrein and Clark 2001, 2003]). In what is perhaps the best known European region, southwestern France, there is an apparent (and possibly universal) dichotomy between cave and rockshelter sites, on the one hand, and open sites, on the other, in placement of sites with regard to basic environmental and topographical features. Most of the former are located in cliff faces in valley walls offering extensive and wide-ranging views of the local landscape, almost invariably in proximity to abundant and high-quality raw materials (Mellars 1996:251–252). As Turq has pointed out (1989:196), they tend to overlook, or to be located on or adjacent to ecotones, with a diversity of habitats which could be easily and efficiently exploited from those locations. Although this view has been contested by Stiner (1991), it has led to the notion that many Middle Paleolithic caves and rockshelters were, in some sense, "central places" from which diverse economic, social, and technological activities were carried out (see also Duchadeau-Kervazo 1984).

A striking feature of Middle Paleolithic open sites is their sheer abundance, greatly exceeding their Upper Paleolithic counterparts (*e.g.*, Marks and Freidel 1977; Duchadeau-Kervazo 1982, 1986; Geneste 1985; Clark 1992). Whereas the locations of cave and rockshelter sites are tightly constrained by the calcareous bedrock formations in which they have formed, which in France extend in a northwest/southeast trending belt through the Périgord, open sites tend to be located on exposed interfluvial *plateaux,* at higher average elevations than the caves, albeit with the densest concentrations also associated with limestone containing high-quality flints Turq (1989:182–196). All the "classic" Bordesian facies are supposedly represented, although MTA sites are most commonly recorded, probably because of the relatively high visibility of the handaxes and their obvious appeal to generations of local collectors. Based on the relative importance of lithic extraction and production activities *vs.* more generalized patterns in tool use and discard, Turq (1988, 1989) has developed a four-part functional classification of

Middle Paleolithic open sites in the Périgord that replicates almost exactly that used to classify their Upper Paleolithic counterparts. His types are (1) extraction and exploitation (quarry) sites, (2) extraction and production (workshop, *atelier*) sites, (3) "mixed strategy" sites, mostly MTA sites with rich and varied lithic assemblages (domestic or residential sites), and (4) episodic or ephemeral sites (small, limited-activity stations with sparse and restricted artifact assemblages).

Finally, there is compelling evidence for "well-organized" Middle (and even Lower) Paleolithic campsites that exhibit all of the features supposedly uniquely associated with the structured use of space noted in ethnographic contexts. These characteristics include (1) open, constructed, paved and excavated hearths (*e.g.*, Grotte Vaufrey, Combe Grenal, Pech de l'Azé II, Grotte du Bison (Arcy), Terra Amata, Hauteroche, Kebara, Ain Difla, Shanidar), (2) stone pavements (*pavages* – *e.g.*, Baume-Bonne, Terra Amata, Aldène, Biache-Saint-Vaast, La Ferrassie), (3) stone walls (*e.g.*, Lazaret, Cueva Morín, Baume des Peyrards, Saint-Vaast-la-Hougue, Terra Amata), (4) intentionally excavated pits (*e.g.*, Combe Grenal, Le Moustier, La Quina, Morín and other sites in southwest France and northern Spain; Ain Difla, Kebara in the Levant), and (5) huts, lean-tos, shelters, postholes and other evidence for intentional, highly patterned behavior indistinguishable from that generated by modern foragers, and extending from western Europe to the southern Levant (*e.g.*, Bilzingsleben, Lazaret, Terra Amata, Grotte du Renne, Les Canalettes, Tor Faraj): for original source material, see de Lumley (1969), Bordes (1972), Rigaud and Geneste (1988:593–611), Mania *et al.* (1980, 1983, 1986), Mellars (1996:269–314), and Henry *et al.* (2004). Although claims for "modern-like" early Paleolithic spatial organization should not be accepted uncritically (Villa 1982, 1983), the weight of evidence seems to indicate that differences between the Middle and Upper Paleolithic are essentially differences in quantity, rather than kind.

The picture is less clear with respect to "art," beads, and organic technologies, although, again, there are suggestions of early Paleolithic examples (*e.g.*, the Châtelperronian levels at Grotte du Renne, the evidence for intentional burial in the Middle Paleolithic, the Tata nummulite, the Berekhet Ram figure; see Duff *et al.* [1992] for a summary of views on the origins of symbolic thought). If correctly interpreted by Mania (1990, 1991; *cf.* Gamble 1999:153–173), the *ca.* 350,000 year old Bilzingsleben open site has yielded evidence of several huts or shelters, an "organized campsite," stone and bone anvils, wooden and bone artifacts, abundant worked stone, hearths, a stone pavement, symbolically engraved bones, specialized predation on rhinos, even human fossil remains, all in a low-energy lakeshore environment, and with only traces of bone-modifying carnivores. Certainly, this is food for thought.

FINAL REMARKS

Our pattern search uncovered many other aspects of Middle Paleolithic material culture that call "the human revolution" into question. Due to space limitations, these lines of inquiry cannot be fully developed here. Taken together, however, the empirical findings we do present constitute strong support for our initial contention that the Middle Paleolithic is not a single "thing," any more than the Upper Paleolithic is, but rather a chimera created by an illusion of technological, typological, and chronological consistency that has little basis in reality. When a broader perspective is adopted that emphasizes the full range of material correlates of human behavior, what emerges from the west Eurasian archaeological record over the interval of 250,000–40,000 years BP is a mosaic of different lithic technologies and typologies, patterns in raw material procurement, reduction and discard, blank types, metrics and frequencies, bone and antler technologies, evidence for symbolic behavior, subsistence strategies and settlement patterns that anticipates the complex patterns of the late Upper Paleolithic.

It is perhaps somewhat ironic, or at least paradoxical, that *The Neanderthal Legacy* (Mellars 1996) was a primary source for this essay. Mellars is very knowledgeable about French Middle Paleolithic archaeology, and the main strength of the book is the definitive literature search which allows the reader to draw his or her own conclusions about the nature of Neandertal adaptations and, in turn, how the Middle Paleolithic might have differed from the Upper Paleolithic. Whatever position is taken on the biological relationship between archaic and modern *Homo sapiens* (Mellars does not discuss the fossil evidence), it is clear and definite from the archaeology that Neandertals represent a long-lasting, successful, adaptive phase immediately preceding "us." Left under-addressed are *why* and *how* the hypothetical replacement event or process that Mellars proposes could have occurred. Although he adopts a moderate position throughout, and does a excellent job of presenting – fully and accurately – alternative viewpoints, Mellars nevertheless argues for near-total biological replacement by claiming (1) that Neandertal technologies, while extremely sophisticated, resulted in a smaller range of formal tools than found in the Upper Paleolithic, (2) that the ranges over which Middle Paleolithic foragers obtained raw materials were smaller than those of their Upper Paleolithic counterparts, (3) that the Neandertals seldom manufactured bone and antler tools, objects of adornment or "art" (and thus lacked cognitive capacities comparable to ours), and (4) that their campsites are not as structured internally as those of the European Upper Paleolithic. The Upper Paleolithic is thus portrayed as an abrupt "cultural leap" when much of his argument rests on the appearance of personal adornment and "art," raising the empirical question of whether or not synchronous changes in other aspects of adaptation also took place.

We should not forget that the divisions of the Paleolithic (indeed, the Paleolithic itself) are "accidents of history" created, for the most part, by French prehistorians between *ca.* 1880 and *ca.* 1940 in order to solve chronological problems, that those divisions are based ultimately on typological systematics, and that they have become reified and essentialized by subsequent workers over time. Although indisputable, and entirely consistent with a broadly scientific, critically self-conscious approach to our discipline, remarks like these have sometimes been taken as (unwarranted) criticisms of European conceptual frameworks and, by implication, the research traditions that produced them – especially those of the "founders" of Paleolithic archaeology, the French (*e.g.*, Marean and Thompson

2003). However, the French were only doing what all scientists do – creating analytical units they deemed relevant and appropriate to some problem they were trying to solve. No one could deny that, if Paleolithic archaeology had arisen somewhere other than where it did (*e.g.*, Africa, instead of Europe), the analytical units would have taken on a very different character (see for example the extended criticism of Eurocentric bias by McBrearty and Brooks [2000]). We archaeologists don't have natural analytical units like the life sciences do. We have to create them, and the only way we can do that is in terms of some problem of interest. But problems are embedded in problem contexts, problem contexts in research traditions, and research traditions in broader intellectual *milieux* (sometimes called metaphysical paradigms) that differ from one another in respect to implicit biases, preconceptions and assumptions about their subject matter, in this case, what the past "was like."

Along with many others, we have also recently examined the material correlates of behavior over the Middle-to-Upper Paleolithic transition and have reached conclusions largely opposed to those of Mellars (*e.g.*, Clark and Lindly 1989; Clark 1997, 2002a; Riel-Salvatore and Clark 2001). In fact, the evidence so painstakingly assembled in *The Neanderthal Legacy* appears to us to lend more support to continuity in adaptation than to the abrupt disjunction implied by the replacement scenarios Mellars favors. It is nevertheless a tribute to Mellars' comprehensive, even-handed treatment of a literature seldom read by American workers that we all can use *The Neanderthal Legacy* to address aspects of Neandertal behavior of common interest to the discipline.

REFERENCES CITED

Ameloot-van der Heijden N. 1993. L'industrie laminaire du niveau CA. In A. Tuffreau (Ed.), *Riencourt-les-Bapaume (Pas-de-Calais): un Gisement du Paléolithique Moyen,* pp. 26–52. Paris: Maison des Sciences de l'Homme.

Anderson-Gerfaud P. 1990. Aspects of behaviour in the Middle Palaeolithic: functional analysis of stone tools from southwest France. In P. Mellars (Ed.), *The Emergence of Modern Humans: an Archaeological Perspective*, pp. 389–418. Edinburgh: Edinburgh University Press.

Barkai R., A. Gopher and C. La Porta 2002. Palaeolithic landscape of extraction: flint surface quarries and workshops at Mt Pua, Israel. *Antiquity* 76: 672–680.

Barton C.M. 1991. Retouched tools, fact or fiction? Paradigms for interpreting Paleolithic chipped stone. In G.A. Clark (Ed.), *Perspectives on the Past: Theoretical Biases in Mediterranean Hunter-Gatherer Research*, pp. 143–163. Philadelphia: University of Pennsylvania Press.

Bar-Yosef O. 1991. Stone tools and social context in Levantine prehistory. In G.A. Clark (Ed.), *Perspectives on the Past: Theoretical Biases in Mediterranean Hunter-Gatherer Research*, pp. 371–395. Philadelphia: University of Pennsylvania Press.

Bar-Yosef O. and S.L. Kuhn 1999. The big deal about blades: laminar technologies and human evolution. *American Anthropologist* 101: 322–338.

Beyries S. 1988. Functional variability of lithic sets in the Middle Paleolithic. In H.L. Dibble and A. Montet-White (Eds.), *The Upper Pleistocene Prehistory of Western Eurasia* (Symposium Series 1), pp. 215–230. Philadelphia: University of Pennsylvania Museum Press.

Bietti A. 1997. The transition to anatomically modern humans: the case of peninsular Italy. In G.A. Clark and C.M. Willermet (Eds.), *Conceptual Issues in Modern Human Origins Research*, pp. 132–147. New York: Aldine de Gruyter.

Binford L.R. and J.A. Sabloff 1982. Paradigms, systematics and archaeology. *Journal of Anthropological Research* 38: 137–153.

Bisson M.S. 2000. Nineteenth century tools for twenty-first century archaeology? Why the Middle Paleolithic Typology of François Bordes must be replaced. *Journal of Archaeological Method and Theory* 7: 1–48.

Boëda E. 1988. Le concept Levallois et evaluation de son champ d'application. In M. Otte (Ed.), *L'Homme de Néandertal, Vol. 4: La Technique*, pp. 13–26. (ERAUL 4) Liège: Université de Liège.

Boëda E. 1993. Le débitage discoïde et le débitage Levallois récurrent centripète. *Bulletin de la Société Préhistorique Française* 90: 392–404.

Boëda E., J.-M. Geneste and L. Meignen 1990. Identification de chaînes opératoires lithiques du Paléolithique ancien et moyen. *Paléo* 2: 43–79.

Bordes F. 1961. *Typologie du Paléolithique ancien et moyen*. Paris: CNRS Editions.

Bordes F. 1963. Le Moustérien à denticulés. *Archeologiki Vestnik* 13–14: 43–49.

Bordes F. 1972. *A Tale of Two Caves*. New York: Harper and Row.

Bordes F. 1968. *The Old Stone Age*. New York: McGraw Hill.

Brantingham P.J., S.L. Kuhn and K.W. Kerry (Eds.) 2004. *The Early Upper Paleolithic Beyond Western Europe*. Berkeley: University of California Press.

Callow P. and R.E. Webb 1981. The application of multivariate statistical techniques to Middle Palaeolithic assemblages from southwestern France. *Revue d'Archéométrie* 5: 129–138.

Chabai, V.P. and K. Monigal (Eds.) 1999. *The Middle Paleolithic of Western Crimea Vol. 2* (ERAUL 87). Liège: Université de Liège.

Chabai V.P., K. Monigal and A.E. Marks (Eds.) *The Middle Paleolithic and Early Upper Paleolithic of Eastern Crimea* (ERAUL 104). Liège: Université de Liège.

Chase P.G. 1986. *The Hunters of Combe Grenal: Approaches to Middle Paleolithic Subsistence in Europe* (BAR International Series 286). Oxford: BAR.

Chase P.G. 1988. Scavenging and hunting in the Middle Paleolithic: the evidence from Europe. In H.L. Dibble and A. Montet-White (Eds.), *The Upper Pleistocene Prehistory of Western Eurasia* (Symposium Series 1), pp. 225–232. Philadelphia: University of Pennsylvania Museum Press.

Chase P.G. 1989. How different was Middle Palaeolithic subsistence? A zooarchaeological perspective on the Middle to Upper Palaeolithic transition. In P. Mellars and C. Stringer (Eds.), *The Human Revolution: Behavioural and Biological Perspectives on the Origins of Modern Humans*, pp. 321–337. Princeton: Princeton University Press.

Clark G.A. 1989a. Romancing the stones: biases, style and lithics at La Riera. In D. Henry and G. Odell (Eds.), *Alternative Approaches to Lithic Analysis* (Archeological Papers of the American Anthropological Association 1), pp. 27–50. Washington: The American Anthropological Association.

Clark G.A. 1989b. Alternative models of Pleistocene biocultural evolution: a response to Foley. *Antiquity* 63: 153–161.

Clark G.A. 1992. Wadi al-Hasa Paleolithic settlement patterns: Negev and south Jordan models compared. In M. Zaghloul (Ed.), *Studies in the History and Archaeology of Jordan, Vol. IV*, pp. 89–96. Amman: Department of Antiquities.

Clark G.A.1993. Paradigms in science and archaeology. *Journal of Archaeological Research* 1: 203–234.

Clark G.A. 1994. Migration as an explanatory concept in Paleolithic archaeology. *Journal of Archaeological Method and Theory* 1: 305–343.

Clark G.A. 1997. The Middle-Upper Paleolithic transition in Europe: an American perspective. *Norwegian Archaeological Review* 30: 25–53.

Clark G.A. 1999. Modern human origins: highly visible, curiously intangible. *Science* 283:2029–2032; 284: 917.

Clark G.A. 2002a. Neandertal archaeology – implications for our origins. *American Anthropologist* 104: 50–68.

Clark G.A. 2002b. American archaeology's uncertain future. In S.D. Gillespie and D.L. Nichols (Eds.), *Archaeology Is Anthropology*, (Archeological Papers of the American Anthropological Association 13), pp. 51–86. Washington: The American Anthropological Association.

Clark G.A. and J.M. Lindly. 1989. Modern human origins in the Levant and Western Asia: The fossil and archeological evidence. *American Anthropologist* 91: 962–983.

Clark J.D.G. 1969. *World Prehistory: a New Outline* (7th Edition). Cambridge: Cambridge University Press.

Crabtree D.E. 1972. The cone fracture principle and the manufacture of lithic materials. *Tebiwa* 15: 29–42.

Crew H. 1976. The Mousterian site of Rosh Ein Mor. In A. E. Marks (Ed.), *Prehistory and Paleoenvironments in the Central Negev, Vol. 1.*, pp. 75–112. Dallas: Southern Methodist University.

David F. and C. Farizy. 1994. Les vestiges osseux: étude archéozoologique. In C. Farizy, F. David and J. Jaubert (Eds.). *Hommes et Bisons du Paléolithique Moyen à Mauran (Haute-Garonne)*, pp. 177–234. Paris: Editions CNRS.

Del Lucchese A., S. Martini, F. Negrino and C. Ottomano. 2000–2001. "I Ciotti" (Mortola Superiore, Ventimiglia, Imperia). Una località di approvigionamento della materia prima per la scheggiatura durante il Paleolitico. *Bullettino di Paletnologia Italiana* 91–92: 1–26.

Dibble H.L. 1984. Interpreting typological variation of Middle Paleolithic scrapers: function, style or sequence of reduction? *Journal of Field Archaeology* 11: 431–436.

Dibble H.L. 1987. Interpretation of Middle Paleolithic scraper morphology. *American Antiquity* 52: 109–117.

Dibble H.L. 1991. Local raw material exploitation and its effects on Lower and Middle Paleolithic assemblage variability. In A. Montet-White and S. Holen (Eds.), *Raw Material Economies Among Prehistoric Hunter-Gatherers* (University of Kansas Publications in Anthropology 19), pp. 33–48. Lawrence: University of Kansas.

Dibble H.L. 1995. Middle Paleolithic scraper reduction: background, clarification, and review of the evidence to date. *Journal of Archaeological Method and Theory* 2: 299–368.

Dibble H.L. and N. Rolland. 1992. On assemblage variability in the Middle Paleolithic of Western Europe: history, perspectives, and a new synthesis. In H.L. Dibble and P. Mellars (Eds.), *The Middle Paleolithic: Adaptation, Behavior and Variability* (Symposium Series 2), pp. 1–28. Philadelphia: University of Pennsylvania Museum Press.

Dibble H.L. and J.C. Whittaker 1981. New experimental evidence on the relation between percussion flaking and flake variation. *Journal of Archaeological Science* 8: 283–296.

Djindjian F., J.K. Kozlowski and F. Bazile. 2003. Europe during the early Upper Palaeolithic (40,000–30,000 BP): a synthesis. In J. Zilhão and F. d'Errico (Eds.), *The Chronology of the Aurignacian and of the Transitional Technocomplexes: Dating, Stratigraphies, Cultural Implications*, pp. 29–48. Lisbon: Instituto Português de Arqueologia.

Doran J.E. and F.R. Hodson 1966. A digital computer analysis of Palaeolithic flint assemblages. *Nature* 210: 688–689.

Duchadeau-Kervazo C. 1982. *Recherches sur l'Occupation Paléolithique du Bassin de la Dronne*. Ph.D. Dissertation, Université de Bordeaux I. Bordeaux.

Duchadeau-Kervazo C. 1984. Influence du substratum sur l'occupation paléolithique du bassin de la Dronne. *Bulletin de la Société Linéenne de Bordeaux* 12: 35–50.

Duchadeau-Kervazo C. 1986. Les sites paléolithiques du bassin de la Dronne (nord de l'Aquitaine): observations sur les modes et les emplacements. *Bulletin de la Société Préhistorique Française* 83: 56–64.

Duff A., G.A. Clark and T. Chadderdon 1992. Symbolism in the early Palaeolithic: a conceptual odyssey. *Cambridge Archaeological Journal* 2: 211–229.

Farizy C. and F. David. 1992. Subsistence and behavioral patterns of some Middle Palaeolithic local groups. In H.L. Dibble and P. Mellars (Eds.), *The Middle Paleolithic: Adaptation, Behavior and Variability* (Symposium Series 2), pp. 87–96. Philadelphia: University of Pennsylvania Museum Press.

Farizy C., F. David and J. Jaubert (Eds.), 1994. *Hommes et Bisons du Paléolithique Moyen à Mauran (Haute-Garonne)*. Paris: Editions CNRS.

Flannery K.V. 1969. Origins and ecological effects of early domestication in Iran and the Near East. In P.J. Ucko and G.W. Dimbleby (Eds.), *The Domestication and Exploitation of Plants and Animals*, pp. 73–100. Chicago: Aldine.

Foley R.A. 1987. Hominid species and stone tools assemblages: how are they related? *Antiquity* 61: 380–392.

Foley R.A. and M.M. Lahr. 1997. Mode 3 technologies and the evolution of modern humans. *Cambridge Archaeological Journal* 7: 3–36.

Freeman L.G. 1994. Kaleidoscope or tarnished mirror? Thirty years of Mousterian investigations in Cantabria. In J. Lasheras (Ed.), *Homenaje al Dr. Joaquin González Echegaray* (Monografía No. 17), pp. 37–54. Museo y Centro de Investigaciones de Altamira.

Gamble Clive. 1999. *The Palaeolithic Societies of Europe.* Cambridge: Cambridge University Press.

Geneste J.-M. 1985. *Analyse lithique d'industries moustériennes du Périgord: une approche technologique du comportement des groupes humains au Paléolithique moyen.* Ph.D. Dissertation, Université Bordeaux I.

Geneste, J.-M. 1988. Les industries de la Grotte Vaufrey: technologie du débitage, économie et circulation de la matière première. In J.-P. Rigaud (Ed.), *La Grotte Vaufrey à Cenac et Saint-Julien (Dordogne): paléoenvironnements, chronologie, activités humaines,* pp. 441–519. Paris: Mémoires de la Société Préhistorique Française.

Geneste J.-M. 1989a. Economie des ressources lithiques dans le moustérien du sud-ouest de la France. In M. Patou-Mathis (Ed.), *L'Homme de Néandertal, Vol. 6: La Subsistance* (ERAUL 33), pp. 75–97. Liège: Université de Liège.

Geneste J.-M. 1989b. Systèmes d'approvisionnement en matières premières au Paléolithique moyen et au Paléolithique supérieur en Aquitaine. In J.K. Kozlowski (Ed.), *L'Homme de Néandertal, Vol. 8: La Mutation* (ERAUL 35) pp. 61–70. Liège: Université de Liège.

Goren-Inbar N., C.S. Feibel, K.L. Verosub, Y. Melamed, M.E. Kslev, E. Tchernov and I. Saragusti 2000. Pleistocene milestones on the out-of-Africa corridor at Gesher Benot Ya'aqov, Israel. *Science* 289: 9444–9447.

Goring-Morris A.N. 1996. Square pegs into round holes: a critique of Neeley and Barton. *Antiquity* 70: 130–135.

Hayden B. 1993. The cultural capacities of Neandertals: a review and re-evaluation. *Journal of Human Evolution* 24: 113–146.

Harrold F.B. and M. Otte 2001. Time, space, and cultural process in the European Middle-Upper Paleolithic transition. In M. Hays and P. Thacker (Eds.), *Questioning the Answers: Re-solving Fundamental Problems of the Early Upper Paleolithic* (BAR International Series 1005), pp. 3–11. Oxford: Archaeopress.

Heinzelin J. de and P. Haesaerts 1983. Un cas de débitage laminaire au Paléolithique ancient: Croix-l'Abbé à Saint-Valéry-sur-Somme. *Gallia Préhistoire* 26: 189–201.

Henry D.O., H.J. Hietala, A. Rosen, Y. Demidenko, V. Usik and T. Armagan 2004. Human behavioral organization in the Middle Paleolithic: were Neanderthals different? *American Anthropologist* 106: 17–31.

Henshilwood C.S. and C.W. Marean 2003. The origin of modern human behavior. *Current Anthropology* 44: 627–652.

Hou Y., R. Potts, B. Yuan, Z. Guo, A. Deino, W. Wang, J. Clark, G. Xie and W. Huang 2000. Mid-Pleistocene Acheulean-like stone technology of the Bose Basin, south China: *Science* 287: 1622–1626.

Howell, F.C. 1998. Evolutionary implications of altered perspectives on hominine demes and populations in the later Pleistocene of western Eurasia. In T. Akazawa, K. Aoki and O. Bar-Yosef (Eds.), *Neandertals and Modern Humans in Western Asia,* pp. 5–28. New York: Plenum Press.

Howell F.C. 1999. Paleo-demes, species clades, and extinctions in the Pleistocene hominin record. *Journal of Anthropological Research* 55: 191–243.

Jaubert J. and J.-P. Brugal 1990. Contribution à l'étude du mode de vie au Paléolithique moyen: les chasseurs d'aurochs de La Borde. In J. Jaubert, M. Lorblanchet, R. Slott-Moller, A. Turq and J.-P. Brugal (Eds.) *Les Chasseurs d'Aurochs de La Borde: un site du Paléolithique moyen (Livernon, Lot),* pp. 128–145. Paris: Maison des Sciences de l'Homme.

Kozlowski J.K. 2000. The problem of cultural continuity between the Middle and Upper Paleolithic in Central and Eastern Europe. In O. Bar-Yosef and D. Pilbeam (Eds.), *The Geography of Neanderthals and Modern Humans in Europe and the Greater Mediterranean* (Peabody Museum of Archaeology and Ethnology Bulletin. 8), pp. 77–106. Cambridge MA: Peabody Museum, Harvard University.

Kuhn S.L. 1991. Unpacking reduction: lithic raw-material economy in the Mousterian of West-Central Italy. *Journal of Anthropological Archaeology* 10: 76–106.

Kuhn S.L. 1992a. On planning and curated technologies in the Middle Paleolithic. *Journal of Anthropological Research* 48: 185–214.

Kuhn S.L. 1992b. Blank form and reduction as determinants of Mousterian scraper morphology. *American Antiquity* 57: 115–128.

Kuhn S.L. 1994. A formal approach to the design and assembly of mobile toolkits. *American Antiquity* 59: 426–442.

Kuhn S.L. 1995. *Mousterian Lithic Technology: an Ecological Perspective*. Princeton: Princeton University Press.

Leroi-Gourhan A. 1964–1965. *Le Geste et la Parole, Vols. 1 and 2*. Paris : A. Michel.

de Lumley H. (Ed.) 1969. *Une cabane acheuléenne dans la Grotte du Lazaret (Nice)* (Memoires de la Société Préhistorique Française 7). Paris: Société Préhistorique Française.

Mania D. 1990. *Auf den Spuren des Urmenschen: Die Funde von Bilzingsleben*. Berlin: Theiss.

Mania D. 1991. The zonal division of the Lower Palaeolithic open-air site Bilzingsleben. *Anthropologie* 29: 17–24.

Mania D., T. Nötzold, V. Toepfer, E. Vlcek and W.D. Heinrich. 1983. *Bilzingsleben II*. Berlin: Veröffentlichungen des Landesmuseums für Vorgeschichte in Halle, Band 36.

Mania D., V. Toepfer and E. Vlcek. 1980. *Bilzingsleben I*. Berlin: Veröffentlichungen des Landesmuseums für Vorgeschichte in Halle, Band 32.

Mania D. and T. Weber (Eds.) 1986. *Bilzingsleben III*. Berlin: Veröffentlichungen des Landesmuseums für Vorgeschichte in Halle, Band 39.

Marean C. and J. Thompson. 2003. Research on the origins of modern humans continues to dominate paleoanthropology. *Evolutionary Anthropology* 12: 165–167.

Marks A.E. and V. Chabai (Eds.) 1998. *The Middle Paleolithic of Western Crimea, Vol. 1* (ERAUL 84). Liège: Université de Liège.

Marks A.E. and D.A. Freidel 1977. Prehistoric settlement patterns in the Avdat/Aqev area. In A.E. Marks (Ed.), *Prehistory and Paleoenvironments in the Central Negev, Israel, Vol. II: The Avdat/Aqev Area, part 2, and the Har Harif*, pp. 131–158. Dallas: Southern Methodist University.

Marks A.E., H.J. Hietala and J.K. Williams. 2001. Tool standardization in the Middle and Upper Paleolithic: a closer look. *Cambridge Archaeological Journal* 11: 17–44.

Mauss M. 1936. Les techniques du corps. *Journal de Psychologie* 32: 271–293.

McBrearty S. and A.S. Brooks. 2000. The revolution that wasn't: a new interpretation of the origin of modern human behavior. *Journal of Human Evolution* 39: 453–563.

Mellars P. 1967. *The Mousterian Succession in South-west France*. Ph.D. Dissertation, University of Cambridge.

Mellars P. 1989. Major issues in the emergence of modern humans. *Current Anthropology* 30: 349–385.

Mellars P. 1996. *The Neanderthal Legacy*. Princeton: Princeton University Press.

Mellars P. 2000. The archaeological records of the Neandertal-modern human transition in France. In O. Bar-Yosef and D. Pilbeam (Eds.), *The Geography of Neanderthals and Modern Humans in Europe and the Greater Mediterranean* (Peabody Museum of Archaeology and Ethnology Bulletin 8), pp. 35–48. Cambridge MA: Peabody Museum, Harvard University.

Movius H.L. 1948. The Lower Paleolithic cultures of southern and eastern Asia. *Transactions of the American Philosophical Society* 38: 329–420.

Neeley M.P. and C.M. Barton. 1994. A new approach to interpreting Late Pleistocene microlith industries in southwest Asia. *Antiquity* 68: 275–288.

Renfrew A.C. 1969. Trade and culture process in European prehistory. *Current Anthropology* 10: 151–169.

Révillon S. 1989. Le débitage du gisement paléolithique moyen de Seclin (Nord). In A. Tuffreau (Ed.), *Paléolithique et Mésolithique du Nord de la France: nouvelles recherches*, pp. 79–90. Lille: Centre d'Etudes et de Recherches Préhistorique.

Riel-Salvatore J. and G.A. Clark 2001. Grave markers: Middle and early Upper Paleolithic burials and the use of chronotypology in contemporary Paleolithic research. *Current Anthropology* 42: 449–480.

Riel-Salvatore J. and C.M. Barton 2004. Late Pleistocene technology, economic behavior and land-use dynamics in southern Italy. *American Antiquity* 69: 257–274.

Rigaud, J.-P. 1997. Scenarios for the Middle to Upper Paleolithic transition: a European perspective. In G.A. Clark and C.M. Willermet (Eds.), *Conceptual Issues in Modern Human Origins Research*, pp. 161–167. New York: Aldine de Gruyter.

Rigaud, J.-P. and J.-M. Geneste 1988. L'utilisation de l'espace dans la Grotte Vaufrey. In J.-P. Rigaud (Ed.), *La Grotte Vaufrey: paléoenvironnement, chronologie, activités humaines* (Mémoires de la Société Préhistorique Française XIX), pp. 593–611. Paris: Société Préhistorique Française.

Roberts M.B. 1986. Excavation of a Lower Palaeolithic site at Amey's Eartham Pit, Boxgrove, West Sussex: a preliminary report. *Proceedings of the Prehistoric Society* 52: 215–245.

Roberts M.B., C.S. Gamble and D.R. Bridgland 1995. The earliest occupation of Europe: the British Isles. In W. Roebroeks and T. van Kolfschoten (Eds.), *The Earliest Occupation of Europe*, pp. 165–192. Leiden: University of Leiden Press.

Sackett J.R. 1988. The Mousterian and its aftermath: a view from the Upper Paleolithic. In H.L. Dibble and A. Montet-White (Eds.), *The Upper Pleistocene Prehistory of Western Eurasia* (Symposium Series 1), pp. 413–426. Philadelphia: University of Pennsylvania Museum.

Sackett J.R. 1991. Straight archaeology French style: the phylogenetic paradigm in historic perspective. In G.A. Clark (Ed.), *Perspectives on the Past: Theoretical Biases in Mediterranean Hunter-Gatherer Research*, pp. 109–140. Philadelphia: University of Pennsylvania Press.

Sackett J.R. 1997. Neanderthal behaviour: the archaeological evidence. *Cambridge Archaeological Journal* 7: 148–149.

Schick K.D. and N. Toth 1994. Early Stone Age technology in Africa: a review and case study into the nature and function of spheroids and subspheroids. In R.S. Corruccini and R.L. Ciochon (Eds.), *Integrative Paths to the Past: Paleoanthropological Advances in Honor of F. Clark Howell*, pp. 429–229. Englewood Cliffs: Prentice Hall.

Schuldenrein J. and G.A. Clark 2001. Prehistoric landscapes and settlement geography along the Wadi Hasa, West-Central Jordan. Part I: Geoarchaeology, human palaeoecology and ethnographic modelling. *Environmental Archaeology* 6: 25–40.

Schuldenrein, J. and G.A. Clark. 2003. Prehistoric landscapes and settlement geography along the Wadi Hasa, West-Central Jordan. Part II: Towards a model of palaeoecological settlement for the Wadi Hasa. *Environmental Archaeology* 8: 1–16.

Scott K. 1986. The bone assemblages of layers 3 and 6. In P. Callow and J.M. Cornford (Eds.), *La Cotte de St. Brelade 1961–1978: Excavations by C.B.M. Burney*, pp. 159–183. Norwich: Geo Books.

Scott K. 1989. Mammoth bones modified by humans: evidence from la Cotte de St Brelade, Jersey, Channel Islands. In R. Bonnichsen and M.H. Sorg (Eds.) *Bone Modification*, pp. 335–346. Orono: Center for the Study of the First Americans.

Siegal S. 1956. *Nonparametric Statistics for the Behavioral Sciences*. New York: McGraw-Hill.

Simpson R.D. 1978. The Calico Mountains archaeological site. In A. Bryan (Ed.), *Early Man in America*, pp. 218–220. Edmonton: University of Alberta.

Simpson R.D. 1982. The Calico Mountains Archaeological Project: a progress report. In J. Ericson, R. Taylor and R. Berger (Eds.), *Peopling of the New World* (Anthropological Papers 23), pp. 181–192. Los Altos: Ballena Press.

Slott-Moller R. 1990. La faune. In J. Jaubert, M. Lorblanchet, R. Slott-Moller, A Turq, and J.-P. Brugal (Eds.), *Les Chasseurs d'Aurochs de La Borde: un site du Paléolithique moyen (Livernon, Lot)*, pp. 33–68. Paris: Maison des Sciences de l'Homme.

de Sonneville-Bordes D. and J. Perrot. 1953. Essai d'adaptation des méthodes statistiques au Paléolithique supérieur. Premiers résultats. *Bulletin de la Société Préhistorique Française* 51: 323–333.

de Sonneville-Bordes D. and J. Perrot. 1954. Lexique typologique du Paléolithique supérieur, outillage lithique. 1. Grattoirs. 2. Outils solutréens. *Bulletin de la Société Préhistorique Française* 51: 327–335.

de Sonneville-Bordes D. and J. Perrot. 1955. Lexique typologique du Paléolithique supérieur, outillage lithique. 3. Outils composites, perçoirs. *Bulletin de la Société Préhistorique Française* 52: 76–79.

de Sonneville-Bordes D. and J. Perrot. 1956. Lexique typologique du Paléolithique supérieur, outillage lithique. 4. Burins. *Bulletin de la Société Préhistorique Française* 53: 408–412, 547–559.

Speth J.D. 1972. Mechanical basis of percussion flaking. *American Antiquity* 37: 34–60.

Speth J.D. 1975. Miscellaneous studies in hard-hammer percussion flaking: the effects of oblique impact. *American Antiquity* 40: 203–207.

Steward J.H. 1936. The economic and social basis of primitive bands. In R.H. Lowie (Ed.), *Essays in Anthropology Presented to A.L. Kroeber*, pp. 331–350. Berkeley: University of California Press.

Stiner M.C. 1991. The community ecology perspective and the redemption of 'contaminated' faunal records. In G.A. Clark (Ed.), *Perspectives on the Past: Theoretical Biases in Mediterranean Hunter-Gatherer Research*, pp. 229–242. Philadelphia: University of Pennsylvania Press.

Stiner M.C. 1994. *Honor among Thieves: a Zooarchaeological Study of Neandertal Ecology*. Princeton: Princeton University Press.

Straus L.G. (Ed.), 2002. *The Role of American Archeologists in the Study of the European Upper Paleolithic* (BAR International Series 1048). Arcaheopress, Oxford.

Straus L.G. 2003. The Aurignacian? Some thoughts. In J. Zilhão and F. d'Errico (Eds.), *The Chronology of the Aurignacian and of the Transitional Technocomplexes: Dating, Stratigraphies, Cultural Implications*, pp. 11–18. Lisbon: Instituto Português de Arqueologia.

Swisher C.C., G.H. Curtis, T. Jacob, A.G. Getty, A. Suprijo and Widiasmoro 1994. Age of the earliest known hominids in Java, Indonesia. *Science* 263: 1118–1121.

Tattersall I. 1998. *Becoming Human: Evolution and Human Uniqueness*. New York: Harcourt Brace.

Toth N. 1985. The Oldowan reassessed: a close look at early stone artifacts. *Journal of Archaeological Science* 12: 101–120.

Toth N. 1987. Behavioral inferences from early stone artifact assemblages: an experimental model. *Journal of Human Evolution* 16: 763–787.

Toth N. and K.D. Schick 1993. Early stone industries. In K.R. Gibson and T. Ingold (Eds.), *Tools, Language, and Cognition in Human Evolution*, pp. 346–362. Cambridge: Cambridge University Press.

Tuffreau A. 1992. Middle Paleolithic settlement in Northern France. In H.L. Dibble and P. Mellars (Eds.), *The Middle Paleolithic: Adaptation, Behavior and Variability* (Symposium Series 2), pp. 59–74. Philadelphia: University of Pennsylvania Museum.

Turq A. 1988. Le Moustérien de type Quina du Roc de Marsal à Campagne (Dordogne): contexte strati-graphique, analyse lithographique et technologique. *Dossiers d'Archéologie Périgourdienne* 3: 5–30.

Turq A. 1989. Exploitation des matières premières lithiques et occupation du sol: l'exemple du Moustérien entre Dordogne et Lot. In H. Laville (Ed.), *Variations des Paléomilieux et Peuplement Préhistorique*, pp. 179–204. Paris: CNRS Editions.

Turq A. 1992. Raw material and technological studies of the Quina Mousterian in Périgord. In H.L. Dibble and P. Mellars (Eds.). *The Middle Paleolithic: Adaptation, Behavior and Variability* (Symposium Series 2), pp. 75–85. Philadelphia: University of Pennsylvania Museum.

Vermeersch P., E. Paulissen and P. van Peer 1997. Extensive Middle Paleolithic chert extraction in the Qena area (Egypt). In R. Schild and Z. Sulgostowska (Eds.), *Man and Flint: Proceedings of the VIIth International Flint Symposium*, pp. 133–142. Warsaw: Institute of Archaeology and Ethnology, Polish Academy of Science.

Villa P. 1982. Conjoinable pieces and site formation processes. *American Antiquity* 47: 276–290.

Villa P. 1983. *Terra Amata and the Middle Pleistocene Archaeological Record of Southern France*. Berkeley: University of California Press.

Winterhalder B. and E.A. Smith 2000. Analyzing adaptive strategies: human behavioral ecology at twenty-five. *Evolutionary Anthropology* 9: 51–72.

Wynn T. 1979. The intelligence of later Acheulean hominids. *Man* 14: 379–391.

Wynn T. 1981. The intelligence of Oldowan hominids. *Journal of Human Evolution* 10: 529–541.

Wynn T. 1985. Piaget, stone tools and the evolution of human intelligence. *World Archaeology* 17: 32–43.

Zilhão, J. and F. d'Errico. 1999. The chronology and taphonomy of the earliest Aurignacian and its implications for the understanding of Neanderthal extinction. *Journal of World Prehistory* 13: 1–68.

Zilhão J. and F. d'Errico (Eds.) 2003. *The Chronology of the Aurignacian and of the Transitional Technocom-plexes: Dating, Stratigraphies, Cultural Implications*. Lisbon: Instituto Português de Arqueologia.

Chapter 4

Testing Retouched Flake Tool Standardization During the Middle Paleolithic
Patterns and Implications

Gilliane Monnier

Department of Anthropology, University of Minnesota, Minneapolis, Minnesota 55455

ABSTRACT

It has long been claimed that retouched flake tools become more standardized throughout the Lower and Middle Paleolithic. Since stone tool standardization has been linked to cognitive abilities, specifically, to the presence of mental templates, the implications of an increase in standardization throughout this time period are that hominid cognitive abilities, including language, became more developed. Such an increase in standardization during this span of time has never been verified empirically, however. In addition, there is reason to question the link between lithic artifact standardization and hominid cognitive abilities. The purpose of this paper is therefore two-fold: first, to empirically test the notion that stone tools become more standardized throughout the late Middle and early Upper Pleistocene, and second, to explore potential causes of standardization more parsimonious than the deliberate imposition of arbitrary form. The results for the first part show no significant increases in standardization among retouched stone tools at three French sites spanning the late Middle and early Upper Pleistocene. The second part yields an interesting new hypothesis regarding circumstances which may lead to standardization among retouched tools, and helps explain why standardization seems to be so much more common after the start of the Upper Paleolithic.

INTRODUCTION

Most research on European pre-Upper Paleolithic stone tools over the past four decades has focused on interpreting assemblage variability and understanding flintknapping technologies. The first venture, best exemplified by the "Great Mousterian Debate" (Binford and Binford 1966; Binford 1973; Bordes and de Sonneville-Bordes 1970; Mellars 1965, 1969, 1973), has led to a better understanding of Middle Paleolithic synchronic variability (*e.g.*, Dibble 1987, 1995; Beyries 1988; Dibble and Rolland 1992; Turq 1992). The second has resulted in the identification of various flintknapping trajectories or *chaînes opératoires*, which may reflect different functions or styles (*e.g.*, Boëda *et al.* 1990; Boëda 1993; Meignen 1993). While both of these approaches have contributed a great deal to our knowledge of typological and technological patterning during this time period, diachronic variability remains remarkably poorly documented, much less understood (for exceptions, see Delagnes and Meignen this volume; Rolland 1986, 1995). One of the main reasons for this has been the lack of an adequate chronology. Now, fortunately, increased application of absolute dating techniques to late Middle and early Upper Pleistocene sites enables us to begin constructing a fairly secure, albeit rudimentary, chronological framework. As chronological resolution increases, it becomes possible to examine diachronic cultural trends across this time period. One such trend is the standardization of retouched flake tools, which has long been claimed to increase throughout this span of time. Since standardization is often argued to reflect cognitive abilities (Gowlett 1984, 1996; Mellars 1989b, 1996b; Wynn 1988; Chazan 1995; see also Marks *et al.* 2001), it is important to verify this claim. This study, therefore, was designed to test whether standardization among retouched flake tools increases throughout the late Middle and early Upper Pleistocene in Western Europe. Second, it explores the causes of standardization, and sets forth a new hypothesis regarding the circumstances which can lead to standardization in stone tools.

The notion that tool standardization increases through time has most recently been applied to the Middle to Upper Paleolithic transition (*e.g.* Mellars 1989a, 1991, 1996b; for rebuttal, see Marks *et al.* 2001). However, it has long been assumed that there is a gradual increase in standardization throughout the Lower and Middle Paleolithic as well. This idea was particularly emphasized at a conference on the Lower to Middle Paleolithic transition held in Haifa, Israel, in 1980 (Ronen 1982). At this conference, for example, Tuffreau (1982:137) characterized retouched stone tools in the Middle Paleolithic as "typologically evolved and well standardized", in contrast to those of the Lower Paleolithic, which he labeled "most of the time rough and typologically little evolved". Valoch echoed this argument, stating that "the shapes of tools were more differentiated" in the Middle Paleolithic than previously (Valoch 1982:193). Finally, Roe characterized Lower Paleolithic retouched flake tools as having "few standardized types or closely repeated shapes," and retouch which is "usually robust and purposeful rather than elegant in appearance" (Roe 1982:180). He described Middle Paleolithic flake tools, on the other hand, as "precisely designed and carefully executed, so that numerous clear types exist (*cf.* Bordes 1961a, *etc.*) and are accurately repeated. There are many different types of retouch, usually accurately and elegantly applied" (Roe 1982:180).

In other words, most participants at the Haifa conference viewed stone tools as evolving from rough precursors during the Lower Paleolithic to perfected forms by the end of the Middle Paleolithic.

Today, although few workers still adhere to a view of unidirectional cultural evolution, most still subscribe to the notion that tools became more standardized and refined through time. For example, in one of the more recent discussions of the subject, Middle Paleolithic lithic assemblages are seen as "characterized by a high proportion of standardised flake-supports and flake tools" (Gamble and Roebroeks 1999:5). In a similar vein, others have emphasized the "more carefully shaped and retouched flake tools" of the Mousterian (Gowlett 1992:353) and the "continued refinement of [its] flake-oriented toolkits" (Trinkaus 1992:349). Tattersall has stated that "the apogee of [flake-tool-making] was achieved by the Neanderthals, whose beautifully crafted Mousterian tools came in a large variety of standardized forms" (Tattersall 1995:244). Callow asserts that Mousterian flake tools are typologically more clearly defined than in preceding periods (Callow 1986:385 as cited in Hayden 1993), and Hayden claims that "classic Mousterian bifaces, points, convergent scrapers, transverse scrapers and other types exhibit degrees of standardization that probably rank among the highest of any flake industry in the world" (Hayden 1993:122). In sum, even today, many archaeologists stress that stone tools become more standardized throughout the Lower and Middle Paleolithic. For the sake of simplicity, the geological period which encompasses these cultural divisions, namely the late Middle to early Upper Pleistocene, is the chronological unit of analysis used here.

THE COGNITIVE IMPLICATIONS OF STONE TOOL STANDARDIZATION

Stone tool standardization has long been regarded as significant in human evolution because it is seen as an indicator of cognitive ability. Most frequently, the presence of standardized artifacts has been interpreted as reflecting the existence of a mental template in the minds of the flintknappers who produced the objects (*e.g.*, Mellars 1989a). The notion of mental template was best described by Deetz (1967:34, emphasis mine): "The idea of the proper form of an object exists in the mind of the maker, and when this idea is expressed in tangible form in raw material, an artifact results. The idea is the *mental template* from which the craftsman makes the object." In other words, when a specific form occurs repeatedly in an assemblage, it is assumed that it represents a desired end-product manufactured according to certain socially defined parameters. These parameters result from mental categories similar to those which represent words, and are symbolic in nature (for a critique of the applicability of mental templates to stone tools, see Chase and Dibble 1987; Dibble 1989).

A similar theme emerges in Holloway's seminal paper, "Culture: A *Human* Domain" (Holloway 1969, italics in the original). Holloway's central argument is that the most important elements of culture, those which distinguish humans from other animals, are arbitrary form and the *imposition* of arbitrary form upon the environment (see also Geertz 1964). The imposition of arbitrary form, according to Holloway, can be detected in stone tools, because "there is no necessary relation between the form of the final product and the original material" (Holloway 1969:401). The shape of stone tools, therefore, is symbolic in nature, according to Holloway, and the appearance of stone tools in the archaeological record signals the emergence of modern human behavior or human culture. Holloway links stone tool-making and language by suggesting that they are "similar, if not identical, cognitive processes" (Holloway 1969:396), not only because both of these activities employ symbolization, but because they are both hierarchically organized processes that depend upon socially mediated rules. The existence and application of explicit rules such as those which define words or set the parameters for a stone tool type, according to Holloway, better accounts for the widespread temporal and spatial distribution of certain tool types, like handaxes, than simple imitative and observational learning (but see Wynn 1995).

Although many of Holloway's ideas are now outdated (for critiques, see Dibble 1989; Noble and Davidson 1991), they laid the foundation for a generation of studies which attempted to trace the evolution of human cognitive abilities on the basis of the archaeological record. For example, Gowlett (1984, 1996) has suggested that standardization among bifaces at the Acheulean site of Kilombe in Africa implies that the makers of the bifaces had a specific mental template which they imposed on the stone, suggesting a certain level of cognitive ability, specifically aptitude for mathematics and art. Another set of studies by Wynn (1985, 1988, 1991) attempts to infer the mental abilities of ancient hominids by seeking evidence in the archaeological record for Piagetian stages of cognitive development. Wynn (1988) has focused on the concept of symmetry in bifaces, which he argues is well developed by 300,000 years ago, indicating the attainment of Piaget's concrete operational intelligence stage. He has also suggested that the standardization of tool types implies that the technology was not *ad hoc* and reflects a certain level of cognitive development (Wynn 1988).

The cognitive implications of standardization and imposition of arbitrary form have been most emphasized by Mellars in relation to the Middle to Upper Paleolithic transition (Mellars 1989a, 1989b, 1991, 1996a:133–136). Mellars argues that Upper Paleolithic stone tools appear to exhibit a better-defined pattern of standardization and imposed form than do their Middle Paleolithic counterparts (Mellars 1989a). Under the assumption that the imposition of arbitrary form and standardization are linked to the presence of mental templates, he concludes that there is greater evidence for a symbolic or cognitive component behind tool-making in the Upper Paleolithic than in the Middle Paleolithic. Another study which examines stone tool standardization across the Middle-to-Upper Paleolithic transition was conducted by Chazan (1995). Chazan posits that stone tool standardization reflects the presence of language, in order to test the hypothesis that the appearance of language was one of the catalysts for the Middle/Upper Paleolithic transition. In a study of assemblages from four sites, he finds no evidence for greater standardization of debitage or selection of blanks for retouch in Upper Paleolithic assemblages and concludes that the language hypothesis for the transition is not supported (Chazan 1995). There are, however, a number of problems with his methodology which throw his results into question (see Monnier 1995).

Many of the other studies mentioned above are also flawed. Some are faulty in the sense that the perceived standardization is actually an artifact of the research methodology. For example, Gowlett interprets the Kilombe bifaces as standardized on the basis of a high correlation between biface length and width (Gowlett 1984, 1996). Another explanation for this phenomenon (observed separately by Alimen and Vignal [1952]) has been proposed by Dibble (1989). Dibble suggests that the high correlation is due to technological constraints on the shapes of bifaces (*e.g.*, it is rare that the length of a biface is ever greater than three times its width), as well as being inherent in the definition of bifaces, whereby length is always greater than width. He demonstrates that an equally high correlation between length and width can be achieved on a random series of computer-generated hypothetical bifaces, as soon as length is set to be greater than width. The apparent standardization of bifaces, therefore, when measured simply as a correlation between length and width, is largely a product of the type definition.

Another fundamental flaw in many of these studies is the strength of the hypothesized link between artifact standardization and symbolic or other cognitive abilities. For example, Chase (1991) has argued that standardization can result from functional and technological factors, and therefore does not require the use of symbols. In fact, he emphasizes that only when standardization can be demonstrated to be unrelated to function, technology, or raw material factors can symboling be inferred. In another study, Dibble (1989) has questioned the link between Bordesian artifact types and mental templates by demonstrating that: (1) there is continuous variation between some Bordesian types (specifically sidescrapers); and, 2) much of this variation represents different degrees of utilization and re-sharpening, which means that artifacts are discarded, worn-out tools rather than desired end-products. He has also shown that, sometimes, types which we consider to be "desired end-products" such as Levallois flakes, are no more standardized than types *not* considered to be "desired end-products," such as biface retouch flakes (Dibble 1989). This challenges the link between standardization and mental templates, and questions whether Lower and Middle Paleolithic stone tool types reflect linguistic categories, or merely other factors such as technology, raw material, and our own classificatory methods (see also Chase and Dibble 1987).

In sum, it is clear that the standardization of stone tools is widely believed to contain significant implications for the cognitive abilities of hominids, especially as they relate to the use of symbols and language. It is also clear, however, that there are significant problems, methodological, theoretical, or both, with many studies which have attempted to reconstruct human cognitive abilities on the basis of stone tool standardization. Despite these difficulties, assertions that retouched tool standardization increases throughout the late Middle and early Upper Pleistocene continue to be made, as described earlier. This study first explores whether standardization of retouched tools increases throughout the late Middle and early Upper Pleistocene, and second examines potential causes of standardization. The first question forms the basis for an empirical study which was carried out as part of a broader work on the Lower to Middle Paleolithic transition in Western Europe (Monnier 2000), and is reported in the main body of this paper. The second question, more theoretical in nature, is treated in the Discussion section.

SAMPLE AND METHODOLOGY

Sample

The assemblages included in this study all come from deeply stratified rock shelters in South-Central and Southwestern France: Combe-Grenal (Bordes 1972), La Chaise (Debénath 1974; Blackwell et al. 1983), and Orgnac 3 (Combier 1967; Moncel and Combier 1992a, 1992b; Moncel 1999). These sites were selected because they are dated by absolute dating methods, were well excavated, span long periods of time, and contain sufficiently large sample sizes. An additional advantage of this sample is that each site used to be considered transitional between the Lower and Middle Paleolithic (e.g., Combier 1967; Bordes 1972; Debénath 1974), and therefore should be expected to show some of the features claimed to reflect an increase in standardization from Lower to Middle Paleolithic in the papers described earlier (e.g., Roe 1982; Tuffreau 1982). Finally, at Orgnac 3 in the Ardèche region of southern France, Moncel and Combier (1992a, 1992b) have argued that retouched flake tools, especially scrapers, become increasingly standardized throughout the sequence. This study can therefore directly verify their claim.

Basic data concerning these assemblages are presented in Table 1. Only assemblages containing sufficient sample sizes were included, and sometimes similar levels were combined in order to increase sample size. In addition, the selection of assemblages at Combe-Grenal was also based on the criteria that they should be well preserved (not weathered or rolled), span a significant portion of the site's occupation, and lastly, be drawn from a variety of industrial types. At La Chaise, which is comprised of two separate but connected rock shelters, comparisons were made from the oldest levels of the Abri Suard to the youngest levels of the Abri Bourgeois-Delaunay. Although each rock shelter has its own formation history, they are connected and are very similar in technology, typology, and raw materials; therefore, they were treated as a single site.

Methodology

The first step in developing a methodology to test the hypothesis of increasing standardization of retouched stone tools throughout the late Middle and early Upper Pleistocene was the operationalization of a definition of standardization that would yield quantitative, testable implications. Next, an attribute analysis was

Table 1. Assemblages used in this study

Site	Levels	N	Dating
Combe-Grenal	22	328	O.I.S. 3 (Bowman and Sieveking 1983, Mellars 1996:39)
	35	416	O.I.S. 4 (*ibid.*)
	56–57	156	O.I.S. 6 (*ibid.*)
	58	289	"
	60–61	146	"
La Chaise (Abri Bourgeois-Delaunay)	9	245	O.I.S. 5d (Blackwell et al. 1983, Schwarcz and Debénath 1979)
	10	49	"
La Chaise (Abri Suard)	51	69	O.I.S. 6 (*ibid.*)
	52–53	77	"
Orgnac 3	1	184	O.I.S. 8 (Moncel and Combier 1992a; Moncel 1999)
	2-3	145	"
	4a–4b	101	"
	5a–6	189	"

designed on the basis of these test implications. The first objective was achieved by specifying the characteristics that a set of standardized tools is expected to exhibit (Table 2). These characteristics were derived in part from existing descriptions of features contributing to standardization, such as "the choice of specific blank forms for distinct artifact categories, the choice of different types of retouch for shaping the tools, the positioning of this retouch at specific points around the margins of the tools, and so on" (Mellars 1989b:358).

Typology and Standardization – Some Considerations

It is clear that the choice of a "set" of tools to be examined for standardization is arbitrary. Such a set could comprise all the lithic artifacts in a particular assemblage, or any subset thereof, such as debitage, retouched tools, or even a particular type of retouched tool. In this study, each set of tools, which formed the unit of analysis that was traced through time, encompasses a number of related Bordes [1961] types, such as single sidescrapers (types 9–11) or double sidescrapers (types 12–17). There are problems with the use of typology in this kind of study, however. The first is that a set of artifacts classified into a type will undoubtedly be less

Table 2. Characteristics of a set of standardized tools

1. They are similar in shape and size.
2. The type of retouch is the same.
3. The location of retouch is similar, and there is a clear separation between retouched and un-retouched portions of the tool.
4. They are often, but not always, symmetrical

variable, and thus more standardized, than artifacts outside of this type. This is because a type, by its very nature, seeks to organize a group of objects containing certain similar, predefined features. This problem is easily corrected by making within-type comparisons only, rather than comparing attributes across types.

The use of typology in within-type comparisons leads to other issues, however. The most serious is the question of whether the archaeological types correspond to the "real," or emic, types. In other words, does it make sense for us to study the patterning of standardization attributes through time within a given tool type, if that tool type does not correspond to a type that the original toolmakers would have recognized? The question of the "reality" of types and whether or not we can identify emic types is the subject of an age-old debate (Spaulding 1953; Ford 1954). Clearly we will never know whether we can identify emic types or not. This study, fortunately, is designed to test claims that standardization increases throughout the late Middle and early Upper Pleistocene, and therefore it does not need to identify emic types, but simply those types used by the archaeologists who made those claims. For this reason, it was deemed appropriate to use Bordesian types (Bordes 1961), which have been widely used in Old World Paleolithic archaeology for over 40 years.

Test Implications

The expected characteristics of a set of standardized tools listed in Table 2 were used to derive four test implications for the hypothesis that retouched stone tools become increasingly standardized throughout the Middle Paleolithic.

1. The variability in **tool size and shape** within a type should become more restricted from older to younger assemblages.
2. The variability in **retouch type** within a tool type should decrease from older to younger assemblages. For example, although a "single straight scraper" (Bordes 1961) is defined as having one edge with rectilinear scraper retouch, in practice such a scraper can have other types of retouch on it (*e.g.*, notches) and still be called a single straight scraper. A set of standardized tools would be expected to show less variability in retouch type than a set of non-standardized tools.
3. The **location of retouch** should become more restricted through time. In other words, it is expected that a set of standardized tools will exhibit retouch on the same portion of the tool (*e.g.*, tip, edge, both edges), and furthermore, that there will be a distinction between the working and non-working edge(s) of the tool. Younger assemblages, if they are indeed more standardized, should therefore exhibit a more consistent location of retouch (within types) than older assemblages, where retouch is expected to be more haphazard.
4. The proportion of **symmetrical tools** should increase through time. Symmetry is often linked to standardization and mental templates (*e.g.*, Wynn 1988, 1991; Mellars 1996b:26), and therefore it is expected that younger

assemblages should have a greater proportion of symmetrical tools than older assemblages. (There are, of course, certain tool types, such as shouldered points, which are asymmetrical yet appear highly standardized, but these are a minority.)

Attribute Analysis Design

An attribute analysis was designed in order to provide quantitative measures of standardization appropriate for application to each of the test implications described above. This was applied to all of the complete, retouched flint tools in each assemblage ("pseudo-tools", such as Bordes' "46-49" category, were not included). The tool classes included in the final analysis are the most common ones: single sidescrapers, double sidescrapers, convergent scrapers, transverse scrapers, notches, and denticulates. A key aspect of the methodology is the orientation of the tools. Each tool included in the study was oriented along the axis of the tool (with the narrower or pointed end up), rather than along the axis of the blank (see Figure 1). Since variability in blank form affects the placement of cutting edges on the tool, this method of orientation makes it more likely that standardization, if present, will be detected. Each tool was then bisected along the longest axis, and again perpendicular to this axis, in order to form four quadrants. These quadrangle lines were then used for measuring tool length and width, respectively, and thickness at the intersection of these lines, relevant to test implication 1. The quadrangle lines were also used as a basis for determining (subjectively) symmetry—longitudinal, transversal, or both—in order to address test implication 4. Test implications 2 and

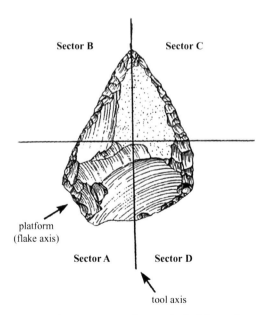

Figure 1. Orientation of Retouched Flake Tools.

Table 3. Major variables used in study

Variable	Description and Attribute States
Length	Measured by caliper along the long axis bisecting the tool (see Fig. 1).
Width	Measured at the midpoint of Length and perpendicular to it.
Thickness	Measured at the intersection of Length and Width.
Retouch Type	Denticulate, Scraper, Notched, Marginal, Abrupt, Quina, Flake, Other.
Location of Retouch	Dorsal Quadrant A, B, C, D, and/or Ventral Quad. A, B, C, D (see Fig. 1).
Amount of Retouch	For each Quadrant: 0%, 1–50%, 51-99%, or 100%. (means were used in the analyses)
Symmetry of Tool	None, Longitudinal, Transversal, Longitudinal and Transversal.

3 were addressed by noting, for each piece and for each quadrant (dorsal as well as ventral), the dominant type of retouch present and the percentage of retouch in that particular quadrant (Table 3). Clearly, retouch attributes are affected by factors such as intensity of utilization (e.g., Dibble and Rolland 1992; Dibble 1995; Holdaway et al. 1996). This, however, does not preclude their use for identifying standardization, the causes of which could reflect intensity of utilization, function, technology, or symbolism.

RESULTS

Size and Shape

The first test implication states that variability in tool size and shape should become more restricted through time. Accordingly, we should expect the coefficient of variation (C.V.; a measure of variability which controls for sample size) of some or all of the metrical attributes (Length, Width, Thickness), as well as that of the ratios (Length/Width and Width/Thickness) to decrease from the older levels to the younger levels within a site. A certain amount of variability is always to be expected in archaeology, so no single tool type is expected to exhibit a perfect pattern of decreasing values of the coefficient of variation (C.V.) from one level to the next. However, if such a pattern is truly present within a given tool type, it is expected that at least two or three of the metrical attributes or ratios should show a *general* trend of decreasing C.V. through time. Accordingly, the results for each attribute were interpreted as significant if the C.V. for four out of five levels at Combe-Grenal, or three out of four levels at Orgnac 3 and La Chaise, decrease consistently through time: in addition, the excluded level must fall within the range of that particular attribute.

Significant patterns are highlighted in bold type in Tables 4a–c. Note that certain tool types could not be included in this analysis when sample sizes fell below five. For this reason, double and convergent scrapers at Orgnac 3 and transverse scrapers at La Chaise were excluded from the analysis. (The exclusion of certain levels in other tests also is a consequence of sample sizes falling below five.) At Combe-Grenal, none of the metrical attributes follows the expected pattern except for single sidescrapers, where the C.V. for three out of five metrical attributes and ratios (specifically, Length, Thickness, and Length/Width) shows a general decrease through time (Table 4a). At Orgnac 3, the only tool type which shows a consistently decreasing C.V. across multiple attributes (Length, Length/Width, Width/Thickness) is again single the sidescraper (see Table 4b). Finally, at La Chaise single sidescrapers are also the only tool type which exhibit a decreasing C.V. across several attributes (Length, Width, and Thickness; see Table 4c). Thus, in all three sites there is some evidence that the size and shape of single sidescrapers become more standardized through time. However, there is no evidence that standardization of size and shape for any of the other tool types increases: double sidescrapers, convergent and transverse scrapers (where tested), notches and denticulates. Test implication 1, therefore, is rejected for all tool types except single sidescrapers.

Table 4a. Coefficient of variation for size and shape attributes at Combe-Grenal (significant patterns are highlighted in bold; see text)

Tool type	Level	N	Length	Width	Thickness	L/W	W/Th
Single Sidescrapers	22	144	**20.54**	24.83	**35.93**	**19.36**	33.87
(Bordes types 9–11)	35	248	**21.32**	23.85	**37.1**	**23.8**	38.13
	56–57	57	**20.92**	25.13	**38.41**	**24.21**	40.79
	58	125	**23.57**	24.86	**35.64**	**28.21**	35.77
	60–61	73	**28.25**	27.45	**46.13**	**21.72**	35.84
Double Sidescrapers	22	20	22.22	18.07	42.07	22.56	34.76
(Bordes types 12–17)	35	35	19.65	23.00	52.37	23.18	34.98
	56–57	6	51.99	22.28	41.48	25.45	40.23
	58	8	17.9	32.51	21.26	29.83	43.04
	60–61	7	19.77	28.15	41.68	21.69	23.96
Convergent Scrapers	22	13	26.29	13.25	34.54	25.29	46.76
(Bordes types 18–20)	35	49	17.70	20.65	32.95	20.59	31.69
	56–57	5	24.21	11.38	31.90	32.73	26.03
	58	6	17.66	14.39	51.32	17.77	45.05
Transverse Scrapers	22	84	17.30	20.61	38.40	19.39	38.24
(Bordes types 22–24)	35	51	20.34	20.56	38.56	17.10	30.53
	56–57	16	33.26	26.14	31.71	21.70	27.74
	58	40	23.36	24.56	32.08	20.62	42.56
	60–61	15	18.59	21.14	46.30	18.37	43.82
Notches	22	23	15.57	17.44	39.34	23.80	35.24
(Bordes type 42)	35	18	27.69	29.95	49.57	29.69	27.21
	56–57	24	19.11	20.31	41.27	23.91	33.59
	58	37	26.87	25.07	34.72	23.60	35.36
	60–61	14	22.45	21.16	24.18	18.50	24.61
Denticulates	22	44	18.23	18.81	35.15	21.99	38.77
(Bordes type 43)	35	15	20.74	31.43	37.12	26.17	29.92
	56–57	48	15.19	20.01	29.42	18.00	36.30
	58	73	18.55	23.57	38.44	22.48	34.98
	60–61	36	21.42	25.23	27.64	20.56	23.68

Table 4b. Coefficient of variation for size and shape metrical attributes at Orgnac 3
(significant patterns are highlighted in bold; see text)

Tool type	Level	N	Length	Width	Thickness	L/W	W/Th
Single Sidescraper	1	68	**19.50**	29.31	38.00	**24.58**	**38.30**
	2–3	54	**25.58**	24.12	36.75	**24.74**	**40.11**
	4a–4b	26	**21.50**	23.06	32.05	**24.89**	**46.55**
	5a–6	81	**25.86**	26.52	37.97	**26.73**	**42.19**
Transverse Scrapers	1	31	20.56	20.88	38.54	**20.49**	42.60
	2–3	28	21.06	17.93	36.50	**17.98**	35.42
	4a–4b	15	18.34	44.11	45.64	**19.25**	45.43
	5a–6	36	29.60	24.20	38.11	**23.77**	32.12
Notches	1	22	26.57	20.88	38.54	20.98	42.60
	2–3	21	22.39	17.93	36.50	28.26	35.42
	4a–4b	28	24.50	44.11	45.64	26.62	45.43
	5a–6	21	22.92	24.20	38.11	25.65	32.12
Denticulates	1	38	21.50	26.62	37.22	22.18	**31.56**
	2–3	31	26.88	32.51	47.45	19.03	**38.94**
	4a–4b	27	24.69	25.00	36.22	27.54	**32.00**
	5a–6	40	25.03	24.22	45.53	23.07	**39.70**

Table 4c. Coefficient of variation for size and shape metrical attributes at La Chaise
(significant patterns are highlighted in bold; see text)

Tool type	Level	N	Length	Width	Thickness	L/W	W/Th
Single Sidescraper	B-D 9	92	**23.50**	23.41	**31.70**	**26.15**	32.73
	B-D 10	19	**20.57**	23.63	**38.48**	**31.79**	37.79
	Suard 51	29	**21.73**	24.19	**35.35**	**23.72**	31.05
	Suard 52–53	36	**24.21**	29.17	**38.62**	**34.65**	32.62
Double Sidescrapers	B-D 9	13	31.32	**17.81**	38.84	23.28	30.79
	Suard 51	11	22.58	**21.82**	19.93	21.57	18.32
	Suard 52–53	8	20.43	**32.80**	37.19	46.07	36.56
Convergent Scrapers	B-D 9	26	27.27	25.43	26.33	19.10	28.72
	B-D 10	5	11.66	18.04	22.23	17.60	14.67
	Suard 52–53	8	28.36	24.49	47.48	26.05	24.78
Notches	B-D 9	24	22.23	28.31	**31.98**	25.46	29.37
	B-D 10	10	21.76	29.83	**38.75**	18.23	25.85
	Suard 51	9	25.06	35.53	**36.62**	28.91	14.29
	Suard 52–53	11	25.02	30.24	**39.64**	24.83	25.07
Denticulates	B-D 9	62	**24.43**	24.75	**34.52**	30.78	37.26
	B-D 10	9	**20.99**	23.48	**20.57**	24.32	21.99
	Suard 51	13	**21.91**	35.42	**43.23**	20.35	27.08
	Suard 52–53	12	**29.48**	31.84	**51.50**	15.98	33.61

Retouch Type

The second test implication in this study is that if standardization increases through time, variability in retouch type within tool types should decrease from older to younger assemblages. This was tested by comparing the mean number of retouch types (other than that which characterizes the type) within each tool type from one level to the next. As can be seen in Tables 5a-b, there is no evidence that the mean number of retouch types decreases through time in any tool class at Combe-Grenal or at Orgnac 3. While it appears that double sidescrapers have a higher mean number of retouch types in levels 2-3 than in level 1 of the latter site, there is no significant difference between these means (Mann-Whitney U = 41,

Table 5a. **Mean number of retouch types within tool types at Combe-Grenal (significant patterns are highlighted in bold; see text)**

Tool type	Level	N	Mean # of Retouch types	Deviation standard
Single Sidescraper	22	144	1.39	.59
	35	248	1.45	.65
	56–57	57	1.70	.76
	58	125	1.66	.73
	60–61	73	1.34	.56
Double Sidescrapers	22	20	1.25	.44
	35	35	1.69	.72
	56–57	6	1.17	.41
	58	8	1.75	.71
	60–61	7	1.29	.49
Convergent Scrapers	22	13	1.08	.28
	35	49	1.61	.70
	56–57	5	1.40	.55
	58	6	1.33	.52
Transverse Scrapers	22	84	1.35	.55
	35	51	1.49	.61
	56–57	16	1.25	.45
	58	40	1.50	.68
	60–61	15	1.20	.41
Notches	22	23	1.30	.47
	35	18	1.33	.59
	56–57	24	1.38	.49
	58	37	1.27	.65
	60–61	14	1.36	.50
Denticulates	22	44	1.34	.48
	35	15	1.87	.74
	56–57	48	1.73	.82
	58	73	1.32	.52
	60–61	36	1.56	.61

Table 5b. Mean number of retouch types within tool types at Orgnac 3 (significant patterns are highlighted in bold; see text)

Tool type	Level	N	Mean # of retouch types	Standard deviation
Single Sidescraper	1	68	1.26	.54
	2–3	54	1.26	.52
	4a–4b	26	1.27	.45
	5a–6	81	1.26	.49
Double Sidescrapers	1	11	1.18	.40
	2–3	8	1.25	.46
Convergent Scrapers	1	14	1.21	.43
	5a–6	8	1.00	.00
Transverse Scrapers	1	31	1.23	.50
	2–3	28	1.29	.46
	4a–4b	15	1.33	.62
	5a–6	36	1.33	.63
Notches	1	22	1.32	.48
	2–3	21	1.10	.30
	4a–4b	28	1.25	.44
	5a–6	21	1.14	.36
Denticulates	1	38	1.32	.66
	2–3	31	1.26	.51
	4a–4b	27	1.19	.40
	5a–6	40	1.23	.42

$n = 19$, $p = 0.726$). For transverse scrapers, a pattern of decreasing mean number of retouch types from older to younger levels is not statistically significant either (Kruskal-Wallis Chi-square $= 0.654$, df $= 3$, $p = 0.884$). Finally, at La Chaise the only instance of decreasing mean number of retouch types through time is found in transverse scrapers, between levels 10 and 9 of the Abri Bourgeois-Delaunay (Table 5c). However, these means are not significantly different (Mann-Whitney U $= 64$, n $= 33$, $p = 0.743$). In sum, there is no evidence for increasing standardization of retouch type through time at these sites, and test implication 2 is rejected.

Location of Retouch

The third test implication states that the location of retouch should be more restricted in standardized tools, and that a distinction between working and non-working edges should be more evident. This was tested by several methods, according to tool type. For example, single sidescrapers, by definition, should have scraper retouch only on one edge. However, in practice, many tools classified as single sidescrapers exhibit retouch on both edges (scraper retouch opposite a

Table 5c. Mean number of retouch types within tool types at La Chaise (significant patterns are highlighted in bold; see text)

Tool type	Level	N	Mean # of retouch types	Standard deviation
Single Sidescraper	B-D 9	92	1.87	.76
	B-D 10	19	2.26	.81
	Suard 51	29	1.93	.65
	Suard 52–53	36	1.64	.68
Double Sidescrapers	B-D 9	13	1.85	.80
	Suard 51	11	2.36	.67
	Suard 52–53	8	1.88	.83
Convergent Scrapers	B-D 9	26	1.88	.86
	B-D 10	5	1.60	.55
	Suard 52–53	8	1.75	.46
Transverse Scrapers	B-D 9	28	1.75	.75
	B-D 10	5	1.80	.45
Notches	B-D 9	24	1.50	.66
	B-D 10	10	1.50	.71
	Suard 51	9	1.89	1.45
	Suard 52–53	11	1.27	.47
Denticulates	B-D 9	62	1.76	.72
	B-D 10	9	2.44	1.33
	Suard 51	13	2.23	.93
	Suard 52–53	12	1.92	.79

notch, for instance). The proportion of such tools should be smaller in a more standardized assemblage; thus it was hypothesized that younger assemblages, if they are more standardized, should contain fewer single sidescrapers exhibiting retouch on *both* edges. Tables 6a-c show the percentage of single sidescrapers containing unilateral *vs.* bilateral retouch. For each site, the percentage of sidescrapers exhibiting only unilateral retouch is expected to rise from the older to the younger levels. There is no such pattern at any of the sites.

Table 6a. Combe-Grenal: Proportion of single sidescrapers with Unilateral vs. Bilateral retouch (significant patterns are highlighted in bold; see text)

Level	Bilateral retouch	Unilateral retouch
22	39 (27.1%)	**105 (72.9%)**
35	76 (30.6%)	**172 (69.4%)**
56–57	19 (33.3%)	**38 (66.7%)**
58	44 (35.2%)	**81 (64.8%)**
60–61	23 (31.9%)	49 (68.1%)

Table 6b. Orgnac 3: Proportion of single
sidescrapers with Unilateral vs. Bilateral
retouch (significant patterns are highlighted in
bold; see text)

Level	Bilateral retouch	Unilateral retouch
1	12 (17.6%)	56 (82.4%)
2–3	6 (11.1%)	48 (88.9%)
4a–4b	5 (19.2%)	21 (80.8%)
5a–6	17 (21.0%)	64 (79.0%)

Table 6c. La Chaise: Proportion of single sidescrapers with
Unilateral vs. Bilateral retouch (significant patterns are
highlighted in bold; see text)

Level	Bilateral retouch	Unilateral retouch
Bourgeois-Delaunay, 9	47 (51.6%)	44 (48.4%)
Bourgeois-Delaunay, 10	12 (63.2%)	7 (36.8%)
Suard, 51	13 (44.8%)	16 (55.2%)
Suard, 52–53	11 (30.6%)	25 (69.4%)

We should also expect that single sidescrapers which contain retouch on **both**
edges should become more lateralized through time. In other words, if standardization increases through time, the distinction between the working edge and the
non-working edge in single scrapers should become stronger. This can be examined
by comparing relative amounts of retouch between both edges. The percentage of
retouch along each edge varies from 0%-100% (see Table 3). The mean difference
in percentage of retouch between each edge was calculated and is presented in
Tables 7a-c. This value is expected to increase from older to younger assemblages
among single sidescrapers, as the working edge becomes more clearly defined.
At Orgnac 3, this value appears to increase across the four major levels in single
sidescrapers (see Table 7b). However, a Kruskal-Wallis test shows no significant
difference between the four means (Chi-square = .341, df = 3, p = 0.952). At La
Chaise and Combe-Grenal, the difference in percentage of retouch between edges
among single sidescrapers does not increase from the older to the younger levels
(see Tables 7a and 7c). In other words, there is no evidence to support the notion
that single sidescrapers become more lateralized, and hence more standardized,
through time.

Increased standardization of retouch location through time can also be tested
on double and convergent scrapers. For these types, the mean difference in retouch amount between edges is expected to decrease through time, since more
standardized double and convergent scrapers, especially the latter, might be expected to exhibit relatively equal amounts of retouch on both edges. However,
as can be seen in Tables 7a-c, this is not the case at either La Chaise, Orgnac 3,

Table 7a. Mean difference in retouch amount between tool edges at Combe-Grenal (significant patterns are highlighted in bold; see text)

Tool type	Level	N	Mean Retouch % difference between edges	Standard deviation	Coefficient of variation
Single Sidescraper	22	39	51.602	22.246	43.11
	35	76	52.467	20.718	39.49
	56–57	19	36.842	24.464	66.40
	58	44	37.784	19.344	51.20
	60–61	23	46.195	18.245	39.50
Double Sidescrapers	22	20	18.125	12.484	68.87
	35	34	23.897	21.622	90.48
	56–57	6	18.750	10.458	55.78
	58	8	12.500	13.363	106.90
	60–61	7	8.929	11.890	133.17
Convergent Scrapers	22	13	25.962	21.324	82.14
	35	49	20.408	16.672	**81.70**
	56–57	5	17.500	16.771	**95.83**
	58	6	12.500	15.811	**126.49**
Transverse Scrapers	22	41	48.781	30.208	61.93
	35	32	42.5781	24.151	56.72
	56–57	5	17.5000	18.957	108.33
	58	19	38.158	24.817	65.04

Table 7b. Mean difference in retouch amount between tool edges at Orgnac 3 (significant patterns are highlighted in bold; see text)

Tool type	Level	N	Mean Retouch % difference between edges	Standard deviation	Coefficient of variation
Single Sidescraper	1	12	46.875	27.760	59.22
	2–3	6	45.833	21.890	47.76
	4a–4b	5	40.000	16.298	40.75
	5a–6	17	41.912	23.775	56.73
Double Sidescrapers	1	11	26.136	17.189	65.77
	2–3	8	21.875	14.562	66.57
Convergent Scrapers	1	14	26.786	13.743	**51.31**
	5a–6	7	17.857	14.174	**79.38**
Transverse Scrapers	1	24	27.083	30.766	113.60
	2–3	14	37.500	29.823	79.53
	4a–4b	5	35.000	29.843	85.27
	5a–6	17	27.206	20.839	76.60

Table 7c. Mean difference in retouch amount between tool edges at La Chaise (significant patterns are highlighted in bold; see text)

Tool type	Level	N	Mean Retouch % difference between edges	Standard deviation	Coefficient of variation
Single Sidescraper	B-D 9	47	38.398	23.226	60.65
	B-D 10	12	53.125	16.101	30.31
	Suard 51	13	46.154	26.213	56.79
	Suard 52–53	11	38.636	30.850	79.85
Double Sidescrapers	B-D 9	13	26.923	21.558	**80.07**
	Suard 51	11	17.045	16.079	**94.33**
	Suard 52–53	8	26.563	26.252	**98.83**
Convergent Scrapers	B-D 9	26	20.192	14.176	70.21
	B-D 10	5	17.500	18.957	108.33
	Suard 52–53	8	12.500	11.573	92.58

or Combe-Grenal. It could be argued, actually, that such a pattern would not necessarily reflect standardization since a set of tools could have asymmetrically retouched edges and still be highly standardized, for example shouldered points. One way that this possibility could be taken into account is by looking at the C.V. of the mean difference in retouch percentage between edges, rather than the mean itself. Even if the mean does not decrease through time, there should be less variability in the difference in retouch amount between edges among a set of standardized tools, therefore one can expect the C.V. to decrease through time. This hypothesis applies to all four scraper classes, including transverse scrapers, which often contain some retouch on the edge opposite the main scraper edge. At Combe-Grenal, the only tool type out of the four which shows a decreasing C.V. through time is convergent scrapers (see Table 7a). At Orgnac 3, the C.V. of level 5a-6 for convergent scrapers is higher than the C.V. of level 1 (see Table 7b). However, since only two levels are included, this pattern has a 50% probability of occurring by chance. At La Chaise, the only pattern out of the four tool types which agrees with the hypothesis is the C.V. for double sidescrapers (see Table 7c). In sum, there is little evidence that the way in which relative amounts of retouch are apportioned between the two edges of scrapers becomes more standardized through time. Test implication 3 is therefore rejected, as well.

Symmetry

Finally, the fourth test implication is that the proportion of symmetrical tools should increase in younger assemblages. This attribute (a subjective assessment of the longitudinal or transverse symmetry of a piece) was noted over all tools within each assemblage, rather than within tool types. Any instance of symmetry, whether longitudinal or transversal, was counted. Tables 8a-c show the proportion of symmetrical to nonsymmetrical tools in each level at Combe-Grenal, Orgnac 3,

Table 8a. Combe-Grenal: Proportion of symmetrical tools (all tool types included) (significant patterns are highlighted in bold; see text)

Level	Non-symmetrical	Symmetrical
22	239 (61.9%)	147 (38.1%)
35	288 (62.6%)	172 (37.4%)
41–42/43	21 (58.3%)	15 (41.7%)
56–57	127 (62.9%)	75 (37.1%)
58	244 (63.7%)	139 (36.3%)
60–61	107 (65.2%)	57 (34.8%)

Table 8b. Orgnac 3: Proportion of symmetrical tools (all tool types included) (significant patterns are highlighted in bold; see text)

Level	Non-symmetrical	Symmetrical
1	153 (68.3%)	71 (31.7%)
2–3	112 (63.6%)	64 (36.4%)
4a–4b	85 (63.9%)	48 (36.1%)
5a–6	168 (72.1%)	65 (27.9%)

Table 8c. La Chaise: Proportion of symmetrical tools (all tool types included) (significant patterns are highlighted in bold; see text)

Level	Non-symmetrical	Symmetrical
Bourgeois-Delaunay, 9	249 (85.3%)	43 (14.7%)
Bourgeois-Delaunay, 10	44 (72.1%)	17 (27.9%)
Suard, 51	74 (77.9%)	21 (22.1%)
Suard, 52–53	80 (83.3%)	16 (16.7%)

and La Chaise, respectively. At none of the sites is there a steady rise in proportion of symmetrical tools through time, and therefore test implication 4 must be rejected.

DISCUSSION

The purpose of this study was to test the long-standing and widely held assumption that retouched flake tool standardization increases throughout the late Middle and early Upper Pleistocene. The results of this study provide very little support for this notion. Test implications 2, 3, and 4 are rejected. Regarding test implication 1, there is weak evidence that one of the tool types, the single sidescraper, becomes more standardized through time in some size and shape attributes. This result is intriguing and certainly merits closer examination and further testing, but as such does not constitute sufficient evidence to support the notion that there is a trend towards increasing stone tool standardization during this time period. These results also reject Moncel and Combier's (1992a, 1992b) claims that retouched tools at Orgnac 3, particularly scrapers and "convergent tools," become more standardized from the oldest to the youngest levels.

The implications of these results must be considered carefully. Some might be tempted to interpret an absence of increase in standardization of tools through time as evidence that hominid cognitive abilities did not evolve throughout this time period. This reasoning, however, would be faulty since the link between standardization and cognitive abilities is tenuous, as discussed earlier. Such a conclusion could only be warranted if we could be sure that the tool types used in the analysis correspond to the mental templates of their makers. As mentioned earlier, it is virtually impossible to be certain we have correctly identified mental templates (see also Marks *et al.* 2001), especially since the variation between so many Paleolithic tool types is continuous (Dibble 1987). On the contrary, it is likely that the impression that retouched tools become more standardized throughout the Middle Paleolithic (and earlier) is an illusion, perhaps resulting from the use of old and highly selected assemblages such as those from Le Moustier, where only the clearest representatives of types have been retained, and which contain abundant examples of aesthetically pleasing, finely retouched and symmetrical tools. In fact, even a cursory inspection of the assemblages used in this study, which are by and large intact (not selected), quickly shows that the retouched flake tools do not become more "refined" or "standardized" through time. If anything, the aesthetic nature of each assemblage seems largely to be determined by the quality of the raw material in that particular assemblage, and the degree to which it was reduced.

It may also be true that there simply were no mental templates for stone tools during the Lower and Middle Paleolithic, or only very general ones (*e.g.*, "flake" *vs.* "core"). It is important to recall that the concept of the mental template was originally based upon North American prehistoric material culture (Deetz 1967), which contains ceramic technology and lithic projectile points, neither of which exists in the Lower and Middle Paleolithic of the Old World (but see Anderson-Gerfaud 1990; Shea 1997). This is significant because ceramics and projectile points, whose overall morphology is important, may be much more amenable to the concept of the mental template than Lower and Middle Paleolithic scrapers (where, I argue, overall morphology is not important). Ethnographic research has clearly shown that within the non-projectile component of lithic technology, contemporary stone-users are rarely concerned with the overall morphology of flake tools. For example, Hayden (1987) found that among contemporary Maya manufacturers of *manos* and *metates* using stone tools, the most important factors are cutting edge and raw material. Among the Aborigines of the Western Desert of Australia, edge morphology within a given functional class can vary widely, across categories that we would describe as scraper, notch, and denticulate (Hayden

1979:13). In addition, most lithic tools used ethnographically are unretouched flakes (*e.g.*, Gould 1977; Hayden 1977), and retouch is applied in order to rejuvenate edges, not to shape the overall piece. In other words, most non-projectile lithic tools are made and used "expediently", to use Binford's (1979) terminology. As summarized by Hayden, "the interest displayed by Aborigines in the modification of most stone tools is approximately equivalent to the amount of interest displayed by most people from developed societies in pencil sharpening" (Hayden 1979:16). In sum, the concept of the mental template clearly does not apply to most flake tools manufactured by contemporary Australian aborigines and other ethnographic stone tool-users.

In many Upper Paleolithic and later assemblages throughout the world (including North America) there are, however, types of tools which in whole or in part do seem to be deliberately "designed," perhaps according to some "mental template." Examples of such tools are highly symmetrical, bifacially retouched objects such as projectile points, and many types of tools made on blades and bladelets (*e.g.*, Châtelperronian and Gravettian points, Uluzzian crescents, *lamelles* Dufour, triangles scalène, geometric microlithis, *etc.*) certain drills (*e.g.*, the microdrills of the Channel Island Chumash of Southern California), and hafted endscrapers. What these tools have in common is the following property: part of the tool is dimensionally restricted in order to make a hole (such as a projectile point or drill) or fit into a hole (such as a haft or shaft). In other words, as shown ethnographically (*e.g.*, Hayden 1979), there is little need to design or shape a flake by retouch in order to accomplish tasks such as cutting, sawing, shaving, chopping, scraping, *etc.* Retouch is needed mainly to re-sharpen and rejuvenate edges, as noted above. Certain other functions, however, such as drilling or perforating, do require modification of flakes through retouch, because most flakes do not naturally have points. Thus, retouch can create a drill bit, the point of an arrowhead, or a burin. Retouch can also shape a tool for hafting, usually by modifying the portion of the tool opposite from the working edge (or tip) in order to enable hafting into a shaft that will be parallel to the application of force, such as an arrow or spear, or perpendicular to it, in the case of axes and adzes, and in composite tools such as sickles.

In sum,*it is hypothesized that whereas overall tool morphology is unimportant in the majority of tasks to which stone tools are put, certain tasks, particularly those involving perforating or hafting, do require a very specific stone tool morphology.* In other words, a mental template may well be required for hafted or perforating tools. This concept is well illustrated in the California Channel Island Chumash shell bead-making industry, which produced millions of shell beads from the mid 12th through the early 19th centuries (Arnold *et al.* 2001). The bead holes were drilled with specialized, hafted chert microdrills which were manufactured by the thousands and are extremely standardized (Arnold 1987; Preziosi 2001); however, no formal sets of tools for roughing out the bead blanks have ever been found, and it is assumed that they were chipped expediently using chert flakes or picks or whatever raw materials were on hand (Arnold, personal communication, 2003). This is a slightly different perspective on standardization and hafting than that presented by Marks *et al.* 2001; they suggest that standardization of the part of the tool that fits into a haft would have an adaptive advantage because it would be more efficient to replace (Marks *et al.* 2001:28). Here I suggest that standardization is a by-product of edge modification designed to enable a blank to fit into a haft or to create holes; in other words, the bases of a set of projectile points are standardized because their shafts are always approximately the same width, rather than they were deliberately standardized for easy replacement. But possibly these are two sides of the same coin.

Although "expedient" and "designed" tools are easily distinguished in this example, it remains to be demonstrated whether they can be identified in prehistoric assemblages on a regular basis (the term "designed" as used here is not equivalent to Binford's term "curated" [Binford 1979], since curated tools as defined by him are not necessarily designed according to a mental template, and, conversely, designed tools are not necessarily curated). To complicate matters, there is no necessary relationship between the categories "designed" and "expedient" and standardized *vs.* unstandardized. In other words, while a set of designed tools will be standardized, a set of expedient tools can be standardized as well. The circumstances most likely to produce standardization among a set of retouched tools are increasing degrees of (1) standardization of blank shape, (2) retouch of blank margins, (3) retouch of blank surfaces, and 4) similarity in size (attributes that are very similar to the "defining characteristics for a set of standardized tools" listed in Table 1). These circumstances can result intentionally from design or unintentionally simply through use and re-sharpening. Thus, certain standardized tools may have been deliberately designed either through retouch (as illustrated above) or "predetermined" through blank technology, such as Levallois points, for example. However, the final form of many other tool types may simply be the product of continual re-use and re-sharpening, leading to a much more standardized appearance at the end of their use-lives than at the beginning, according to the principles of the scraper reduction model (Dibble 1995). This fact, combined with possible pressure on raw material availability through time leading to more intensive utilization (Dibble 1988), could well be the explanation for the weak trend in increasing standardization observed among the single scrapers in this study (in test implication 1).

To summarize, using stone tool standardization as a proxy for the development of cognitive abilities is problematic for a host of reasons, including the facts that (1) most stone tools were probably *not* designed according to a mental template, and (2) standardization can result from a number of circumstances, and does not necessarily reflect the application of mental templates.

Finally, another reason why retouched stone tool standardization is not a good indicator of cognitive abilities is that the role of stone tools within the overall technological domain may well have changed throughout the Paleolithic. If the hypothesis described above, which states that stone tools are most likely to be designed when they need to fit into something, is confirmed, then the presence or absence of stone tools standardized by "design" could simply indicate the relative degree to which these functions were filled by stone tools as opposed to tools made of other materials. In other words, perforating tools such as spears were certainly made by Neandertals and earlier hominids, but these were made out of wood rather than stone (*e.g.*, the Schöningen hunting spears, Thieme 1997). Indeed, claims for hafted stone projectile points during the Middle Paleolithic (Beyries 1988; Shea 1988, 1997; Anderson-Gerfaud 1990) remain controversial (Holdaway 1989; Plisson and Beyries 1998; Boëda *et al.* 1999). It is possible that one of the differences between Upper and Middle Paleolithic technology is that stone and bone replaced wood for certain types of tools, although this is, of course, difficult to prove except circumstantially. In other words, the differences between the two periods' technologies may be due less to changes in tool types or functions than to changes in raw materials. The shift from wood to stone and bone could represent significant technological advancements, adaptations to changes in raw material availability, or simply historical contingency.

In conclusion, there are two main components to this paper. First of all, it tests the long-voiced claim that standardization among retouched flake tools increases throughout the late Middle and early Upper Pleistocene. Until just recently it has not been possible to study diachronic trends throughout this time period due to the lack of a chronology. Since standardization has long been linked to hominid cognitive abilities, it was deemed important to (1) verify the claim that standardization increases over time, and (2) examine the strength of the link between standardization and cognition. The first goal was accomplished by studying the retouched tools from three well-excavated, deeply stratified, and absolutely dated sites in France. Numerous different measures of standardization revealed no significant increases in standardization through time. It is concluded that the impression that flake tools become more standardized through time is misguided and is ultimately based upon outdated notions of progressive cultural evolution, compounded by the use of old collections which are highly selected, and therefore portray later Mousterian assemblages as more uniform than they really are. Scraper frequencies do increase throughout the time period included in this study (Monnier n.d.), and may become more reduced through time, which may also contribute to the impression of greater standardization and "clarity" of types. The second objective was based on a more theoretical approach which tries to determine why standardization, and specifically the concept of the mental template which links stone tool morphology to cognitive abilities, is so difficult to identify prior to the Upper Paleolithic. The paper makes a functional distinction between everyday or "expedient" tools, and projectile points and other types which are designed in order to create a hole or to fit into a haft. It is hypothesized that the overall morphology of most expedient lithic tools is unimportant (a claim supported by extensive ethnographic studies), whereas the morphology of tools designed to perforate and/or to fit into a haft has significant functional constraints. In other words, prehistoric flintknappers may not have needed a mental template for expedient tools, but did need one for perforating/hafted tools. There is inconsistent evidence for stone perforating or hafted tools prior to the Upper Paleolithic, as mentioned earlier. Mental templates for stone tools may simply not have existed prior to the Upper Paleolithic, and, hence, there can be no standardization based upon mental templates prior to that time period.

ACKNOWLEDGEMENTS

The author wishes to thank Jean-Jacques Cleyet-Merle, Jean Combier, André Debénath, Henry de Lumley, Denise de Sonneville-Bordes, Jean-François Tournepiche, and Paola Villa for providing access and permission to study the collections; and Harold Dibble, Erella Hovers, Steve Kuhn, and Gilbert Tostevin for providing useful comments on earlier versions of this paper. Funding for the data collection was provided by a Traveling Fellowship from the French Institute for Culture and Technology at the University of Pennsylvania.

REFERENCES CITED

Alimen H. and A. Vignal 1952. Étude statistique de bifaces acheuléens. *Bulletin de la Société Préhistorique Française* 49: 56–72.

Anderson-Gerfaud P. 1990. Aspects of behaviour in the Middle Paleolithic: functional analysis of stone tools from Southwest France. In P. Mellars (Ed.), *The Emergence of Modern Humans*, pp. 389–418. Edinburgh: Edinburgh University Press.

Arnold J.E. 1987. *Craft Specialization in the Prehistoric Channel Islands, California*. Berkeley: University of California Press.

Arnold J.E., A.M. Preziosi and P. Shattuck 2001. Flaked stone craft production and exchange in Island Chumash Territory. In J.E. Arnold (Ed.), *The Origins of a Pacific Coast Chiefdom: The Chumash of the Channel Islands*, pp. 113–132. Salt Lake City: University of Utah Press.

Beyries S. 1988. Functional variability of lithic sets in the Middle Paleolithic. In H. Dibble and A. Montet-White (Eds.), *Upper Pleistocene Prehistory of Western Eurasia* (Symposium Series 1), pp. 213–224. Philadelphia: University Museum Press.

Binford L. 1973. Interassemblage variability – The Mousterian and the functional argument. In C. Renfrew (Ed.), *The Explanation of Culture Change*, pp. 227–254. London: Duckworth.

Binford L. 1979. Organization and formation processes: looking at curated technologies. *Journal of Anthropological Research* 35: 255–73.

Binford, L. and S. Binford 1966. A preliminary analysis of functional variability in the Mousterian of Levallois facies. *American Anthropologist* 68: 238–295.

Blackwell, B., H. Schwarcz and A. Debénath 1983. Absolute dating of hominids and Paleolithic artefacts of the Cave of La Chaise-de-Vouthon (Charente), France. *Journal of Archeological Science* 10: 493–513.

Boëda E. 1993. Le débitage discoïde et le débitage Levallois récurrent centripète. *Bulletin de la Société Préhistorique Française* 90: 392–404.

Boëda E., J.-M. Geneste, C. Griggo, N. Mercier, S. Muhesen, J.L. Reyss, A. Taha and H. Valladas 1999. A Levallois point embedded in the vertebra of a wild ass (*Equus africanus*): hafting, projectile and Mousterian hunting weapons. *Antiquity* 73: 394–402.

Boëda E., J.-M. Geneste and L. Meignen 1990. Identification de chaînes opératoires lithiques du paléolithique ancien et moyen. *Paléo* 2: 43–80.

Bordes F., 1961. *Typologie du Paléolithique ancien et moyen*. Paris: Centre National de la Recherche Scientifique.

Bordes F. 1972. *A Tale of Two Caves*. New York: Harper and Row.

Bordes F. and D. de Sonneville-Bordes 1970. The significance of variability in Paleolithic assemblages. *World Archaeology* 2: 61–73.

Bowman S. and G. Sieveking 1983. Thermoluminescence dating of burnt flint from Combe Grenal. *Journal of the European Study Group on Physical, Chemical and Mathematical Techniques Applied to Archaeology* 9: 253–268.

Callow P. and J. Cornford (Eds.) 1986. *La Cotte de St. Brelade 1961–1978: Excavations by C.B.M. McBurney*. Norwich: Geo Books.

Chase P.G. 1991. Symbols and Paleolithic artifacts: style, standardization, and the imposition of arbitrary form. *Journal of Anthropological Archaeology* 10: 193–214.

Chase, P.G. and H. Dibble 1987. Middle Paleolithic symbolism: a review of current evidence and interpretations. *Journal of Anthropological Archaeology* 6:263–296.

Chazan M. 1995. The language hypothesis for the Middle-to-Upper Paleolithic transition. *Current Anthropology* 36: 749–68.

Combier J. 1967. *Le Paléolithique de l'Ardèche dans son Cadre Paléoclimatique* (Memoire no. 4). Bordeaux: Publications de l'Institut de Préhistoire de l'Université de Bordeaux.

Debénath A. 1974. *Recherches sur les terrains Quaternaires Charentais et les industries qui leur sont associées.* Thèse de Doctorat d'Etat et Sciences Naturelles, Université de Bordeaux.

Deetz, J. 1967. *Invitation to Archaeology.* Garden City, NY: The Natural History Press.

Dibble H. 1987. The interpretation of Middle Paleolithic scraper morphology. *American Antiquity* 52: 109–117.

Dibble H. 1988. Typological aspects of reduction and intensity of utilization of lithic resources in the French Mousterian. In H. Dibble and A. Montet-White (Eds.), *Upper Pleistocene Prehistory of Western Eurasia* (Symposium Series 1), pp. 181–187. Philadelphia: University Museum Press, Philadelphia.

Dibble H. 1989. The implications of stone tool types for the presence of language during the Middle Paleolithic. In P. Mellars and C.B. Stringer (Eds.), *The Human Revolution: Behavioural and Biological Perspectives on the Origins of Modern Humans,* pp. 415–432. Edinburgh: Edinburgh University Press.

Dibble H. 1991. Local raw material exploitation and its effects on Lower and Middle Paleolithic assemblage variability. In A. Montet-White and S. Holen (Eds.), *Raw Material Economies Among Prehistoric Hunter-Gatherers* (University of Kansas Publications in Anthropology 19), pp. 33–48. Lawrence: University of Kansas.

Dibble H. 1995. Middle Paleolithic scraper reduction: background, clarification, and review of evidence to date. *Journal of Archaeological Method and Theory* 2: 299–368.

Dibble H. and N. Rolland 1992. On assemblage variability in the Middle Paleolithic of Western Europe: history, perspectives and a new synthesis. In H. Dibble and P. Mellars, (Eds.), *The Middle Paleolithic: Adaptation, Behavior and Variability* (Symposium Series 2), pp. 1–20. Philadelphia: University Museum Press.

Ford J. 1954. On the concept of types. *American Anthropologist* 56: 42–54.

Gamble C. and W. Roebroeks, 1999. The Middle Paleolithic: a point of inflection. In W. Roebroeks and C. Gamble (Eds.), *The Middle Palaeolithic Occupation of Europe,* pp. 3–22. Leiden: University of Leiden.

Geertz C. 1964. The transition to humanity. In S. Tax (Ed.), *Horizons of Anthropology.* Aldine: Chicago.

Gould R. 1977. Ethno-archaeology: or, where do models come from? In R.V.S. Wright (Ed.), *Stone Tools as Cultural Markers: Change, Evolution and Complexity,* pp. 162–168. Canberra: Australian Institute of Aboriginal Studies.

Gowlett J.A.J. 1984. Mental abilities of Early Man: A look at some hard evidence. In R.A. Foley (Ed.), *Hominid Evolution and Community Ecology: Prehistoric Human Adaptation in Biological Perspective,* pp. 167–192. New York: Academic Press.

Gowlett J.A. 1992. Tools - the Paleolithic record. In S. Jones, R.D. Martin and D. Pilbeam (Eds.), *The Cambridge Encyclopedia of Human Evolution,* pp. 350–360. Cambridge: Cambridge University Press.

Gowlett J.A. 1996. Mental abilities of early *Homo:* Elements of constraint and choice in rule systems. In P. Mellars and K. Gibson (Eds.), *Modeling the Early Human Mind,* pp. 191–216. Cambridge: McDonald Institute for Archaeological Research.

Hayden B. 1977. Stone tool functions in the Western Desert. In R.V.S. Wright (Ed.), *Stone Tools as Cultural Markers: Change, Evolution and Complexity,* pp. 178–188. Canberra: Australian Institute of Aboriginal Studies.

Hayden B. 1979. *Palaeolithic Reflections: Lithic Technology and Ethnographic Excavation Among Australian Aborigines.* New Jersey: Humanities Press Inc.

Hayden B. 1987. *Lithic Studies Among the Contemporary Highland Maya.* Tucson: University of Arizona Press.

Hayden B. 1993. The cultural capacities of Neandertals: a review and re-evaluation. *Journal of Human Evolution* 24: 113–146.

Holdaway S. 1989. Were there hafted projectile points in the Mousterian? *Journal of Field Archaeology* 16: 79–85.

Holdaway S., S. McPherron and B. Roth 1996. Notched tool reuse and raw material availability in French Middle Paleolithic sites. *American Antiquity* 61: 377–89.

Holloway R. 1969. Culture: a human domain. *Current Anthropology* 10: 395–412.

Holloway R. 1981. Culture, symbols, and brain evolution: A synthesis. *Dialectical Anthropology* 5: 287–303.

Marks A.E., H. Hietala and J.K. Williams 2001. Tool standardization in the Middle and Upper Paleolithic: a closer look. *Cambridge Archaeological Journal* 11: 17–44.

Meignen L. 1993. *L'abri des Canalettes: un habitat moustérien sur les Grands Causses (Nant, Aveyron). Fouilles 1980–1986.* Paris: Centre National de la Recherche Scientifique.

Mellars P. 1965. Sequence and development of the Mousterian traditions in Southwestern France. *Nature* 205: 626–627.

Mellars P. 1969. The chronology of Mousterian industries in the Perigord region. *Proceedings of the Prehistoric Society* 35: 134–171.

Mellars P. 1973. The character of the Middle-Upper Paleolithic transition in South-West France. In C. Renfrew (Ed.), *The Explanation of Culture Change*, pp. 255–276. Pittsburgh: University of Pittsburgh Press.

Mellars P. 1989a. Major issues in the emergence of modern humans. *Current Anthropology* 30: 349–385.

Mellars P. 1989b. Technological changes at the Middle-Upper Palaeolithic transition: economic, social and cognitive perspectives. In P. Mellars and C.B. Stringer (Eds.), *The Human Revolution*, pp. 338–365. Edinburgh: Edinburgh University Press.

Mellars P. 1991. Cognitive changes and the emergence of modern humans in Europe. *Cambridge Archaeological Journal* 1: 63–76.

Mellars P. 1996a. *The Neanderthal Legacy: An Archaeological Perspective from Western Europe*. Princeton: Princeton University Press.

Mellars P. 1996b. Symbolism, language, and the Neanderthal mind. In P. Mellars and K. Gibson (Eds.), *Modeling the Early Human Mind*, pp. 15–31. Cambridge: McDonald Institute for Archaeological Research.

Moncel M.-H. 1999. *Les assemblages lithiques du site pleistocène moyen d'Orgnac 3 (Ardèche, Moyenne Vallée du Rhone, France)* (ERAUL 89). Liège :Université de Liège.

Moncel M.-H. and J. Combier 1992a. Industrie lithique du site pleistocène moyen d'Orgnac 3 (Ardèche). *Gallia Préhistoire* 34: 1–55.

Moncel M.-H. and J. Combier 1992b. L'outillage sur éclat dans l'industrie lithique du site pléistocène moyen d'Orgnac 3 (Ardèche, France). *L'Anthropologie* 96: 5–48.

Monnier G. 1995. Comment on "The language hypothesis for the Middle-to-Upper Paleolithic transition" by Michael Chazan. *Current Anthropology* 36: 761–762.

Monnier G. 2000. *A Re-evaluation of the Archaeological Evidence for a Lower/MiddlePaleolithic Division in Western Europe*. Ph.D. Dissertation, University of Pennsylvania.

Monnier G. n.d.. A re-examination of the Archaeological Evidence for a Lower/Middle Paleolithic Division in Western Europe. Manuscript in possession of the author.

Noble W. and I. Davidson 1991. The evolutionary emergence of modern human behaviour: language and its archaeology. *Man* 26: 223–253.

Plisson H. and S. Beyries 1998. Pointes ou outils triangulaires? Données fonctionnelles dans le Moustérien levantin. *Paléorient* 24: 5–24.

Preziosi A. 2001. Standardization and specialization: The island Chumash microdrill industry. In J.E. Arnold (Ed.), *The Origins of a Pacific Coast Chiefdom: The Chumash of the Channel Islands*, pp. 151–164. Salt Lake City: University of Utah Press.

Roe D.A. 1982. Transition from lower to middle Palaeolithic, with particular reference to Britain. In A. Ronen (Ed.), *The Transition from Lower to Middle Paleolithic and the Origin of Modern Humans* (BAR International Series 151), pp. 177–190. Oxford: BAR.

Rolland N. 1986. Recent findings from La Micoque and other sites in South-Western and Mediterranean France: their bearing on the Tayacian problem and Middle Paleolithic emergence. In G.N. Bailey and P. Callow (Eds.), *Stone Age Prehistory*, pp. 121–151. Cambridge: Cambridge University Press.

Rolland N. 1995. Levallois technique emergence: single or multiple? In H. Dibble and O. Bar-Yosef (Eds.), *The Definition and Interpretation of Levallois Technology* (Monographs in World Archaeology 23), pp. 333–360. Madison: Prehistory Press.

Ronen A. (Ed.) 1982. *The Transition from Lower to Middle Paleolithic and the Origin of Modern Human* (BAR International Series 151). Oxford: BAR.

Schwarcz H. and A. Debénath 1979. Datation absolue de restes humains de La Chaise-de-Vouthon (Charente), au moyen du dés-equilibre des séries d'Uranium. *Compte Rendu de l'Académie des Sciences Paris* 288: 1155–1157.

Shea J.J. 1988. Spear points from the Middle Paleolithic of the Levant. *Journal of Field Archaeology* 15: 441–450.

Shea J.J. 1997. Middle Paleolithic spear point technology. In H. Knecht (Ed.), *Projectile Technology*, pp. 79–106. New York: Plenum Press.

Spaulding A.C. 1953. Statistical techniques for the discovery of artifact types. *American Antiquity* 18: 305–13.

Tattersall I. 1995. *The Fossil Trail*. New York: Oxford University Press.

Thieme H. 1997. Lower Paleolithic hunting spears from Germany. *Nature* 385: 807–810.

Trinkaus E. 1992. Evolution of human manipulation. In S. Jones, R.D. Martin and D. Pilbeam, D. (Eds.) *The Cambridge Encyclopedia of Human Evolution*. Cambridge: Cambridge University Press.

Tuffreau A. 1982. The transition from Lower to Middle Palaeolithic in Northern France. In A. Ronen (Ed.) *The Transition from Lower to Middle Palaeolithic and the Origin of Modern Man* (BAR International Series 151), pp. 137–149. Oxford: BAR.

Turq A. 1992. Raw material and technological studies of the Quina Mousterian in Périgord. In H. Dibble and P. Mellars (Eds.), *The Middle Paleolithic: Adaptation, Behaavior, and Variability* (Symposium Series 2), pp. 75–85. Philadelphia: University Museum Press.

Valoch K. 1982. The Lower/Middle Palaeolithic transition in Czechoslovakia. In A. Ronen (Ed.), *The Transition from Lower to Middle Palaeolithic and the Origin of Modern Man* (BAR International Series 151), pp. 193–201. Oxford: BAR.

Wynn T. 1985. Piaget, stone tools and the evolution of human intelligence. *World Archaeology* 17: 32–42.

Wynn T. 1988. Tools and the evolution of human intelligence. In R.W. Byrne and A. Whiten (Eds.), *Machiavellian Intelligence*, pp. 271–84. Oxford: Clarendon Press.

Wynn T. 1991. Archaeological evidence for modern intelligence. In R. Foley (Ed.), *The Origins of Human Behavior*, pp. 52–66. London: Unwin Hyman.

Wynn T. 1995. Handaxe enigmas. *World Archaeology* 27: 10–24.

Chapter **5**

Diversity of Lithic Production Systems During the Middle Paleolithic in France
Are There Any Chronological Trends?

Anne Delagnes

Institut de Préhistoire et de Geologie du Quaternaire UMR 5199–PACEA/Université Bordeaux I
FRANCE a.delagnes@ipgq.u-bordeauxl.fr

Liliane Meignen

C.N.R.S/CEPAM, Sophia Antipolis, Valbonne FRANCE meignen@cepam.cnrs.fr

ABSTRACT

The technological approaches developed in Western Europe during the last two decades aim to define different systems of debitage (used here as a noun to denote the process of producing blanks). For the Middle Paleolithic, the best documented are the Levallois debitage system, the laminar production system, the discoidal debitage system, and the Quina debitage system. Their geographical and chronological distributions show some general trends: a greater diversity of the production systems coexisting within the same region (especially in Southwestern France) at the end of the Middle Paleolithic; an increased use of the systems characterized by a low degree of blank predetermination (Quina and discoidal systems, Levallois recurrent centripetal method), and the emergence of a flexible, multifunctional toolkit with a high curation potential. These changes can be attributed to groups with different technical traditions who kept their own fundamental technical identity but who also adopted similar mobility patterns during the unstable climatic period at the end of the Middle Paleolithic, resulting in shared forms of socioeconomic behavior (frequent population moves and increased residential mobility).

INTRODUCTION

Ever since the first half of the 20th century, when Breuil defined the Middle Paleolithic as a period of flake-based industries characterized by a notable stability in tool types, it has been widely accepted that this period remained remarkably uniform both geographically and chronologically. However, the Middle Paleolithic of Western Europe, and more particularly the French Middle Paleolithic, is actually highly diversified. This notion of diversity was already implicit in the typological approach advocated by Bordes (1950), which led to the recognition of five Mousterian facies based on the relative proportions of retouched tool types (Bordes 1953, 1981). Recently the perception of this diversity in Western Europe has been greatly refined by the development of technological approaches. Despite the fact that technical traditions persisted longer in the Middle Paleolithic than in later time periods, it is now quite obvious that the idea of the Middle Paleolithic being a homogeneous period should be dismissed, at least for Western Europe.

Over the last two decades, approaches based on the concept of *chaîne opératoire* (Cresswell 1982; Lemonnier 1986; Karlin *et al.* 1991) have aimed to characterize lithic production systems in terms of production methods, blank morphology, and transformation of these blanks into tools. Using a systemic approach of lithic production, these studies reveal a diversity of technical strategies for the Middle Paleolithic that is probably as wide as the diversity recorded in the Upper Paleolithic, although differently structured. Indeed, despite the fact that a relatively limited number of sites have been analyzed with this focus on technical systems, results already demonstrate the range and diversity of stone tool production systems. How this diversity is patterned in time and space is precisely what we will now discuss.

The technological approaches (the so-called *"chaînes opératoires"* approach in the French literature) have allowed scholars not only to recognize various stages in lithic tool making (a topic not developed in this paper) but also to investigate the basic conceptual processes which underlie the sequence of manufacturing steps in stone tool production. Different ways of organizing and exploiting cores in three dimensions (*i.e.*, *"conceptions volumétriques"* in the French literature) have been identified, along with their respective end-products and by-products. The pioneering work carried out by Boëda (1986, 1994) focused initially on the Levallois concept and its variability, as expressed in different reduction modalities. This work was followed later by the identification of other production methods: "discoidal method" (Boëda 1993), "alternating platform technique" (Ashton 1992) or "clactonian method" (Forestier 1993), "Quina method" (Bourguignon 1996, 1997), "laminar production system" (Boëda 1990; Revillion 1994), the "Kombewa-like Les Tares method" (Geneste and Plisson 1996), the "Pucheuil-type method" (Delagnes 1993) and the "bifacial shaping method" (*"chaîne opératoire de façonnage bifacial"*.) The latter strategy aims at the production of bifaces with different roles: depending on the assemblages, the bifaces have been used as long use-life tools, as "cores" (Soressi 2002), or as tool-blanks (Boëda *et al.* 1990, 1996). Since the mid-1980s, many lithic assemblages have been studied within this conceptual framework, which has helped to expand our knowledge of the internal variability within each system (Geneste 1988; Turq 1989; Boëda et al. 1990; Boëda 1991; Delagnes 1992; Jaubert 1993; Meignen 1993; Locht and Swinnen 1994; Jaubert and Farizy 1995; Texier and Francisco-Ortega 1995; Delagnes and Ropars 1995; Geneste et al. 1997, among others). In fact, these lithic production systems are far from rigid, and due to their inherent flexibility, the various flaking modalities recognized do not always match up to the limits of our conventional technological categories (see below). For example, it is clear that the traditional binary opposition "Levallois"/non-Levallois" or "elaborated/non-elaborated debitage" should be abandoned.

In this paper, we will deal with the four main debitage systems (ignoring for the moment the bifacial shaping system) that are the best documented in the Middle Paleolithic: the Levallois debitage system, the laminar production system, the discoidal debitage system and the Quina debitage system. The Levallois system has been extensively studied and its internal variability is now well known (outside of Europe as well), while the Quina concept, more recently described, is much less thoroughly documented. This must be kept in mind when we compare the spatial and chronological distribution of these lithic technical systems.

DIVERSITY OF MIDDLE PALEOLITHIC PRODUCTION SYSTEMS

Levallois Debitage System

Based on experimental and archaeological studies, Boëda (1994, 1995) described a specific volumetric organization of the core which he used to define the Levallois concept. The core is first shaped in order to get two asymmetrical convex intersecting surfaces. These two surfaces do not have the same function: one is used for the production of predetermined flakes (flaking surface from which the Levallois blanks are struck), while the other is used as a striking platform surface. Creating the lateral and distal convexities of the flaking surface allows the knapper to produce Levallois blank(s) with a controlled morphology. The fracture planes for detachment of Levallois blanks are parallel or subparallel to the plane of intersection between the two surfaces (Figure 1). Blanks can be produced following different methods: the recurrent methods (with either unidirectional, bidirectional, or centripetal removals), through which several predetermined flakes are produced from the same flaking surface, and the preferential method in which a single Levallois blank is produced from each flaking surface.

The blanks produced by these different methods are quite diversified in terms of morphology and size. Nevertheless all flakes possess long cutting edges with very acute edge angles and more or less symmetrical shapes and cross-sections. Uni- and bidirectional recurrent methods focus on the production of quadrangular blanks, sub-triangular when the unidirectional removals are convergent. Less standardized and more diversified end-products result from the centripetal recurrent method, while the preferential methods lead to more rigidly predetermined shapes (large

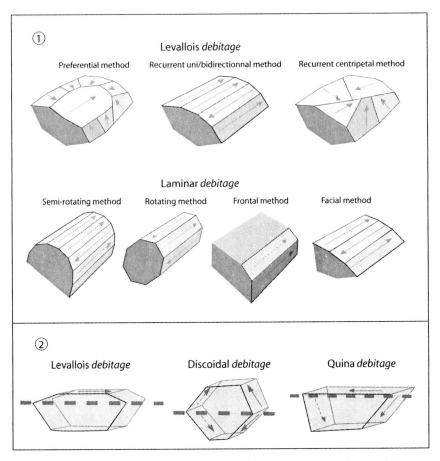

Figure 1. The major methods of production related to the Levallois and laminar *debitages*; 2. schematic representation of the volumetric conception for the Levallois, the discoidal and the Quina *debitages* (redrawn after Bourguignon 1997).

oval Levallois flakes or Levallois points, depending on how the core was initially prepared).

In some assemblages, the Levallois flakes are produced in order to closely fit the planned morphology of the final tools, especially in the case of preferential or recurrent uni/bidirectional flaking methods described, for instance, in the assemblages of Biache-St-Vaast IIA (Boëda 1988a) and Vaufrey, levels VII and VIII (Geneste 1988). In these cases, the Levallois products are either lightly retouched (a type of retouch that enhances the original morpho-functional attributes) or left unretouched (and probably used as such). On the other hand, other assemblages are characterized by blanks that are quite diversified in shape and size, requiring more investment in retouch in order to get the intended morpho-functional characteristics, for instance in the assemblages of the Abri Suard at La Chaise-de-Vouthon (Delagnes 1991).

Laminar Production System

Laminar production is the main production system in several Middle Paleolithic sites, characterized by various flaking strategies (Ameloot-Van der Heijden 1993b; Revillion 1994; Revillion and Tuffreau 1994a; Delagnes 1996a; Locht 2002). Boëda (1988a, 1990) pointed out some critical features which distinguish blade production strategies from those of the Levallois system. Most importantly, the core-volume organization is radically different: the active surface of the core from which the removals are struck extends along most, if not all the core's periphery rather than being restricted to one delimited surface (see Figure 1).

Blade cores can be reduced according to four different strategies: semi-rotating method, rotating method, frontal method and facial method (Delagnes 2000 and references therein). These different options may occur in full or partial combination in the archaeological assemblages, the semi-rotating method being most common. Variability is also expressed in the number of striking platforms present on the cores (one or two opposed). The method of core reduction (recurrent unidirectional or bidirectional) generally involves the production of crested blades, although this is not an absolute rule. Usually, Middle Paleolithic blade cores are only minimally prepared, and the volume is not thoroughly shaped out before starting the production of blades. The blades were detached with a hard hammer and consequently show significant variation in shape and size.

In Middle Paleolithic assemblages, blade production is generally found in combination with flakes produced following the Levallois concept, the later being in most cases the dominant mode of reduction (*e.g.*, the sites of Lailly/le domaine de Beauregard B and Bettencourt-Saint-Ouen, level N2B3: Locht and Swinnen 1994; Locht 2002). The Levallois recurrent uni/bidirectional methods are most commonly associated with laminar production systems in Mousterian assemblages. The need to produce quadrangular elongated blanks which implied the use of this peculiar method could have contributed in the same assemblages to the emergence of a blade production. The few blades that are retouched are modified through marginal retouch. In fact, the laminar production in the Middle Paleolithic is a unique phenomenon, clearly distinct from Upper Paleolithic blade production in the striking technique used (direct percussion with a stone hammer) as well as in the way core volume was exploited, in the characteristics of the end-products and in its systematic association with flake production.

Discoidal System

Defined by Boëda (1993) and given a rather different meaning from the discoidal/Mousterian debitage described by Bordes (1961), the discoidal core reduction strategy has been recognized in many sites, and a significant amount of variability noted (Jaubert 1993; Locht and Swinnen 1994; Peresani 1998; Pasty 2000). In a classic discoid system the core possesses two highly convex surfaces, but unlike Levallois, neither assumes priority over the other: both surfaces can alternately be used for flake detachment or as striking platform. Most often this strategy is based on a recurrent centripetal reduction of the core, with the removals struck from platforms extending around the core's entire periphery. In distinction to the Levallois system, both surfaces, highly convex, intersect each other at a relatively high angle (see Figure 1). Such a volumetric construction often results in cores with a bi-pyramidal (eventually pyramidal) morphology. The end-products of discoid production systems are generally short and asymmetrical. They include *pseudo-Levallois* points, short *débordant* flakes, and quadrangular flakes.

Quina System

Recently defined by Bourguignon in a study based on several Quina Mousterian assemblages (Bourguignon 1996, 1997), this reduction strategy is not yet well documented and many other Quina assemblages should be re-examined. This reduction strategy is more flexible than the previous ones (see Turq 1989; Bourguignon 1997), but all variants clearly share the principle that the core is reduced by exploiting two surfaces which intersect at a low angle. Like the discoidal method, neither surface takes priority over the other, and both are alternately used as flaking and striking platform surfaces. The core reduction is mostly recurrent, in that many blanks are detached, and the series of removals are unidirectional, following fracture planes alternatively secant and parallel to the intersection of the two surfaces (see Figure 1). As a result of the absence of initial core shaping end-products are frequently cortical. They are generally short and thick, with a triangular cross-section and are characterized by a wide butt that is oriented at an obtuse angle to the ventral face. In most Quina Mousterian assemblages, these blanks were used mainly for the production of various sidescrapers on the lateral and transversal edges, some of them characterized by fairly heavy invasive retouch (the "Quina retouch"), creating a convex working edge with a remarkably constant steep angle (Bourguignon 1997). Re-sharpening, recognized by characteristic flakes, is a frequent activity (Lenoir 1986; Meignen 1988). Interestingly, these flakes are sometimes themselves recycled into scrapers. All the Quina assemblages studied are globally characterized by high ratios of retouched tools (see Rolland 1981). In a few cases, however, the diagnostic Quina blanks were not shaped by heavy Quina retouches but left unretouched or lightly modified into sidescrapers and/or denticulates, as observed in Sclayn layer 5 and Combe-Capelle Bas (Dibble and Lenoir 1995; Bourguignon 1998).

The degree of predetermination of the end-products, *i.e.*, the control of their morpho-functional characteristics, varies between all these flaking systems. The level of predetermination is relatively high in the preferential Levallois method, the laminar system and in the Levallois recurrent uni/bidirectional methods. The morphology of the end-products is predetermined to a lesser degree in the Levallois recurrent centripetal method and in the Quina and the discoidal systems.

It is worth noting that these four major reduction strategies, as well as several other lithic production systems previously mentioned, are sometimes associated in the same assemblage (Tables 1 and 2), each of them presumably associated with different functional applications, as for instance at Riencourt-les Bapaume in level CA (Beyries 1993). Moreover, in some assemblages, the coexisting flaking

Table 1. List of the major sites illustrating the diversity of the production systems during the Middle Paleolithic in Northern and Southwestern France (only sites subjected to chronological and technological studies have been reported)

Site (levels)	Chronology* (isotopic stage)	Dominant production system	Secondary production system	Mousterian facies	References
		North/Northwestern France			
Salouel	stages 8-beginning 7	LP	LRU		Ameloot-van der Heidjen et al. 1996
Le Pucheuil (C-A)	end stage 8-beginning 7	LRU	BS		Delagnes, 1996a
Bagarre (7)	stages 8 to 6	LP			Boëda, 1994; Tuffreau et al., 1975
Longavesnes	stages 8 to 6	LRU	LRC		Ameloot-van der Heidjen, 1993a
Champvoisy	stage 7	LRU		F	Tuffreau, 1989
Biache-Saint-Vaast (IIA, IIbase)	end stage 7-beginning 6	LRU		F	Boëda, 1988, 1994; Tuffreau and Marcy, 1988
Le Pucheuil (B)	beginning stage 6	LP, LRU			Delagnes, 1996b
Etouvie	stage 6	LP			Tuffreau, 1995
Querqueville	stage 5e	LRU	BS	M	Clet et al., 1991
Roisel	stage 5e	LP	LRC, LRU		Gautier, 1989
Vinneuf (N1)	stages 5d-c	BP	BS	M	Gouedo et al., 1994
Seclin	stages 5d-c	BP	LRC, LRU		Révillion, 1994
Saint-Germain-des-Vaux I	stages 5d-c	LRU, LRC, LP, BP			Révillion and Cliquet, 1994
Riencourt-les-Bapaume (CA)	stage 5c	BP	LRC		Ameloot-van der Heijden, 1993b
Etoutteville	stages 5b-a	LRU, BP			Delagnes, 1996c
Lailly/le domaine de Beauregard (B)	stage 5a	LRU	BP, BS		Locht and Ferdouel, 1994
Molinons/le Grand Chanteloup	stage 5a	LRU	BS	MTA or T ?	Locht et al., 1994
Bettencourt-Saint-Ouen (N2B3)	stage 5a	LRU	BP		Locht ed., 2002
Auteuil	stage 5	LRU	LRC, LP		Swinnen et al., 1996
Le Petit Saule (2)	stage 5	LRU	LRC, BP	T	Locht, 1997

(Continued)

Table 1. (*Continued*)

Site (levels)	Chronology* (isotopic stage)	Dominant production system	Secondary production system	Mousterian facies	References
Saint-Vaast-La-Hougue (inf.)	stage 5	LRU		D	Guette, 2002
Champlost	stage 5	LRU, LP, LRC	BS	M	Gouedo, 1988
Houppeville	stage 5	LRU	LRC	T	Vallin, 1992
Goareva	stage 5 or 4 ?	LRU, LRC			Huet, 2002
Hermies (sup.)	stage 4	LP			Masson and Vallin, 1993
Lailly/Le Fond de la Tourmerie (1)	stage 4	LRU	LRC, BS	MTA or T ?	Depaepe and Brassinne, 1994
Bois du Rocher	stage 4	D	BS		Molines et al., 2001
Beauvais	end stage 4 or stage 3	D		T	Locht and Swinnen, 1994
Corbehem	stage 3	LRC		T	Boëda, 1994; Tuffreau, 1979
Butte d'Arvigny	stage 3	LRU, LRC, BP			Gouedo et al., 1994
Hénin-sur-Cojeul (G)	stage 3	LRC	LRU	T	Marcy et al., 1993
South-Western France					
Moulin du Milieu (VIII to XI)	stages 8 to 6 ?	LRC	BS	MTA	Turq, 2000
Grotte Vaufrey (VII, VIII)	stage 6	LRU		T	Geneste, 1985; Rigaud ed., 1988
Abri Suard	stage 6	LRU		T	Delagnes, 1990, 1992
Coudoulous I	stage 6	D	LRC		Jaubert and Mourre, 1996
Fontéchevade (EI)	stage 5e ?	D		.	Meignen et al., Tournepiche : unpublished
La Borde	older than stage 5b	D	LRC	D	Jaubert et al., 1990; Jaubert and Farizy, 1995
Le Rescoundudou (C1)	stage 5	LRC	LRU		Jaubert et al., 1992
Abri Bourgeois-Delaunay (10, 9)	stage 5	LRU		T	Delagnes, 1992
Coursac	stage 5	LRU	LRC, BS	MTA (A)	Geneste, 1985
Artenac (7)	stage 5	Q			Delagnes : unpublished
Artenac (6c)	stage 5	LRC		F	Delagnes et al., 1999

Site	Chronology*				Reference
Coupe-Gorge/Montmaurin	stage 5	D			Gaillard, 1982; Jaubert and Bismuth, 1996
Combe-Grenal (38)	stage 5	LRC	BS	D	Delagnes, 1992
Combe-Grenal (36)	stage 5a	LRC		T	Turq, 2000
Les Canalettes (2 to 4)	stage 5a	LTC	LRU	T	Meignen, 1993
La Plane	stage 5 or 4?	LRC	LRU, BS	MTA	Turq, 2000
Les Forêts	post. stage 5	D	BS	M	Folgado et al., 1997; Brenet and Folgado, in press
Champs de Bossuet	post. stage 5 or 7?	D		D	Bourguignon et al., 2000
Combe-Grenal (35)	stage 4	LRC	LRU	F	Delagnes, 1992
Combe-Grenal (31 to 28)	stage 4	LRC		T	Turq, 2000
La Quina (3, G3-N)	older than stage 3	Q		Q	Bourguignon, 1997; Debénath et al., 1998
Mauran	end stage 4 or stage 3	D		D	Farizy et al., 1994
Marillac (9, 10)	stage 4 or 3?	Q		Q	Meignen, 1988; Bourguignon, 1997
Hauteroche (C)	stage 4 or 3?	Q		Q	Bourguignon, 1997
Combe-Grenal (22)	stage 3	Q		Q	Turq, 2000
Combe-Grenal (14)	stage 3	D		D	Bourguignon and Turq, in press
Combe-Grenal (6, 7)	stage 3	LRC		T	Turq, 2000
Fonseigner (F, E, DMI)	stage 3	LRC	LRU	T	Geneste, 1985
Fonseigner (Dsup)	stage 3	LRC	LRU, BS	MTA (A) or T?	Geneste, 1985, 1990
Le Moustier	stage 3	LRU	BS	MTA (A)	Soressi, 1999
Pech-de-l'Azé I (4)	stage 3	LRU	BP, BS	MTA (A)	Soressi, 2002
Espagnac	stage 3	D	Q	Q	Jaubert et al., 2001
Sous les Vignes	stage 3	D	Q	Q	Turq et al., 1999
Roc de Marsal	stage 3	Q		Q	Turq, 2000
Camiac	stage 3	D		D	Lenoir, 1980
Saint-Césaire	stage 3	D		D	Guilbaud, 1993
Fréchet	stage 3	D		T	Jaubert and Bismuth, 1996

*based on chrono/biostratigraphy and/or radiometric datations.

LRU: Levallois recurrent unidirectional; LRC: Levallois recurrent centripetal; LP: Levallois preferential; BP: Blade production; D: Discoidal debitage; Q: Quina debitage; BS: bifacial shaping; T: Typical; F: Ferrassie; Q: Quina; D: Denticulates; MTA: Mousterian of Acheulean Tradition; M: Micoquian.

Table 2. List of the major sites illustrating the diversity of the production systems during the Middle Paleolithic in Southeastern France (only sites subjected to chronological and technological studies have been reported)

Site (levels)	Chronology* (isotopic stage)	Dominant production system	Secondary production system	Mousterian facies	References
		South-Eastern France			
Orgnac 3 (3, 2)	stages 10, 9	LRC	LP		Moncel and Combier, 1992
Orgnac 3 (1)	stages 10, 9	LP	LRC		Moncel and Combier, 1992
Les Mourets	stages 6 or 5e ?	LRU	LRC		Bernard-Guelle, 1998–1999
Bérigoule (I)	stage 5 ?	LRU, LRC		F	Texier and Francisco-Ortega, 1995
Saint-Marcel d'Ardèche	end stage 5 or stage 3 ?	D		T	Moncel, 1998
Abri du Maras (8 to 4)	stages 4 or 3 ?	LRC	LRU	T or F ?	Moncel, 1996
Abri du Maras (1)	stages 4 or 3 ?	LRU	LRC	F or Q ?	Moncel, 1996
LHortus	stages 4, 3	LRC		T	de Lumley de and Licht, 1972
Grotte Mandrin (1 to 4)	stages 4, 3	LRU			Yvorra and Slimak, 2001
Esquicho-Grapaou	stage 3	Q		Q	Bourguignon, 1997
La Roquette	stage 3	Q		Q	Meignen, 1981

*based on chrono/biostratigraphy and/or radiometric datations.

LRU: Levallois recurrent unidirectional; LRC: Levallois recurrent centripetal; LP: Levallois preferential; BP: Blade production; D: Discoidal debitage; Q: Quina debitage; Q: Quina; D: Denticulates; MTA: Mousterian of Acheulean Tradition; M: Micoquian. F: Ferrassie; Q: Quina; D: Denticulates; MTA: Mousterian of Acheulean Tradition; M: Micoquian.

methods were carried out on different types of raw material. For instance, at Sclayn layer 5 in Belgium, discoidal, Quina and Levallois products were manufactured from three different types of raw materials (Moncel 1998b). At Coudoulous I, les Fieux, and La Borde, discoidal debitage was used mostly on quartz/quartzite and Levallois method applied to flint (Jaubert and Farizy 1995; Jaubert and Mourre 1996). All these examples clearly illustrate the complexity and variability of the lithic technical systems within the Western European Middle Paleolithic.

GEOGRAPHIC AND CHRONOLOGICAL DISTRIBUTIONS

We now turn to the geographic and chronological distributions of these four technical systems in order to better understand their meaning. As we have stressed previously, it must be kept in mind that our understanding of these production systems suffers from the limited number of sites that have been studied from a technological perspective, as well as from the lack of reliable chronological data. Only the assemblages with large samples and for which technological and chronological information is available are taken into consideration here.

The Levallois concept is the most widespread set of Middle Paleolithic production systems. While the Levallois concept covers a large geographic area (Figure 2), it should be noted that this reduction strategy is absent or rare in regions with low quality raw materials (Pyrenees, Eastern and Central France, Brittany), but remarkably well represented in the three large areas discussed here: Northern, Southwestern and Southeastern France. Assemblages from Northern France are dominated by the recurrent uni- and bidirectional patterns of exploitation while the centripetal method is quite rare. To the contrary, the latter is very common in lithic industries from Southwestern France. The preferential method (one blank per prepared surface), present in Northern France, has not been identified as the dominant method in any southern assemblage. No trends are recognized in Southeastern France, but this may result from the relatively small sample of well-studied sites in this region. The Levallois concept is documented throughout the entire Middle Paleolithic period, but may have appeared earlier in the northern area (Tables 1 and 2).

No clear break in the chronological distribution of the different Levallois methods is apparent, but some general trends may be pointed out (Figure 3). First, the uni- and bidirectional modalities prevailed during the Early Middle Paleolithic and lasted until the end of the period. This trend, already emphasized by Geneste (1990), is best expressed in the northern region, where the Levallois recurrent centripetal modality is quite rare during the Early Middle Paleolithic. In contrast, this strategy became largely dominant after Oxygen Isotope Stage 5, mainly in Southwestern France.

The blade production system, relatively circumscribed in space and time, is limited to more or less 10 sites (and only five, if we consider only the sites where this production is abundantly represented). Most Mousterian sites with blade technology are located in the western part of the North-European plain (Northern France,

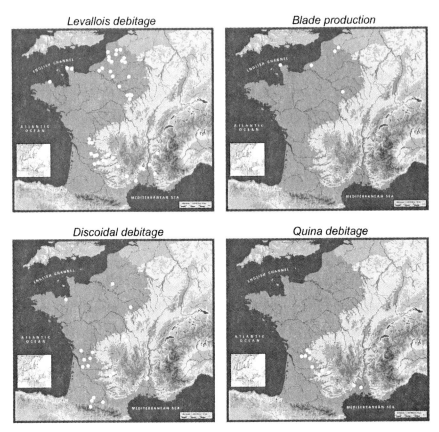

Figure 2. Geographical distribution of the 4 production systems (the sample of sites corresponds to the list detailed in tables 1 and 2).

Southern Belgium and Western Germany; see Figure 2), and span a relatively short chronological period (see Figure 3). Blade production systems appeared first in early Middle Paleolithic industries during the penultimate glaciation (Oxygen Isotope Stage 6), and are particularly well represented at the very beginning of the last Glacial (Oxygen Isotope Stage 5).

In the context of the Middle Paleolithic in Northern France, blade production should be considered as a technical phenomenon with a very restricted distribution in time, and unrelated, on the basis of the available data, with Early Upper Paleolithic blade production (Delagnes 2000). However, this situation may be entirely different in Southwestern France. In a few assemblages attributed to the Mousterian of Acheulean Tradition (for instance, Pech de l'Aze I, level 4), dated to the end of the Late Middle Paleolithic (Isotope Stage 3), elongated flakes were struck from semi-rotating cores following a reduction strategy close to the laminar concept (Soressi 2002). The hypothesis of a technical link with the Châtelperronian had been suggested by several authors (Pelegrin 1995; Soressi 2002).

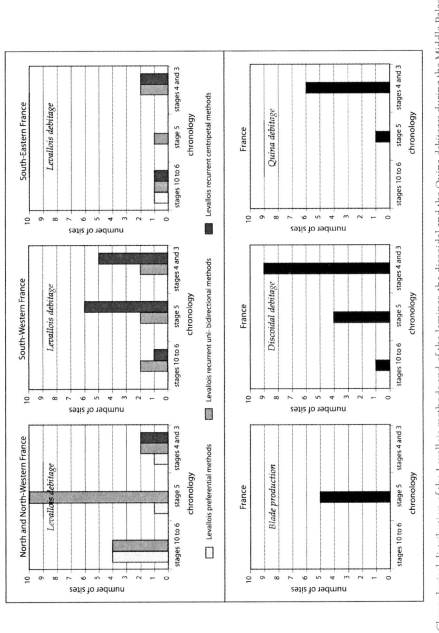

Figure 3. Chronological distribution of the Levallois methods and of the laminar, the discoidal and the Quina *debitages* during the Middle Paleolithic.

The discoidal method, less widely spread than Levallois, is common in regions where flint is scarce, such as the Pyrenees area and Catalonia in Spain (Jaubert and Farizy 1995) but also in Charente and Perigord where flint resources are abundantly available (see Figure 2). This system is frequently associated with raw materials of poor quality such as quartz or quartzite. However, this correlation is only partial, and discoidal assemblages made on flint are also documented in regions with high-quality raw materials, as seen in Northern (e.g., Beauvais [Locht and Swinnen 1994]) and Southwestern France (e.g., Saint Césaire [Guilbaud 1993]; Champs de Bossuet [Bourguignon 2000; Bourguignon and Turq 2003]). The discoidal production system spans a large block of time (see Figure 3), from at least Oxygen Isotope Stage 6 through Isotope Stage 3: it is particularly common at the very end of the Middle Paleolithic (Stage 3).

Geographic and chronological distributions for the Quina system are probably underestimated in our study due to the limited number of technological studies of these assemblages. The Quina system has been recorded in many areas of Southern and Central France (see Figure 2), as well as in Belgium, but only sporadically in Spain. This method is totally absent in Northern France. This production system seems to appear at the end of Oxygen Isotope Stage 5 (e.g., Artenac level 7), but without the characteristic Quina retouch, and becomes more common during the Later Middle Paleolithic (mostly in Isotope Stage 3, see Figure 3).

DISCUSSION

The analysis presented here highlights the diversity of technical behaviors in tool manufacture and management during the Middle Paleolithic. This diversity is first seen in the development of very different types of lithic production systems, with their own respective goals and constraints. The morphological, functional characteristics of the tools—mainly the forms and angles of working edges and the morphology of zones suitable for prehension—were controlled by Middle Paleolithic tool makers, sometimes from the beginning of the reduction sequence. This diversity is also reflected by the combination of different types of reduction sequence (as well as bifacial shaping), with their own respective goals, within a single assemblage.

Due to space constraints, we will not attempt to review all the factors lying behind this intra- and inter-site variability. However, it is important to note that the observed diversity is probably the result of the interaction of several factors: raw material availability, the intended function of the tool (in relation with the site function within a territory), and the range of technical knowledge available to be used by Middle Paleolithic groups in response to the previous two factors. The role played by each of these factors has generated several debates, summarized by Mellars (1996). In this regard, the variability observed cannot be simply reduced to environmental or functional factors. The tool morphology—seen not from a typological standpoint, but rather from a technological perspective, that is, taking into account the entire shape of the tool—certainly fits the intended function, but the particular way artifacts were made (*i.e.*, the production methods) stemmed from a socially meaningful body of knowledge transmitted from generation to generation (Mauss 1936; Levi-Strauss 1976; Rogers 1988; Pelegrin 1990; Lemonnier 1992; Dobres and Hoffman 1994). Methods of blank production and transformation following specific processes represent in our opinion the best markers for identifying groups who shared a set of technical traditions.

At a broad regional scale, the results discussed here also show the coexistence *sensu lato* (taking into account the low degree of chronological resolution) of several lithic production systems. Southwestern France, and more specifically Perigord, is a good example: very different production systems, such as the Levallois, the discoidal, the Quina, and the bifacial shaping methods, were present at the same time, especially during Isotope Stage 3. If it is true that common production systems resulted from technical knowledge socially transmitted by groups that shared comparable technical behaviors, the previous propositions indicate that human groups with different technical traditions coexisted, at least in certain areas. During the Middle Paleolithic, population density was probably generally low, which would explain the existence of "separate patterns of technological development fostered by the variable degrees of social distance maintained between the human populations involved" (Mellars 1996).

It also seems that in Southwestern France, groups with different technical traditions occupied the same rockshelters or caves, replacing each other over time, a pattern that was recognized previously based on the identification of typological facies in sites like Combe Grenal and Pech de l'Aze. These results suggest frequent large-scale population moves within this region. Such moves appear to have been less numerous in Southeastern France where the stratigraphic sequences are technologically more homogeneous. This pattern, especially obvious in Perigord, is probably related to the specific local climatic and ecological conditions of Southwestern France (Mellars 1996; Turq 1999). The influence of the oceanic system on the climate, resulting in comparatively mild winters, would have increased the development of plant resources during the year, which in turn would have had a major impact on the overall regional carrying capacity in animal herds (Mellars 1996). Moreover, the contrasting topographic zones, the abundance of river valleys functioning as migration trails, as well as the availability of rockshelters/caves and good quality raw materials would have represented attractive factors for hunter-gatherer groups throughout the Middle Paleolithic period (Mellars 1996; Turq 1999 and references therein).

Are there chronological trends within the Middle Paleolithic? We can unequivocally answer "yes": we do observe chronological trends in lithic production systems during the Middle Paleolithic. However, given the lack of precision of radiometric dating for this period, only rough chronological trends can be proposed.

The most significant chronological pattern is found at the end of the Middle Paleolithic, during Oxygen Isotope Stage 3 and possibly in late Stage 4. These changes consist of a diversification of the production systems (see Tables 1 and 2; Figure 3), and an increased use of these systems characterized by a low degree of blank predetermination, especially the Quina and discoidal systems and the

Levallois recurrent centripetal method. This diversity in production methods is especially clear in Southwestern France, where it is associated with an increased number of occupied sites. During the same period, the great plains of Northern France were depopulated (Tuffreau 1992; Roebroeks and Tuffreau 1999; Antoine *et al.* 2003). Indeed, human occupation in these northern regions is mostly limited to the temperate climatic phases and the beginning of the glacial episodes. The area was abandoned when the climate got more rigorous.

The territory of France, located at the extremity of the European continent, was characterized by topographic and ecological diversity. This region may have been the source of several population shifts as human groups moved from unfavorable areas to more bountiful ones during the most rigorous climatic oscillations. The overall severe conditions of Isotope Stage 4 and the short and dramatic fluctuations during Stage 3, as suggested by ice-core data (Dansgaard *et al.* 1993), may have triggered these displacements and/or replacements of populations. Instability in the availability of plant and animal resources may have been associated with a higher level of mobility.

This last point is confirmed by studies of lithic raw material transport used in toolkit manufacture. According to Féblot-Augustins (1993, 1999), raw material transfers over medium to long distances were more frequent during the Late Middle Paleolithic in Europe. The chronological trends we observed towards the use of lithic production systems characterized by a low degree of end-product predetermination during the late Middle Paleolithic could have been related to the mobility patterns of the Neandertal groups, following the model proposed by Binford (1980). According to this model, high residential mobility would have led to the production of a portable, multifunctional toolkit, intended for general use and requiring a low degree of predetermination but likely subject to much retouch and re-sharpening (Hovers 1997 and references therein).

Indeed, in some industries, blanks showing a lower level of investment in predetermination during core reduction are associated with tools with high use, recycling and/or curation potential. Tools of the Quina type, their large blanks allowing the successive transformation of the working edges, are excellent examples of this principle. In other industries, blanks were transformed into tools with little additional modification. These tools are common, for example, in assemblages including a discoid reduction sequence, like the Denticulate Mousterian, and in some assemblages with a recurrent Levallois reduction sequence. These characteristics fit with "the lithic technologies of residentially mobile groups which are geared toward the production of highly portable assemblages dominated by blanks meant to be used for immediate purposes and then re-sharpened as needs arise" (Adler 2002).

Thus, at the end of the Middle Paleolithic, the Western part of Europe may have been frequented by prehistoric groups carrying different technical traditions but who nonetheless adopted the same kind of mobility pattern in response to environmental factors. The observed diversity in lithic production systems as well as an increased residential mobility at the end of the Middle Paleolithic have no counterparts in areas with less strongly fluctuating climatic conditions and more stable animal resources, such as the Central Levant. The available data for the latter area show a greater homogeneity in lithic production systems, in that assemblages with Levallois reduction sequences dominate the picture from Stage 5 on, albeit exhibiting the full variability of this particular lithic production system. Moreover, evidence points to a relatively low level of residential mobility during the Late Middle Paleolithic (based on radiating system) (Meignen *et al.* this volume). These results underline the adaptive capacities of Neandertal hunter-gatherer groups. Confronted with an unstable climate they nevertheless kept the same fundamental technical identity (as seen in their lithic production systems), but modified their raw material economies, and the composition and management of their toolkits as a function of the local economic conditions.

ACKNOWLEDGEMENTS

We thank Erella Hovers and Steve L. Kuhn for their helpful editing comments made on this paper.

REFERENCES CITED

Adler D. 2002. *Late Middle Palaeolithic Patterns of Lithic Reduction, Mobility and Land-use in the Southern Caucasus.* Ph.D. Dissertation, Harvard University.

Ameloot-Van der Heijden N. 1993a. L'ensemble lithique du gisement de Longavesnes (Somme): illustration d'un problème de reconnaissance du débitage Levallois dans une industrie à bifaces de la phase ancienne du Paléolithique moyen. *Bulletin de la Société Préhistorique Française* 90: 257–263.

Ameloot-Van der Heijden N. 1993b. L'industrie laminaire du niveau CA. In A. Tuffreau (Ed.). *Riencourt-les-Bapaume (Pas-de-Calais): un gisement du Paléolithique moyen* (Documents d'Archéologie Française 37), pp. 26–52. Paris: Maison des Sciences de l'Homme

Ameloot-Van der Heijden N., C. Dupuis, N. Limondin, A. Munaut and J.J. Puissegur 1996. Le gisement Paléolithique moyen de Salouel (Somme, France). *L'Anthropologie* 100: 555–573.

Antoine P., N. Limondin-Lozouet, P. Auguste, A. Lamotte, J.J. Bahain, C. Falguères, M. Laurent, P. Coudret, J.L. Locht, P. Depaepe, J.P. Fagnart, M. Fontugne, C. Hatté, N. Mercier, M. Frechen, A.M. Moigne, A.V. Munaut, P. Ponel and D.D. Rousseau 2003. Paléoenvironnements pléistocènes et peuplements paléolithiques dans le bassin de la Somme (Nord de la France). *Bulletin de la Société Préhistorique Française* 100: 5–28.

Ashton N.M. 1992. The High Lodge flint industries. In N. Ashton, J. Cook, S.G. Lewis and J. Rose (Eds.), *High Lodge. Excavations by G. de Sieveking, 1962–8 and J. Cook, 1988*, pp. 124–168. London: British Museum Press.

Bernard-Guelle S. 1998–1999. Le gisement moustérien de plein air des Mourets (Villard de-Lans, Isère): une nouvelle analyse de l'industrie. *Préhistoire Anthropologie Méditerranéennes* 7–8: 53–61.

Beyries S. 1993. Analyse fonctionnelle de l'industrie lithique du niveau CA: rapport préliminaire et directions de recherche. In A. Tuffreau (Ed.), *Riencourt-les-Bapaume (Pas-de-Calais): un gisement du Paléolithique moyen* (Documents d'Archéologie Française 37), pp. 53–61. Paris: Maison des Sciences de l'Homme.

Binford L.R. 1980. Willow smoke and dogs' tails: hunter-gatherer settlement systems and archaeological site formation. *American Antiquity* 45: 4–20.

Boëda E. 1986. *Approche technologique du concept Levallois et évaluation de son champ d'application.* Thèse Doctorat, Université Paris X- Nanterre.

Boëda E. 1988a. Biache-St-Vaast. Analyse technologique du débitage du niveau IIA. In A. Tuffreau and
    J. Sommé (Eds.), Le gisement Paléolithique moyen de Biache-St-Vaast (Pas-de-Calais) (Mémoires de
    la Société Préhistorique Française 21), pp. 185–214. Paris: Société Préhistorique Française.

Boëda E. 1988b. Le concept laminaire: rupture et filiation avec le concept Levallois. In J.K. Kozlowski
    (Ed.), L'Homme de Néandertal: La mutation (ERAUL 35), pp. 41–59. Liège: Université de Liège.

Boëda E. 1990. De la surface au volume. Analyse des conceptions des débitages Levallois et laminaire.
    In C. Farizy (Ed.), Paléolithique moyen récent et Paléolithique supérieur ancien en Europe (Mémoires
    du Musée de Préhistoire d'Ile-de-France 3), pp. 63–68. Nemours: APRAIF.

Boëda E. 1991. Approche de la variabilité des systèmes de production lithique des industries du
    Paléolithique inférieur et moyen: chronique d'une variabilité attendue. Techniques et Culture
    17–18: 37–79.

Boëda E. 1993. Le débitage discoïde et le débitage Levallois récurrent centripète. Bulletin de la Société
    Préhistorique Française 90: 392–404.

Boëda E. 1994. Le concept Levallois: variabilité des méthodes (Monographie du CRA 9). Paris: CNRS
    Editions.

Boëda E. 1995. Levallois: A Volumetric Construction, Methods, a Technique. In H.L. Dibble and O.
    Bar-Yosef (Eds.), The Definition and Interpretation of Levallois Technology (Monographs in World
    Archaeology 23), pp. 41–68. Madison: Prehistory Press.

Boëda E., J.-M. Geneste and L. Meignen 1990. Identification de chaînes opératoires lithiques du
    Paléolithique ancien et moyen. Paléo 2: 43–80.

Boëda E., B. Kervazo, N. Mercier and H. Valladas 1996. Barbas C'3 base (Dordogne), une industrie
    bifaciale contemporaine des industries du Moustérien ancien: une variabilité attendue. Quaternaria
    Nova VI: 465–504.

Bordes F. 1950. Principes d'une méthode d'étude des techniques de débitage et de la typologie du
    Paléolithique ancien et moyen. L'Anthropologie 54: 19–34.

Bordes F. 1953. Essai de classification des industries "moustériennes". Bulletin de la Société Préhistorique
    Française 50: 457–467.

Bordes F. 1961. Typologie du Paléolithique ancien et moyen (Publications de l'Institut de Préhistoire de
    l'Université de Bordeaux). Bordeaux: Delmas.

Bordes F. 1981. Vingt-cinq ans après: le complexe moustérien revisité. Bulletin de la Société Préhistorique
    Française 78: 77–87.

Bourguignon L. 1996. La conception de débitage Quina. Quaternaria Nova VI: 149–166.

Bourguignon L. 1997. Le Moustérien de type Quina: Nouvelle Définition d'une Entité Technique. Thèse
    Doctorat, Université Paris X-Nanterre.

Bourguignon L. 1998. Le débitage Quina de la couche 5 de Sclayn: éléments d'interprétation. In
    M. Otte, M. Patou-Mathis and D. Bonjean (Eds.), Recherches aux Grottes de Sclayn (ERAUL 79),
    pp. 249–276. Liège: Université de Liège.

Bourguignon L. 2000. Saint-Denis-de-Pile: le gisement moustérien de Champs de Bossuet (Gironde). DFS
    sauvetage urgent, AFAN.

Bourguignon L. and A. Turq 2003. Une chaîne opératoire de débitage discoïde sur éclat du Moustérien
    à denticulés aquitain: les exemples de Champ de Bossuet et de Combe-Grenal c.14. In M. Peresani
    (Ed.), Advancements and Implications in the Study of the Discoid Technology (BAR International Series
    1120), pp. 131–152. Oxford: Archaeopress.

Brenet M. and M. Folgado 2003. Le débitage discoïde du gisement des Forêts à Saint-Martin-de-
    Gurçon (Dordogne). In M. Peresani (Ed.), Advancements and Implications in the Study of the Discoid
    Technology (BAR International Series 1120), pp. 153–177. Oxford: Archaeopress.

Clet M, D. Cliquet, J.P. Coutard, G. Fosse, P. Maubray, J.C. Ozouf and G. Vilgrain 1991. Le gisement
    paléolithique moyen de Querqueville (Manche). In A. Tuffreau (Ed.), Paléolithique et Mésolithique
    du Nord de la France: nouvelles recherches II (Publications du CERP 3), pp. 81–93. Lille: Université
    des Sciences et Techniques.

Cresswell R.C. 1982. Transferts de techniques et chaînes opératoires. Techniques et culture 2: 143–163.

Dansgaard W., S.N. Johnsen, H.B. Clausen, D. Dahl-Jensen, N.S. Gundestrup, C.U. Hammer, C.S.
    Hvidberg, J.P. Steffensen, A.E. Sveinbjornsdottir, J. Jouzel and G. Bond 1993. Evidence for general
    instability of past climate from a 250-kyr ice-core record. Nature 364: 218–220.

Debénath A. and A.J. Jelinek 1998. Nouvelles fouilles à La Quina (Charente). *Gallia Préhistoire* 40: 29–74.

Delagnes A. 1990. Analyse technologique de la méthode de débitage de l'abri Suard (La Chaise-de-Vouthon, Charente). *Paléo* 2: 81–88.

Delagnes A. 1991. Mise en évidence de deux conceptions différentes de la production lithique au Paléolithique moyen. In *25 Ans d'études technologiques en Préhistoire*, pp.125–137. Juan-Les-Pins: APDCA.

Delagnes A. 1992. *L'organisation de la production lithique au Paléolithique moyen: approche technologique à partir de l'étude des industries de La Chaise-de-Vouthon (Charente)*. Thèse Doctorat, Université Paris X - Nanterre.

Delagnes A. 1993. Un mode de production inédit au Paléolithique moyen dans l'industrie du niveau 6e du Pucheuil (Seine-Maritime). *Paléo* 5: 111–120.

Delagnes A. 1996a. Le site d'Etoutteville (Seine-Maritime): l'organisation technique et spatiale de la production laminaire à Etoutteville. In A. Delagnes and A. Ropars (Eds.), *Paléolithique moyen en Pays de Caux (Haute-Normandie): Le Pucheuil, Etoutteville: deux gisements de Plein air en milieu loessique* (D.A.F. 56), pp. 164–228. Paris: Maison des Sciences de l'Homme.

Delagnes A. 1996b. Le site du Pucheuil à Saint-Saëns (Seine-Maritime): l'industrie lithique de la série B du Pucheuil. In A. Delagnes and A. Ropars (Eds.), *Paléolithique moyen en Pays de Caux (Haute-Normandie): Le Pucheuil, Etoutteville: deux gisements de plein air en milieu loessique* (D.A.F. 56), pp. 59–130. Paris: Maison des Sciences de l'Homme.

Delagnes A. 1996c. Le site du Pucheuil à Saint-Saëns (Seine-Maritime): l'industrie lithique des séries A et C du Pucheuil. In A. Delagnes and A. Ropars (Eds.), *Paléolithique moyen en Pays de Caux (Haute-Normandie): Le Pucheuil, Etoutteville: deux gisements de plein air en milieu loessique* (D.A.F. 56), pp. 131–144. Paris: Maison des Sciences de l'Homme.

Delagnes A. 2000. Blade production during the Middle Paleolithic in Northwestern Europe. *Acta Anthropologica Sinica* 19 (supplement): 181–188.

Delagnes A., J.F. Tournepiche, D. Armand, E. Desclaux, M.F. Diot, C. Ferrier, V. Le Fillatre and B. Vandermeersch 1999. Le gisement Pléistocène moyen et supérieur d'Artenac (Saint-Mary, Charente): premier bilan interdisciplinaire. *Bulletin de la Société Préhistorique Française* 96(4): 469–496.

Depaepe P. and L. Brassinne 1994. Lailly/Le Fond de la Tournerie (vallée de la Vanne). In V. Deloze, P. Depaepe, J.M. Gouédo, V. Krier and J.L. Locht (Eds.), *Le Paléolithique moyen dans le Nord du Sénonais (Yonne)* (D.A.F. 47), pp. 163–202. Paris: Maison des Sciences de l'Homme.

Dibble H. and M. Lenoir 1995. *The Middle Paleolithic Site of Combe-Capelle Bas (France)*. Philadelphia: The University Museum-University of Pennsylvania.

Dobres A.M. and C.R. Hoffman 1994. Social agency and the dynamics of prehistoric technology. *Journal of Archaeological Method and Theory* 1: 211–258.

Féblot-Augustins J. 1993. Mobility strategies in the late Middle Paleolithic of Central Europe and Western Europe: elements of stability and variability. *Journal of Anthropological Archaeology* 12: 211–265.

Féblot-Augustins J. 1999. Raw material transport patterns and settlement systems in the European Lower and Middle Palaeolithic: continuity, change and variability. In W. Roebroeks and C. Gamble (Eds.), *The Middle Palaeolithic Occupation of Europe*, pp. 193–214. Leiden: University of Leiden.

Folgado M. 1997. *Saint-Martin-de-Gurçon, "Les Forêts"*. DFS sauvetage urgent, DRAC Aquitaine.

Forestier H. 1993. Le Clactonien: mise en application d'une nouvelle méthode de débitage s'inscrivant dans la variabilité des systèmes de production lithique du Paléolithique ancien. *Paléo* 5: 53–82.

Gaillard C. 1982. L'industrie lithique du Paléolithique inférieur et moyen de la grotte de Coupe-Gorge à Montmaurin (Hte Garonne). *Gallia Préhistoire* 25: 79–105.

Gautier C. 1989. Technologie de l'industrie moustérienne de Roisel (Somme). In A. Tuffreau (Ed.), *Paléolithique et Mésolithique du Nord de la France: nouvelles recherches* (Publications du CERP 1), pp. 61–68. Lille: Université des Sciences et Techniques.

Geneste J.M. 1985. *Analyse lithique d'industries moustériennes du Périgord: une approche technologique du comportement des groupes humains au Paléolithique moyen*. Thèse Doctorat, Université de Bordeaux I.

Geneste J.M. 1988. Les industries de la Grotte Vaufrey: technologie du débitage, économie et circulation de la matière première. In J.P. Rigaud (Ed.), *La Grotte Vaufrey: paléoenvironnement, chronologie, activités humaines* (Mémoires de la Société Préhistorique Française XIX), pp. 441–517. Paris: Société Préhistorique Française.

Geneste J.M. 1990. Développement des systèmes de production lithique au cours du Paléolitique moyen en Aquitaine septentrionale. In C. Farizy (Ed.), *Paléolithique Moyen Récent et Paléolithique Supérieur Ancien en Europe* (Mémoires du Musée de Préhistoire d'Ile-de-France 3), pp. 203–213. Nemours: APRAIF.

Geneste J.M., J. Jaubert, M. Lenoir, L. Meignen and A. Turq 1997. Approche technologique des Moustériens charentiens du Sud-ouest de la France et du Languedoc oriental. *Paléo* 9: 101–142.

Geneste J.M. and H. Plisson 1996. Production et utilisation de l'outillage lithique dans le Moustérien du sud-ouest de la France: les Tares, à Sourzac, Vallée de l'Isle, Dordogne. *Quaternaria Nova* VI: 343–368.

Gouédo J.M. 1988. Etude préliminaire de la technologie de l'industrie de Champlost: exemples de la chaîne opératoire Levallois et des racloirs à retouches bifaces. In A. Tuffreau (Ed.), *Cultures et industries paléolithiques en milieu loessique*. Revue Archéologique de Picardie (1–2 n° spécial), pp. 149–155. Amiens,.

Gouédo J.M., P. Alix, S. de Beaune, V. Krier and J.L. Locht 1994a. Etudes archéologiques: Vinneuf/ Les Hauts Massous (plateau du Sénonais). In V. Deloze, P. Depaepe, J.M. Gouédo, V. Krier and J.L. Locht (Eds.), *Le Paléolithique moyen dans le Nord du Sénonais (Yonne)* (D.A.F. 47), pp. 83–118. Paris: Maison des Sciences de l'Homme.

Gouédo M., J.C. Bats,V. Krier, P. Pernot and J.L. Ricard 1994b. Le gisement moustérien de la "Butte d'Arvigny" commune de Moissy-Cramayel (Seine-et-Marne), premiers résultats. *Bulletin de la Société Préhistorique Française* 91: 369–377.

Guette C. 2002. Révision critique du concept de débitage Levallois à travers l'étude du gisement moustérien de Saint-Vaast-la-Hougue/le Fort (chantier I-III et II, niveaux inférieurs) (Manche, France). *Bulletin de la Société Préhistorique Française* 99: 237–248.

Guilbaud M. 1993. Debitage from the Upper Castelperronian level at Saint Césaire. In F. Lévêque, A.M. Baker and M. Guilbaud (Eds.), *Context of a Late Neandertal*, (Monographs in World Archae-ology16), pp. 39–58. Madison: Prehistory Press.

Hovers E. 1997. *Variability of Levantine Mousterian Assemblages and Settlement Patterns: Implications for Understanding the Development of Human Behavior*. Ph.D. Dissertation, The Hebrew University of Jerusalem.

Huet B. 2002. Une industrie à composante lithologique mixte: le gisement paléolithique moyen de Goaréva (île de Bréhat, Côtes-d'Armor). *Bulletin de la Société Préhistorique Française* 99: 699–716.

Jaubert J. 1993. Le gisement paléolithique moyen de Mauran (Haute-Garonne): techno-économie des industries lithiques. *Bulletin de la Société Préhistorique Française* 90(5): 328–335.

Jaubert J. 2001. Un site moustérien de type Quina dans la vallée du Célé (Pailhès à Espagnac-Sainte-Eulalie, Lot). *Gallia Préhistoire* 43: 1–99.

Jaubert J. and T. Bismuth 1996. Le Paléolithique moyen des Pyrénées centrales: esquisse d'un schéma chronologique et économique dans la perspective d'une étude comparative avec les documents ibériques. In H. Delporte and J. Clottes (Eds.), *Pyrénées préhistoriques. Arts et Sociétés. Actes du 118ème Congrès national des Sociétés Historiques et Scientifiques,* pp. 9–26. Paris: Editions du CTHS.

Jaubert J. and C. Farizy 1995. Levallois debitage: exclusivity, absence or coexistence with other operative schemes in the Garonne Basin, Southwestern France. In H.L. Dibble and O. Bar-Yosef (Eds.), *The Definition and Interpretation of Levallois Technology* (Monographs in World Archaeology 23), pp. 227–248. Madison: Prehistory Press.

Jaubert J., B. Kervazo, Y. Quinif, J.-P. Brugal and W. O'yl 1992. Le site paléolithique moyen du Rescoundudou (Aveyron, France). Datations U/Th et interprétation chronostratigraphique. *L'Anthropologie* 96: 103–112.

Jaubert J., M. Lorblanchet, H. Laville, R. Slott-Moller, A. Turq and J.-P.Brugal 1990. *Les Chasseurs d'Aurochs de La Borde, un site du Paléolithique moyen* (Livernon, Lot) (D.A.F. 27). paris: Maison des Sciences de l'Homme.

Jaubert J. and V. Mourre V. 1996. Coudoulous, Le Rescoundudou, Mauran: diversité des matières premières et variabilité des schémas de production d'éclats. *Quaternaria Nova* VI: 313–341.

Karlin C., P. Bodu and J. Pelegrin 1991. Processus techniques et chaînes opératoires. Comment les préhistoriens s'approprient un concept élaboré par les ethnologues. In H. Balfet (Ed.), *Observer l'action technique: des chaînes opératoires, pour quoi faire?* pp. 101–117. Paris: CNRS Editions.

Lemonnier P., 1986. The study of material culture today: toward an Anthropology of technical systems. *Journal of Anthropological Archaeology* 5: 147–186.

Lemonnier P. 1992. *Elements for an Anthropology of Technology* (Anthropological papers 88).Ann Arbor: Museum of Anthropology, University of Michigan.

Lenoir M. 1980. Fouilles de sauvetage dans un gisement du Pléistocène supérieur en Gironde: le gisement de la Cimenterie Despiet à Camiac et Saint Denis (Gironde). *Revue d'Histoire et d'Archéologie du Libournais* XXLVIII: 41–51.

Lenoir M. 1986. Un mode d'obtention de la retouche "Quina" dans le Moustérien de Combe-Grenal (Domme, Dordogne). *Bulletin de la Société d'Anthropologie du Sud-Ouest* XXI: 153–160.

Levi-Strauss C. 1976. *Structural Anthropology.* University of Chicago Press, Chicago.

Locht J.L. (Ed.) 2002. *Bettencourt-Saint-Ouen (Somme). Cinq occupations paléolithiques au début de la dernière glaciation* (D.A.F. 90). Paris: Maison des Sciences de l'Homme.

Locht J.L., V. Deloze, P. Pihuit and E. Teheux 1994. Molinons/Le Grand Chanteloup (vallée de la Vanne). In V. Deloze, P. Depaepe, J.M. Gouédo, V Krier and J.L. Locht (Eds.), *Le Paléolithique moyen dans le Nord du Sénonais (Yonne)* (D.A.F. 47), pp. 119–138. Paris: Maison des Sciences de l'Homme.

Locht, J.L., and F. Ferdouel 1994. Lailly/Le Domaine de Beauregard (vallée de la Vanne). In V. Deloze, P. Depaepe, J.M. Gouédo, V Krier and J.L. Locht (Eds.), *Le Paléolithique moyen dans le Nord du Sénonais (Yonne)* (D.A.F. 47), pp. 139–162. Paris: Maison des Sciences de l'Homme.

Locht J.L. and C. Swinnen 1994. Le débitage discoïde du gisement de Beauvais (Oise): aspects de la chaîne opératoire au travers de quelques remontages. *Paléo* 6: 89–104.

de Lumley H. and M.H. Licht 1972. Les industries moustériennes de la grotte de l'Hortus (Valflaunès, Hérault). In H. de Lumley (Ed.), *La grotte moustérienne de l'Hortus (Valflaunès, Hérault)*, pp. 387–487. Marseille: Université de Provence.

Marcy J.-L., P. Auguste, M. Fontugne, A.V. Munaut and B. Van Vliet-Lanoë 1993. Le gisement moustérien d'Hénin-sur-Cojeul (Pas-de-Calais). *Bulletin de la Société Préhistorique Française* 90: 251–256.

Masson B. and L. Vallin 1993. Un atelier de débitage Levallois intact au sein des loess weichseliens du Nord de la France à Hermies (Pas-de-Calais). *Bulletin de la Société Préhistorique Française* 90: 265–268.

Mauss M. 1936 (translated 1979). *Les techniques du corps. Sociologie et psychologie.* London: Routledge and Kegan Paul.

Meignen L. 1988. Un exemple de comportement technologique différentiel selon les matières premières: Marillac couches 9 et 10. In M. Otte (Ed.), *L'Homme de Néandertal: la Technique* (ERAUL 31), pp. 71–79. Liège: Universite de Liège.

Meignen L. 1993. Les industries lithiques de l'abri des Canalettes: couche 2. In L. Meignen (Ed.), *L'abri des Canalettes. Un habitat moustérien sur les Grands Causses (Nant, Aveyron)* (Monographie du CRA 10), pp. 239–328. Paris: CNRS Editions.

Mellars P. 1996. *The Neanderthal Legacy. An Archaeological Perspective from Western Europe.* Princeton: Princeton University Press.

Molines N., S. Hinguant and J.L. Monnier 2001. Le Paléolithique moyen à outils bifaciaux dans l'ouest de la France: synthèse des données anciennes et récentes. In D. Cliquet, (Ed.), *Les industries à outils bifaciaux du Paléolithique moyen d'Europe occidentale* (ERAUL 98), pp. 107–114. Liège: Université de Liège.

Moncel M.H. 1996. L'industrie lithique du Paléolithique moyen de l'abri du Maras (Ardèche) (fouilles de René Gilles et de Jean Combier): la question des moustériens tardifs et du débitage laminaire au Paléolithique moyen. *Gallia Préhistoire* 38: 1–41.

Moncel M.H. 1998a. Les niveaux moustériens de la grotte de Saint-Marcel (Ardèche). Fouilles René Gilles. Reconnaissance de niveaux à débitage discoïde dans la vallée du Rhône. *Bulletin de la Société Préhistorique Française* 95: 141–170.

Moncel M.H. 1998b. L'industrie lithique de la grotte Scladina (Sclayn)- La couche moustérienne éémienne. In M. Otte, M. Patou-Mathis and D. Bonjean (Eds.), *Recherches aux grottes de Sclayn* (ERAUL 79), pp. 181–247. Liège: Université de Liège.

Moncel M.H. and J. Combier 1992. L'industrie lithique du site pleistocène moyen d'Orgnac 3 (Ardèche). *Gallia Préhistoire* 34: 1–55.

Pasty J.F. 2000. Le gisement Paléolithique moyen de Meillers (Allier): un exemple de la variabilité du débitage Discoïde. *Bulletin de la Société Préhistorique Française* 97(2): 165–190.

Pelegrin J. 1990. Prehistoric lithic technology: some aspects of research. *Archaeological Review from Cambridge* 9: 116–125.

Pelegrin J. 1995. *Technologie lithique: le Chatelperronien de Roc-de-Combe (Lot) et de La Côte (Dordogne)* (Cahiers du Quaternaire 20). Paris: CNRS Editions.

Peresani M. 1998. La variabilité du débitage discoïde dans la grotte de Fumane (Italie du Nord). *Paléo* 10: 123–146.

Révillion S. 1994. *Les industries laminaires du Paléolithique moyen en Europe septentrionale. L'exemple des gisements de Saint-Germain-des-Vaux/Port Racine (Manche), de Seclin (Nord)et de Riencourt-les-Bapaume (Pas-de-Calais)* (Publications du CERP 5). Lille: Université des Sciences et Technologies.

Révillion S. and A. Tuffreau 1994a. *Les industries laminaires au Paléolithique moyen* (Dossier de Documentation Archéologique 18). Paris: CNRS Editions.

Révillion S. and A. Tuffreau 1994b. Valeur et signification du débitage laminaire du gisement paléolithique moyen de Seclin (Nord). In S. Révillion and A. Tuffreau (Eds.), *Les industries laminaires au Paléolithique moyen* (Dossier de Documentation Archéologique 18), pp. 19–43. Paris: CNRS Editions.

Rigaud J.P. (Ed.) 1988. *La Grotte Vaufrey: paléoenvironnement, chronologie, activités humaines* (Mémoire de la Société préhistotirque Française, XXIX). Paris: Société Préhistorique Française.

Roebroeks W. and A. Tuffreau 1999. Paleoenvironment and settlement patterns of the Northwest European Middle Palaeolithic. In W. Roebroeks and C. Gamble (Eds.), *The Middle Palaeolithic Occupation of Europe*, pp. 121–138. Leiden: University of Leiden.

Rogers A.R. 1988. Does biology constrain culture? *American Anthropologist* 90: 819–831.

Rolland N. 1981. The interpretation of Middle Palaeolithic variability. *Man* 16: 15–42.

Soressi M. 1999. Variabilité technologique au Moustérien: analyse comparée du débitage Levallois MTA A du Moustier (Dordogne, France). *Paléo* 11: 111–134.

Soressi M. 2002. *Le Moustérien de Tradition Acheuléenne du Sud-ouest de la France. Discussion sur la signification du faciès à partir de l'etude comparée de quatre sites: Pech de l'Azé I, Le Moustier, La Rochette et la Grotte XVI*. Thèse Doctorat, Université Bordeaux 1.

Swinnen C., J.L. Locht and P. Antoine 1996. Le gisement moustérien d'Auteuil (Oise). *Bulletin de la Société Préhistorique Française* 93: 173–182.

Texier P.J. and I. Francisco-Ortega 1995. Main technological and typological characteristics of the lithic assemblage from level I at Bérigoule (Murs-Vaucluse, France). In H.L. Dibble and O. Bar-Yosef (Eds.), *The Definition and Interpretation of Levallois Technology* (Monographs in World Archaeology 23), pp. 213–248. Madison: Prehistory Press.

Tuffreau A. 1979. Le gisement moustérien du Château d'Eau à Corbehem (Pas-de-Calais). *Gallia Préhistoire* 22(2): 371–389.

Tuffreau A. 1986. Biache-Saint-Vaast et les industries moustériennes du Pléistocène moyen récent dans la France septentrionale. In A. Tuffreau and J. Sommé (Eds.), *Chronostratigraphie et faciès culturels du Paléolithique inférieur et moyen dans l'Europe du Nord-Ouest*, pp. 197–204. Bulletin de l'A.F.E.Q (Supplement).

Tuffreau A. 1989. Le gisement paléolithique moyen de Champoisy (Marne). In A. Tuffreau (Ed.), *Paléolithique et Mésolithique du Nord de la France: nouvelles recherches* (Publications du C.R.E.P. 1), pp. 69–77. Villeneuve d'Asq: CREP.

Tuffreau A. 1992. Middle Paleolithic settlement in Northern France. In H.L. Dibble and P. Mellars (Eds.), *The Middle Paleolithic: Adaptation, Behavior and Variability* (University Museum symposium series 2), pp. 59–73. Philadelphia: University of Pennsylvania.

Tuffreau A. 1995. Variability of Levallois technology in Northern France and neighboring areas. In H.L. Dibble and O. Bar-Yosef (Eds.), *The Definition and Interpretation of Levallois Technology* (Monographs in World Archaeology 23), pp. 413–431. Madison: Prehistory Press.

Tuffreau A., Y. Zuate and J. Zuber 1975. La terrasse fluviatile de Bagarre (Etaples, Pas-de-Calais) et ses industries: note préliminaire. *Bulletin de la Société Préhistorique Française* 72: 229–235.

Turq A. 1989. Approche technologique et économique du faciès Moustérien de type Quina: étude préliminaire. *Bulletin de la Société Préhistorique Française* 86(8): 244–256.

Turq A. 1999. Reflections on the Middle Palaeolithic of the Aquitaine Basin. In W. Roebroeks and C. Gamble (Eds.), *The Middle Palaeolithic Occupation of Europe*, pp. 107–120. Leiden: University of Leiden.

Turq A. 2000. *Paléolithique inférieur et moyen entre Dordogne et Lot.* Les Eyzies: SAMRA.

Turq A., J.L. Guadelli and A. Quintard 1999. A propos de deux sites d'habitat moustérien de type Quina à exploitation du bison: l'exemple du Mas-Viel et de Sous-les-Vignes. In J.-P. Brugal, F. David, J.G. Enloe and J. Jaubert (Eds.), *Le Bison: gibier et moyen de subsistance des hommes du Paléolithique aux Paléoindiens des Grandes Plaines*, pp. 143–157. Antibes: APDCA.

Vallin L. 1992. Le gisement moustérien d'Houppeville-les Hautes Terres Sud (Seine-Maritime): étude d'un assemblage lithique en milieu loessique. *Revue Archéologique de l'Ouest* 9: 5–37.

Yvorra P. and L. Slimak 2001. La grotte Mandrin à Malataverne (Drome). Prèmiers éléments pour une analyse spatiale des vestiges en contexte moustérien. *Bulletin de la Société Préhistorique Française* 98: 189–206.

Chapter **6**

Trajectories of Change in the Middle Paleolithic of Italy

Steven L. Kuhn

Dept. of Anthropology, University of Arizona, Tucson, AZ 85721-0030

ABSTRACT

This paper examines the idea that there are few if any long-term cultural evolutionary trends in the Middle Paleolithic. First, the general notion of Mousterian stasis is examined. Second, patterns of directional change in lithic technology (laminarity) in two Italian Middle Paleolithic sequences are discussed. Trajectories of change over time trend in opposite directions in the two cases and show very different relationships with the succeeding Upper Paleolithic. Results from this and other papers suggest that Middle Paleolithic hominids were more than capable of altering their behavior, but that there is no generalized tendency for Mousterian industries to develop in the direction of the Upper Paleolithic. This conclusion is difficult to reconcile with progressive views of human cultural evolution. The concept of rugged fitness landscapes may provide a more satisfactory explanatory framework.

INTRODUCTION

Conventional wisdom among many scholars has been that the Middle Paleolithic was an interval of remarkable stasis, a period during which there were few if any significant evolutionary developments in hominid behavioral tendencies or capacities (Mithen 1996: 123; Kuhn and Stiner 1998a; Gamble 1999:422–423; Klein 1999:442). But what is really meant by this? The Middle Paleolithic in its broadest sense encompasses a set of behavioral adaptations and technological strategies that persisted for more than 150,000 years in the face of a wide range of environmental conditions and profound shifts in climate. It is simply inconceivable that Mousterian hominids could have been successful in occupying territory from the Persian Gulf to the Russian Plain without being able to alter their ways of doing things. Moreover, there is quite a bit of temporal and spatial variation in the archaeology of the Middle Paleolithic and in Mousterian technology: the explanation of "Mousterian assemblage variability" has been a major point of contention for Paleolithic archaeologists over the past 50 years (*e.g.*, Bordes 1961; Binford and Binford 1969; Rolland and Dibble 1990). The mere existence of such variation implies differentiation, which means that some kind of change had to have occurred.

In emphasizing the static nature of the Middle Paleolithic, I believe that scholars actually make two separate, and unequally defensible, assertions. One is that no major technological innovations occurred during the Middle Paleolithic, that nothing significant was added to the human technological repertoire (Kuhn and Stiner 1998a). This would seem to be a fairly safe claim within the limits of current knowledge. Virtually the entire technological and behavioral repertoire documented at the end of the Middle Paleolithic around 35,000 years ago was already in place 200,000 years earlier at the end of the Lower Paleolithic. For the most part, Mousterian variability represents the recombination of a variety of behaviors with great time depth. Arguably the only real technological novelties associated with the Middle Paleolithic are the use of ochre and the hafting of projectile points and other stone elements (Callow and Cornford 1986; Shea 1988), though some researchers assert that these practices can also be found in the late Lower Paleolithic (*e.g.*, Barham 2002). So, from this perspective, the stasis of the Mousterian relates mainly to the lack of novelty.

A second aspect to claims about stasis during the Middle Paleolithic is that there are few if any sustained directional trends in technological evolution. As a result of the fundamental work of F. Bordes on the Mousterian in Western Europe, it is commonly believed that though Mousterian assemblages may vary through time within any one stratified site, there is little or no consistent directionality to these changes. In other words, while the Mousterian may have changed over time it was not going anywhere in particular. This view is far from universal, however. In the eastern Mediterranean Levant there is clearly a highly generalized pattern of change over time in Levallois technology (Garrod and Bate 1937; Jelinek 1981; Bar-Yosef 1998), and some researchers have long argued that at least limited temporal trends in technology and typology can be found in western Europe as well (Mellars 1970, 1986). Perhaps more importantly though, even where trends can be detected the question remains as to whether they anticipated the Upper Paleolithic. For example, in the well-known sequence from Tabun Cave in Israel, it is actually the earliest assemblages that seem most Upper Paleolithic in character, due largely to the presence of blades. Similarly, many of the more recent Middle Paleolithic assemblages in southwest Europe are characterized as Quina or Denticulate Mousterian (Mellars 1970, 1996), neither of which is known for high frequencies of Upper Paleolithic elements.

This paper, like many others in this volume, is concerned mainly with the second claim, relating to long-term, directional trends in Middle Paleolithic technology. In considering the problem it is important to separate the question of whether trends *per se* exist from the question of whether they anticipate the Upper Paleolithic. Simply asking whether there is evidence for directional change within Middle Paleolithic technologies mainly implicates the general adaptive and behavioral capacities of the hominids. It is an entirely different issue to ask whether any changes observed anticipated the direction of specific Upper Paleolithic cultural trends. In principle we should not be surprised to find that Mousterian hominids (Neandertals and anatomically modern *Homo sapiens*) were fully capable of change and even some level of innovation but that they were following evolutionary trajectories quite different from those documented for hominids in Eurasia after 50,000 years ago. The distinction can be illustrated by looking at two Middle Paleolithic sequences from Italy. Both show definite technological trends. However, those trends are in rather different directions, and appear to have rather different relationships to the Upper Paleolithic industries that followed.

STUDY SAMPLES

Two study samples are discussed below, one from a series of sites in coastal Latium, in the west-central part of the Italian peninsula, and the other from a single site on the northern Ligurian coast. I would not argue that the assemblages from this small sample of caves are representative of the entire range of variation within the Italian Middle Paleolithic. The samples are chosen to illustrate just a part of the variability present in the Mousterian sequences of this area.

The sample from Latium includes a series of Mousterian assemblages from several sites in the region southwest of Rome. They represent a time range between Oxygen Isotope Stage 5a and roughly 36,000 years BP. The assemblages all belong to the so-called "Pontinian," a distinctive regional variant of the Mousterian manufactured using small flint pebbles from fossil marine beaches and characterized by diminutive artifacts and an abundance of heavily reduced scrapers. Results from research on the assemblages from Latium have been extensively published elsewhere (Kuhn 1992, 1995a, 1995b; Kuhn and Stiner 1992). A limited amount of data is also available for a single early Upper Paleolithic (Aurignacian) assemblage, from layer 21 at the site of Grotta del'Fosselone (Blanc and Segre 1953). The Aurignacian at Fossellone has yielded a single conventional ^{14}C date of *ca.* 27,000 years BP, but this determination is somewhat suspect.

The second sample discussed here comes from the site of Riparo Mochi. Riparo Mochi is located in the Balzi Rossi near Ventemiglia, very close to the French/Italian border, and is one of the complex of sites often referred to as the "Grimaldi caves." Riparo Mochi, which preserved a deep sequence of Middle and Upper Paleolithic deposits, was excavated on and off between 1939 and 1959 by L. Cardini of the Istituto Italiano di Paleontologia Umana. The Mousterian at Riparo Mochi has been exposed over a depth of more than 4 m. Although strata drawings indicate that much finer sedimentary subdivisions could be made (Kuhn and Stiner 1992), the entire Middle Paleolithic sequence was given a single stratigraphic designation (layer I). Unlike the Upper Paleolithic deposits at the site, the Middle Paleolithic at Riparo Mochi was excavated in arbitrary 10 cm levels instead of along natural stratigraphic divisions. No dates are currently available for the Middle Paleolithic at Riparo Mochi. However, the overlying layer G, yielding an early Upper Paleolithic (proto-Aurignacan) industry (Laplace 1977) is dated to between 35,000 and 36,000 years BP, roughly the same age as the most recent Mousterian layers in Latium (Kuhn and Stiner 1998b; Kuhn and Bietti 2000). There may have been a brief hiatus in the occupation of Riparo Mochi, represented by sparse, mixed remains in layer H, but there is no major disconformity in the stratigraphic sequence. Based on geological criteria it has been argued that the Mousterian sequence at Mochi fits into the later half of the Upper Pleistocene, that is into Oxygen Isotope Stages 4 and 3 (de Lumley 1969). Chronologically it probably corresponds roughly with the last half of the Latium sequence.

The technological trends discussed in this paper involve changes in blank form and core reduction technology. Of particular interest for the present discussion are changes over time within each area in the degree of laminarity, the numbers of blades and blade-like pieces, as well as associated technological strategies. Blade blanks are not exclusive to the Upper Paleolithic, and their presence in the Mousterian is itself no surprise (Bar-Yosef and Kuhn 1999). However, blade technology of one form or another *is* a widely shared feature of the early Upper Paleolithic in Eurasia. This paper examines blade production not because it is somehow essentially modern, but because that is the direction lithic technologies in western Eurasia eventually followed subsequent to the Mousterian. Typological trends in the Italian Mousterian have been discussed by other researchers. Mussi (1990) and others (*e.g.*, Palma di Cesnola 1996) recognize an increase in the numbers of denticulate-dominated assemblages over time in the peninsula as a whole, although the trend is not clearly expressed in the Latium area.

Two kinds of observations are summarized below. One concerns the frequencies of different dorsal scar patterns. Parallel, longitudinal scar patterns with previous removals originating from the proximal or distal parts of a blank are hallmarks of blade technologies, whether prismatic or Levallois, whereas multidirectional scar patterns are more typical of discoid and centripetal Levallois blank production methods. The second set of observations concerns a simple index of elongation of complete flakes and blanks, the length/width ratio. Obviously, one can and should examine technological practices in much greater detail than this: there is more to it than just the shape of the blanks and the orientation of dorsal scars (for more detailed analysis, see Bietti and Grimaldi 1995; Kuhn 1995a, 1995b). Nonetheless, these are commonly recorded variables with a fair degree of technological significance.

In both Mochi and the Latium sites there are distinct trends in the relative degree of elongation and frequencies of parallel dorsal scar patterns in the Middle Paleolithic assemblages (Figures 1 and 2). In neither sample are the trends absolutely monotonic, nor should they be expected to be: nonetheless, they do represent statistically significant trends. More interestingly, however, the trends observed are in opposite directions. In Latium there is a distinct increase in laminarity in the Middle Paleolithic assemblages over time (Figure 1a, 1b). This is a result of heavier emphasis on unidirectional cores, both Levallois and non-Levallois, and

a.

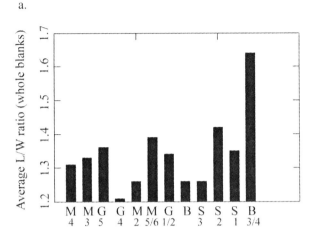

b.

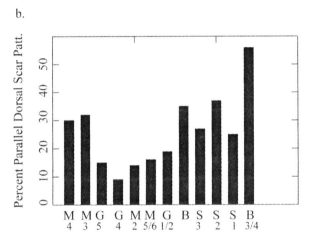

Figure 1. Technological trends in Latium Middle Paleolithic. Bars indicate: a. average length/width ratios of retouched pieces; b. percent blanks with parallel, longitudinal dorsal scar patterns. Age decreases from left to right. Key to assemblage designations: M = Grotta dei Moscerini; G = Grotta Guattari; S = Grotta di Sant'Agostino; B = Grotta Breuil.

a decreasing emphasis on centripetal Levallois and bipolar technology through time (Kuhn 1995a). In contrast, at Riparo Mochi the highest levels of laminarity occur in the lower part of the sequence: over time there is a shift away from heavy reliance on unidirectional Levallois technology to almost exclusive use of discoid technology at the top of the Mousterian sequence (Figure 2a, 2b). It is not clear whether the comparatively low frequencies of blades and parallel scar patterns in the earliest levels (cuts 72-68) are genuine or an artifact of very small sample sizes.

Interestingly, parallels can be found for both of these trends in other Italian sites. There is a general (though not universal) tendency for discoid core technology to dominate late Mousterian assemblages, particularly in northern Italy (Kuhn

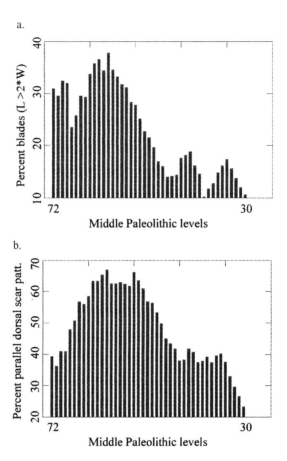

Figure 2. Technological trends in Middle Paleolithic of Riparo Mochi. Bars indicate running averages over ranges of five arbitrary 10 cm levels for : a. proportion technical blades (length > 2*width); and, b. proportion blanks with parallel longitudinal dorsal scar patterns. Depth increases from right to left.

and Bietti 2000; Peresani 1995–96). On the other hand, a few so-called "terminal Mousterian" assemblages from outside the Pontinian area, such as the one from the open-air site of San Francesco in Liguria (Tavoso 1988) are distinctively laminar in their blank production.

It is also important to point out that the trends in laminarity in both study areas seem to represent shifts in the frequency of different technological elements, not the appearance of entirely new forms of technology. There is evidence that many if not all of the basic manufacture strategies were present throughout both Middle Paleolithic sequences. Discoid reduction is strongly represented throughout the Mochi sequence, even in the earliest layers with the highest incidence of blades and parallel dorsal scar patterns. Likewise, something akin to centripetal recurrent Levallois method is found in all of the assemblages from Latium, even the most recent. In other words, the observed trajectories of change represent shifting emphases within a set of alternatives rather than the introduction of entirely new sets of technological procedures.

It is clear that trends in laminarity in Latium and Liguria differ in direction. They also differ in their relationship with the succeeding Upper Paleolithic. Interestingly, however, in neither region does the early Upper Paleolithic seem to represent a further extension of trends that began in the Middle Paleolithic, at least in this feature of lithic technology. In Latium, the earliest Upper Paleolithic (from Fossellone and Grotta Barbara), which is not in fact very early, has a relatively low frequency of blades, especially in that portion of the assemblages manufactured using the local pebble raw materials. In fact, blanks from Fossellone are somewhat less elongate on average than the more recent Mousterian assemblages (Figure 3a). So although the frequency of blades increases over time in the Mousterian of Latium, it does not continue to do so in the Aurignacian. At Riparo Mochi,

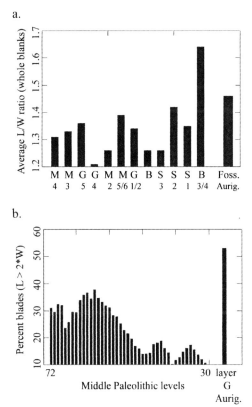

Figure 3. Middle Paleolithic technological trends compared with early Upper Paleolithic: a. average length/width ratios of retouched pieces from Latium Mousterian sites and Aurignacian of Riparo Salvini; b. a. proportion technical blades (length > 2*width) in Mousterian and "proto-Aurignacian" of Riparo Mochi.

there is an abrupt and pronounced reversal of the Mousterian trend away from laminarity with the earliest Upper Paleolithic. The industry of layer G, classified as "proto-Aurignacian", is typified by high frequencies of retouched bladelets and blade blanks (Figure 3b).

DISCUSSION AND CONCLUSION

Compared to later time periods, the Middle Paleolithic does appear to be an interval of relative stasis, at least with respect to the generation of novel forms of technological behavior. However, the Neandertals and their contemporaries were not locked into a single way of doing things. Given the range of habitats and climates they inhabited, Middle Paleolithic hominids must have been highly flexible. That flexibility seems to have been manifest mainly though redeploying and recombining a limited range of technological options, and not as the development of entirely new technological solutions. Moreover, as this paper and many others in the current volume demonstrate, many sites and regional sequences do in fact show evidence for sustained, directional trends in technology and perhaps in foraging as well. However, as is the case in Italy, the trajectories of technological change seem to vary from region to region, and even from site to site. Moreover they do not necessarily lead towards classical Upper Paleolithic patterns. The general trend in Latium is towards a pattern of blank production that is similar to Upper Paleolithic prismatic blade technology in its general features, though quite different in its specifics. At Riparo Mochi, the trend is for a greater emphasis over time on typically Middle Paleolithic technological options. Yet no one would suggest that Neandertals in Latium were on the road toward the Upper Paleolithic whereas the occupants of Riparo Mochi were only becoming more "Mousterian" over time.

The inconsistent directions of local trajectories of change do not necessarily mean that Neandertals and their contemporaries were simply taking a random walk through the Upper Pleistocene. Instead we are probably seeing a trend towards increasing regional diversity in the Middle Paleolithic over the course of the Upper Pleistocene, behavioral differentiation in response to specific ecological, demographic and social conditions. The trends documented here and elsewhere probably represent responses to localized environmental and demographic conditions, within constraints imposed by raw materials as well as the technological knowledge base of local populations. In Latium, the changes in technology seem to be linked to shifts in land-use at a regional scale. The increasing emphasis over time on relatively efficient methods for producing laminar blanks is accompanied by declining levels of scraper reduction and lower retouch frequencies, as well as by evidence for increasing provisioning of sites with hunted game. These results are interpreted as reflecting an overall increase in the duration of individual site occupation events and concomitantly lower levels of residential mobility, responses to changes in the terrestrial habitat brought on by declining sea levels (see Stiner and Kuhn 1992; Stiner 1994; Kuhn 1995a). At Riparo Mochi we currently lack independent evidence from faunal remains or other sources in the Middle Paleolithic layers that might help to reconstruct activities. I suspect the patterns observed in the Mochi sequence reflect very local changes in how Mousterian hominids used this particular shelter, which is part of an extensive complex of caves and shelters in the surrounding Balzi Rossi. However, the fact that late Mousterian assemblages in the northern Mediterranean are often dominated by discoid reduction suggests that there may be a larger, regional trend as well.

Of course, there are many other elements of behavior that we could measure and compare across regions over the course of the Upper Pleistocene, and we should also expect to see different kinds of trends, played out at different spatial scales, when looking at different variables. For example, frequencies of retouched pieces and the intensity of retouch/reduction both decline over time in **both** Riparo Mochi and the Latium caves. This could indicate broadly similar trends in patterns of site use, though much more research would be needed to test such an hypothesis. Long-term tendencies in large game acquisition may show greater local and regional diversity over this same interval simply because these are so closely conditioned by the abundance of game animals (Grayson and Delpech 1998; Grayson *et al.* 2001; Stiner 2002). Even so, some very broadly expressed trends in things such as patterns of small game exploitation (*e.g.*, Stiner *et al.* 2000; Stiner 2002) may express the influence of more global ecological and demographic factors.

If this and the other contributions to the present volume share a single general theme, it is that the changes associated with the transition from Middle to Upper Paleolithic in Eurasia do not necessarily represent a shift from one stable state to another. Both the Middle and the Upper Paleolithic are dynamic and variable, although the dynamism may be expressed at different temporal and spatial scales and in different domains of behavior. Another theme that develops out of the results presented here, as well as of those discussed in other papers, is that the Mousterian could change without necessarily becoming the Upper Paleolithic.

This second notion is rather more difficult to reconcile with common perceptions of the long-term evolution of Paleolithic cultures. Prevailing views of cultural evolution tend to be "accretive" and progressive. Earlier culture complexes are treated as incomplete or impoverished versions of later ones, lacking certain key characteristics, the addition of which mark major transitions in cultural evolution. The history of human cultural achievement can be represented as a single time line, punctuated by major innovations or thresholds in human culture. Change ("progress") in the Middle Paleolithic is thus measured in terms of its distance from the Upper Paleolithic and "modern human behavior". Such a view is almost certainly a legacy of early culture evolutionist thinking, and it diverges radically from modern notions of evolution as a historically contingent process based on random production and subsequent reduction of novelty. Moreover, it does little to help us understand such variation and change as existed within the earlier phases of human cultural evolution.

The concept of fitness landscapes may be more useful in understanding the dynamism of the Middle Paleolithic. The term was originally coined by Wright (1932) and has been much elaborated over the intervening 70 years (*e.g.*, Perelson and Kaufman 1991). A fitness landscape is a theoretical topographic construct describing the influence of a range of different factors on the fitness of a population of organisms. High points on the landscape represent adaptive configurations of relatively greater fitness, whereas topographic low points represent areas of reduced fitness. In a simple fitness landscape, all factors converge to create a single Mt. Fuji-like peak, a single behavioral and/or physical phenotype that provides a near-optimal adaptive solution to a wide range of environmental problems. Organisms that can maintain higher levels of fitness will be evolutionarily successful, so selection will tend to drive populations toward the single peak from anywhere in the simple fitness landscape.

A more interesting, and probably more widely applicable construct is the rugged fitness landscape (*e.g.*, Palmer 1991). Rugged fitness landscapes are characterized by many fitness peaks of varying heights (local sub-optima) separated by "valleys" representing adaptive states of lower fitness. Selection will still drive populations towards adaptive configurations that result in higher levels of fitness, but on a rugged landscape the populations will tend to climb the peak closest to their starting position. This may or may not be the highest peak on the landscape. However, once a population has begun to ascend a particular fitness peak it is very difficult for it to shift to another, even one that provides greater maximum fitness, because shifting between peaks necessarily involves a reduction in fitness, something that evolutionary processes do not generally promote. Fortunately for the denizens of rugged fitness landscapes, severe environmental or demographic perturbations may serve to dislodge a population from its current sub-optimal fitness peak, providing at least the opportunity for it to begin climbing an even higher one that happens to be accessible.

The notion of rugged fitness landscapes may help us understand how on one hand the Mousterian could have been changeable and dynamic, yet on the other how it seems to show so few consistent trends in the direction of the subsequent Upper Paleolithic. If we conceive of the fitness landscape inhabited by Upper Pleistocene hominids as consisting of a single, Fuji-like peak, then the fact that few if any Middle Paleolithic populations successfully climbed to the level of the Upper Paleolithic would have to mean that they were simply incapable of changing, and that nothing much really happened in Eurasia between 250,000 and 40,000 years ago. If, on the other hand, we imagine a very rugged fitness landscape, with many peaks and troughs, then the evidence makes more sense. Middle Paleolithic populations were in fact evolving behaviorally, their fitness was increasing locally, but as it happens they happened to be ascending a peak (or more likely several peaks) different from the one that anatomically modern Upper Paleolithic populations eventually climbed. In other words, the Middle Paleolithic was not just an unfinished version of the Upper: despite the historical course of the Middle-to-Upper Paleolithic transition, there were many different evolutionary trajectories that Mousterian populations could have followed, and in fact did follow. Ultimately, learning what happened to the hominids responsible for the Middle Paleolithic is much more than a matter of deciding whether they could or could not change, or where it was situated on the slopes of "Mt. Modernity".

It requires that we understand the particular local fitness peaks that particular Middle Paleolithic populations occupied, the evolutionary trajectories they might have been following, and the difficulty of making the transition from one peak or trajectory to another. This seems a daunting task, but as many of the contributions to this volume attest, we may already have a great deal more basic evidence than seems at first.

ACKNOWLEDGEMENTS

Research in Italy was supported by the L.S.B. Leakey Foundation, Fulbright Fellowship programs, and an N.S.F/NATO postdoctoral fellowship. I am grateful to my co-editor Erella Hovers and to the many participants in this symposium and volume for their insights and stimulating ideas.

REFERENCES CITED

Barham L. 2002. Systematic pigment use in the Middle Pleistocene of south-central Africa. *Current Anthropology* 43: 181–190.

Bar-Yosef O. 1998. The chronology of the Middle Paleolithic in the Levant. In T. Akazawa, K. Akoi and O. Bar-Yosef (Eds.), *Neandertals and Modern Humans in Western Asia*, pp. 39–56. New York: Plenum Press.

Bar-Yosef O. and S.L. Kuhn 1999. The big deal about blades: laminar technologies and human evolution. *American Anthropologist* 101: 322–338.

Blanc A.C. and A. Segre 1953. *Le Quaternaire du Mont Circé*. IV Congress INQUA, guide à l'excursion au mont Circé. Rome.

Bietti A. and S. Grimaldi 1995. Levallois debitage in central Italy: technical achievements and raw material procurement. In H.L. Dibble and O. Bar-Yosef (Eds.), *The Definition and Interpretation of Levallois Technology* (Monographs in World Prehistory 23), pp. 125–142. Madison: Prehistory Press.

Binford S. and L. Binford 1969. Stone tools and human behavior. *Scientific American* 220: 70–82.

Bordes F. 1961. Mousterian cultures in France. *Science* 134: 803–10.

Callow P. and J.M. Cornford 1986. *La Cotte de St. Brelade, Jersey: Excavations by C.B.M. McBurney, 1961–1978*. Norwich: Geo Books.

Gamble C. 1999. *The Paleolithic Societies of Europe*. New York: Cambridge University Press.

Garrod D.A.E. and D.M.A. Bate 1937. *The Stone Age of Mount Carmel*. Vol. 1. Oxford: Clarendon Press.

Grayson, D. and F. Delpech 1998. Changing diet breadth in the early Upper Palaeolithic of southwestern France. *Journal of Archaeological Science* 25: 1119–1129.

Grayson D., F. Delpech, J.-P. Rigaud and J. Simek 2001. Explaining the development of dietary dominance by a single ungulate taxon at Grotte XVI, Dordogne, France. *Journal of Archaeological Science* 28: 115–125.

Jelinek A. 1981. The Middle Paleolithic of the Levant from the perspective of Tabun cave. In J. Cauvin and P. Sanlaville (Eds.), *Préhistoire du Levant*, pp. 265–80. Paris: CNRS Editions.

Klein R. 1999. *The Human Career: Human Biological and Cultural Origins*. 2nd Edition. Chicago: University of Chicago Press.

Kuhn S.L. 1992. Blank form and reduction as determinants of Mousterian scraper morphology. *American Antiquity* 57: 115–28.

Kuhn S.L. 1995a. *Mousterian Lithic Technology: An Ecological Perspective*. Princeton: Princeton University Press.

Kuhn S.L. 1995b. A Perspective on Levallois from a "non-Levallois" assemblage: the Mousterian of Grotta di Sant'Agostino (Gaeta, Italy). In H.L. Dibble and O. Bar-Yosef (Eds.), *The Definition and Interpretation of Levallois Technology* (Monographs in World Prehistory 23), pp. 157–170. Madison: Prehistory Press.

Kuhn S.L. and A. Bietti 2000. The late Middle and early Upper Paleolithic in Italy. In O. Bar-Yosef and D. Pilbeam (Eds.), *The Geography of Neandertals and Modern Humans in Europe and the Greater Mediterranean*, pp. 49–76. Cambridge MA: Peabody Museum, Harvard University.

Kuhn S.L. and M.C. Stiner 1992. New Research on Riparo Mochi, Balzi Rossi (Liguria): Preliminary Results. *Quaternaria Nova* (Italy) 2: 77–90.

Kuhn S.L. and M.C. Stiner 1998a. Middle Paleolithic creativity: reflections on an oxymoron? In S. Mithen (Ed.), *Creativity in Human Evolution and Prehistory*, pp. 146–164. London: Routledge.

Kuhn S.L. and M.C. Stiner 1998b. The earliest Aurignacian of Riparo Mochi (Liguria, Italy). *Current Anthropology* 39 (supplement): S175–S189.

Laplace G. 1977. Il Riparo Mochi ai Balzi Rossi di Grimaldi (Fouilles 1938–1949): les industries leptolithiques. *Rivista di Scienze Preistoriche* 32: 3–131.

de Lumley H. 1969. *Le Paléolithique inférieur et moyen de midi Méditerranén dans son cadre geologique.* Gallia Préhistoire (Supplement 5). Paris: CNRS Editions.

Mellars P. 1970. The chronology of Mousterian industries in the Périgord region of south-west France. *Proceedings of the Prehistoric Society* 35: 134–170.

Mellars P. 1986. A new chronology for the Mousterian period. *Nature* 322: 410–411.

Mellars P. 1996. *The Neanderthal Legacy: An Archaeological Perspective from Western Europe.*, Princeton: Princeton University Press.

Mithen S. 1996. *The Prehistory of the Mind: A Search for the Origins of Art, Religion and Science.* London: Thames and Hudson.

Mussi M., 1990. Le peuplement de l'Italie a la fin du Paléolithique moyen et au début du Paléolithique supérieur. In C. Farizy (Ed.), *Paléolithique moyen récent et paléolithique supérieur ancien en Europe* (Mémoirs du Musée de Préhistoire d'Ille de France no. 3), pp. 251–262. Nemours: APRAIF.

Palma di Cesnola A. 1996. *Le Paléolithique inférieur et moyen en Italie.* Grenoble: Grenoble: Jérôme Millon.

Palmer R. 1991. Optimization on rugged fitness landscapes. In E. Perelson and S. Kaufman (Eds.), *Molecular Evolution on Rugged Fitness Landscapes*, pp. 3–25. Redwood City CA: Addison.

Perelson E. and S. Kaufman (Eds.) 1991. *Molecular Evolution on Rugged Fitness Landscapes.* Redwood City, CA: Addison: .

Peresani M. 1995–96. Sistemi tecnici di produzione litica nel Musteriano d'Italia. *Rivista di Scienze Preistoriche* 47: 79–167.

Rolland N. and H.L. Dibble 1990. A new synthesis of Mousterian variability. *American Antiquity* 55: 480–99.

Shea J.J. 1988. Spear points from the Middle Paleolithic of the Levant. *Journal of Field Archaeology* 15: 441–450.

Stiner M. 1994. *Honor among Thieves: Zooarchaeological Perspectives on Neandertal Foraging Ecology.*, Princeton: Princeton University Press.

Stiner M. 2002. Carnivory, coevolution and the geographic spread of the genus *Homo. Journal of Archaeological Research* 10: 1–63.

Stiner M.C. and S.L. Kuhn 1992. Subsistence, technology, and aadaptive variation in the Middle Paleolithic. *American Anthropologist* 94: 306–39.

Stiner M.C., N. Munro and T. Surovell 2000. The tortoise and the hare: small game use, the broad spectrum revolution, and Paleolithic demography. *Current Anthropology* 41: 39–73.

Tavoso A. 1988. L'outillage du gisment de San Francesco à San Remo (Ligurie, Italie): nouvel examen. In J.K. Kozlowski (Ed.), *L'Homme de Neanderthal: La Mutation* (ERAUL 35), pp. 193–210. Liège: Université de Liège.

Wright S. 1932. The roles of mutation, inbreeding, crossbreeding and selection in evolution. *Proceedings of the 6th International Congress on Genetics* 1: 356–366.

Chapter **7**

Stasis and Change During the Crimean Middle Paleolithic

Anthony E. Marks

Southern Methodist University, Dallas, TX, USA 75275-0116

Victor P. Chabai

Institute of Archaeology, Crimean Branch, Simferopol, Ukraine 95007

ABSTRACT

During the late Middle Paleolithic (*ca.* 50,000 BP to *ca.* 28,000 BP), the Crimea was occupied by two groups with distinctly different material cultures: the Crimean Micoquian and the Western Crimean Mousterian. The Crimean Micoquian, firmly associated with Neandertals, used an unchanging bifacial and a unifacial discoidal lithic technology to produce heavily retouched bifacial and unifacial points and scrapers. The Western Crimean Mousterian, on the other hand, utilized a technology initially based on both unifacial Levallois and volumetric core reductions that, through time, evolved into an almost wholly volumetric, blade producing reduction strategy. Tools, however, remained constant, with elongated points and scrapers most common and with Upper Paleolithic types very rare. The Crimean Micoquian exhibited only limited mobility, while the Western Crimean Mousterian appears to have had a highly mobile settlement system, extending over a very large area. Both exploited the same range of large steppe animals, but Western Crimean Mousterian sites are all highly ephemeral, while those of the Crimean Micoquian range from highly ephemeral to longer occupied sites with a range of structures, such as fireplaces, storage pits, burials, *etc.* The reasons for these differences are considered, if not fully elucidated.

INTRODUCTION

In Crimea, the Middle Paleolithic is both as old and as young as anywhere in Eastern Europe. Appearing first during the Last Interglacial, at its end it coexisted with the Upper Paleolithic, as recently as 28,000 BP. One Middle Paleolithic group, the Crimean Micoquian, appears to have been present, often if not continually, during this almost 100,000 years, while another group, the Western Crimean Mousterian, seems to have first appeared in Crimea no earlier than 50,000 years ago but lasted till the same time as the Crimean Micoquian. Unlike in Western Europe, where different Mousterian industries are recognized by different proportional occurrences of commonly shared technological and typological traits (Bordes 1961b; Rolland 1981; Dibble 1987) and, perhaps, by temporal sequencing (Mellars 1969), in Crimea these two Middle Paleolithic groups clearly were co-existent for about 20,000 years, while sharing virtually no technological or typological characteristics. On the other hand, from 50,000 to 30,000 BP, they did have similar adaptive patterns, if not similar settlement systems (Marks and Chabai 2001). In spite of this, one group, the Crimean Micoquian, while exhibiting some proportional variability typologically (Kolosov et al. 1993), underwent virtually no significant, patterned diachronic change during its long presence in Crimea. The Western Crimean Mousterian, on the other hand, exhibited marked technological change over its mere 20,000 year duration.

This paper will examine these two Middle Paleolithic groups, their adaptive patterns, and environmental contexts within Crimea to see whether stasis or change may be linked to one or more factors and if there were any adaptive or other patterns, of either group, which suggest developmental movement toward any "Upper Paleolithic" status.

CRIMEA IN SPACE AND TIME

The Crimean peninsula (ca.27,500 sq. km) is situated in southern Eastern Europe and is surrounded by the Black Sea on the west and south and by the Azov Sea on the east. Crimea consists of two major parts: a steppe zone and a mountainous region, with the latter representing less than 30% of the peninsula (Figure 1). The Crimean Mountains are subdivided into three ranges. The Main (First) Range occupies the southern bank of the peninsula and consists of relatively high (ca.1000 m) plateaus with steep slopes, some caves, and rare flint outcrops. The Internal Range (ca.600-300 m) is situated to the north of the Main Range, and has cuesta landscapes, numerous rockshelters, and outcrops of flint located mostly along the north edge of this range. All known outcrops of high quality flint are situated on the slopes of the Internal Range. The External Range is a chain of low hills (ca.300 m) on the border with the steppe zone, with some rockshelters and flint outcrops.

Two main geographical changes took place in the course of the Crimean Upper Pleistocene. During the Last Interglacial, due to global climatic warming

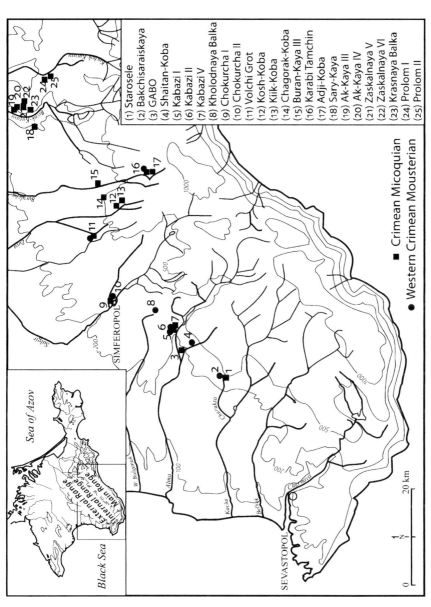

Figure 1. Map of the distribution of Crimean Middle Paleolithic sites by industry.

and rising sea levels, Crimea was an island. The climatic fluctuation of the following glacial period made Crimea a part of the Northern Black Sea Plain that stretched from southern Romania to the Northern Caucasus. The beginning of this process corresponds with the Moershoofd Interstadial, during which major river valley down-cutting began. On the other hand, no marine deposits dated from the Last Interglacial to the glacial maximum have been found in the Azov Sea (Alekseev *et al.* 1986). That is, the Azov Sea did not exist and Crimea was connected to the Northern Caucasus during most of the Upper Pleistocene.

The first 100,000 years of Upper Pleistocene climatic fluctuations did not have much effect in Crimea, for there was neither arcto-boreal flora nor fauna (Gerasimenko 1999). Although remains of reindeer and polar fox appear incidentally, they do not dramatically change the composition of the known faunal complexes, which mainly were based on such steppe and forest-steppe species as *Equus hydruntinus* and *Saiga tatarica*. Finds of red deer, mammoth, wooly rhino, *Bovidae*, and giant deer are rare and do not negate the dominance of steppe and/or forest-steppe environments. The available microfauna and malacofauna data also support the inference of steppe and forest-steppe landscapes during the Middle Paleolithic stage of the Upper Pleistocene (Markova 1999; Mikhailesku 1999). The climatic conditions varied then from continental during the stadials to moderate continental during interstadials. The former corresponded to steppe and/or semi-desert environments, while the latter corresponded mainly to forest-steppe environments. Thus, while the Crimean climate during the Middle Paleolithic was continental, at the same time it was relatively milder than conditions in neighboring northern territories, such as the middle Dniester and mid-Don Valleys, where arcto-boreal forms of both flora and fauna were abundant under both stadial and interstadial conditions (Bolikhovskaya and Pashkevich 1982; Ivanova 1982, 1987; Maliasova and Spiridonova 1982).

The majority of some 30 stratified Crimean Middle Paleolithic sites are situated in rockshelters or open-air locations within the Internal Range of the Crimean Mountains (Figure 1). There are just four Middle Paleolithic-age rockshelters known in the Main Range (Kiik-Koba, Karabi Tamchin, Kosh-Koba and Adji-Koba), the last two exhibiting only very vague traces of human occupation. The Crimean Micoquian and Western Crimean Mousterian are found in the same geographical and topographical situations. There are three sites where both occur together: the open-air site of Kabazi II and the rockshelters of Shaitan-Koba in the Internal Range, and Karabi Tamchin in the Main Range of the Crimean Mountains. In all cases, the Western Crimean Mousterian occupations stratigraphically overlay the Crimean Micoquian. In short, while there are more Crimean Micoquian sites than Western Crimean Mousterian sites known at present, they appear to have had essentially the same geographic distributions.

CHRONOLOGY

The chronological positions of the Crimean Micoquian and Western Crimean Mousterian were ascertained from biostratigraphic information as well as radiometric methods of dating (Table 1) (Hedges *et al.* 1996; McKinney and Rink 1996; Gerasimenko 1999; Markova 1999; McKinney 1998; Pettitt 1998; Rink *et al.* 1998, in press; Mikhailesku 1999). Three relatively well-studied and stratigraphically long sequences at the sites of Kabazi II (13 m), Starosele (4 m), and Zaskalnaya V (4.5 m) serve as the basis for the chronological framework of the Crimean Middle Paleolithic (Chabai *et al.* 1998, 1999). Moreover, the stratigraphical succession seen at Kabazi II includes the whole known Western Crimean Mousterian sequence and the early period of Crimean Micoquian evolution. At the same time, late Crimean Micoquian assemblages are known from Starosele, Zaskalnaya V and VI, Prolom I,

Table 1. The chronology of the Crimean Middle Paleolithic (thousand years BP)

	Western Crimean MOUSTERIAN	Crimean MICOQUIAN
Arcy (Denekamp)		Siuren I, H: 28.2±.4[3]
	Kabazi II, A₃A-A₄	Buran-Kaya III, B1: 28.52±.46[3]
		28.84±.46[3]
STADIAL	Kabazi II, II/1A: 32.1±6.5[1]	Prolom I, upper: 30.51+.58/−.53[3]
	30±20[2]	31.3+.63/−.58[3]
	Kabazi II, II/1: 31.55±0.6[3]	
	40.1±5[1]	Zaskalnaya VI, II: 30.11±.63[3]
	Kabazi II, II/2: 35.1±0.85[3]	Zaskalnaya VI, III: 35.25±.9[4]
	Kabazi II, II/4: 32.2±0.9[3]	Zaskalnaya VI, IIIa: 39.1±1.5[4]
	Kabazi II, II/5: 33.4±1[3]	Zaskalnaya VI, IIIa: 30.76±.69[3]
Les Cottes	Kabazi II, II/7: 46.5±8[1]	
	Kabazi II, II/7AB: 36±3[2]	Zaskalnaya V, II: 41.8±3.1[2]
	38±4[2]	
Hengelo	Kabazi II, II/8: 44±5[2]	Starosele, level 1: 41.2±1.8[3]
	Kabazi II, II/8C	42.5±3.6[3]
	Kabazi II, IIA/1	41.2±3.6[2]
STADIAL	Kabazi II, IIA/2	Zaskalnaya V, III
		Kabazi II, IIA/2-3
Moershoofd		Starosele, level 2: 47.5+13/−11[1]
		63+5/−4[1]
		Kabazi II, IIA/₃-IIA₄B
		Kabazi V, II/₃-II/₄A
		Kabazi V, II/7 (?)
STADIAL		Kabazi II, III/1A-III/1
		Starosele, level 3: av. of 3:67.5[1]
		Kabazi V, III/1: 73.3±6[1]
Odderade		Starosele, level 4: av. of 4:80[1]
Brorup		Kabazi II, III2: av. of 3:74−85[2]
Amersfoort		Zaskalnaya V, V
STADIAL		Kabazi II, III/2A-III/3
Last Interglacial		Kabazi II, VI/1-VI/17

[1]U-series; [2]ESR; [3]AMS; [4]AMS tripetide.

Buran-Kaya III, and Siuren I. On the basis of biostratigraphic evidence and numerous radiometric dates, the time range for the Crimean Micoquian appears to extend from the Last Interglacial to the Arcy (Denekamp) Interstadial inclusively. The time range for the Western Crimean Mousterian appears to extend from the stadial preceding Hengelo to Arcy inclusively (see Table 1). That is, the Western Crimean Mousterian and the Crimean Micoquian chronologically coexisted on the Crimean territory during at least 20,000 years (Chabai *et al.* 1998, 1999).

THE MIDDLE PALEOLITHIC GROUPS

The Western Crimean Mousterian and the Crimean Micoquian are mainly and strikingly contrasted by their different approaches to raw material reduction, knapping technology, and typology. In addition, they appear to have quite different geographic connections and origins.

Crimean Micoquian

Raw material reduction in the Crimean Micoquian was largely bifacial, whether utilizing plaquettes, nodules, or even flakes to produce blanks (Marks *et al.* 1996; Chabai 1998b, 1999). True core reduction was rare and, in fact, absent in most assemblages. When present, cores tend to be simple and highly variable in form, from radial and discoidal to unidirectional and multidirectional. There was no Levallois technology. Regardless of final form, cores lacked complex prepared flaking and striking surfaces and blanks from these tend to be short flakes and only an occasional, fortuitous blade. The blanks obtained from core reduction and from bifacial tool production are very similar, although those from bifacial reduction tend to be thinner and have somewhat more complex striking platforms. These patterns can be seen in the average of technological indices for the Crimean Micoquian: Ilam = 12; IFs = 25; IF = 40.

The dominant bifacial reduction, whether in the preform or final stage, was of plano-convex type (Figure 2, nos.1, 2, 9, 12, 13), with almost no presence of bi-convex bifacial tools. A variety of instruments were employed to reduce raw material, both from cores and as bifacial reduction: sandstone pebbles, tuffaceous stones, as well as sandstone and bone retouchers of different shapes and sizes used for retouching blanks.

In spite of the diachronically consistent reduction technology, not unexpectedly, there was some typological variability in tool assemblages and in tool size, as well. Here, as in Western Europe, variability is mainly in the proportional occurrence of shared forms, both unifacial and bifacial, rather than the presence or absence of specific forms through time and/or space. These differences were used to divide the Crimean Micoquian assemblages into three facies: the Ak-Kaya, the Staroselian, and the Kiik-Koba (Kolosov *et al.* 1993; Chabai 1999). It must be noted, however, that the morphological range of both Crimean Micoquian bifacial and unifacial tools, including numerous forms of bifacial knives, foliates, points and scrapers, as well as a whole range of quite complex unifacial scraper forms, often with inverse thinning (see Figure 2), far exceeds that recognized for Western Europe (cf. Bordes 1961a and Gladilin 1976; Chabai and Demidenko 1998).

On one end of the spectrum, the Ak-Kaya facies has the highest percentages of bifacial tools, simple scrapers, and large tools (Figure 3), but the lowest percentage of unifacial convergent tools, while the Kiik-Koba facies has the lowest percentage of bifacial tools, simple scrapers, and the highest percentage of convergent tools (Chabai 1999). In addition, the Kiik-Koba facies has the smallest tools (see Figure 2). The Staroselian falls intermediate between the other two for all of these attributes (Marks and Monigal 1998). For the most part, the differences in proportional occurrences are only moderate; for instance, while the Ak-Kaya may have simple scrapers accounting for up to 60% of the unifacial tools, this falls to just 45% in the Staroselian and to 30% in the Kiik-Koba. A somewhat greater spread exists for bifacial tools, with the extremes going from Ak-Kaya with 50% to Kiik-Koba with only 12%, but the averages are much less marked (Chabai 2000).

The presently available chronological controls indicate an absence of any temporal patterning to these Crimean Micoquian typological facies, at least, for the later part of the Middle Paleolithic where both sites and absolute dates are abundant. From about 40,000 to 30,000 BP, all three facies were represented at a number of occupations in the adjacent river valleys of the Internal Range of the Crimean Mountains (Chabai et al. 1998).

This variability may be explained most parsimoniously as reflecting differences in duration and intensity of occupation, as well as distance from raw material sources (Chabai 1999; Chabai et al. 1999; Marks and Chabai 2001). Specifically, the differences between the Ak-Kaya and the Kiik-Koba facies may merely reflect different site usages. On the one hand, the Ak-Kaya assemblage "type" seems to represent ephemeral/short-term occupations with limited, mainly primary and/or secondary butchering activities, the Staroselian representing short-term secondary butchering camps, while the Kiik-Koba represents repeatedly occupied, short-term secondary butchering camps in areas with little available raw material (Chabai 1999).

Together, these "facies" form a rather complex settlement system for the Crimean Micoquian (Marks and Chabai 2001). The most peculiar settlement type is the highly ephemeral, Equus hydruntinus primary butchering loci at Kabazi II Unit III and, probably, at Sary-Kaya, as well. In spite of variable distances to raw material sources (less than 100 m in the case of Sary-Kaya and more than 7 km in the case of Kabazi II), those present at both loci brought only finished tools with them, producing none on-site (Chabai 1999). Neither fireplaces, nor other kinds of constructions were found in association with these loci. At the same tine, the different types of short-term occupations demonstrate the wide range of economic and social activities that are reflected in a number of on-site constructions, such as pit caches of bifacial tools (Zaskalnaya VI, II), burials (Kiik-Koba, upper level and Zaskalnaya VI, IIIa), numerous hearths, at times surrounded by limestone blocks (Kabazi I, Kabazi V Unit III) (Bonch-Osmolowski 1940; Formozov 1959; Kolosov 1986). This settlement system, along with the lithic typology and technology,

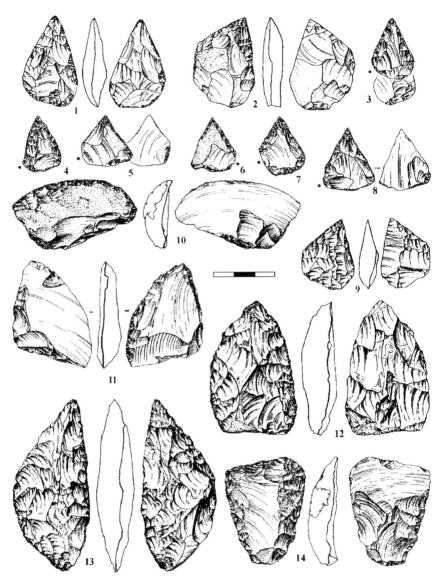

Figure 2. Crimean Micoquian: Kiik-Koba (1-9) and Ak-Kaya (10-14) facies. The artifacts from Prolom I (1-9); Kabazi II, levels IIA/4 (10), III/2 (11), VI/3 (14); Chokurcha I, levels IV/i (12) and IV/g (13). Bifacial points: leaf-shaped (1, 12); sub-trapezoidal (2, 9); sub-crescent (13). Points: leaf-shaped with thinned base (3); sub-trapezoidal (4, 7); semi-trapezoidal (5, 6); sub-triangular with thinned base (8). Scrapers: transverse-convex with thinned base (10); convex with thinned back (11); sub-trapezoidal with thinned base (14).

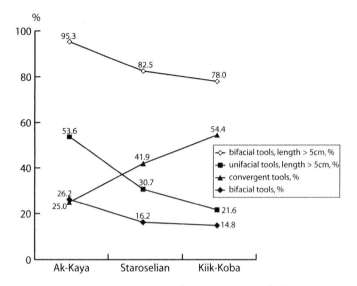

Figure 3. Crimean Micoquian: a correlation of tool size and morphology by industry facies.

remains remarkably stable through the shifting environmental conditions from the Last Interglacial to the Arcy Interstadial (Chabai 2003).

Western Crimean Mousterian

The Western Crimean Mousterian is strikingly different from the Crimean Mousterian in its technology and typology. Most importantly, it lacks even the slightest traces of bifacial reduction. Instead, there was a developmental evolution in core reduction strategies. During the early stage, a number of different core reductions were utilized, including Levallois Tortoise (Figure 4:6), as well as uni- and bidirectional volumetric and non-volumetric strategies. For the early stage of Western Crimean Mousterian evolution, three main core reduction methods were reconstructed: Levallois, Biache (following Boëda 1988), and volumetric (Chabai 1998a, 2000). By the late stage, the Levallois strategy had disappeared, leaving mainly volumetric reduction (Figure 4:5). During both stages, all cores were flaked by hard hammer percussion. The exploitation of volumetric cores included the use of crested blades and core tablets, while at the same time complex platform faceting was highly developed: IFs = 31 − 58; IF = 53 − 69. The increasing use of volumetric reduction during this late stage led to almost a doubling of blade proportioned blanks and is reflected in extremely high blade indices: Ilam = 38-40.

The late Western Crimean Mousterian core reduction strategies include traditional aspects of both Middle Paleolithic (hard hammer percussion and platform faceting) and Upper Paleolithic (volumetric exploitation of core flaking surfaces, crested blades, and core tablets) modes of knapping.

In spite of the significant shift in primary flaking technology, there was no comparable change in tool typology. Both early and late stage assemblages have the same typological structure. The only difference might be seen in blank type selected for tool production. The early Western Crimean Mousterian assemblages have about equal numbers of blade and flake tool blanks, including Levallois (Figure 4:2, 3), while the late Western Crimean Mousterian mostly has tools made on blade blanks (Figure 4:1, 4). The most distinctive tool types are points, which usually account for about a quarter of all tools. Among these are distal (Figure 4:1, 3), lateral, and obliquely retouched points, all made on blades. Simple scrapers dominate the tool assemblages, while convergent scrapers are rare. Unlike in the Crimean Micoquian, ventral thinning is virtually non-existent. Other tools include small numbers of denticulates and notches. While the very extensive use of blade blanks in tool production might suggest the presence of Upper Paleolithic tool types, in fact they occur only sporadically (Chabai 1998a, 2000).

Two main site types are known (Chabai 2000). There are highly ephemeral *Equus hydruntinus* primary butchering stations at Kabazi II Units II and IIA (upper part) and two short-term camps with secondary butchering activity at

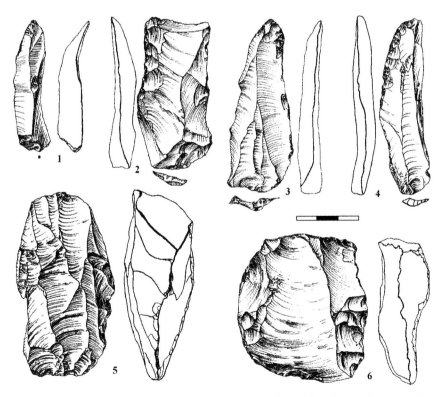

Figure 4. Western Crimean Mousterian: early (1, 4, 5) and late (2, 3, 6) stages. The artifacts from Kabazi II, levels II/1 (4, 5), II/2 (1), II/7A (3), II/7C (2), II/8 (6). Points, distal (1, 3). Scrapers: concave (2) on Levallois blank and convex (4) on blade. Cores: bi-directional (5) and Levallois Tortoise (6).

Shaitan-Koba and Karabi Tamchin (Patou-Mathis 1999; Marks and Chabai 2001; Patou-Mathis and Chabai 2003). These latter two sites exhibit a wider range of large game exploitation, including *Saiga tatarica* and *Cervus elaphus.* The two short-term camps differ from one another in being in distinct environmental zones (Shaitan-Koba in the second Mountain Range and Karabi Tamchin at the edge of a high plateau in the highest mountain range) but, also, probably, by seasonality (Yevtushenko *et al.* 2003). Neither constructions nor traces of fire were found in association with the ephemeral loci, whereas in each of the two short-term camps a number of burned bones were recovered. Yet, no clear fireplaces or other constructions were found. In addition, all of the assemblages, regardless of site type or environmental zone, contain the same typological structure. Yet, the distance of Karabi Tamchin from a raw material source (*ca.* 30 km) resulted in the importation of blanks and finished tools into the site, while Shaitan Koba, near to raw material sources, exhibited the full range of lithic reduction and tool production.

Thus, the adaptation to different environmental zones was based on a relatively simple but effective settlement system, which emphasized highly specialized hunting of steppe/forest-steppe ungulates. In the framework of this unchanging adaptation, however, the Western Crimean Mousterian exhibits a clear technological shift toward abundant blade production.

DISCUSSION

Within Eastern and Central Europe, the Crimean Micoquian appears to have the longest chronological sequence of about 100,000 years. The chronological sequence of the Western Crimean Mousterian is much shorter, only some 20,000 years. During this 20,000 year period, however, it "coexisted" with the Crimean Micoquian in the Crimean Mountains (Table 1). Such "coexistence" did not result in any technological, typological, or other kinds of archeologically visible interactions. During its 20,000 year presence in Crimea, the Western Crimean Mousterian underwent marked technological change. In contrast, the Crimean Micoquian, during its whole 100,000 year duration, maintained incredible technological and typological stability. In addition, it apparently maintained a constant Crimean presence. While Crimea was the northwestern zone of a larger Micoquian distribution, including the northern Caucasus, it does not appear that the Crimean Micoquian population ever left the Crimea, even during Interglacial conditions, when Crimea would have been cut off from areas to the southeast. On the other hand, the number, types, and distribution of Western Crimean Mousterian sites suggest a pattern of mobility that transcended Crimea and may have included much of the Northern Black Sea Plain. Therefore, the Crimean data include two quite different situations: for the Crimean Micoquian we probably have a full picture of a regionally limited settlement system through time, with all its variability. For the Western Crimean Mousterian, we may be seeing only a small portion of its geographic range and, therefore, of its overall settlement system. Still, the contrasts between the two groups in the Crimea are striking. How might this difference be understood?

In spite of a traditional tendency to assume that all European Middle Paleolithic was made by Neandertals, for Eastern Europe, at least, the only association between fossil type and culture type clearly links the Crimean Micoquian with Neandertals at a number of sites in Crimea and the Northern Caucasus (Chabai *et al.* 2004). There are no hominid fossils associated with the Western Crimean Mousterian, the "Levallois-Mousterian" of the Dniester region and the mid-Dnieper area (Meignen *et al.* 2004), or with the Blade Mousterian of eastern Ukraine (Kolesnik 1994). All these industries share tendencies for Levallois and/or blade production and there is not the slightest evidence for what fossil human type made them. While it might be tempting to assign these related industries to a non-Neandertal maker, in light of their tendency for the production of "progressive" elongated blanks, it is now abundantly clear that blade production is situational and unrelated to fossil type (Bar-Yosef and Kuhn 1999). More likely, the technological and typological stasis seen in the Crimean Micoquian, as opposed to the technological change seen in the Western Crimean Mousterian, may be understood as reflections of differing settlement systems. In particular, the difference between the localized mobility of the Crimean Micoquian and the apparent inter-regional mobility of the Western Crimean Mousterian, may account for what is seen in Crimea.

In the case of the Crimean Micoquian, long-term residency meant that all locations of basic needed resources (water, fuel, animals, and raw materials) were well known and, therefore, predictable. While raw material was not always available immediately adjacent to other resources that were seasonally abundant, such as wild ass in the Crimean Highlands (Burke 2004), the closest raw material sources were known, and adjustments were made for scarcity through blank size reduction, and more intense rejuvenation of blanks, resulting in a greater than usual proportion of retouched tools (Yevtushenko 2004). With such adjustments, no changes in technological patterns were required and none took place.

For the Western Crimean Mousterian/Levallois Mousterian (of the Prut-Dniester region), the situation was quite different. Its distribution is much greater than that of the Crimean Mousterian and includes areas that experienced greater aridity and cold than did Crimea. In addition, these areas had much greater distances between clusters of needed resources, perhaps necessitating greater mobility with less certainty as to where specific resources might be found. While water and animals may well be predictable, based upon topography, the presence of lithic raw materials is not so easily known. Therefore, the greater efficiency of blade production, per unit weight of flint, might well have carried adaptive value. If the shift toward blade technology in the Western Crimean Mousterian was due to increasing mobility during the arid stadial climatic conditions following the Les Cottés interstadial, this technological adaptation might be comparable to that described for the Negev under warmer but comparably arid conditions (Marks 1988). This is not to say that mobility requires blade production, merely that blade production is one adaptation that makes movement into new areas with unknown lithic resources, or with widely scattered lithic resources, less hazardous.

To sum, from 50,000 to 30,000 BP, the Western Crimean Mousterian and the Crimean Micoquian exploited the same range of steppe-forest large animals in the same environmental zones. It is clear, however, that each had quite different settlement systems, one highly mobile, and the other, at least, regionally restricted, as well as markedly different lithic technologies and typologies. In short, there were two very distinct Middle Paleolithic groups in Crimea during the late Middle Paleolithic, one exhibiting extreme consistency in settlement systems, technological patterning, and typological patterning, and the other exhibiting marked technological change but within an otherwise consistent settlement system and unchanging typological pattern. Such a difference within a single region during the Middle Paleolithic is highly unusual. However, only the Crimean Micoquian was local and fully adapted to the resource distributions of Crimea. The Western Crimean Mousterian exploited the Crimea as only one part of a presumably much larger territory. Such a large territory called for considerable mobility and the adjustments such mobility encourages, if not requires. Therefore, the Crimean data reflect two historically quite different adaptations. A small region with reasonably closely clustered, predictable resources may be exploited with only the limited mobility of the Crimean Micoquian but, as in the case of the Western Crimean Mousterian, it may also be exploited, as part of a larger range, by highly mobile groups.

REFERENCES CITED

Alekseev M.N., A.A. Chistiakov and F.A. Scherbakov 1986. *Chetvertichnaya Geologia Materikovyh Okrain*. Moscow: Nedra.

Bar-Yosef O. and S.L. Kuhn 1999. The big deal about blades: laminar technologies and human evolution. *American Anthropologist* 101: 322–338.

Boëda E. 1988. Analyse technologique du débitage du niveau IIA. In A. Tuffreau and J. Sommé (Eds.), *Le gisement paléolithique moyen de Biache-Saint-Vaast (Pas-de-Calais): stratigraphie, environnement, études archéologiques, 1 Partie*. Monographie de la Société Préhistorique Française 21, pp. 185–214. Paris: Société Préhistorique Française.

Bolikhovskaya N.S. and G.A. Pashkevich 1982. Dinamika rastitelnosti v okrestnostiah stoianki Molodova I v pozdnem Pleistocene. V knige. In G.I. Goretsky. G.I. and I.K. Ivanova (Eds.), *Molodova I. Unikalnoe musterskoe poselenie na Srednem Dnestre*, pp. 120–145. Moscow: Nakua.

Bonch-Osmolowski G.A. 1940. *Paleolit Kryma. Grot Kiik-Koba*. Moscow–Leningrad: Vypusk 1.

Bordes F. 1961a. *Typologie du Paléolithique Ancien et Moyen*. Bordeaux.: Delmas.

Bordes F. 1961b. Mousterian cultures in France. *Science* 134: 803–810.

Burke A. 2004. Karabi Tamchin: faunal remains. In V.P. Chabai, K. Monigal and A.E. Marks, (Eds.), *The Middle Paleolithic and Early Upper Paleolithic of Eastern Crimea* (ERAUL 104), pp. 283-288. Liège: Université de Liège.

Chabai V.P. 1998a. Kabazi II: the Western Crimean Mousterian assemblages of Unit II, levels II/7-II/8C. In A.E. Marks and V.P. Chabai (Eds.), *The Middle Paleolithic of Western Crimea, vol. 1* (ERAUL 84), pp. 201–252. Liège: Université de Liège.

Chabai V.P. 1998b. Kabazi II, Units IIA-III: artifacts. In A.E. Marks and V.P. Chabai (Eds.), *The Middle Paleolithic of Western Crimea, vol. 1* (ERAUL 84), pp. 253–272. Liège: Université de Liège.

Chabai V.P. 1999. Akkaitsy v zapadnom Krymu: Kabazi II, sloi III. *Arheologicheskiy Almanah* 8: 51–76.

Chabai V.P. 2000. The evolution of Western Crimean Mousterian industry. In J. Orschiedt and G.-Ch. Weniger (Eds.), *Neandertals and Modern Humans – Discussing the Transition: Central and Eastern Europe from 50.000 – 30.000 B.P.*, pp. 196–211. Mettmann: Neandertal Museum.

Chabai V.P. 2003. Kabazi II, kulturnye sloi V i VI: mikok vremeni poslednego intergliaciala. *Arheologicheskiy Almanah* 12: 81–127.

Chabai V.P. and Y.E. Demidenko 1998. The classification of flint artifacts. In A.E. Marks and V.P. Chabai (Eds.), *The Middle Paleolithic of Western Crimea vol. 1* (ERAUL 84), pp. 31–51. Liège: Université de Liège.

Chabai V.P., Y.E. Demidenko and A.I. Yevtushenko 2000. *Paleolit Kryma: Metody Issledovaniy I Konceptualnye Podhody*. Simferopol-Kiev.

Chabai V.P., A.E. Marks and K. Monigal 1999. Western Crimean Middle Paleolithic paleoenvironment and paleoeconomy. In V.P. Chabai and K. Monigal (Eds.), *The Middle Paleolithic of Western Crimea, vol. 2* (ERAUL 87), pp. 211–233. Liège: Université de Liège.

Chabai V.P., A.E. Marks and K. Monigal 2004. Crimea in the context of the Eastern European Middle Paleolithic and Early Upper Paleolithic. In V.P. Chabai, K. Monigal and A. E. Marks (Eds.), *The Middle Paleolithic and Early Upper Paleolithic of Eastern Crimea* (ERAUL 104), pp. 419–460. Liège: Université de Liège.

Chabai V.P., A.E. Marks and M. Otte 1998. Variabelnost srednego I rannei pory pozdnego paleolita Kryma (predvaritelnye itogi mezdunarodnogo archeologicheskogo proekta). *Arheologia* 4: 19–47.

Dibble H. 1987. Reduction sequences in the manufacture of Mousterian implements of France. In O. Soffer (Ed.), *The Pleistocene of Old World: Regional Perspectives*, pp. 33–45. New York: Plenum Press.

Formozov A.A. 1959. Musterskaya stoianka Kabazi v Krymu. Sovetskaya arheologia. *Sovetskaya Arheologia* XXIX – XXX: 143–158.

Gerasimenko N. 1999. Late Pleistocene vegetational history of Kabazi II. In V.P. Chabai and K. Monigal (Eds.), *The Middle Paleolithic of Western Crimea, vol. 2* (ERAUL 87), pp. 115–141. Liège: Université de Liège.

Gladilin V.N. 1976. *Problemy rannego paleolita Vostochnoi Evropy*. Kiev: Naukova Dumka.

Hedges R.E.M., R.A. Housley, P.B. Pettitt, C. Bronk Ramsey and G.J. Van Klinken 1996. Radiocarbon dates from Oxford AMS system: *Archaeometry* date list 21. *Archaeometry* 38: 181–207.

Ivanova I.K. 1982. Geologia I paleogeografia musterskogo poselenia Molodova I. In G.I. Goretsky and I.K. Ivanova, I.K. (Eds.), *V knige: Molodova I. Unikalnoe Musterskoe Poselenie na Srednem Dnestre*, pp. 188–235. Moscow: Nauka.

Ivanova I.K. 1987. Paleogeografia i paleoecologia sredy obitania ludei kamennogo veka na srednem Dnestre. Stoyanka Molodova V. In: I. K. Ivanova and S.M. Tseitlin (Eds.), *V knige: Mnogosloinaya Paleoliticheskaya Stoyanka Molodova V. Ludi Kamennogo Veka i Okruzshauschaya Sreda*, pp. 94–123. Moscow: Nauka.

Kolesnik A.V. 1994. Mousterian industries' evolution of southeastern Ukraine. *European Prehistory* 6: 175–186.

Kolosov Y.G. 1986. *Akkaiskaya musterskaya kultura*. Naukova Dumka, Kiev.

Kolosov Y.G. Stepanchuk, V.N., Chabai, V.P., 1993. *Ranniy paleolit Kryma*. Naukova Dumka, Kiev.

Maliasova Y.S. and Y.A. Spiridonova 1982. Paleogeografia Kostenkovsko-Borshchevskogo raiona po dannym palinologicheskogo analiza. In N.D. Praslov and A.N. Rogachev (Eds.), *V knige: Paleolit Kostenkovsko-Borshchevskogo raiona na Donu 1879–1979. Nekotorye itogi polevyh issledovaniy*, pp. 234–235. Leningrad: Nauka.

Markova A. 1999. Small mammal fauna from Kabazi II, Kabazi V, and Starosele: paleoenvironments and evolution. In V.P. Chabai and K. Monigal (Eds.), *The Middle Paleolithic of Western Crimea, vol. 2* (ERAUL 87), pp. 75–95. Liège: Université de Liège.

Marks A.E. 1988. The Middle to Upper Paleolithic transition in the Southern Levant: technological change as an adaptation to increasing mobility. In J.K. Kozlowski (Ed.), *L'Homme de Neandertal: La Mutation* (ERAUL 35), pp. 109–123. Liège: Université de Liège.

Marks A.E. and V.P. Chabai 2001. Constructing Middle Paleolithic settlement system in Crimea: potentials and limitations. In N.J. Conard (Ed.), *Settlements Dynamics of the Middle Paleolithic and Middle Stone Age*, pp. 179–204. Tübingen: Kerns Verlag.

Marks A.E. and K. Monigal 1998. Starosele: The lithic artifacts. In A.E. Marks and V.P. Chabai, (Eds.), *The Middle Paleolithic of Western Crimea, vol 1* (ERAUL 84), pp. 117–165. Liège: Université de Liège.

Marks A.E., Y.E. Demidenko, V.I. Usik, K. Monigal and M. Kay 1996. The "chaîne opératoire" in the Middle Paleolithic of level 1, Starosele, Crimea. *Quaternaria Nova* VI: 57–82.

McKinney C. 1998. U-series dating of enamel, dentine, and bone from Kabazi-II, Starosele, Kabazi-V, and GABO. In A.E. Marks and V.P. Chabai (Eds.), *The Middle Paleolithic of Western Crimea, vol. 1* (ERAUL 84), pp. 341–353. Liège: Université de Liège.

McKinney C. and W.J. Rink 1996. The absolute chronology of the Middle Paleolithic of the Crimea. Paper presented at the 61st Annual Meeting of the Society of American Archaeology April, 11, 1996. New Orleans.

Meignen L., J-M. Geneste, L. Koulakovskaia and A. Sytnik. 2004. Koulichivka and its place in the Middle-Upper Paleolithic transition in Eastern Europe. In P.J. Brantingham, S.L. Kuhn and K.W Kerry (Eds.), *The Early Upper Paleolithic beyond Western Europe*, pp. 50–63. Berkeley: University of California Press.

Mellars, P. 1969. The chronology of Mousterian industries in the Périgord region of south-west France. *Proceedings of the Prehistoric Society* 35: 134–171.

Mikhailesku C. 1999. Malacology and paleoenvironments of Western Crimea. In V.P. Chabai and K. Monigal (Eds.), *The Middle Paleolithic of Western Crimea, vol. 2* (ERAUL 87), pp. 99–114. Liège: Université de Liège.

Patou-Mathis M. 1999. Archeozoologic analysis of the Middle Paleolithic fauna from selected levels of Kabazi II. In V.P. Chabai and K. Monigal (Eds.), *The Middle Paleolithic of Western Crimea, vol. 2* (ERAUL 87), pp. 41–74. Liège: Université de Liège.

Patou-Mathis M. and V.P. Chabai 2003. Kabazi II (Crimée, Ukraine): un site d'abattage et de boucherie du Paléolithique moyen. *L'Anthropologie* 107: 223–253.

Pettitt P.B. 1998. Middle Palaeolithic and Early Upper Palaeolithic: the radiocarbon chronology, In M. Otte (Ed.), *Préhistoire d'Anatolie. Genèse de deux mondes. vol. 2* (ERAUL 85), pp. 329–338. Liège: Université de Liège.

Rink W.J., C.R. Ferring, and V.P. Chabai in press. Coupled ESR/Mass Spectrometric U-Series dating of the Middle Paleolithic site of Kabazi II, Southwestern Crimea, Ukraine. *Journal of Field Archaeology*.

Rink, W. J., H.-K. Lee, J. Rees-Jones, and K.A. Goodger 1998. Electron Spin Resonance (ESR) and mass spectrometric U-series (MSUS) dating of teeth in Crimean Paleolithic sites: Starosele, Kabazi II and Kabazi V. In A.E. Marks and V .P. Chabai (Eds.). *The Middle Paleolithic of Western Crimea, vol. 1* (ERAUL 84), pp. 323–340. Liège: Université de Liège.

Rolland N. 1981. The interpretation of Middle Palaeolithic variability. *Man* 16: 15–42.

Yevtushenko A.I. 1998. Kabazi V: assemblages from selected levels. In A.E. Marks and V.P. Chabai (Eds.), *The Middle Paleolithic of Western Crimea, vol. 1* (ERAUL 84), pp. 287–322. Liège: Université de Liège.

Yevtushenko A.I. 2004. Karabi Tamchin: lithic assemblages from selected levels. In V.P. Chabai, K. Monigal and A.E. Marks (Eds.), *The Middle Paleolithic and Early Upper Paleolithic of Eastern Crimea* (ERAUL 104), pp. 307–342. Liège: Université de Liège.

Yevtushenko A., A. Burke, C.R. Ferring, V. Chabai and K. Monigal 2003. Karabi Tamchin: the Middle Paleolithic site in Crimean Mountains. *Proceedings of the Prehistoric Society* 69: 137–159.

Chapter **8**

Monospecific or Species-Dominated Faunal Assemblages During the Middle Paleolithic in Europe

Sabine Gaudzinski

Römisch-Germanisches Zentralmuseum Mainz, Forschungsbereich Altsteinzeit, Schloss Monrepos, 56567 Neuwied, GERMANY

ABSTRACT

Monospecific or species-dominated faunal assemblages are a common phenomenon especially during the Upper Pleistocene in Europe. Analysis of these assemblages indicated hunting by Neandertals and moreover point to a variety of exploitation tactics used which can be interpreted in terms of a highly flexible subsistence strategy. Though these assemblages provide an excellent source for our understanding of Neandertals' subsistence, the coarse chronological resolution during the Pleistocene prevents further and far-reaching conclusions concerning evolutionary behavioural trends during the Middle Paleolithic.

INTRODUCTION

The last decades have seen considerable debate about the ways in which Neandertals obtained their food. Much progress has been made in this domain. There is growing evidence that Late Middle Paleolithic hominids were capable hunters (Stiner 1994; Gaudzinski 1995; Shea 1998; Boëda *et al.* 1999; Speth and Tchernov 2001). Even more so than Middle Upper Paleolithic anatomically modern humans, it appears that Late Neandertals were top-level carnivores at the dominating end of the food chain (Bocherens *et al.* 1999; Richards *et al.* 2000, 2001). However, the nature of their strategy of biomass exploitation remains debatable as detailed results of archaeozoological analysis seldom permit a consideration of this point.

Current research suggests that Neandertals were highly mobile, a feature seen in their raw material transfer patterns (Féblot-Augustins 1999; Roebroeks and Tuffreau 1999) as well as in the spatial structuring of their sites (Kolen 1999). High mobility might have enabled Neandertals to successfully deal with the sometimes highly unstable conditions of Pleistocene biotopes. Climatic shifts and the resulting variety of environmental responses could have led to continuous fluctuations in quality and quantity of ungulate biomass in any given area. Efficient hominid adaptation to these conditions would put a premium on high flexibility. A number of synthetic analyses of regional subsistence (Boyle 2000; Conard and Prindiville 2000; Patou-Mathis 2000) emphasize flexibility in subsistence tactics. Common to these analyses is the interpretation of high species diversity as reflecting flexibility.

The present paper will demonstrate that so-called monospecific Middle Paleolithic faunal assemblages can likewise be interpreted in terms of flexible subsistence strategies. It will suggest that the term "monospecific" possibly masks important variation in the activities that led to the accumulation of these faunal assemblages. This issue will be discussed in a broader context, with reference to the temporal chronology of these faunas.

MONOSPECIFIC FAUNAL ASSEMBLAGES

Sites with monospecific faunas are characterized by the high dominance of remains of a single species, represented by minimum numbers of individuals of up to over 100 animals, associated with lithic artifacts. These assemblages occur in numerous open-air sites (Farizy *et al.* 1994) but also in caves (Valensi 2000). From the early Weichselian onwards, monospecific or species-dominated faunal assemblages are found all over Europe (Figure 1). The list of species at these sites includes herd animals such as bovids (Gaudzinski 1996), equids (Pillard 1972; Ulrix-Closset 1975; Chase 1986), cervids (Pillard 1972; Valensi 2000), reindeer (Gaudzinski 1999; Moigne and Barsky 1999) and saiga (Formozov 1959) but also species with a solitary life style such as rhinoceros (Bratlund 2000).

Human exploitation of the fauna is shown by cut marks and hammerstone-induced impact notches on bones. Although monospecific faunal records could result from natural catastrophic events without any hominid interference, the regularity with which they occur in association with anthropogenic artifacts in open-air sites as well as in caves during the last Glacial is more suggestive of primary hominid interference, and analysis of some of these assemblages points to hominid hunting (Gaudzinski 1996).

Unfortunately this important source for our understanding of Middle Paleolithic subsistence suffers from the fact that taphonomic analyses have been undertaken only in a few cases. However, recently excavated faunal assemblages,

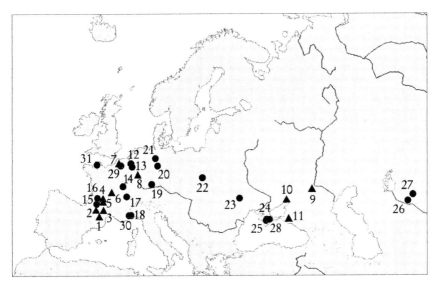

Figure 1. Monospecific or species dominated faunal assemblages: 1 Mauran (Farizy *et al.* 1994), 2 La Borde (Jaubert *et al.* 1990), 3 Coudoulous (Brugal 1999), 4 Les Fieux (Brugal and Jaubert 1996), 5 Le Roc (Brugal and Jaubert 1996), 6 Champlost (Farizy and David 1992) 7 Hénin-sur-Cojeul (Marcy *et al.* 1993), 8 Wallertheim (Gaudzinski 1995), 9 Sukhaja Mečetka (Vereščagin and Kolbutov 1957), 10 Rozhok (Praslov 1968), 11 Ilskaja (Hoffecker *et al.* 1991), 12 L'abri Sandron (Fraiport and Tihon 1896), 13 Grotte du Docteur (Ulrix-Closset 1975), 14 Genay (Patou 1987), 15 Combe Grenal 22, Combe Grenal 50 (Bordes and Prat 1965, Chase 1986), 16 Haute Roche 1 (Bouchud 1966), 17 La Chaise de Vouthon (Bouchud 1966), 18 Grotte du Lazaret (Valensi 2000), 19 Vogelherd VII (Lehmann 1954), 20 Taubach (Bratlund 2000), 21 Salzgitter Lebenstedt (Gaudzinski 1999), 22 Zwoleń (Schild *et al.* 2000), 23 Ripičeni-Izvor (Paunescu 1965), 24 Čocurča (Formozov 1959), 25 Starosel'e (Gabori 1976), 26 Tesik Tas (Gromova 1940), 27 Aman Kutan (Bibikova 1958), 28 Kabazi (Burke 1999), 29 Biache St. Vaast (Auguste 1995), 30 Caune d'Arago (Moigne 1999), 31 La Cotte de St. Brelade (Callow and Cornford 1986).

as well as assemblages for which recent taphonomic re-evaluation was undertaken, indicate that the fact that these thanatocoenoses appear quite similar does not imply that the exploitation strategies behind them are necessarily identical. This will be shown by the following examples.

Bovid-Dominated Faunal Assemblages

Numerous large bovid-dominated faunas are known from the earlier part of the Weichselian throughout Europe, e.g., Mauran (Farizy *et al.* 1994), La Borde (Jaubert *et al.* 1990) in France or Wallertheim in Germany (Gaudzinski 1995) (see Figure 1). The sites are spread across Europe, showing that bovid dominance is not regionally restricted. All these sites (Figure 1) have been interpreted as kill sites. Their lithic assemblages consist mainly of unmodified flakes, denticulates, and simple scrapers produced *ad hoc* from locally available raw material. Zooarchaeological studies of bovid age patterns at these sites have indicated dominance of individuals at the height of their reproductive life, with only a low proportion of very old bovids. Where data are available, sex composition is typical of a living herd during rutting season.

The exploitation of the bovid carcasses by hominids followed a uniform strategy of bone breakage for marrow extraction. A comparative consideration of hammerstone-induced impact notches associated with marrow processing illustrates a uniform strategy across geography and time. Blows were positioned at the weakest part of the bone so as to take advantage of natural bone fracture properties. This method of bone fracture for the extraction of marrow can be seen into the Holocene (Gaudzinski 1996).

Data from bovid ethology as well as the prime age composition of the thanatocoenoses suggest that these assemblages may reflect selective, controlled, and systematic exploitation of bovids over what might have been a long period of time, indicating that the occupants of these sites were capable of repeated communal hunts (Gaudzinski 1996). For Mauran, the excavators estimate that the site must contain the remains of approximately 4,000 bison (Farizy *et al.* 1994). Where data are available, there are no indications for seasonally restricted hunting, nor an apparent preference for a particular topographic position of the sites.

The Exploitation of Rhinos at Taubach

That subsistence tactics behind monospecific faunal assemblages were variable is indicated by the Eemian, Oxygen Isotope Stage (OIS) 5e travertine site of Taubach in Germany (see Figure 1). Taubach is located *ca.* 4 km south-east of Weimar. The site's long history of investigation started in the 19th century, when the travertine exposure, covering merely 0.2 km^2, was still exploited (Kahlke 1977).

The faunal assemblage studied to date consists of approximately 4,500 bones, among which the following species are represented: *Castor fibber, Canis lupus, Ursus arctos, Ursus spelaeus, Meles meles, Lutra lutra, Crocuta crocuta, Lynx lynx, Panthera pardus* ssp., *Panthera leo spelaea* or *cf. spelaea, Elephas antiquus, Equus taubachensis, Stephanorhinus kirchbergensis, Stephanorhinus hemitoechus, Sus scrofa, Megaloceros giganteus, Dama dama, Cervus elaphus, Alces latifrons, Capreolus capreolus, Bison priscus* and *Bos primigenius.* The faunal assemblage was collected over several years from the same location and was not uncovered during excavations. The sample is definitely biased against certain species and skeletal elements. *Stephanorhinus kirchbergensis* (Number of Identifiable Specims [NISP] 1,224, Minimum Number of Individuals [MNI] = 76) and *Ursus arctos* (NISP 1,537, MNI = 51) dominate, followed by bison (NISP = 533, MNI = 17) and beaver (NISP = 319, MNI = 10). Numerous bones with cut marks (rhinoceros NISP with cut marks: 99 ~ MNI = 10; brown bear NISP with cut marks: 292 ~ MNI = 9; bison NISP with cut marks:

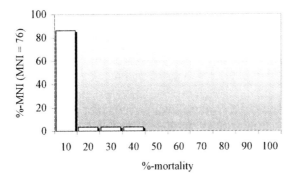

Figure 2. Taubach. Age profile for rhinoceros. Data from Bratlund (2000).

25 ~ MNI = 2; beaver NISP with cut marks: 10 ~ MNI = 2) point to extensive exploitation of these resources by hominids (Bratlund 2000).

The Taubach sequence yielded an undisturbed archaeological horizon represented by a sandy travertine formation. From this layer 900 artifacts were recovered as well as numerous large mammal bones. The presence of several hearths was reported. The mammal bones were obviously deposited in close association with the hearths, as indicated by a number of calcined and burned bones (Bratlund 2000).

This assemblage is dominated by an animal with a predominantly solitary life-style—*Stephanorhinus kirchbergensis*—which is represented by at least 76 individuals. As shown by Bratlund's (2000) recent detailed study of the Taubach assemblage, bones of this rhinoceros bear abundant traces of hominid interference, especially in the form of cut marks.

According to Bratlund (2000) the age structure for rhino is striking, and is characterized by a very high percentage of young and sub-adult individuals (Figure 2). Juveniles or young sub-adults between 1 and 1.5 years old are present with an MNI of 44 in addition to 7 older sub-adults. Only 25 old sub-adults are represented, and old individuals are absent. On the basis of the age structure Bratlund argues that an accumulation such as the one seen at Taubach has to be explained by selective hominid hunting activities of one individual at a time and repeated visits to the travertine lake area over quite a long period of time.

Exploitation of Reindeer at Salzgitter Lebenstedt

The German site of Salzgitter Lebenstedt indicates a subsistence pattern quite different from the one outlined above. For Salzgitter Lebenstedt we have indications that larger numbers of animals might have been taken at the same time, and that during subsequent processing of the slaughtered game Neandertals focused on better quality animals and prime anatomical parts.

Salzgitter Lebenstedt is situated in northern Germany (see Figure 1), about 50 km south-east of Hanover. The site is located where a narrow and steep valley joins the wide and flat glacial valley of the Fuhse, in a transitional zone between the *Mittelgebirge* and the North German plain. The site is dated to the earlier part of the last Glacial (OIS 5-3). Salzgitter Lebenstedt was excavated in 1952 and *ca.* 3,000 faunal specimens together with *ca.* 800 tools were uncovered.

With an MNI of 86, *Rangifer tarandus* (reindeer) dominated the fauna. Based on age estimates from analysis of complete mandibles, their age distribution was characterized by a high proportion of 8-year-old individuals (MNI = 20) as well as a relatively stable presence of pre-8-year-old animals (Gaudzinski and Roebroeks 2000). Mandibles yielded an MNI of 7 animals younger than 30 months corresponding well with the presence of 8 complete antler frontlets from juvenile reindeer as well as an MNI of 9 individuals younger than 30 months revealed by the study of 195 reindeer bones with unfused epiphyses.

Metric analysis of antler bases indicated that adult males were best represented in this assemblage (Figure 3). Given the condition of antler bases it was concluded that these animals probably died within a relatively short span of time during

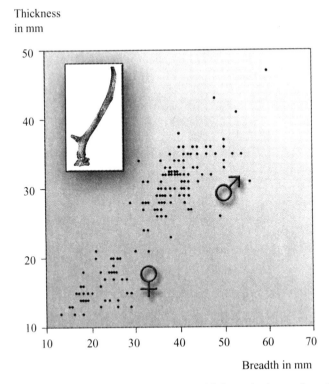

Figure 3. Salzgitter Lebenstedt. Thickness vs. Breadth for antler beams (n = 135). For position of measurements taken see Sturdy (1975, Figure 1, position 2).

Figure 4. Salzgitter Lebenstedt. Reindeer radius-ulna showing cut marks due to meat processing.

September- early October. This conclusion was supported by the state of dentition of young animals.

The reindeer remains display abundant evidence of meat processing and of very standardized marrow processing (Figure 4). During marrow processing there was a clear selection against sub-adults as well as against parts with low marrow content. This is indicated by the proportion of exploited long bones from adult individuals to unexploited long bones from juvenile/sub-adult animals. While adults were clearly preferred, adult bones with low marrow content were excluded from use (Gaudzinski and Roebroeks 2000).

Traces of carnivore modification were only marginally present, and the faunal remains are characterized by homogeneous and excellent preservation. The best explanation for the evidence seems to be that we are dealing with seasonal but unselective killing of animals with subsequent selective exploitation of only high quality nutritional resources.

The topographic setting of Salzgitter in a small, steep valley which joins a major wide river valley is extremely well suited for hunting reindeer: in that it is comparable to the German Late Glacial Upper Paleolithic sites of Meiendorf and Stellmoor. These Late Glacial assemblages also show a remarkable degree of similarity to Salzgitter in the physical treatment of reindeer prey (Gaudzinski and Roebroeks 2000).

Salzgitter provides indications of seasonally restricted exploitation of prey. This behavior is also recognized in other sites where prey specialization is evident. Burke's (2000) analysis of different occupation levels at the Crimean site of Starosel'e suggests a seasonal exploitation of family bands of *Equus hydruntinus* which, most interestingly, remained the subsistence strategy through time despite climatic changes and local evolution of the landscape.

DISCUSSION AND CONCLUSION

Even though monospecific faunal assemblages share some major characteristics, subsistence tactics which led to these accumulations were obviously quite varied. For the bovid-dominated assemblages, selective long-term exploitation of herd animals can be proposed, whereas at Taubach we see selective exploitation of rhinoceros, an animal with a predominantly solitary life style. Finally, exploitation of larger herds of reindeer, interpreted as mass-hunting, can be proposed for Salzgitter Lebenstedt.

Differences in exploitation strategies can be interpreted in terms of flexible resource utilization against a background of unstable environmental conditions. In terms of behavioral evolutionary models, the flexibility observed in subsistence tactics allows equivocal interpretations. It could reflect very efficient hominid adaptation to the environment, mere opportunism, or a combination of both.

However, in the case of Salzgitter Lebenstedt we could in fact show that at least the physical treatment and exploitation of reindeer prey characteristic for the Late Glacial were already practiced during the Late Middle Paleolithic (Gaudzinski and Roebroeks 2000). This does not necessarily imply that subsistence tactics were similar in the two periods. Data from other regions indicate that during the Late Glacial reindeer hunts must have been situated in a wider array of hunting site types and base camps (Baales 1996).

The frequent occurrence of monospecific assemblages during the Upper Pleistocene is striking, whereas such evidence is rare for the Middle Pleistocene.

For the entire Middle Pleistocene period only a handful of such assemblages (see Figure 1) is known. These include the French red deer-dominated Grotte du Lazaret (OIS 6) (Valensi 2000), the bovid-dominated open-air assemblage Biache St. Vaast (OIS 7c) (Auguste 1995), the reindeer- dominated fauna from level L of Caune d'Arago (OIS 14) (Moigne and Barsky 1999), and the mammoth-dominated fauna from La Cotte de St. Brelade on Jersey (OIS 7) (Callow and Cornford 1986).

To the extent that taphonomic studies have been carried out at these sites, it is obvious that subsistence tactics outlined for the Upper Pleistocene can also be found during the Middle Pleistocene. Mass mammoth hunting by driving is postulated for both levels 3 and 6 at the Saalian site of La Cotte, which are separated by intervening interstadial conditions. Quite in line with Upper Pleistocene bovid-dominated faunas, the record at Biache St. Vaast is considered to display selective and long-term exploitation of bovids. However, the current state of research does not enable an evaluation of whether subsistence tactics behind these assemblages are exceptional or representative for the entire Middle Pleistocene period. The differences in evidence before, during, and after OIS 7 correspond to major ecological changes during OIS 7 (*e.g.*, Kahlke 1994), which could have resulted in shifts in hominid subsistence tactics. It is equally possible that post-depositional taphonomic destruction is responsible for the observed changes over time. Though the majority of monospecific faunal assemblages is dated to the earlier part of the Weichselian, the sites may in fact be separated by thousands of years. It is this relatively coarse chronological resolution which hampers more accurate evaluation of the mode and tempo of change, or even recognition of evolutionary trends in subsistence tactics from Middle Paleolithic monospecific faunal assemblages.

REFERENCES CITED

Auguste P. 1995. Chasse et charognage au Paléolithique moyen: l'apport du gisement de Biache-Saint-Vaast (Pas-de-Calais). *Bulletin de la Société Préhistorique Française* 92: 155–167.

Baales M. 1996. *Umwelt und Jagdökologie der Ahrensburger Rentierjäger im Mittelgebirge*. Bonn: Habelt.

Bibikova V.I. 1958. Nekotorye žamečanija po faune iz must' erskoj peščery Aman-Kutan I. *Sovetskaja Archeologija* 3: 229–233.

Bocherens H., D. Billiou, A. Mariotti, M. Patou-Mathis, M. Otte, D. Bonjean and M.Toussaint 1999. Palaeoenvironmental and paleodietary implications of isotope biochemistry of last interglacial Neandertal and mammal bones in Scladina Cave (Belgium). *Journal of Archaeological Science* 26: 599–607.

Boëda E., J.-M. Geneste, C. Griggo, N. Mercier, S. Muhesen, J.L. Reyss, A. Taha and H. Valladas 1999. A Levallois point imbedded in the vertebra of a wild ass (*Equus africanus*): hafting, projectiles and Mousterian hunting weapons. *Antiquity* 73: 394–402.

Bordes F. and F. Prat 1965. Observations sur les faunes du Riss et du Würm I en Dordogne. *L'Anthropologie* 69: 31–45.

Bouchud J. 1966. *Essai sur le Renne et la Climatologie du paléolithique moyen et supérieur*. Périgeux: Magne.

Boyle K.V. 2000. Reconstructing Middle Palaeolithic subsistence strategies in the south of France. *International Journal of Osteoarchaeology* 10: 336–356.

Bratlund B. 2000. Taubach revisited. *Jahrbuch des Römisch-Germanischen Zentralmuseums Mainz* 46: 61–174.

Burke A. 1999. The fauna of Kabazi I: a Mousterian rock shelter. In V.P. Chabai and K. Monigal (Eds.), *Palaeolithic of Western Crimea*, Vol. 2 (ERAUL 87), pp. 1–27. Liège: Université de Liège.

Burke A. 2000. The view from Starosele: faunal exploitation at a Middle Palaeolithic site in Western Crimea. *International Journal of Osteoarchaeology* 10: 325–335.

Brugal J.-P. 1999. Middle Palaeolithic subsistence on large bovids: La Borde and Coudoulous I (Lot, France). In *The Role of Early Humans in the Accumulation of European Lower and Middle Palaeolithic Bone Assemblages* (Monographien des Römisch-Germanisches Zentralmuseums 42), pp. 263–266. Bonn: Habelt Verlag.

Brugal J.-P. and J. Jaubert 1996. Stratégie d'exploitation et mode de vie des populations du Paléolithique moyen: exemples des sites du sud de la France. *La Vie Préhistorique*, pp. 148–155. Paris: Editions Faton.

Callow P. and J.M. Cornford 1986. *La Cotte de St. Brelade 1961–1978*. Norwich: Geo Books.

Chase P.G. 1986. *The Hunters of Combe Grenal. Approaches to Middle Paleolithic subsistence in Europe.* (BAR International Series 285). Oxford: BAR.

Conard N.J. and T.J. Prindiville 2000. Middle Palaeolithic hunting economies in the Rhineland. *International Journal of Osteoarchaeology* 10: 286–309.

Farizy C. and F. David 1992. Subsistence and behavioural patterns of some Middle Paleolithic local groups. In H.L. Dibble and P. Mellars (Eds.), *The Middle Paleolithic: Adaptation, Behavior and Variability*, pp. 87–96. Philadelphia: The University Museum, University of Pennsylvania.

Farizy C., F. David, F. and J. Jaubert 1994. *Hommes et bisons du Paléolithique moyen à Mauran (Haute Garonne)*. Paris: CNRS Editions

Féblot-Augustins J. 1999. Raw material transport patterns and settlement systems in the European Lower and Middle Palaeolithic: continuity, change and variability. In W. Roebroeks and C. Gamble (Eds.), *The Middle Palaeolithic Occupation of Europe*, pp. 193–214. Leiden: Leiden University Press.

Formozov A.A. 1959. Issledovanija po kamennomu veku Kryma v 1956 godu. Kratkie soobščenija o dokladach i polevych issledovanijach instituta istorii material'noj kul' tury 73: 39–41.

Gabori M. 1976. *Les civilisations du Paléolithique moyen entre les Alpes et l'Oural*. Budapest: Akadémiai Kiadó.

Gaudzinski S.1995. Wallertheim revisited: a re-analysis of the fauna from the Middle Palaeolithic site of Wallertheim (Rheinhessen, Germany). *Journal of Archaeological Science* 22: 51–66.

Gaudzinski S. 1996. On bovid assemblages and their consequences for the knowledge of subsistence patterns in the Middle Palaeolithic. *Proceedings of the Prehistoric Society* 62: 19–39.

Gaudzinski S. 1999. Knochen und Knochengeräte der mittelpaläolithischen Fundstelle Salzgitter Lebenstedt. *Jahrbuch des Römisch-Germanischen Zentralmuseums Mainz* 45: 163–220.

Gaudzinski S. and W. Roebroeks 2000. Adults only. Reindeer hunting at the Middle Palaeolithic site Salzgitter Lebenstedt, Northern Germany. *Journal of Human Evolution* 38: 497–521.

Gromova V.I. 1940. Ostatki Mlekopitajušcich iž Peščery Tesik-Tas. Moskva: Trudy Akademia Nauk SSSR.

Hoffecker J.F., G. Baryshnikov and O. Potapova 1991. Vertebrate remains from the Mousterian site of Il'skaya I (Northern Caucasus, U.S.S.R.): new analysis and interpretation. *Journal of Archaeological Science* 18: 113–147.

Jaubert J., M. Lorblanchet, H. Laville, R. Slot-Moller, A. Turo and J.-P. Brugal 1990. *Les Chasseurs d'Aurochs de La Borde*. Paris: Editions de la Maison des Sciences de l'Homme..

Kahlke H.-D. 1977. *Das Pleistozän von Taubach bei Weimar*. Berlin: Akademie Verlag.

Kahlke R.-D. 1994. *Die Entstehungs-, Entwicklungs-, und Verbreitungsgeschichte des Oberpleistozänen Mammuthus-Coelodonta-Faunenkomplexes in Eurasien (Großsäuger)*. Frankfurt: Abhandlungen der Senckenbergischen Naturforschenden Gesellschaft.

Kolen J. 1999. Hominids without homes: on the nature of Middle Palaeolithic settlement in Europe. In W. Roebroeks and C. Gamble (Eds.), *The Middle Palaeolithic Occupation of Europe*, pp. 139–176. Leiden: Leiden University Press.

Lehmann U. 1954. Die fauna des "Vogelherds" bei stetten im Lohnetal (Württemberg). *Neues Jahrbuch für Geologie und Paläontologie, Abhandlungen* 99: 33–146.

Marcy J.-L., P. Auguste, M. Fontugne, A.V. Munaut and B. Van Vliet-Lanoë 1993. Le gisement moustérien d'Hénin-sur-Cojeul (Pas-de-Calais). *Bulletin de la Société Préhistorique Française* 90: 251–256.

Moigne A.-M. and D. Barsky 1999. Large mammal assemblages from Lower Palaeolithic sites in France: La Caune de L'Arago, Terra-Amata, Orgnac 3 and Cagny L'Epinette. In *The Role of Early Humans in the Accumulation of European Lower and Middle Palaeolithic Bone Assemblages* (Monographien des Romisch-Germanisches Zentralmuseums 42), pp. 219–235. Bonn: Habelt Verlag.

Paunescu A. 1965. Sur la succession des habitats paléolithiques et post-paléolithiques de Ripičeni-Izvor. *Dacia* 9: 5–31.

Patou M. 1987. La grande faune de la Brèche de Genay (Cote d'Or). Fouilles de L'Abbé Joly. *L'Anthropologie* 91: 97–108.

Patou-Mathis M. 2000. Neandertal subsistence behaviours in Europe. *International Journal of Osteoarchaeology* 10: 379–395.

Pillard B. 1972. La faune des grands mammifères du Würmien II. In H. de Lumley (Ed.), *La grotte moustérienne de l'Hortus (Valflaunès, Hérault)*, pp 163–206. Marseille: Etudes Quaternaires 1.

Praslov N.D. (1968). *Rannij Paleolit Severo-Vostočnogo Priazov'ja i Nižnego Dona*. Leningrad: Akademii Nauk SSSR.

Richards M.P., P.B. Pettitt, E. Trinkaus, E.H. Smith, M. Paunovic and I. Karavanic 2000. Neandertal diet at Vindija and Neandertal predation: the evidence from stable isotopes. *Proceedings of the National Academy of Sciences USA* 97: 7663–7666.

Richards M.P., P.B. Pettitt, M.C. Stiner and E. Trinkaus 2001. Stable isotope evidence for increasing dietary breadth in the European Mid-Upper Palaeolithic. *Proceedings of the National Academy of Sciences USA* 98: 6528–6532.

Roebroeks W. and A. Tuffreau 1999. Palaeoenvironment and settlement patterns of the northwest European Middle Palaeolithic, In W. Roebroeks and C. Gamble (Eds.), *The Middle Palaeolithic Occupation of Europe*, pp. 121–138. Leiden: Leiden University Press.

Schild R., A.J. Tomaszewski, Z. Sulgostowska, A. Gautier, A. Bluszcz, B. Bratlund, A.M. Burke, H. Juel Jensen, H. Królik, A. Nadachowski, E. Stworzewicz, J.H. Butrym, J. Maruszczak and J.E. Mojski 2000. The Middle Palaeolithic kill-butchery site of Zwoleń, Poland. In A. Ronen and M. Weinstein-Evron, (Eds.), *Toward Modern Humans: Yabrudian and Micoquian 400 - 50 k Years Ago* (BAR International Series 850), pp. 189–207. Oxford: Archaeopress.

Shea J. 1998. Neandertal and early modern human behavioral variability. *Current Anthropology* 39 (Supplement.): 45–78.

Speth J.D. and E. Tchernov 2001. Neandertal hunting and meat processing in the Near East: evidence from Kebara Cave (Israel). In C.B. Stanford and H.T. Bunn (Eds.), *Meat-Eating and Human Evolution*, pp. 52–72. Oxford: Oxford University Press.

Stiner M. 1994. *Honor among Thieves: Zooarchaeological Perspectives on Neandertal Foraging Ecology*. Princeton: Princeton University Press.

Sturdy D.A. 1975. Some reindeer economies in prehistory. In E.S. Higgs (Ed.), *Palaeoeconomy*, pp. 55–95. Cambridge: Cambridge University Press.

Ulrix-Closset M. 1975. *Le Paléolithique moyen dans le Bassin Mosan en Belgique*. Wetteren: Universal.

Valensi P. 2000. The archaeozoology of Lazaret Cave (Nice, France). *International Journal of Osteoarchaeology* 10: 357–367.

Vereščagin N.K. and A.A. Kolbutov 1957. Ostatki životnych na must'erskoj stojanke pod Stalingradom i stratigrafičeskoe položenie paleolitičeskogo sloja. *Trudy Zoologičeskogo instituta Akademii Nauk, SSSR* 22: 75–89.

Chapter **9**

Middle Paleolithic Settlement Patterns in the Levant

Liliane Meignen

CEPAM-CNRS, Sophia-Antipolis, 06560 Valbonne, France

Ofer Bar-Yosef

Dept. of Anthropology, Harvard University, Cambridge, MA 02138, USA

John D. Speth

Museum of Anthropology, University of Michigan, Ann Arbor, MI 48109-1079, USA

Mary C. Stiner

Dept. of Anthropology, University of Arizona, Tucson, AZ 85721-0030, USA

ABSTRACT

Drawing on a variety of lithic and faunal data from Hayonim, Kebara, Amud, and other well-documented sites in the Levant and adjacent areas, as well as information on numbers of sites, intensity of occupations, and internal structure of occupations, this paper explores broad changes in the nature of settlement patterns over the roughly 200,000 years of the Levantine Middle Paleolithic. The most readily visible differences between the early and late Mousterian are about numbers of people on the landscape—rates and timing of visitation and, perhaps, the sizes of the social groups present. From the point of view of site structure, we see substantive contrasts between Hayonim and Kebara caves and the successive phases of the Mousterian that they represent. Hayonim seems to be characterized by redundant, spot-specific use of domestic space, whereas Kebara displays a more rigidly partitioned and persistent spatial pattern, probably in response to higher rates of debris generation and more frequent visitation. Convincing indications of more people in the later Mousterian appear as two spatial aspects of the archaeological record: internal differentiation in site structure during the later Mousterian and, on a geographic scale, greater numbers of sites that may also be richer in material. Our principal conclusion, best viewed at this stage as a working hypothesis, is that the changes in settlement patterns between the early and the late Middle Paleolithic reflect an increase in regional population, as well as shifts in forager mobility in response to seasonal and eventually long-term changes in resource distribution and abundance. We believe that these settlement changes are most parsimoniously accounted for by reference to a combination of demographic and paleoecological factors rather than by positing a change in the cognitive capacities of local or intrusive populations.

INTRODUCTION

It is commonplace to view the daily, seasonal, and annual mobility patterns of foragers as reflecting the distribution of resources in their territory, as well as the degree of availability, predictability, reliability, and accessibility of these resources. Social structure and mating systems are also interwoven into the spatial network of contiguous territories. The geographic position, topography, and climatic regime of the region under discussion—the Near Eastern Levant—determine the distribution and seasonality of the available resources (Zohary 1973). However, optimal exploitation depends on resource accessibility, and this is where social constraints, such as defensive territoriality by neighboring bands, could be a limiting factor. At low population densities, a region rich in resources might be adequate to meet the needs of a discrete social unit with relatively limited mobility. Under the same conditions, increasing population densities might necessitate the implementation of a very different mobility system. The diachronic sequence of the Middle Paleolithic in the Levant may indicate such a process, as suggested in the following discussion (see also Hovers 2001).

The Levant encompasses a series of topographic and climatic features with both west-east and north-south trends. The coastal plain is wider in the south and narrower along the Lebanese-Syrian and Turkish shoreline, a configuration that persisted throughout cycles of sea level fluctuations. Mountain ranges are oriented more or less parallel to the shoreline. The first or westernmost range is generally higher in the north and lower in the south. Moving eastward, next comes the Orontes-Jordan Rift Valley, which is generally less than 15 km wide. East of the Rift the major Syro-Arabian plateau descends into Mesopotamia and the Arabian peninsula. Winter rains decrease from west to east, with higher amounts in the mountains and lower amounts on the eastern plateau. The vegetation belts follow the same pattern, with Mediterranean vegetation to the west, the Irano-Turanian open oakland next, and the steppic to arid zone (Saharo-Arabian) in the east. Mediterranean vegetation dwindles in the south (the Negev), and the Irano-Turanian and the Saharo-Arabian prevail over most of the Sinai peninsula. Food and water resources are available almost all year round in the Mediterranean vegetational belt, are more seasonal in the steppic zone, and ephemeral in the arid region. The typical annual resource cycle in the Mediterranean zone involves a great abundance of seeds and fruits from February through November, and a period of stress for both plants and mammals during the winter—December through February. On the basis of these rudimentary observations, one can predict a settlement pattern with high mobility in the desert and steppic zone and less frequent movements in the Mediterranean belt.

The Middle Paleolithic period as dated currently by the Thermoluminescence (TL) and Electon Spin Resonance (ESR) techniques lasted from about 270,000/250,000 through 50,000/48,000 BP, hence almost 200,000 years (Schwarcz and Rink 1998; Valladas *et al.* 1998; Meignen *et al.* 2001b). During this period we witness evidence for climatic changes which roughly correspond to Oxygen Isotope Stages (OIS) 7, 6, 5, 4 and the early part of OIS 3. One might expect that the climatic changes that occurred over this long time interval had an impact on the environments and carrying capacity of the subregions of the Levant and therefore also impacted the mobility patterns of Middle Paleolithic humans. But it must be stressed that climatic and animal community changes in the Levant were never as striking as those in northern Europe (*e.g.*, Tchernov 1992, 1994). The most important change was the degree of humidity. The Upper Pleistocene climate was generally cooler and more humid than at present, and the contrasts between mild and drier episodes not very strong, at least along the coast. But the situation could have been quite different in the southern and eastern Levant, as shown by pollen analyses (Horowitz 1988), calcite deposits in the Negev (Avigour *et al.* 1992), and speleothems in caves (Bar-Matthews *et al.* 1998, 1999, 2000), which indicate that the woodland and steppe phytozones must have shifted frequently in this area.

Building models for Middle Paleolithic settlement patterns is far from being an easy task (Bar-Yosef 1995). As stated by Van Peer (2001), "a settlement system refers to a regional system of behavior (Binford 1983) which is archaeologically visible as a set of related, contemporaneous sites in a landscape." Operationalizing such a definition, however, poses serious methodological problems, because the degree to which the Middle Paleolithic occupations are synchronous is difficult to establish, given the poor chronological resolution of our record and the small number of sampled sites in each region. In fact, studies of settlement patterns, which have become increasingly common over the last two decades (Conard 2001, and references therein), are generally based on sites that are only broadly contemporaneous (when chronometric dates are available) and/or culturally related. This is the position adopted here, since we have compressed sites covering thousands of years into the same model.

Our studies take into account site size, intensity, duration and nature of occupation, as well as information concerning the exploitation of food resources and raw materials (Bar-Yosef 2000). Throughout, we use the concept of *"chaîne opératoire"* (Cresswell 1982; Lemonnier 1986, 1992; Boëda *et al.* 1990; Karlin *et al.* 1991), a methodological framework which helps to elucidate the nature and sequencing of technological and functional activities carried out by the Middle Paleolithic groups. It relies on the assertion that human activities are part of a dynamic system, in which the different phases of resource exploitation (acquisition, production and use/maintenance/discard of stone tools—the "reduction stream" to use the term coined by Henry [1995a]—as well as acquisition, processing and consumption of animal resources) were organized and carried out in different places and at different times, as people moved across the landscape (Geneste 1988, 1991; Henry 1989, 1995b). Identifying the portions of these exploitation sequences (mainly lithic raw material techno-economy and nature and composition of faunal assemblages) that are represented in a particular site allows us to decipher the subsistence activities that were carried out by the site's occupants, and to identify the site's function within the system of territory exploitation. Specific occupations are then examined for their internal patterning as they may relate to available resources and to the ways those resources were exploited. With this approach, different patterns of site use can be defined, and used to reconstruct reasonable, if not fully documented, settlement systems (Marks and Chabai 2001).

Needless to say, employing the known variability in land-use patterns of recent hunter-gatherers as the basis for the reconstruction of Middle Paleolithic settlement patterns is problematic. Several models of hunter-gatherer mobility and land-use strategies have been proposed, but none of these models is sophisticated enough to encompass the great diversity of changes in environment and resource distribution that must have occurred during the Late Pleistocene. Binford (1980), in a pioneering systematization of mobility patterns, defined two end points in a continuum of hunter-gatherer mobility and land-use strategies but, at the same time, acknowledged that "logistical and residential variability are not to be viewed as opposing principles . . . but as organizational alternatives which may be employed in varying mixes in different settings" (Binford 1980).

Concerning the lithic tools of Paleolithic hunter-gatherers, Kuhn (1992, 1995) has introduced a model of "technological provisioning", which is based on the assumption that the aim of any technological system is "to make tools available where and when they are needed." The concept of "provisioning" crosscuts the more familiar terms of "curation" and "expediency" (used by Binford 1977, 1979). It refers to the depth of planning in artifact production, transport and maintenance, and the strategies by which potential needs are met (Kuhn 1995:22). Modern foragers cope with anticipated demands for tools in a variety of different ways. Kuhn (1992, 1995) recognizes two principal modes of provisioning which ensure the availability of tools in advance. "Provisioning of individuals" with "personal gear" (Binford 1977, 1979) is a strategy in which people always have at least a limited toolkit in hand. Implements are manufactured, and then transported and maintained in anticipation of varied exigencies, in the form of specialized tools if specific needs have been anticipated, or as generalized tools (or even raw material in the form of cores) for more general needs. The strategy of "provisioning places" consists of supplying those places where anticipated activities will occur with necessary raw material and/or implements. This strategy requires some prior knowledge of both the timing and the probable locations of future needs. Its utility depends on residential stability, on the duration of use of habitation sites (Kuhn 1995). The relative importance of each provisioning strategy should vary with the magnitude of residential mobility. Short-duration occupations yield relatively large numbers of tools carried by individuals, while places occupied for longer periods are more likely to be mostly provisioned with raw materials. As the duration of site use increases, the large quantities of debris from manufacturing tools on site will rapidly swamp the transported toolkit, which is always less numerous (Kuhn 1995). Since mobility patterns among modern hunter-gatherers vary over the course of a year and spatially within their territory (Bamforth 1991), foragers often practiced a mixture of technological strategies (Kuhn 1992, 1995; Henry 1998), creating an archaeological record that will be very difficult to decipher.

Flexibility in human group mobility in response to changes in the local physical and social environment is assumed in the models put forward by most researchers (e.g., Henry 1989, 1995a, 1998; Lieberman and Shea 1994; Kuhn 1995; Hovers 1997; Bar-Yosef 2000; Marks and Chabai 2001). With this picture in mind, in our research we simply compare the archaeological data with the global expectations deduced from ethnological models in order to identify the most plausible interpretation of site use and function in Middle Paleolithic mobility systems.

Moreover, in order to test the possibility of diachronic changes in mobility patterns, we have grouped together, in a schematic way, data collected from sites spanning tens of thousands of years. We rely heavily on patterns evident in two sites that we have studied in considerable detail (Hayonim cave for the early Middle Paleolithic; and Kebara cave for the late Middle Paleolithic). These patterns allow us to identify very general trends in forager mobility, the validity of which can then be explored further using data from other roughly contemporaneous Levantine sites. (see also application by Stiner and Kuhn 1992, on the Italian Middle Paleolithic). In painting this tentative picture, we are fully aware of the oversimplification of such a presentation and of the need for additional studies. The current paper is thus a preliminary step in what we feel is a useful direction.

EARLY MIDDLE PALEOLITHIC/LATE MIDDLE PALEOLITHIC MOBILITY PATTERNS: THE CASES OF HAYONIM AND KEBARA CAVES

Our presentation and discussion are mostly based on the results of the excavations carried out by an interdisciplinary team during the last 20 years in Hayonim and Kebara caves. From Hayonim cave we selected layer F and the base of layer E, about 180,000–215,000 years ago, and from Kebara cave, units IX to XI dated to about 57,000–60,000 years ago Each of these cases reflects different site functions and land-use patterns as will be shown below.

Hayonim Cave (Layers F and Lower E = Units 10 to 4)

Hayonim is located 13 km from the present Mediterranean coast, in Western Galilee, at an elevation of about 250 m asl, in a limestone cliff along the right bank of Nahal Meged. The cave overlooks a small valley which leads to the coastal plain.

The occupations in this cave were repetitive (units 4 to 10 are more than 3 m thick) but ephemeral, as shown by the low density of artifacts (between 200 and 320 pieces larger than 2 cm per m^3 of deposit, depending on the level), in spite of a slow rate of sedimentation. Each cubic meter accumulated over 10–15,000 years (based on the TL dates). This type of ephemeral habitation facilitated nesting by barn owls and thus most of the sediments are rich in microfauna, mainly rodents. The ephemeral character of the occupations is also expressed in the nature of the hearths, which generally are thin (in contrast to those at Kebara) when still visible to the naked eye. Micromorphological, mineralogical and phytolith analyses clearly show that the deposits are mainly anthropogenic, with remains of ashes that have been heavily trampled (Weiner et al. 1995, 2002; Goldberg and Bar-Yosef 1998; Albert et al. 2003). In fact, fireplaces had been numerous but in general were too thin to be preserved. The abundance of phytoliths of wood/bark and also leaves in the hearth sediments suggests that the main type of fuel used by Mousterian groups at Hayonim was often small branches probably derived from trees and bushes (Albert et al. 2003); the use of the latter is supported by the presence of minute baked clay balls seen in thin-sections of hearths, probably resulting from the uprooting of bushes (P. Goldberg, personal communication). Very likely the twigs used for fuel at Hayonim were collected in the immediate surroundings of the cave. The lack of evidence for systematic collection of fire wood from trees supports the view that the occupations were short-term and opportunistic in nature. Such opportunistic collection of fire wood, similarly linked with short-term occupations, has been described in other Middle Paleolithic sites as well (Théry-Parisot 2002; Théry-Parisot and Texier in press).

Although the intensity of occupation appears to have been low in the different units, all stages of stone tool production were carried out in the cave, employing nodules of different flint raw materials, most of which were collected within a distance of 10–15 km of the site (i.e., within the probable daily foraging range). Numerous Eocene and Cenomanian outcrops of good quality raw material were available in the vicinity of the cave, most of them strictly local (less than 7 km). However, a few of the recovered artifacts testify to an origin some 20 km to the south of Hayonim (Zomet Hamovil area), and a few appear to come from distances as great as 30–40 km (Mount Carmel to the southwest, Nahal Dishon area to the northeast) (Delage et al. 2000). These exotic materials constitute more than 10% of the assemblage in some units. But the imported blanks were not exclusively introduced in the form of finished products. Levallois and laminar blanks were brought in, but also debitage byproducts. Thus, it seems that this nonlocal flint component should be seen as reflecting a larger exploitation territory, not as the result of a specific curation strategy.

Different core reduction strategies were used in lithic production. Throughout the sequence, a specific laminar technology aimed at the production of elongated blanks was employed, together with a form of Levallois core reduction designed to obtain short and elongated products (Meignen 1998, 2000). The former is more developed in the lower units (units 10 to 7 or layer F). Numerous diversified retouched blanks (e.g., characteristic elongated retouched points or so-called

"Abu Sif points", retouched blades, sidescrapers and inversely retouched scrapers on Levallois blanks, typical burins) are present, but only in the lower units. For example, in unit 7 these elements are more abundant at the entrance of the cave than in the central area of the interior, which suggests some sort of spatial separation of activities within the site.

The analysis of the animal bones indicates low intensity exploitation of ungulates and tortoises (Stiner *et al.* 2000), pointing to low densities of human populations for much or all of the Mousterian period. Mortality patterns dominated by prime-age adults and anatomically balanced body part profiles of wild cattle (*Bos primigenius*), fallow deer (*Dama mesopotamica*), and mountain gazelle (*Gazella gazella*) clearly indicate that these game animals were obtained by hunting (Stiner this volume), and that these hominids enjoyed narrow diets rich in high-yield game types (Stiner 2001). Site-specific data for Hayonim cave indicate ephemeral occupations overall (Stiner 2005). The minimum number of individual ungulates (MNI) is consistently small in the Mousterian faunal assemblages preserved in Layer E (little to no fauna was preserved in the underlying layer F). Evidence of carnivore activity in Hayonim cave is virtually nonexistent, despite the presence of hyenas and canids in Middle Pleistocene ecosystems of the region (Tchernov 1992, 1994). Though conjectural, the lack of gnawing damage in this case may be another indication that refuse accumulation in the site was minimal and widely scattered in time, perhaps insufficient to attract large carnivores with any regularity.

In conclusion, the evidence from the lower layers in Hayonim cave (the complete sequence of tool manufacture and maintenance activities in the site, but with low densities of archaeological remains) reflects residential camps of short duration within a strategy of high mobility. This interpretation is supported by the presence of imported exotic raw materials from different directions at distances between 30–40 km. Complete on-site core reduction, together with a diversified toolkit, do not support the view that Hayonim was used primarily as a locus for highly task-specific activities. A strategy of high residential mobility would most likely occur in the Mediterranean belt when population densities were low.

Kebara Cave (Units XI to IX)

The nature of the occupations in Kebara, located close to the present-day Mediterranean coast on the western face of Mt. Carmel (Bar-Yosef *et al.* 1992), especially those in units XI–IX, were very different from those at Hayonim. Kebara's occupations were systematically repetitive over the entire 2-m-thick sequence of deposits that comprise these three units, a sequence that probably spans about 3,000 years from *ca.* 60,000 through *ca.* 57,000 years ago. Evidence of intensive human use of the cave is reflected by the paucity of small-sized rodent remains (*e.g.*, Tchernov 1996). The density of occupations is also clearly demonstrated by the large number of artifacts (1,000–1,200) per m^3 of deposit, which based on TL dates, accumulated over roughly 1,500 years. The same is true for the animal bones. The astounding "kitchen midden" (Schick and Stekelis 1977) along the north wall in Units XI–IX (see also Speth this volume) demonstrates the frequent hunting activities of the cave's occupants, and the recurrent processing of carcasses at the site (see also Speth and Tchernov 1998, 2001). Such spatial patterning at the margin of the occupation area recalls the gradual accumulation of trash along the peripheries of habitation areas observed among contemporary hunter-gatherers, a pattern that becomes increasingly apparent the longer the occupation (O'Connell 1987).

The hearths are well developed, and are often the result of numerous phases of use in the same place (Meignen *et al.* 1989, 2001a). Wood collected on the slopes of Mt. Carmel (*Quercus calliprinos*, *Q. ithaberensis*, *Crataegus* sp. and *Pistacia* sp.) was employed as the principal fuel, as shown by both charcoal and phytolith analyses (Baruch *et al.* 1992; Albert *et al.* 2000).

The mobility system in the case of Kebara was based on repetitive occupation of the same place by groups who shared the same global lithic tradition. No drastic changes in lithic technical reduction strategies can be detected across stratigraphic units XI–IX (Meignen and Bar-Yosef 1991, 1992). The same observation holds for the spatial organization of the central area in the cave. In units XI to IX there is a clear distinction between the central zone, where *in situ* fireplaces as well as flintknapping and animal processing activities occurred, and the dumping zone near the northern wall, where many of the larger debitage products and high densities of broken bones accumulated, forming what Stekelis many years ago referred to as the "kitchen midden" (Schick and Stekelis 1977; Speth this volume).

The study of the animal bones and carbonized plant remains from units XI–IX (Speth and Tchernov 2001; Lev *et al.* 2005) appears to reflect late fall, winter and spring/early summer occupations. Hunting of gazelles and fallow deer was carried out during winter and/or early spring, with male and female animals being taken in proportions broadly similar to their occurrence in wild populations (Speth and Tchernov 2001). Legume seeds, mostly various species of *Vicia* and lentils (*Lens* sp.), occur in all three layers, implying occupations of the cave in spring to early summer time, while pistachio nuts and acorn shells may indicate the presence of humans in the fall (Lev *et al.* 2005).

In units XI–IX rich faunal assemblages, mostly composed of ungulates of different sizes, result from hunting activities rather than scavenging, as demonstrated by Speth and Tchernov (1998). Differential treatment of the carcasses has been recognized, with large-sized game (red deer and aurochs) represented by elevated proportions of elements of high marrow utility, and medium- and small-sized game (fallow deer and gazelles) represented by more complete carcasses, including many elements of only moderate to low marrow utility. Transport decisions were also strongly conditioned by bulk, such that crania and pelves of the largest taxa were much less often brought to the cave than their counterparts from smaller ungulates (Speth and Tchernov 2001). Intense butchery activities, including dismembering, defleshing, and marrow extraction, as well as cooking, took place in the cave (Speth and Tchernov 2001).

All stages of lithic production were carried out inside the cave, as shown by the proportions of by-products (especially cortical products), ordinary flakes and cores (Meignen and Bar-Yosef 1991, 1992). Blocks of flint were imported from a maximum distance of 10–15 km (within the catchment area), as the nodules that were employed occur in abundance, both to the north and south of the site, in Mt. Carmel Cretaceous and Eocene formations (Shea 1991). Cores, most highly exhausted, were discarded at the site. All of these characteristics evoke a strategy of provisioning places (Kuhn 1995).

Flaking was most often done using the unidirectional convergent Levallois technique directed towards the production of triangular blanks (Meignen 1995). These blanks were rarely retouched, even though use-wear analysis demonstrates that some were repeatedly used. The tool characteristics were most often directly the result of the flaking technique, the desired morphologies of the end-products being controlled by means of the manner in which the core was shaped (Levallois blanks). As shown by the low percentage of retouched tools, the low intensity of retouching on each piece, and the observed pattern of use-wear, it is obvious that tools, with or without retouch, were not intensively utilized. In fact, few tools exhibit wear referable to prolonged use (Shea 1991). Such casual raw material exploitation, with little evidence of recycling, has been described in the context of base camps in ethnographic studies (Parry and Kelly 1987). The tools, retouched and non-retouched, were used in the cave for a series of diversified activities, including butchery (*e.g.*, dismembering, defleshing, slicing) and maintenance tasks (*e.g.*, wood working, cutting hard materials, scraping hard and medium materials, wedging or splitting). Even the retouched component of the assemblage does not demonstrate prolonged cycles of use and recycling; this category was often involved in maintenance activities, with high edge-attrition rates mostly related to wood working (Shea 1991). While Beyries (Plisson and Beyries 1998) concluded that pointed Levallois blanks were mostly multifunctional (multipurpose tools involved in butchery activities and wood working), Shea suggested that the design and the presence of impact fractures imply that they were often hafted as spear points (Shea 1988; Shea *et al.* 1998). The discovery of a broken point in a wild ass vertebra in the Middle Paleolithic site of Umm el Tlel in the El-Kowm basin in northeast Syria (Boëda *et al.* 1999) demonstrates that at least some of the Middle Paleolithic points were made as hunting devices, but were also, as with Neolithic arrowheads (Moss 1983), used in butchery activities. The same combination spear-knife is often observed in ethnographically documented hunter-gatherer groups (Oswalt 1976).

The absence of artifacts made of imported exotic raw material implies that the availability of good quality raw material from local sources was known in advance by the Mousterian occupants of the cave. This, as well as the complete reduction sequence of cores on site, the high densities of stone tools and animal bones, the numerous well-defined and often superimposed fireplaces, the development of a substantial midden along the site's northern periphery, and the redundancy of spatial patterning—all point to the conclusion that the cave was occupied by Middle Paleolithic groups on a regular and anticipated basis. In short, the occupations at Kebara during units XI–IX suggest relatively long-term encampments with formalized internal structure involving spatially differentiated activities and even human burials. The entire set of indicators tells us that the degree of residential mobility was comparatively low. The predominant lithic supply strategy in units XI–IX was the provisioning of place, the supply of raw material in the form of blocks that for the most part came from flint sources within the catchment area. The position of the cave, at the confluence of erosional gullies and adjacent to the coastal plain and the hills of Mt. Carmel, facilitated the exploitation of animal and vegetal resources from a diversity of habitats. Kebara's location is entirely compatible with its interpretation as a base camp, as such settlements are often situated at locations of compromise between widely dispersed resource concentrations (Harpending and Davis 1977; Jochim 1979; Hovers 1997). To sum, during the time of deposition of units XI–IX, Kebara functioned as a major cool-season base camp where a wide range of maintenance and extractive tasks took place, including a substantial amount of hunting in both open lowland habitats and more dissected, forested uplands.

It is worth noting a slight but intriguing change in units VIII and VI, in the later occupations of the cave. While the lithic activities appear to remain more or less the same (*i.e.*, high densities of artifacts, complete core reduction sequences *in situ*, but a more diversified Levallois production), evidence for hunting declines and is differently organized. During these later visits to the cave, either a narrower range of carcass parts, of lower average food utility, was brought back to the site, or, as seems more likely, many of the carcass parts that did make it to Kebara during these occupations were butchered and processed only to the extent necessary to prepare the higher-utility parts for transport elsewhere, leaving behind mostly lower-utility skeletal parts that had been culled and discarded. Moreover, the timing of hunting activity appears to have changed as well. Whereas in units XI–IX most hunting may have taken place during the winter and early spring, in the later Middle Paleolithic occupations, and during those of the earliest Upper Paleolithic, most hunting appears to have taken place later in the year—in the late spring or even during the warmer summer months. Thus, while the lithic data suggest the same kind of dense occupations as in units XI–IX, the faunal data point to a shift in site function and a shift in the seasonality of those activities as well. While these contrasts must still be regarded as tentative, they highlight the value of considering the lithic and faunal data together rather than as completely independent data sets.

We can now posit the question of whether the observed changes in mobility patterns hypothesized on the basis of Hayonim and Kebara simply reflect different site functions or have broader diachronic significance in the region. Unfortunately, evaluation of this hypothesis is handicapped by the limited amount of available information. Even though the data from the Levant are better than from many other geographical areas, the information is still insufficient to disclose a clear picture. But tentatively the following observations can be made.

Early Middle Paleolithic

On the whole, the limited published evidence of a few quantitative studies concerning raw material economy, occupation densities, and dating, seems to indicate that a high degree of residential mobility characterized the early Middle

Paleolithic period in the Levant. For example, in the cave of Abu Sif (Judean Desert), the low densities of lithics (suggested by Neuville 1951:54 in a footnote), the introduction of finished tools (retouched and non-retouched), and the low proportions of debitage by-products (primary flakes and especially very few cores), suggest that the occupations were short, and that most knapping activities were conducted away from the cave (Neuville 1951:54). Provisioning of individuals, based on carrying one's toolkit as personal gear, was probably the principal strategy employed by the site's inhabitants. Together with the impressive homogeneity of the toolkit, characterized by elongated retouched points together with shorter triangular tools, the former (Abu Sif points) being the most frequent, the composition of these assemblages could also evoke a task-specific location. In the laminar assemblage of Tabun IX, as described by Jelinek (1982), "the Levallois products (including blades) outnumber the non Levallois elements, a fact meaning the former's import into the site as finished blanks." This pattern may reflect short-term occupations of the cave, confirmed by low densities of artifacts (bed 39: 170 pieces per m^3, Jelinek 1977: table 2). Relatively high proportions of retouched tools, indicative of heavy blank curation, and eventually recycling, are observed in Tabun IX (19.6%, Jelinek 1982:92), Hummal Ia (*ca.* 18%, Copeland 1985), and probably in Abu Sif (Neuville 1951). These limited data, taken together, suggest a pattern of high residential mobility in which people carried over the landscape at least a limited toolkit (and see Hovers 2001).

Conversely, excavations at two large sites (Rosh Ein Mor, Nahal Aqev) as well as tests and surface collections at several smaller sites in the Negev highlands, an area rich in water sources and outcrops of good quality raw material, allowed Marks and his colleagues (Munday 1976, 1979; Marks and Friedel 1977) to propose, for the wetter periods, a relatively stable settlement/procurement pattern in which base camps (Rosh Ein Mor and Nahal Aqev) were occupied over extended periods and provisioned logistically by what they called "radiating mobility" from short-term camps (Henry 1995a). Unfortunately, the lack of preservation of faunal remains prevents us from a more detailed discussion of these Negev sites.

Late Middle Paleolithic

Not surprisingly, the late Middle Paleolithic is a richer period with many more excavated sites, and a range of site functions can be identified. The excavations at Amud cave have produced evidence for dense occupations (1,000 lithics/m^3, over 1,000–1,500/m^3 in layers B1–B2) with numerous hearths, even if not well preserved (Hovers 2001). A pattern of repeated occupations is suggested by temporal consistency in the use of designated parts of the cave as a depository for human remains (Hovers *et al.* 1995). These preliminary results are congruent with the behavior of groups moving regularly over familiar tracts of territories, the size of which allowed frequent returns to the same locale (Hovers 2001).

The intrasite patterns observed in a series of other sites of the late Middle Paleolithic (Quneitra, Farah II, Umm el Tlel) suggest relatively short encampments tied to butchery, meat-processing and initial raw-material processing. The open-air site of Quneitra, on the Golan, amidst lava flows and next to a pond, is seen as a temporary seasonal hunting camp which was repeatedly occupied within a logistical system (Goren-Inbar 1990; Hovers 1990). Located in a landscape scarce in sedimentary rocks, good quality flint could have been a critical resource for Quneitra's inhabitants. Most of the raw materials originated from distances of 10–18 km, probably beyond the daily foraging range of the site's inhabitants (Hovers 1990); part of the primary knapping of the material took place elsewhere (at the flint source or at another site). According to Hovers (1990), raw material provisioning probably required special trips (*i.e.*, procurement was probably not an "embedded" strategy); hence, once brought to the site, raw materials were intensively exploited (exhausted cores).

Farah II in the Negev is an open-air site located near water sources (Nahal Besor) and above a conglomerate rich in flint cobbles and pebbles (constituting a strictly local raw material source). It is interpreted by the authors as a short-term encampment with on-site lithic production and carcass exploitation. The main prey animals were large ungulates, possibly forming big aggregations near watering places during dry periods, and a comparatively predictable resource for people to hunt (Gilead and Grigson 1984). Hovers (1997: 246–247) suggested that at Farah II activities rather than places were provisioned, implying unanticipated tool needs, where "lithic production focused on obtaining cutting edges through knapping a large number of flakes, the shape and size of which were of little relevance." The idea of such fortuitous behavior seems contradicted both by the predictability of prey animals congregating near watering places (emphasized by the authors) and the likely predictability of the lithic resources at the site. Processing and consumption of animal resources (large ungulates) at Farah II, close to the hunting place (Gilead and Grigson 1984:89), as well as the production of a toolkit on the spot, would seem instead to suggest an expedient strategy in which "time and place of use are highly predictable so that a minimized technological effort is required" (Nelson 1991, quoted in Hovers 1997). Thus, Farah II could be considered as a residential camp in a context of high mobility (as previously indicated by Gilead and Grigson who suggested the occupation represent a duration probably not exceeding a few weeks (Gilead and Grigson 1984). While the toolkit is clearly the result of an expedient strategy, the lithic reduction strategy used by the occupants could have been more sophisticated than it seems. Levallois points, even if not numerous, are present in the site and the low ratio of Levallois products could be due to their export to other places, not surprising in a context of high residential mobility. This hypothesis of mobile end-products has also been considered by Hovers (1997: 247).

In the site of Umm el Tlel (El Kown basin), located in the present-day desertic zone (Boëda *et al.* 2001), numerous successive levels of Middle Paleolithic occupations accumulated quite rapidly in a changing environment, from steppic arid to open grassland with patches of trees, but always next to a permanent water source. The function of each occupational level varies and many appear to be logistically-based task-specific horizons. This variability is neatly expressed in the three following examples.

Layer VI3b'1 – these occupations, in a steppic environment, occurred near a lake. Meat processing for delayed consumption was the main activity as demonstrated by the transport of large numbers of high-utility parts of wild camels to the site. Intense butchery activities occurred at the site and, taking into account the large quantities of meat processed, the authors considered the hypothesis of de-layed consumption as the most plausible interpretation of the observed data. Part of the toolkit was brought in as personal gear (large Levallois points and elongated blanks), completed by on-site lithic production. The site was also provisioned with raw material in the form of large flakes and small blocks that were obtained from flint outcrops that occur in the vicinity of the site (1–5 km). The duration of site use must have been relatively short as the debris of tool-manufacture using the local raw material has not overwhelmed evidence of provisioning of individuals (Kuhn 1995). Such a combination of different provisioning strategies has also been identified in other Middle Paleolithic sites such as Qafzeh (Hovers 1997) and Tor Sabiha (Henry 1995a, 1995b, 1998). Of course, it is also commonplace among modern hunter-gatherers who often prepare at least part of their toolkit in advance of use (Kuhn 1992, 1995, and references therein).

Layer VI1a0 – in this occupation, also in a steppic arid environment, the site was used as a hunting station and for primary butchery activities as shown by the abundance of low-utility body parts. It is also characterized by a very low density of stone tools (n = 18 in an area of 20 m^2), with few Levallois products carried into the place as personal gear. These characteristics (very low density of lithics, strategy of provisioning individuals) suggest a task-specific location.

Layer V2ba – in this layer, lithic and faunal studies point to encampments of longer duration in a quite different environment (open grassland with patches of trees). Although the densities of lithics are not very high, core reduction was done on-site from nodules already roughly shaped at the raw material outcrops more than 5 km away (a strategy of provisioning places). The toolkit, mainly Levallois flakes and points, was suitable for a diversity of activities. The tools were rarely resharpened. Animal carcasses (mostly equids and *Camelus* sp.) were brought into the site for consumption.

In the lower levels at Kebara cave (units XIII–XII), in contrast with the unit XI–IX occupations described previously, the composition of the lithic assemblage as well as the faunal remains suggest that the cave was used on a short-term basis, probably as a hunting station. Surprisingly, despite exceptionally low den-sities of artifacts in unit XIII, huge fireplaces have been observed in the central area. In unit XII, Neandertals introduced Levallois end-products as personal gear and completed their toolkit by on-site flintknapping. As previously described, a combination of both strategies of provisioning (provisioning of individual and place) testifies to the flexibility of Middle Paleolithic organizational behavior at Kebara.

The late Middle Paleolithic examples presented above often point to systems of low residential mobility, with some occupations resembling task-specific activ-ity loci, others much longer-term repetitive occupations (base camps?), and some varying over time, as in the cases of the long stratigraphic sequences at Kebara and Umm el Tlel. A similar diachronic change in site occupation behavior has been observed in Qafzeh cave (Hovers 1997, 2001) during OIS 5. In southern Jordan, the available information from Tor Faraj and Tor Sabiha, two sites located along the southern edge of the Jordanian plateau, point to a combination of radiating and circulating settlement patterns (Henry 1995b). In Tor Sabiha, situated at 1,300 m asl on the plateau, the composition of the stone tool assemblage (introduction of large Levallois points as personal gear and local raw material reduction on site), together with low densities of occupation, seem to reflect "ephemeral high elevation summer camps provisioned opportunistically from resources found within their catchment" (Henry 1998:128). But the development of final processing activities (tool fabrication, maintenance and rejuvenation) could also suggest a task-specific locale. Levallois points, often considered as hunting/butchering implements, could have been imported to the site in anticipation of such specialized activities. In Tor Faraj, positioned at 900 m asl, spatially organized and repeated occupations have been documented, which often have the characteristics of base camps in a logistical strategy (provisioning of place with raw material from within and outside the site catchment; complete reduction sequence on site; Henry 1995b, 1998). But lithic densities remain low (123 to 205 /m^3; Henry 1995b: table 7.6), indicative of relatively brief occupations even if longer than in Tor Sabiha. Considering these two sites as roughly contemporaneous and in spite of the lack of fauna or plant remains, Henry (1995) interpreted Tor Faraj as winter occupations in the lowlands and Tor Sabiha as summer stations at higher elevation. In this interpretation, the topography and absolute altitude structured the nature of the mobility system.

The early Middle Paleolithic sites in the Negev, although within the steppic belt, possibly represent occupations during periods of greater precipitation when this sub-region fell within the vegetational belt of the open parkland, and not the semiarid zone. Thus, if these Middle Paleolithic occupations took place in conditions resembling those of Mt. Carmel, we may expect similar mobility patterns that range from residential through logistical strategies, and perhaps more often the combination of the two.

CONCLUSIONS

Most Levantine Mousterian sites are located within the present distribution of the Mediterranean woodland ecozone (Bar-Yosef 1995), and this belt was even more extensive during the early Upper Pleistocene (Horowitz 1979). Conversely, sites are less common in the steppic southern and eastern parts of the Levant. In our current knowledge, late Middle Paleolithic occupations are more numerous than occupations of early Middle Paleolithic age, and they often occur in multilayered sites occupied recurrently over the course of thousands of years. In addition, many late Middle Paleolithic sites also seem to be more densely occupied (e.g., Kebara, Amud). Hence, the available evidence suggests either changes in mobility patterns or demographic increase or some combination of the two during the Middle Paleolithic. To date, no early Middle Paleolithic sites have been described which demonstrate an intensity and permanence of occupation comparable to what is seen in the late Mousterian sequence in Kebara cave. Admittedly, however, very few early Middle Paleolithic sites are known. Consequently, it is quite difficult to evaluate the proposed hypothesis of a change in human population size per territory from the early to the late Middle Paleolithic (see also discussion in Hovers 2001).

Nevertherless, during the onset of OIS 4, it is probable that some population increase did occur, due perhaps to a combination of local population growth and an influx of people from the Anatolian plateau (Bar-Yosef 2000). Stiner *et al.* (1999, 2000) present evidence, based on changes in dietary breadth, predator-prey computer simulation modeling, and an observed decline in mean body sizes of Late Pleistocene tortoises, that human populations in the Levant may have grown somewhat toward the end of the Middle Paleolithic, after about 55,000 years ago, thereby reopening the door to discussions of late Neandertal hunting pressure on the larger ungulates, albeit on a subtle scale if compared to later human impacts on Pleistocene environments (Stiner 2001).

Evidence for population increase is also suggested by the more numerous and diversified late Middle Paleolithic sites and the more intensive and repetitive use of the caves as described above. It is in fact possible that these changes began first during the occupation of Qafzeh cave, as proposed by Hovers (2001), namely during the early part of the Upper Pleistocene.

The Kebara faunal data provide additional though tentative evidence for demographic increase in the late Middle Paleolithic (Speth 2004). A striking feature of Kebara's faunal record is the monotonic decline of the principal larger-bodied animals – red deer and aurochs – over the entire four-meter-deep Middle Paleolithic sequence and continuing into the early Upper Paleolithic. Particularly noteworthy is the fact that this decline continues unabated across several major swings in regional paleoclimate that are clearly evident in the speleothem-based oxygen-isotope record from Soreq Cave in Israel (Bar-Matthews *et al.* 1998, 1999; Speth and Tchernov 2002). A long-term trend of similar nature is documented for the Wadi Meged faunal sequence, spanning the early Middle Paleolithic, Upper Paleolithic and Epipaleolithic from the sites of Hayonim cave and Meged rockshelter (Stiner this volume). Here, changes in ungulate prey sizes are examined from the standpoint of biomass-corrected data and indicate that large mammal communities may have been affected by human predation as early as the late Middle Paleolithic, and certainly by the early Upper Paleolithic. More robust findings on this subject in the Wadi Meged thus far come from the small game data.

In light of the Soreq Cave record, it seems very unlikely that the "phasing out" of the two largest-bodied taxa at Kebara can be attributed in any simple or direct way to changes in paleoclimate. Instead, increasing predator pressure seems to have contributed to the trend, the predator of course being the late Neandertal inhabitants of the region and/or the influx of Upper Paleolithic populations to adjoining regions (see Davis *et al.* 1988 for an earlier discussion of overhunting). Most paleoanthropologists assume, for the most part implicitly, that pre-modern human population densities in the eastern Mediterranean would have been too sparse to have had such an impact on these animals. Kebara, however, provides a few other pieces of evidence that may also point to overhunting in the later part of the Middle Paleolithic. For example, mean crown heights of the lower 4th premolars and third molars of adult gazelles increase steadily (*i.e.*, the teeth are less heavily worn) from the beginning of the sequence right into the early Upper Paleolithic indicating that, over time, Kebara's Neandertal hunters focused ever more heavily on younger adult gazelles, a possible sign of subsistence intensification. Moreover, not only were Kebara's hunters making increasing use of juvenile and young adult gazelles, prey that would have ranked lower than their prime-adult counterparts, other data such as relative skeletal completeness and the number of heads compared to postcranial parts that were transported back to the cave, suggest that the hunters had to travel longer distances to procure game, further indication of subsistence intensification during the latter part of the Middle Paleolithic.

Thus, Kebara's faunal evidence may point to overhunting of the largest mammalian taxa and intensified procurement of lower-ranked gazelles. This trend appears to be unrelated to the climatic changes that were affecting the region at the same time. Human demographic pressure, therefore, seems to have been a contributing cause. However, even if we accept a demographic explanation for the patterning, by itself Kebara does not demonstrate that the phenomenon affected the entire region. Hence, at this stage we must regard the Kebara evidence as suggestive rather than conclusive.

One may argue from the above observations that the most readily visible differences between the early and late Mousterian are about numbers of people on a landscape—rates and timing of visitation and, perhaps, the sizes of the social groups present. From the point of view of site structure, we see substantive contrasts between Hayonim and Kebara caves and the successive phases of the Mousterian that they represent. Hayonim seems to be characterized by redundant, spot-specific use of domestic space, whereas Kebara displays a more rigidly partitioned spatial pattern, probably in response to higher rates of debris generation. Finer variations in resource scheduling may also be apparent in the late Mousterian, but this is less certain due to the limitations of the Hayonim sample sizes. What indications we find of predator pressure on large mammals are subtle. The ungulate mortality evidence is suggestive but as yet unclear with respect of variation within the Mousterian. Evidence of pressure on small game resources seems clear. Convincing indications of more people in the later Mousterian appear as two spatial aspects of the archaeological record: internal differentiation in site structure during the later Mousterian and, on a geographic scale, greater numbers of sites that may also be richer in material.

Our principal conclusion, perhaps best viewed at this stage as a working hypothesis, is that the changes in settlement patterns between the early and the late Middle Paleolithic reflect an increase in regional population, as well as shifts in forager mobility in response to seasonal and eventually long-term changes in resource distribution and abundance. We believe that these settlement changes are most parsimoniously accounted for by reference to a combination of demographic and paleoecological factors rather than by positing a change in the cognitive capacities of local or intrusive populations.

REFERENCES CITED

Albert R.M., O. Bar-Yosef, L. Meignen and S. Weiner 2003. Quantitative phytolith study of hearths from the Natufian and Middle Palaeolithic levels of Hayonim Cave (Galilee, Israel). *Journal of Archaeological Science* 30: 461–480.

Albert R.M., S. Weiner S., O. Bar-Yosef and L. Meignen 2000. Phytoliths in the Middle Palaeolithic deposits of Kebara cave, Mt Carmel, Israel: sudy of the plant materials used for fuel and other purposes. *Journal of Archaeological Science* 27: 931–947.

Avigour A., M. Magaritz and A. Issar 1992. Pleistocene paleoclimate of the arid region of Israel as recorded in calcite deposits along regional transverse faults and in veins. *Quaternary Research* 37: 304–314.

Bamforth, D.B. 1991. Population dispersion and Paleoindian technology at the Allen Site. In A. Montet-White and S. Holen (Eds), *Raw Material Economies among Prehistoric Hunter-Gatherers*, pp. 357–374. Lawrence: University of Kansas.

Bar-Matthews M., A. Ayalon and A. Kaufman 1998. Palaeoclimate evolution in the eastern Mediterranean region during the last 58,000 years as derived from stable isotopes of speleothems (Soreq Cave, Israel). *Isotope Techniques in the Study of Environmental Change* (Proceedings of an International Symposium on Isotope Techniques in the Study of Past and Current Environmental Changes in the Hydrosphere and the Atmosphere), IAEA-SM-349/17. pp. 673–682. Vienna: International Atomic Energy Agency,

Bar-Matthews M., A. Ayalon and A. Kaufman 2000. Timing and hydrogeological conditions of sapropel events in the Eastern Mediterranean, as evident from speleothems, Soreq Cave, Israel. *Chemical Geology* 169: 145–156.

Bar-Matthews M., A. Ayalon, A. Kaufman and G.J.Wasserburg 1999. The eastern Mediterranean paleoclimate as a reflection of regional events: Soreq Cave, Israel. *Earth and Planetary Science Letters* 166: 85–95.

Bar-Yosef O. 1995. The Lower and Middle Paleolithic in the Mediterranean Levant: chronology, and cultural entities. In H. Ullrich (Ed.), *Man and Environment in the Palaeolithic*, pp. 247–263. (ERAUL 62). Liège: Université de Liège.

Bar-Yosef O. 1998. The chronology of the Middle Paleolithic of the Levant. In T. Akazawa, K. Aoki and O. Bar-Yosef (Eds.), *Neandertals and Modern Humans in Western Asia*, pp. 39–56. New York: Plenum Press.

Bar-Yosef O. 2000. The Middle and Upper Paleolithic in Soutwest Asia and neighboring regions. In O. Bar-Yosef and D. Pilbeam (Eds.), *The Geography of Neandertals and Modern Humans in Europe and the Greater Mediterranean*, pp. 107–156. Cambridge MA: Peabody Museum of Archaeology and Ethnology, Harvard University.

Bar-Yosef O., B. Vandermeersch, B. Arensburg, A. Belfer-Cohen, P. Goldberg, H. Laville, L. Meignen, Y. Rak, J.D. Speth, E. Tchernov, A.-M. Tillier and S. Weiner 1992. The excavations in Kebara cave, Mt Carmel. *Current Anthropology* 33: 497–550.

Baruch U., E. Werker and O. Bar-Yosef 1992. Charred wood remains from Kebara Cave, Israel: preliminary results. *Bulletin de la Société Botanique Francaise* 139: 531–538.

Binford L.R. 1977. Forty-seven trips: a case study in the character of archaeological formation processes. In R.V.S. Wright (Ed.), *Stone Tools As Cultural Markers*, pp. 24–36. Canberra: Australian Institute of Aboriginal Studies.

Binford L.R. 1978. *Nunamiut Ethnoarchaeology*. New York: Academic Press.

Binford L.R. 1979. Organization and formation processes: looking at curated technologies. *Journal of Anthropological Research* 35: 255–273.

Binford L.R. 1980. Willow smoke and dogs' tails: hunter-gatherer settlement systems and archaeological site formation. *American Antiquity* 45: 4–20.

Binford L.R. 1983. *In Pursuit of the Past*. London: Thames and Hudson.

Boëda E., J.-M. Geneste, C. Griggo, N. Mercier, S. Muhesen, J.-L Reyss, A. Taha and H. Valladas 1999. A Levallois point imbedded in the vertebra of a wild ass (*Equus africanus*): hafting, projectiles and Mousterian hunting weapons. *Antiquity* 73: 394–402.

Boëda E., J.-M. Geneste and L. Meignen 1990. Identification de chaînes opératoires lithiques du Paléolithique ancien et moyen. *Paléo* 2: 43–80.

Boëda E., C. Griggo and S. Noel-Soriano 2001. Différents modes d'occupation du site d'Umm el Tlell au cours du Paléolithique moyen (El Kowm, Syrie centrale). *Paléorient* 27: 13–28.

Conard N. J. 2001. Advances and problems in the study of Paleolithic settlement systems. In N. Conard (Ed.), *Settlement Dynamics of the Middle Paleolithic and Middle Stone Age*, pp. VII–XX. Tübingen: Kerns Verlag.

Copeland L. 1985. The pointed tools of Hummal Ia (El Kowm, Syria). *Cahiers de l'Euphrate* 4: 177–189.

Cresswell R.C. 1982. Transferts de techniques et chaînes opératoires. *Techniques et Cultures* 2: 143–163.

Davis S.J.M., R. Rabinovich and N. Goren-Inbar 1988. Quaternary extinctions and population increase in western Asia: the animal remains from Biq'at Quneitra. *Paléorient* 14: 95–105.

Delage C., L. Meignen and O. Bar-Yosef 2000. Chert procurement and the organization of lithic production in the Mousterian of Hayonim cave (Israel). *Journal of Human Evolution* 38: A10–A11.

Geneste J.-M. 1988. Systèmes d'approvisionnement en matières premières au Paléolithique moyen et au Paléolithique supérieur en Aquitaine. In J.K. Kozlowski (Ed.), *L'Homme de Néandertal: La Mutation* (ERAUL 35), pp. 61–70. Liège: Université de Liège.

Geneste J.-M. 1991. Systèmes techniques de production lithique: variations techno-économiques dans les processus de réalisation des outillages paléolithiques. *Techniques et cultures* 17–18: 1–35.

Gilead I. and C. Grigson 1984. Far'ah II: a middle Palaeolithic open-air site in the northern Negev, Israel. *Proceedings of the Prehistoric Society* 50: 71–97.

Goldberg P. and O. Bar-Yosef 1998. Site formation processes in Kebara and Hayonim Caves and their significance in Levantine prehistoric caves. In T. Akazawa, K. Aoki and O. Bar-Yosef (Eds.), *Neandertals and Modern Humans in Western Asia*, pp. 107–125. New-York: Plenum Press.

Goren-Inbar N. 1990. *Quneitra: a Mousterian Site on the Golan heights* (Qedem 31). Jerusalem: Institute of Archaeology, The Hebrew University of Jersualem.

Harpending H. and H. Davis 1977. Some implications for hunter-gatherer ecology derived from the spatial structure of resources. *World Archaeology* 8: 275–286.

Henry D. 1989. Correlations between reduction strategies and settlement patterns. In D. Henry and G. Odell (Eds.), *Alternative Approaches to Lithic Analysis*, pp. 139–155. Washington D.C.: Archeological Papers of the American Anthropological Association.

Henry D. 1995a. The Influence of mobility levels on Levallois point production, late Levantine Mousterian, Southern Jordan. In H.L. Dibble and O. Bar-Yosef (Eds.), *The Definition and Interpretation of Levallois Technology* (Monographs in World Prehistory 23), pp. 185–200. Madison: Prehistory Press.

Henry D.O. 1995b. *Prehistoric Cultural Ecology and Evolution. Insights from Southern Jordan*. New York: Plenum Press.

Henry D.O. 1998. Intrasite spatial patterns and behavioral modernity: indications from the late Levantine Mousterian rockshelter of Tor Faraj, southern Jordan. In T. Akazawa, K. Aoki and O. Bar-Yosef (Eds.), *Neandertals and Modern Humans in Western Asia*, pp. 127–142. New York: Plenum Press.

Horowitz A. 1979. *The Quaternary in Israel*. New York: Academic Press.

Horowitz, A., 1988. Quaternary environments and paleogeography in Israel. In Y. Yom-Tov, and E. Tchernov (Eds.), *The Zoogeography of Israel*, pp. 35–58. Dordrecht: Junk.

Hovers E. 1990. The exploitation of raw material at the Mousterian site of Quneitra. In N. Goren-Inbar (Ed.), *Quneitra: a Mousterian Site on the Golan heights* (Qedem 31), pp. 150–167. Jerusalem: Institute of Archaeology, The Hebrew University.

Hovers E. 1997. *Variability of Levantine Mousterian Assemblages and Settlement Patterns: Implications for Understanding the Development of Human Behavior*. Ph.D. dissertation, The Hebrew University of Jerusalem.

Hovers E. 2001. Territorial behavior in the Middle Paleolithic of the Southern Levant. In N.J. Conard (Ed.), *Settlement Dynamics of the Middle Paleolithic and Middle Stone Age*, pp. 123–152. Tübingen: Kerns Verlag.

Hovers E., Y. Rak, R. Lavi and W.H. Kimbel 1995. Hominid remains from Amud cave in the context of the Levantine Middle Paleolithic. *Paléorient* 21: 47–61.

Jelinek A.J. 1977. A preliminary study of flakes from the Tabun Cave, Mount Carmel. In B. Arensburg and O. Bar-Yosef (Eds), *Moshe Stekelis Memorial Volume* (Eretz-Israel: Archaeological, Historical and Geographical Studies 13), pp. 87–96. Jerusalem: The Israel Exploration Society.

Jelinek A.J. 1982. The Middle Paleolithic in the Southern Levant, with comments on the appearance of modern *Homo sapiens*. In A. Ronen (Ed.), *The Transition from Lower to Middle Paleolithic and the Origin of Modern Man* (BAR International Series 151), pp. 57–104. Oxford: BAR.

Jochim M.B. 1979. Breaking down the system: recent ecological approaches in archaeology. In M.B. Schiffer (Ed.), pp. 77–118. *Advances in Archeological Method and Theory*. New York: Academic Press.

Karlin C., P. Bodu and J. Pelegrin 1991. Processus techniques et chaînes opératoires. Comment les préhistoriens s'approprient un concept élaboré par les ethnologues. In H. Balfet (Ed.), *Observer l'action technique: des chaînes opératoires, pour quoi faire?*, pp. 101–117. Paris: Editions du CNRS.

Kuhn S.L. 1992. On planning and curated technologies in the Middle Paleolithic. *Journal of Anthropological Research* 48: 185–213.

Kuhn S.L. 1995. *Mousterian Lithic Technology. An ecological perspective*. Princeton: Princeton University Press.

Lemonnier P. 1986. The study of material culture today: toward an anthropology of technical systems. *Journal of Anthropological Archaeolog* 5: 147–186.

Lemonnier P. 1992. *Elements for an Anthropology of Technology*. (Anthropological Paper 88). Ann Arbor: University of Michigan, Museum of Anthropology.

Lev E., M.E. Kislev and O. Bar-Yosef 2005. Mousterian vegetal food in Kebara Cave, Mt. Carmel. *Journal of Archaeological Science* 32: 475–484.

Lieberman D.E. and J.J. Shea 1994. Behavioral differences between Archaic and modern humans in the Levantine Mousterian. *American Anthropologist* 96: 300–332.

Marks A.E. and V.P. Chabai 2001. Constructing Middle Paleolithic settlement systems in Crimea: potentials and limitations. In N. Conard (Ed.), *Settlement Dynamics of the Middle Paleolithic and Middle Stone Age*, pp. 179–204. Tübingen: Kerns Verlag.

Marks A.E. and D.A. Friedel 1977. Prehistoric settlement patterns in the Avdat/Aqev area. In A.E. Marks (Ed.), *Prehistory and Paleoenvironments in the Central Negev, Israel*, pp. 131–158. Dallas: Southern Methodist University Press.

Meignen L. 1995. Levallois lithic production systems in the Middle Palaeolithic of the Near East: The case of the unidirectional method. In H. Dibble and O. Bar-Yosef (Eds.), *The Definition and Interpretation of Levallois Technology*, pp. 361–380. Madison, WI: Prehistory Press.

Meignen L. 1998. Hayonim cave lithic assemblages in the context of the Near Eastern Middle Palaeolithic: a preliminary report. In T. Akazawa, K. Aoki and O. Bar-Yosef (Eds.), *Neandertals and Modern Humans in Western Asia*, pp. 165–180. New York: Plenum Press.

Meignen L. 2000. Early Middle Palaeolithic blade technology in southwestern Asia. *Acta Anthropologica Sinica* 19 (Supplement): 158–168.

Meignen L. and O. Bar-Yosef 1991. Les outillages lithiques moustériens de Kebara (fouilles 1982–1985): premiers résultats. In O. Bar-Yosef and B. Vandermeersch (Eds.), *Le Squelette Moustérien de Kebara 2*, pp. 49–75. Paris: Editions du CNRS.

Meignen L. and O. Bar-Yosef 1992. Middle Palaeolithic variability in Kebara Cave (Mount Carmel, Israel). In T. Akazawa, K. Aoki and T. Kimura (Eds.), *The Evolution and Dispersal of Modern Humans in Asia*, pp. 129–148. Tokyo: Hokusen-Sha.

Meignen L., O. Bar-Yosef and P. Goldberg 1989. Les structures de combustion moustériennes de la grotte de Kébara, Mont Carmel, Isräel. In M. Olive and Y. Taborin Y. (Eds.), *Nature et Fonction des Foyers Préhistoriques*, pp. 141–146. Nemours: APRAF.

Meignen L., O. Bar-Yosef, P. Goldberg and S. Weiner 2001a. Le feu au Paléolithique moyen: recherches sur les structures de combustion et le statut des foyers. L'exemple du Proche-Orient. *Paléorient* 26: 9–22.

Meignen L., O. Bar-Yosef, N. Mercier, H. Valladas, P. Goldberg and B. Vandermeersch. 2001b. Apport des datations au problème de l'origine des hommes modernes au Proche-Orient. In J.N. Barrandon, P. Guilbert and V. Michel (Eds.), *Datation*. (XXI° Rencontres Intern. d'archéologie et d'histoire d'Antibes), pp. 295–313. Antibes: A.P.D.C.A.

Meignen L., S. Beyries, J.D. Speth and O. Bar-Yosef 1998. Acquisition, traitement des matières animales et fonction du site Paléolithique moyen dans la grotte de Kébara (Israël): approche interdisciplinaire. In J.-P. Brugal, L. Meignen and M. Patou-Mathis (Eds.), *Economie préhistorique: les
comportements de subsistance au Paléolithique*, pp. 227–258. Sophia-Antipolis: A.P.D.C.A.

Moss E. 1983. The functions of burins and tanged points from Tell Abu Hureira (Syria). In M.C. Cauvin
(Ed.), *Traces d'utilisation sur les outils néolithiques du Proche-Orient*, pp. 143–161. Lyon: Travaux de
la Maison de l'Orient.

Munday F.C. 1976. Intersite variability in the Mousterian of the Central Negev. In A.E. Marks (Ed.),
Prehistory and Paleoenvironment in the Central Negev, Israel. vol. 1, pp. 113–140. Dallas: Southern
Methodist University Press.

Munday F.C. 1979. Levantine Mousterian technological variability: a perspective from the Negev.
Paléorient 5: 87–104.

Nelson M. 1991. The study of technological organization. In M. Schiffer (Ed.), *Archaeological Method
and Theory*, pp. 57–100. Tucson: University of Arizona Press.

Neuville R. 1951. La grotte d'Abou Sif. In *Le Paléolithique et le Mésolithique de Judée* (Archives de l'IPH,
vol. 24), pp. 47–60. Paris: Masson et cie.

O'Connell J.F. 1987. Alyawara site structure and its archaeological implications. *American Antiquity* 52:
74–108.

Oswalt W. 1976. *An Anthropological Analysis of Food-Getting Technology*. New York: John Wiley.

Parry W.J. and R.L. Kelly 1987. Expedient core technology and sedentism. In J.K. Johnson and T.A.
Morrow (Eds.), *The Organization of Core Technology*, pp. 285–309. Boulder: Westview Press.

Plisson H. and S. Beyries 1998. Pointes ou outils triangulaires? Données fonctionnelles dans le
moustérien Levantin. *Paléorient* 24: 5–24.

Schick T. and M. Stekelis 1977. Mousterian assemblages in Kebara cave, Mount Carmel. In B. Arensburg
and O. Bar-Yosef, O. (Eds.), *Moshe Stekelis Memorial Volume* (Eretz-Israel: Archaeological, Historical
and Geographical Studies 13), pp. 97–149. Jerusalem: The Israel Exploration Society.

Schwarcz H.P. and W.J. Rink 1998. Progress in ESR and U-Series chronology of the Levantine Paleolithic.
In T. Akazawa, K. Aoki and O. Bar-Yosef (Eds.), *Neandertals and Modern Humans in Western Asia*,
pp. 57–68. New York: Plenum Press.

Shea J. 1988. Spear points from the Middle Paleolithic of the Levant. *Journal of Field Archaeology* 15:
441–450.

Shea J. 1991. *The Behavioral Significance of Levantine Mousterian Industrial Variability*. Ph.D. Dissertation,
Harvard University.

Shea J. 1998. Neandertal and early modern human behavioral variability. A regional-scale approach to
lithic evidence for hunting in the Levantine Mousterian. *Current Anthropology* 39 (Supplement):
S45–S78.

Shea J. A. Marks and J.-M. Geneste 1998. Commentaires sur l'article de H. Plisson et S. Beyries "Pointes
ou outils triangulaires? Données fonctionnelles dans le Moustérien levantin". *Paléorient* 24: 5–24.

Speth J.D. 1983. *Bison Kills and Bone Counts: Decision Making by Ancient Hunters*. Chicago: University
of Chicago Press.

Speth J.D. 2004. Hunting pressure, subsistence intensification, and demographic change in the Levantine late Middle Paleolithic. In N. Goren-Inbar and J.D. Speth (Eds.), *Human Paleoecology in the
Levantine, Corridor*, pp. 149–166. Oxford: Oxbow Press.

Speth J.D. and E. Tchernov 1998. The role of hunting and scavenging in Neanderthal procurement
strategies: new evidence from Kebara Cave (Israel). In T. Akazawa, K. Aoki and O. Bar-Yosef (Eds.),
Neanderthals and Modern Humans in West Asia, pp. 223–240. New York: Plenum Press.

Speth J.D. and E. Tchernov 2001. Neandertal hunting and meat-processing in the Near East: evidence
from Kebara Cave (Israel). In C.B. Stanford and H.T. Bunn (Eds.), *Meat Eating and Human Evolution*,
pp. 52–72. Oxford: Oxford University Press.

Speth J.D. and E. Tchernov 2002. Middle Paleolithic tortoise use at Kebara Cave (Israel). *Journal of
Archaeological Science* 29: 471–483.

Stiner M.C. 2005. *The Faunas of Hayonim Cave (Israel): A 200,000 Year Record of Paleolithic Diet, Demography and Society*. American School of Prehistoric Research, Cambridge, MA: Peabody Museum
Press, Harvard University.

Stiner M.C. 2001. Thirty years on the "Broad Spectrum Revolution" and paleolithic demography. *Proceedings of the National Academy of Sciences USA* 98: 6993–6996.

Stiner M.C. and S.L. Kuhn 1992. Subsistence, technology, and adaptive variation in Middle Paleolithic Italy. *American Anthropologist* 94: 12–46.

Stiner M.C., N.D. Munro and T.A. Surovell 2000. The tortoise and the hare: small game use, the Broad Spectrum Revolution, and Paleolithic demography. *Current Anthropology* 41: 39–73.

Stiner M.C., N.D. Munro, T.A. Surovell, E. Tchernov and O. Bar-Yosef 1999. Paleolithic population growth pulses evidenced by small animal exploitation. *Science* 283: 190–194.

Tchernov E. 1992. Biochronology, paleoecology, and dispersal events of hominids in the southern Levant. In T. Akazawa, K. Aoki and T. Kimura (Eds.), *The Evolution and Dispersal of Modern Humans in Asia*, pp. 149–188. Tokyo: Hokusen-Sha.

Tchernov E. 1994. New comments on the biostratigraphy of the Middle and Upper Pleistocene of the southern Levant. In O. Bar-Yosef and R.S. Kra (Eds.), *Late Quaternary Chronology and Paleoclimates of the Eastern Mediterranean*, pp. 333–350. Tucson: University of Arizona.

Tchernov E. 1996. Rodent faunas, chronostratigraphy and paleobiogeography of the southern Levant during the Quaternary. *Acta Zoologica Cracov* 39: 513–530.

Théry-Parisot I. 2002. Gathering of firewood during the Palaeolithic. In S. Thiébault (Ed.), *Charcoal Analysis. Metodological Approaches, Palaeoecological Results and Wood Uses*, pp. 243–249. Oxford: Archeopress.

Théry-Parisot I. and P.-J. Texier in press. La collecte du bois de feu dans le site moustérien de la Combette (Bonnieux, Vaucluse). Implications paléoéconomiques et paléoécologiques. Approche morphométrique des charbons de bois. *Buletin de la Société Préhistorique Française*.

Valladas H., N. Mercier, J.L. Joron and J.L. Reyss 1998. GIF Laboratory dates for Middle Paleolithic Levant. In T. Akazawa, K. Aoki and O. Bar-Yosef (Eds.), *Neandertals and Modern Humans in Western Asia*, pp. 69–76. New York: Plenum Press.

Van Peer P. 2001. The Nubian complex settlement system in Northeast Africa. In N.J. Conard (Ed.), *Settlement Dynamics of the Middle Paleolithic and Middle Stone Age*, pp. 45–63. Tübingen: Kerns Verlag.

Weiner S., S. Schiegl and O. Bar-Yosef 1995. Recognizing ash deposits in the archaeological record: a mineralogical study at Kebara and Hayonim caves, Israel. *Acta Anthropologica Sinica* 14: 340–351.

Weiner S., P. Goldberg and O. Bar-Yosef 2002. Three-dimensional distribution of minerals in the sediments of Hayonim cave, Israel: diagenetic processes and archaeological implications. *Journal of Archaeological Science* 29: 1289–1308.

Zohary M. 1973. *The Geobotanical Foundations of the Middle East*. Stuttgart: Fischer Verlag.

Chapter *10*

Housekeeping, Neandertal-Style
Hearth Placement and Midden Formation in Kebara Cave (Israel)

John D. Speth

Museum of Anthropology, University of Michigan, Ann Arbor, Michigan 48109-1079 USA

ABSTRACT

This paper shows that Neandertals used the Middle Paleolithic site of Kebara Cave (Israel) in a manner that is consistent with the way that modern hunter-gatherers might use such a cave. More specifically, I review evidence showing that these hominids (1) repeatedly built or rekindled their hearths in more or less the same place over a period of several thousand years; (2) periodically emptied their fireplaces and cleared the habitation area of larger lithic and faunal debris; and (3) disposed of hearth cleanings and other debris in a substantial midden that accumulated along the cave's north wall. These observations, while in no way proving that Neandertals were the cognitive equals of their Upper Paleolithic successors, should nonetheless help to counter the pervasive image of these hominids as bumbling dimwits whose habitations lacked human-like internal patterning or structure.

INTRODUCTION

The interpretation of Neandertal lifeways has probably never been as polarized as it is today. At one extreme are many archaeologists and biological anthropologists, and quite a few geneticists, who see Neandertals as belonging to a species other than our own, most often a decidedly inferior one in terms of both behavior and cognitive wherewithal (*e.g.*, Mellars 1996, 2000; Krings *et al.* 1997; Stringer and McKie 1997; Harpending *et al.* 1998; Hublin 2000; Klein 2000). At the other extreme are quite a few archaeologists, together with the so-called "multiregionalists" and a much smaller but growing contingent of geneticists, who see Neandertals as close cousins, perhaps "technologically challenged" but definitely not lacking in essential cognitive machinery (e.g., Frayer et al. 1993; Templeton 1993, 2002; Wolpoff and Caspari 1997; Clark 1997; Duarte et al. 1999; Zilhão and d'Errico 1999; Wolpoff et al. 2000, 2001; Zilhão 2000). Of course, this is an exaggerated picture of reality, as one can find scholars occupying a spectrum of positions between the two extremes (see discussions in Trinkaus and Shipman 1993; Relethford 2001), but the endpoints are by far the most visible and certainly have attracted the lion's share of media attention (Wong 1999).

So as not to keep the reader guessing, my position lies closer to the latter endpoint, the view that sees Neandertals as cousins, not as a separate species. From this perspective, I tend to see the so-called "creative explosion" of the Upper Paleolithic (Pfeiffer 1982) more as the visible (and geographically patchy) expression of a long period of social, demographic, economic, and technological intensification (e.g., Hayden 1993; Kuhn and Stiner 1998) rather than as the product of a newly emergent hominid with qualitatively superior mental abilities (Klein 2000).

I recognize, however, that there are cogent arguments for and against both positions, and that in reality the issue remains far from resolved. For archaeologists, the Neandertal conundrum ultimately stems from the fact that our frameworks and explanations can be drawn from two very different theoretical domains, and we presently lack a basis for deciding which one is most appropriate. On the one hand, we know that more complex cognitive and symbolic capacities did in fact evolve during the past two and a half million years, so why not expect such changes toward the end of the Middle Paleolithic? On the other hand, in the archaeological record left by unquestionably fully modern humans, there are many instances where clear-cut material expressions of their complex symbolic capabilities are simply not manifest, perhaps because the requisite social or economic stresses, or opportunities, that might favor such expression were insufficient or lacking. Thus, for example, parietal and mobile art, the traits most often thought to herald the emergence of fully modern humans, appear quite suddenly in Western Europe in the early Upper Paleolithic, but are conspicuously absent throughout most of the Upper Paleolithic in both Southwestern Asia and the Far East, yet no one would seriously suggest that these Asian areas were occupied by a different hominid species with inferior cognitive abilities. After all, the Near East and China, despite their striking artistic silence throughout much of the Upper Paleolithic, went on to become two of the world's earliest centers of plant and animal domestication, sedentary village life, and complex civilizations. It seems that archaeologists may have great difficulty settling the question of whether or not Neandertals were cognitively challenged, so long as we continue to demand as proof of such capacity nothing short of cave paintings, carved ivory plaques, or ochre-encrusted aurochs skulls. Unfortunately, by equating "humanness" with traits such as these, or with more problematic ones like blade-making, bone-working, building huts, collecting shellfish, or hunting dangerous prey (see discussions in Hayden 1993; Wolpoff and Caspari 1997; Bar-Yosef and Kuhn 1999; McBrearty and Brooks 2000), even many Holocene cultural entities would almost certainly fail to qualify as products of cognitively modern humans (e.g., Belfer-Cohen and Hovers 1992). If one were to follow this line of reasoning to its logical conclusion, we would be forced to demote much of the Paleo-Indian and early Archaic record of both eastern and western North America to the realm of the pre-human!

So where does this leave us? In the work that has been done at the Israeli Middle Paleolithic site of Kebara Cave, no one has encountered evidence of ochre-encrusted skulls, carved ivory plaques, or paintings on the cave walls. Not surprisingly, therefore, we are unable to conclude that Levantine Neandertals were the cognitive equals of their artistically mute Upper Paleolithic successors. What I can do here is far more modest, and that is to show that Neandertal occupation in Kebara Cave was anything but random or haphazard, and that instead these hominids used the cave in a manner that is consistent with the way that modern hunter-gatherers might use such a cave. More specifically, I will show that Neandertals (1) repeatedly built or rekindled their hearths in more or less the same place over a period of several thousand years; (2) repeatedly emptied their fireplaces and cleared the habitation area of larger lithic and faunal debris; and (3) disposed of hearth cleanings and other debris in a midden that accumulated along the cave's north wall. Needless-to-say, these are not particularly earth-shattering observations, but they should help in some small measure to counter the surprisingly pervasive and tenacious image of Neandertals as bumbling dimwits, whose behavior was unplanned and whose habitations lacked internal patterning or structure (*e.g.*, Pettitt 1997; Kolen 1999).

KEBARA AND ITS FAUNA

Kebara is a large cave on the western face of Mt. Carmel (Israel), about 30 km south of Haifa and 2.5 km east of the present-day Mediterranean shoreline. Two major excavations at the site, the first conducted by Moshe Stekelis between 1951 and 1965 (Schick and Stekelis 1977), the second by a French-Israeli team codirected by Ofer Bar-Yosef and Bernard Vandermeersch between 1982 and 1990 (Bar-Yosef 1991; Bar-Yosef *et al.* 1992), yielded thousands of animal bones and stone tools from a 4-m deep sequence of Middle Paleolithic deposits dating between approximately 60,000 and 48,000 years ago (Valladas *et al.* 1987).

Stekelis's excavations were conducted within 2 × 2-m grid squares by arbitrary horizontal levels (spits), typically 10–20 cm in thickness. Almost all of the excavated deposits were screened and all faunal material, including unidentifiable bone fragments, were kept. Depths for levels were recorded in cm below a fixed datum. In the more recent work at the site, directed by Bar-Yosef and Vandermeersch, the excavators employed 1-m grid units (often divided into smaller subunits), many items (including fauna) were piece-plotted, and wherever possible they followed the natural stratigraphy of the deposits, using levels that seldom exceeded 5 cm in thickness. Depths were again recorded in cm below datum, using the same reference point that Stekelis had used. The newer excavations recognized nine natural stratigraphic levels (units) within the Mousterian sequence: unit XIII (bottom) to unit V (top). The early Upper Paleolithic levels begin with unit IV.

While both approaches–horizontal spits and natural stratigraphic levels–result in the pooling of material from more than one occupational episode, I focus here on materials from the newer excavations in order to minimize the distortion that may arise from the use of aggregated samples.

Results are evaluated statistically using the following methods. For testing the significance of the difference between two percentages, I use the arcsine transformation (t_s), as defined by Sokal and Rohlf (1969:607–610); and to evaluate differences between means I use standard unpaired t-tests (t).

Most of the larger mammal remains derive from two taxa – mountain gazelle (*Gazella gazella, ca.* 60%) and Persian fallow deer (*Dama mesopotamica, ca.* 21%). Other animals, represented by small numbers of specimens, include roe deer (*Capreolus capreolus*, < 1%), red deer (*Cervus elaphus*, 6%), wild goat (*Capra* cf. *aegagrus*, 1%), wild boar (*Sus scrofa*, 5%), and aurochs (*Bos primigenius*, 7%). Small numbers of equid remains are also present (Davis 1977; Eisenmann 1992; Speth and Tchernov 1998, 2001).

Nearly half of Kebara's Middle Paleolithic ungulate remains came from an extremely dense concentration of bones which accumulated within a roughly 2-m to 4-m-wide zone close to the cave's north wall, and particularly from stratigraphic units IX–XI. In the central floor area of the cave, separated by a gap of several meters from the north wall accumulations, and most clearly evident in unit X (the so-called "*décapage*"), bones were encountered in small, discrete concentrations or patches, separated from each other by zones with few or no bones (see Meignen *et al.* 1998:230–231). Studies of the sediments on the cave floor, using on-site Fourier transform infrared spectrometry, indicate that these localized bone concentrations reflect the original burial distribution, not the end-product of selective dissolution following burial (Weiner *et al.* 1993).

While there is clear evidence throughout the cave's Middle Paleolithic sequence for the intermittent presence of carnivores, most notably spotted hyenas (*Crocuta crocuta*), the modest numbers of gnawed and punctured bones, the scarcity of gnaw-marks on midshaft fragments (Marean and Kim 1998:S84–S85), and the hundreds of cut marked and burned bones, as well as hearths, ash lenses, and large numbers of lithic artifacts, clearly testify to the central role played by humans in the formation of the bone accumulations (Bar-Yosef *et al.* 1992; Speth and Tchernov 1998, 2001).

HEARTHS

Let me begin by briefly considering the nature and placement of hearths at Kebara. As these fascinating features have been discussed elsewhere in detail (Meignen *et al.* 1989, 2001; Bar-Yosef *et al.* 1992), I present here only a brief summary. Most of the fireplaces occur out on the floor of the cave, well away from the walls. In this central area, the sequence of superimposed and often overlapping hearths and ash lenses attains the remarkable thickness of nearly four meters. Most of the hearths were built directly on the surface, with no trace of a pit or basin.

Others, however, are classic basin-shaped features that were set in shallow pits excavated below the surrounding surface. Most of the hearths, whether on the surface or in basins, are round to oval features, and average between 30 cm and 60 cm in diameter. A few, however, are much larger, with diameters exceeding 80 cm to 100 cm. One of the striking aspects of Kebara's hearths is their consistent internal stratigraphy. Most have a 3-cm to 5-cm-thick, brownish black to black organic horizon at the base, often containing small pieces of wood charcoal and a surprising number of charred legume seeds (Baruch *et al.* 1992; Lev *et al.* 2005). This dark horizon is overlain by a 5-cm to 8-cm-thick lens of yellowish to whitish ash. In addition, the sediments directly beneath many of the hearths have been altered to a distinctly reddish brown or orange color, almost certainly the result of intense or prolonged heat. Stratigraphic and micromorphological studies of the sediments in the hearths indicate that many of these features were rekindled more than once. Moreover, scores of hearths are superimposed on top of each other, either directly, or in closely overlapping, almost imbricated, succession, making it clear that their placement stayed highly localized within the central area of the cave for millennia, a pattern that is anything but haphazard or unstructured (Figure 1).

MIDDEN

Now let us turn to evidence showing that Kebara's Neandertal inhabitants repeatedly cleaned faunal debris from the habitation area and dumped it along the north wall of the cave, over time forming a substantial midden. This, by the way, is not a new conclusion. Stekelis, who excavated in Kebara nearly half a century ago, was struck by the sheer volume of bone along the north wall, and concluded that it probably represented "... the kitchen midden of the Mousterian inhabitants" (Schick and Stekelis 1977:102). The stone tools found there are consistent with Stekelis's view, as the assemblage is "comprised of larger pieces than elsewhere in the cave and includes an abundance of cores, cortical elements, flakes, and other waste ... " (Bar-Yosef *et al.* 1992:526).

Keeping habitation areas clear of debris is, of course, commonplace among contemporary hunter-gatherers. In modern forager camps, trash tends to accumulate along the peripheries of the habitation area, a pattern that becomes increasingly apparent the longer the occupation (*e.g.*, O'Connell 1987). Here, I present in summary form several lines of faunal evidence supporting the view that the concentration of bones along the north wall does, in fact, represent a Middle Paleolithic midden consisting largely of secondary refuse that accumulated during extended periods of intensive occupation of the cave by Neandertals.

1. Most of the Middle Paleolithic faunal remains are concentrated vertically within three principal stratigraphic units, IX, X, and XI, denoting the principal period of midden formation. There is a smaller but nonetheless distinct peak in unit VII, which probably marks a period of renewed though less intense midden development (see Figure 2; Number of Identifiable

Figure 1. Part of Kebara's west profile, showing superimposed Middle Paleolithic hearths.

Specimens or NISP). The attenuated nature of the peak in unit VII may also be accentuated somewhat by the smaller scale of excavations in this unit.

2. In units IX through XI, and again in unit VII, nearly 60% of all ungulate dentitions (intact tooth rows and isolated teeth) are concentrated close to the north wall, not out on the floor of the cave (see Figure 3; NISP). In contrast, in units V, VI, VIII, and XII, the proportion of dentitions that occur near the wall is exceedingly small.

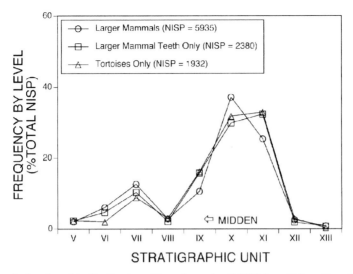

Figure 2. Stratigraphic distribution of faunal remains (NISP) from Kebara Cave (larger mammals include gazelle, fallow deer, wild boar, red deer, and aurochs).

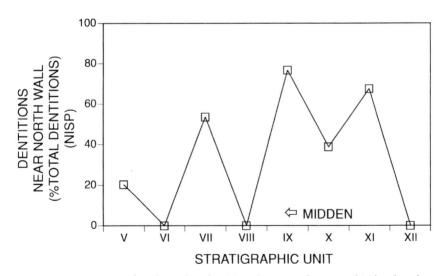

Figure 3. Proportion of total ungulate dentitions (intact tooth rows and isolated teeth; NISP = 6531) that occur in the midden zone close to cave's north wall.

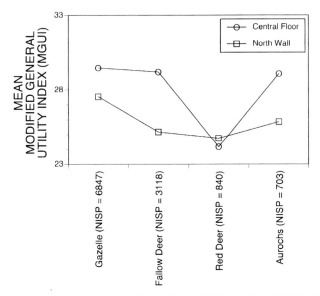

Figure 4. Comparison of average Modified General Utility Index (MGUI) of ungulate faunal remains in north wall concentration and central cave floor.

3. Detailed taphonomic studies of the bones in the north wall accumulation indicate that humans, not hyenas, were the principal agents in its formation. Evidence for this includes the modest number of gnawed and punctured bones; the scarcity of gnaw-marks on midshaft fragments, indicating that marrow had been removed from most bones before hyenas had access to them (Marean and Kim 1998:S84–S85); and the presence of hundreds of cut marked and burned bones (see Speth and Tchernov 1998, 2001).

4. In three of the four major ungulate taxa at Kebara (i.e., gazelle, fallow deer, aurochs), the average utility (using Binford's [1978] Modified General Utility Index or MGUI) of the bones in the north wall assemblage is significantly lower than the value for bones from the central floor area, suggesting disposal of less-valued carcass parts of these animals in the midden (Figure 4; gazelle, t = −4.965, p < .0001; fallow deer, t = −7.086, p < .0001; aurochs, t = −3.208, p = .001; Binford 1978:74).

5. The average length (cm) of bone fragments found near the north wall is significantly greater than in the central floor area in all taxa but fallow deer, and the difference becomes more pronounced the larger the animal (see Figure 5; all taxa combined, t = 4.267, p < .0001; gazelle, t = 3.540, p < .001; fallow deer, t = 0.954, p > .05; wild boar, t = 3.058, p < .01; red deer, t = 3.004, p < .01; aurochs, t = 4.508, p < .0001). Again, this result is compatible with the view that less heavily processed parts were discarded in the midden area. The smaller size of fragments on the cave floor might be due to more intense trampling but, as discussion below will attempt to show, this is probably not the case.

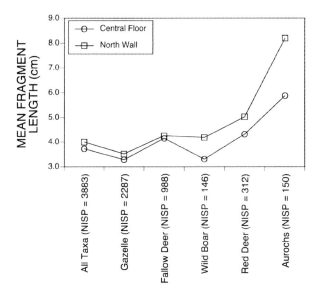

Figure 5. Comparison of mean length (cm) of bone fragments in north wall concentration and central cave floor.

6. Heads (maxillae, mandibles, isolated teeth, and miscellaneous cranial parts), the bulkiest part of the ungulate carcass, are proportionately (and absolutely) more abundant in the midden area than out on the floor of the cave (see Figure 6). On average, roughly half (51.0%) of all bone fragments in the midden derive from crania compared to only 37.6% in the habitation area ($t_s = 16.10$, $p < .0001$). Significant differences are seen in all five taxa and, not surprisingly, the magnitude of the difference is greatest in the larger ones (gazelle, $t_s = 7.09$, $p < .0001$; fallow deer, $t_s = 11.07$, $p < .0001$; wild boar, $t_s = 6.40$, $p < .0001$; red deer, $t_s = 5.80$, $p < .0001$; aurochs, $t_s = 7.87$, $p < .0001$).

7. Cut marks, reflecting both dismemberment and defleshing, are significantly more common on bones in the habitation area than on bones that had been tossed into the midden (see Figure 7; 12.1% vs. 9.2%, $t_s = 5.59$, $p < .0001$). The difference is significant, or nearly so, in four of the five major taxa (gazelle, $t_s = 2.33$, $p < .05$; fallow deer, $t_s = 4.25$, $p < .0001$; wild boar, $t_s = 0.63$, $p > .05$; red deer, $t_s = 1.81$, $p = .07$; aurochs, $t_s = 2.82$, $p < .01$). I see these results as evidence that material in the midden received less intensive processing prior to discard than material that remained on the floor of the cave.

8. The proportion of complete first and second phalanges, two potentially important marrow bones, is greater in the midden than out on the floor of the cave (see Figure 8; all taxa combined, $t_s = 6.35$, $p < .0001$). While comparisons within individual taxa are handicapped by small sample sizes, the contrast between midden and floor is significant, or nearly so, in three of the five taxa (gazelle, $t_s = 4.82$, $p < .0001$; fallow deer, $t_s = 1.81$,

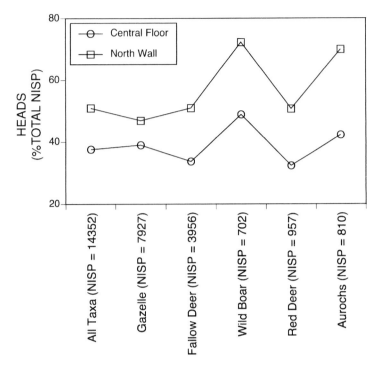

Figure 6. Cranial remains as a proportion of total NISP in north wall concentration and on cave floor.

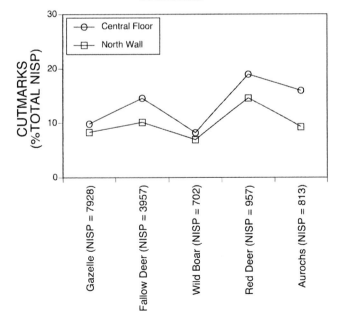

Figure 7. Proportion of cut marked remains in north wall concentration and on cave floor.

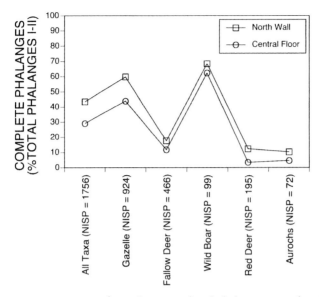

Figure 8. Proportion of complete 1st and 2nd phalanges in north wall
concentration and on cave floor.

$p = .07$; wild boar, $t_s = 0.62$, $p > .05$; red deer, $t_s = 2.35$, $p = .05$;
aurochs, $t_s = 0.92$, $p > .05$). Again, the suggestion is that bones tossed
into the midden were less intensively processed, on average, than those that
remained behind in the habitation area. One might argue, of course, that
more foot traffic on the floor of the cave accounts for the higher incidence
of breakage there (as well as the smaller average fragment size, noted
before). Fortunately, the condition of the crania may help us determine
whether the breakage in phalanges derives more from trampling or from
food-processing. If trampling were the principal source of fragmentation,
skulls, being one the most fragile elements in the ungulate skeleton, should
be more highly fragmented in the habitation area than in the midden.
This is not the case, however. The proportion of isolated teeth compared
to teeth that remain socketed in mandibles and maxillae is significantly
higher in the midden (81.9% vs. 66.4%, $t_s = 13.23$, $p < .0001$), a breakage
pattern opposite to the one seen in phalanges. It therefore seems unlikely
that higher fragmentation in the phalanges, bones that should stand up
to attrition better than crania, can be attributed to trampling. Marrow
extraction would seem to be a much more likely explanation.
9. One of the most interesting results to emerge from the study of spatial
    patterning concerns the distribution of burned bones. Before discussing
    this patterning, however, I need to digress briefly to point out that bones
    became burned at Kebara largely as a result of cooking, not accidental
    post-discard exposure to fire. This conclusion is suggested by four prin-
    cipal observations (see Speth and Tchernov 2001:63): first, burning is

concentrated on limb epiphyses (5.6%) rather than on midshafts (2.3%; $t_s = 2.83$, $p < .01$); second, burning is more common on elements of mature animals (5.6%) than on those of juveniles (3.6%; $t_s = 2.02$, $p < .05$); third, in adults, the proportion of burned bones varies in a systematic fashion across anatomical units, such that limbs are more often burned than heads, axial elements, or feet (see Speth and Tchernov 2001:62); and finally within the limbs, the average marrow utility (Binford 1978:27) of those limb elements that are burned (63.1 ± 26.7) is significantly greater than the average utility of those that are not (54.8 ± 29.3; $t = -3.29$, $p = .001$; gazelle and fallow deer combined).

Now let us return to the spatial distribution of burned bones at Kebara. Burned bones comprise a significantly greater proportion of the faunal assemblage in the north wall midden than in the remains out on the cave floor (5.8% vs. 4.1%, excluding isolated teeth; $t_s = 3.69$, $p < .001$). When looked at by species, sample sizes decline precipitously in all but two taxa, gazelle and fallow deer; in these two animals, however, the relationship persists and remains significant (see Figure 9; gazelle, $t_s = 2.65$, $p < .01$; fallow deer, $t_s = 2.61$, $p < .01$). The higher incidence of

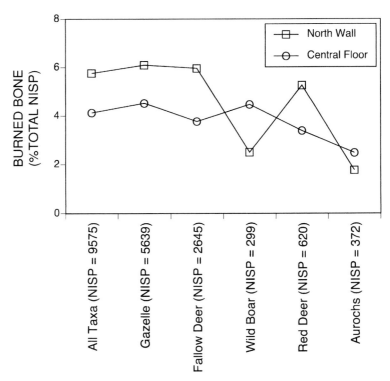

Figure 9. Proportion of burned bones in north wall concentration and on cave floor (isolated teeth are excluded from calculations).

burned bones close to the wall of the cave at first seems counterintuitive in light of the fact that most of the fireplaces are located well away from the wall. One could argue that, like the breakage in phalanges, this result is an artifact of attritional processes. I have already noted that the proportion of isolated teeth is greater in the midden area than out on the cave floor. This could indicate that fragmentation of skulls, by sediment compaction or other attritional processes, was more intense near the north wall. And, since burned bones are far more fragile than unburned ones, the higher proportion of charred items in the midden could simply indicate that more of the burned elements in this part of the site had broken apart into smaller pieces. In order to check this, I recomputed the percentages of burned bones in the two areas of the cave, but this time looking only at *complete* elements (*e.g.*, carpals, tarsals, phalanges, etc.). The difference between midden and floor area persists, despite the reduction in sample size. Along the north wall, nearly 6.4% of the complete bones are burned compared to only 4.1% on the cave floor, a difference that remains statistically significant ($t_s = 2.63$, $p < .01$).

If one accepts that the concentration of bones close to the north wall does in fact represent a midden, and if one also accepts that much of the burning is the result of cooking activities, not accidental post-discard exposure of bones to fire, then the higher incidence of burned bone close to the north wall indicates that Kebara's Neandertal inhabitants periodically cleaned out their cooking and eating areas and dumped this debris in the midden. While such behavior is commonplace in long-term encampments of contemporary foragers, this evidence of fastidiousness may come as a surprise to those who view Neandertals as subhuman dimwits.

CONCLUSIONS

I think it is safe to conclude, on the basis of the evidence presented here, that the late Middle Paleolithic encampments in Kebara Cave display reasonably clear-cut evidence of internal order and structure. Other Neandertal sites in the Near East, such as Amud (Hovers *et al.* 1991:156), Tabun (Albert *et al.* 1999), and Tor Faraj (Henry *et al.* 2004), and sites like Abric Romaní at the far western edge of the Neandertal world (Pastó *et al.* 2000; Vaquero *et al.* 2001), are revealing equally compelling evidence of internal structure.

What do the findings at Kebara and elsewhere have to say about the Middle to Upper Paleolithic "transition"? For one thing, they tell us that the transition, at least in so far as it is reflected in patterned use of living space, did not occur at the traditional boundary between the Middle and Upper Paleolithic, but squarely within the former, perhaps as much as 60,000 years ago, possibly more. This of course is problematic, because one must either conclude that (1) late Neandertals possessed the mental capacities that many would like to reserve for modern humans, or (2) the criterion is inappropriate for identifying modernity (*e.g.*, Pettitt 1997). This, at least, is the way many archaeologists would dichotomize this dilemma. I can't resolve it, but I can muddy the water a little more. I think there is a third alternative, where (1) and (2) are both true, that needs to be considered, if for no other reason than to falsify it. Let me explain this third possibility by means of an example drawn from the much younger archaeological record of North America.

Human presence in North America begins about 12,000 years ago, some would say earlier. These first inhabitants of the New World are generally known as "Paleo-Indians." Many Paleo-Indian sites, particularly in the mid-continent region of North America, testify to the considerable prowess of these early hunters, tackling mammoths and perhaps mastodons, as well as a large and now-extinct form of bison. By about 8,000 years ago, these big-game hunters gave way to much less newsworthy Archaic-period foragers, who eked out a meager existence harvesting seeds, nuts and smaller animals in the vast deserts, prairies, and forests of North America.

The relevance of the North American record to the question of Neandertal's organizational and mental capacities is simply this: most archaeological sites that date to the Paleo-Indian and early Archaic periods—periods that together last some 5,000 to 6,000 years and represent nearly half of the securely known occupation span of the New World—have little or no evident internal structure. Most are just "patches" or "scatters" of artifacts and bones, with few if any formal hearths: isolated patches and lenses of ash are much more the norm for thermal features. Moreover, most sites from these periods have little or nothing in the way of ornaments or grave accompaniments; huts are generally absent or very controversial; and art of any non-perishable sort is virtually non-existent. They certainly didn't paint cave walls; in fact, we are hard-put in most cases to find anything that even remotely smacks of symbolism. If we were to use the same criteria that we apply to Neandertals, we would have to conclude that the inhabitants of North America up until only a few thousand years ago were "cognitively challenged." The parallels with the record of the Middle Paleolithic are even more striking if we exclude from consideration the few dry caves in western North America and waterlogged sites in Florida of late Paleo-Indian and early Archaic age which have miraculously preserved traces of basketry, textiles, and other unusual and highly perishable items.

Then in the late Archaic, around 5,000 years ago give or take a millennium, came North America's counterpart to Eurasia's Upper Paleolithic "revolution." We suddenly see an explosion of art–intricately shaped and often engraved "exotica" of shell, antler, bone, stone, tortoise shell, and native copper, including cups, tubes, pendants, beads, pins, rattles, atlatl hooks and weights, and gorgets; there are also remnants of elaborately decorated textiles and baskets, and almost ubiquitous red ochre. Many of the raw materials came from distant lands–marine shell from the Gulf of Mexico, shark's teeth from the mid-Atlantic states, copper from the Lake Superior region of Michigan, galena and mica from Illinois and the Appalachians. This is also the time when we begin to see large numbers of burials clustered together in real cemeteries, not just a few peppered here and there over the archaeological landscape; and for the first time many of these burials are elaborately decked out with ornaments and other "exotica," so much so at times that we begin to speculate about the beginnings of prestige enhancement and wealth display, about "big men," about reduced mobility and increasing conflict, about the growing importance of intergroup exchange and political alliances, about the very seeds of societal inequality and hierarchy. This is the bread and butter of North American archaeology. And while there is lots to argue about (particularly about what is "cause" and what is "effect"), everyone seems to agree that in some form or other what we are seeing over the course of the Archaic is the playing out of gradually increasing populations that were slowly filling in the landscape, reducing people's ability to "vote with their feet" when things got tough, and thereby compelling them to begin playing with alternative economic, social and political strategies for maintaining the delicate balance between war and peace—in a word, social, technological, economic, and political *intensification*. No one, of course, would believe for a nanosecond that in the artless and style-devoid silence of the early Archaic we are dealing with a cognitively impaired proto-human.

In fact, many of North America's regional archaeological sequences bear witness to the same general developmental trajectory: the sequences almost invariably begin with some variant of an "early archaic" stage, characterized by small, highly mobile populations; little or no evidence of patterned use of space in sites; almost no evidence of long-distance exchange; very little in the way of non-perishable art; and artifact assemblages that display little spatial or temporal stylistic differentiation. Late in the sequences, populations have grown much larger; mobility is greatly curtailed; sites begin to display much more clear-cut evidence of internal structure; long-distance trade has become much more evident and involves large quantities of ornately decorated and "exotic" items; and stylistic differentiation in projectile points, but especially in ceramics, reaches the point where nearly every valley has its own distinctive styles, and time-slices sometimes as short as 25–50 years can be distinguished on stylistic grounds alone. What I have just described could easily serve, in broad outline, as a description of the major contrasts between the Middle and Upper Paleolithic. There is at least enough similarity here to be cause for concern.

Given this scenario, the "transition" taking place during the Levantine late Middle Paleolithic might be seen as broadly analogous to the changes that characterize the "intermediacy" of the middle Archaic period in eastern North America: a variety of faunal evidence points to a noticeable demographic upswing in local, perhaps regional, human populations (Stiner *et al.* 2000; Speth and Tchernov 2002; Speth in press); burials become an expectable part of the archaeological record; and the deeply stratified sequences of hearths and ash lenses found in sites like Kebara, Tabun, and Amud reflect seasonally declining residential mobility and more structured use of living space (*e.g.*, Hovers *et al.* 1991; Albert *et al.* 1999). Looking farther afield, one might be tempted to see the appearance of ornaments, bone tools, and occasional huts in the Châtelperronian as a reflection of a similar trend toward social and economic intensification (*e.g.*, d'Errico *et al.* 1998, 2003). There is at least some food for thought here.

As I indicated at the outset, nothing that I do in this brief paper will prove that Levantine Neandertals were the cognitive equals of their Upper Paleolithic successors, though this remains a viable possibility, but I hope that I have at least helped to show that there is nothing distinctly "unhuman" about the spatial structure of Neandertal habitation in Kebara Cave.

ACKNOWLEDGEMENTS

I thank O. Bar-Yosef, A. Belfer-Cohen, S. J. M. Davis, T. Dayan, P. Goldberg, N. Goren-Inbar, L. K. Horwitz, E. Hovers, S.L. Kuhn, L. Meignen, R. Rabinovich, M. B. Schiffer, M. C. Stiner, E. Tchernov, and two anonymous reviewers for their helpful suggestions in the development of the ideas presented here. Partial support for this research was received from the U.S.-Israel Binational Science Foundation, L. S. B. Leakey Foundation, National Endowment for the Humanities Fellowship for University Teachers, Hebrew University (Jerusalem), and the University of Michigan's Museum of Anthropology, Office of the Vice-President for Research, and Horace H. Rackham School of Graduate Studies.

REFERENCES CITED

Albert R.M., O. Lavi, L. Estroff, S. Weiner, A. Tsatskin, A., Ronen and S. Lev-Yadun 1999. Mode of occupation of Tabun Cave, Mt. Carmel, Israel during the Mousterian period: a study of the sediments and phytoliths. *Journal of Archaeological Science* 26: 1249–1260.

Baruch U., E. Werker and O. Bar-Yosef 1992. Charred wood remains from Kebara Cave, Israel: preliminary report. *Bulletin de la Société Botanique de France* 139: 531–538.

Bar-Yosef O. 1991. The history of excavations at Kebara Cave. In O. Bar-Yosef and B. Vandermeersch (Eds.), *Le Squelette Moustérien de Kébara 2*, pp. 17–27. Paris: Éditions CNRS.

Bar-Yosef O. and S.L. Kuhn 1999. The big deal about blades: laminar technologies and human evolution. *American Anthropologist* 101: 322–338.

Bar-Yosef O., B. Vandermeersch, B. Arensburg, A. Belfer-Cohen, P. Goldberg, H. Laville, L. Meignen, Y. Rak, J.D. Speth, E.Tchernov, A.-M. Tillier and S. Weiner 1992. The excavations in Kebara Cave, Mt. Carmel. *Current Anthropology* 33: 497–550.

Belfer-Cohen A. and E. Hovers 1992. In the eye of the beholder: Mousterian and Natufian burials in the Levant. *Current Anthropology* 33: 463–471.

Binford L.R. 1978. *Nunamiut Ethnoarchaeology*. New York: Academic Press.

Clark G.A. 1997. Through a glass darkly: conceptual issues in Modern Human Origins research. In G.A. Clark and C.M. Willermet (Eds.), *Conceptual Issues in Modern Human Origins Research*, pp. 60–76. Hawthorne NY: Aldine de Gruyter.

Davis S.J.M. 1977. The ungulate remains from Kebara Cave. In B. Arensburg and O. Bar-Yosef (Eds.), *Moshe Stekelis Memorial Volume* (Eretz-Israel: Archaeological, Historical and Geographical Studies 13), pp. 150–163. Jerusalem: The Israel Exploration Society.

d'Errico F., J. Zilhão, M. Julien, D. Baffier and J. Pelegrin 1998. Neanderthal acculturation in Western Europe? A critical review of the evidence and its interpretation. *Current Anthropology* 39(Supplement): S1–S44.

d'Errico F., M. Julien, D. Liolios, M. Vanhaeren and D. Baffier 2003. Many awls in our argument: bone tool manufacture and use in the Châtelperronian and Aurignacian levels of the Grotte du Renne at Arcy-sur-Cure. In J. Zilhão and F. d'Errico (Eds.), *The Chronology of the Aurignacian and of the Transitional Technocomplexes: Dating, Stratigraphies, Cultural Implications* (Trabalhos de Arqueologia 33), pp. 247–270. Lisbon: Istituto Português de Arqueologia.

Duarte C., J. Maurício, P.B. Pettitt, P. Souto, E. Trinkaus, H. van der Plicht and J. Zilhão 1999. The early Upper Paleolithic human skeleton from the Abrigo do Lagar Velho (Portugal) and modern human emergence in Iberia. *Proceedings of the National Academy of Sciences USA* 96: 7604–7609.

Eisenmann V. 1992. Systematic and biostratigraphical interpretation of the equids from Qafzeh, Tabun, Skhul and Kebara (Acheulo-Yabrudian to Upper Paleolithic of Israel). *Archaeozoologia* 5: 43–62.

Frayer D.W., M.H. Wolpoff, A.G. Thorne, F.H. Smith and G.G. Pope 1993. Theories of modern human origins: the paleontological test. *American Anthropologist* 95: 14–50.

Harpending H.C., M.A. Batzer, M. Gurven, K.B. Jorde, A.R. Rogers and S.T. Sherry 1998. Genetic traces of ancient demography. *Proceedings of the National Academy of Sciences USA* 95: 1961–1967.

Hayden B. 1993. The cultural capacities of Neandertals: a review and re-evaluation. *Journal of Human Evolution* 24: 113–146.

Henry D.O., H.J. Hietala, A.M. Rosen, Y.E. Demidenko, V.I. Usik and T.L. Armagan 2004. Human behavioral organization in the Middle Paleolithic: were Neanderthals different? *American Anthropologist* 106: 17–31.

Hovers E., Y. Rak and W.H. Kimbel 1991. Amud Cave – 1991 season. *Journal of the Israel Prehistoric Society* 24: 152–157.

Hublin J.-J. 2000. Brothers or cousins? Climate change and competition from modern humans led to the demise of the Neandertals. *Archaeology* 53: 49–54.

Klein R.G. 2000. L'art est-il né d'une mutation génétique? *La Recherche Hors-Série* 4: 18–21.

Kolen J. 1999. Hominids without homes: on the nature of Middle Palaeolithic settlement in Europe. In W. Roebroeks and C. Gamble (Eds.), *The Middle Palaeolithic Occupation of Europe*, pp. 139–175. Leiden: University of Leiden.

Krings M., A. Stone, R.W. Schmitz, H. Krainitzki, M. Stoneking and S. Pääbo 1997. Neandertal DNA sequences and the origin of modern humans. *Cell* 90: 19–30.

Kuhn S.L. and M.C. Stiner 1998. Middle Palaeolithic 'creativity': reflections on an oxymoron? In S. Mithen (Ed.), *Creativity in Human Evolution and Prehistory*, pp. 143–164. London: Routledge.

Lev E., M.E. Kislev and O. Bar-Yosef 2005. Mousterian vegetal food in Kebara Cave, Mt. Carmel. *Journal of Archaeological Science* 32: 475–484.

Marean C.W. and S.Y. Kim 1998. Mousterian large mammal remains from Kobeh Cave: behavioral implications for Neanderthals and early modern humans. *Current Anthropology* 39 (Supplement): S79–S113.

McBrearty S. and A.S. Brooks 2000. The revolution that wasn't: a new interpretation of the origin of modern human behavior. *Journal of Human Evolution* 39: 453–563.

Meignen L., O. Bar-Yosef and P. Goldberg 1989. Les structures de combustion moustériennes de la grotte de Kébara (Mont Carmel, Israël). In M. Olive and Y. Taborin (Eds.), *Nature et fonction des foyers préhistoriques* (Mémoires du Musée de Préhistoire d'Ile de France 2), pp. 141–146. Nemours: Association pour la Promotion de la Recherche Archéologique en Ile de France.

Meignen L., S. Beyries, J.D. Speth and O. Bar-Yosef 1998. Acquisition, traitement des matières animales et fonction du site au paléolithique moyen dans la grotte de Kébara (Israël): approche interdisciplinaire. In J.-P. Brugal, L. Meignen and M. Patou-Mathis (Eds.), *Économie préhistorique: les comportements de subsistance au Paléolithique*, pp. 227–24. Sophia Antipolis: Éditions APDCA

Meignen L., O. Bar-Yosef, P. Goldberg and S. Weiner 2001. Le feu au paléolithique moyen: recherches sur les structures de combustion et le statut des foyers. L'exemple du Proche-Orient. *Paléorient* 26: 9–22.

Mellars P.A. 1996. Models for the dispersal of anatomically modern populations across Europe: theoretical and archaeological perspectives. In M. Piperno, O. Bar-Yosef and L.L. Cavalli-Sforza (Eds.), *The Origin of Modern Man*, pp. 225–235. Forli: A.B.A.C.O.

Mellars P.A. 2000. The archaeological records of the Neandertal-modern human transition in France. In O. Bar-Yosef and D. Pilbeam (Eds.), *The Geography of Neandertals and Modern Humans in Europe and the Greater Mediterranean*, pp. 35–47. Cambridge MA: Peabody Museum of Archaeology and Ethnology, Harvard University.

O'Connell J.F. 1987. Alyawara site structure and its archaeological implications. *American Antiquity* 52: 74–108.

Pastó I., E. Allué and J. Vallverdú 2000. Mousterian hearths at Abric Romaní, Catalonia (Spain). In C.B. Stringer, R.N.E. Barton and J.C. Finlayson (Eds.), *Neanderthals on the Edge: Papers from a Conference Marking the 150th Anniversary of the Forbes' Quarry Discovery, Gibraltar*, pp. 59–67. Oxford: Oxbow Books.

Pettitt P.B. 1997. High resolution Neanderthals? Interpreting Middle Palaeolithic intrasite spatial data. *World Archaeology* 29: 208–224.

Pfeiffer J.E. 1982. *The Creative Explosion: an Inquiry into the Origins of Art and Religion.* New York: Harper and Row.

Relethford J.H. 2001. *Genetics and the Search for Modern Human Origins.* New York: John Wiley and Sons.

Schick T. and M. Stekelis 1977. Mousterian assemblages in Kebara Cave, Mount Carmel. In B. Arensburg and O. Bar-Yosef (Eds.), *Moshe Stekelis Memorial Volume* (Eretz-Israel: Archaeological, Historical and Geographical Studies 13), pp. 97–149. Jerusalem: The Israel Exploration Society.

Sokal R.R. and F.J. Rohlf 1969. *Biometry: The Principles and Practice of Statistics in Biological Research.* San Francisco: W.H. Freeman.

Speth J.D. in press. Hunting pressure, subsistence intensification, and demographic change in the Levantine Late Middle Paleolithic. In N. Goren-Inbar and J.D. Speth (Eds.), *Human Paleoecology in the Levantine Corridor.* Oxford: Oxbow Press.

Speth J.D. and E. Tchernov 1998. The role of hunting and scavenging in Neandertal procurement strategies: new evidence from Kebara Cave (Israel). In T. Akazawa, K. Aoki and O. Bar-Yosef (Eds.), *Neandertals and Modern Humans in Western Asia,* pp. 223–239. New York: Plenum Press.

Speth J.D. and E. Tchernov 2001. Neandertal hunting and meat-processing in the Near East: evidence from Kebara Cave (Israel). In C.B. Stanford and H.T. Bunn (Eds.), *Meat Eating and Human Evolution,* pp. 52–72. Oxford: Oxford University Press.

Speth J.D. and E. Tchernov 2002. Middle Paleolithic tortoise use at Kebara Cave (Israel). *Journal of Archaeological Science* 29: 471–483.

Stiner M.C., N.D. Munro and T.A. Surovell 2000. The tortoise and the hare: small game use, the Broad Spectrum Revolution, and Paleolithic demography. *Current Anthropology* 41: 39–73.

Stringer C.B. and R. McKie 1997. *African Exodus: The Origins of Modern Humanity.* London: Pimlico.

Templeton A.R. 1993. The "Eve" hypothesis: a genetic critique and reanalysis. *American Anthropologist* 95: 51–72.

Templeton A.R. 2002. Out of Africa again and again. *Nature* 416: 45–51.

Trinkaus E. and P. Shipman 1993. *The Neandertals: Changing the Image of Mankind.* New York: Alfred A. Knopf.

Valladas H., J.-L. Joron, G. Valladas, B. Arensburg, O. Bar-Yosef, A. Belfer-Cohen, P. Goldberg, H. Laville, L. Meignen, Y. Rak, E. Tchernov, A.-M. Tillier and B. Vandermeersch 1987. Thermoluminescence dates for the Neanderthal burial site at Kebara in Israel. *Nature* 330: 159–160.

Vaquero M., G. Chacón, C. Fernández, F. Martinez and J.M. Rando 2001. Intrasite spatial patterning and transport in the Abric Romani Middle Paleolithic site (Capellades, Barcelona, Spain). In N.J. Conard (Ed.), *Settlement Dynamics of the Middle Paleolithic and Middle Stone Age,* pp. 573–595. Tübingen: Kerns Verlag.

Weiner S., P. Goldberg, and O. Bar-Yosef 1993. Bone preservation in Kebara Cave, Israel using on-site Fourier Transform Infrared Spectrometry. *Journal of Archaeological Science* 20: 613–627.

Wolpoff M.H. and R. Caspari 1996. Why aren't Neandertals modern humans? In M. Piperno, O. Bar-Yosef and L.L. Cavalli-Sforza (Eds.), *The Origin of Modern Man,* pp. 133–156. Forli: A.B.A.C.O.

Wolpoff M.H. and R. Caspari 1997. What does it mean to be modern? In G.A. Clark and C.M. Willermet (Eds.), *Conceptual Issues in Modern Human Origins Research,* pp. 28–44. Hawthorne NY: Aldine de Gruyter.

Wolpoff M.H., J. Hawks and R. Caspari 2000. Multiregional, not multiple origins. *American Journal of Physical Anthropology* 112: 129–136.

Wolpoff M.H., J. Hawks, D.W. Frayer and K. Hunley 2001. Modern human ancestry at the peripheries: a test of the replacement theory. *Science* 291: 293–297.

Wong K. 1999. Is Out of Africa going out the door? *Scientific American* 281(2):13–14.

Zilhão J. 2000 Fate of the Neandertals. *Archaeology* 53: 24–31.

Zilhão J. and F. d'Errico 1999. The chronology and taphonomy of the earliest Aurignacian and its implications for the understanding of Neandertal extinction. *Journal of World Prehistory* 13: 1–68.

Chapter 11

The Middle Paleolithic of the Levant
Recursion and Convergence

John J. Shea

Anthropology Department, Stony Brook University Stony Brook, NY USA 11794-4364

ABSTRACT

Improved geochronology for the Middle Paleolithic Levant reveals a "recursive" trajectory to several important dimensions of archaeological variability. This paper argues these recursions stem from repeated turnovers of Levantine hominin populations. Neandertals and early modern humans appear to have occupied the Levant at different times. Nevertheless, the similar lithic assemblages associated with these humans are seen by many researchers as evidence for cultural contacts and evolutionary continuity. Closer examination suggests they arise from convergence in hominin behavioral evolution, probably in the context of competition for the same ecological niche.

INTRODUCTION

Our ability to infer trajectories of culture change depends heavily on chronology. Improved chronology has dramatically altered our understanding of Middle Paleolithic (MP) biological and cultural evolution in the East Mediterranean Levant (the territory corresponding to the modern states of Lebanon, Syria, Israel, Jordan, and the Sinai Peninsula). From the 1950s to the mid-1980s, when chronological relationships among MP assemblages were inferred primarily from land-sea stratigraphic correlations, biostratigraphy, and the archaeological sequences at "type-sites" such as Tabun Cave, the Levant MP record was seen as furnishing strong fossil evidence for the gradual origin of modern humans out of "progressive" Neandertal ancestors (Howell 1958; Brace 1964; Wolpoff 1980:304–309; Trinkaus 1984). That both Neandertals and early modern humans were associated with very similar "Levalloiso-Mousterian", or alternatively "Levantine Mousterian", assemblages supported the hypothesis of evolutionary continuity between these hominins in this region. Archaeological studies of Levantine MP variability during this time identified changes in settlement patterns and lithic industries that were thought to reflect this evolutionary transition (Binford 1968; Brose and Wolpoff 1970; Jelinek 1982).

During the 1980s–1990s, new Thermoluminescence (TL), Electron Spin Resonance (ESR) and Uranium-series dates reversed the chronological relationship between Levantine Neandertals and early modern humans (Bar-Yosef 1989; for a complete listing of these dates, see Shea 2003a:337–343). The most recent Levantine MP humans are Neandertals dating to between 70,000 and 45,000 BP at Kebara and Amud. These Neandertals were preceded in the Levant between 80,000 and 130,000 years BP by early modern humans from Skhul and Qafzeh. Recent direct dating of the Tabun C1 Neandertal (112 or 143 thousand years BP, depending on the dating model used) points to a still earlier Neandertal presence (Grün and Stringer 2000). Rak *et al.* (2002) report that the Tabun C2 mandible, stratified below Tabun C1 and dating to more than 120,000 to 140,000 years (ESR) or 165,000 years BP (TL), lacks uniquely derived Neandertal morphologies, but other researchers consider its affinities ambiguous (Quam and Smith 1998). The new dates have effectively falsified the longstanding hypothesis of a simple Neandertal-modern human evolutionary transition in the Levant. Several researchers have accommodated these new dates to models of the Levant as a "Contact Zone" in which gene flow occurred between Eurasian Neandertals and African early modern humans (Simmons 1994; Hawks and Wolpoff 2001). Yet, there is thus far no stratigraphic evidence for the prolonged sympatry between Neandertals and modern humans that would be necessary for such gene flow to occur (Bar-Yosef 2000; Shea 2003a). The most parsimonious reading of the dating evidence (the one requiring the least number of assumptions about hypothetical cultural contacts and interbreeding), is that of ecological vicarism, alternating Neandertal and early modern human occupations correlated with patterns of regional climate change (Rak 1993). These developments reinforce the model of Neandertals and modern humans as separate species (Tattersall and Schwartz 1999; Klein 2003; Cooper *et al.* 2004), who, if they interacted at all, did so as competitors for the same ecological niche (Shea 2003b).

The implications of these new dates and reformed models of Neandertal-modern human evolutionary relationships have not yet been fully integrated into models of human cultural evolution during the MP of the Levant. This paper examines the trajectory of behavioral evolution in the Levant during MP times. I argue that the pattern of culture change in the Levant involves two phenomena, recursion and convergence. Recursion is when novel adaptive strategies do not persist in the archaeological record (and see Hovers and Belfer-Cohen this volume). Some of these recursive behaviors, such as blade production and exosomatic symbol use, foreshadow Upper Paleolithic adaptations. Others, such as the bulk production of stone spear points, do not. Convergence is when the adaptive strategies of different entities, in this case Neandertals and early modern humans, grow to resemble one another in response to similar evolutionary forces. Both of these phenomena, recursion and convergence, are distinctive features of the Levantine MP. I argue here that both arise from the same ultimate cause, repeated turnovers of human populations living in the Levant corridor in Late Pleistocene times.

(Author's Note: In the interest of bibliographic brevity, for primary documentation of chronology, paleontology, and lithic evidence, I refer the reader to recently published tabular summaries in Shea [2003a]).

THE LEVANTINE MIDDLE PALEOLITHIC SEQUENCE

The Middle Paleolithic period in the Levant lasted between approximately 250,000 and 45,000 BP, spanning marine Oxygen Isotope Stages (OIS) 7 through early OIS 3. The beginning of this period has been established by TL and ESR dates for Late Lower Paleolithic ("Acheulo-Yabrudian") and early Middle Paleolithic contexts at Tabun, Hayonim, Yabrud, and Qesem Caves, 'Ain Difla, and Rosh Ein Mor (for a recent review of the dating evidence, see Shea 2003a). The "Levantine Mousterian" is the principal MP industrial entity in the Levant. It contrasts with the preceding Acheulo-Yabrudian industry primarily in a broader geographic distribution in the southern Levant, increased use of recurrent Levallois core reduction techniques, and decreased frequencies (indeed absence) of handaxes and steeply retouched scrapers. Jelinek (1982) proposed that the Early MP developed out of the Acheulo-Yabrudian, but subsidence and sediment redeposition in the relevant sections of Tabun Cave call into question the geological underpinnings of this transition scenario (Bar-Yosef 1994:254; Tsatskin 2000).

Levantine MP faunal assemblages preserve evidence for effective hunting of many large woodland-dwelling species, most notably aurochs, red deer, fallow deer, and boar, as well as smaller species and taxa associated with steppe vegetation, including ibex, gazelle, and various equids (horse, onager). Remains of both territorial woodland species and migratory steppe species occur in MP faunal assemblages, suggesting a degree of tactical variability in MP food procurement strategies (see Shea 2003a:351–354). Limited faunal assemblages from Acheulo-Yabrudian contexts make it difficult to tell if this is a novel aspect of MP human adaptation. Comparison with Upper Paleolithic faunal assemblages suggests no major differences in large mammal exploitation (Kaufman 2002). Levantine MP humans did not exploit small game (birds, tortoises, small mammals) to nearly the same extent as Upper Paleolithic humans. This is thought to reflect relatively smaller MP group sizes (Stiner et al. 2000).

The principal MP lithic industry in the Levant is the Levantine Mousterian. Since the mid-1970s the internal cultural variability of the MP period in the Levant

Table 1. Archaeological Chronology for the Levant Late Lower Paleolithic, Middle Paleolithic, and Initial Upper Paleolithic

Period & Dates (Kyr)1	Marine OIS & Levantine Climate	Hominids & Lithic Industries	Representative archaeological contexts
Late Lower Paleolithic 250-350 Kyr	OIS 8-7 Cold, then warmer	*Homo* sp. indet. with Late Acheulean & Acheulo-Yabrudian	Hummal Well Ib Masloukh Bezez Level C Yabrud Shelter 1, Levels 11–25 Zuttiyeh Tabun Units X–XII
Early MP 250-128 Kyr	OIS 7-6 Warm, then colder	*Homo* sp. indet. with Tabun D-type/Phase 1 Levantine Mousterian	Douara Level IV Hummal Well Level 6b? Hayonim Level E Tabun Units II–IX (& lower Unit I?) 'Ain Difla (WHS 634) Rosh Ein Mor (D15)
Middle MP 128-71 Kyr	OIS 5. Initially warm and humid but growing colder, more arid	Neandertals and early modern humans with Tabun C-Type/Phase 2 Levantine Mousterian	Douara Level IIIB Naamé Nahr Ibrahim Tabun Unit I Skhul Level B Qafzeh Units XVII–XXIV
Late MP 71-< 47 Kyr	OIS 4-early 3. Cold and dry.	Neandertals with Tabun B-type/Phase 3 Levantine Mousterian	Umm el Tlel Unit III2a Jerf Ajla Level C Biqat Quneitra Amud Levels B1–B4 Kebara Units VI–XII Tor Faraj Level C Tor Sabiha Level C Far'ah II
Initial UP 47-32 Kyr	Mid-late OIS 3 Cold and dry	Unknown humans with IUP, modern humans with Ahmarian industry.	Üçagizli Locus II, Level H Umm el Tlel Unit III2a-b Ksar Akil Levels XXV–XVI Kebara Units III–VI Boker Tachtit Levels 1–4 Boker A Lagama Sites VII & VIII Abu Noshra Sites I & II

has usually been described in terms of Garrod's stratigraphy of Tabun Cave Levels B-D (Copeland 1975; Meignen 1988; Bar-Yosef 1995). Though it is highly improbable that such a coarse division of the Tabun sequence can serve as a model for the entire region, recent dates for MP contexts tend to support correlations between the major Tabun-based divisions of the Levantine Mousterian and a three-part division of the MP based on patterns of climate change (Shea 2003a:345–348) (See Table 1).

The Early Middle Paleolithic lasted from around 250,000 to 128,000 years BP (OIS 7-6). Marine sediments and pollen evidence from the East Mediterranean and Jordan Valley indicate a shift from warm humid conditions supporting extensive temperate *Quercus-Pistachia* woodlands in OIS 7 to cold dry conditions and increased *Artemisia* steppe-desert vegetation during OIS 6 (Horowitz 1987; Cheddadi and Rossignol-Strick 1995). The Early MP witnessed the extinction of several archaic Middle Pleistocene rodent species and an infusion of African fauna (Tchernov 1998). Early MP (Levantine Mousterian "Tabun D-Type" or "Phase 1") assemblages include Tabun Units II–IX (Garrod's layer D), Rosh Ein Mor, Hayonim Level E, and 'Ain Difla (WHS 634). These assemblages feature products of recurrent unidirectional-parallel and bidirectional-opposed Levallois core reduction. Many of these reduction by-products are elongated flakes and blades. "Upper Paleolithic" tool types such as endscrapers, burins, backed knives, and perforators are common. No human fossils of diagnosable morphology are associated with Early MP assemblages.

The Middle MP lasted between about 128,000 to 71,000 thousand years BP, roughly conterminously with OIS 5 or the Last Interglacial *sensu lato*. This period witnessed an abrupt increase in temperatures and humidity during the Last Interglacial (OIS 5e, 128,000–115,000 years BP) followed by a general cooling trend punctuated by wide alternations between cold dry and warm humid conditions. The overall impact of these changes was a reduction in woodland vegetation cover in favor of steppe-desert. "Tabun C-Type" or "Phase 2" Levantine Mousterian assemblages dating to this period include Tabun Unit I (Garrod's layer C), Skhul Level B, the beach deposits at Naamé, Nahr Ibrahim, and Qafzeh Units XVII–XXIV. The MP levels of Ras el-Kelb, Lebanon, are also assigned to this period on stratigraphic grounds. Centripetal methods dominate Levallois core reduction in Middle MP assemblages. Flakes are typically more common than either points or blades. Retouched tools include numerous sidescrapers on large oval flakes. Both Neandertals and early modern humans appear to have been in the Levant during this period, though Neandertal fossils are restricted to the uppermost surfaces of Tabun layer C. Some researchers, including the original excavator (Garrod 1937: 64) consider these Neandertal remains intrusive from Tabun layer B (Bar-Yosef and Callendar 1999). The Middle MP ends around 71,000 years BP with the rapid transition between nearly full-interglacial conditions during OIS 5a and the onset of Main Würm Stadial (OIS 4).

The Later MP spans the period 71,000–47,000 years BP. Following the rapid establishment of cold dry conditions during OIS 4, the climate of the Levant varied widely between cooler and warmer conditions. Steppe-desert conditions predominated throughout the Levant, but decreased evaporation resulted in the formation of large lakes in the Jordan Valley, on the Golan Heights, in Syria and in Jordan. Archaeological contexts dating to this period include Kebara Units VII–XII, Amud Level B, Tor Faraj Level C, Biqat Quneitra, and Umm El Tlel Unit IIIA. Levantine Mousterian "Tabun B-Type" or "Phase 3" lithic assemblages from these contexts typically feature high percentages unidirectional-convergent core-reduction strategies. Many assemblages reflect bulk production of both large and small isosceles Levallois points. Only Neandertal fossils have been found in association with Late MP assemblages.

Initial Upper Paleolithic (IUP) assemblages appear in the Levant *ca.* 47,000–40,0000 years BP. This period witnessed a short, but profound increase in aridity, registered by a drop in level of Lake Lisan (the Pleistocene precursor to the Dead Sea) to −350 m below sea level (Bartov *et al.* 2002; Haase-Schramm *et al.* 2004). Examples of IUP assemblages include Üçagizli Cave Levels F-H, Umm el Tlel Units III2a-b, Ksar Akil Levels XXV–XVI, Kebara Units III–VI, Boker Tachtit Levels 1–4, and Tor Sadaf Levels A-B (Marks 1983; Azoury 1986; Bar-Yosef 2000; Fox and Coinman 2004; Kuhn *et al.* 2004). There are numerous typological continuities between IUP and Late MP assemblages, most notably in the production of Emireh points (Levallois points and blades with basal retouch) and *chanfrein* endscrapers (flakes and blades retouched distally by an oblique or "tranchet" flake removal). The main technological difference between IUP and Late MP assemblages is decreased use of Levallois techniques and increased use of prismatic blade core technology. No human fossils are associated with IUP assemblages, however, *Homo sapiens* fossils are associated with Early Upper Paleolithic "Ahmarian" assemblages at Qafzeh Cave and Ksar Akil Level XVII (Ronen and Vandermeersch 1972:201; Bergman and Stringer 1989:106; Gilead 1991:191).

RECURSIVE BEHAVIORAL CHANGE IN THE LEVANT MP

What is the trajectory of human behavioral evolution during the MP in the Levant? The answer to this question depends on the particular behaviors that comprise one's definition of behavioral modernity (Henshilwood and Marean 2003) and the degree to which one accepts rare instances of a particular behavior as indicating a general pattern of adaptation. One of the advantages of improved chronology for the MP Levant is that it allows us to examine change and variability in evidence for particular components of "behavioral modernity." This paper examines two of the most commonly cited attributes of "behavioral modernity", blade production and exosomatic symbol use. It also examines stone spear point production, a behavior that is thought to link Later MP assemblages to the IUP. In each of these behaviors, there is neither a steady increase in frequency nor is there a steady state without apparent change. Rather, each follows a recursive trajectory, an increase followed by a decrease, without clear evidence of continuity in subsequent periods.

Blade Technology

The value attached to blade technology in modern human origins research almost certainly reflects the historical priority of Paleolithic research in Europe, where consistent evidence for blade production and modern human fossils appeared together in the early Upper Paleolithic. We now know that blade production occurred episodically in Europe, Africa, and the Levant from mid-Middle Pleistocene times onward (Bar-Yosef and Kuhn 1999). Unlike such earlier blade technologies, blades from Levantine Mousterian contexts are typically large, generally cortex-free, and feature carefully prepared striking platforms (Wiseman 1993; Monigal 2001). Systematic blade production of the kind seen in the MP Levant also has a significant energetic payoff in terms of both increased morphological consistency among debitage products and, theoretically, increased cutting edge recovery (Leroi-Gourhan 1993:134–137; Whittaker 1994:119–231). This sort of blade production speaks to a greater degree of planning depth and technical skill than any of the other core reduction strategies in use among Late Middle Pleistocene hominins. If there was a trend towards more complex tool making strategies through the course of the MP in the Levant, it ought to be reflected in increased blade production.

As monitored by laminar indices (Ilam, see Table 2) blade production peaks among Early MP assemblages, declines in the Middle MP, then rebounds among some Late MP assemblages (see also Hovers 1998:155; Monigal 2001:15). This pattern can be seen through the Tabun sequence, the one site with assemblages representing Early, Middle and Late MP. However, it should be noted, that Ilam values for Tabun are consistently higher (by two or more standard deviations) than the mean for assemblages of the same MP period. Furthermore, some Later MP assemblages, such as Kebara and Amud, exhibit essentially opposite trends in blade production. Blades increase through time at Amud and decrease through time at Kebara (Hovers 1998:155). Blade production increases across the Middle-to-Upper Paleolithic transition in the Levant, but the particular methods of blade production seen in IUP and early Upper Paleolithic "Ahmarian" assemblages differ from those predominating in Late MP contexts (Monigal 2001). Instead, they have their strongest affinities with blade production techniques seen in Early MP (*e.g.*, Rosh Ein Mor), more than 100,000 years earlier (Marks and Monigal 1995).

Exosomatic Symbols

The use of exosomatic symbols, colorants, personal adornment, mortuary structures, and the like are behavioral universals among recent humans. While there are some sporadic hints of a symbolic capacity among Neandertals (d'Errico 2003), the earliest clear and convincing evidence for exosomatic symbolic behavior appears in contexts associated with African early modern humans (McBrearty and Brooks 2000; Henshilwood *et al.* 2004;). After 40,000 to 50,000 years BP, evidence for such symbolic behavior tracks the global dispersal of *Homo sapiens* (Klein and Edgar 2002). If there was either a steady increase or a sudden revolution in modern humans' symbolic capacity, it should be reflected in the chronological distribution of exosomatic symbols through the MP Levant (Table 3).

The Early MP has, thus far, no claimed evidence for exosomatic symbolic behavior. In contrast, Middle MP contexts feature several different indications of exosomatic symbol use, including incised patterns on stone tools, transport

Table 2. Laminar Indices and Percentages of Points among Levallois products for Middle
Paleolithic assemblages by period

Assemblage (Site & Level)	I Lam	%LP	Source
Early MP			
Tabun Unit IX	76	34	Jelinek (1982)
Rosh Ein Mor	20	33	Crew (1976)
Ksar Akil XXVIIIA	24	44	Marks and Volkman (1986)
Ksar Akil XXVIIIB	28	41	Marks and Volkman (1986)
WHS 634/'Ain Difla	42	17	Lindly and Clark (1987)
Bezez B Unit M150	20	17	Copeland (1983)
Bezez B Unit M151	30	28	Copeland (1983)
Bezez B Unit V200	33	24	Copeland (1983)
Bezez B Unit D44/G44	31	26	Copeland (1983)
Nahal Aqev/D35 Level 3	25	41	Munday (1976)
Middle MP			
Tabun Unit I, Beds 18–26	36	8	Jelinek (1982)
Ksar Akil Level XXVIA	24	0	Marks and Volkman (1986)
Ksar Akil Level XXVIB	20	7	Marks and Volkman (1986)
Ksar Akil Level XXVIIA	25	0	Marks and Volkman (1986)
Ksar Akil Level XXVIIB	26	19	Marks and Volkman (1986)
Qafzeh Unit XIX	8	1	Hovers (1997)
Qafzeh Unit XVII	11	2	Hovers (1997)
Qafzeh Unit XV	17	15	Hovers (1997)
Ras el-Kelb Rail Level D	21	3	Copeland (1998)
Ras el-Kelb Rail Level C	10	3	Copeland (1998)
Ras el-Kelb Rail Level B	18	2	Copeland (1998)
Ras el-Kelb Tunnel Level O)	9	5	Copeland (1998)
Ras el-Kelb Tunnel Level N	13	0	Copeland (1998)
Ras el-Kelb Tunnel Level M	7	3	Copeland (1998)
Ras el-Kelb Tunnel Level L	11	1	Copeland (1998)
Ras el-Kelb Tunnel Level K	5	1	Copeland (1998)
Ras el-Kelb Tunnel Level J	6	0	Copeland (1998)
Naamé Upper Level	3	4	Fleisch (1970) and Copeland (1998)
Naamé Lower Level	4	6	Fleisch (1970) and Copeland (1998)
Late MP			
Tabun Unit I, Beds 1–17	64	28	Jelinek (1982)
Kebara Unit VII	12	7	Meignen and Bar-Yosef (1989)
Kebara Unit VIII	11	5	Meignen and Bar-Yosef (1989)
Kebara Unit IX	10	14	Meignen and Bar-Yosef (1989)
Kebara Unit X	13	18	Meignen and Bar-Yosef (1989)
Kebara Unit XI	20	8	Meignen and Bar-Yosef (1989)
Kebara Unit XII	23	11	Meignen and Bar-Yosef (1989)
Keoue Unit I	26	26	Nishiaki and Copeland (1992)
Keoue Unit II	21	31	Nishiaki and Copeland (1992)
Keoue Unit III	27	32	Nishiaki and Copeland (1992)
Tor Sabiha Level C	37	37	Henry (1995)
Tor Faraj Level C	17	62	Henry (1995)
Amud Level B1	32*	8	Hovers (1998)
Amud Level B2	22	34	Hovers (1998)
Amud Level B4	10	38	Hovers (1998)

*I Lam values for Amud B1 estimated from Hovers 1998, Figure 7.

Table 3. Levantine Middle Paleolithic Symbolic behavior by periods

Context	Description	Interpretation	Source
Middle MP			
Qafzeh XVII	Core fragment with repetitive linear markings.	Unknown	Hovers (1997)
Ras el-Kelb Tunnel Trench Level F	Flint flake with linear incisions on the dorsal surface.	Unknown	Moloney (1998)
Qafzeh XVII	Incised blocky fragment of red ochre, numerous ochre pellets, ochre-stained stone tools.	Color symbolism	Vandermeersch (1966), Hovers *et al.* (2003)
Qafzeh XXI–XXIV	Shells of the marine mollusc, *Glycymeris*.	Personal adornment? Pigment use, long-distance (>30) transport of non-utilitarian objects.	(Taborin 2003)
Qafzeh XVII	Antlers and frontal bone of a fallow deer clasped to the upper chest of Qafzeh 11.	Mortuary ritual	Vandermeersch (1970)
Qafzeh IX	Double burial of a child (Qafzeh 10) and a young adult female (Qafzeh 9).	Mortuary ritual	Vandermeersch (1981)
Skhul B	Boar mandible under left forearm of Skhul 5.	Mortuary ritual	McCown (1937:100)
Skhul B	Mollusc shells	Transport of non-utilitarian objects?	(Bate 1937: 224–225)
Nahr Ibrahim	Fallow deer skeleton with red ochre	Unknown/Mortuary ritual?	(Solecki 1975: 290)
Tabun B/C	Adult female Neandertal (C1) accompanied by an unrecovered neonate.	Mortuary ritual	Garrod (1937)
Late MP			
Biqat Quneitra	Tabular flint block with concentric elliptical incised marks.	Unknown	Marshack (1996)
Amud B	Red deer maxilla on the pelvis of Amud 7.	Mortuary ritual	Hovers *et al.* (1995)
Dederiyeh 11	Infant skeleton accompanied by limestone slab, flint flake.	Mortuary ritual?	Akazawa, *et al.* (1995)
Kebara XII	Cranium of Kebara 2 removed after burial.	Mortuary ritual?	Bar-Yosef and Vandermeersch (1991)

of nonutilitarian objects (possibly for personal adornment), collection and use of mineral pigments, and mortuary ritual (Shea 2003a:359). Artifacts with repetitive linear markings have been reported from Qafzeh Unit XVII and Ras el-Kelb Tunnel Trench Level F (Hovers *et al.* 1997; Moloney 1998). Shells of the marine molluscs found more than 30 km inland at Qafzeh is evidence for the long-distance transport of nonutilitarian objects (Taborin 2003). Numerous fragments of red ochre from Qafzeh gathered from diverse geological sources also point to color symbolism (Hovers *et al.* 2003). This conclusion is reinforced by identifications of ochre and manganese oxide traces on two of the Qafzeh shells (Walter 2003). Skhul Level B also preserves shells of several mollusc species (Bate 1937:224–225) that are considered unlikely to have been transported for food (Daniella Bar-Yosef Meyer, personal communication 7/12/04).

Perhaps the clearest evidence for Middle MP symbolic behavior, however, are human burials, largely complete skeletons preserved in anatomical articulation (Skhul 1, 4, 5, and 9, Qafzeh 8–11, 13, and 15 and Tabun C1)(Garrod 1937; McCown 1937; Vandermeersch 1981). Two of these (Qafzeh 9 & 10) appear to have been a double burial. Two others were buried with foreign objects clasped to their chests, a red deer antler with Qafzeh 11 and a boar mandible with Skhul 5. There is even a report of a fallow deer skeleton accompanied by red ochre from Nahr Ibrahim Cave (Solecki 1970).

Evidence for symbolic behavior decreases in the Late MP, even though the number of recently excavated Late MP contexts vastly outnumbers those of Middle MP ones. A single flint fragment with concentric markings is reported from the Biqat Quneitra open-air site (Goren-Inbar 1990:238; Marshack 1996). Three Late MP burials, in themselves indications for symbolic behavior, possibly show evidence of mortuary ritual, but each is problematical. The cranium of Kebara 2 was removed several months after its death, but it is unclear if this activity was symbolic, as what was done with it next remains unknown. A complete red deer maxilla on the pelvis of Amud 7 is the only claimed instance of Late MP mortuary furniture (Rak *et al.* 1994). Though red deer complete anatomical elements are not common, fragmentary red deer remains do occur in the same level as Amud 7 (Rabinovich and Hovers 2004:292), and thus the possibility of a fortuitous non-symbolic juxtapositioning cannot be ruled out (see detailed discussion in Gargett 1999, 2000; Hovers *et al.* 2000). Similarly, the Dederiyeh 1 child's skeleton is associated with a limestone slab (near its head) and a triangular flake (on its abdomen), but both limestone slabs and triangular flakes are common components of the archaeological "background" at this site (Akazawa *et al.* 1995). In this respect, the burials of the Later MP have rather more in common with the ambiguous mortuary structures seen with European Neandertals (Gargett 1989) than they do with their immediate precursors in the Levant. Burials with grave goods, perforated shells, and red ochre do not again become common components of the Levantine archaeological record until Upper Paleolithic and Epipaleolithic times (D. Bar-Yosef 1989; Belfer-Cohen and Hovers 1992; Bar-Yosef 1997; Kuhn *et al.* 2001), long after the extinction of Levantine Neandertal populations (Hovers *et al.* 2003).

Spear Point Production

Systematic use of hafted weapon armatures is among the emergent features of modern behavior seen in the African Middle Stone Age (McBrearty and Brooks 2000:496–497; Brooks *et al.* this volume). Hafting in general, and hafted points in particular, are rare in European MP contexts (Mellars 1996:116–117). A link between Levallois point/triangular flake production and the use of hafted stone spear points in the MP Levant is supported by microwear analysis, an ecogeographically-patterned distribution, and morphometric comparisons with experimental tools, and a point fragment embedded in an equid vertebra all point to (Shea 1988, 1998; Boëda *et al.* 1999; Shea *et al.* 2001). Although Meignen (1995) cites the systematic production of subtriangular flakes by unidirectional convergent methods as a main characteristic of the Levantine Mousterian, this method of point production is not distributed evenly through time. Bulk production of triangular flakes is vastly more common among Early and Late MP assemblages than in Middle MP assemblages (see Table 2).

Levantine Initial and Early Upper Paleolithic contexts feature many pointed stone artifacts that are thought to have been hafted weapon armatures (Bergman 1981; Bergman and Newcomer 1983), and it could be argued that these represent a development out of Late MP technological strategies. Emireh points, for example, are made on Levallois points in Later MP contexts and on blades in Initial Upper Paleolithic contexts. However, even a cursory examination of such Initial and Early Upper Paleolithic points reveals telling morphometric and functional differences. Upper Paleolithic stone points are significantly narrower and thinner in cross-sectional area than their MP precursors (Shea 2003a:370). They are also more extensively retouched and retouched in different ways (*i.e.*, backed) than MP points. These differences suggest that Upper Paleolithic stone points were true projectile points while most MP points were designed for use with close-quarters weapons (*i.e.*, thrusting spears or hand-cast spears). There is no necessary reason to see this projectile technology as an indigenous development out of the Late MP. It may just as well reflect the immigration of human populations from a region in which projectile technology has a much greater antiquity, such as Africa.

In terms of each of the behaviors examined, the pattern of cultural change in the Levantine MP is "recursive." Blade production, exosomatic symbol use, and spear point production appear, flourish, then either disappear or decline markedly in frequency during subsequent periods. These and other elements of behavioral modernity really only begin to appear consistently in the Levant only after the onset of the Initial Upper Paleolithic, ca. 40,000–47,000 years BP.

These "recursions" might reflect changes in the costs and benefits attending particular behavioral strategies of a stable Levantine human population. However, the new chronology for human fossils in the Levant suggests an alternative explanation–changes in the hominin populations occupying the region. Neandertals and early modern humans originated on different continents, in different habitats. It seems reasonable to expect that there would have been differences in the ways that each of them adapted to the Levant.

"EVERYBODY LOSES": A DISCONTINUITY HYPOTHESIS

In order to understand the course of MP culture change in this region, we need to understand the ecogeographic forces shaping its biological community. Throughout the Pleistocene, the Levant was a biogeographic corridor linking Eurasia and Africa. The North-South alignment of the Levant's principal topographic features, the Jordan Rift Valley and the Anti-Lebanon Mountains, facilitated dispersals of mammal species from Western Asia and North Africa into the Levant (Tchernov 1992). Neandertals and early *Homo sapiens* appear in the fossil records of western Eurasia and northeastern Africa, respectively, in late Middle Pleistocene times, *ca.* 250,000–130,000 years BP (Klein 1999). As global climate changes periodically expanded fertile oak-terebinth woodlands out of their refugia along the East Mediterranean coast and upslope into the formerly steppe-desert interior (Cheddadi and Rossignol-Strick 1995), Eurasian Neandertal and African human populations would have been drawn into the Levant.

Although the Levant's corridor-like structure encouraged dispersal, it may also have been a particularly inimical place for long-term stability in human populations. The Levant is a small region circumscribed to the north by mountains, to the west by the Mediterranean Sea, and to the south and east by the Arabian Desert. Geographic circumscription increases the risks of extinction to small populations of large mammals with slow reproductive rates (Gilpin and Soulé 1986), characteristics that almost certainly describe all hominin populations. These risks would have increased during periods of rapid climate change, increasing aridity, and declining temperatures during Marine OIS 5-3 (Lister 1997; Finlayson 2004). There were many rapid climate shifts in the Levant during Late Pleistocene times. It is interesting, perhaps telling, that several of these, the OIS 6-5e deglaciation (*ca.* 128,000 years BP), the rapid onset of glacial conditions in OIS 5a-4 (*ca.* 71,000 years BP) and an episode of hyper-aridity at *ca.* 40,000–47,000 years BP, all mark major changes in the character of MP archaeological assemblages.

The stability of a large mammal population in a particular region is in large part a function of population size. A rough estimate of Levantine MP population size can be constructed using data on recent human hunter-gatherer population densities (Kelly 1995:224–225) and the known distribution of MP sites. Hunter-gatherers living in temperate woodland habitats comparable to those associated with most Levantine MP sites do so at population densities ranging between 1–38 people per 100 km^2, with a median value of 7. Projecting this median population density value onto a 120,000 km^2 polygon enclosing all known MP sites in Lebanon, Syria, Jordan and Israel yields a population estimate of 8400 people. This number almost certainly over estimates actual MP population. Only the Early MP appears to have coincided with widespread temperate woodland. For much of the Middle and Late MP (from OIS 5d-3, 115,000–45,000 years BP) the region was dominated by steppe and desert vegetation (Cheddadi and Rossignol-Strick 1995). The range of population densities for hunter-gatherers living in temperate deserts ranges less widely, 1–19 people per 100 km^2, with a median value of 4.75. Projecting this figure onto the MP Levant polygon yields a population of only 5700 people; yet, even this may be an overestimate.

Faunal assemblages from contexts associated with Neandertals and early modern humans consistently point to these populations as having been less effective at collecting smaller game than recent human hunter-gatherers (Stiner *et al.* 1999; Klein *et al.* 2004). Such limited foraging efficiency would have further reduced population densities. If we use the lowest population density figures for recent human hunter-gatherers living in temperate woodlands and temperate deserts (1.0 in both cases), the projected Levantine MP human population at any one point in time would be only 1200 people. By any standard, these figures suggest that Levantine MP humans' risks of encountering minimum viable population thresholds were much greater than those of MP humans living in less-circumscribed regions to the north and south of the Levant.

Although we archaeologists often infer continuity between MP contexts widely separated in time and space, we must also be aware that there are circumstances that make discontinuity more likely than continuity. In such a small region as the Levant, geographic circumscription combined with rapid climate change and increased aridity through much of the early Upper Pleistocene, probably kept MP humans close to the verge of extinction. When these populations became extinct, the success of subsequent attempts to recolonize the Levant would have depended in large part on the nature of the environment at the time. Colder conditions would have favored cold-tolerant Neandertals; warmer conditions would have favored Africans (Figure 1). There undoubtedly were times when both Neandertals and modern humans were both present in the Levant, but these periods were probably brief and marked by intense competition for the same ecological niche (Shea 2003b). This is an admittedly grim scenario, a "nobody wins" model

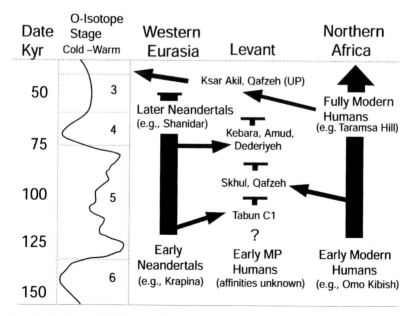

Figure 1. Middle Paleolithic population movement and relationships in the Levant and adjacent regions.

for the Levantine MP cultural sequence, but it is more realistic, better-grounded in general ecological principles, and more consistent with the facts than alternative models of Levantine MP cultural evolution.

ARCHAEOLOGICAL EVIDENCE FOR CONVERGENT BEHAVIORAL EVOLUTION

The hypothesis of discontinuity between Neandertals and early modern humans in the Levant is also consistent with ever-growing body of evidence indicating they were separate species (Tattersall and Schwartz 1999; Klein 2003; Cooper *et al.* 2004). Comparisons between Neandertal DNA and DNA of both European Upper Paleolithic and recent humans show no evidence of interbreeding or any particularly close relationship between Neandertals and living western Eurasian human populations (Caramelli *et al.* 2003). These same DNA comparisons suggest that Neandertals' and early modern humans' last common ancestor lived 300,000–500,000 years ago, long before either of its descendants appeared in the Levant. The body shapes of Levantine Neandertals and the Skhul/Qafzeh humans suggest origins in differing temperature regimes (Holliday 2000). Craniofacial differences between Neandertals and modern humans are comparable in scale to those between different living primate species (Harvati *et al.* 2004). It is not as easy to distinguish Southwest Asian Neandertals and the Skhul/Qafzeh humans from each other as it is to distinguish between European Neandertals and Upper Paleolithic humans (Hawks and Wolpoff 2001), but this may reflect the greater closeness of the Skhul/Qafzeh humans to their and the Neandertals' last common ancestor (Pearson 2000), as well as the relatively small number of well-preserved Levantine human fossils.

The principal argument against seeing extinction and turnover in hominin populations as the principal mechanism underlying Levantine MP cultural evolution is that similarities in the lithic assemblages associated with Neandertals and early modern humans suggest cultural continuity, and by implication evolutionary continuity, among the Neandertals and early modern humans associated with them (Jelinek 1982:99; Wolpoff 1989:136; Clark 1992:194; Hawks and Wolpoff 2001:42; Kaufman 2001).

Middle MP assemblages associated with the Skhul/Qafzeh humans and the Late MP assemblages associated with Levantine Neandertals are similar to one another, both technologically and typologically. They have a similar range of core reduction techniques, similar inventories of artifact types, and overlapping values for major technological and typological indices (Shea 2003a:333–335). These similarities have led some researchers to combine them into a single highly variable "Later Levantine Mousterian" industry (Ronen 1979:303; Jelinek 1982; Clark and Lindly 1989:973; Marks 1992:133; Hovers 1998:156). Other researchers point to differences in relative frequencies of tools and core reduction techniques (*chaînes opératoires*) to support making a distinction between them (Meignen 1998:686; Kaufman 1999:32–33; Bar-Yosef 2000:116). Regardless of what position one takes on this taxonomic issue, the central question is whether similarities among these assemblages are sufficient to infer cultural continuity among the hominins stratigraphically associated with them. I argue that this is not the case, and that an alternative mechanism, behavioral convergence, is a better explanation for these similarities.

Most retouched tools from Middle and Late MP assemblages are simple flakes or blades with minimal modification. In the author's experience, a competent modern human flintknapper equipped with the proper raw materials can replicate any of these artifacts in a minute or less. Such simplicity carries with it a high likelihood of convergence, of different hominin populations producing similar tools in response to similar technological challenges. Not surprisingly, artifacts morphologically identical to those found in the Middle and Late MP of the Levant can be found in countless Eurasian MP and African Middle Stone Age (MSA) assemblages. This broad distribution suggests that these tools were products of cognitive and manual skills that were evolutionarily primitive among Middle Pleistocene *Homo* (Wynn 1989). Neandertals and early modern humans had similar metabolic needs (Sorenson and Leonard 2001) and they seem to have met them with similar energetic costs, at least as registered by skeletal indices (Lieberman 1998). It is not surprising that they responded with similar technological strategies when faced with similar terrain, raw material availability, and prey species. Thus viewed, Neandertals' and early modern humans' similar lithic archaeological associations in the Levant can be recognized as by-products of convergent behavioral evolution. To see them as evidence for contact and cultural exchange requires one to assume contemporaneity between these hominins that is not supported by the chronological and stratigraphic evidence.

Further evidence against accepting similarities among Middle and Late MP assemblages as evidence for Neandertal-modern human cultural continuity can be found in detailed studies of variability in core reduction techniques. There are many equally-effective ways to produce the various flakes, blades, and points that served as blanks for Levantine MP tools (Shea 2001:44). It would be a strong argument against the "discontinuity" model proposed here if separate Neandertal and early modern human populations chose precisely the same sets of core reduction techniques. Given the limited number of ways that there are to align flake scars across the surface of a Levallois core, there are, predictably, overlaps in the ranges of core preparation techniques seen in all Middle and Late MP assemblages. However, there are important differences in modalities between Middle and Late MP assemblages (Meignen 1998). By-products of radial/centripetal Levallois core reduction dominate Middle MP assemblages associated with early modern humans in Qafzeh Units XVII–XXIV (Boutié 1989:219). Late MP assemblages associated with Neandertals at Kebara and Amud are dominated by convergent and bipolar Levallois techniques (Meignen and Bar-Yosef 1992; Hovers 1998:148). (Comparisons involving the Skhul Level B and Tabun Level C assemblages are complicated by much of these assemblages having been discarded in the field, by the remainder having been dispersed to over a dozen different institutions, and by the possibly intrusive status of the Tabun C1 burial.) If the choice among functionally equivalent core-reduction techniques arises from patterns of learned, socially transmitted "traditions" (Meignen and Bar-Yosef 1988:88; Hovers 1997), then these technological differences suggest Levantine Neandertals and early modern humans maintained different lithic technological traditions. Such differences support the discontinuity hypothesis.

Many of the same criticisms leveled here against the assumption of continuity in the MP can also be applied to the Middle-to-Upper Paleolithic transition. It is frequently assumed that IUP populations were modern humans, but no hominin fossils are thus far associated with IUP assemblages. Indeed, the immediate precursors of the IUP in much of the region appear to have been Neandertals. The situation as it stands raises several interesting questions. If the ancestors of the Levant's Upper Paleolithic modern human populations were present in the Levant during Late MP times, why are they archaeologically invisible? Could it be that Late MP Neandertal populations experienced their own Middle-to-Upper Paleolithic transition in the Levant in much the same way as their European counterparts appear to have done in Europe (d'Errico 2003)? Might there be more than one hominin species undergoing such a transition to Upper Paleolithic adaptations in the Levant at the same time? Do the Levant's Upper Paleolithic human populations reflect a later dispersal following an extinction of Late MP Neandertals, in a manner similar to that proposed for Iberia (Finlayson 2004)? Alternatively, does the IUP represent modern humans having finally developed effective strategies for outcompeting Neandertals for the "human niche" in the Levant (Shea 2003b)? These questions can only be answered by further archaeological fieldwork and improvements in geochronology.

CONCLUSION

Most of our explanations for the long sweep of Paleolithic prehistory are optimistic ones. We interpret incremental changes in successive industries as evidence for cultural and biological continuity. Most, if not all, trajectories of culture change lead to modern humans and our global ecological dominion. Non-ancestral hominins are portrayed as static "bench-warmers" in the grand narrative of human evolution (Landau 1991). The contrast with models of biological evolution could hardly be starker. There, continuity is the exception, not the rule. Most species we know from the fossil record are extinct. Only a fraction of species extant today will likely have descendants 100,000 years from now. There is no question that we have ancestors who lived in Middle Paleolithic times, but estimating whether these ancestors were among those humans who lived in a particular part of the world requires us to make a clear-eyed assessment of the likelihood of their long-term success. Humans have no exemption from extinction, and some parts of the Pleistocene world were more likely than others to create evolutionary "dead ends." The Levant is one such region.

The East Mediterranean Levant is a tough neighborhood. It must have been tougher still during the MP, when rival human species competed there for the same human niche. During humid periods like the Early MP, the Levant was a corridor linking Africa and Eurasia. During periods of aridity and desert growth, such as the Middle and Late MP, it was a barrier. African populations who dispersed into the Levant during humid periods probably became trapped there during arid periods, and dwindled to extinction. Neandertals who moved into the region during cooler periods, probably met a similar fate, isolation followed by extinction. The human fossil and archaeological record of the Levant provides no support for a gradual indigenous transition to modern human adaptations. Rather, what we see is a recursive pattern, one that reflects cyclical human dispersals into the Levant driven by the wide swings of the Pleistocene climatic pendulum. Neandertals appear to have displaced early modern humans at least once in the Levant, after 71,000 years ago. It was not until after 40,000 years ago, more than 200,000 years after the beginning of the MP, that *Homo sapiens* populations broke this evolutionary stalemate, dispersing north into western Eurasia. Their success in this dispersal may owe much to the rigors they faced in successfully transiting the Levant biogeographic corridor.

ACKNOWLEDGEMENTS

I thank Steve L. Kuhn and Erella Hovers for their editorial suggestions. The ideas in this paper germinated in the course of discussions with many researchers, most notably Ofer Bar-Yosef, Eitan Tchernov, Dan Lieberman, and Dan Kaufman. I alone am responsible for the opinions expressed here.

REFERENCES CITED

Akazawa T., S. Muhesen, Y. Dodo, O. Kondo, Y. Mizoguchi, Y. Abe, Y. Nishiaki, S. Ohta, T. Oguchi and J. Haydal 1995. Neanderthal infant burial from the Dederiyeh Cave in Syria. *Paléorient* 21: 77–86.

Azoury I. 1986. *Ksar Akil, Lebanon. A Technological and Typological Analysis of the Transitional and Early Upper Paleolithic Levels at Ksar Akil and Abu Halka* (BAR international Series 289). Oxford: BAR.

Bar-Yosef D.E. 1989. Late Paleolithic and Neolithic marine shells as cultural markers. In *Proceedings of the 1986 Shell Bead Conference,* pp. 169–174. Rochester NY: Rochester Museum and Science Center.

Bar-Yosef O. 1989. Geochronology of the Levantine Middle Paleolithic. In P.A. Mellars and C.B. Stringer (Eds.), *The Human Revolution,* pp. 589–610. Edinburgh: Edinburgh University Press.

Bar-Yosef O. 1994. The Lower Paleolithic of the Near East. *Journal of World Prehistory* 8: 211–265.

Bar-Yosef O. 1995. The origins of modern humans. In T.E. Levy (Ed.), *Archaeology of Society in the Holy Land,* pp. 110–123. New York: Facts on File.

Bar-Yosef O. 1997. Symbolic expressions in later prehistory of the Levant: why are they so few? In M. Conkey, O. Soffer, D. Stratmann and N. Jablonski (Eds.), *Beyond Art: Pleistocene Image and Symbol* (Publication No. 23 of the California Academy of Science), pp. 161–187. San Francisco: California Academy of Sciences.

Bar-Yosef O. 2000. The Middle and Early Upper Paleolithic in Southwest Asia and neighboring regions. In O. Bar-Yosef and D. Pilbeam (Eds.), *The Geography of Neandertals and Modern Humans in Europe and the Greater Mediterranean,* pp. 107–156. Cambridge MA: Peabody Museum of Archaeology and Ethnology, Harvard Univesity.

Bar-Yosef O. and J. Callendar 1999. The woman from Tabun: Garrod's doubts in historical perspective. *Journal of Human Evolution* 37: 879–885.

Bar-Yosef O. and S.L. Kuhn 1999. The big deal about blades: laminar technologies and human evolution. *American Anthropologist* 101: 322–338.

Bar-Yosef O. and B. Vandermeersch (Eds.) 1991. *Le Squelette moustérien de Kébara 2, Mt. Carmel, Israël.* Paris: Editions du CNRS.

Bartov Y., M. Stein, Y. Enzel, A. Agnon and Z. Reches 2002. Lake levels and sequence stratigraphy of Lake Lisan, the Late Pleistocene precursor of the Dead Sea. *Quaternary Research* 57: 9–21.

Bate D.M.A. 1937. Part II – Palaeontology: The fossil fauna of the Wady el-Mughara Caves. In D.A.E. Garrod and D.M.A. Bate (Eds.), *The Stone Age of Mount Carmel, Vol. 1: Excavations in the Wady el-Mughara*, pp. 136–233. Oxford: Clarendon.

Belfer-Cohen A. and E. Hovers 1992. In the eye of the beholder: Mousterian and Natufian burials in the Levant. *Current Anthropology* 33: 463–471.

Bergman C.A. 1981. Point types in the Upper Palaeolithic sequence at Ksar Akil, Lebanon. In J. Cauvin and P. Sanlaville (Eds.), *Préhistoire du Levant*, pp. 319–330. Paris: C.N.R.S.

Bergman C. and M.H. Newcomer 1983. Flint arrowhead breakage: examples from Ksar Akil, Lebanon. *Journal of Field Archaeology* 10: 238–243.

Bergman C.A. and C.B. Stringer 1989. Fifty years after: Egbert, an Early Upper Paleolithic juvenile from Ksar Akil, Lebanon. *Paléorient* 15: 99–112.

Binford L.R., 1968. Early Upper Pleistocene adaptations in the Levant. *American Anthropologist* 70: 707–717.

Boëda E., J.-M. Geneste, C. Griggo, N. Mercier, S. Muhesen, J.L. Reyss, A. Taha and H. Valladas 1999. A Levallois point embedded in the vertebra of a wild ass (*Equus africanus*): hafting, projectiles and Mousterian hunting weapons. *Antiquity* 73: 394–402.

Boutié P. 1989. Étude technologique de l'industrie moustérienne de la grotte de Qafzeh (près de Nazareth, Israël). In O. Bar-Yosef and B. Vandermeersch (Eds.), *Investigations in South Levantine Prehistory/Préhistoire du Sud-Levant* (BAR International Series 497), pp. 213–230. Oxford: BAR.

Brace C.L. 1964. The fate of the "classic" Neandertals: a consideration of hominid catastrophism. *Current Anthropology* 5: 3–43.

Brose D.S. and M.H. Wolpoff 1970. Early Upper Paleolithic man and Middle Paleolithic tools. *American Anthropologist* 73: 1156–1194.

Caramelli D., C. Lalueza-Fox, C. Vernesi, M. Lari, A. Casoli, F. Mallegni, B. Chiarelli, I. Dupanloup, J. Bertranpetit, G. Barbujani and G. Bertorelle 2003. Evidence for a genetic discontinuity between Neandertals and 24,000-year-old anatomically modern Europeans. *Proceedings of the National Academy of Sciences USA* 100: 6593–6597.

Cheddadi R. and M. Rossignol-Strick 1995. Eastern Mediterranean Quaternary paleoclimates from pollen isotope records of marine cores in the Nile cone area. *Paleoceanography* 10: 291–300.

Clark G.A. 1992. Continuity or replacement? Putting modern humans in an evolutionary context. In H.L. Dibble and P.A. Mellars (Eds.), *The Middle Paleolithic: Change, Adaptation, and Variability*, pp. 183–206. Philadelphia: University of Pennsylvania Museum Press.

Clark, G.A. and J. Lindly 1989. Modern human origins in the Levant and Western Asia: the fossil and archeological evidence. *American Anthropologist* 91: 962–985.

Cooper A., A.J. Drummond and E. Willersley 2004. Ancient DNA: would the real Neandertal please stand up? *Current Biology* 14: R431–R433.

Copeland L. 1975. The Middle and Upper Palaeolithic of Lebanon and Syria in the light of recent research. In F. Wendorf and A.E. Marks (Eds.), *Problems in Prehistory: North Africa and the Levant*, pp. 317–350. Dallas: Southern Methodist University Press.

Copeland L. 1983. The Levalloiso-Mousterian of Bezez Cave Level B. In D.A. Roe (Ed.), *Adlun in the Stone Age* (BAR International Series 159(i)), pp. 261–324. Oxford: BAR.

Copeland L. 1998. The Middle Palaeolithic flint industry of Ras el-Kelb. In L. Copeland and N. Moloney (Eds.), *The Mousterian Site of Ras el-Kelb, Lebanon* (BAR International Series 706), pp. 73–175. Oxford: Archaeopress.

Crew H. 1976. The Mousterian site of Rosh Ein Mor. In A.E. Marks (Ed.), *Prehistory and Paleoenvironments in the Central Negev, Israel, Vol. 1*, pp. 75–112. Dallas: SMU Press.

d'Errico F. 2003. The invisible frontier. A multiple species model for the origin of behavioral modernity. *Evolutionary Anthropology* 12: 188–202.

Finlayson C. 2004. *Neanderthals and Modern Humans: An Ecological and Evolutionary Perspective.* Cambridge: Cambridge University Press.

Fleisch H. 1970. Les habitats du paléolithique moyen à Naamé (Liban). *Bulletin de la Musée de Beyrouth* 23: 25–93.

Fox J.R. and N.R. Coinman 2004. Emergence of the Levantine Upper Paleolithic: evidence from the Wadi al-Hasa. In P.J. Brantingham, S.L. Kuhn and K.W. Kerry (Eds.), *The Early Upper Paleolithic beyond Western Europe*, pp. 97–112. Berkeley: University of California Press.

Gargett R.H. 1989. Grave shortcomings: the evidence for Neandertal burial. *Current Anthropology* 30: 157–190.

Gargett R.H. 1999. Middle Palaeolithic burial is not a dead issue: the view from Qafzeh, St. Césaire, Kebara, Amud, and Dederiyeh. *Journal of Human Evolution* 37: 27–90.

Gargett R.H. 2000. A response to Hovers, Kimbel and Rak's argument for the purposeful burial of Amud 7. *Journal of Human Evolution* 39: 261–266.

Garrod D.A.E. 1937. Et-Tabun: description and archaeology. In D.A.E. Garrod and D.M.A. Bate (Eds.), *The Stone Age of Mount Carmel, Vol. 1: Excavations in the Wady el-Mughara*, pp. 57–70. Oxford: Clarendon Press.

Gilead I. 1991. The Upper Paleolithic in the Levant. *Journal of World Prehistory* 5: 105–154.

Gilpin M.E. and M.E. Soulé 1986. Minimum viable populations: processes of species extinction. In M.E. Soulé (Ed.), *Conservation Biology: The Science of Scarcity and Diversity*, pp. 19–34. Sutherland MA: Sinauer Associates.

Goren-Inbar N. 1990. *Quneitra: A Mousterian Site on the Golan Heights.* Jerusalem: Institute of Archaeology, Hebrew University.

Grün R. and C. Stringer 2000. Tabun revisited: revised ESR chronology and new ESR and U-series analyses of dental material from Tabun C1. *Journal of Human Evolution* 39: 601–612.

Haase-Schramm A., S. Goldstein and M. Stein 2004. U-Th dating of Lake Lisan (Late Pleistocene Dead Sea) aragonite and implications for glacial east Mediterranean climate. *Geochimica et Cosmochimica Acta* 68: 985–1005.

Harvati K., S.R. Frost, K.P. McNulty 2004. Neanderthal taxonomy reconsidered: Implications of 3D primate models of intra- and interspecific differences. *Proceedings of the National Academy of Sciences USA* 101: 1147–1152.

Hawks J.D. and M.H. Wolpoff 2001. The four faces of Eve: hypothesis compatibility and human origins. *Quaternary International* 75: 41–50.

Henry D.O. 1995. The Middle Paleolithic sites. In D.O. Henry (Ed.), *Prehistoric Cultural Ecology and Evolution: Insights from Southern Jordan*, pp. 49–84. New York: Plenum Press.

Henshilwood C., F. d'Errico, M. Vanhaeren, K. van Niekerk and Z. Jacobs 2004. Middle Stone Age shell beads from South Africa. *Science* 304: 404.

Henshilwood C.S. and C.W. Marean 2003. The origin of modern human behavior. *Current Anthropology* 44: 627–651.

Holliday T.W. 2000. Evolution at the crossroads: modern human emergence in Western Asia. *American Anthropologist* 102: 54–68.

Horowitz A. 1987. Subsurface palynostratigraphy and paleoclimates of the Quaternary Jordan Rift Valley Fill, Israel. *Israel Journal of Earth Sciences* 36: 31–44.

Hovers E. 1997. *Variability of Levantine Mousterian Assemblages and Settlement Patterns: Implications for Understanding the Development of Human Behavior.* Ph.D. Dissertatioh, The Hebrew University of Jerusalem.

Hovers E. 1998. The lithic assemblages of Amud Cave: implications for understanding the end of the Mousterian in the Levant. In T. Akazawa, K. Aoki and O. Bar-Yosef (Eds.), *Neandertals and Modern Humans in Western Asia*, pp. 143–164. New York: Plenum Press.

Hovers E., Y. Rak, R. Lavi and W.H. Kimbel 1995. Hominid remains from Amud Cave in the context of the Levantine Middle Paleolithic. *Paléorient* 21: 47–61.

Hovers E., B. Vandermeersch and O. Bar-Yosef 1997. A Middle Palaeolithic engraved artefact from Qafzeh Cave, Israel. *Rock Art Research* 14: 79–87.

Hovers E., W.H. Kimbel and Y. Rak 2000. The Amud 7 skeleton–still a burial. Response to Gargett. *Journal of Human Evolution* 39: 253–260.

Hovers E., S. Ilani, O. Bar-Yosef and B. Vandermeersch 2003. An early case of color symbolism: ochre use by modern humans in Qafzeh Cave. *Current Anthropology* 44: 491–522.

Howell F.C. 1958. Upper Pleistocene men of the Southwest Asian Mousterian. In G.H.R. von Koenigswald (Ed.), *Hundert Jahre Neanderthaler*, pp. 185–198. Utrecht: Kemik en Zoon.

Jelinek A.J. 1982. The Middle Paleolithic in the Southern Levant with comments on the appearance of modern *Homo sapiens*. In A. Ronen (Ed.), *The Transition from Lower to Middle Paleolithic and the Origins of Modern Man* (BAR International Series 151), pp. 57–104. Oxford: BAR.

Kaufman D. 1999. *Archaeological Perspectives on the Origins of Modern Humans: A View from the Levant.* Westport, CT: Bergin & Garvey.

Kaufman D. 2001. Comparisons and the case for interaction among Neanderthals and early modern humans in the Levant. *Oxford Journal of Archaeology* 20: 219–240.

Kaufman D. 2002. Re-evaluating subsistence skills of Levantine Middle and Upper Palaeolithic hunters: a comparison of the faunal assemblages. *Oxford Journal of Archaeology* 21: 217–230.

Kelly R. 1995.*The Foraging Spectrum: Diversity in Hunter-Gatherer Lifeways.* Washington, DC: Smithsonian Institution Press.

Klein R.G. 1999. *The Human Career* (Second Edition). Chicago: University of Chicago Press.

Klein R.G. 2003. Whither the Neanderthals? *Science* 299: 1525–1527.

Klein R.G., G. Avery, K. Cruz-Uribe, D. Halkett, J.E. Parkington, T. Steele, T.P. Volman and R. Yates 2004. The Ysterfontein 1 Middle Stone Age site, South Africa, and early human exploitation of coastal resources. *Proceedings of the National Academy of Sciences USA*: 5708–5715.

Klein R.G. and B. Edgar 2002. *The Dawn of Human Culture.* New York: Nevramont.

Kuhn S.L., M.C. Stiner and E. Güleç 2004. New Perspectives on the Initial Upper Paleolithic: the view from Üçagizli Cave, Turkey. In P.J. Brantingham, S.L. Kuhn and K.W. Kerry (Eds.), *The Early Upper Paleolithic beyond Western Europe*, pp. 113–128. Berkeley: University of California Press.

Kuhn S.L., M.C. Stiner, D.S. Reese and E. Güleç, E. 2001. Ornaments of the earliest Upper Paleolithic: new insights from the Levant. *Proceedings of the National Academy of Sciences USA* 98: 7641–7646.

Landau M.L. 1991. *Narratives of Human Evolution.* New Haven: Yale University Press.

Leroi-Gourhan A. 1993. *Gesture and Speech.* Cambridge, MA: MIT Press.

Lieberman D.E. 1998. Neandertal and early modern human mobility patterns: comparing archaeological and anatomical evidence. In T. Akazawa, K. Aoki and O. Bar-Yosef (Eds.), *Neandertals and Modern Humans in Western Asia*, pp. 263–276. New York: Plenum Press.

Lindly J. and G.A. 1987. A preliminary lithic analysis of the Mousterian site of 'Ain Difla (WHS Site 634) in the Wadi Ali, West-Central Jordan. *Proceedings of the Prehistoric Society* 53: 279–292.

Lister A.M. 1997. The evolutionary response of vertebrates to Quaternary environmental change. In B. Huntley, W. Cramer, A.V. Morgan, H.C. Prentice and J.R.M. Allen (Eds.), *Past and Future Rapid Environmental Changes*, pp. 287–302. Berlin: Springer Verlag.

Marks A.E. (Ed.) 1983. *Prehistory and Paleoenvironments in the Central Negev, Israel, Vol. III: The Avdat/Aqev Area, Part 3.* Dallas: SMU Press.

Marks A.E. 1992. Typological variability in the Levantine Middle Paleolithic. In H.L. Dibble and P.A. Mellars (Eds.), *The Middle Paleolithic: Adaptation, Behavior and Variability*, pp. 127–141. Philadelphia: University of Pennsylvania Museum Press.

Marks A.E. and K. Monigal 1995. Modeling the production of elongated blanks from the Early Levantine Mousterian at Rosh Ein Mor. In H.L. Dibble and O. Bar-Yosef (Eds.), *The Definition and Interpretation of Levallois Technology* (Monographs in World Archaeology 23), pp. 267–277. Madison: Prehistory Press.

Marks A. and P. Volkman 1986. The Mousterian of Ksar Akil: Levels XXVIA through XXVIIIB. *Paléorient* 12: 5–20.

Marshack A. 1996. A Middle Paleolithic symbolic composition from the Golan Heights: the earliest known depictive image. *Current Anthropology* 37: 357–365.

McBrearty S. and A.S. Brooks 2000. The revolution that wasn't: a new interpretation of the origin of modern human behavior. *Journal of Human Evolution* 39: 453–563.

McCown T.D. 1937. Mugharet es-Skhul. Description and excavations. In D.E.A. Garrod and D.M.A. Bate (Eds.), *The Stone Age of Mount Carmel, Vol. 1: Excavations in the Wady el-Mughara*, pp. 91–112. Oxford: Clarendon Press.

Meignen L. 1988. Le Paléolithique moyen du Levant: synthese. *Paléorient* 14: 168–173.

Meignen L. 1995. Levallois lithic production systems in the Middle Paleolithic of the Near East: the case of the unidirectional method. In H.L. Dibble and O. Bar-Yosef (Eds.), *The Definition and Interpretation of Levallois Technology* (Monographs in World Archaeology 23), pp. 361–380. Madison: Prehistory Press.

Meignen L. 1998. Le Paléolithique moyen au Levant sud et central: que nous apprennent les données recentes? In M. Otte (Ed.), *Préhistoire d'Anatolie: Genèse de deux mondes/Anatolian Prehistory: At the Crossroad of Two Worlds* (ERAUL 85), pp. 685–708. Liège: Université de Liège.

Meignen L. and O. Bar-Yosef 1988. Variabilité technologique au Proche Orient: l'example de Kebara. In M. Otte (Ed.) *L'Homme de Néanderthal: La Téchnique* (ERAUL 31), pp. 81–95. Liège: Université de Liège.

Meignen L. and O. Bar-Yosef 1989. Nouvelles récherches sur la paléolithique moyen d'Israël: la grotte de Kebara, Unités VII à XII. In O. Bar-Yosef and B. Vandermeersch (Eds.), *Investigations in South Levantine Prehistory/Préhistoire du Sud-Levant* (BAR International Series 497), pp. 169–184. Oxford: BAR.

Meignen L. and O. Bar-Yosef 1992. Middle Paleolithic lithic variability in Kebara Cave, Mount Carmel, Israel. In T. Akazawa, K. Aoki and T. Kimura (Eds.), *The Evolution and Dispersal of Modern Humans in Asia*, pp. 129–148. Tokyo: Hokusen-Sha.

Mellars P.A. 1996. *The Neanderthal Legacy: An Archaeological Perspective from Western Europe*. Princeton: Princeton University Press.

Moloney N. 1998. Ochre and incised flint from Ras el-Kelb. L. Copeland and N. Moloney (Eds.), *The Mousterian Site of Ras el-Kelb, Lebanon* (BAR International Series 706), pp. 181–185. Oxford: Archaeopress.

Monigal K. 2001. Lower and Middle Paleolithic blade industries and the dawn of the Upper Paleolithic in the Levant. *Archaeology, Ethnology, and Anthropology of Eurasia* 1: 11–24.

Munday F.C. 1976. Nahal Aqev (D35): a stratified, open-air Mousterian occupation in the Avdat/Aqev Area. In A.E. Marks (Ed.), *Prehistory and Paleoenvironments in the Central Negev, Israel, Vol. 2: The Avdat/Aqev Area, Part 2 and the Har Harif*, pp. 35–60. Dallas: SMU Press.

Nishiaki Y. and L. Copeland 1992. Keoue Cave, Northern Lebanon, and its place in the context of the Levantine Mousterian. In T. Akazawa, K. Aoki and T. Kimura (Eds.), *The Evolution and Dispersal of Modern Humans in Asia*, pp. 107–128. Tokyo: Hokusen-sha.

Pearson O.M. 2000. Postcranial remains and the origin of modern humans. *Evolutionary Anthropology* 9: 229–247.

Quam R.M. and F.H. Smith 1998. A reassessment of the Tabun C2 mandible. In T. Akazawa, K. Aoki and O. Bar-Yosef (Eds.), *Neandertals and Modern Humans in Western Asia*, pp. 405–422. New York: Plenum Press.

Rabinovich R. and E. Hovers 2004. Faunal analysis from Amud Cave: preliminary results and interpretations. *International Journal of Osteoarchaeology* 14: 287–306.

Rak Y. 1993. Morphological variation in *Homo neanderthalensis* and *Homo sapiens* in the Levant: a biogeographic model. In W.H. Kimbel and H.L. Martin (Eds.), *Species, Species Concepts, and Primate Evolution*, pp. 523–536. New York: Plenum Press.

Rak Y., A. Ginzburg and E. Geffen 2002. Does *Homo neanderthalensis* play a role in modern human ancestry? The mandibular evidence. *American Journal of Physical Anthropology* 119: 199–204.

Rak Y., W.H. Kimbel and E. Hovers 1994. A Neandertal infant from Amud Cave, Israel. *Journal of Human Evolution* 26: 313–324.

Ronen A. 1979. Paleolithic industries. In A. Horowitz (Ed.), *The Quaternary of Israel*, pp. 296–307. New York: Academic Press.

Ronen A. and B. Vandermeersch 1972. The Upper Palaeolithic sequence in the cave of Qafza (Israel). *Quaternaria* XVI: 189–202.

Shea J.J. 1988. Spear points from the Middle Paleolithic of the Levant. *Journal of Field Archaeology* 15: 441–450.

Shea J.J. 1998. Neandertal and early modern human behavioral variability: a regional-scale approach to the lithic evidence for hunting in the Levantine Mousterian. *Current Anthropology* 39 (Supplement): S45–S78.

Shea J.J. 2001. The Middle Paleolithic: Neandertals and early modern humans in the Levant. *Near Eastern Archaeology* 63: 38–64.

Shea J.J. 2003a. The Middle Paleolithic of the East Mediterranean Levant. *Journal of World Prehistory* 17: 313–394.

Shea J.J. 2003b. Neandertals, competition, and the origin of modern human behavior in the Levant. *Evolutionary Anthropology* 12: 173–187.

Shea J.J., Z. Davis and K. Brown 2001. Experimental tests of Middle Paleolithic spear points using a calibrated crossbow. *Journal of Archaeological Science* 28:807–816.

Simmons T. 1994. Archaic and modern *Homo sapiens* in the contact zones: evolutionary schematics and model predictions. In M.D. Nitecki and D.V. Nitecki (Eds.), *Origins of Anatomically Modern Humans*, pp. 201–225. New York: Plenum Press.

Solecki R. 1970. Summary report of the Columbia University prehistoric investigations in Lebanon, Season 1969. *Bulletin de la Musée de Beyrouth* 23: 95–128.

Solecki R. 1975. The Middle Paleolithic site of Nahr Ibrahim (Asfourieh Cave) in Lebanon. In F. Wendorf and A.E. Marks (Eds.), *Problems in Prehistory: North Africa and the Levant*, pp. 283–295. Dallas: SMU Press.

Sorenson M.V. and W.R. Leonard 2001. Neandertal energetics and foraging efficiency. *Journal of Human Evolution* 40: 483–495.

Stiner M.C., N.D. Munro and T.A. Surovell 2000. The tortoise and the hare: small game use, the broad spectrum revolution, and Paleolithic demography. *Current Anthropology* 41: 39–73.

Stiner M.C., N.D. Munro, T.A. Surovell, E. Tchernov and O. Bar-Yosef 1999. Paleolithic population growth pulses evidenced by small animal exploitation. *Science* 283: 190–194.

Taborin Y. 2003. La mer et les premiers hommes modernes. In B. Vandermeersch (Ed.), *Echanges et diffusion dans la préhistoire Méditerranéenne*, pp. 113–122. Paris: Editions du Comité des Travaux Historiques et Scientifiques.

Tattersall I. and J.H. Schwartz 1999. Hominids and hybrids: the place of Neanderthals in human evolution. *Proceedings of the National Academy of Sciences USA* 96: 7117–7119.

Tchernov E. 1992. Eurasian-African biotic exchanges through the Levantine corridor during the Neogene and Quaternary. In W. von Koenigswald and L. Werdelin (Eds.), *Mammalian Migration and Dispersal Events in the European Quaternary*, pp. 103–125. Frankfurt: Courier Forschungsinstitut Senckenberg.

Tchernov E. 1998. The faunal sequences of the southwest Asian Middle Paleolithic in relation to hominid dispersal events. In T. Akazawa, K. Aoki and O. Bar-Yosef (Eds.), *Neandertals and Modern Humans in Western Asia*, pp. 77–90. New York: Plenum Press.

Trinkaus E. 1984. Western Asia. In F.H. Smith and F. Spencer (Eds.), *The Origins of Modern Humans*, pp. 251–293. New York: Alan R. Liss.

Tsatskin A. 2000. Acheulo-Yabrudian sediments of Tabun: a view from the microscope. In A. Ronen and M. Weinstein-Evron (Eds.), *Toward Modern Humans: Yabrudian and Micoquian, 400–50 k Years Ago* (BAR International Series 850), pp. 133–142. Oxford: Archaeopress.

Vandermeersch B. 1966. Decouverte d'un objet en ocre avec traces d'utilisation dans le moustérien de Qafzeh (Israël). *Bulletin de la Société Préhistorique Française* 66: 157–158.

Vandermeersch B. 1970. Une sepulture moustérienne avec offrandes decouverte dans la grotte de Qafzeh. *Comptes Rendues de L'Academie des Sciences Paris* Serie D 270: 298–301.

Vandermeersch B. 1981. *Les Hommes Fossiles de Qafzeh (Israël)*. Paris: Editions CNRS.

Walter P. 2003. Caractérisation des traces rouges et noires sur les coquillages perforés de Qafzeh. In B. Vandermeersch (Ed.), *Echanges et Diffusion dans la Préhistoire Méditerranéenne*, pp. 122. Paris: Editions du Comité des Travaux Historiques et Scientifiques.

Whittaker J.C. 1994. *Flintknapping: Making and Understanding Stone Tools*. Austin: University of Texas Press.

Wiseman M.F. 1993. Lithic blade elements from the southern Levant: a diachronic view of changing technology and design processes. *Journal of the Israel Prehistoric Society* 25: 13–102.

Wolpoff M.H. 1980. *Paleoanthropology*. New York: Alfred A. Knopf.

Wolpoff M.H. 1989. The place of Neanderthals in human evolution. In E. Trinkaus (Ed.), *The Emergence of Modern Humans*, pp. 97–114. Cambridge: Cambridge University Press.

Wynn T. 1989. *The Evolution of Spatial Competence*. Urbana: University of Illinois Press.

Chapter **12**

Middle Paleolithic Subsistence Ecology in the Mediterranean Region

Mary C. Stiner

Department of Anthropology, Building 30, University of Arizona, Tucson, AZ 85721-0030, U.S.A.
Email: mstiner@email.arizona.edu

ABSTRACT

The assertion that Middle Paleolithic humans were large game hunters is almost certainly true, but this statement reveals little about subsistence organization, land use, and demography, some of which was unique to the period. In addition to hunting large game, Middle Paleolithic humans made considerable use of small animals in the Mediterranean region, but only those species that were relatively easy to collect. These early humans maintained remarkably narrow diets, even in habitats characterized by high species diversity. Few subsistence trends are apparent *within* the Middle Paleolithic, with the possible exceptions of (a) somewhat greater use of highland taxa (ibex), (b) mild harvesting pressure on slow-turnover prey populations after about 50,000 years ago, and (c) accelerated debris build-up in later sites. Middle Paleolithic populations were small, experiencing only minor increases at the close of this period. Hominid niche boundary shifts cluster at 500 thousand years ago (KYA), at 250 KYA with the onset of the Middle Paleolithic, and in rapid succession between 50,000 and 10,000 years ago. A categorical shift in human predator-prey dynamics in concert with human demographic expansion occurred around the time of the Middle-Upper Paleolithic cultural boundary in the eastern Mediterranean area between 40,000 and 50,000 years ago and somewhat later to the west.

INTRODUCTION

The hunting-scavenging debate of the Middle Paleolithic (Mousterian) is by now a rather old horse. Plenty of large game hunting took place back then, but, more to the point, this is only one of several important dimensions of the hominid predatory niche during this long and remote culture period. Here I review in bold strokes what I have come to understand about Middle Paleolithic existence from the zooarchaeological record, and to note what changes may have occurred within the period as opposed to after it. Three Paleolithic trends are evidenced by the zooarchaeological and related data based on (1) ungulate exploitation, (2) small game use and its demographic correlates, and (3) some seemingly counter-intuitive aspects of technology that relate to acquiring and processing game. The Mousterian is not noted for rapid change or for pronounced regional variation in technology and subsistence. There is, however, a widely acknowledged increase in Middle Paleolithic site numbers after about 60,000 years ago in several regions (van Andel *et al.* 2003), and there are hints of new pressures on human populations and their traditional food supplies toward the close of the Middle Paleolithic period.

BACKGROUND

Some early Mousterian sites dating to the middle Pleistocene are thick with the bones of large, medium, and some small ungulates, and these remains clearly represent the products of human hunting. One example of an obviously hunted ungulate fauna from the Levant, composed mostly of fallow deer (*Dama mesopotamica*), mountain gazelle (*Gazella gazella*), and aurochs (*Bos primigenius*), comes from Hayonim Cave in the Galilee (Stiner and Tchernov 1998). Later Middle Paleolithic examples of ungulate hunting from the same region are many more in number and include assemblages from Kebara Cave (Bar-Yosef *et al.* 1992; Speth and Tchernov 1998) and Qafzeh Cave (Rabinovich and Tchernov 1995). Comparable situations are reported for continental Europe, such as in Italy (Tozzi 1970; Cassoli and Tagliacozzo 1991; Stiner 1994), France (Chase 1986; David and Poulain 1990; Jaubert *et al.* 1990), Germany (Gaudzinski 1995), and Russia (Hoffecker *et al.* 1991), leaving little doubt about the general hunting capabilities of these foragers. Relatively complete body part representation, mortality patterns, and tool marks on bones indicate that Middle Paleolithic humans at times enjoyed consistent, direct access to large game.

Without concluding that Middle Paleolithic foraging habits were wholly equivalent to modern predatory adaptations, it is fair to say that the faunal record includes some straightforward evidence of ungulate hunting. However, the Middle Paleolithic faunal record presents other facets that are less easy to interpret, because they diverge from what we expect based on knowledge of recent hunter-gatherers and Upper Paleolithic peoples (Binford 1983, 1990; Gamble 1986, 1999; Mellars 1989; Kuhn and Stiner 2001). Small prey were exploited at lower latitudes by Middle Paleolithic humans, but these activities were confined largely to "gatherable" types such as marine molluscs, tortoises, legless lizards, and ostrich eggs (Palma di

Cesnola 1965, 1969; Klein and Scott 1986; Stiner 1994; Stiner and Tchernov 1998; Barton *et al.* 1999; Stiner *et al.* 2000; Speth and Tchernov 2001). Occasional scavenging, primarily of ungulate head parts in spring, is associated with small game use in the multiple layers of Grotta dei Moscerini (Italy), indicating more than anything a strong emphasis on gathered foods during these particular occupations (Stiner 1994). Many of the zooarchaeological manifestations of large game exploitation in the Middle Paleolithic nonetheless are consistent with what one would expect to see if hunting were a regular part of human subsistence (reviewed in Stiner 2002). In addition, the products of foraging were deliberately aggregated in some Middle Paleolithic sites—processed and consumed by multiple persons—evidence, it seems, of a rather close-knit social life that centered on the use of large prey.

TREND 1, HUMANS AS UNGULATE PREDATORS

Considerable overlap in the foraging interests of Pleistocene hominids and carnivores is apparent from the exploitation of hoofed animals, and it seems that the niches of ungulate predators were shaped in part by the risks of interference competition for large resource packages. A theoretical outcome of inter-specific competition is differentiation, or character displacement, which relieves the stresses of potential conflict among consumers who must coexist (MacArthur and Levins 1967; Pianka 1978). As hunters of ungulates, hominids appear always to have been of the ambushing sort. The impact of hominids' hunting tactics on ungulate populations with time grew increasingly distinct from the ways of coeval large cats, spotted hyenas, and large canids. Specifically, humans are the only predator that frequently targets the reproductive core (prime adults) of ungulate populations (Stiner 1990). Because spotted hyenas and large canids generally focus on the juvenile and old adult age groups in the same prey species, and most cats apart from the cheetah tend to take prey more randomly, humans' focus on prime adult prey is ecologically unprecedented.

Figure 1 illustrates in tripolar format the averaged ungulate mortality patterns for Paleolithic humans and various nonhuman predators, framed against natural variation in the structures of living prey populations and the mortality patterns that arise from nonviolent causes (from Stiner 1990, 1994). The ungulate mortality patterns generated by cursorial predators, such as spotted hyenas, wolves, and cape hunting dogs, overlap completely with death patterns resulting from attritional factors such as disease, malnutrition, and old age. Predators that ambush their prey, such as lions and tigers, tend to hunt non-selectively with respect to prey age, unless the quarry is exceptionally large, and the resulting death patterns therefore resemble the age structure of living prey populations. The extent to which predators scavenge for ungulate carcasses seems to push the mean value higher on the old age axis, as is the case for Indian tigers in this comparison. Middle Paleolithic, Upper Paleolithic, and more recent human cases generally fall on the "ambush" side of the distribution. They also display a notable "preference" for (or mild bias to) prime adult prey in commonly hunted artiodactyl species.

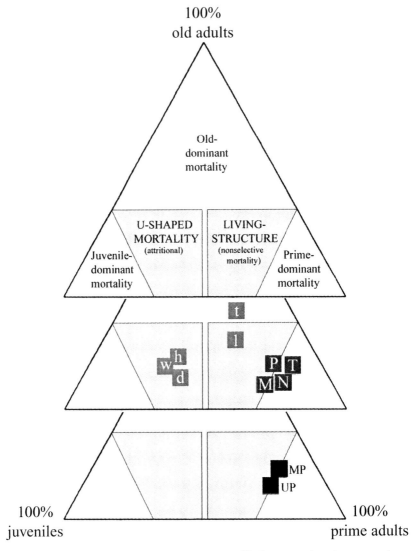

Figure 1. Mean ungulate mortality patterns generated by human and nonhuman predators. Shading represents natural variation in the age structure of living ungulate populations (right panel); mortality patterns caused by attritional factors, such as disease, accidents, and malnutrition (left panel). Predators that ambush their prey are [t] tigers and [l] lions. Cursorial or long-chase hunters are [h] spotted hyenas, [w] wolves and [d] African wild dogs. Corners of the graph represent strong biases toward the designated prey age groups. Darker gray squares are Holocene humans: Paleoindian/Archaic [P], Mississippian farmers [M], Nunamiut Eskimo [N], trophy hunters in modern game parks [T]. MP is the mean for Middle Paleolithic hunted faunas and closely resembles that for the Upper Paleolithic (UP).

Numerous colleagues have applied the method described above to yet other cases. While results vary in some of their details, the larger patterns and observations about Paleolithic hunting niche appear to be well supported. The emphasis on prime-adult prey is geographically and temporally widespread from the Middle Paleolithic through the Holocene (*e.g.*, Smith 1974; Jaubert *et al.* 1990; Stiner 1990; Gaudzinski 1995; Enloe 1997; Speth and Tchernov 1998; Pike-Tay 1999; Rick and Moore 2001); the possibility that these patterns are explained by differential decomposition of young ungulate teeth is refuted by a variety of taphonomic observations (*e.g.*, Stiner 1994, 2005). Human hunting effects thus are distinct on average from those of nonhuman predators, strong evidence of niche separation as a result of hominids' membership in ungulate predator guilds. We might conclude that this tendency is a Middle Paleolithic development at the very latest.

Somewhat counter-intuitively, prime-biased ungulate hunting is largely insensitive to regional and temporal variation in weapons technology. What is more, prime-biased ungulate hunting can be a relatively fragile predator-prey relationship because reproductive-aged adults are disproportionately sought, including females. Seemingly antithetical to "prudent predation" models (Pianka 1978:210), such a relationship may only be feasible for omnivorous predators that can switch to other foods when the densities of favored prey decline (Stiner 1994; Winterhalder and Lu 1997). Neandertal populations nonetheless appear to have been quite carnivorous, at least in Europe, based on stable carbon and nitrogen isotope evidence (*e.g.*, Richards *et al.* 2000). Small quantities of burned seeds or nuts have been found in some Mediterranean Mousterian sites (*e.g.*, Barton *et al.* 1999), and fruit consumption is very likely, but there currently is no evidence that Neandertals obtained a high proportion of their total energy from plant sources, or that they engaged in high-investment processing of plant seeds.

That hominids' tendency to harvest prime-adult bovids and cervids was well established by the Late Pleistocene raises the question of when it first evolved. Current evidence places this behavior in the middle Pleistocene, some 250,000 years ago or earlier (Stiner 2005). It is clearly in evidence in the early Middle Paleolithic of Hayonim Cave (Figure 2; also Meignen *et al.* this volume), suggesting ecological specialization by this time and, as well, a deeper history for more generalized forms of ungulate hunting by hominids (*e.g.*, Bunn 2001). It seems likely on theoretical grounds and from limited empirical evidence that a more basic adaptation for ungulate hunting had evolved in hominids by at least 500,000 years ago. Unfortunately, there are relatively few cases available for comparison from the earlier time range, and most are subject to many more questions about site formation history. To the extent that non-confrontational scavenging is evidenced in the Middle Paleolithic, it obviously was just one facet of a more complex array of foraging behaviors (Stiner and Kuhn 1992; Stiner 1994). The subject of ungulate mortality patterns merits continued investigation. Apart from still incomplete knowledge of seasonality in resource exploitation (*e.g.*, Speth and Tchernov 2001), the information yield of ungulate mortality data seems to be nearing a plateau, making data on small game use and changes in prey emphasis from the perspective of biological productivity increasingly attractive.

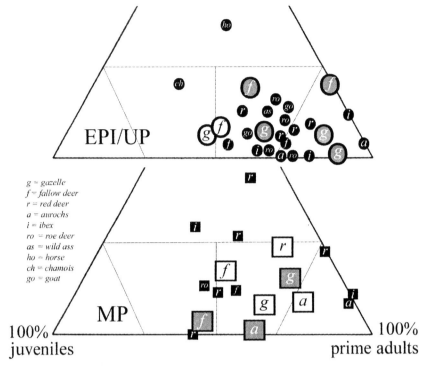

Figure 2. Ungulate mortality patterns, Mousterian (squares) and Upper/Epi-Paleolithic (circles), from Mediterranean sites in Israel and Italy. Artiodactyl ungulate taxa are (g) mountain gazelle, (r) red deer, (f) fallow deer, (a) aurochs. Large gray-filled symbols are from Hayonim Cave, Israel; large white-filled symbols are from Kebara Cave (Kebara data taken from Speth and Tchernov 1998).

TREND 2, SMALL GAME USE AND PALEODEMOGRAPHY

While all Paleolithic humans lived by hunting and collecting wild foods, subsistence diversification is expected to occur whenever and wherever foragers put undue pressure on staple food resources. Perhaps the clearest signal of increasing dietary breadth is greater proportional evenness among high-ranked and low-ranked prey items in response to the declining availability of the preferred types. A predator can afford to ignore lower quality prey, if the chance of finding a superior type in the near future is high, leading to a narrower diet. As the supply of preferred prey dwindles, broadening the diet to include common but lower yield prey types maximizes a predator's returns per unit expenditure by reducing search time (Pianka 1978; Stephens and Krebs 1986). This reasoning assumes that resources can be ranked in the energetic terms of the predator. Ancient criteria for ranking prey cannot be inferred from the decisions of recent peoples, but the relative values (pay-offs) of prey can be evaluated in a general way from the adaptations of the types of animals whose bones occur in archaeofaunas. Interestingly, some distantly related small taxa are nearly equivalent from the viewpoint of handling costs on

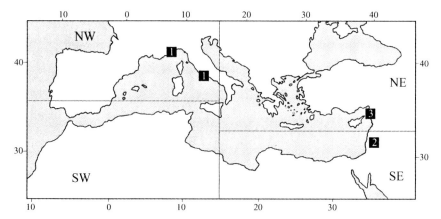

Figure 3. Geographic origins of the three Mediterranean faunal series: (1) Italy; (2) Israel; (3) Turkey (from Stiner 2001). Four ecological quadrants are distinguished on the basis of endemic species distributions and dominant habitat structures (base map after Blondel and Aronson 1999:38).

account of their locomotor habits or ways of avoiding predators: both tortoises and rock-dwelling marine shellfish are sluggish or immobile and thus easily captured; hares and partridges, though similar in body weight to tortoises or an arm full of shellfish, contrast greatly from the first group in being quick and maneuverable.

Small animals were important to human diets in lower latitude areas such as the Mediterranean Basin (Figure 3) from at least the early Middle Paleolithic onward. The relative emphasis that humans placed on three general types of small animals changed dramatically with time—these are slow-moving, easily collected types (tortoises and shellfish), fast-running mammals (hares and rabbits), and quick-flying game birds. Remarkably, Mousterian foragers seldom bothered with small prey unless they could be obtained easily. The situation changed greatly from the Upper Paleolithic and onward.

A simple measure of evenness in the prey types eaten—the Reciprocal of Simpson's Index, or $1/\Sigma(\rho_i)^2$, where ρ represents the proportion of each prey type for array $_i$ in an assemblage—reveals significant expansion in human dietary breadth, beginning 40–50,000 years ago (Figure 4) in the eastern end of the Mediterranean Basin (Stiner 2001). Eighteen small game assemblages from shelter sites in Israel (200,000-11,000 years BP), Italy (110,000-9,000 years BP), and Turkey (41,000-17,000 years BP), representing three relatively distinct ecogeographic zones (following Blondel and Aronson 1999), display a clear trend toward more *even* dependence on high-ranked sluggish animals and low-ranked quick-moving prey types ($r = 0.606$, $p = .01$, n = 18). Most of the dietary expansion took place during a time of climate cooling (Oxygen Isotope Stages 3 and especially 2, following Martinson *et al.* 1987). This is the opposite of what would be expected to result from climate-driven changes in animal community composition, since resident species diversity generally increases as effective latitude decreases (Pianka 1978). The evidence indicates a categorical change in how humans

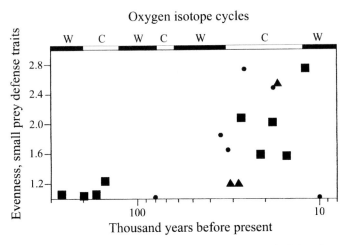

Figure 4. Evenness among three small game categories in Paleolithic faunas, based on prey defense mechanisms (slow game, quick-running terrestrial mammals and quick-flying birds) (3 = most even, 1 = least even). Symbols are for assemblages from Italy (circle), Israel (square), and Turkey (triangle). Time is expressed on a logged scale, as are oxygen isotope climate cycles; (c) cold stage, (w) warm stage (from Stiner 2001).

interacted with small animal populations just prior to or with the Middle-to-Upper Paleolithic transition. The proportion of slow animals within the small game fraction of each assemblage declines with time ($r = 0.572$, $.02 < p < .01$, $n = 18$) (Figure 5) due to the increased reliance on small quick animals. In this view of the data, the large-to-small body size contrast in the three Mediterranean series appears trendless ($r = 0.276$, $p = 1$, $n = 18$).

Another way to view the archaeofaunal data is in terms of the relative productivity of different prey types. Biomass-corrected prey counts (Minimum Numbers of Individuals multiplied by mean body weight for each taxon) indicate that Paleolithic humans of the Mediterranean Basin obtained most of their meat from ungulates until very late in the Pleistocene (Figure 6). Medium to large-sized ungulates remained the preferred prey types in the Upper and Epi-Paleolithic culture periods, but the biomass-corrected prey abundance data in Figure 7 indicate greater use of lower-ranked, faster-reproducing species with time, including smaller ungulates as well as lagomorphs and game birds. Exploitation of resources other than large game seems to have accelerated with the late Epi-Paleolithic, rising to 17% or greater.

Differential productivity is also a key to understanding the trend in small game exploitation (Stiner *et al.* 2000). In the Mediterranean Basin, a simple distinction in the "catchability" of small animals happens to correspond to great differences in prey population resilience, the latter governed mainly by the rates at which individual prey animals mature. Slow-moving tortoises, maturing at 8–12 years, and certain shellfish (*e.g.*, limpets maturing at 1–5 years) are especially susceptible to overharvesting (see also Klein and Cruz-Uribe 1983 on the Middle-Late Stone Age subsistence transition in South Africa). It is striking that Mousterian foragers

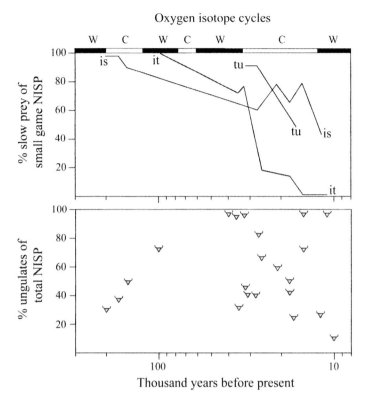

Figure 5. Regional trends (lines) in the percentage of slow small prey within the small game fraction of each assemblage in (is) Israel, (it) Italy, and (tu) Turkey; and the percentage of ungulate remains in the total count of each assemblage (from Stiner 2001).

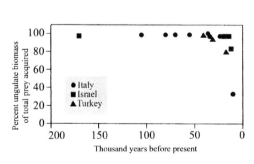

Figure 6. Percentage of total ungulate biomass consumed over time in three distinct Mediterranean faunal series (biomass = bone-based MNI multiplied by average individual prey weight in kg) (from Stiner 2005).

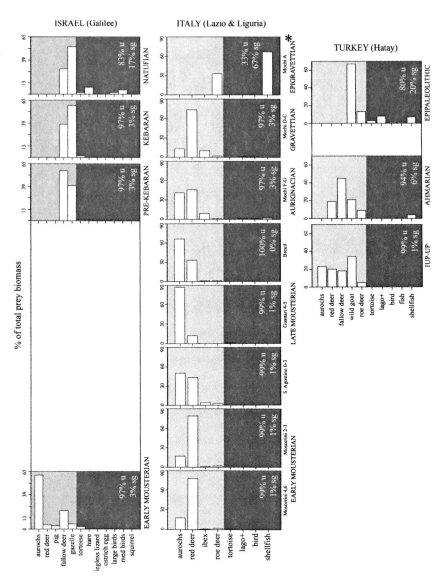

Figure 7. Percentage of total prey biomass for size-ordered prey species in three Mediterranean faunal series (biomass = bone-based MNI multiplied by average individual prey weight in kg) (from Stiner 2005). Only relatively common prey species are considered. (u) total ungulate percentage; (sg) total small game percentage; (*) Riparo Mochi A in the Italian series represents an extreme situation but is still fairly typical of coastal occupations for the period; all Turkish data are from Üçağızlı Cave (Hatay coast); Israeli sites are Hayonim Cave and Meged Rockshelter in the Wadi Meged (western Galilee).

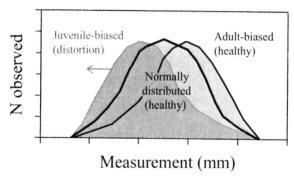

Figure 8. Modeled patterns of size (= age) skewing and implications for population state based on a morphometric trait in a K-selected, continuously growing animal species such as tortoises. Normally distributed (bell-shaped) size/age patterns and those biased toward older adults are indications of healthy population structure, because adult mortality rates are very low in natural settings and juvenile mortality high. A bias toward juveniles (skewing to the left of the normal distribution) reflects abnormal distortion of the size/age structure, due to unusually high adult mortality, and is known to result from heavy predation of adult animals (from Stiner 2005).

tended to use slow-growing prey types consistently, when they bothered with small game at all. Overharvesting of tortoises causes *diminution* or a reduction in the mean size of individuals available to foragers from one generation to the next. Diminution occurred for tortoises by the earliest Upper Paleolithic in Israel (≥44 thousand years ago) or by very late Middle Paleolithic (Stiner *et al.* 2000; see also Speth and Tchernov 2002), and the diminution effect was sustained over multiple climate cycles thereafter. While mean size declined significantly with time, the maximum body sizes attained by long-lived individual tortoises remained about the same. Size skewing toward juveniles in the later part of the series confirms that predator-induced distortion is the cause of mean size reduction (Figures 8 and 9), and that this is not the result of species replacement or environmental change. The timing and duration of body size suppression in the tortoises are largely independent of global climate trends—which would be the other potential cause of diminution. Thus the data point largely to a human cause.

An important quality of small prey populations that rebound quickly is their greater reliability as a food source. Any forager population that can grow faster on low value but more resilient foods will have a demographic advantage over competing populations. Warm-blooded small animals, mainly partridges, hares, and rabbits, mature in ≤1 year, and their populations rebound easily from heavy hunting by humans. Predator-prey computer simulations indicate that hare and partridge populations can support seven to ten times the annual off-take that tortoise populations can support (Stiner *et al.* 2000). Thus greater dependence on slow-growing animals during the Middle Paleolithic, and on larger individual prey, implies that these early human populations were very small and dispersed. Foragers' emphasis on slow (highly ranked) and quick (lower ranked) small prey

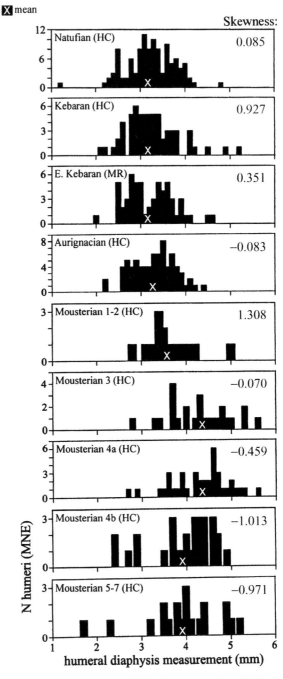

Figure 9. Size skewing in tortoise humeral diaphysis mean breadth for the Wadi Meged series, from the early Mousterian through Natufian periods, Galilee, Israel. (HC) Hayonim Cave; (MR) Meged Rockshelter. Negative and near-zero values indicate normal population structures, positive values indicate significant distortion from heavy predation on adults.

grew more "even" with time, the predicted outcome of hunting pressure and demographic increase, particularly in the absence of a correlation with climate warming. The zooarchaeological evidence of expanding dietary breadth testifies to several demographic pulses over the course of the Late Pleistocene, the intensity of which increased after the Last Glacial Maximum. Of greatest relevance to this discussion is the first pulse, occurring between 40–50,000 years ago, at the threshold of the Middle-to-Upper Paleolithic cultural transition. It stands to reason that some late Mousterian populations were also affected, if only indirectly.

TREND 3, PALEOLITHIC FORAGING TECHNOLOGY

While there is considerable evidence for large game hunting in the Middle Paleolithic period, very few Middle Paleolithic tools can reasonably be called hunting weapons. Stone-tipped weapons appear late in the Eurasian Mousterian and are not widespread (Kuhn and Stiner 1998), and bone-working, and bone-tipped weapons designed specifically for hunting generally are confined to the Upper Paleolithic and later cultures, when rapid radiations in weapons and other material culture took place (*e.g.*, Knecht 1997). A certain "inventiveness" with respect to weapon heads cannot be denied for some later Middle Paleolithic cases in Eurasia, where bifacial (blastspitzen, Müller-Beck 1988) and mounted Levallois-type stone points (Shea 1989) occur. Bifacial stone and bone points are also reported for some Middle Stone age sites in Africa (*e.g.*, Brooks *et al.* 1995; d'Errico *et al.* 2001; Wrinn and Rink 2003).

A paradox exists nonetheless in that humans routinely hunted medium-sized and large ungulates long before the undisputed or regular appearance of stone-tipped and bone-tipped weapons in Paleolithic records anywhere. Prime-age focused ungulate hunting is evidenced in cases as old as 200–250,000 years ago, about the time that earliest Middle Paleolithic technologies first evolved and well before every indisputable innovation in weapons technology save the simple wooden spear (*e.g.*, Lehringen *ca.* 200 thousand years ago, Jacob-Friesen 1956; Schöningen *ca.* 400 thousand years ago, Thieme 1997). The elaborate weapons traditions of the Eurasian Upper Paleolithic and African Late Stone Age are separated from the emergence of prime-focused ungulate hunting by some 150,000 years. Even the remarkable and apparently precocious examples from Middle Stone Age sites are much too young to close this temporal gap. The lag in technological change suggests that cooperation among hunters was essential for the capture of game. It also indicates that shifts in the rate of technological change, including hunting weapons designs, was largely independent of the evolution of humans' capacity to bring down large prey.

Many of the changes in weapons design of the later Paleolithic certainly were connected to humans' dietary interest in large and small game, but less directly than one might imagine. Improvements in weapons design and efficiency do not necessarily raise the number of large prey animals available to Paleolithic hunters. Improvements in weapons efficiency are more likely to reduce individual's procurement time and risk per foray, and possibly also the minimum hunting party size needed to capture large animals (Kuhn and Stiner 2001; Stiner 2002). This implies a change in the value of forager's time—time that could be allocated to other tasks (*sensu* Pianka 1978:258; Hames 1992). Larger scale resource pooling could favor greater individual task specialization, albeit to the extent that human population densities allow. Thus, while weapons innovations may be driven partly by a need for greater mechanical efficiency, the incentives for doing so may originate from the pressures of time allocation for diverse social or foraging concerns. These changes in foraging equipment and organization seem to be confined to the Upper Paleolithic period. Few if any changes in hunting agendas are apparent within the Middle Paleolithic period.

A very different side of the technological record concerns carcass processing innovations and increases in nutrient consumption efficiency. Bone cracking with stone hammers and anvils is remarkably efficient, if compared to the energy and time that large-jawed carnivores must spend to open the same kinds of large bones. Carcass-processing routines of the Paleolithic grew much more complex with time, including grease rendering via stone boiling, evidenced by the thick litter of fire-cracked stones in some later Upper Paleolithic sites such as in France, Germany, and Portugal (Audouze 1987; Weniger 1987; Stiner 2003). Heat-in-liquid techniques raise the protein and fat yields per carcass well beyond what is possible from cold-extraction techniques (Binford 1978; Brink 1997; Lupo and Schmitt 1997). Yet only cold-extraction techniques that focus on the concentrated marrow reserves encased in large bone medullary cavities were employed during the Middle Paleolithic. More efficient harvesting of quick small game generally antedates or accompanies the changes in marrow processing of large mammal carcasses.

CONCLUSION

The assertion that Middle Paleolithic humans were large game hunters is almost certainly true, but this statement obscures much about human subsistence organization, predator-prey interactions, or demography. Middle Paleolithic humans in the Mediterranean region made considerable use of small animals, but normally only those species that were relatively easy to collect. These early humans maintained remarkably narrow diets across a wide range of latitudes, even in habitats where animal species diversity was high. Ungulate remains dominate archaeofaunas of the Middle Paleolithic period, and the mortality patterns of many Middle Paleolithic assemblages are biased toward prime adult prey, a tendency that also distinguishes human hunting patterns from those of all other large predators. Marrow processing in the Middle Paleolithic was efficient within the limits of cold-extraction methods, but it never intensified beyond this.

Few subsistence trends are apparent within the Middle Paleolithic, with the exceptions of possible mild harvesting pressure on slow-turnover prey populations after about 50,000 years ago and accelerated debris build-up in late Middle Paleolithic sites. Human populations were exceptionally small during the Middle Paleolithic, and perhaps easily swamped by a faster growing human population new to the region. A categorical shift in human predator-prey dynamics accompanied by human demographic expansion occurred around the time of the Middle-Upper Paleolithic cultural boundary. This process began earlier in the eastern Mediterranean area than to the north and west. The strangely liberal use of slow-moving, slow-growing small prey populations that do not rebound easily from heavy exploitation prior to this transition is striking. It is ironic as well that, while Middle Paleolithic humans frequently hunted large game animals, stone-tipped weapons surface only by the Middle Paleolithic, and weapon heads were substantially elaborated upon only within the Upper and Epipaleolithic periods. Regular hunting of large animals under the earlier set of conditions implies high levels of cooperation within what must have been small foraging groups.

The Middle Paleolithic is remarkably consistent internally, especially if its long duration and wide geographic distribution are taken into account. There seems to have been a lack of pressure or economic incentive for squeezing more out of traditional food supplies—little if any selection, it seems, for greater foraging efficiency. The hunting equipment of the Middle Paleolithic was modest, changing little over 250,000 years. Analysts most familiar with later culture periods might ask why there was so little change in the Middle Paleolithic. On the other hand, why should there be change if the system works well for a highly carnivorous and mobile predator population? More difficult to explain are the downward shifts in trophic level from the Upper Paleolithic onward—mainly diversification via the inclusion of lower-ranked foodstuffs. Related to this are increases in human population densities and/or larger networks for spreading risk that may have put some populations at advantage.

The signals of change discussed here are mainly zooarchaeological in nature and imply a demographic process. Humans had fewer options for solving problems of resource availability via mobility as early as the Upper Paleolithic. These changes in the condition of human existence intensified greatly with the Epi-Paleolithic, as first noted by Binford (1968, see also 1999) and Flannery (1969). The patterns of large and small game exploitation in the Mediterranean Paleolithic record suggest increasing dependence on more biologically "productive" or resilient prey populations. This trend may or may not have allowed people to obtain more meat per unit habitat area, but prey population resilience can affect the reliability and the diversity of meat sources to which a population has access, particularly if the costs of acquisition or processing can be reduced with technology. A more consistent supply of animal protein and fats can significantly improve child survivorship and inadvertently swell the ranks of a human population. Populations using Middle Paleolithic technology may not have been the source of pressure on resources 40–50,000 years ago, but they had to have been feeling it indirectly by the close of this period.

ACKNOWLEDGEMENTS

I owe thanks to a great many colleagues for their valuable comments and assistance during the many stages of this research, not least to L.R. Binford, H. Harpending, L.G. Straus, and S.L. Kuhn. In addition, I am very grateful to O. Bar-Yosef, A. Belfer-Cohen, L. Grossman, E. Hovers, L. Meignen, J.D. Speth, and E. Tchernov in connection with my work in Israel; F. Alhaique, A. Bietti, P. Cassoli, A. Recchi, A. Segre, E. Segre-Naldini, and C. Tozzi in Italy; and E. Güleç, A. Açikkol, and C. Pehlevan in Turkey. This research was supported by a CAREER grant from the National Science Foundation Archaeology Program (SBR-9511894).

REFERENCES CITED

Audouze F. 1987. The Paris Basin in Magdalenian times. In O. Soffer (Ed.), *The Pleistocene Old World: Regional Perspectives*, pp. 183–200. New York: Plenum Press.

Barton R.N.E., A.P. Currant, Y. Fernandez-Jalvo, J.C. Finlayson, P. Goldberg, R.Macphail, P.B. Pettitt and C.B. Stringer 1999. Gilbraltar Neanderthals and results of recent excavations in Gorham's, Vanguard and Ibex Caves. *Antiquity* 73: 13–23.

Bar-Yosef O., B. Vandermeersch, B. Arensburg, A. Belfer-Cohen, P. Goldberg, H. Laville, L. Meignen, Y. Rak, J.D. Speth, E. Tchernov, A.-M. Tillier and S. Weiner 1992. The excavations in Kebara Cave, Mt. Carmel. *Current Anthropology* 33: 497–550.

Binford L.R. 1968. Post-Pleistocene adaptations. In S.R. Binford and L.R. Binford (Eds.), *New Perspectives in Archaeology*, pp. 313–341. Chicago: Aldine.

Binford L.R. 1978. *Nunamiut Ethnoarchaeology*. New York: Academic Press.

Binford L.R. 1983. *In Pursuit of the Past*. London: Thames and Hudson.

Binford L.R. 1990. Isolating the transition to cultural adaptations: an organizational approach. In E. Trinkaus (Ed.), *The Emergence of Modern Humans: Biocultural Adaptations in the Later Pleistocene*, pp. 18–41. New York: Cambridge University Press.

Binford L.R. 1999. Time as a clue to cause? *Proceedings of the British Academy* 101: 1–35.

Blondel J. and J. Aronson 1999. *Biology and Wildlife of the Mediterranean Region*. Oxford: Oxford University Press.

Brink J.W. 1997. Fat content in leg bones of *Bison bison*, and applications to archaeology. *Journal of Archaeological Science* 24: 259–274.

Brooks A.S., D.M. Helgren, J.S. Cramer, A. Franklin, W. Hornyak, J.M. Keating, R.G. Klein, W.J. Rink, H. Schwarcz, J.N.L.Smith, K. Stewart, N.Todd, J. Verniers and J.E. Yellen, 1995. Dating and context of three middle Stone Age sites with bone points in the upper Semliki Valley, Zaire. *Science* 268: 548–553.

Bunn H.T. 2001. Hunting, power scavenging, and butchering by Hadza foragers and by Plio-Pleistocene *Homo*. In C.B. Stanford and H.T. Bunn (Eds.), *Meat-Eating and Human Evolution*, pp. 199–218. Oxford: Oxford University Press.

Cassoli P.F. and A. Tagliacozzo 1991. Consideraziooni paleontologiche, paleoecologiche e archeozoologiche sui macromammiferi e gli uccelli dei livelli del pleistocene superiore del Riparo di Fumane (VR) (scavi 1988–91). *Bolletino di Museo Civico e Storia Naturale, Verona* 18: 349–445.

Chase P.G. 1986. *The Hunters of Combe Grenal: Approaches to Middle Paleolithic Subsistence in Europe* (BAR International Series 286), Oxford: BAR.

David F. and T. Poulain 1990. La faune de grands mammifères des niveaux XI et XC de la Grotte du Renne a Arcy-sur-Cure (Yonne): Etude préliminaire. In C. Farizy (Ed.), *Paléolithique moyen récent et paléolithique supérieur ancien en Europe* (Mémoires du Musée de Préhistoire, no. 3), pp. 319–323. Nemours: APRAI.

d'Errico F., C. Henshilwood and P. Nilssen 2001. Engraved bone fragment from ca. 70,000-year-old Middle Stone Age levels at Blombos Cave, South Africa: implications for the origin of symbolism and language. *Antiquity* 75: 309–318.

Enloe J.G. 1997. Seasonality and age structure in remains of *Rangifer tarandus*: Magdalenian hunting strategy at Verberie. *Anthropozoologica*: 25–26, 95–102.

Flannery K.V. 1969. Origins and ecological effects of early domestication in Iran and the Near East. In P.J. Ucko and G.W. Dimbleby (Eds.), *The Domestication and Exploitation of Plants and Animals*, pp. 73–100. Chicago: Aldine.

Gamble C. 1986. *The Palaeolithic Settlement of Europe.* Cambridge: Cambridge University Press.

Gamble, C. 1999. The Hohlenstein-Stadel revisited. In E. Turner and S. Gaudzinski (Eds.), *The Rrole of Early Humans in the Accumulation of European Lower and Middle Palaeolithic Bone Assemblages*, pp. 305–324. Mainz: Monographien des Romisch-Germanischen Zentralmuseums 42.

Gaudzinski S. 1995. Wallertheim revisited: a re-analysis of the fauna from the Middle Palaeolithic site of Wallertheim (Rheinhessen/Germany). *Journal of Archaeological Science* 22: 51–66.

Hames R. 1992. Time allocation. In E.A. Smith and B. Winterhalder (Eds.), *Evolutionary Ecology and Human Behavior*, pp. 203–235. New York: Aldine de Gruyter.

Hoffecker J.F., G. Baryshnikov and O. Potapova 1991. Vertebrate remains from the Mousterian site of Il'skaya I (northern Caucasus, U.S.S.R.): new analysis and interpretation. *Journal of Archaeological Science* 18: 113–147.

Jacob-Friesen K.H. 1956. Eiszeitliche elephantenjäger in der Lüneburger Heide. *Jarbüch des Römisch-Germanischen Zentralmuseums Mainz* 3: 1–22.

Jaubert J., M. Lorblanchet, H. Laville, R. Slott-Moller, A. Turq and J.-P. Brugal 1990. *Les Chasseurs d'Aurochs de La Borde* (Documents d'Archéologique Français, no. 27), Paris: Editions de la Maison des Sciences de L'Homme.

Klein R.G. and K. Cruz-Uribe 1983. Stone age population numbers and average tortoise size at Bynesdranskop Cave 1 and Die Kelders Cave 1, Southern Cape Province, South Africa. *The South African Archaeological Bulletin* 38: 26–30.

Klein R.G. and K. Scott 1986. Re-analysis of faunal assemblages from the Haua Fteah and other Late Quaternary archaeological sites in Cyrenaican Libya. *Journal of Archaeological Science* 13: 515–542.

Knecht H. (Ed.) 1997. *Projectile Technology.* New York: Plenum Press.

Kuhn S.L. and M.C. Stiner 1998. Middle Paleolithic "creativity": Reflections on an oxymoron? In S. Mithen (Ed.), *Creativity in Human Evolution and Prehistory*, pp. 143–164. London: Routledge.

Kuhn S.L. and M.C. Stiner 2001. The antiquity of hunter-gatherers. In C. Panter-Brick, R.H. Layton and P. Rowley-Conwy (Eds.), *Interdisciplinary Perspectives on Hunter-Gatherers*, pp. 99–142. Cambridge: Cambridge University Press.

Lupo K.D. and D.N. Schmitt 1997. Experiments in bone boiling: Nutritional returns and archaeological reflections. *Anthropozoologica* 25–26: 137–144.

MacArthur R.H. and R. Levins 1967. The limiting similarity, convergence, and divergence of coexisting species. *The American Naturalist* 101: 377–385.

Martinson D.G., N.G. Pisias, J.D. Hays, J. Imbrie, T.C. Moore and N.J. Shackleton 1987. Age dating and the orbital theory of the ice ages: development of a high-resolution 0 to 300,000-year chronostratigraphy. *Quaternary Research* 27: 1–29.

Mellars P. 1989. Major issues in the emergence of modern humans. *Current Anthropology* 30: 349–385.

Müller-Beck H. 1988. The ecosystem of the "Middle Paleolithic" (late Lower Paleolithic) in the Upper Danube region: a stepping stone to the Upper Paleolithic. In H.L. Dibble and A. Montet-White (Eds.), *Upper Pleistocene Prehistory in Western Eurasia* (University Museum Monograph, no. 54), pp. 233–254. Philadelphia: University of Pennsylvania.

Palma di Cesnola A. 1965. Notizie preliminari sulla terza campagna di scavi nella Grotta del Cavallo (Lecce). *Rivista di Scienze Preistoriche* 25: 3–87.

Palma di Cesnola A. 1969. Il musteriano della Grotta del Poggio a Marina di Camerota (Salerno). *Estratto dagli Scritti sul Quaternario in Onore di Angelo Pasa*, pp. 95–135. Venosa: Museo Civico di Storia Naturale di Venosa.

Pianka E.R. 1978. *Evolutionary Ecology*. New York: Harper and Row.

Pike-Tay A. 1999. Seasonal variations of the Middle-Upper Paleolithic transition at El Castillo, Cueva Morin and El Pendo (Cantabria, Spain). *Journal of Human Evolution* 36: 283–317.

Rabinovich R. and E. Tchernov 1995. Chronological, paleoecological and taphonomical aspects of the Middle Paleolithic site of Qafzeh, Israel. In H. Buitenhuis and H.-P. Uerpmann (Eds.), *Archaeozoology of the Near East, II*, pp. 5–44. Leiden: Backhuys Publishers.

Richards M.P., P.B. Pettitt, E. Trinkaus, F.H. Smith, M. Paunovic and I. Karavanic 2000. Neandertal diet at Vindija and Neandertal predation. The evidence from stable isotopes. *Proceedings of the National Academy of Sciences USA* 97: 7663–7666.

Rick J. and K.M. Moore 2001. Specialized meat-eating in the Holocene: an archaeological case from the frigid topics of high altitude Peru. In C.B. Stanford and H.T. Bunn (Eds.), *Meat Eating and Human Evolution*, pp. 237–260. Oxford: Oxford University Press.

Shea J. 1989. A functional study of the lithic industries associated with hominid fossils in the Kebara and Qafzeh caves, Israel. In P. Mellars and C.B. Stringer (Eds.), *The Human Revolution*, pp. 611–625. Princeton: Princeton University Press.

Smith B.D. 1974. Predator-prey relationships in the southeastern Ozarks—A. D. 1300. *Human Ecology* 2: 31–43.

Speth J.D. and E. Tchernov 1998. The role of hunting and scavenging in Neanderthal procurement strategies: new evidence from Kebara Cave (Israel). In T. Akazawa, K. Aoki and O. Bar-Yosef (Eds.), *Neanderthals and Modern Humans in West Asia*, pp. 223–239. New York: Plenum Press.

Speth J.D. and E. Tchernov 2001. Neandertal hunting and meat-processing in the Near East: evidence from Kebara Cave (Israel). In C.B. Stanford and H.T. Bunn (Eds.), *Meat-Eating and Human Evolution*, pp. 52–72. Oxford: Oxford University Press.

Speth J.D. and E. Tchernov 2002. Middle Paleolithic tortoise use at Kebara Cave (Israel). *Journal of Archaeological Science* 29: 471–483.

Stephens D.W. and J.R. Krebs 1986. *Foraging Theory*. Princeton: Princeton University Press.

Stiner M.C. 1990. The use of mortality patterns in archaeological studies of hominid predatory adaptations. *Journal of Anthropological Archaeology* 9: 305–351.

Stiner M.C. 1994. *Honor among Thieves: A Zooarchaeological Study of Neandertal Ecology*. Princeton: Princeton University Press.

Stiner M.C. 2001. Thirty years on the "Broad Spectrum Revolution" and Paleolithic demography. *Proceedings of the National Academy of Sciences USA* 98: 6993–6996.

Stiner M.C. 2002. Carnivory, coevolution, and the geographic spread of the genus *Homo*. *Journal of Archaeological Research* 10: 1–63.

Stiner M.C. 2003. Zooarchaeological evidence for resource intensification in Algarve, southern Portugal. *Promontoria* 1: 27–61.

Stiner M.C. 2005. *Paleolithic Diet and Demography: A 200,000-Year Record from Hayonim Cave (Levant)*. Cambridge, MA: Peabody Museum Press, Harvard University.

Stiner M.C., N.D. Munro and T.A. Surovell 2000. The tortoise and the hare: small game use, the Broad Spectrum Revolution, and Paleolithic demography. *Current Anthropology* 41: 39–73.

Stiner M.C. and S.L. Kuhn 1992. Subsistence, technology, and adaptive variation in Middle Paleolithic Italy. *American Anthropologist* 94: 12–46.

Stiner M.C. and E. Tchernov 1998. Pleistocene species trends at Hayonim Cave: changes in climate versus human behavior. In T. Akazawa, K. Aoki and O. Bar-Yosef (Eds.), *Neanderthals and Modern Humans in West Asia*, pp. 241–262. New York: Plenum Press.

Thieme H. 1997. Lower Palaeolithic hunting spears from Germany. *Nature* 385: 807–810.

Tozzi C. 1970. La Grotta di S. Agostino (Gaeta). *Rivista di Scienze Preistoriche* 25: 3–87.

van Andel T.H., W. Davies, B. Weninger and O. Jöris 2003. Archaeological dates as proxies for the spatial and temporal human presence in Europe: a discourse on the method. In T.H. van Andel and W. Davies (Eds.), *Neandertals and Modern Humans in the European Landscape during the Last Glaciation*, pp. 21–29. Cambridge: McDonald Institute for Archaeological Research, University of Cambridge.

Weniger G.-C. 1987. Magdalenian settlement pattern and subsistence in Central Europe: the southwestern and central German cases. In O. Soffer (Ed.), *The Pleistocene Old World: Regional Perspectives*, pp. 201–215. New York: Plenum Press.

Winterhalder B. and F. Lu 1997. A forager-resource population ecology model and implications for indigenous conservation. *Conservation Biology* 11: 1354–1364.

Wrinn P.J. and J.W. Rink 2003. ESR dating of tooth enamel from Aterian levels at Mugharet el 'Aliya (Tangier, Morocco). *Journal of Archaeological Science* 30: 89–99.

Chapter *13*

Projectile Technologies of the African MSA
Implications for Modern Human Origins

Alison S. Brooks
Lisa Nevell
George Washington University, Washington DC 20052

John E. Yellen
National Science Foundation, Arlington, Virginia 22230

Gideon Hartman
Harvard University, Cambridge, Massachusetts 02138

ABSTRACT

One of the most significant barriers to understanding the emergence of Late Palaeolithic adaptations is the absence of a comparative analytical framework encompassing African MSA/LSA and Eurasian Middle/Late Palaeolithic industries. Projectile armatures, varying widely in time and space, constitute many of the original "fossiles directeurs" of the Eurasian Upper Palaeolithic, and their development may have been important in the eventual dominance of anatomically modern humans across this region. At an earlier date, the African MSA is distinguished from most Middle Palaeolithic industries of Eurasia by the complexity and patterned variation of projectile armatures, as well as by their numerical dominance in many industries. This paper will review the patterning of projectile armatures in Africa, discuss alternative approaches to analysis, and present a comparative study of armatures from two African regions and the Levant. We argue that the small size of many MSA points implies the existence of a complex projectile technology rather than simple spears.

INTRODUCTION

Middle Stone Age (MSA) assemblages of Africa, especially those from sub-Saharan regions, have rarely been compared directly to Middle Paleolithic (MP) assemblages outside Africa. Until very recently, results of excavations in Middle Stone Age (MSA) sites were mostly published in regional journals or local presses, and often included only limited illustrations. Even more complete and well-illustrated publications did not furnish easy comparisons with assemblages from the Near East and elsewhere in Eurasia. African archaeologists almost never followed examples from the Levant in using Bordes' (1961) typology or another European typology, modified as necessary, to describe their finds.

For much of the MSA, the Bordes typology and others like it would obscure fundamental regional differences, as well as the major differences between the MSA and the MP outside Africa. This is because the focus of Bordes' typology is on scrapers, which often form the dominant and most elaborated category in European MP assemblages. Many of the more formal categories of tools in MSA assemblages from tropical Africa are points, not scrapers (Figure 1). Carefully retouched bifacial and unifacial points may dominate the retouched or formal tool component, while scrapers, although sometimes more numerous, often form a far more heterogeneous grouping, many of them recycled from points, or manufactured from a similar template and using similar techniques of retouch. Initial reports on Blombos in South Africa, for example, noted that 52% of the retouched stone tools were bifacial points and fragments (Henshilwood and Sealey 1997, n.d.). Points were used to define the original MSA and its variants (Goodwin 1928), and are present at early sites like Gademotta and Kukeleti (Wendorf and Schild 1974).

The focus of this paper is the distinctiveness of the African MSA; however it is important to note that the patterning of points in the MSA does have implications for two aspects of the debate on behavioral modernity. First, the MSA points' complexity and their clear use as projectile armatures (*e.g.*, Volman 1984; Harper 1994; Würz 1997; Milo 1998) in what may have been a variety of specialized compound artifacts implies cognitive sophistication. The process of assembling diverse elements into a compound artifact such as a projectile could be seen as analogous to the process of assembling words into a sentence. There is a grammar and an order to the tool assembly process that is partly universal and partly culturally specific; furthermore, each element of the tool can be exchanged for a different one, changing the meaning and the function of the resulting product.

The second contribution of MSA stone points to the behavioral modernity debate is the regional and chronological specificity of MSA points, which has implications for the social organization of the producers. Wilmsen (1974) has argued that the form of projectile points is more tightly constrained by aerodynamic requirements than the form of other stone tools is constrained by function; consequently, he argues that points are the most likely candidates to reflect regional "styles". Projectile armatures must be able to replace broken armatures, so the haft into which they are placed also imposes limitations on the projectile size and form. Having a system of exchange within social networks further encourages similarity of point form so that the product remains interchangeable within a

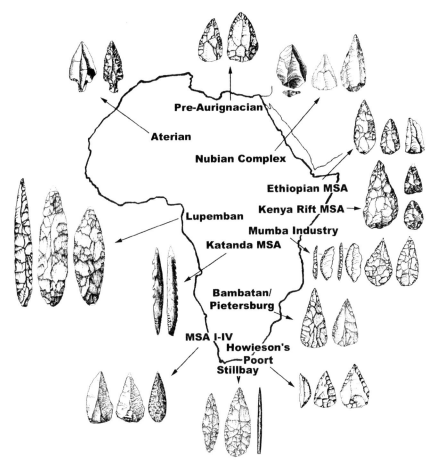

Figure 1. African points of the Middle Stone Age [adapted from McBrearty and Brooks (2000)].

cultural group. Wiessner (1983) argued from ethnographic data that even where forms were extremely limited by raw materials regional styles emerged (*e.g.*, fence wire in Wiessner's ethnographic example). Men hunt well for only a few years but continue to make arrow points for most of their lives; consequently, arrows are frequently given to hunters in exchange for a claim on the eventual kill. Hunting success is influenced by the hunter's familiarity with an armature; this kind of social trade network would therefore be expected to encourage homogeneity in the size and shape of projectile points. Thus social organization, especially the development of exchange networks, constrains point styles and creates sharp discontinuities at social boundaries, whether these boundaries are linguistic, ethnic or simply a result of an empty buffer zone between group ranges.

In 1988, Desmond Clark wrote an important summary entitled "The Middle Stone Age of East Africa and the beginnings of regional identity". Much of the "regional identity" of his title concerned not only ways in which the East African MSA was distinctive, but differences within East Africa, especially in the forms of points. Within the Horn of Africa alone, Clark (1988:297) contrasted ".... the markedly subtriangular points of Gorgora [in the north], the pointed leaf-shaped forms at Porc Epic and Gademotta [both in the Ethiopian Rift], and the Levallois points at Midhishi in Somalia."

Point variants were also used to define different regional and chronological variants of the South African MSA, including the Stillbay points of the Cape coast, with their pointed bases, the Howiesons Poort geometrics of the Cape Province and surrounding regions, the elongated Pietersburg points of the Transvaal and the triangular Bambata points of Botswana and western Zimbabwe. Many of these point types are similar in size and are made with a similar range of raw materials including local quartz and quartzites, as well as exotic silcretes and other silicified materials. As Clark (1988) argued (see Figure 1), East Africa also includes several regional and chronological variants. At Mumba in Tanzania, for example, small triangular points occur throughout the long MSA sequence and are joined in the later "Mumba" industry (*ca.* 65–45 thousand years ago) levels by a group of highly formalized medium-sized crescent-shaped geometric points (Mehlman 1979, 1989, 1991). North African points also exhibit regional and chronological variants, including Nubian point types in the Nile Valley, and various tanged and leaf-shaped Aterian points throughout the Sahara and North African littoral. In the Central African region, not only is there a range of elongated Lupemban points, but also assemblages of miniature triangular points such as those described by Mercader and Marti (1999) for Cameroon and by Robbins *et al.* (2000) for Rhino shelter in northern Botswana.

In addition to lithic points, MSA sites have also yielded bone points from two different regions of Africa in association with MSA lithics and which are dated to early Oxygen Isotope Stage (OIS) 4, approximately 70,000–90,000 years ago. The cylindrical points of Blombos and Klasies on the South African coast (Henshilwood and Sealey 1997) and the barbed points of Katanda in the Rift Valley of eastern Congo (Yellen 1988; Brooks *et al.* 1995, 2004; Yellen *et al.* 1995; Brooks and Yellen 2004) are markedly different in style, yet may both be associated with a new economic activity, fishing.

The study of excavated assemblages with MSA points from two different regions of sub-Saharan Africa demonstrates how these differ from each other and from points described for the Levantine Mousterian. MSA points may also have been used in fundamentally different ways from Levantine examples.

THE SAMPLE

≠Gi Site, Botswana

The first region to be compared is in the Kalahari Desert of Western Botswana, on the Namibian border (Figure 2). The MSA-LSA site of ≠Gi , with MSA horizons dated to *ca.* 77,000 years BP, is located on the eastern edge of the deepest pan

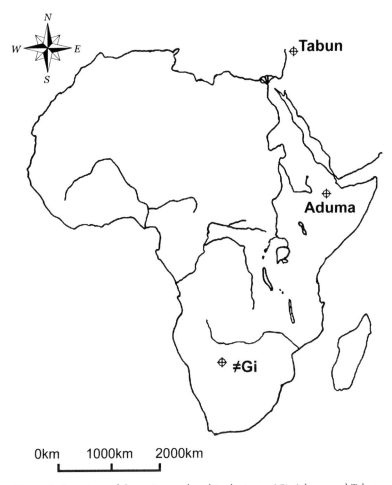

Figure 2. Locations of three sites analyzed in the text, ≠Gi, Aduma and Tabun.

or depression in the area (Brooks *et al.* 1980, 1990; Brooks and Yellen 1987; Brooks 1998). To the present day (2003) the pan serves as an ambush hunting venue, whose use is limited to the end of the rainy season when water scarcity concentrates game around this one remaining water source. In the site's LSA levels, crescents, which are interpreted as arrow armatures, far outnumbered scrapers. In the underlying MSA levels, points were the dominant tool class, constituting 41% of the *ca.* 1,500 retouched pieces. Many additional points had been recycled into scrapers and knives.

The points at ≠Gi are predominantly small, triangular, and bifacial, averaging *ca.* 41 mm in length, with some examples close to 30 mm. Bases are heavily thinned and modified, presumably for hafting. Although some points are entirely unifacial, most have some degree of bifacial working, either just at the base, over part of the edge, or over the entire ventral surface (Figure 3). Maximum width, usually at the base, was tightly controlled (Figure 4). This was in spite of the use of a wide

≠Gi Bifacial Points

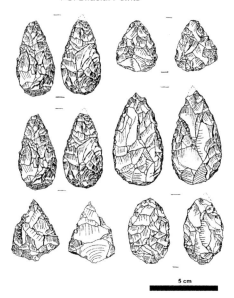

5 cm

≠Gi Partly Bifacial Points

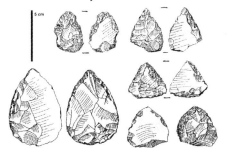

5 cm

≠Gi Unifacial Points

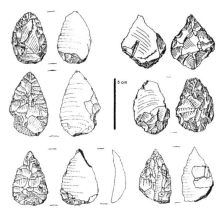

5 cm

Figure 3. ≠Gi points.

238

Figure 4. Photo of ≠Gi points.

range of raw materials including chert, jasper, chalcedony and quartzite. These materials occurred in both tabular form in local outcrops and in medium to large size cobbles in the conglomerate below the MSA horizons. Since they are made on discoidal cores, the flakes' bulbs and striking platforms are frequently on the corner rather than in the center of the base. Not only are the platforms heavily modified or removed by retouch, but we noted that the side opposite the one ending in a striking platform is often slightly wider, as if in an effort to compensate for the increased mass on the striking platform side. We began to develop a measurement system to detect this asymmetry, in addition to reflecting differences in size, shape and process of manufacture.

≠Gi points are markedly smaller than typical MP points from outside Africa, although mean thickness is slightly greater (14.1 mm) since this is a discoidal rather than a Levallois technology. Point bases are heavily retouched and width is controlled, suggestive of hafting. In addition, the ≠Gi sample exhibits multiple examples of projectile impact damage, including hinge fractures, broken tips, and burination spalls (shown in Figure 5), and micro-striations, the latter possibly due to hafting wear. Their size places them at the lower limits of ethnographically known spear armatures and within the range of ethnographically known spear thrower darts and larger arrowheads, as well as in the lower range of non-microlithic projectile points (Thomas 1976). It is perhaps not surprising that the associated ≠Gi MSA faunal remains suggest commonalities with South African LSA hunters, such as those at Nelson's Bay Cave (Klein 1989, 1992, 1999).

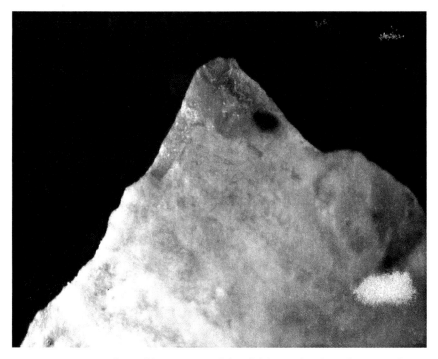

Figure 5. Microphoto of burination spall (X40) [photo taken by Robin Teague].

Aduma Sites, Middle Awash, Ethiopia

Our second point sample comes from the region of Aduma, in the Middle Awash Valley of Ethiopia (Haile-Selassie *et al.*, 2004; Yellen *et al.* in press). Here we excavated a series of sealed archaeological occurrences spread over 15 km² of small relict erosional hills on the west bank of the river. The dominant feature of the Aduma landscape is a massive series of silts lacking any marked soil horizons, overlying the cobble pavement at the A-1 site, and interstratified elsewhere with sands and fine gravels towards the base. This silt unit is termed "Ardu II". We have divided the rest of our sites, for comparative purposes, into three groups: the sand/fine gravel/basal silt layers (Ardu II-base), the massive silts above (Ardu II), and the site A-5 soil horizon at the Ardu II/III contact between the massive silts and the overlying dark colluvial level. Based on a preliminary assessment, the entire sequence appears to represent a relatively short interval, dating to late OIS 5 or early OIS 4, and is almost certainly older than 70,000 years BP. The A-1 lag surface is likely to be considerably older, possibly representing a hyper-arid period of deflationary activity during OIS 6, or earlier, paralleling the expansion of African arid zones during OIS 4 and 2.

At site A-1, a lag of MSA materials rested on an old cobble pavement incorporating multiple erosional cycles. An excavated sample was recovered from the base of silts overlaying a cobble layer. Variants of Levallois technology dominate the lithic assemblage, although discoidal and small blade cores are also present. The points and cores include forms typical of later horizons, but are dominated by unique types not seen in the overlying levels. These include large bifacial points or small bifaces (Figure 6:F), and large "Mousterian" type points on big Levallois flakes (Figure 6:E). Obsidian is used for approximately half the points and for at least one extremely large pointed "biface" core; other materials include fine

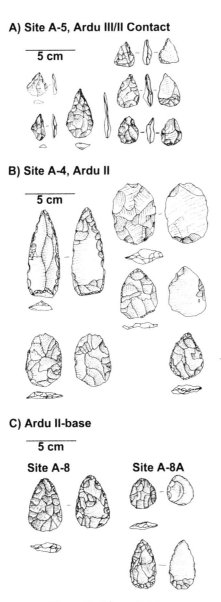

Figure 6. Aduma Points.

D) Aduma
Classic MSA Points

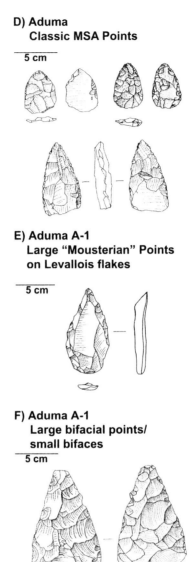

E) Aduma A-1
Large "Mousterian" Points
on Levallois flakes

F) Aduma A-1
Large bifacial points/
small bifaces

Figure 6. (*Continued*)

volcanics and cherts. The presence of types identical to those found higher in the sequence could signal stratigraphic admixture. Unfortunately, we have not been able to derive a date for this horizon consistent with those suggested for the later horizons.

Seventy-six to 93% of all points in these later levels are made of obsidian. The dominant point types of Ardu II (silt) and Ardu II base (gravel) include classic

Table 1. Point type percentage

	Tabun B (n=9)	Tabun C (n=10)	Tabun D (n=31)	Aduma 1 (n=16)	A8 Gravel (n=69)	A4 Silt (n=33)	Aduma 5 (n=39)
Point biface	0	0	0	6.3	0	0	0
Mousterian Point	0	10	26	31.3	0	0	0
Levallois Point	100	60	42	18.8	0	0	2.6
Classic MSA Point	0	0	0	18.8	12.7	36.4	5.1
Short Broad Point	0	0	0	0	19.7	33.3	7.7
Small Blunt Point	0	0	0	0	0	0	10.3
Pointed blade	0	10	32	0	1.4	6.1	0
Acute tip Point	0	20	0	0	8.5	9.1	23.1
Pint/Perforator	0	0	0	6.3	18.3	0	15.4
Perforator	0	0	0	6.3	23.9	3	28.2
Miscellaneous	0	0	0	12.5	9.9	12.1	5.1
Perforator-borer	0	0	0	0	0	0	0
Unknown	0	0	0	0	0	0	2.6
Broken	0		0	18.8	14.5	0	0

MSA points with trimmed bases and highly invasive bifacial and unifacial retouch (FIG 6:D). These are much less common in the uppermost horizon, which is dominated by small acute-tip and blunt points and point-perforators (Figure 6:A, Table 1). Point-perforators and perforators are also found in the Ardu II base. This probably reflects differences in landscape and site function. A group of short broad points also appears in this basal level and diminishes in frequency thereafter. The uppermost level (Ardu II/III) is distinguished by the very small size of the point component with some points measuring less than 2 cm in length. Like the ≠Gi points, the average Ardu II and II/III points fall within the ethnographic spear thrower dart and large arrow range in length, but the Ardu II/III points are so small that they do not overlap at all with the range of length of ethnographic spear points.

Tabun Cave, Israel

Because the points from Aduma were made to a large extent on Levallois flakes and flake/blades, we compared them to a series of 56 points from levels at Tabun B, C, and D in the Levant to explore the differences between African points and Levantine Mousterian points. The upper horizons, Tabun B and C, are probably roughly contemporary with the Ardu II and II/III, while Tabun D may be older than or approximately contemporary with the very early Aduma A-1 assemblage. The Tabun B and C points were classed predominantly as Levallois points; Mousterian and acute-tip points as well as pointed blades were somewhat more common in the underlying Tabun layer D (Table 1). We note, however, that the Tabun sample was taken from old collections excavated by Garrod (Garrod and Bate 1937) held at the National Museum of Natural History, Smithsonian

Institution. This collection is biased in favor of complete and aesthetically pleasing artifacts, and this comparison should be regarded as only suggestive.

RESULTS

Our point measurement system involves a total of 25 variables describing attributes of the blank, the divergence and shape of the sides, point asymmetry, marginal retouch, and treatment of the base. In this comparison we will focus on only a few of these: overall dimensions, the angle described by the sides of the point from the tip to the maximum distance of each side from the midline, the marginal retouch pattern, and treatment of the butt (Figure 7, Table 2). Points which lay more than two standard deviations from the mean were considered outliers. African hunter-gatherers today use bows and arrows in addition to larger tool types and by analogy we propose that projectile technology in the MSA was adopted as part of a broad toolkit; diagrams representing trends in point size and shape do not depict outliers. The number of points measured and the number of outliers excluded is reported for each analysis (Figures 8, 9, 10 and 11), as is the sample size, mean, and standard deviation of the total sample (Table 2).

Tabun points (Figure 8a) become markedly shorter through time from layers D to B, but width is held remarkably constant over time so that the youngest points are very broad for their length. Note that the average length of Tabun points varies

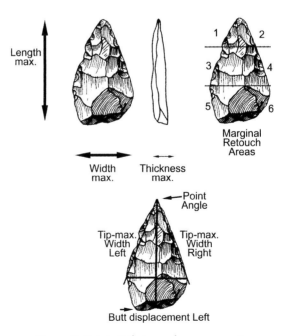

Figure 7. Point attributes and measurements.

Table 2. Metric values of points at Tabun, Aduma and ≠Gi

	Length (mm)	Width (mm)	Thickness (mm)	Angle (degrees)	Weight/ predicted (g)
Tabun B N	8	9	9	9	9
Mean	53.6	36.7	7.2	55.6	12.6
Std. Deviation	11.1	7.6	1.9	8.8	6.0
Tabun C N	16	16	16	10	14
Mean	67.8	34.4	8.3	46.0	16.8
Std. Deviation	12.5	8.1	2.4	11.7	11.9
Tabun D N	31	31	31	31	31
Mean	71.9	35.9	8.7	45.5	19.0
Std. Deviation	13.9	8.9	2.3	10.3	9.6
≠Gi N	16	16	16	16	16
Mean	74.0	46.8	14.1	55.3	50.1
Std. Deviation	24.9	14.7	3.8	11.8	43.9
Aduma 1 N	68	69	69	68	68
Mean	35.4	27.4	9.0	61.2	8.8
Std. Deviation	7.4	10.0	2.3	15.6	6.0
Aduma 8 N	32	33	33	32	32
Mean	48.5	32.8	10.7	57.3	19.7
Std. Deviation	16.3	10.8	4.7	19.1	20.2
Aduma 4 N	39	39	39	37	39
Mean	32.5	23.9	7.3	55.8	6.6
Std. Deviation	11.0	8.6	2.7	13.9	6.8
Aduma 5 N	299	299	260	299	299
Mean	40.2	30.1	10.2	70.5	11.8
Std. Deviation	8.4	6.1	2.7	10.6	7.2

from *ca.* 70 mm in the lower levels to *ca.* 50 mm in Level B, well within the range of ethnographic spear heads. The comparable distributions at Aduma and ≠Gi are shown in Figure 8b. In general, at Aduma, both length and width decrease regularly through time and in constant relation to each other.

The relationship between thickness and width is compared between the two regions and follows a pattern similar to the relationship between length and width. At Tabun, (Figure 9a) thickness decreases slightly from D up to B, but width is held relatively constant. On the other hand, at Aduma (Figure 9b), thickness and width both decrease through time in a constant ratio. As a result of maintaining a constant width through time while decreasing length and thickness, the point angle at Tabun becomes duller over time (Figure 10a). One interpretation of this pattern is that the hafting requirements remained constant, without regard for the functional quality of the point itself. At Aduma on the other hand (Figure 10b) the point angle is relatively invariant through time, averaging between 55 and 60 degrees, suggesting that consistency in the functional attributes of the point itself was more important than consistency of the hafting scheme.

Perhaps the most important attribute in the development of a projectile technology is weight, since Newton's second law predicts that a lighter projectile must

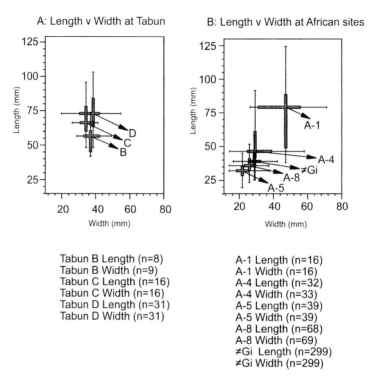

A: Length v Width at Tabun

B: Length v Width at African sites

Tabun B Length (n=8)
Tabun B Width (n=9)
Tabun C Length (n=16)
Tabun C Width (n=16)
Tabun D Length (n=31)
Tabun D Width (n=31)

A-1 Length (n=16)
A-1 Width (n=16)
A-4 Length (n=32)
A-4 Width (n=33)
A-5 Length (n=39)
A-5 Width (n=39)
A-8 Length (n=68)
A-8 Width (n=69)
≠Gi Length (n=299)
≠Gi Width (n=299)

Cross plot sample size included sample (# of outliers not shown)	late		early	early			late
	Tabun B	Tabun C	Tabun D	≠Gi	Aduma 1	Aduma 8	Aduma 4	Aduma 5
Length	8(0)	16(0)	31(0)	285(14)	16(0)	67(1)	32(0)	36(3)
Width	9(0)	14(2)	31(0)	290(9)	16(0)	67(2)	33(0)	37(2)
Thickness	9(0)	15 (1)	31(0)	257(3)	15(1)	65(4)	32(1)	38(1)
Angle	9(0)	10(0)	30(1)	299(0)	16(0)	68(0)	32(0)	36(1)
Weight/Predicted Weight	9(0)	12(2)	30(1)	282(17)	15(1)	64(4)	31(1)	35(4)

Figure 8. Distribution of Length vs. Width at Tabun (A) and African sites (B). Box plots show the mean and one standard deviation, whiskers show 1 to 2 standard deviations. Outliers not shown.

be propelled with greater acceleration to achieve the same force or penetration (or, conversely, a more forceful propulsion system allows use of a lighter projectile). While the haft certainly contributed a major part of total projectile weight, functional considerations would require that haft and point weights be related, so that a large heavy haft would tend to be armed with a large heavy point. Point weight decreases through time in both Africa and the Levant, but much more so in the African sample, reaching averages of as low as 6.6 grams at some of the Aduma sites (Figure 11a, b).

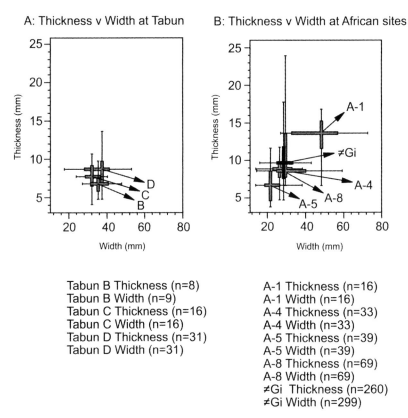

A: Thickness v Width at Tabun   B: Thickness v Width at African sites

Tabun B Thickness (n=8)
Tabun B Width (n=9)
Tabun C Thickness (n=16)
Tabun C Width (n=16)
Tabun D Thickness (n=31)
Tabun D Width (n=31)

A-1 Thickness (n=16)
A-1 Width (n=16)
A-4 Thickness (n=33)
A-4 Width (n=33)
A-5 Thickness (n=39)
A-5 Width (n=39)
A-8 Thickness (n=69)
A-8 Width (n=69)
≠Gi Thickness (n=260)
≠Gi Width (n=299)

Figure 9. Distribution of Thickness vs. Width at Tabun (A) and African sites (B). Box and whisker plots as in Figure 8. In figure 9A: Tabun B thickness and width (n = 9 for each measurement); Tabun c thickness and width (n = 16 each); Tabun D thickness and width (n = 31 each); figure 9B: A-1 thickness and width (n = 16 for each measurement); A-4 thickness and width (n = 33 each); A-5 thickness and width (n = 39 each); A-8 thickness and width (n = 69 each); ≠Gi thickness (n = 260); ≠Gi width (n = 299).

While all pieces from ≠Gi and Tabun were weighed on an O-Haus triple beam balance, weights of points at Aduma were estimated from the volume. We used the total of 0.5 times maximum width times maximum length times maximum thickness (0.5 W × L × Th) as a proxy for the volume of a roughly triangular point. For the ≠Gi sample, the regression formula calculated for weight against this volume was

$$\text{Weight (g)} = 0.750 + (\text{Volume in mm}^3 \text{ times } 0.001684).$$

The adjusted r^2 value (0.944) was significant beyond 0.001 level, indicating that the formula accounts for 94% of the variance in the ≠Gi point sample. We used this regression formula to predict the weights of points from Aduma for which we did not have direct measurement of the weight. Since the obsidian of

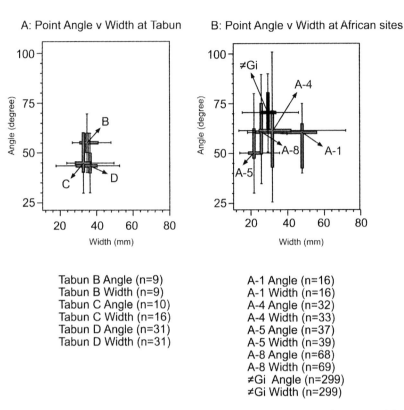

Figure 10. Distribution of Point angle vs. Width at Tabun (A) and African sites (B).
Box and whisker plots as in Figure 8.

the Aduma points is lighter than the quartzite and silcrete of the ≠Gi points, the actual values are likely to be even lower than the estimated ones. For Tabun, the comparable formula was

$$\text{Weight} = 0.426 + (\text{Volume} \times 0.001571).$$

The adjusted r^2 value was 0.914, which accounts for 91% of the variation and is significant to the .000 level. Regression formulae which predict the mass based on the area of a point were derived separately using comparative material from either Africa or the Levant, both formulae describe a large potion of the variation in the samples, both formulae are highly significant, and both formulae provide reasonable estimates of the mass of Aduma points.

Marginal retouch is another area in which Aduma MSA points are distinguished from Tabun points (Figure 12). Each piece was divided into six retouch areas, three per side, and the presence, position and nature of the retouch, if any, were noted for each area While some points from the earliest Tabun sample are retouched, a greater portion of Aduma points are retouched in every level. The pieces that are retouched at Aduma are more completely retouched (retouched in

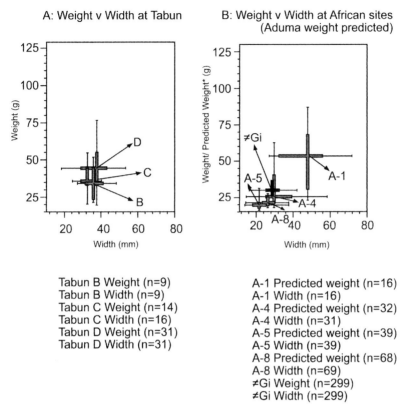

A: Weight v Width at Tabun

B: Weight v Width at African sites (Aduma weight predicted)

Tabun B Weight (n=9)
Tabun B Width (n=9)
Tabun C Weight (n=14)
Tabun C Width (n=16)
Tabun D Weight (n=31)
Tabun D Width (n=31)

A-1 Predicted weight (n=16)
A-1 Width (n=16)
A-4 Predicted weight (n=32)
A-4 Width (n=31)
A-5 Predicted weight (n=39)
A-5 Width (n=39)
A-8 Predicted weight (n=68)
A-8 Width (n=69)
≠Gi Weight (n=299)
≠Gi Width (n=299)

Figure 11. Distribution of Weight *vs.* Width at Tabun (A) and African sites (B). Box and whisker plots as in Figure 8.

more areas of each piece) than the Tabun points. While inverse, or ventral, retouch is rare throughout, it is actually most common in Tabun D. Bifacial retouch, on the other hand, is virtually absent in the Tabun sample and present at significant frequencies throughout the Aduma sample, except for the uppermost level. Invasive retouch, a hallmark of the classic MSA, is found at low levels in Tabun D (although not in B or C), but at Aduma, it rises along with the frequency of classic MSA points to a maximum in the Ardu II silt sites, then decreases slightly at the top.

Finally, striking platforms of complete pieces are virtually unmodified in the Tabun assemblage but up to 50% are thinned or removed on the Aduma points. Overall, the earliest Aduma points from A-1 are most similar to the Tabun points from Level D. If one were to argue from the points for a moment of contact or expansion in either direction, this time period represents the most likely candidate. The later points in both areas dating to late OIS 5 and early OIS 4 are increasingly divergent in style.

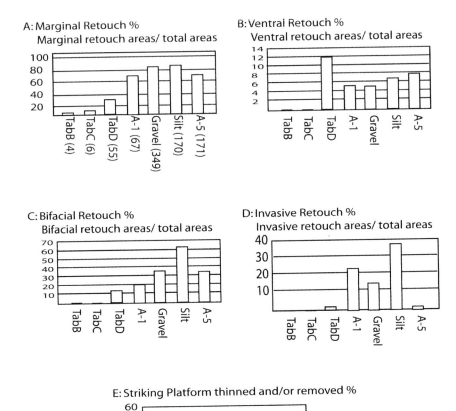

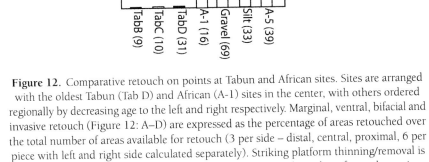

Figure 12. Comparative retouch on points at Tabun and African sites. Sites are arranged with the oldest Tabun (Tab D) and African (A-1) sites in the center, with others ordered regionally by decreasing age to the left and right respectively. Marginal, ventral, bifacial and invasive retouch (Figure 12: A–D) are expressed as the percentage of areas retouched over the total number of areas available for retouch (3 per side – distal, central, proximal, 6 per piece with left and right side calculated separately). Striking platform thinning/removal is expressed as number of modified striking platforms over total number of complete points.

ETHNOGRAPHIC COMPARISONS

While it is difficult to reconstruct the entire projectile system from the lithic remains, North American archaeologists have used ethnographic examples to derive correlations between lithic attributes and projectile systems. This type of correlation, of course, does not encompass the possibility of now-vanished projectile systems relating to an earlier evolutionary stage. The most cited study is that of D.H. Thomas (1976) who examined 142 stone-tipped projectiles from ethnographic contexts housed at the American Museum of Natural History. His results showed that while some arrowheads were large and weighed between 11 and 17 g, most were very small, and weighed 4 g or less. Spear thrower darts, on the other hand, varied between *ca.* two and eight grams.

The Aduma points tend increasingly toward the dimensions of spear thrower darts or arrows, and hold point angle constant. Although ethnographic and archaeological examples of spear throwers are not known from any African site, spear throwers are present at a much later date on all the other inhabited continents and begin to appear at a time when African LSA armatures already fall within the size range of modern arrowheads (at < 1.5 g). The early diminution of African stone armature may indicate that Africa passed through a spear thrower stage at an earlier date.

DISCUSSION AND CONCLUSIONS

In summary, the regional and chronological diversity and specificity of MSA points, their small size, the emphasis on control and standardization of basal morphologies, and point angles, and the extensive use of bifacial retouch can be thought of as a complex of features; this complex distinguishes MSA points after 100,000 years ago from those of the Levantine Mousterian. The decrease in point size and weight within the MSA suggest concomitant development of a system that could propel projectiles over greater distances, increasing hunting success while decreasing risk to the hunter. The projectile system, whether a bow and arrow or more likely, a spear thrower, would have involved organic materials that have not survived. In both Europe and North America, the use of spear throwers may have preceded in some instances the use of the bow and arrow. Since the early Upper Paleolithic of Europe is also characterized by small and/or light (bone) projectile armatures (*e.g.*, Bricker *et al.* 1995; Brooks *et al.* 1995; Cattelain 1997; Perpère 1997; Hays and Lucas 2001, *etc.*) several authors have argued for early use of a complex projectile system, despite the absence of actual examples of either bows or spear throwers.

The adoption of a complex projectile system during the MSA, in combination with the development of complex economic, social and symbolic systems signified by such finds as increased use of marine and lacustrine resources (Brooks *et al.* 1995; Yellen *et al.* 1995; Henshilwood and Sealey 1997; Crawford *et al.* 1999; Poeggenpohl 1999), regional point "styles" (Clark 1988; McBrearty and Brooks

2000), incised ocher plaques (Henshihlwood *et al.* 2002), long distance transport of raw materials (Merrick *et al.* 1994), and beads (Hare *et al.* 1993; Kuhn *et al.* 2001) would have resulted in lowered risk to individual hunters and increased survivorship of both individuals and populations (McBrearty and Brooks 2000). Increased survivorship, in turn, could explain the successful expansion of anatomically modern humans out of Africa at *ca.*60,000 years BP. The apparent similarity of even earlier point technologies in Africa and the Near East to one another, exemplified respectively by Aduma A-1 and Tabun D, could also explain the failure of earlier anatomically modern African populations to expand beyond the Near East, as well as the absence of significant technological differences over time between the earliest modern humans and Neandertals in the Near East. Apart from possible comparisons to a few small points from the Later MP of the Caucasus (*e.g.*, Doronichev and Galovanova 2003), European MP bifacial point technologies are closer in size to the A-1 and Tabun assemblages than to the evolved MSA points of sub-Saharan Africa.

ACKNOWLEDGEMENTS

The research in Botswana and Ethiopia was supported by NSF grants to Brooks and Yellen, and to Brooks and Clark, as well as by grants from the National Geographic Society, L.S.B. Leakey Foundation, Smithsonian Institution, and the George Washington University Committee on Research. We would like to acknowledge the assistance of Robin Teague and Paul Constantino of the George Washington University Hominid Paleobiology Program, in collecting information, photos and preparing materials for this paper. The drawings of points were done by Wendy Bruneau (≠Gi) and Fekru Haile Mariam (Aduma). In addition, we would like to express our gratitude to Tim White, the late Desmond Clark, Yonas Beyene and the other directors of the Middle Awash Project, and especially the governments and peoples of Botswana and Ethiopia, who made possible the excavations on which the paper was based. Lisa Nevell and Gideon Hartman were supported by an NSF IGERT grant and by a George Washington Presidential Fellowship to GH.

REFERENCES CITED

Bordes F. 1961. *Typologie du Paléolithique ancien et moyen.* Bordeaux : Delmas.
Bricker H.M., A.S. Brooks, R.B. Clay and N. 1995. Les fouilles de H.L. Movius Jr. à *l'abri Pataud:* généralités. In H.M. Bricker (Ed.), *Le Paléolithique supérieur de l'abri Pataud (Dordogne): les fouilles de H.L. Movius Jr: suivi d'un inventaire analytique des sites Aurignaciens et Périgordiens de Dordogne,* pp. 11–30. Paris: Editions de la Maison des Sciences de l'Homme.
Brooks A.S., A.L. Crowell and J.E. Yellen 1980. ≠Gi: a Stone Age archaeological site in the northern Kalahari Desert, Botswana. In R.E.F. Leakey and B.A. Ogot, (Eds.), *Proceedings of the Eighth Panafrican Congress of Prehistory and Quaternary Studies (Nairobi, 1977),* pp. 304–309. Nairobi: The International Louis Leakey Memorial Institute for African Prehistory.

Brooks A.S. and J.E. Yellen 1987. The preservation of activity areas in the archaeological record: ethnoarchaeological and archaeological work in northwest Ngamiland, Botswana. In S. Kent (Ed.), *Method and Theory of Activity Area Research: An Ethnoarchaeological Approach*, pp. 63–106. New York: Columbia University Press.

Brooks A.S., P.E. Hare, J.E. Kokis, G.H. Miller, R.D. Ernst and F. Wendorf 1990. Dating Pleistocene archaeological sites by protein diagenesis in ostrich eggshell. *Science* 248: 60–64.

Brooks A.S., D.M. Helgren, J.M. Cramer, A. Franklin, W. Hornyak, J.M. Keating, R.G. Klein, W.J. Rink, H.P. Schwarcz, J.N.L. Smith, K. Stewart, N.E. Todd, J. Verniers and J.E. Yellen 1995. Dating and context of three Middle Stone Age sites with bone points in the upper Semliki Valley, Zaire. *Science* 268: 548–553.

Brooks A.S. 1998. Open air sites in the Middle Stone Age of Africa. In N. Conard and F. Wendorf (Eds.), *Middle Paleolithic and Middle Stone Age Settlement Systems*, pp. 249–253. Forli: A.B.A.C.O.

Brooks A.S. and J.E.Yellen 2004. Bones of contention: bone tools and the emergence of modern human behavior. *Abstracts of the 69th Annual Meeting of the Society for American Archaeology, Montreal Canada*, p. 65. Washington DC: Society for American Archaeology.

Brooks A.S., F.J. Feathers, G. Hartman, N. Tuross, F. d'Errico and J.E. Yellen 2004. Middle Stone Age bone points from Katanda (D.R. Congo): new perspectives on age and association. Poster presented at the Annual Meeting of the Palaeoanthropology Society, Montreal Canada, March 30–31, 2004.

Cattelain P. 1997. Hunting during the Upper Paleolithic: bow, spearthrower, or both? In H. Knecht, (Ed.), *Projectile Technology*, pp. 213–240. New York: Plenum.

Clark J.D. 1988. The Middle Stone Age of East Africa and the beginnings of regional identity. *Journal of World Prehistory* 2: 235–305.

Crawford M.A., M. Bloom, C.L. Broadhurst, W.F. Schmidt, S.C.G.C. Cunnane, K. Gehbresmeskel, F. Linseisen, J. Lloyd-Smith and J. Parkington 1999. Evidence for the unique function of docasahexaenoic acid during the evolution of the modern human brain. *Lipids* 34 (Supplement): S39–S47.

Doronichev V. and L. Golovanova 2003. Bifacial tools in the Lower and Middle Paleolithic of the Caucasus. In M. Soressi and H.L. Dibble (Eds.), *Multiple Approaches to the Study of Bifacial Technologies*, pp. 77–107. Philadelphia: Museum of Archaeology and Anthropology, University of Pennsylvania.

Garrod D. 1937. The Near East as a gateway of prehistoric migration. In G.G. MacCurdy (Ed.), *Early Man, as Depicted by Leading Authorities at the International Symposium, the Academy of Natural Sciences, Philadelphia, March 1937*, pp. 33–40. Philadelphia: J.B. Lippincott Company.

Garrod D.A.E. and D.M. Bate 1937. *The Stone Age of Mount Carmel*. Oxford: Clarendon Press.

Goodwin A.J.H. 1928. An introduction to the Middle Stone Age in South Africa. *South African Journal of Science* 25: 410–418.

Haile Selassie Y., B. Asfaw and T.D. White 2004. Hominid cranial remains from Upper Pleistocene deposits at Aduma, Middle Awash, Ethiopia. *American Journal of Physical Anthropology* 123: 1–10.

Hare P.E., G.A Goodfriend, A.S. Brooks, J.E. Kokis, and D.W. von Endt 1993. Chemical clocks and thermometers: diagenetic reactions of amino acids in fossils. *Carnegie Institute Washington Yearbook* 92: 80–85.

Harper P.T. 1994. *The Middle Stone Age Sequence at Rose Cottage Cave: A Search for Continuity and Discontinuity*. Ph.D. Dissertation, University of the Witwatersrand.

Hays M.A. and G. Lucas 2001. Experimental investigations of Aurignacian Dufour bladelets. In M.A. Hays and P.T. Thacker (Eds.), *Questioning the Answers: Re-solving Fundamental Problems of the Early Upper Paleolithic* (BAR International Series S1005), pp. 109–116. Oxford: Archaeopress.

Henshilwood C. and J.C. Sealey 1997. Bone artefacts from the Middle Stone Age at Blombos Cave, Southern Cape, South Africa. *Current Anthropology* 38: 890–895.

Henshilwood C. and J.C. Sealey (n.d.). *Blombos Cave, South Africa*. Unpublished excavation report. Department of Archaeology, University of Cape Town.

Henshilwood C.S., F. d'Errico, R. Yates, Z. Jacobs, C. Tribolo, G.A.T. Duller, N. Mercier, J.C. Sealey, H. Valladas, I. Watts, I. and A.G. Wintle 2002. Emergence of modern human behaviour: Middle Stone Age engravings from South Africa. *Science* 295:1278–1280.

Klein R.G. 1989. Biological and behavioral perspectives on modern human origins in Southern Africa. In P. Mellars and C.B. Stringer (Eds.), *The Human Revolution: Behavioral and Biological Perspectives on the Origins of Modern Humans*, pp. 529–546. Edinburgh: Edinburgh University Press.

Klein R.G. 1992. The archaeology of modern human origins. *Evolutionary Anthropology* 1: 5–14.

Klein R.G. 1995. Anatomy, behavior, and modern human origins. *Journal of World Prehistory* 9: 167–198.

Klein R.G. 1998. Why anatomically modern people did not disperse from Africa 100,000 years ago. In T. Akazawa, K. Aoki and O. Bar-Yosef (Eds.), *Neandertals and Modern Humans in Western Asia*, pp. 509–522. New York: Plenum.

Klein R.G. 1999. *The Human Career.* 2nd Edition. Chicago: University of Chicago Press.

Klein R.G. 2000. Archaeology and the evolution of human behavior. *Evolutionary Anthropology* 9: 17–36.

Knecht H. 1993. Early Upper Palaeolithic approaches to bone and antler projectile technology. In G.L. Petersen, H.M. Bricker and P. Mellars, (Eds.) *Hunting and Animal Exploitation in the Later Palaeolithic and Mesolithic of Eurasia,* pp. 33–47. Washington DC: Archaeological Papers of the American Anthropological Association.

Knecht H. 1997. Projectile points of bone, antler, and stone: experimental explorations of manufacture and use. In H. Knecht (Ed.), *Projectile Technology*, pp. 191–212. New York: Plenum.

Kuhn S.L., M.C. Stiner, D.S. Reese and E. Güleç 2001. Ornaments of the earliest Upper Paleolithic: new insights from the Levant. *Proceedings of the National Academy of Sciences USA* 98: 7641–7646.

McBrearty S. and A.S. Brooks 2000. The revolution that wasn't: A new theory of the origin of modern human behavior. *Journal of Human Evolution* 39: 453–563.

Mehlman M.J. 1979. Mumba-Höhle revisited: the relevance of a forgotten excavation to some current issues in East African prehistory. *World Archaeology* 11: 80–94.

Mehlman M.J. 1989. *Late Quaternary Archaeological Sequences in Northern Tanzania*. Ph.D. Dissertation, University of Illinois, Urbana.

Mehlman M.J. 1991. Context for the emergence of modern man in Eastern Africa: some new Tanzanian evidence. In J.D. Clark (Ed.), *Cultural Beginnings: Approaches to Understanding Early Hominid Lifeways in the African Savanna* (Römisch-Germanisches Zentralmuseum, Monographien 19), pp. 177–196. Mainz: Forschunginstitut fur Vor-und Fruhgeschichte.

Mercader J. and R. Marti 1999. Archaeology in the tropical forest of Banyang-Mbo, SW Cameroon. *Nyame Akuma* 52: 17–24.

Merrick H.V. and F.H. Brown 1984. Obsidian sources and patterns of source utilization in Kenya and northern Tanzania: some initial findings. *African Archaeological Review* 2: 129–152.

Merrick H.V., F.H. Brown and W.P. Nash 1994. Use and movement of obsidian in the Early and Middle Stone Ages of Kenya and northern Tanzania. In S.T. Childs (Ed.), *Society, Culture, and Technology in Africa* (MASCA 11 [Supplement]), pp. 29–44. Philadelphia: Museum of Archaeology and Anthropology, University of Pennsylvania.

Milo R.G. 1998. Evidence for hominid predation at Klasies river mouth, South Africa, and its implications for the behaviour of early modern humans. *Journal of Archaeological Science* 25: 99–133.

Perpère M. 1997. Les pointes de la Gravette de la couche 5 de l'abri Pataud: réflexions sur les armes de pierre dans les outillages *Périgordiens*. *Colloque International: la chasse dans la Préhstoire, Treignes 1990* (ERAUL), pp. 9–15. Liège: Université de Liège.

Poeggenpohl C. 1999. *Workshop 5: Fish Remains in Archaeological Sites*. Capetown: World Archaeological Congress.

Robbins L.H., G.A. Brook, M.L. Murphy, A.C. Campbell and A.C. Melear 2000. Late Quarternary archaeological and palaeoenvironmental data from sediments at Rhino Cave, Tsodilo hills, Botswana. *South African Field Archaeology* 9: 17–31.

Shea J.J. 1988. Spear points from the Middle Paleolithic of the Levant. *Journal of Field Archaeology* 15: 441–450.

Shea J.J. 1997. Middle Paleolithic spear point technology. In H. Knecht (Ed.), *Projectile Technology*, pp. 79–106. New York: Plenum.

Thomas D.H. 1978. Arrowheads and atlatl darts: how the stones got the shaft. *American Antiquity.* 43: 461–472.

Volman T.P. 1984. Early prehistory of southern Africa. In R.G. Klein (Ed.), *Southern African Prehistory and Paleoenvironments*, pp. 169–220. Rotterdam: Balkema.

Wendorf F. and R. Schild 1974. *A Middle Stone Age Sequence from the Central Rift Valley, Ethiopia*. Wroclaw: Zaklad Narodowy im. Ossolinskich.

Wiessner P. 1983. Style and social information in Kalahari San projectile points. *American Antiquity* 48: 253–276.

Wilmsen E.N. 1974. *Lindenmeier: A Pleistocene Hunting Society.* New York: Harper & Row.

Würz S. 1997. *The Howiesons Poort at Klasies River: From Artefacts to Cognition.* M.A thesis, University of Stellenbosch.

Würz S. 1999. The Howiesons Poort backed artifacts from Klasies River: an argument for symbolic behavior. *South African Archaeological Bulletin* 54: 38–50.

Yellen J.E. 1998. Barbed bone points: tradition and continuity in Saharan and sub-Saharan Africa. *African Archaeological Review* 15: 173–198.

Yellen J.E., A.S. Brooks, E. Cornelissen, M.H. Mehlman and K. Stewart 1995. A Middle Stone Age worked bone industry from Katanda, Upper Semliki Valley, Zaire. *Science* 268: 553–556.

Yellen J.E., A.S. Brooks, D.M. Helgren, M. Tappen, S. Ambrose, R. Bonnefille, J. Feathers, G. Goodfriend, K. Ludwig, P. Renne and K. Stewart in press. The archaeology of Aduma: a Middle Stone Age site in the Awash Valley, Ethiopia. *PalaeoAnthropology.*

Chapter **14**

From Acheulean to Middle Stone Age in the Kapthurin Formation, Kenya

Sally McBrearty

Department of Anthropology, U-2176, University of Connecticut, Storrs, CT 06269 USA

Christian Tryon

Department of Anthropology, Smithsonian Institution, NHB 343 Washington, DC 20560 USA

ABSTRACT

The Acheulean to Middle Stone Age (MSA) transition is examined from an evolutionary perspective. The replacement of Acheulean handaxes by MSA points represents a shift from hand-held to hafted technology, but the timing and nature of this process are poorly understood due to the rarity of sites from the early MSA (EMSA), here defined as the portion of the MSA predating 130,000 years ago. The well-calibrated sequence in the Kapthurin Formation, Kenya, spans the transition, and shows that MSA technology was present before 285,000 years ago. This date coincides with the age of known African fossils that most likely represent the earliest members of the *Homo sapiens* lineage. Occurrences with characteristic Acheulean and EMSA artifacts are interstratified in the Kapthurin Formation, demonstrating that the transition was not a simple, unidirectional process. A variety of flake production techniques is present at both Acheulean and MSA sites in the formation. The Levallois tradition begins before 285,000 BP in an Acheulean context; Levallois production methods diversify in the MSA. The precocious appearance of blades, grindstones, and pigment in the Kapthurin Formation before 285,000 BP shows that the array of sophisticated behaviors known in the later MSA (LMSA) began at the Acheulean to MSA transition, and it is suggested that such technological changes are among the causes or consequences of the origin of our species.

257

INTRODUCTION

During the later Middle Pleistocene in Africa, large bifaces disappear from the archaeological record and are replaced by smaller points, marking the transition from the Acheulean to the Middle Stone Age (MSA). New dates from the Kapthurin Formation establish that the transition was underway in East Africa before 285,000 years ago. We examine here data relevant to understanding the significance of this large scale archaeological change. The difference between the Acheulean and the MSA is poorly understood because most well documented MSA sites date to the later Middle Stone Age (LMSA) after 130,000 years BP. We therefore concentrate upon the early MSA (EMSA), which we define as that part of the MSA lying within the Middle Pleistocene, that is, before 130,000 years BP. This period has greater relevance for understanding the transition and provides the basis for understanding later behavioral developments within the MSA.

In the first part of this paper we examine general issues relating to the transition, including functional contrasts between handaxes and points, and the influence that different methodological and analytical approaches have upon inferences regarding the nature and timing of archaeological change. In the second part we discuss the transition as seen in the Middle Pleistocene Kapthurin Formation of Kenya where a number of well-dated sites span the transition. We examine the Kapthurin Formation record from the point of view of diagnostic formal tools as well as methods of flake production. In the third section, we introduce the African fossil hominids of this period, in order to establish the evolutionary context of the technological change. We suggest that the abandonment of Acheulean technology is part of a package of increasingly complex hominid behaviors that appears with the earliest members of the *H. sapiens* lineage.

THE NATURE OF THE TRANSITION

Handaxes and the Acheulean

The handaxe is emblematic of the Acheulean. Its wide geographic distribution (Africa, Europe and parts of Asia), and longevity (~1.3 million years) demonstrate that the handaxe was a successful adaptive device useful in a wide range of environments and situations (see papers in Petraglia and Korisettar 1998). Current interpretations suggest that handaxes were handheld, portable, multipurpose implements, and possibly sources of flakes (Clark 1994; McBrearty 2001). Experimental work and microwear analyses of edge damage have shown the handaxe to have been used for a variety of purposes, including butchery and woodworking (*e.g.*, Jones 1980; Binneman and Beaumont 1992; Roberts and Parfitt 1999; Dominguez-Rodrigo *et al.* 2001). In cases of exceptional preservation, traces of a several tasks may be preserved on different edges of the same piece, as reported by Keeley (1993).

Chronological or geographic patterning among Acheulean sites remains poorly understood, and it is possible that the ubiquity of the handaxe masks other important aspects of variability. For example, cleavers are frequent in Africa, but are not common in European sites; cleavers made on Kombewa flakes have been used as a marker for out-of-Africa emigration in the Levant (Goren-Inbar 1992; Goren-Inbar *et al.* 2000). Cleavers and handaxes are produced by a variety of flaking methods and techniques, as is the flake, core and small tool component at Acheulean sites (Clark 1994, 2001c; Roche and Texier 1995; McBrearty 2001). There is clear evidence for raw material selection at some Acheulean sites, although predominantly durable, locally available types were used (Clark 1980; Féblot-Augustins 1990; Jones 1994; Merrick *et al.* 1994; Raynal *et al.* 1995). Finally, archaeological projects at Isimila, Tanzania, and Olorgesailie, Kenya, document local hominid landscape use, and have shown variable patterns of Acheulean site distribution and composition that can be broadly correlated with paleoecological features (Kleindienst 1961; Hansen and Keller 1971; Cole and Kleindienst 1974; Isaac 1977; Potts 1994; Potts *et al.* 1999).

Points and the Middle Stone Age

The point is the characteristic implement of the MSA. The presence of points rather than handaxes in the MSA is significant because points represent the replacement of handheld artifacts by hafted, composite tools (Clark 1988; McBrearty and Brooks 2000). They show the development of complex hunting armatures, and unlike Acheulean handaxes, they show regional diversity in shape.

Direct evidence for hafted points includes tangs on Aterian implements (Clark 1970), the basal thinning of many other African stone points (Brooks, this volume), and grooves at the base of bone harpoons from sites at Katanda, Zaire (Yellen 1998). Points, and possibly backed crescents found at some MSA sites, were most likely designed as weapons to dispatch game or rival humans, as components of stabbing or throwing spears, and possibly as arrows (McBrearty and Brooks 2000; Waweru 2004). Impact damage consistent with the use of stone points as projectiles has been observed on the tips of MSA points from ≠Gi, Botswana (Kuman 1989). Importantly, these weapons convey the ability to inflict "death at a distance," supplying an adaptive advantage to the hunters using them by reducing their risk of injury through close physical encounters with large menacing animals (Berger and Trinkaus 1995; Cattelain 1997; Churchill 2002).

MSA points are made of bone as well as stone, and are produced using a variety of technological approaches. Some MSA stone points are unifacial, others bifacial. Levallois points, retouched or unretouched, are found in some regions. Bone points may be fashioned through several possible combinations of incision, grinding and polishing (Yellen 1998; Henshilwood *et al.* 2001a; Barham *et al.* 2002). Stylistic variation among points shows geographic patterning, often corresponding to broad paleoecological zones, suggesting regional traditions (Clark 1988, 1993; McBrearty and Brooks 2000).

Chronological change, as described below, is detected within the MSA at some locations. Variety in raw material use likewise reflects new approaches to resource procurement. Lithic source data suggest increased hominid ranging areas, with a selective shift towards finer-grained material, frequently from distant sources (Clark 1980; Merrick *et al.* 1994; Raynal *et al.* 1995). Similarly, MSA sites occur in a number of previously unoccupied, often water-poor environments, with a sophisticated strategy of landscape use implied by occupation of ecotones to maximize resource access (Helgren 1997; Ambrose 2001). Specialized hunting and fishing sites were recurrently used, possibly on a seasonal basis (Brooks *et al.* 1995; Yellen *et al.* 1995; Marean 1997; Clark 2001a; Henshilwood *et al.* 2001b).

The Sangoan and Fauresmith Industries

In Africa, the Sangoan and Fauresmith industries were at one time considered "intermediate" between the Acheulean and the MSA (Clark 1957a:xxxiii). The "intermediate" terminology was formally abandoned at the 1965 Burg Wartenstein symposium (Bishop and Clark 1967:987), but discussion of these industries remains central to understanding the Acheulean-to-MSA transition. Both the Sangoan and Fauresmith industries are poorly dated, but the Sangoan, characterized by heavy-duty tools, has been found to overlie the Acheulean and to underlie the MSA at a number of sites (*e.g.*, Cole 1967; McBrearty 1988; Clark 2001b). McBrearty (1991) and Clark (2001b) have argued for the status of the Sangoan as an independent entity, though Clark (1982) formerly regarded it as an activity variant of either the Acheulean or the MSA, and Sheppard and Kleindienst (1996) consider it part of the MSA. The Fauresmith, characterized by small, well-made handaxes, is considered a phase of the final Acheulean (Sampson 1974; Binneman and Beaumont 1992). The Sangoan has long been considered a forest or woodland adaptation, whereas the Fauresmith has been thought confined to savanna zones (Clark 1988), though this dichotomy has been questioned by McBrearty (1992; McBrearty *et al.* 1996).

Methodological Challenges

We argue here that the replacement of handaxes by points and other hafted implements is significant, but the attempt to pin down the timing and circumstances of this process suffers from a number of conceptual and practical difficulties. Chronological issues are discussed below. A serious concern is definition of the term MSA itself. As originally conceived by Goodwin and Van Reit Lowe (1929), the MSA is characterized by the absence of the handaxes of the preceding Acheulean and the absence of microliths of the succeeding Later Stone Age (LSA), and by the presence of points. The ambiguity of the term "Middle Stone Age" has long been recognized (Clark *et al.* 1966). In part this ambiguity stems from its definition as both a typological-technological unit and a temporal unit. The equation of the MSA with Clark's (1977) Mode 3 is inaccurate, as not all MSA sites exhibit Levallois technology, and some contain blades (Mode 4) or microliths

(Mode 5) (see McBrearty and Brooks 2000). Furthermore, prepared core (Mode 3) and blade (Mode 4) elements are sometimes found in Acheulean (Mode 2) contexts (*e.g.*, Leakey *et al.* 1969; McBrearty *et al.* 1996; Kuman 2001). While arguably a semantic issue, it is important to emphasize that simplified terminology (Acheulean *versus* MSA) creates the impression that the transition to the MSA was a well-defined event, rather than a process of adaptive change. Furthermore, rates of technological change, artifact discard, and sediment deposition vary independently, and our inferences about the nature of the transition are founded on rare, possibly non-representative sites scattered across time and space.

Because the definitions of Acheulean and MSA emphasize handaxes and points, a practical challenge for the archaeologist lies in the fact that many sites lack large numbers of diagnostic formal tools. In part this is due to variable recovery and preservation, but it also reflects functional and environmental factors operating in the past. Formal tools are vastly outnumbered at nearly all sites by flakes, cores, and expedient tools, and the basic flake and core artifact inventories of the Acheulean, MSA, Sangoan, and Fauresmith are in many cases indistinguishable. Many methods of direct percussion flake detachment were mastered by early hominids practicing Oldowan technology, and were retained in some cases until quite recent times, rendering them inappropriate as chronological markers (Clark *et al.* 1994; Roche *et al.* 1999). Also, some *fossiles directeurs* may not be truly temporally diagnostic. Although the handaxe and point are characteristic of the Acheulean and MSA, there may be a size continuum between them, and there are no formal criteria for distinguishing small handaxes from large bifacially flaked points. Functional approaches that may provide distinguishing criteria, such as those of breakage patterns, wear traces, and metrical features (*e.g.*, Thomas 1978; Shea 1988; Dockall 1997; Shott 1997; Hughes 1998), have not been widely applied in Africa. Although picks and other heavy-duty tools are characteristic of the Sangoan, similar tools also occur in Acheulean, MSA and even LSA contexts (Clark 2001b), and the qualities formerly thought to render Fauresmith handaxes unique may derive from physical properties imposed by the raw material (Humphreys 1970).

Despite its flaws, the *fossile directeur* approach has not yet been supplanted as a means to compare African Acheulean with MSA occurrences or MSA sites with each other. Statistical comparison of artifact class frequencies (*e.g.*, Mason 1962) has not proved fruitful. The method of Bordes (1961, *cf.* Debènath and Dibble 1994), although widely used in European and Levantine sites, relies heavily upon the presence of retouched tools, and, as mentioned previously, retouched pieces are rare or absent at many African Acheulean and MSA sites. A factor contributing to the rarity of retouched tools is the durability of the lava and metamorphic rocks available in sub-Saharan Africa, compared to the flint used elsewhere. While comparison of large cutting tools documents differences in raw material selection and artifact discard patterns between Acheulean and Sangoan assemblages at Kalambo Falls (Sheppard and Kleindienst 1996), few significant differences between Acheulean and MSA sites have been detected through comparison of flake and core metric attributes (*e.g.*, McBrearty 1981; Sheppard and Kleindienst 1996). This observation stands in contrast to the diminution in artifact dimensions through time seen within long MSA sequences such as Mumba, Klasies River, or Cave of Hearths (Sampson 1974; Thackeray and Kelly 1988; Mehlman 1989; see Brooks *et al.* this volume). Systematic comparisons of other shared tool classes, such as scrapers, are rare, although McBrearty (1986) reports differences in the degree and placement of retouch between Sangoan-Lupemban and overlying MSA horizons at Muguruk, Kenya.

The *chaîne opératoire* approach focuses upon the method, rather than the product, of stone tool fabrication (*e.g.*, Pelegrin *et al.* 1988; Boëda *et al.* 1990; Inizan *et al.* 1999; Bar-Yosef 2000:113–116). The emphasis is shifted from archaeological types to analysis of the entire process of core reduction, from raw material acquisition to eventual discard. Importantly, it does not rely on the presence of *fossiles directeurs.* Analyses of European material have shown that variability in modes of flake production and tool shaping may crosscut traditional industrial categories such as Acheulean or Mousterian (*cf.* Boëda 1991; Tuffreau *et al.* 1997). Application of the approach in Africa, however, remains rare (but see Roche and Texier 1995; Roche *et al.* 1999; Würz 2002; Pleurdeau 2003).

The Timing of Archaeological Change

The earliest dates for the African MSA are derived from the Kapthurin Formation sequence, where points predate 285,000 years BP (Deino and McBrearty 2002; Tryon and McBrearty 2002). This date is in general agreement with the age of the earliest MSA layers at Florisbad, South Africa, estimated by Electron Spin Resonance (ESR) on overlying units at ∼280,000 years BP (Grün *et al.* 1996; Kuman *et al.* 1999), but is considerably older than age estimates of 235,000 years BP from Gademotta, Ethiopia (Wendorf *et al.* 1994), and ≥230,000 years BP from Twin Rivers, Zambia (Barham and Smart 1996). The switch from handheld to hafted technology most likely did not occur at the same time everywhere, and the tradition of biface manufacture appears to have persisted later in some parts of the continent than in others (*cf.* Clark *et al.* 1994). For example, handaxes are present in the Herto Member of the Bouri Formation in the Middle Awash, Ethiopia as late as 160,000 years BP (Clark *et al.* 2003).

The MSA is replaced across most of the African continent by sites attributed to the LSA at about 40,000 years BP (*e.g.*, Ambrose 1998; McBrearty and Brooks 2000). The time span of the MSA therefore exceeds 240,000 years. However, the majority of documented MSA assemblages post-date the onset of the Last Interglacial (Oxygen Isotope Stage 5) at ∼130,000 years BP (Klein 1999; McBrearty and Brooks 2000). Our information for the preceding ∼155,000 years, or more than half the duration of the MSA, is derived from a handful of sites scattered across over 13 million km^2 of the African continent (Figure 1). Furthermore, at many localities, the Acheulean and MSA layers are separated by unconformities, and chronological resolution is generally poor (see Clark 1982; Tryon and McBrearty 2002 for recent reviews). Combined, these gaps have a clear effect on our perceptions of change. In this paper we stress the role of information from the EMSA in clarifying the situation.

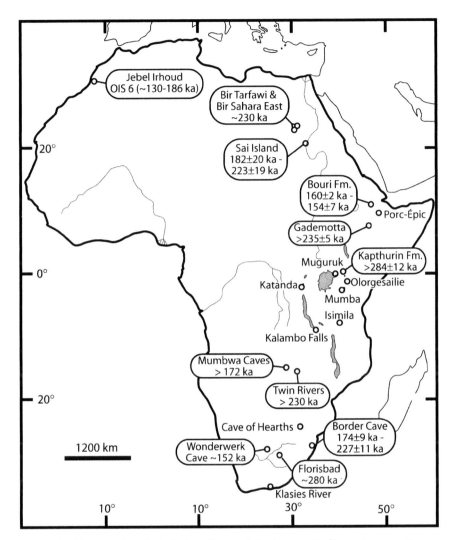

Figure 1. African archaeological sites discussed in the text. Radiometric age estimates shown for all Early Middle Stone Age (EMSA) sites. Data from Barham (2000), Barham and Smart (1996), Clark et al. (2003), Deino and McBrearty (2002), Grün and Beaumont (2001), Grün et al. (1996), Hublin (2001), Kuman et al. (1999), Van Peer et al. (2003), Vogel (2001), Wendorf et al. (1993, 1994).

Regionalization in artifact traditions (Clark 1988), as well as change through time, can be seen in the latter half of the MSA, but due to the lack of data for the EMSA we can only speculate about when they began. Regionalization of MSA lithic industries results in different trajectories of change in each area. For example, the South African Later Pleistocene MSA (LMSA) succession, based largely upon the sequence at Klasies River, illustrates a number of quantitative and qualitative

changes. These include trends towards shorter, wider flake-blades (*e.g.*, Thackeray
and Kelly 1988), variation in raw material choice, and a succession of different
methods of flake, blade, and point production. These methods vary in the means
of preparation of the core's flaking surface, the volume of the core exploited, and
the degree of tool retouch (Würz 2002). The Kalambo Falls (Zambia) sequence
shows the incremental addition of blades and diverse point forms from early to
late MSA (Clark 2001b). In contrast, Porc-Épic Cave in Ethiopia shows a high
degree of technological variability within each stratigraphic unit, but reveals no
clear trend through its long, essentially undated sequence (Pleurdeau 2003). Few
generalizations can be made from these data about the nature of temporal variation
on a continent-wide scale or when and how this regionalization first appeared.
There is some indication that local traditions of flake and tool manufacture already
existed among late Acheulean sites. This phenomenon is suggested by the presence
of geographically restricted methods of large flake production at some Acheulean
sites, including the Tabelbala-Tachengit method of the northwestern Sahara (Tixier
1957; Alimen and Zuarte y Zuber 1978), the *hoenderbek* cores and flakes found in
South Africa (McNabb 2001), and blades and large Levallois cores in the Kapthurin
Formation (Leakey *et al.* 1969; McBrearty 1999). What is required to resolve these
issues is documentation of well-calibrated EMSA sequences that can be compared
with known Acheulean and LMSA occurrences.

THE KAPTHURIN FORMATION

The Geological and Archaeological Sequence

Our data from the Kapthurin Formation are critical to addressing these issues
of hominid behavioral change. The deposits span much of the Middle Pleistocene,
contain a succession of archaeological sites chronologically ordered by tephrostratigraphy, and demonstrate considerable diversity in hominid adaptations in the
use of a variety of shaped or retouched tools and flake production strategies. The
formation also spans the Acheulean-to-MSA transition, and includes EMSA sites.
Some stratigraphic levels preserve multiple archaeological sites that make it possible to assess contemporaneous inter-assemblage variability. These factors allow us
to examine the nature of behavior in the MSA, especially EMSA, and to compare
it with behavior seen in the Acheulean.

The Kapthurin Formation forms the Pleistocene portion of the sedimentary
sequence in the Tugen Hills in the Kenya Rift Valley west of Lake Baringo (Figure 2).
The formation is about 125 m thick and is exposed over an area of about 150 km^2.
More than 70 archaeological and fossil sites are now documented in the formation
(Leakey *et al.* 1969; Cornelissen *et al.* 1990; Cornelissen 1992; McBrearty *et al.*
1996; McBrearty 1999, 2001; Tryon 2002). The basic stratigraphic succession as
defined by Martyn (1969) and Tallon (1976, 1978) includes three fluviolacustrine
members (K1, K3, and K5) separated by two major tephra members, the Pumice
Tuff Member (K2), and the Bedded Tuff Member (K4). An additional, unnumbered

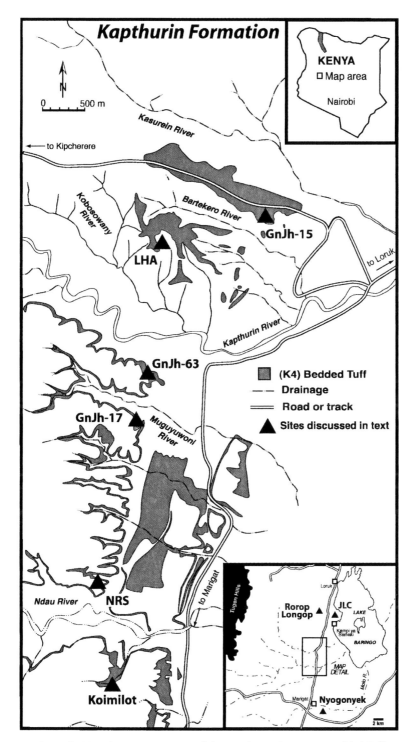

Figure 2. Map showing exposures of the Kapthurin Formation Bedded Tuff Member and the sites discussed in the text.

tephra, the Grey Tuff, lies within K3. Three additional lavas, the Upper and Lower Kasurein Basalts and the Baringo Trachyte, are intercalated with Kapthurin Formation sediments. These volcanic units have now been successfully dated by $^{40}Ar/^{39}Ar$, using both incremental heating of multi-grain samples with a broad-beam CO_2 laser (LIH method), and fusion of individual phenocrysts by laser in a single step (SCTF method) (Deino and McBrearty 2002).

Materials relevant to the Acheulean-to-MSA transition lie above the Grey Tuff, dated to 509,000 ± 9,000 years BP, and within and immediately below the Bedded Tuff Member (K4). The Bedded Tuff Member is a complex of tephra horizons deposited during a period of intermittent volcanism. Intercalated sediments, incipient paleosols, and root casts mark former stable land surfaces upon which assemblages of artifacts and fossil fauna accumulated. On a macro scale, defining these ancient land surfaces and comparing archaeological sites is accomplished using the widespread bracketing layers of tuff. However, it can be problematic to establish stratigraphic relations among sites within K4 exposed over a large area of heavily eroded topography by field mapping alone, and geochemical analysis was used as a basis for tephrostratigraphic correlation among disparate Kapthurin Formation outcrops (see Figure 2) (Tryon and McBrearty 2002; Tryon 2003).

Individual tephra units of the Bedded Tuff Member (K4) were analyzed both petrographically and geochemically with a wavelength dispersive electron microprobe. The Bedded Tuff Member consists of two distinct lithologies: (1) widespread beds of fine-grained mafic ash, overlain by (2) sparse deposits of felsic, locally pumiceous material. Stratigraphic and geochemical trends suggest that the Bedded Tuff Member deposits derive from a single volcanic source that underwent progressive magma compositional change. Periods of quiescence were punctuated by multiple, brief eruptive events. These trends provide a robust correlation tool for tephra deposits and associated sites within the formation (Tryon and McBrearty 2002). $^{40}Ar/^{39}Ar$ age estimates of 235,000 ± 2,000 and 284,000 ± 12,000 years BP from two layers of an upper, pumiceous unit (Deino and McBrearty 2002) date the latest eruptive phases of the Bedded Tuff Member. Most archaeological sites associated with the Bedded Tuff Member occur within, beneath, or immediately above beds of the lower, basaltic ash, which lack material suitable for $^{40}Ar/^{39}Ar$ dating. The date of 284,000 ± 12,000 years BP on the upper, pumiceous unit of K4 at the NRS sampling locality therefore provides a minimum age for these Kapthurin Formation Acheulean and EMSA sites (Figure 3).

Stratigraphic ordering of Kapthurin Formation sites through tephra correlation demonstrates the interstratification of sedimentary units containing Acheulean, Sangoan, Fauresmith, and MSA artifacts (see Figure 3). These findings show that the Acheulean-to-MSA transition predates 284,000 ± 12,000 years BP in this part of the Rift Valley, and that it was not a simple, unidirectional process (Tryon and McBrearty 2002). Instead, this record may represent competition among a number of hominid groups with different technological traditions, or the presence of hominids with broad technological competence responding to differing local contingencies.

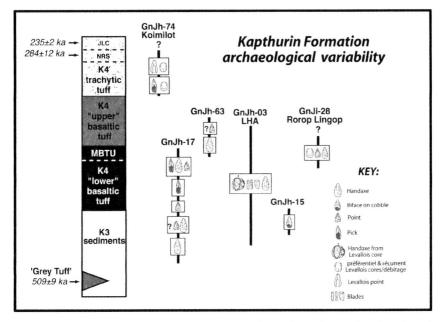

Figure 3. Schematic diagram showing stratigraphic relationships of archaeological assemblages in the Kapthurin Formation, emphasizing typological and technological variability among later Middle Pleistocene sites containing diagnostic artifacts. Modified from Tryon and McBrearty (2002).

Interpretation of the Kapthurin Formation Sequence

Our comparative analysis of Kapthurin Formation site function is in its very early stages. Most presently known Kapthurin Formation sites appear to have been flake production sites. Retouched tools are rare. Plausible sources of the fine-grained lava cobbles that were used for flake production in many cases lie within a few hundred meters of the sites, and exotic raw materials are infrequent.

We examine change through time here by comparing sites from two stratigraphic intervals, the portion of Middle Silts & Gravels Member (K3) above the Grey Tuff, and the overlying Bedded Tuff Member (K4) (see Figure 2). Late Acheulean and EMSA sites are most numerous in the Middle Silts & Gravels Member above the Grey Tuff. One element common to all these sites is a simple flake and core component, characterized by discoidal and opportunistically flaked single and multiple platform cores. In some excavated assemblages, such as the upper paleosol at GnJh-17, these are the only methods of flake production present. Other sites contain additional distinctive items. Blades, Levallois debitage, grindstones, and traces of pigment are found at site GnJh-15. At the Acheulean site of LHA (GnJh-03), large (~10–20 cm) Levallois flakes were struck by the *préférential* method from centripetally prepared boulder cores and sometimes retouched into handaxes or scrapers. Several refitted series from LHA show regular blade production by both Levallois and non-Levallois methods (Leakey *et al.* 1969; Texier 1996; McBrearty 1999). At site GnJh-52, split lava boulders and cobbles were transformed into scrapers or cores. In the upper paleosol from site GnJh-17, picks or core-axes and scrapers were manufactured from elongated cobbles, as shown by extensive refitting (Cornelissen 1992).

The overlying Bedded Tuff Member (K4) contains fewer sites, but they too show great variety. All share the simple flake and core component seen at K3 sites, but most feature additional distinctive elements. For example Rorop Lingop (GnJi-28) contains small Levallois cores, diminutive handaxes reminiscent of the Fauresmith, and rare points. Site GnJh-63 preserves a single handaxe together with an industry based on the flaking of small cobbles by a number of methods, including bipolar flaking. Recent excavations at Koimilot (GnJh-74) have produced an assemblage containing *préférentiel* and *récurrent* Levallois cores with centripetal preparation, including refitted cores and flakes and an implement resembling a pick or core-axe. This assemblage is overlain by a horizon characterized by large (~10 cm) unretouched Levallois points or elongated flakes with a dorsal scar pattern suggesting predominantly unidirectional flaking during core preparation (Tryon 2002, 2003). Two additional sites, Nyogonyek (GoJh-1) and Locality 92, contain large amounts of Levallois flakes and cores, and few if any formal retouched tools, though their precise position in the stratigraphy is as yet unresolved.

In summary, Acheulean and EMSA assemblages in the Kapthurin Formation show variation both among contemporary sites and through time. However, a Levallois concept of flaking is present in each, suggesting a shared technological tradition. There is a reduction in size of the Levallois flakes through time, and an increase in the variety of the flake production methods (*cf.* Van Peer 1992; Böeda 1994; Inizan *et al.* 1999). Furthermore, items usually thought characteristic of later prehistory, such as blades, grindstones, and pigment, occur in the Middle Silts and Gravels Member of the Kapthurin Formation where they predate 285,000 years BP.

HUMAN EVOLUTIONARY CONTEXT

Behavioral Change

It has been repeatedly asserted that MSA toolmakers lacked cognitive sophistication, and that a late, sudden genetic mutation at 40,000 to 50,000 years ago explains the modern behavior seen in the LSA (*e.g.*, Diamond 1992; Klein 1992, 1995, 1998; Mithen 1994; Mellars and Gibson 1996; Klein and Edgar 2002). But many behaviors once thought to postdate 40,000 years ago are in fact found in the MSA. These behavioral advances include blade and microlithic technology, formal bone tools, increased geographic range, specialized hunting, the use of aquatic resources, long-distance trade or transport of raw materials, systematic processing and use of pigment, art and decoration, and the habitation of previously unoccupied water-poor environments (Deacon and Deacon 1999;

Klein 1999; McBrearty and Brooks 2000; Henshilwood *et al.* 2002). The evidence that we have discussed here shows that some of these technological innovations appeared as early as the late Acheulean. Thus the record of behavioral change commenced at or immediately before the Acheulean-MSA boundary, and continued to accumulate over the entire time span of the MSA. This evidence leads to the conclusion that hominids living as early as 250,000–300,000 years ago possessed the cognitive and technical ability to invent sophisticated items of material culture. The Acheulean-to-MSA transition marks the beginning of an increasingly complex hominid adaptive pattern, the archaeological signature of expanding hominid populations who developed diversified tool kits as a means of coping with novel problems. Hominid postcranial remains from this period show a mosaic of modern and archaic features, indicating that some patterns of modern positional, locomotor, and manipulative behavior are present by 300,000 BP and probably earlier (Pearson 2000; Fisher and McBrearty 2002). It is very likely that technological changes at the Acheulean-to-MSA transition are intimately linked to these anatomical changes.

Taxonomic Issues

The central unresolved issue in understanding the Acheulean-to-MSA transition is the taxonomic identity of the hominids responsible for the formation of the Middle Pleistocene archaeological record. Evidence from both nuclear and mitochondrial DNA strongly supports an African origin for *H. sapiens* (Howell 1999; Relethford 2001; Tishkoff and Williams 2002). Most investigators include African hominid fossils predating ∼500,000, such as Bodo (550,000–650,000 BP), Ndutu (500,000–600,000 BP), and Saldhana (400,000–800,000 BP), in *H. erectus*, but opinion is divided as to the status of other, perhaps slightly later specimens, such as Kabwe (>400,000 BP), for which the names *H. heidelbergensis* or *H. rhodesiensis* are used. The oldest securely dated specimens formally ascribed to our species are the three crania from the Herto Member of the Bouri Formation in the Middle Awash region of Ethiopia, dated to ∼160,000 years BP, attributed to the subspecies *H. sapiens idaltu* (White *et al.* 2003). Other early African representatives of *H. sapiens* predating 100,000 include Omo I from the Kibish Formation, Ethiopia, and the sample from Klasies River, South Africa (see McBrearty and Brooks 2000, for a review of the fossil and dating evidence). For the purposes of understanding the Acheulean-to- MSA transition, the taxonomic identity of specimens dating to ∼200,000–300,000 years BP are critical. Lahr (1996; Lahr and Foley 1998) sees some of the African fossils, including Florisbad (260,000 years BP) and Ngaloba, as representing a distinct species, *H. helmei*, but Stringer (1996, 2002) sees this group as subsumed under *H. sapiens,* though perhaps representing a somewhat archaic form. If specimens of *H. helmei* in fact represent early *H. sapiens,* then our species appeared simultaneously in Africa with MSA technology between 250,000 and 300,000 years BP.

Discussion

Historically the divide between the Acheulean and the MSA was an arbitrary distinction for the convenience of archaeologists (Goodwin and Van Riet Lowe 1929). If the appearance of the MSA and the *H. sapiens* lineage coincide, however, then the Acheulean-to-MSA transition acquires evolutionary significance. Early *Homo* is assumed to be the maker of Oldowan artifacts, and *H. erectus* is thought to be the maker of Acheulean tools because the first appearances of the hominids in the fossil record roughly coincides with that of the artifacts. In similar fashion, members of early *H. sapiens* were no doubt the makers of some Middle Pleistocene assemblages. Speciation assumes separation of populations that formerly belonged to the same reproductive community. The resulting daughter species may coexist in time with the ancestral stock for a considerable period. We can expect these close relatives to share many features of behavior in common, and thus to produce similar archaeological traces (*cf.* Lieberman and Shea 1994). Technological innovation also builds upon existing knowledge, and primitive forms often survive together with newer inventions. Populations of *H. rhodesiensis* may have survived well into the late Middle Pleistocene and created a body of archaeological remains, and we are at present often unable to assign assemblage to maker with any certainty. Our challenge is to detect the signature of the emerging adaptation of early *H. sapiens.*

CONCLUSIONS

The Acheulean-to-MSA transition is a large scale behavioral change that is significant when viewed in an evolutionary context. If, as seems very likely, fossils dating to 200,000–300,000 years BP are in fact early representatives of *H. sapiens,* then the origin of our species occurred simultaneously with the appearance of MSA technology. Linking technological and evolutionary change requires information from the EMSA, which is at present poorly known. Some of the hallmarks of the MSA are seen first in the late Acheulean of East Africa, where they probably represent the behavior of the ancestors of *H. sapiens.* Blades, grindstones, and pigment, for example, appear in the Kapthurin Formation before 285,000 years BP. Technological innovations can be seen as the causes or consequences of anatomical changes that reflect new habitual positional, manipulative, or locomotor behaviors. Reconsideration of the MSA itself reveals evidence of sophisticated behaviors previously thought to appear much later in time during the LSA. The items of material culture known to the LSA hunting and gathering groups required time to invent. The Acheulean-to-MSA transition, marked by new stone tool technology, is among the first visible signs in a record of continuous behavioral development in the African Middle Pleistocene that continued to accumulate over the course of the next 250,000 years.

ACKNOWLEDGEMENTS

Work in the Kapthurin Formation has been funded by grants to the senior author from the US National Science Foundation (BCS-0217728), the L.S.B. Leakey Foundation, and the University of Connecticut Research Foundation. Her research was conducted under a research permit issued by the Government of the Republic of Kenya and an excavation permit from the Minister for Home Affairs and National Heritage, both issued to Andrew Hill and the Baringo Palaeontological Research Project. She would like to thank personnel of the Archaeology Division of the National Museums of Kenya for facilitating her research, and to acknowledge the contribution of her collaborators to the ideas presented here, among them Alison Brooks, Els Cornelissen, Alan Deino, Andrew Hill, John Kingston, and Pierre-Jean Texier. Tryon's research in the Kapthurin Formation was funded by the US National Science Foundation (BCS-0118345), the L.S.B. Leakey Foundation, the Wenner-Gren Foundation for Anthropological Research, Inc., the University of Connecticut Research Foundation, and the Bill Bishop Memorial Trust, UK. His research in Kenya was conducted under a research permit from the Government of the Republic of Kenya (MOEST 13/001/30C 229) and an exploration and excavation permit from the Ministry for Heritage and Sports. Portions of the text were written while a post-doctoral fellow sponsored by the Fyssen Foundation (Paris). Support from the Archaeology Division of the National Museums of Kenya, the Tryon and Acree families and Rhonda Kauffman made the research possible. Both authors would like to thank the editors of this volume for the invitation to contribute. Their thoughtful comments on our original manuscript, as well as those of two anonymous reviewers, are likewise much appreciated.

REFERENCES CITED

Alimen H. and J. Zuate y Zuber 1978. *L'evolution de l'acheuléen au Sahara Nord-occidental (Saoura-Ougarta-Tabelbala)*. Meudon: Centre National de la Recherche Scientifique.

Ambrose S.H. 1998. Chronology of the Later Stone Age and food production in East Africa. *Journal of Archaeological Science* 25: 377–392.

Ambrose S.H. 2001. Middle and Later Stone Age settlement patterns in the Central Rift Valley, Kenya: comparisons and contrasts. In N.J. Conard (Ed.), *Settlement Dynamics of the Middle Paleolithic and Middle Stone Age*, pp. 21–44. Tübingen: Kerns Verlag,

Bar-Yosef O. 2000. The Middle and Upper Paleolithic in Southwest Asia and neighboring regions. In O. Bar-Yosef and D. Pilbeam (Eds.), *The Geography of Neanderthals and Modern Humans in Europe and the Greater Mediterranean*, pp. 107–156. Cambridge MA: Peabody Museum of Archaeology and Ethnology, Harvard University.

Barham L.S. 2000. *The Middle Stone Age of Zambia, south-central Africa*. Bristol: Western Academic & Specialist Press.

Barham L.S. and P. Smart 1996. Early date for the Middle Stone Age of central Zambia. *Journal of Human Evolution* 30: 287–290.

Barham L.S., L. Pinto and C. Stringer 2002. Bone tools from Broken Hill (Kabwe) cave, Zambia, and their evolutionary significance. *Before Farming* 2: 1–16.

Berger T.D. and E. Trinkaus 1995. Patterns of trauma among the Neanderthals. *Journal of Archaeological Science* 22: 841–852.

Binneman J. and P. Beaumont 1992. Use-wear analysis of two Acheulian handaxes from Wonderwerk Cave, Northern Cape. *South African Field Archaeology* 1: 92–97.

Bishop W.W. and J.D. Clark (Eds.) 1967. *Background to Evolution in Africa*. Chicago: University of Chicago Press.

Boëda E. 1991. Approche de la variabilité des systèmes de production lithique des industries du paléolithique inférieur et moyen: chronique d'une variabilité attendue. *Techniques et Culture* 17–18: 37–79.

Boëda, E. 1994. *Le concept Levallois: variabilité des méthodes*. Paris: CNRS Editions.

Boëda E., J.-M. Geneste and L. Meignen 1990. Identification de chaînes opératoires lithiques du Paléolithique ancien et moyen. *Paléo* 2: 43–80.

Bordes F. 1961. *Typologie du Paléolithique ancien et moyen* 2 Vols. Memoires de L'Institut Prehistorique de l'Université de Bordeaux 1. Bordeaux: Delmas.

Brooks A.S., D.M. Helgrem, J.S. Cramer, A. Franklin, W. Hornyak, J.M. Keating, R.G. Klein, W.J. Rink, H.P. Schwarcz, J.N. Smith, K. Stewart, N.E. Todd, J. Verniers and J.E. Yellen 1995. Dating and context of three Middle Stone Age sites with bone points in the upper Semliki Valley, Zaire. *Science* 268: 548–553.

Cattelain P. 1997. Hunting during the Upper Paleolithic: bow, spearthrower, or both? In H. Knecht (Ed.), *Projectile Technology*, pp. 213–240. New York: Plenum Press.

Churchill S.E. 2002. Of assegais and bayonets: reconstructing prehistoric spear use. *Evolutionary Anthropology* 11: 185–186.

Clark J.D. (Ed.) 1957.*Proceedings of the Third Panafrican Congress on Prehistory, Livingstone, 1955*. London: Chatto & Windus.

Clark J.D. 1970. *The Prehistory of Africa*. New York: Praeger.

Clark J.D. 1980. Raw material and African lithic technology. *Man and the Environment* 4: 44–55.

Clark J.D. 1982. The transition from Lower to Middle Palaeolithic in the African continent. In A. Ronen (Ed.), *The Transition From Lower to Middle Palaeolithic and the Origin of Modern Man* (B.A.R. International Series 151), pp. 235–255. Oxford: BAR.

Clark J.D. 1988. The Middle Stone Age of East Africa and the beginnings of regional identity. *Journal of World Prehistory* 2: 235–305.

Clark J.D. 1993. African and Asian perspectives on the origins of modern humans. In M.J. Aitken, C.B. Stringer and P.A. Mellars (Eds.), *The Origin of Modern Humans and the Impact of Chronometric Dating*, pp. 148–178. Princeton: Princeton University Press.

Clark J.D. 1994. The Acheulian Industrial Complex in Africa and elsewhere. In R.S. Corrucini and R.L. Ciochon (Eds.), *Integrative Pathways to the Past*, pp. 451–470. Englewood Cliffs NJ: Prentice-Hall.

Clark J.D. 2001a. Ecological and behavioral implications of the siting of Middle Stone Age rockshelter and cave settlements in Africa. In N.J. Conard (Ed.), *Settlement Dynamics of the Middle Paleolithic and Middle Stone Age*, pp. 91–98. Tübingen: Kerns Verlag.

Clark J.D. (Ed.) 2001b. *Kalambo Falls Prehistoric Site, vol. 3*. Cambridge: Cambridge University Press.

Clark J.D. 2001c. Variability in primary and secondary technologies of the Later Acheulian in Africa. In S. Milliken and J. Cook (Eds.), *A Very Remote Period Indeed: Papers on the Paleolithic Presented to Derek Roe*, pp. 1–18. Oxford: Oxbow Books.

Clark D.J., Y. Beyene, G., WoldeGabriel, W. Hart, P.R. Renne, H. Gilbert, A. Defleur, G. Suwa, S. Katoh, K.R. Ludwig, J.-R. Boisserie, B. Asfaw and T.D. White 2003. Stratigraphic, chronological and behavioral contexts of Pleistocene *Homo sapiens* from the Middle Awash, Ethiopia. *Nature* 423: 747–752.

Clark J.D., G.H. Cole, G.L. Isaac and M.R. Kleindienst 1966. Precision and definition in African archaeology. *South African Archaeological Bulletin* XXI: 114–121.

Clark J.D., J. de Heinzelin, K.D. Schick,W.K. Hart, T.D. White, G. WoldeGabriel, R.C. Walter, G. Suwa, B. Asfaw, E. Vrba and Y. Selassie 1994. African *Homo erectus*: old radiometric ages and young Oldowan assemblages in the Middle Awash Valley, Ethiopia. *Science* 264: 1907–1910.

Clark J.G.D. 1977. *World Prehistory: A New Outline*. Cambridge: Cambridge University Press.

Cole G.H. 1967. The later Acheulian and Sangoan of southern Uganda. In W.W. Bishop and J.D. Clark (Eds.), *Background to Evolution in Africa*, pp. 481–528. Chicago: University of Chicago Press.

Cole G.H. and M.R. Kleindienst 1974. Further reflections on the Isimila Acheulian. *Quaternary Research* 4: 346–355.

Cornelissen E. 1992. *Site GnJh-17 and Its Implications for the Archaeology of the Middle Kapthurin Formation, Baringo, Kenya* (Annales, Sciences Humaines 133). Tervuren: Musée Royale de l'Afrique Centrale.

Cornelissen, E., A. Boven, A. Dabi, J. Hus, K. Ju Yong, K., E. Keppens, R. Langohr, J. Moeyersons, P. Pasteels, M. Pieters, H. Uytterschaut, F. Van Note and H. Workineh 1990. The Kapthurin Formation revisited. *African Archaeological Review* 8:23–76.

Deacon H.J. and J. Deacon 1999. *Human Beginnings in South Africa: Uncovering the Secrets of the Stone Age*. Capetown: David Philip.

Debènath A. and H.L. Dibble 1994. *Handbook of Paleolithic Typology. Volume One: Lower and Middle Paleolithic of Europe*. Philadelphia: University Museum, University of Pennsylvania.

Deino A. and S. McBrearty 2002. ^{40}Ar/^{39}Ar chronology for the Kapthurin Formation, Baringo, Kenya. *Journal of Human Evolution* 42: 185–210.

Diamond J. 1992. *The Third Chimpanzee*. New York: Harper Collins.

Dockall J.E. 1997. Wear traces and projectile impact: a review of the experimental and archaeological evidence. *Journal of Field Archaeology* 24: 321–331.

Dominguez-Rodrigo M., J. Serralonga, J. Juan-Tresserras, L. Alcala and L. Luque 2001. Woodworking activities by early humans: a plant residue analysis on Acheulian stone tools from Peninj (Tanzania). *Journal of Human Evolution* 40: 289–299.

Féblot-Augustins J. 1990. Exploitation des matières premières dans l'acheuleen d'Afrique: Perspectives comportementales. *Paléo* 2: 27–42.

Fisher R.E. and S. McBrearty 2002. The comparative morphology of hominin postcranial remains from the Kapthurin Formation, Baringo District, Kenya. *American Journal of Physical Anthropology* 34 (Supplement): 70.

Goodwin A.J.H. and C. Van Riet Lowe 1929. The Stone Age cultures of South Africa. *Annals of the South African Museum* 27: 1–289.

Goren-Inbar N. 1992. The Acheulian site of Gesher Benot Ya'aqov: an African or Asian entity? In T. Akazawa, K. Aoki and T. Kimura (Eds.), *The Evolution and Dispersal of Modern Humans in Asia*, pp. 67–82. Tokyo:Hokusen-sha.

Goren-Inbar N., C.S. Feibel, K.L. Verosub, Y. Melamed, M.E. Kislev, E. Tchernov and I. Saragusti 2000. Pleistocene milestones on the out-of-Africa corridor at Gesher Benot Ya'aqov, Israel. *Science* 289: 944–947.

Grün R., J.S. Brink, N.A. Spoor, L. Taylor and C.B. Stringer 1996. Direct dating of Florisbad hominid. *Nature* 382: 500–501.

Grün R. and P.B. Beaumont 2001. Border Cave revisited: a revised ESR chronology. *Journal of Human Evolution* 40: 467–482.

Hansen C.L. and C.M. Keller 1971. Environment and activity patterning at Isimila korongo, Iringa district, Tanzania: a preliminary report. *American Anthropologist* 73: 1201–1211.

Helgren D.M. 1997. Locations and landscapes of paleolithic sites in the Semliki Rift, Zaire. *Geoarchaeology* 12: 337–361.

Henshilwood C.S., F. d'Errico, C.W. Marean, R.G. Milo and R. Yates 2001a. An early bone tool industry from the Middle Stone Age at Blombos Cave, South Africa:implications for the origins of modern human behaviour, symbolism and language. *Journal of Human Evolution* 41: 631–678.

Henshilwood C.S., J.C. Sealy, R. Yates, K. Cruz-Uribe, P. Goldberg, F.E. Grine, R.G., Klein, C. Poggenpoel, K. van Niekerk and I. Watts 2001b. Blombos Cave, Southern Cape, South Africa: preliminary report on the 1992–1999 excavations of the Middle Stone Age levels. *Journal of Archaeological Science* 28: 421–448.

Henshilwood C.S. F. d'Errico, R. Yates, Z. Jacobs, C. Tribolo, G.A.T. Duller, N. Mercier, J.C. Sealy, H. Valladas, I. Watts and A.G. Wintle 2002. Emergence of modern human behavior: Middle Stone Age engravings from South Africa. *Science* 295: 1278–1280.

Howell F.C. 1999. Paleo-demes, species clades, and extinctions in the Pleistocene hominin record. *Journal of Anthropological Research* 55: 191–243.

Hublin J.J. 2001. Northwestern African Middle Pleistocene hominids and their bearing on the emergence of *Homo sapiens*. In L.S. Barham and K. Robson-Brown (Eds.), *Human Roots: Africa and Asia in the Middle Pleistocene*, pp. 99–121. Bristol: Western Academic & Specialist Press.

Hughes S.S. 1998. Getting to the point: evolutionary change in prehistoric weaponry. *Journal of Archaeological Method and Theory* 5: 345–408.

Humphreys A.J.B. 1970. The role of raw material and the concept of the Fauresmith. *South African Archaeological Bulletin* 25: 139–144.

Inizan M.-L., H. Roche and J. Tixier 1999. *Technology and Terminology of Knapped Stone*. Nanterre: CREP.

Isaac G. 1977. *Olorgesailie: Archaeological Studies of a Middle Pleistocene Lake Basin in Kenya*. Chicago: University of Chicago Press.

Jones P.R. 1980. Experimental butchery with modern stone tools and its relevance for Paleolithic archaeology. *World Archaeology* 12: 153–175.

Jones P.R. 1994. Results of experimental work in relation to the stone industries of Olduvai Gorge. In M.D. Leakey and D.A. Roe (Eds.), *Olduvai Gorge, Vol. 5: Excavations in Beds III, IV and the Masek Beds, 1968–1971,* pp. 254–298. Cambridge: Cambridge University Press.

Keeley L.H. 1993. The utilization of lithic artifacts. In R. Singer, B.G. Gladfelter and J.J. Wymer (Eds.), *The Lower Paleolithic Site of Hoxne, England,* pp. 129–149. Chicago: University of Chicago Press.

Klein R.G. 1992. The archaeology of modern human origins. *Evolutionary Anthropology* 1: 5–14.

Klein R.G. 1995. Anatomy, behavior, and modern human origins. *Journal of World Prehistory* 9: 167–198.

Klein R.G. 1998. Why anatomically modern people did not disperse from Africa 100,000 years ago. In T. Akazawa, K., Aoki and O. Bar-Yosef (Eds.), *Neandertals and Modern Humans in Western Asia,* pp. 509–522. New York: Plenum Press.

Klein R.G. 1999. *The Human Career*, 2nd Edition. Chicago: University of Chicago Press.

Klein R.G. and B. Edgar 2002. *The Dawn of Human Culture*. New York: John Wiley.

Kleindienst M.R. 1961. Variability within the Late Acheulian assemblages in Eastern Africa. *South African Archaeological Bulletin* 16: 35–52.

Kuman K.A. 1989.*Florisbad and ≠Gi: the Contribution of Open-Air Sites to the Study of the Middle Stone Age in Southern Africa*. Ph.D. Dissertation, University of Pennsylvania, Philadelphia.

Kuman K. 2001. An Acheulean factory site with prepared core technology near Taung, South Africa. *South African Archaeological Bulletin* 173–174: 8–22.

Kuman K., M. Inbar and R.J. Clarke 1999. Palaeoenvironments and cultural sequence of the Florisbad Middle Stone Age hominid site, South Africa. *Journal of Archaeological Science* 26: 1409–1426.

Lahr M. 1996. *The Evolution of Modern Human Diversity: A Study of Cranial Variation*. Cambridge: Cambridge University Press.

Lahr M.M. and R. Foley 1998. Towards a theory of modern human origins: geography, demography, and diversity in recent human evolution. *Yearbook of Physical Anthropology* 41: 137–176

Leakey M., P.V. Tobias, J.E. Martyn and R.E.F. Leakey 1969. An Acheulian industry with prepared core technique and the discovery of a contemporary hominid mandible at Lake Baringo, Kenya. *Proceedings of the Prehistoric Society* 3: 48–76.

Lieberman D. and J.J. Shea 1994. Behavioral differences between archaic and modern humans in the Levantine Mousterian. *American Anthropologist* 96: 300–332.

Marean C.W. 1997. Hunter-gatherer foraging strategies in tropical grasslands: model-building and testing in the East African Middle and Later Stone Age. *Journal of Anthropological Archaeology* 16: 189–225.

Martyn J.E., 1969. *The Geological History of the Country between Lake Baringo and the Kerio River, Baringo District, Kenya*. Ph.D. Dissertation. University of London.

Mason R.J., 1962. *Prehistory of the Transvaal*. Johannesburg: Witswatersrand University Press.

McBrearty S. 1981. Songhor: A Middle Stone Age site in western Kenya. *Quaternaria* 23: 171–190.

McBrearty S. 1986. *The Archaeology of the Muguruk Site, Western Kenya*. Ph.D. Dissertation, University of Illinois, Urbana.

McBrearty S. 1988. The Sangoan-Lupemban and Middle Stone Age sequence at the Muguruk site, western Kenya. *World Archaeology* 19: 379–420.

McBrearty S. 1991. Recent research in western Kenya and its implications for the status of the Sangoan industry. In J.D. Clark (Ed.), *Cultural Beginnings: Approaches to Understanding Early Hominid Lifeways in the African Savanna* (Forschunginstitut fur Vor- und Fruhgeschichte, Monographien 19), pp. 159–176. Bonn: Römisch-Germanisches Zentralmuseum.

McBrearty S. 1992. Sangoan technology and habitat at Simbi, Kenya. *Nyame Akuma* 38: 29–33.

McBrearty S. 1999. Archaeology of the Kapthurin Formation. In P. Andrews and P. Banham (Eds.), *Late Cenozoic Environments and Hominid Evolution: a Tribute to Bill Bishop*, pp. 143–156. London: Geological Society.

McBrearty S. 2001. The Middle Pleistocene of East Africa. In L.H. Barham and K. Robson-Brown (Eds.), *Human Roots: Africa and Asia in the Middle Pleistocene*, pp. 81–97. Bristol: Western Academic & Specialist Press.

McBrearty S. and A. Brooks 2000. The revolution that wasn't: A new interpretation of the origin of modern human behavior. *Journal of Human Evolution* 39: 453–563.

McBrearty S., L. Bishop and J. Kingston 1996. Variability in traces of Middle Pleistocene hominid behavior in the Kapthurin Formation, Baringo, Kenya. *Journal of Human Evolution* 30: 563–580.

McNabb J. 2001. The shape of things to come. A speculative essay on the role of the Victoria West phenomenon at Canteen Koppie, during the South African Earlier Stone Age. In S. Milliken and J. Cook (Eds.), *A Very Remote Period Indeed: Papers on the Paleolithic Presented to Derek Roe*, pp. 37–46. Oxford: Oxbow Books.

Mehlman M.J. 1989. *Late Quaternary Archaeological Sequences in Northern Tanzania*. Ph.D. dissertation, University of Illinois, Urbana.

Mellars P.A. and K. Gibson (Eds.) 1996. *Modeling the Early Human Mind*. Oxford: McDonald Institute Monographs & Oxbow Press.

Merrick H.V., F.H. Brown and W.P. Nash 1994. Use and movement of obsidian in the Early and Middle Stone Ages of Kenya and northern Tanzania. In S.T. Childs (Ed.), *Society, Culture, and Technology in Africa*, MASCA 11 (supplement), pp. 29–44.

Mithen S. 1994. From domain-specific to generalized intelligence: a cognitive interpretation of the Middle/Upper Paleolithic transition. In C. Renfrew and E. Zubrow (Eds.), *The Ancient Mind: Elements of a Cognitive Archaeology*, pp. 29–39. Cambridge: Cambridge University Press.

Pearson O.M. 2000. Postcranial remains and the origin of modern humans. *Evolutionary Anthropology* 9: 229–247.

Pelegrin J., C. Karlin and P. Bodu 1988. Chaînes opératoires: un outil pour le préhistorien. In J. Tixier (Ed.), *Technologie Préhistorique,* (Notes et mongraphies techniques 25), pp. 55–62. Paris, CNRS/CRA.

Petraglia M.D. and R. Korisettar (Eds.) 1998. *Early Human Behavior in Global Context: The Rise and Diversity of the Lower Paleolithic Record.* London: Routledge.

Pleurdeau D. 2003. Le Middle Stone Age de la grotte du Porc-Épic (Dire Dawa, Éthiopie): gestion des matières premières et comportements techniques. *L'Anthropologie* 107: 15–48.

Potts R. 1994. Variables versus models of early Pleistocene hominid land use. *Journal of Human Evolution* 27: 7–24.

Potts R., A.K. Behrensmeyer and P. Ditchfield 1999. Paleolandscape variation and Early Pleistocene hominid activities: Members 1 and 7, Olorgesailie Formation, Kenya. *Journal of Human Evolution* 37: 747–788.

Raynal J.-P., L. Magoga, F.Z. Sbihi-Alaoui and D. Geraads 1995. The earliest occupation of Atlantic Morocco: the Casablanca evidence. In W. Roebroeks and T. Van Kolfschoten (Eds.), *The Earliest Occupation of Europe*, pp. 255–262. Leiden: University of Leiden.

Relethford J.H. 2001. *Genetics and the Search for Modern Human Origins*. New York: Wiley-Liss.

Roberts M.B. and S.A. Parfitt 1999. *Boxgrove: A Middle Pleistocene Hominid Site at Eartham Quarry, Boxgrove, West Sussex* (English Heritage Archaeological Report 17). London: English Heritage.

Roche H., A. Delagnes, J.-P. Brugal, C.S. Feibel, M.Kibunjia, V. Mourre and P.-J. Texier 1999. Early hominid stone tool production and technical skill 2.34 myr ago in West Turkana, Kenya. *Nature* 399: 57–60.

Roche H. and P.-J. Texier 1995. Evaluation of technical competence of *Homo erectus* in East Africa during the Middle Pleistocene. In J.R.F. Bower and S. Sartono, (Eds.), *Evolution and Ecology of* Homo Erectus, pp. 153–167. Leiden: Royal Netherlands Academy of Arts and Sciences Pithecanthropus Centennial Foundation.

Sampson C.G. 1974. *The Stone Age Archaeology of Southern Africa.* New York: Academic Press.

Shea J.J. 1988. Spear points from the Middle Paleolithic of the Levant. *Journal of Field Archaeology* 15: 441–450.

Sheppard P.J. and M.R. Kleindienst 1996. Technological change in the Earlier and Middle Stone Age of Kalambo Falls (Zambia). *African Archaeological Review* 13: 171–195.

Shott M.J. 1997. Stones and shafts redux: the metric discrimination of chipped-stone dart and arrow points. *American Antiquity* 62: 86–101.

Stringer C.B.1996. Current issues in modern human origins. In W.E. Meikle, F.C. Howell and N.G. Jablonski (Eds.), *Contemporary Issues in Human Evolution,* pp. 115–134. San Francisco: California Academy of Sciences.

Stringer C.B. 2002. Modern human origins: progress and prospects. *Philosophical Transactions of the Royal Society of London B* 357: 563–579.

Tallon P.W.J. 1976. *The Stratigraphy, Palaeoenvironments and Geomorphology of the Pleistocene Kapthurin Formation, Kenya.* Ph.D. Dissertation, Queen Mary College, London.

Tallon P.W.J. 1978. Geological setting of the hominid fossils and Acheulian artifacts from the Kapthurin Formation, Baringo District, Kenya. In W.W. Bishop (Ed.), *Geological Background to Fossil Man,* pp. 361–373. Edinburgh: Scottish Academic Press.

Texier P.-J. 1996. Production en série: la débitage de lames de pierre à 250.000 ans. *Pour la Science* 223: 22.

Thackeray A.I. and A.J. Kelly 1988. A technological and typological analysis of Middle Stone Age assemblages antecedent to the Howiesons Poort at Klasies River Main Site. *South African Archaeological Bulletin* 43: 15–26.

Thomas D.H. 1978. Arrowheads and atlatl darts: how the stones got the shaft. *American Antiquity* 43: 461–472.

Tishkoff S. and S. Williams 2002. Genetic analysis of African populations: human evolution and complex disease. *Nature Reviews of Genetics* 3: 611–621.

Tixier J. 1957. Le hachereau dans L'Acheuléen nord-africain. *Congrès Préhistorique de France, Comptes Rendus de la XVe Session 1956,* pp. 914–923. Poitiers: Angoulême.

Tryon C.A. 2002. Middle Pleistocene sites from the "southern" Kapthurin Formation of Kenya. *Nyame Akuma* 57: 6–13.

Tryon C.A. 2003. *The Acheulian to Middle Stone Age Transition: Tephrostratigraphic Context for Archaeological Change in the Kapthurin Formation, Kenya.* Ph.D. dissertation, University of Connecticut, Storrs.

Tryon C.A. and S. McBrearty 2002. Tephrostratigraphy and the Acheulian to Middle Stone Age transition in the Kapthurin Formation, Baringo, Kenya. *Journal of Human Evolution* 42: 211-235.

Tuffreau A., A. Lamotte and J.-L. Marcy 1997. Land-use and site function in Acheulean complexes of the Somme Valley. *World Archaeology* 29: 225–241.

Van Peer P. 1992. *The Levallois Reduction Strategy.* Madison: Prehistory Press.

Van Peer P., R. Fullagar, S. Stokes, R.M. Bailey, J. Moeyersons, F. Steenhoudt, A. Geerts, T. Vanderbeken, M. De Dapper and F. Geus 2003. The Early to Middle Stone Age transition and the emergence of modern human behavior at site 8-B-11, Sai Island, Sudan. *Journal of Human Evolution* 45: 187–194.

Vogel J.C. 2001. Radiometric dates for the Middle Stone Age in South Africa. In P.V. Tobias, M. Raath, J. Maggi-Cecchi and G. Doyle (Eds.), *Humanity from African Naissance to Coming Millennia: Colloquia in Human Biology and Paleoanthropology,* pp.261–268. Florence: Florence University Press.

Waweru V. 2004. Functional analysis of points from Cartwright's site, Kenya: bow and arrow or spear technology and implications for modern human behavior. Paper presented at the annual meeting of the New England Biological Anthropology Society, New Haven.

Wendorf F., A.E. Close and R. Schild 1994. Africa in the period of *Homo sapiens neanderthalensis* and contemporaries. In: S.J. De Laet, A.H. Dani, J.L. Lorenzo, and R.B. Nunoo (Eds.), *History of Humanity,* vol. 1: *Prehistory and the Beginnings of Civilization,* pp. 117–135. New York: Routledge & UNESCO.

Wendorf F., R. Schild and A.E. Close 1993. *Egypt During the Last Interglacial.* New York: Plenum Press.

White, T.D., B. Asfaw, D. DeGusta, H. Gilbert, G.D. Richards, G. Suwa and F.C. Howell 2003. Pleistocene *Homo sapiens* from Middle Awash, Ethiopia. *Nature* 423: 742–747.

Würz S. 2002. Variability in the Middle Stone Age lithic sequence, 115,000–60,000 years ago at Klasies River, South Africa. *Journal of Archaeological Science* 29: 1001–1015.

Yellen J.E. 1998. Barbed bone points: tradition and continuity in Saharan and sub-Saharan Africa. *African Archaeological Review* 15: 173–198.

Yellen J.E., A.S. Brooks, E. Cornelissen, M.H. Mehlman and K. Stewart 1995. A Middle Stone Age worked bone industry from Katanda, Upper Semliki Valley, Zaire. *Science* 268: 553–556.

Chapter **15**

The Use of Space in the Late Middle Stone Age of Rose Cottage Cave, South Africa
Was There a Shift to Modern Behavior?

Lyn Wadley

School of Geography, Archaeology and Environmental Studies, University of the Witwatersrand, Private Bag 3, WITS, 2050 SOUTH AFRICA. email: wadleyl@geoarc.wits.ac.za

INTRODUCTION

Perhaps the use of space is always linked to social organization. Relationships among African great apes guide their nest building: individuals nest closest to those with whom they are most familiar; gorilla females build higher than males and low-ranking individuals nest on the periphery of the group (Fruth and Hofmann 1996:232). There are even marked seasonal differences in the way that apes use space: in the dry season in Senegal favored sites are re-used, while this is not the case in the wet season (McGrew 1992:210). Apes also maintain basic hygiene principles because they climb out of their nests to defecate. These great ape examples warn us not to rely only on sleeping or feeding arrangements, seasonality or issues of basic hygiene when we are looking for spatial patterns that we believe can be attributed to humans. Since great apes use space socially it is particularly challenging to define a uniquely human use of space. Maybe it is not possible to distinguish the use of space by great apes and early hominids. Indeed, Sept's (1992) research at Koobi Fora suggests that their records are indistinguishable.

Binford (1998) sees the contemporaneous duplication of "modules" (domestic areas) as a characteristic of modern hunter-gatherers. This is a useful definition that may imply discrete kin groupings within a larger band. However, it is probably the use of symbolism in space, as well as in other lifeways, that distinguishes people

279

with modern cognition from other hominids and even the great apes. Modern people use space symbolically to demarcate their cultural environment and to codify their relationships with strangers and with kin. Almost all modern people order space in their dwelling places (Kolen 1999:141). Seating arrangements at a formal dinner provide a good example in complex western societies. Cynics could comment that such landscaping is based on status and is not dissimilar from the ranking of gorillas in their nests. However, physical strength, the attribute important to gorilla society, is no longer as closely linked to status in modern human society.

Of course, the symbolic use of space is not restricted to complex cultures like our own because modern hunter-gatherers also use space to arrange their world. The Ju/'hoansi (!Kung) have separate seating places for men and women during their aggregation phase: men sit to the right of the fire facing the hut, while women sit to the left (Marshall 1976:88, 249). Public and private spaces are also demarcated during the aggregation phase: each family hut has its own fireplace, but there is a central hearth where communal activities such as story-telling and dancing take place. Space can thus be used to group people by gender, age, kinship, or status; space reflects social organization that can be simple, but may also be complex. In Kalahari camps, social groupings or work stations can occasionally be recognized through segregated clusters of material culture. Thus it is sometimes possible to recognize behavior that implicates public or private space and bead or arrow manufacturing areas. However, where Kalahari Ju'hoansi live for extended periods in aggregation camps, a great deal of household debris accumulates and it is not possible to disentangle activity areas (Brooks 1984).

The type of social classification evident in Kalahari spatial patterns, where smudging has not been an issue, is probably not recognizable in the deep past, first because the archaeological record does not usually have sufficient resolution for such interpretations. Secondly and more importantly, we should not make the assumption that the link between categories of material culture and human groups was the same in the deep past as it is today. We should not, for example, make gender attributions based on our present understanding of hunter-gatherer behavior because cultural mores can change through time. Women in the Kalahari make beads today, but this need not mean that men did not make them in the deep past. Nonetheless, it is still useful to study spatial patterning in the deep past even if we cannot interpret its precise meaning. In particular, it is essential to examine trends in the distributions of material culture items and the placement of features such as hearths. Galanidou (2000:272) suggests that, instead of trying to construct individual moments of spatial use in cave or rock shelter sites, archaeologists could profitably look for redundant patterns, that is, patterns that run through more than one event of occupation. This is precisely what I shall attempt to do here and I shall use the intra-site study of three final Middle Stone Age (MSA) layers from Rose Cottage to examine the possibility that there were directional trends towards modern hunter-gatherer spatial patterns. While it will not necessarily be possible to point to the moment in time when people began to use space symbolically, it should be possible to recognize increasing complexity of spatial use through time.

My framework for recognizing different kinds of spatial behavior is simple and it is built on expectations encouraged by hunter-gatherer ethnography. I anticipate that people who do not deliberately use space for symbolic purposes may, like the great apes, have simple, repetitive spatial patterning in their campsites. This patterning may (or may not) include separating sleeping and working space and may include disposal of trash. Once fire is controlled and is regularly used for cooking and heating, it is likely to have become an important and complicating part of the spatial equation. Hearths vary in size because of the number of users and the frequency of use; a hearth can be used as the focus for all activities or as the focus of a specialized single activity. Hearths can be widely spaced or close together. Hearths can be for private or for public use.

My expectation is that the use of space would have become more complex through time and that this complexity can be identified archaeologically even where specific activities cannot be spatially recognized. Hunter-gatherers who use space symbolically (and are therefore modern) will be recognizable in Stone Age sites because: (1) there will sometimes be evidence for segregated work stations, for example, bead making, bone processing, whittling of wood or grinding of plant foods; and, (2) there will sometimes be discrete hearths with indications that they were used for special rather than general activities. Segregated activities will not always be recognizable because of the potential smudging of artifacts and hearths in camps with repeated long-term occupancy. Thus, even in periods when space is already used symbolically, there may be some sites where discrete activity patterns are unrecognizable. Even so, it should be possible to discern trends through time from consistently simple spatial patterns in the deep past to greater complexity and a variety of configurations in the more recent past. In any such study, large sample sizes are preferable to show trends clearly. Sadly, there are relatively few sites that have data available for detailed spatial examination.

Few spatial studies have been carried out at MSA sites in South Africa, perhaps because only a handful of sites have been excavated on a large enough scale for this purpose. Rose Cottage Cave is one such site. Rose Cottage Cave was first excavated in the 1940s by Malan and in the early 1960s by Beaumont; the more recent excavations by Wadley have taken place since 1987 (Wadley 1997). Rose Cottage is just five km from Ladybrand in the eastern Free State (29° 13′ S; 27° 28′E). The cave is about 20 m long and 10 m wide and it is concealed by a great boulder that encloses the front of the cave, leaving a skylight and narrow eastern and western entrances (Figure 1). Wadley's excavations into the Later Stone Age (LSA) were conducted in a 32 m^2 grid, but the grid was reduced to 23 m^2 for the Middle Stone Age (MSA) layers that are discussed here. An additional small excavation into the MSA deposits abutting the Malan excavation was made by Harper (1997) under Wadley's supervision.

Rose Cottage was habitually occupied during the MSA and LSA with the result that the deposit is more than 6 m deep. The last occupation was dated

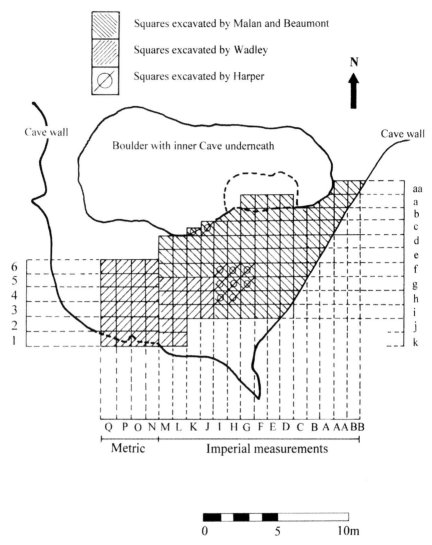

Figure 1. Plan of Rose Cottage Cave showing the area of the Wadley excavation discussed in this paper.

to approximately 500 B.P. and the earliest occupation was during the MSA, at approximately 100,000 years ago (Woodborne pers. comm.). The oldest layers of the site have a pre-Howiesons Poort MSA stone industry containing points, knives (straight scrapers in the Bordes classification [Bordes 1961; Debénath & Dibble 1994]), sidescrapers and blades (Wadley and Harper 1989; Harper 1997). A rich Howiesons Poort industry with backed tools made on small blades is sandwiched between the early occupations and later ones that contain yet another point, knife and scraper industry. The site also has a suite of late MSA assemblages dated to between 30,800 and 27,700 years ago, a Transitional MSA/LSA industry dated to about 20,600 years ago, and a long LSA sequence (Wadley 1997). The change in technology from the MSA to LSA seems to have been a gradual process (Clark 2000) and the Transitional MSA/LSA industry encompasses MSA retouched tools, such as knives, points, large sidescrapers and denticulates, as well as MSA radial cores and LSA bladelets and irregular bladelet cores. Three late MSA layers Dy, Dc and Ru are discussed in this paper. The earliest of these layers, Dy (called YD in Allott 2000), is dated to 30,800 ± 200 years ago. Layer Dc produced a date of 27,200 ± 350 years ago, but this date should probably be rejected because Dc lies below layer Ru, which has three dates: 27,700 ± 480 years ago, 27,800 ± 1700 years ago and a basal date of 28,800 ± 450 years ago.

THE SPATIAL ANALYSIS

The spatial study of MSA layers uses lithics because organic preservation is poor and only scraps of bone survive beyond about 20,000 years ago. The high density of small lithics at the site made it impractical, indeed impossible, to point plot each piece during excavation, therefore the contents of hearths, pits, and ash smears were kept separately, but finds collected outside of features were curated by meter-square. This technique has obviously set limitations on the resolution that can be obtained from the spatial studies. Layer Dy holds 2.7 m^3 of deposit, which is the largest volume of deposit in the three MSA layers discussed here. Layer Dc comprises 2.4 m^3 of deposit, and layer Ru comprises 1.91 m^3 of deposit. Sediment formation and site formation processes at Rose Cottage seem to have been predominantly anthropogenic (Smith 1997), a factor which has important implications for spatial studies.

The lithic distributions were plotted using unconstrained clustering, a technique that produces contours (isopleths) based on the percentages of items in each square meter of the grid (Whallon 1984).

Layer Dy

Layer Dy, the oldest of the three MSA layers, has 48 hearths littered across the grid (Figure 2). Some of the Dy hearths overlap or abut their neighbours. Several hearths are small pits of up to 200 mm in depth and this type of hearth seems to be unique to layer Dy. Most hearths in Rose Cottage are flat or slightly convex with no built structures, although, by 20,600 years ago, a few hearths have stone surrounds. The largest Dy hearths are in the western part of the grid. Between these western hearths and those forming an eastern cluster in squares K4/K5 and L4/L3 there is a small divide that provides the first suspicion that the eastern and western features might be the result of two separate occupations. The eastern

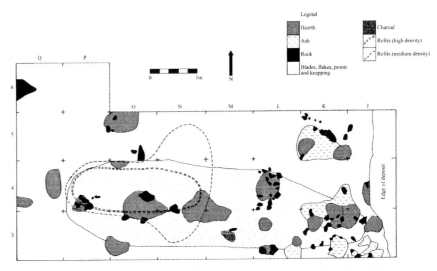

Figure 2. Rose Cottage Cave: Plan of layer Dy hearths, isopleths for refitted lithics and isopleths for all other lithics.

cluster contains large smears of ash that are not present in the western part of the grid. Few lithics were recovered from any of the hearths.

Layer Dy contains 7,659 pieces of worked stone, of which 74 are retouched. This is one of the smallest assemblages at the site and the volume density of lithics is far lower (2836.7 lithics per m^3) than that in the two younger MSA layers. Layer Dc has 3.5 times as many lithics per m^3 and layer Ru has 11.3 times as many lithics per m^3.

There are 14 classes of retouch in Dy. Miscellaneously retouched pieces and broken pieces predominate in the assemblage. Knives make up 12% of the retouched assemblage. Only 57 blades and bladelets (blades with lengths shorter than 26 mm) are present compared to 1,072 whole flakes. This means that blades and bladelets constitute only 5% of the total of whole blades, bladelets, and flakes.

The highest densities of lithics are in the western section of the excavation grid (Allott 2000:56) (see Figure 2) where all types of retouch, flakes, blades, chips (here classified as debitage with dimensions of less than 10 mm) and chunks are inextricably entangled. Thus no separate activity areas can be distinguished. A detached, minor concentration of mixed lithics occurs in the eastern part of the grid (see Figure 2) on the edge of Malan's excavation from the 1940s. This cluster may once have formed part of a larger area of occupation debris like the one in the western section of the grid, but the information is now lost because the Malan excavation did not record spatial data. In order to explore the relationship between the eastern and western lithic accumulations, Lucy Allott attempted a refitting exercise in Dy. Twenty-six refits, involving 60 pieces, were made. Most conjoins were found in different squares, although natural breaks and fire-popped refits were found close to each other in the same squares (Allott 2000:51–52). This suggests that there has been little postdepositional site disturbance (Allott 2000:52), but this interpretation must be made cautiously because cave deposits are notorious for allowing the downward travel of lithic pieces (Richardson 1992) and no vertical conjoining of pieces has yet been attempted at Rose Cottage.

The majority of refits lie in the western part of the excavation grid within the dense concentration of lithics (see Figure 2). No refits occurred between the eastern and western isopleths and the western and eastern artifact clusters were therefore unlikely to have been contemporary (Allott 2000:59). A similar interpretation was made from the refitting of lithics at Mousterian sites on the edge of the Parisian Basin (Depaepe 2001) and several differentiated occupations were shown to have occurred on a single site surface.

Layer Dc

Twenty hearths with a mean inter-hearth distance of 0.4 m were excavated in layer Dc (Figure 3). The eastern hearths are generally smaller than those in the west and, as is the case in layer Dy, there are several ash smears in the eastern part of the grid, but none in the west. The two largest hearths, spanning squares O4/O3 and N4/N3/M4/M3, each measure about one meter across. The hearths contain relatively few pieces of stone and those present are mostly small. However, in the areas immediately surrounding the hearths, knapping debris in the form of chips, chunks, cores, and broken flakes and blades, is intermixed with whole flakes and blades, retouched pieces, and coloring material, so that no independent activity clusters can be detected. A slightly higher concentration of lithics occurs in the

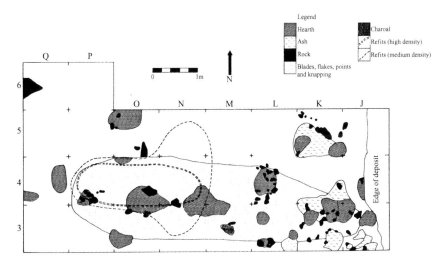

Figure 3. Rose Cottage Cave: Plan of layer Dc hearths, isopleths for refitted lithics and isopleths for all other lithics.

center of the excavation (see Figure 3), but a single isopleth links the hearths in the west and the east.

Layer Dc has 23,531 lithics of which 259 are retouched and 14 are ground. Thus the 23 formal tool classes make up 1.2% of the total assemblage. Cores are mostly bipolar (45%), core-reduced (17.6%) or irregular forms (33.2%) and only 2.6% of cores appear to have been used for blade or bladelet production. It is therefore not surprising that the layer yielded only 223 whole blades and bladelets compared with 3,117 whole flakes. Blades and bladelets accordingly make up 6.7% of the total of whole debitage in the sample. Backed tools and scrapers are notably rare. Amongst the points are some small, standardized white opaline examples that have no parallel elsewhere in the site, or indeed (to my knowledge), elsewhere in southern Africa. Some of these points have backing rather than retouch forming the points. Knives are another prominent category of retouch. The burin/awl category is rather problematic from a typological perspective, but all the pieces appear to have worn tips consistent with piercing or graving. Some of the tools have definite burin spall removals, but others are split flakes that have had their chisel ends exploited. Artifact density is high (9804.6 lithics per m^3).

Refitting of lithic artifacts was attempted by A. Field and L. Winter and refits from widely spaced squares have been conjoined (Figure 4). The majority of pieces that were refitted in layer Dc came from squares O4 and N4, that is, in the area surrounding the two largest hearths. It makes sense that this concentration of refits (see Figure 4) is within the highest density cluster of lithics. The majority of refits is in close proximity (in the same or adjacent squares) suggesting that no major postdepositional disturbance was taking place. The 21 fire-popped fragments, for example, lay next to each other in a single square. Thus, where refits were made

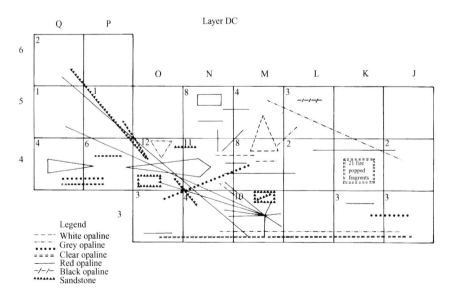

Figure 4. Rose Cottage Cave: Plan of layer Dc refitted lithics. Each line connects conjoins.

across several squares we can infer that they represent deliberate human transport. Distant refits were made between square M3 and squares Q6 and Q5, and between square J3 and N3 and O3 (see Figure 4). Unlike layer Dy, layer Dc has some refits between the western and eastern sections of the grid. Refits were, for example, made between squares O3 and J3, N3 and J3, M5 and J4. None of the Dc hearths can, therefore, be shown to be independent of each other and this is quite a different situation from the one in Dy. Some pieces may have been recycled during separate occupations of the same layer, but the high density of lithics in Dc implies that recycling may not have been favored. People who left their lithics on the Dc surface used a larger area of the grid floor than was the case on the Dy surface. Of course this does not necessarily mean that the Dc occupation floor was larger because the archaeological grid limits sampling, yet the high density of lithics in Dc does tend to support the idea of an extensive occupation compared to the one in Dy.

Winter (pers. comm. 2000) refitted a blade core with nine retrieved removals. The green core was originally larger than the refitted version (Winter pers. comm.) and it may therefore have yielded many more blades than those recovered during the refitting exercise. The knapping process appears to have begun with a single platform core; later the platform was rejuvenated and the core size was reduced. The core was subsequently inverted to provide a new platform. Most of the conjoined pieces are not intended blade products, but are instead rejects, with hinge terminations and thick flake platforms, resulting from a combination of knapping inaccuracies and raw material flaws (Winter pers. comm.). The discarded core was found in square M3 together with four of the refits and there is no evidence that the core moved from this position during the three phases of the knapping procedure. Unfortunately, the core tablet is missing. The remaining green core refits were found in the western part of the grid in squares Q5, O4, N4 and N3. None of the core's refits came from the eastern part of the excavation grid.

Excluding the 21 fire-popped refits in a single square, only 87 refits were found in Dc. When unworked chunks are removed from the stone inventory, this means that only 0.4% of the 20,644 lithics could be refitted. This is an exceptionally low percentage of refits compared to the refits that have been obtained in some European Palaeolithic open-air sites (Conard et al. 1998), and several reasons are possible for this. First, the vast size of the collection makes the task extremely difficult and, secondly, the small size of individual pieces is an added problem (13,222 pieces are smaller than one centimeter). The color of the pieces from a single nodule can also be quite variable and color is not always a useful refitting attribute. Thirdly, although there are 768 cores in the layer, most are tiny bipolar or core-reduced forms that are almost impossible to refit. Fourthly, pieces could be trampled from Dc into the layer below, a hypothesis that has not yet been tested. Lastly, some pieces may have been transported outside of the excavation grid, or even off-site. Interestingly, a higher percentage of refits (0.9%) was obtained from layer Dy than from level Dc, notwithstanding a vast investment of time in the Dc refitting exercise and a relatively small investment of time in the Dy refitting exercise. This suggests that the large size of the Dc collection is an important consideration when assessing the low percentage of conjoins.

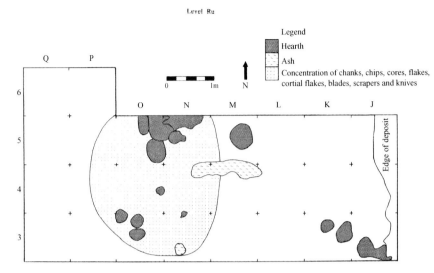

Figure 5. Rose Cottage Cave: Plan of layer Ru hearths and isopleths for all lithics.

Layer Ru

A behavioral change is implied in the youngest of the three layers, Ru, because there are far fewer hearths here than in layers Dy and Dc (Figure 5). Only 14 hearths and two ash spreads are found in Ru. There is an accumulation of overlapping hearths in squares O5 and N5 which appears to encapsulate the main burning area. The round hearth in M5 was one of the few Rose Cottage hearths with a white capping, black, charcoal-rich center and a chestnut-colored, burnt earth base. There is a large open space between the eastern and western clusters of hearths and another space to the west of the O row of squares (see Figure 5). In layer Dy there was also a space between the eastern and western sections of the grid, but it was not nearly as pronounced as the one in Ru.

When the unconstrained clustering technique is applied to the spatial distribution of lithics in Ru, no separate activity areas can be discerned, but the densest smudge of artifactual material occurs between grouped or smudged hearths in rows O and N (see Figure 5).

Layer Ru has a density of artifacts considerably greater than that in layer Dc because 61,193 lithics occur in Ru (Clark 2000) in only 1.91 m³ of deposit (32,038 lithics per m³). This enormous density of lithics implies that multiple occupations may be represented. Two hundred and sixty-one formal tools (only 0.4% of the total stone) separate into 24 classes and a wide range of activities must be represented by this distribution. Knives are the primary retouched category (Clark 2000) and they comprise 37% of the retouched assemblage. Points, scrapers and backed tools occur in smaller frequencies with each class making up about 10% of the retouched assemblage. Only 290 whole blades and bladelets are in the assemblage, compared to 5,622 whole flakes. Thus blades and bladelets comprise only 4.9% of the total of whole blades, bladelets and flakes. This is not surprising since only 4.6% of the cores are blade or bladelet forms. In all, 61% of cores are irregular, 18.6% are core-reduced, 13.7% are bipolar and 2% are radial cores. No refitting has been undertaken in Ru because of the intimidating size of the collection.

DISCUSSION

The spatial patterns of the three Rose Cottage Cave final MSA layers dating between 30,800 and 27,700 years ago share several features. First, they have no discrete knapping or other independent activity areas. Instead, they have a widespread, undifferentiated distribution of lithics encompassing hearths. Knapping, tool use and a variety of tasks seem to have taken place together with a disregard for spatial differentiation, but it is possible that the pattern arose because of recurrent occupation of the same space. As might be expected, relatively few of the lithics are in the hearths themselves, most pieces are peripheral. This pattern was also noted at Klithi, Greece (Galanidou 1999:151). Secondly, each Rose Cottage layer contains tightly packed or overlapping hearths that lack structure such as stone linings or surrounds. At the Greek rockshelter Kastritsa there is a high density of hearths in Stratum 5, dated to $19,900 \pm 370$ years ago, and Galanidou (1999:155) has suggested that the spatial uniformity in the composition of the lithic assemblage could be attributed to the lack of consistency with which the hearths were located. The smudging of the Rose Cottage MSA lithic distribution might also correlate with the high density of hearths, although there is as much smudging in Ru as in Dy, even though there are far fewer hearths in Ru.

Notwithstanding that a relatively short period is covered by the three final MSA layers, it is possible to trace a few intra-site differences. First, hearth density decreases through time. The earliest layer, Dy, has the most hearths (48 hearths in 23 m^2; 1 hearth for every 0.06 m^3), while the most recent layer, Ru, has the fewest hearths (14 hearths in 23 m^2; 1 hearth for every 0.14 m^3). Secondly, there is a greater variety of hearth types early on. Layer Dy has tiny pit hearths in addition to flat or saucer-shaped hearths, but no pit hearths occur more recently. Thirdly, the volume density of lithics becomes greater through time together with tool class richness. Layer Dy has the lowest volume density of lithics (2836.7 per m^3) and only 14 retouched tool classes, while layer Dc has 23 retouched tool classes and 9804.6 lithics per m^3 and Ru has 24 retouched tool classes and 32,038 lithics per m^3.

At first glance the concentration of hearths makes layer Dy look like a long-term or high density occupation. This is contradicted by its low richness of artifact types and its low volume density of lithics compared with the other two MSA layers (which contain far fewer hearths even though their lithic assemblages are far larger than the one in Dy). This evidence suggests that Dy represents short-term occupations and/or that the group size was small. It seems likely that people occupying the Dy floor repeatedly made new fireplaces instead of reusing older ones. Ethnoarchaeological studies illustrate that re-using old hearths or making new ones is a cultural decision (Gorecki 1991) that need not reflect group size. A large number of hearths in an archaeological context cannot, then, automatically be assumed to correlate with large groups of people.

The refitting exercise in Dy showed that there were no conjoins between the eastern and western lithic concentrations (Allott 2000) and it would therefore appear that two separate occupations are represented within the archaeological grid. This is an important observation, for the contemporaneous duplication of domestic areas could indicate a modular pattern, which Binford (1998) believes is characteristic of modern hunter-gatherers. Modular patterns are, according to Binford, absent from Middle Palaeolithic sites. In layer Dy, the lack of duplicated modules and the low density of artifacts scattered with no apparent preference for spatial activity areas also suggest that modern hunter-gatherer camps may not be an appropriate model for the period.

In contrast to Dy, layer Ru has only 14 hearths, but eight times as many lithics as Dy. The high density of lithics seems to imply that Ru represents a long-term occupation, or a palimpsest of occupation horizons, or the debris left by a relatively large group of hunter-gatherers, or some or all of these options. Undifferentiated areas of household debris have been recorded in modern Kalahari open-air sites where San live for extended periods in aggregation camps (Brooks 1984). It is also true that the longer San stay in a camp, the more activities are likely to be represented and the richer the artifact inventory is likely to become. Indeed it could be argued that the Ru spatial pattern is not unlike that of a Kalahari long-term aggregation camp. This is a difficult argument to support or counter, not least because of the lack of organic preservation in the Rose Cottage MSA. In addition, details of the spatial arrangements at Kalahari aggregation camps remain unpublished and we therefore do not know whether smudging occurs over an entire camp or whether separate contemporary "modules" (Binford's 1998 terminology) are still recognizable. Certainly no contemporary "modules" are recognizable in any of the Rose Cottage Cave MSA layers, but they are recognizable in the LSA layers. Another important observation is that layer Dy's small assemblage of lithics has the same unstructured pattern as the large lithic assemblage from Ru. This suggests that people living in caves in the late MSA may have been unconcerned about ordering their activities spatially.

Notwithstanding this common factor, there is evidence for a directional trend between the earlier layer Dy and the later layer Ru: there is a reduction in the number of hearths through time, a proclivity that continued into the LSA of Rose Cottage, where layers quite commonly contain fewer than five hearths, even where lithic density is exceptionally high (in excess of 25,000 pieces).

The late MSA spatial patterns described here differ from each other much less than they differ from the LSA ones in younger layers of Rose Cottage (Wadley 2001). When lithics, bone waste, coloring material and other debris from LSA layers are plotted spatially, there is a tendency for some groups of items to be isolated from the main hearth clusters. This suggests that selected activities took place away from centralized activity areas (Wadley 1996, 2000, 2001). Examples of segregated activities around their own hearths or in a discrete area of the cave include grinding of plant foods, the preparation and use of coloring material, the use of backed tools, and the processing of bone. The number of substantial LSA7 hearths is limited and their greater thickness relative to earlier MSA hearths suggests that the former were consistently reused. What is noteworthy is that discrete activity areas are observable in all of the 20 LSA horizons, but in none of the MSA layers. This difference occurs even though there is no apparent discrepancy in the way that the MSA and LSA sediments were formed (Smith 1997), even though the LSA and MSA deposits are of similar depths, even though both the LSA and MSA layers are probably palimpsests, and even though the density of artifacts is similarly high in MSA (excluding layer Dy) and Later Stone Age layers. Behavioral differences seem to provide the best explanation for the contrasting MSA and LSA spatial patterns.

It appears that when LSA people re-used the cave they paid attention to the spatial arrangements of the previous LSA occupants. They seem to have adopted old hearths and perhaps they duplicated some work areas. Even though band fluidity and mobility would have affected spatial organization through various phases of site occupation, I argue that the Rose Cottage LSA data imply that space was being ordered for social purposes. Kolen's (1999) "mythical ordering of space" seems to have operated in the LSA, but not in the MSA of Rose Cottage Cave. Spatial site structure in caves and rockshelters could serve the same purpose as style does in material culture (Galanidou 2000:272), in that it might communicate messages about group identity. If this is the case then it seems that people in the MSA of Rose Cottage were less interested in communicating group identity through space than people who lived in the LSA.

A few other sites in South Africa have spatial information although there are presently no other published intra-site spatial studies. Bone and artifactual material was scattered in an unstructured way around a single hearth on the ca.121,000-year-old occupation floor at the open site of Florisbad (Kuman 1989). New detailed spatial analyzes at Florisbad (Brink and Henderson 2001; Henderson 2001), based on a study of 4,171 lithics and 1,723 bone fragments, provides more information. The patterning of the conjoining lithics reconfirms a concentration around the hearth area, but also implies a knapping area to the north of the hearth (Henderson 2001:14). The distribution of the faunal remains suggests that there was a disarticulation or processing area separate from a consumption area (Henderson 2001:14). Since Rose Cottage Cave has no bone preservation in the MSA layers, no comparison can be made, but the possible presence of a distinct knapping area at Florisbad is certainly a different pattern from the one depicted at Rose Cottage. However, as Brooks (1996:253) points out, open-air and cave sites sample very different parts of a settlement pattern. It may be unwise to compare spatial patterns in caves and open-air sites directly because there are constraints on space in caves. This limitation may force people to behave differently from the way that they behave when space is unconstrained. At Klasies River Shelter 1B, in MSA layers thought to date between 80,000 and 70,000 years ago, shellfish were cooked and some shells were dumped away from the hearths. Apart from this, there were no recognizable activity areas at the site (Henderson 1992). At Strathalan B, in a MSA layer dated 29,000 years ago, there were dispersed scatters of bone and lithic artifacts near hearths, and in grass concentrations (Opperman 1996) that may represent sleeping quarters. Data from these sites, together with information from Rose Cottage, suggest that unstructured camp organization with a clutter of artifacts and food waste, usually in close association with hearths, may be the norm for MSA cave or shelter sites in South Africa. Similar spatial configurations occur in the Middle Palaeolithic, where they are not considered modern (Mellars 1996). For example, jumbled hearths are a feature of occupation floors in the Middle Palaeolithic of Europe (Stringer and Gamble 1993). In Abric Romaní, Spain, refuse areas were apparent, but hearths played a key role in settlement strategies. There was a regular association of hearths, lithic scatters from *in situ* reduction sequences, and small bones, but no specialized task groups were recognized (Vaquero *et al.* 2001:591). Although it would be rash to emphasize similarities between African MSA and European Middle Palaeolithic behaviors that were produced by two different hominid types, it is also impossible to avoid making the comparison.

Because of the lack of fine resolution in Stone Age sites it is neither valid nor especially useful to attempt to reconstruct cameos or "moments in time" in the cave's history; rather it seems important to paint broad brush strokes that exhibit change through time. Although the spatial arrangement in the final MSA layer, Ru, implies a directional trend towards LSA spatial patterns, the Rose Cottage data suggest that MSA spatial patterns are less complex than LSA ones. It seems that people living in the cave during the final MSA were not concerned about emphasizing group identity, in other words they were probably not using space symbolically. There is also no evidence for contemporary modules in the late MSA of Rose Cottage, whereas they are evident in all LSA layers. This distinction needs to be explored at other African sites because the database is currently small. The lack of evidence for symbolism in the use of space in late MSA occupations of Rose Cottage does not, however, imply that symbolism was absent from other aspects of life at this time. Style in Rose Cottage lithics seems present earlier than formal spatial patterns (Wadley 2001). McBrearty and Brooks (2000) suggest that modern behavior did not appear as a package in the MSA and the Rose Cottage data seem to support this view. The evidence for an uneven chronology in symbolic evolution is even clearer in some other African sites. Personal ornamentation is undoubtedly symbolic and ostrich eggshell beads are present at 40,000 years ago in Enkapune Ya Muto, Kenya (Ambrose 1998). Even earlier beads made from shells seem to be present *ca.*75,000 years ago at Blombos Cave, South Africa (Henshilwood *et al.* 2004). Thus symbolism appears to be expressed in personal ornamentation thousands of years before its spatial expression. It will be interesting to see whether this interpretation of the trend is still valid after several other African sites have been analyzed spatially.

ACKNOWLEDGEMENTS

I thank Wendy Voorvelt for redrawing the figures, Stephan Woodborne for the unpublished Rose Cottage Cave date, and Annabel Field and Luke Winter for the refitting analysis of layer Dc. Funding for the Rose Cottage project was provided by the University of the Witwatersrand and the Center for Scientific and Industrial Research. Opinions expressed and conclusions arrived at are those of the author and are not necessarily to be attributed to the University or the CSIR.

REFERENCES CITED

Allott L.F. 2000. *Spatial analysis of YD Layer at Rose Cottage Cave near Ladybrand, South Africa*. M.Sc. research report, University of the Witwatersrand.

Ambrose S.H. 1998. Chronology of the Later Stone Age and food production in East Africa. *Journal of Archaeological Science* 25: 377–392.

Binford L.R. 1998. Hearth and home: the spatial analysis of ethnographically documented rock shelter occupations as a template for distinguishing between human and hominid use of sheltered space. In N.J. Conard and F. Wendorf (Eds.), *Middle Palaeolithic and Middle Stone Age Settlement Systems*, pp. 229–239. Forli: ABACO.

Bordes F. 1961. *Typologie du Paléolithique ancien et moyen*. Bordeaux: Delmas.

Brink J.S. and Z.L. Henderson 2001. A high-resolution Last Interglacial MSA horizon at Florisbad in the context of other open-air occurrences in the central interior of southern Africa: an interim statement. In N. Conard (Ed.), *Settlement Dynamics of the Middle Palaeolithic and Middle Stone Age*, pp. 1–20. Tübingen: Kerns Verlag.

Brooks A. 1984. San land-use patterns, past and present: implications for southern African prehistory. In M. Hall, G. Avery, D.M. Avery, M.L. Wilson and A.J.B. Humphreys (Eds.), *Frontiers: Southern African Archaeology Today* (BAR International Series 207), pp. 40–52. Oxford: BAR.

Brooks A. 1996. Open air sites in the Middle Stone Age of Africa. In N.J. Conard and F. Wendorf (Eds.), *Middle Palaeolithic and Middle Stone Age Settlement Systems*, pp. 249–253. Forli: ABACO.

Clark A.M.B. 2000. *A Technological and Behavioural Interpretation of the Change From the Middle Stone Age to the Later Stone Age in South Africa*. Ph.D. Dissertation, University of the Witwatersrand.

Conard N.J., T. Prindeville and D.S. Adler 1998. Refitting bones and stones as a means of reconstructing Middle Paleolithic subsistence in the Rhineland. In J.-P. Brugal, L. Meignen and M. Patou-Mathis (Eds.), *Économie préhistorique: les comportements de subsistance au Paléolithique*, pp. 273–290. Sophia Antipolis: APDCA.

Debénath A. and H.L. Dibble 1994. *Handbook of Palaeolithic Typology*. Philadelphia: University of Pennsylvania.

Depaepe P. 2001. A comparison of spatial analyses of three Mousterian sites: new methods, new interpretations. In N. Conard (Ed.), *Settlement Dynamics of the Middle Palaeolithic and Middle Stone Age*, pp. 337–360. Tübingen: Kerns Verlag.

Fruth B. and G. Hofmann 1996. Nest building behaviour in the great apes: the great leap forward? In W.C. McGrew, L.F. Marchant and T. Nishida (Eds.), *Great Ape Societies*, pp. 225–240. Cambridge: Cambridge University Press.

Galanidou N. 1999. Regional settlement and intra-site spatial patterns in Upper Palaeolithic Epirus. In G.N. Bailey, E. Adam, E. Panagopoulou, C. Perlès and K. Zachos (Eds.), *The Palaeolithic Archaeology of Greece and Adjacent Areas*, pp. 148–158. London: The British School at Athens Studies.

Galanidou N. 2000. Patterns in caves: foragers, horticulturists, and the use of space. *Journal of Anthropological Archaeology* 19: 243–275.

Gorecki P.P. 1991. Horticulturalists as hunter-gatherers: rock shelter usage in Papua New Guinea. In C.S. Gamble and W. A. Boismier, (Eds.), *Ethnoarchaeological Approaches to Mobile Campsites*, pp. 237–262. Ann Arbor: International Monographs in Prehistory.

Harper P.T. 1997. The Middle Stone Age sequences at Rose Cottage Cave: a search for continuity and discontinuity. *South African Journal of Science* 93: 470–475.

Henderson Z. 1992. The context of some Middle Stone Age hearths at Klasies River Shelter 1B: implications for understanding human behaviour. *South African Field Archaeologist* 1: 14–26.

Henderson Z. 2001. The integrity of the Middle Stone Age horizon at Florisbad, South Africa. *Navorsinge van die Nasionale Museum, Bloemfontein* 17: 26–52.

Henshilwood C., F. d'Errico, M. Vanhaeren, K. van Niekerk and Z. Jacobs 2004. Middle Stone Age shell beads from South Africa. *Science* 304: 404.

Kolen J. 1999. Hominids without homes: on the nature of Middle Palaeolithic settlement in Europe. In W. Roebroeks and C. Gamble (Eds.), *The Middle Palaeolithic Occupation of Europe*, pp. 139–163. Leiden: University of Leiden.

Kuman K.A. 1989. *Florisbad and /Gi: The Contribution of Open-air Sites to Study of the Middle Stone Age in Southern Africa*. Ph.D. Dissertation, University of Pennsylvania.

Marshall L. 1976. *The !Kung of Nyae Nyae*. Cambridge, MA: Harvard University Press.

McBrearty S. and A.S. Brooks 2000. The revolution that wasn't: a new interpretation of the origin of modern human behavior. *Journal of Human Evolution* 39: 453–563.

McGrew W.C. 1992. *Chimpanzee Material Culture: Implications for Human Evolution*. Cambridge: Cambridge University Press.

Mellars P. 1996. *The Neanderthal Legacy: An Archaeological Perspective from Western Europe*. Princeton: Princeton University Press.

Opperman H. 1996. Strathalan Cave B, north-eastern Cape Province, South Africa: evidence for human behaviour 29,000–26,000 years ago. *Quaternary International* 33: 45–53.

Richardson N. 1992. Conjoin sets and stratigraphic integrity in a sandstone shelter: Kenniff Cave (Queensland, Australia). *Antiquity* 66: 408–418.

Sept J.M. 1992. Was there no place like home? A new perspective on early hominid archaeological sites from the mapping of chimpanzee nests. *Current Anthropology* 33:187–207.

Smith J. 1997. *Stable Isotope Analysis of Fauna and Soils from Sites in the Eastern Free State and Western Lesotho, Southern Africa: A Palaeoenvironmental Interpretation*. M.Sc. thesis, University of Cape Town.

Stringer C.B. and C. Gamble 1993. *In Search of the Neanderthals*. London: Thames and Hudson.

Vaquero M., G. Chacón, C. Fernández, K. Martínez and J.M. Rando 2001. Intrasite spatial patterning and transport in the Abric Romaní Middle Paleolithic site (Capellades, Barcelona, Spain). In N. Conard (Ed.), *Settlement Dynamics of the Middle Palaeolithic and Middle Stone Age*, pp. 573–595. Tübingen: Kerns Verlag.

Wadley L. 1996. The Robberg industry of Rose Cottage Cave, eastern Free State: the technology, spatial patterns and environment. *South African Archaeological Bulletin* 51: 64–74.

Wadley L. 1997. Rose Cottage Cave: Archaeological work 1987 to 1997. *South African Journal of Science* 93: 439–444.

Wadley L. 2000. The use of space in a gender study of two South African Stone Age sites. In M. Donald and L. Hurcombe (Eds.),*Gender and Material Culture in Archaeological Perspective*, pp. 153–168. Basingstoke: Macmillan Press.

Wadley L. 2001. What is cultural modernity? A general view and a South African perspective from Rose Cottage Cave. *Cambridge Archaeological Journal* 11: 201–221.

Wadley L. and P.T. Harper 1989. Rose Cottage Cave revisited: Malan's Middle Stone Age collection. *South African Archaeological Bulletin* 44: 23–32.

Whallon R. 1984. Unconstrained clustering for the analysis of spatial distributions in archaeology. In H. Hietala (Ed.), *Intrasite Spatial Analysis in Archaeology*, pp. 242–277. Cambridge: Cambridge University Press.

Chapter *16*

"Now You See it, Now You Don't"—Modern Human Behavior in the Middle Paleolithic

Erella Hovers
Anna Belfer-Cohen

Institute of Archaeology, The Hebrew University of Jerusalem, Mt. Scopus, Jerusalem 91905, ISRAEL

ABSTRACT

An intriguing phenomenon of the Middle Paleolithic archaeological record is the sporadic occurrence of traits commonly associated with alleged modern behavior. Given the antiquity in the hominin lineage of the organic systems that control such behaviors, the question of interest is not whether Middle Paleolithic people were *capable* of such behaviors, but rather why its occurrence is so haphazard and irregular. We suggest that the archaeological finds reflect only those elements of human knowledge that have been accepted and incorporated into societal norma- tive behaviors, stored and kept for repeated use through canonization and rituals. Instability of demographic systems and population crashes prevented the con- tinuous accumulation of such knowledge in certain regions of the Old World, dictating that technological and symbolic innovations be "re-invented" time and again throughout the Middle Paleolithic period.

INTRODUCTION

To many researchers, the Middle Paleolithic period is "the muddle in the mid- dle" of prehistoric times (Stringer and Gamble 1993, after G. Isaac). Though shorter than the previous Lower Paleolithic, this period still comprises some 200,000 years. The technological variability recognized through this time interval is claimed to reflect shifts in mobility and subsistence modes, which were in turn responsive to changing ecological circumstances. In contrast, temporal variability in tool morphology, if observed at all, occurs at a slow pace, lending the Middle Paleolithic (and the Middle Stone Age) a monotonous appearance (Kuhn and Stiner 1998; Bar-Yosef 2000; Würz 2002). The latter was often explained by the contention that the brains of Middle Paleolithic hominins were organized differently from those of modern humans. In consequence, these archaic humans were lacking in the cognitive abilities that are the prerequisites for invention and innovations (e.g., Mithen 1996).

For a long time, archaeological wisdom advocated a straightforward approach to the question of human cognitive capacities: *what you see is what there was*. To wit, it was assumed that human potential for modern cognitive behavior must be attested to in the archaeological record, and that the evidence for its existence would be unequivocal (e.g., parietal and mobile art [Noble and Davidson 1996; Mellars 1996; but see Humphrey 1998]). A different outlook had implications too difficult to face. Indeed, if one delved too deeply into the idea of *latent* cognitive potential, not expressed in the archaeological evidence, hypotheses concerning stages and tempo of evolution of behavior and culture would stand on shaky ground, at best. For example, in order to overcome the epistemological difficulty of actualization of latent capacities, Leroi-Gourhan incorporated in his studies of human technology the somewhat arbitrary notion of a "driving force" that perpetuated a *continuous* realization of the cognitive potential (and see Audouze 2002).

For the purpose of the ongoing discussion, we use the term "modern" in its basic meaning as "of, relating to, or characteristic of the present or the immediate past" (Mish 1996), with no *a priori* evolutionary connotations. According to this definition, modern behavior is not necessarily unique to the present, and its presence in the past does not distract from its modernity.

Clear-cut evidence for modern behavior (in the sense discussed above) seemed to occur in Europe as an integrated, normative system only at the beginning of the Upper Paleolithic, seemingly hand in hand with the arrival of modern humans who replaced the local Neandertals. Due to its sudden emergence and characteristics, this evidence was taken to reflect a revolutionary event. And due to the Eurocentric worldview of prehistoric research at the time, this postulated occurrence (which was not observed outside of western Europe) was perceived as a turning point in human evolution.

Since the formulation of this paradigm, pre-Upper Paleolithic finds, of the kind typically considered as evidence for modern cognitive abilities, have time and again dented this notion (e.g., Goren-Inbar 1986, 1990; Marshack 1989, 1991, 1996; Bednarik 1994; d'Errico et al. 1998; Hovers et al. 1997, 2003; Gaudzinski 1999 [and see discussion in Villa and d'Errico 2001]; d'Errico and Nowell 2000; Henshilwood et al. 2001, 2002). Concurrently, it has become evident that Anatomically Modern Humans coexisted with (and sometimes preceded) the Neandertals (Vandermeersch 1982; Smith et al. 1999; and see papers in Bar-Yosef and Pilbeam

2000). The accumulated evidence from various domains of research, recovered from widespread geographical regions, and from different time periods, now suggests that the presence of Middle Paleolithic symbolic or cognitive behavior is not tethered to the existence of Anatomically Modern Humans (Belfer-Cohen 1988).

As part of the on-going process of "coming of age" in anthropological thought, archaeological theory came to accept the notion that the material record provides but fragmentary and partial evidence of past human cognitive capacities (Preucel and Hodder 1996). Where there had been certainty, skepticism arose: does the archaeological record depict the total cognitive capacity of hominins at any given time? Or do the observed phenomena reflect a *realized* segment (randomly preserved) of far more expansive abilities?

The issue is farther complicated since archaeological data are often open to wide, sometimes contradictory yet equally valid interpretations. Clearly, questions about human cognition in the past cannot be resolved from within the archaeological domain exclusively. The input from other disciplines can, and indeed should, serve in evaluating our ideas concerning prehistoric cognitive abilities and their evolution through time.

Paleo-neurological studies (and to a lesser extent, evolutionary psychology) indicate that the neural substructure for human cognitive abilities does indeed go very far back (Humphrey 1976; Barkow *et al.* 1992; Deacon 1997a, and references therein). For example, there is evidence to indicate that the limbic system, which dictates many of the behaviors considered markedly human, has not changed structurally, at least since the Middle Pleistocene (*e.g.*, Maclean 1982; Eccles 1989). Similarly, the neuro-anatomical configuration enabling language, a marker of modernity, seems to appear very early in human evolution (Deacon 1989, 1997b; Calvin and Bickerton 2000). Given the antiquity of these neural systems, it is plausible that Middle Paleolithic hominins possessed much of the cerebral hardware pertaining to modern behavior, regardless of their taxonomic/genetic affinities.

Here, we interpret the concept of "human behavior" as encompassing both the actualization of certain types of behavior as well as the latent capacity for such behaviors. Borrowing from biology, we refer to these as "phenotypic" and "genotypic" components, respectively. As is the case with many biological phenotypes, some behaviors will become apparent only on the cue of particular stimuli (*e.g.*, Ridley 1993). The implications are twofold: (1) contrary to the notion that "instant" neurological mutations are immediately expressed "phenotypically" (*e.g.*, Klein 2000), the first recognizable appearance of a behavior probably does not signify that the cognitive potential for this behavior had emerged just shortly before; and (2) because stimuli are circumstance-dependent, we should not expect behaviors of discrete populations to be necessarily or absolutely similar, even if they possess similar cognitive abilities (for example, the polemic concerning Neandertals and Anatomically Modern Humans).

In our view, the fascinating question as regards the long Middle Paleolithic record is related neither to the feasibility of modern cognitive behavior, nor to its first appearance in the archaeological record (see Hovers 1997 for discussion). Rather, we are concerned here with the sporadic mode of manifestation of this behavior, and its possible causative processes. The following discourse is an attempt to understand these phenomena, taking into consideration the interaction of demographic and social circumstances and their effects on systems of human communication.

A NOTE ON THE NATURE OF HUMAN KNOWLEDGE

It is important to bear in mind that any given cognitive behavior is an expression of inherent ("genotypic") potential and its interaction with *knowledge*. Given the existence of a potential for cognitive behavior in Middle Paleolithic hominins, it is useful to consider here the properties of knowledge, the second prerequisite for a manifest behavior.

A sometimes overlooked, but nonetheless fundamental property of human knowledge is its accretionary nature (Jacob 1973). Knowledge connotes past experience as well as the "proclivity to experiment with new ideas, techniques, devices, and strategies to make inventions into innovations" (*i.e.*, "innovativeness"; Sundbo 1998:20). It is through these properties that knowledge acts to expand future frames of reference.

Inventions are "the discovery or achievement by an individual of a new process, whether deliberate or by chance" (Renfrew 1978:90 and references therein). Inventions often stem from "brain storms", independent of existing knowledge and/or of means to "test" and implement them—Leonardo da Vinci's inventions are a case in point. However, inventions become full-fledged innovations, which are part of an observable behavioral repertoire, only when adopted by a large number of individuals (Renfrew 1978; Schiffer and Skibbo 1987; Kuhn and Stiner 1998). In such a process, knowledge acts as a pre-adaptive matrix. New ideas operate and are tested within the range of possibilities defined by any given state of knowledge.

Certain forms of social, physical, and organizational infrastructure are required to promote the diffusion of technological knowledge that supports the use of innovative technologies (Burt 1980; Wallace 1982; Doloreux 2002). Thus Leonardo's inventions, being divorced from the engineering realities of their time, remained technological fantasies for hundreds of years. In non-industrial societies, the spread of knowledge may occur less formally, but is nonetheless indispensable. Knowledge provides an element of familiarity that is needed to overcome the inherent human reluctance, more pronounced in traditional societies, to adopt novelties (*e.g.*, Renfrew 1978; Spratt 1989; Lepowsky 1991; Saidel 2000).

THE ARCHAEOLOGICAL RECORD

We emphasize here, at the risk of being redundant, that the first-ever, original invention underlying any innovation is most likely untraceable archaeologically. A novel behavior that is archaeologically observable necessarily implies that an invention had already been transformed into an innovation through complex processes of spread and adoption.

That said, we posit that by the Middle Paleolithic, the "blueprint" underlying modern behavior (*i.e.*, the biological potential and the practical knowledge) had already been in place. Thus, behaviors commonly accepted as modern can be observed consistently throughout the duration of the Middle Paleolithic (for example, big-game hunting and its social and technological implications; see Stiner 2002 for a recent discussion). Other facets of modern behavior, though sporadically attested to, are implied by uncommon finds (*e.g.*, ochre, bone tools, engraved bone and stone items, see references above) as well as by the appearance of burials (see Belfer-Cohen and Hovers 1992; Defleur 1993; Hovers *et al.* 2000).

Overall, the late Middle-early Upper Pleistocene record speaks against the emergence of "modernity" as a global, one-time event associated solely with *Homo sapiens sapiens*. Judging by the criteria commonly used to identify cultural modernity, the African Middle Stone Age appears to portray the emergence of human modernity as an incremental process, beginning some 280,000 years ago (McBrearty and Brooks 2000 and references therein). By the same criteria, we will have to conclude that in the Levant, the full-fledged modern behavioral package appeared abruptly only at the close of the Pleistocene, with the emergence of the Natufian cultural entity (*ca.* 13,000 BP) (Bar-Yosef 1998 and references therein). Thus the archaeological evidence indicates that the tempo and mode of modern behavior appearance throughout the Middle Paleolithic differ over time and across geographical spaces, crosscutting the taxonomic boundaries of contemporaneous human groups.

DISCUSSION

Why then does the emergence of behavioral and cultural modernity seem chaotic and particularistic in nature? We have argued above that behavior becomes archaeologically visible only after appropriate cues in the social and physical environments have triggered the passage from latent potential, to actualized behavior, to prevalent norms. Once the initial trigger kicks in, the particular behavior appears. However, in order for such a behavior to *persist*, the pertinent knowledge must be retained and transmitted down the generations.

The triggers (or lack thereof) stimulating innovations that led to what we define as modern behavior have been discussed extensively in the anthropological literature. Often, they were identified in demographic circumstances. Ecological conditions are suggested to have led to convergence of human groups in limited regions of the Levant, leading to increased technological variability at the end of the Middle Paleolithic (Hovers 1997, 2001). Increased population densities in *refugia* areas in western Europe are argued to have stimulated the occurrence of parietal art (Jochim 1983). By the same token, social pressures and increased occupation densities are said to have led to sedentism and agriculture at the end of the Pleistocene (Keeley 1995; Belfer-Cohen and Bar-Yosef 2000).

Here we focus not so much on the stimulants of modern behavior expressions. Rather, we look at the mechanisms that might have led to the persistence of such behavior *after* it had been triggered. As a rule, cultural information (*i.e.*, the sets of beliefs, ideas, and practices that allow one to identify oneself with a broader community) has to be remembered and transmitted again and again with little or no alteration, or else the accumulation of alteration will compromise the very existence of culture (Sperber and Hirschfeld 2004).

In non-literate societies, information is stored by means of oral tradition and shared through extensive networks of lateral and vertical cultural transmissions. Information needed for mediating mundane subsistence and social needs, and to cope with frequent and recurrent stress events, is used constantly. It is therefore easily accessible, efficiently retained, but at the same time responsive to small-scale changes in the circumstances to which this information is pertinent. On the other hand, information needed for negotiating rare crises is in danger of being forgotten in parts or as a whole, because it is put to use only very infrequently. In this case, there is a premium on resistance to change, namely on the capacity to maintain information intact through time, despite the "noise" introduced into the process of transmission as either random or systemic phenomenon (K. P. Smith 1988:99–100). As a means to prevent the loss of such knowledge, it is incorporated into rites and myths, and canonized as part of the group's cultural heritage and social identity. Smith (1988:87) suggested that ritual is particularly appropriate for the storage of information necessary for long-term group survival. Significantly, ritual also epitomizes fundamental constituents of a group's social self-image and regulates its very social structure. Changes to ritual are risky not only in terms of ecological balance; they entail a heavy social toll and endanger the group's existence as a social unit. It is for these reasons that rites and symbols are strictly adhered to and perpetuated at the cost of heavy social investment. This central role of ritual in the retention and transfer of information is amply illustrated ethnographically (Minc 1986; Minc and Smith 1989; Kosse 1990; Owens and Hayden 1997; Sobel and Bettles 2000).

It is the information stored in, and transmitted through, ritual and myth that serves as a foundation on which additional knowledge is accrued. The mechanisms that maintain information transmission are dependent upon critical population size and density (Kosse 1990). If networks of storage and transmission are *not* available or fail when facing a sudden, unexpected crisis, the group will come up with an innovative behavior—or perish.

The archaeological evidence commonly cited as indicating modern behavior (see details above) relates both to technological efficiency (*e.g.*, introduction of bone tools, composite weapons, *etc.*) as well as to ritual contexts that do not reflect directly the daily "business of living." It seems to us that, at least in the framework of the present argument, the mundane and ritual domains are interrelated. In fact, social retention of the former may have been dependent on the existence of the latter. This interpretation is justified, given the contexts of similar occurrences in later prehistory and in modern ethnographic records (Turner 1970; Conkey 1980; Jochim 1983; Sagona 1994).

We suggest that the sporadic expressions of modern behavior in the Middle Paleolithic reflect a situation where systems of knowledge retention were rather unstable. Recurrent demographic crashes would operate to eradicate much of the socially stored knowledge. Such crashes in the Upper Pleistocene are indeed postulated by genetic studies (*e.g.*, Semino *et al.* 2000; Caramelli *et al.* 2003). Thus we should not be surprised that a particular behavior appeared in the Middle Paleolithic record either sporadically or suddenly. Fluctuations in the ability of Middle Paleolithic human groups to store knowledge also constitute a parsimonious explanation for the different trajectories of establishment and growth of modern behavior in various geographical regions (*e.g.*, Africa *vs.* Europe *vs.* the Levant). These are the expected patterns when a behavior is "invented" anew time and again.

To conclude, the hindrance to modern human behavior in the Middle Paleolithic may have resulted not from evolutionary biological limitations, namely, inferior mental capacities. Rather, the impediment to the perseverance of full-fledged cultural modernity lies in demographic constraints on the formation of an appropriate matrix of "innovativeness". The processes of change that took place within the Middle Paleolithic sometimes go unrecognized because they were not progressive in nature, *i.e.*, did not lead linearly from a given situation to a specific end (Hovers 1997). Viewed from this perspective, the Middle Paleolithic should not be regarded as a period of cultural stasis. Conversely, the processes of change in the course of this time span were the background for the crystallization of Upper Paleolithic modern behavior (*e.g.*, Gilman 1984). The spread and persistence of modern behavior is a tale of historical contingency rather than a gradual evolutionary culture change or an Upper Paleolithic innovation *sensu stricto*.

ACKNOWLEDGEMENTS

We thank Steve L. Kuhn for insightful discussions of various issues raised by us and for his comments on an earlier draft. We also thank Yehuda Cohen and two anonymous reviewers for their comments during various stages of writing this paper.

REFERENCES CITED

Audouze F. 2002. Leroi-Gourhan, a philosopher of technique and evolution. *Journal of Archaeological Research* 10: 277–306.

Barkow J.H., L. Cosmides and J. Tooby 1992. *The Adapted Mind. Evolutionary Psychology and the Generation of Culture.* Oxford: Oxford University Press.

Bar-Yosef O. 1998. The Natufian culture in the Levant, threshold to the origins of agriculture. *Evolutionary Anthropology* 6: 159–177.

Bar-Yosef O. 2000. The Middle and Early Upper Paleolithic in Southwest Asia and neighboring regions. In O. Bar-Yosef and D. Pilbeam (Eds.), *The Geography of Neandertals and Modern Humans in Europe and the Greater Mediterranean*, pp. 107–156. Cambridge MA: Peabody Museum of Archaeology and Ethnography, Harvard University.

Bar-Yosef O. and D. Pilbeam (Eds.) 2000. *The Geography of Neandertals and Modern Humans in Europe and the Greater Mediterranean.* Cambridge, MA: Peabody Museum of Archaeology and Ethnology, Harvard University.

Bednarik R. G. 1994. The Pleistocene Art of Asia. *Journal of World Prehistory* 8(4): 351–375.

Belfer-Cohen A. 1988. The appearance of symbolic expression in the Upper Pleistocene of the Levant as compared to Western Europe. In O. Bar-Yosef (Ed.), *L'Homme de Néanderthal: La Pensé* (ERAUL 32), pp. 25–29. Liège: Université de Liège.

Belfer-Cohen A. and E. Hovers 1992. In the eye of the beholder: Middle Palaeolithic and Natufian burials in the Levant. *Current Anthropology* 33: 463–471.

Belfer-Cohen A. and O. Bar-Yosef 2000. Early sedentism in the Near East—a bumpy ride to village life. In I. Kuijt (Ed.), *Life in Neolithic Farming Communities. Social Organization, Identity, and Differentiation,* pp. 19–38. New York: Kluwer Academic/Plenum.

Burt R.S. 1980. Innovation as a structural interest: rethinking the impact of network position on innovation adoption. *Social Networks* 2: 327–355.

Calvin W.H. and D. Bickerton 2000. *Lingua ex Machine: Reconciling Darwin and Chomsky with the Human Brain.* Cambridge, MA: MIT Press.

Caramelli D., C. Lalueza-Fox, C. Vernesi, M. Lari, A. Casoli, F. Mallegni, B. Chiarelli, I. Dupanloup, J. Bertanpetit, G. Barbujani and G. Bertorelle 2003. Evidence for a genetic discontinuity between Neandertals and 24,000-year-old anatomically modern Europeans. *Proceedings of the National Academy of Science USA* 100: 6593–6597.

Conkey M.W. 1980. The identification of prehistoric hunter-gatherer aggregation sites: the case of Altamira. *Current Anthropology* 21: 609–631.

Deacon T.W. 1989. The neural circuitry underlying primate calls and human language. *Human Evolution* 4: 367–401.

Deacon T. W. 1997a. *The Symbolic Species: The Co-Evolution of Language and the Human Brain.* London: Allen Lane, The Penguin Press.

Deacon T.W. 1997b. What makes the human brain different? *Annual Review of Anthropology* 26: 337–357.

Defleur A. 1993. *Les sepultures moustériennes.* Paris: Editions CNRS.

Doloreux D. 2002. What we should know about regional systems of innovation. *Technology in Society* 24: 243–263.

Eccles J.C.1989. *Evolution of the Brain. Creation of the Self.* London: Routledge.

d'Errico F. and A. Nowell 2000. A new look at the Berekhat Ram figurine: implications for the origins of symbolism. *Cambridge Archaeological Journal* 10: 123–167.

d'Errico, F., J. Zilhão, M. Julien, D. Baffier and J. Pelegrin 1998. Neanderthal acculturation in Western Europe? a critical review of the evidence and its interpretation. *Current Anthropology* 39 (Supplement): S1–S44.

Gaudzinski S. 1999. Middle Paleolithic bone tools from the open-air site Salzgitter-Lebenstedt (Germany). *Journal of Archaeological Science* 26: 125–141.

Gilman A. 1984. Explaining the Upper Palaeolithic revolution. In M. Spriggs (Ed.), *Marxist Perspectives in Archaeology,* pp. 115–126. Cambridge: Cambridge University Press.

Goren-Inbar N. 1986. A figurine from the Acheulean site of Berekhat Ram. *Journal of the Israel Prehistoric Society* 19: 7–11.

Goren-Inbar N. 1990. *Quneitra - A Mousterian Site on the Golan Heights* (Qedem 31). Jerusalem: Institute of Archaeology, The Hebrew University.

Henshilwood C.S., F. d'Errico, C.W. Marean, R.G. Milo and R. Yates 2001. An early bone tool industry from the Middle Stone Age at Blombos Cave, South Africa: implications for the origins of modern human behaviour, symbolism and language. *Journal of Human Evolution* 41: 631–678.

Henshilwood C.S., F. d'Errico, R. Yates, Z. Jacobs, C. Tribolo, G.A.T. Duller, N. Mercier, J.C. Sealy, H. Valladas, I. Watts and A.G. Wintle 2002. Emergence of modern human behavior: Middle Stone Age engravings from South Africa. *Science* 295: 1278–1280.

Hovers E. 1997. *Variability of Levantine Mousterian Assemblages and Settlement Patterns: Implications for Understanding the Development of Human Behavior.* Ph.D Dissertation, The Hebrew University, Jerusalem.

Hovers E. 2001. Territorial behavior in the Middle Paleolithic of the Southern Levant. In N. Conard (Ed.), *Settlement Dynamics of the Middle Paleolithic and Middle Stone Age*, pp. 123–152. Tübingen: Kerns Verlag.

Hovers E., B. Vandermeersch and O. Bar-Yosef 1997. A Middle Palaeolithic engraved artefact from Qafzeh Cave, Israel. *Rock Art Research* 14: 79–87.

Hovers E., W.H. Kimbel and Y. Rak 2000. The Amud 7 skeleton - still a burial. Response to Gargett. *Journal of Human Evolution* 39: 253–260.

Hovers E., S. Ilani, O. Bar-Yosef and B. Vandermeersch 2003. An early case of color symbolism: ochre use by early modern humans in Qafzeh Cave, Israel. *Current Anthropology* 44: 491–522.

Humphrey N. 1976. The social function of intellect. In P.P.G. Bateson and A.R. Hinde (Eds.), *Growing Points in Ethology*, pp. 303–317. Cambridge: Cambridge University Press.

Humphrey N. 1998. Cave art, autism, and the evolution of the human mind. *Cambridge Archaeological Journal* 8: 165–191.

Jacob F. 1973. *The Logic of Life: a History of Heredity*. New York: Pantheon Books.

Jochim M. 1983. Palaeolithic art in ecological perspective. In G. Bailey (Ed.), *Hunter-Gatherer Economy in Prehistory*, pp. 212–219. Cambridge: Cambridge University Press.

Keeley L.H. 1995. Protoagricultural practices among hunter-gatherers: a cross-cultural survey. In T.D. Price and A.-B. Gebauer (Eds.), *Last Hunters - First Farmers*, pp. 243–272. Santa Fe: School of American Research Press.

Klein R.G. 2000. Archeology and the evolution of human behavior. *Evolutionary Anthropology* 9: 17–36.

Kosse K. 1990. Group size and societal complexity: thresholds in the long-term memory. *Journal of Anthropological Archaeology* 9: 275–303.

Kuhn S.L. and M.C. Stiner 1998. Middle Paleolithic 'creativity': reflections on an oxymoron? In S. Mithen (Ed.), *Creativity in Human Evolution and Prehistory*, pp. 143–164. London: Routledge.

Lepowsky M. 1991. The way of the ancestors: custom, innovation, and resistance. *Ethnology* XXX: 217–235.

Maclean P.D. 1982. Evolution of the psychoencephalon. *Zygon* 17: 187–211.

Marshack A. 1989. Evolution of the human capacity: the symbolic evidence. *Yearbook of Physical Anthropology* 32: 1–34.

Marshack A. 1991. *The Roots of Civilization. The Cognitive Beginnings of Man's First Art, Symbol and Notation*. 2nd edition. New York: Moyer Bell Limited.

Marshack A. 1996. A Middle Paleolithic symbolic composition from the Golan Heights: the earliest known depictive image. *Current Anthropology* 37: 357–365.

McBrearty S. and A.S. Brooks 2000. The revolution that wasn't: a new interpretation of the origin of modern human behavior. *Journal of Human Evolution* 39(5): 453–563.

Mellars P. 1996. *The Neanderthal Legacy: an Archaeological Perspective from Western Europe*. Princeton: Princeton University Press.

Minc L. 1986. Scarcity and survival: The role of oral tradition in mediating subsistence crises. *Journal of Anthropological Archaeology* 5: 39–113.

Minc L. and K. Smith 1989. The spirit of survival: cultural responses to resource variability in North Alaska. In P. Halstead and J. O'Shea (Eds.), *Bad Year Economics: Cultural Responses to Risk and Uncertainty*, pp. 8–39. Cambridge: Cambridge University Press.

Mish F.C. 1996. *Merriam-Webster Collegiate Dictionary*. 10 edn. Springfield, MA: Merriam-Webster, Incorporated.

Mithen S. 1996. *The Prehistory of the Mind. A Search for the Origins of Art, Religion and Science*. London: Thames and Hudson.

Noble W. amd I. Davidson 1996. *Human Evolution, Language, and Mind: a Psychological and Archaeological Inquiry*. Cambridge: Cambridge University Press.

Owens D.A. and B. Hayden 1997. Prehistoric rites of passage: a comparative study of transegalitarian hunter-gatherers. *Journal of Anthropological Archaeology* 16: 121–161.

Preucel R.W. and I. Hodder (Eds.), 1996. *Contemporary Archaeology in Theory: A Reader*. Oxford: Blackwell Publishers Inc.

Renfrew C. 1978. The anatomy of innovation. In C. Renfrew (Ed.), *Approaches to Social Archaeology*, pp. 390–418. Cambridge, MA: Harvard University Press.

Ridley M. 1993. *The Red Queen: Sex and the Evolution of Human Nature*. New York: Macmillan Publishing Company.

Sagona A. (Ed.) 1994. *Bruising the Red Earth: Ochre Mining and Ritual in Aboriginal Tasmania*. Melbourne: Melbourne: University Press.

Saidel B.A. 2000. Matchlocks, flintlocks, and saltpeter: the chronological implications of the use of matchlock muskets among Ottoman-period Bedouins in the southern Levant. *International Journal of Historical Archaeology* 4:191–216.

Schiffer M.B. and J.M. Skibbo 1987. Theory and experiment in the study of technological change. *Current Anthropology* 28: 595–622.

Semino O., J. Passarino, P.J. Oefner, A.A. Lin, S. Arbuzova, L.E. Beckman, G. de Benedictis, P. Francalacci, A. Kouvatsi, S. Umborska, M. Marcikiae, A. Mika, B. Mika, D. Primorac, A.S. Santachiara-Benerecetti, L.L. Cavalli-Sforza and P.A. Underhill 2000. The genetic legacy of Paleolithic *Homo sapiens* in extant Europeans: a Y-chromosome perspective. *Science* 210: 1155–1159.

Smith F.H., E. Trinkaus, P.B. Pettitt, I. Karavanic and M. Paunovic 1999. Direct radiocarbon dates for Vidija G1 and Velika Pecina Late Pleistocene hominid remains. *Proceedings of the National Academy of Science USA* 96: 11281–11286.

Smith K.P. 1988. Ritual and resource variability: mechanisms for the transmission and storage of information regarding low-frequency resource cycles in hunter-gatherer societies. In B.V. Kennedy and G.M. LeMoine (Eds.), *Diet and Subsistence: Current Archaeological Perspectives* (Proceedings of the Chacmool Annual Conference), pp. 86–107. Calgary: The University of Calgary, Archaeological Association.

Sobel E. and G. Bettles G. 2000. Winter hunger, winter myths: subsistence risk and mythology among the Klamath and Modoc. *Journal of Anthropological Archaeology* 19: 276–316.

Spratt D.A. 1989. Innovation theory made plain. In S.E. van der Leeuw and R. Torrence (Eds.), *What's New? A Closer Look at the Process of Innovation*, pp. 245–257. London: Unwin Hyman.

Sperber D. and L.A. Hirschfeld 2004. The cognitive foundations of cultural stability and diversity. *Trends in Cognitive Sciences* 8: 40–46.

Stiner M.C. 2002. Carnivory, coevolution, and the geographic spread of the Genus *Homo*. *Journal of Archaeological Research* 10: 1–63.

Stringer C.B. and C.S. Gamble 1993. *In Search of the Neanderthals: Solving the Puzzle of Human Origins*. New York: Thames and Hudson.

Sundbo J. 1998. *The Theory of Innovation: Enterpreneurs, Technology and Strategy*. Cheltenham, UK: E. Elgar.

Turner V. 1970. *The Forest of Symbols: Aspects of Ndembu Ritual*. New York: Cornell University Press.

Vandermeersch B. 1982. The first *Homo sapiens sapiens* in the Near East. In A. Ronen (Ed.), *The Transition from Lower to Middle Palaeolithic and the Origins of Modern Man* (BAR International Series 151), pp. 297–299. Oxford: BAR.

Villa P. and F. d'Errico 2001. Bone and ivory points in the Lower and Middle Paleolithic of Europe. *Journal of Human Evolution* 41: 69–112.

Wallace A.F.C. 1982. *The Social Context of Innovation: Bureaucrats, Families, and Heroes in the Early Industrial Revolution, as Foreseen in Bacon's New Atlantis*. Princeton: Princeton University Press.

Würz S. 2002. Variability in the Middle Stone Age lithic sequence, 115,000–60,000 years ago at Klasies River, South Africa. *Journal of Archaeological Science* 29: 1001–1015.

Chapter 17

Between Observations and Models

An Eclectic View of Middle Paleolithic Archaeology

Ofer Bar-Yosef

Dept. of Anthropology, Harvard University, Cambridge MA 02138, USA

OPENING REMARKS

While it is the domain of "fossil hunting" that receives immediate media attention, Paleolithic archaeology entails no minor commitment to adequately explore issues of site formation processes, stone artifacts, human and animal bone taphonomy, spatial distribution of various elements—all of which are components in reconstructing past societies. Going through the papers in this volume, readers undoubtedly will recognize that we, Paleolithic archaeologists, are improving our understanding of some processes of human evolution and, in particular, of those related to the emergence of what we call "modern behavior." Encouragingly, even a cursory examination of the literature published since the 1950s shows an exponential increase in the number of investigators, regions examined and sites excavated. The removal of geopolitical boundaries in eastern Europe and most of Asia, the rapidly growing number of projects in many countries, including China, and the increase in communication and diffusion of ideas and techniques (in part due to the World Wide Web), all facilitate the advancement of Paleolithic research and make room for a lot of optimism about the possibilities and abilities of our discipline.

While several questions raised by previous generations remain on the Paleolithic agenda, the ever-increasing available data provide a wider basis for rephrasing old queries and adding new ones. In trying to sort out the data into what we believe are meaningful units of information, from which we can piece together an improved insight into past cultural processes, Middle Paleolithic research struggles with difficulties familiar to archaeologists of later periods as well as to historians. These inquiries raise the following basic issues:

1. The choice and use of classificatory terminology and its meaning. This includes the subdivision of recorded information into units of analysis such as assemblages, industries, cultures, technocomplexes, or the definitions of knapping techniques and their internal variability.
2. The need to affirm the "when" and "where" of observable major cultural or economic changes that could also be labeled as "revolutions," and in particular those changes that we view as meaningful transformations in site size, tool types, diet, mortuary practices, artistic expressions, and the like.
3. The assessment of the time span required by human societies to learn or adopt new tools and other elements of behavior. Based on the historical experience we recognize that human societies tend to keep their traditions expressed in technical knowledge, belief systems, and social structure. Hence, technical, economic, and organizational changes occur at different paces, depending on the particular history of each human society.
4. The speculation of "why" a well-documented change occurred, assuming we agree that it was a major change, such as the onset of the Upper Paleolithic or the Neolithic Revolution, remains the domain of endless arguments, often based on concepts held by the involved scholars.
5. The search for an adequate explanation for the observed regional differences among the Middle Paleolithic entities across the Old World leads us into the realms of geography, genetics, technology, and—I suggest—language as a societal attribute.

Readers of this volume may notice that not all investigators share the same research goals. Some have solely the humble desire of reporting archaeological observations when studying a Middle Paleolithic site. Others would like to conclude with the entire story of the evolution of humankind—from the Middle Paleolithic to the 21st century. Between the least and the most ambitious aims stands the question: how do we know what we know? However, I have no intention of elaborating on the epistemology of archaeology, and only in passing, while discussing briefly a few selected topics, will I refer to "constructing frameworks of reference" (see Binford 2001).

USE AND ABUSE OF TERMINOLOGY

Taxonomy is the classification of organisms (or other phenomena) in an ordered hierarchical system, which indicates a natural relationship. During the 19th century the pioneers of prehistoric research viewed animals, humans, and stone artifacts as part of a natural order, tied to the geochronology of the Quaternary

(Sackett 1981). Following the Pleistocene geological stratigraphy, on which relative chronology was based, investigators coined the terms Lower, Middle, and Upper Paleolithic, later adding the terms Mesolithic and Neolithic. Eschewing the Greek, English-speaking prehistorians in Africa introduced the terms Early Stone Age (ESA), Middle Stone Age (MSA) and Late Stone Age (LSA). The fact that we still use the latter terms when referring to Africa reflects our need to be politically correct. If the rules of paleontology that concern the primacy of names for species do apply to archaeology, only one set of terms should be used, namely that which was introduced first.

Equally ambiguous and problematic are terms coined by Graham Clark (1970) in relation to the lithic industries. Clark assigned to particular configurations of lithic production a status that he called a "mode." However, these generalized, essentially technological modes have been confounded with temporal determinations (see McBrearty and Tyron this volume). For example, core and flake assemblages ("Mode 1"), including the Oldowan, the Clactonian or the industry of Gran Dolina in Atapuerca, are chronologically dated to the Lower and Middle Pleistocene (*e.g.*, Carbonell *et al.* 1999). In southeast Asia these flake-and-core industries are of Upper Paleolithic age or date even to the Neolithic (*e.g.*, in south China). "Mode 2" represents the Acheulean or all biface industries. One may wonder about the "Mousterian of Acheulean Tradition," which was produced by European Neandertals and was chronologically incorporated within "Mode 3" in a major literature survey (Foley and Lahr 1997). It would seem that those who prefer to use Clark's terms should adhere to the technological scheme. But in fact it was G. Clark himself who introduced the confusion when suggesting that "Mode 4" is Upper Paleolithic, "Mode 5" is the Mesolithic period and "Mode 6" is the Neolithic. Thus his scheme is not different from the old notion of evolutionary cultural progress in Prehistory, an association that the chronological subdivisions within the Paleolithic sequence do not carry. I therefore suggest that we abandon Clark's terminology and continue to enjoy the traditional, boring and harmless terminology.

STRATIGRAPHY AND RADIOMETRIC AGE ESTIMATES

Chronological control is necessary for all archaeological investigations, let alone one that attempts to look at the tempo and mode of cultural evolution. Since the establishment of radiocarbon dating, radiometric techniques have replaced the relative chronologies based on bio-zones. Crossing the chronological boundary of 40,000 years BP is crucial for research concerned with the emergence of early modern humans which seems to occur at an earlier age. The most common techniques today for directly dating late Middle Paleolithic burned flints, animal teeth, and quartz grains in the deposits are luminescence (thermoluminescence [TL], Optical Stimulation Luminescence [OSL]) and electron spin resonance (ESR) techniques (*e.g.*, Wagner 1998; Rink 2001). Other methods such as U-series (*e.g.*, TIMS) are used in dating speleothems.

This progress, however, comes with price tags. We often accept without reservation radiometric dates provided by specialists who obtain their samples from either an excavation or museum collections. It is my personal observation that we rarely bother to check the dates against the stratigraphic information, or to consider carefully the possible effects of bioturbation and intrusions, or the impact of immeasurable amounts of U-rich water in both caves and open-air sites. Accepting or rejecting the dates without detailed scrutiny, relying on one's predispositions towards the questions under study, results in misinterpretations of the chronometric positions of sites, assemblages, and human fossils and leads to endless published debates that are a waste of energy, time, and paper.

We should have learned a few lessons from the early days of radiocarbon research! More caution is warranted. Editors should demand that reported radiometric dates be associated clearly with stratigraphic information. Similarly, we must be on guard when old museum collections are being used for dating purposes. A good example is the first series of ESR dates from Tabun (Grün et al. 1991). These dates, obtained from teeth in museum collections without a detailed stratigraphic context within each layer, did not correspond to the TL dates obtained later from artifacts located in situ in the deposits (Mercier 1992; Mercier et al. 1995). I expressed my doubts concerning the relatively younger ESR dates of Tabun cave (Bar-Yosef 1998a) after assessing the reasonable time correlation between the ESR and TL readings from the caves of Kebara and Qafzeh as well as the preliminary ones from Amud (Valladas et al. 1987, 1988; Grün and Stringer 1991; Mercier 1992; Mercier et al. 1995). Such doubts were later confirmed by a larger set of dates (Valladas et al. 1999; Rink et al. 2001). The recent ESR readings from layer E in Tabun led Rink et al. (2004) to suggest that the previously published ESR dates are probably too young due to the effects of U-enriched water. This also casts doubt on the mass spectrometric U-series dates produced by McDermott et al. (1993). Similar doubts exist concerning open-air or terrace sites, such as Quneitra and 'Ain Difla, where the only available dates are ESR readings (Goren-Inbar 1990; Clark et al. 1997) or OSL measurements obtained from an exposure only tentatively correlated with the archaeological horizon such as the Acheulean context at Holon (Porat et al. 1999).

To these reservations we may add a recently mounting discrepancy between the TL and ESR dates for the Acheulo-Yabrudian in Tabun cave and much younger U-series dates on speleothems from the top of an Acheulo-Yabrudian sequence at Qesem Cave (Barkai et al. 2003). The younger speleothem dates in Qesem Cave indicate a certain contemporaneity with the TL dates of the early Levantine Mousterian ("Tabun-D type") in Tabun Cave, where this kind of Mousterian overlies the Acheulo-Yabrudian. One can already predict that a suggested explanation will support the cultural contemporaneity of these two entirely different industries. On the other hand, further dating (with more than one dating technique) of sites currently under excavation may clarify the chronological ordering of the industries. I will return to this issue below in discussing territoriality among Middle Paleolithic groups.

OPERATIONAL SEQUENCE (*CHAÎNE OPÉRATOIRE*) STUDIES

By determining the source of lithic raw materials, analyzing the core reduction sequence and the shaping of retouched stone tools, and recording their discard patterns, we learn about the minds of prehistoric knappers and their daily behavior. This familiar concept has been known in the literature for about twenty years and was adopted by investigators across Europe and the Levant (*e.g.*, Geneste 1985; Boëda *et al.* 1990; Pigeot 1991; Bar-Yosef and Meignen 1992; Van Peer 1992, 1998; Boëda 1995; Kuhn 1995; Meignen 1995; Sellet 1995; Schlanger 1996; Kerry and Henry 2000).

For most Middle Paleolithic Levantine cases, the reduction sequence was reconstructed from the study of the blanks (*e.g.*, Meignen 1995; Goren-Inbar and Belfer-Cohen 1998), but in Western Europe there are growing numbers of refitted cores from Mousterian assemblages (*e.g.*, Locht 2002). The by now famous Levantine example of Boker Tachtit level 1 (Volkman 1983; Marks 1993) is unfortunately an industry of the Initial Upper Paleolithic and not truly Mousterian. Farah II (Gilead 1988) provides too small a sample from which to draw conclusions, though the case studies from Umm el-Tlel furnish additional information (Boëda *et al.* 2001). We are therefore left with the option of studying the operational sequences by reading the superposition of flake negatives on blanks, then classifying them into a rudimentary type-list of cortical elements, core rejuvenation pieces, flakes, blades, *etc.*, at the same time identifying the blanks chosen for further modification. A question rarely asked is how we might determine the dominant and less dominant methods of detachment employed by Middle Paleolithic knappers. Quantification is rarely used (but see for example Hovers 1998, 2001). Do we need to include in our calculations all the classified elements or only those that could fall into a usable size category (with or without retouch)?

Previously (*e.g.*, Bar-Yosef 1998a) I have suggested that we should ignore the discarded cores and examine only the first one-third or one-half of the blanks removed following the core's decortication. Often these are the pieces that were usable blanks. Although I did not provide quantitative data it seemed to me that researchers commonly attribute considerable importance to the study of the discarded cores without assessing the possible effects of equifinality. The scar pattern of an exhausted core, when compared with the primary post-decortication blanks, reflect changes in the sequence of the knapper's actions. For example, it may happen that a "unidirectional recurrent Levallois core" was modified into a "centripetal" one in its final stage of exploitation (*e.g.*, Meignen and Bar-Yosef 1991; Hovers 1998). Indeed, in the course of studying and describing most Middle Paleolithic lithic assemblages we should ask ourselves who was responsible for the core exploitation at the final phase, especially those in which the scars of the discarded cores reflect a change in the reduction strategy. It is not an easy question to answer. One possible explanation is that a change in the reduction sequence during the final exploitation of a given core had a different purpose than obtaining the first and often largest blanks for uses such as butchering or whittling. It could be that the shift was implemented by the same knapper in the course of practice sessions while teaching younger members of the group, or that the final removals were done by small children imitating without supervision of adult artisans.

One problem with drawing conceptual conclusions from discarded cores is that it is impossible for us to know whether the change in the organization of the removals was implemented by the original knapper, though perhaps the personal continuity in the detachment of blanks is of no importance. Each Middle Paleolithic reduction system possesses an intrinsic variability, and therefore, unless a series of cores from a closed context are refitted, identifying a particular individual is impossible. The same issue was addressed in the study of the Magdalenian lithics by the late Sylvie Ploux (1991). Similarly, the excavation of a limited area, portraying a single occupation horizon, in a Mousterian site in the Nile Valley (as yet unpublished), yielded cores that were almost fully refitted, thus indicating the presence of a single knapper (Van Peer, personal communication).

In sum, I suggest that we should hesitate to accept without further scrutiny the classification of discarded Middle Paleolithic cores and by extension the inferences about their quantitative role in defining the dominant operational sequences. In a more restricted sense, the final forms of the cores should be regarded as the result of equifinality, unless they conform to the original design of the primary blank reduction after decortication (Hovers 1997, 1998).

STABILITY AND RETENTION OF THE LEARNING PROCESSES

We should now turn to examine the issue of *chaîne opératoire* during the Middle Paleolithic in a diachronic context. In conducting this investigation two questions need to be addressed:

1. How should we interpret essentially the same, or several, *chaînes opératoires* being employed for extended periods, as long as 40,000 to 50,000 years or more (*e.g.*, Bar-Yosef 2000)?
2. Why, if one or two *chaînes opératoires* are optimal under certain circumstances, do we suddenly witness a change and the adoption of a different method or methods?

Each of these questions can be exemplified by several Middle Paleolithic cases. The documented high frequencies of particular operational sequences among Levantine Middle Paleolithic assemblages served as the basis for clustering assemblages into industrial groups (*e.g.*, Meignen and Bar-Yosef 1991; Bar-Yosef 1992; Meignen 1995). As stressed elsewhere (Bar-Yosef 1998a, 1998b, 2000) there is definitely a degree of technological variability among Mousterian assemblages such as those clustered, regardless of their local environment, under the term "Tabun B-type" (Tabun B, Geula, Kebara, Amud, and Tor Faraj). An instance of a minor variability is documented in Kebara Cave. The frequencies of blades increase and the triangular Levallois points decrease in units VIII–VII compared to the earlier

Units X–IX (Meignen and Bar-Yosef 1991; Meignen 1998a). However, through the entire sequence the "convergent recurrent Levallois method" remains the dominant method for obtaining blanks. Similar cases for intrinsic variability are reported in other sites, for example in Tor Faraj and Amud (Henry 1995, 1998, 2004; Hovers 1998).

Understanding the sources of the recorded variability within assemblages produced mainly by a single operational sequence has two faces. On one hand the sources of the observed variability are not easily explained. Possibly "God is in the details"—but what do the details mean, exactly, in the context of technology? We do not have the terms of reference needed to provide a paleoanthropological interpretation for this variability even when it is quantified by frequencies. For example, what does it mean that blade percentages increase from 15% to 25%? Is it possible that during the earlier time blades were taken away while later they were mostly used in place, and thus their frequency in the cave increased but production remained the same?

On the other hand, without refitting numerous cores (an effort hard to accomplish in the rich Late Mousterian cave sites in the Levant), the boundaries between the "recurrent convergent," "bidirectional," and "centripetal" sequences could be blurred. These operational sequences, which designate either the "Tabun C-type" (*e.g.*, Qafzeh; Hovers 1997) or the "Tabun B-type" (*e.g.*, Kebara, Amud, *etc.*), are quite distinctive when compared to the "Tabun D-type" core reduction. However, when the latter industry, dominated by elongated products many of which are true blades, was produced through the Levallois concept, it bears of course resemblance to the "recurrent convergent" type. Due to this superficial similarity some assemblages of "Tabun B-type" in the Negev or southern Jordan, for example Tor Faraj, were considered as "Tabun D-type". This in turn led to claims for temporal continuity between the two types of assemblages in the semiarid belt (*e.g.*, Marks 1990, 1992; Henry 1995).

Some of the ambiguities in defining the dominant operational sequences emerge from the common claim among researchers of Middle Paleolithic assemblages that the prehistoric knappers had comprehensive knowledge (*savoir-faire*) of all of the available methods and techniques. According to this view, knappers made choices during their lifetime or as they responded to changing practical needs in diverse environments. To me the assumption that Middle Paleolithic artisans mastered the entire array of Levallois methods remains unproven. The same would be true for the knowledge of all non-Levallois techniques or for a wider knowledge incorporating both non-Levallois and Levallois methods. Under such circumstances the most parsimonious explanation is that the variability within isolated and stratified assemblages was the expression of the individual abilities and capacities in a given, rather rigid system of learning and teaching (Hovers 1997).

As mentioned above, the specific "life histories" of refitted cores can hardly be understood in caves or open-air sites where there are no identifiable living floors. Instead we can identify the trends in reconstructed *chaînes opératoires*, as well as calculate the number of items per time of sediment accumulation. Investigating the densities of the occupation requires us to identify the agencies of site formation processes and make sure we are not comparing oranges and apples when comparing sites. An example used in previous papers compares the difference between 3,000 to 15/10,000 years per m³ of deposit in the cases of Kebara and Hayonim caves (Bar-Yosef 1998a, 2000). In the case of Kebara the number of pieces larger than 2 cm per m³ was about 1000–1200. Hayonim provided about 270–300 lithic specimen per m³. Kebara cave had a very meager accumulation of rodents, often resulting from the deterioration of barn owl pellets. Hayonim cave was extremely rich in this category of material. Hence, not only did the TL and ESR dates document rapid *versus* slow rates of accumulation, but the activities of the barn owl also provided clues about different intensities of human habitation in the two caves. As the Middle Paleolithic deposits in each cave site are at least 4m thick, it follows that the dominant knapping methods lasted for at least 15,000 years in Kebara and 50,000 years at Hayonim cave.

Hence, it appears that the right question to ask is what kind of learning or teaching processes imposed the rigid retention of operational sequences, each with minor technical variability over such long time spans. If we assume that prehistoric societies tend to be more conservative than historical ones, then the once successful or imposed technical knowledge had to be taught again and again as the only socially accepted way of making stone tools. As these artifacts were instrumental for the physical survival of the group, keeping the tradition was imperative. It seems that in guarding a traditional way of life the Middle Paleolithic period provides many instances of long time spans during which the same tool types were used and are thus different from the records for the Upper Paleolithic. This rigidity in the pattern of knapping behavior is altogether amazing, especially today when most scholars accept that Middle Paleolithic hominids used spoken language. I dare say that the geographic distribution of lithic variability seen across Africa and Eurasia probably reflects the presence of different languages. This contention leads us to discuss the issues involved in the possible identification of "paleo-cultures" (Jelinek 1977).

TERRITORIALITY DURING THE MIDDLE PALEOLOITHIC

By identifying the common lithic operational sequences through time and space in various assemblages, together with the particular tool types such as Aterian points, Stillbay points, bifaces of Mousterian of Acheulean Tradition, bifacial points or foliates of the eastern Micoquian, and the like, we can cluster assemblages and sites into entities or "paleo-cultures" across Eurasia and Africa. It would seem then that the old "*fossile directeur*" approach, which for a long time has been out of archaeological favor, comes into vogue again. While several of the cultural labels remain the same as in the first half of the 20th century, today they can be used in reference to both the predominant *chaîne opératoire* (when studied) and the distinctive tool types.

The spatial definition of each "paleo-culture" can be based on a series of published dated assemblages assuming the full information is provided. Temporary boundaries between entities are delineated when the chronological and geographic information is available. Not surprisingly we note that certain "paleocultures" overlap in space. This phenomenon is not different from the results of historical dispersals, diffusions, and acculturations whether expressed only in material elements, languages, gradual population expansion or migration. History demonstrates that all these various phenomena may occur in variable combinations.

More than ten years ago I advocated, following earlier studies, the use of maps of Middle Paleolithic social geography (Bar-Yosef 1990), but failed to produce the maps. Others, such as the late Desmond Clark (1992: figure 1) were able to render a cartographic representation of the distributions of different lithic types in the African MSA, employing elements that served as "*fossiles directeurs*" in the lack of information concerning core reduction strategies. A far-ranging review was carried out by Foley and Lahr (1997), who mapped the so-called "Mode 3" occurrences (*i.e.*, Middle Paleolithic; see above) with the intention to tie the archaeological information with human fossils. Indeed, with the advancement in dating techniques and proliferation of published lithic studies, it is now possible to produce a map of Middle Paleolithic social geography by employing the geographic distribution of the sites in order to identify boundaries. Figure 1 in this paper is the result of such an attempt, illustrating as it does the spread of Late Mousterian entities. As the following examples demonstrate, clear boundaries emerge.

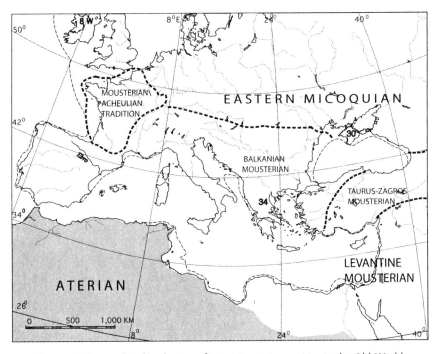

Figure 1. Geographic distribution of Late Mousterian entities in the Old World.

While Aterian tanged and bifacial points could have been attractive to other hunters, we see no evidence for their imitation either in the Nile Valley or farther east in the Levant or the Arabian peninsula. The distribution of the Aterian assemblages is limited to a vast region west of the Nile Valley. We may propose that if bearers of the Aterian culture met their contemporaries, it was only infrequently. Or such encounters may have been similar to those of Holocene contacts between New Guinean bow users and Australians who hunted with spear-throwers and boomerangs. In the latter case, no introduction of the New Guinean bow and arrow into the Australian continent was noted.

In a similar way one may interpret the boundary within the Middle Paleolithic world in the Caucasus region. On the northern slopes of the mountains and into the Russian plains the Eastern Micoquian (Mousterian) sites dominate as an extension from northern and eastern Europe. This Mousterian Micoquian is characterized by bifacial points that occur together with numerous side scrapers, as is the case at Mezmaskaya and other neighboring sites (Golovanova and Doronichev 2003). On the southern slopes of the Caucasus the late Mousterian is characterized only by sidescrapers and retouched flake points as in Ortvale Klde or Bronze cave (Adler 2003). This is the current distribution of types through the entire region south of the Caucasus including the rest of Georgia, Armenia, and Azarbeijan as reported by V. Lubin, D. Toushabramashvili, and Golovanova and Doronichev (2003), as well as in the Crimea (Marks and Chabai this volume).

A third example for a Middle Paleolithic boundary would be during the time of the late Levantine Mousterian. The typical "Tabun B type" industry stretches from Southern Jordan (Henry 1995, 2004) through the hilly flanks of the Taurus in southeast Turkey, but is not present in the Zagros ranges (e.g., papers in Olszewski and Dibble 1993), or farther in the western Taurus as shown by the excavations at Karain cave (Yalçinkaya et al. 1993).

A fourth example indicates that some cultural boundaries could be traced already in the Middle Pleistocene. This contention is based on the limited territorial distribution of the Acheulo-Yabrudian in the Levant. Artifacts such as the thick Quina-type scrapers of this industry are easily recognized in the field; yet they were never found during the extensive surveys in the Negev in southern Israel. On the other hand, the Acheulo-Yabrudian is well known from the area between El-Kowm in Syrian and the Yarkon River in the central coastal plain of Israel. If the Yarkon River was the real physical boundary between two populations of foragers, one may suggest that some of the Late Acheulean assemblages from the southern coastal plain, the Negev and inland basins in Jordan were broadly contemporary with the Acheulo-Yabrudian (Copeland 1991, 1998; Bar-Yosef 1998b).

All these examples are based on a general analogy with the territorial behavior of foragers as recorded, for example, in Australia and North America (Birdsell 1971). Similar archaeological examples among farming communities in southwestern Asia can be cited (e.g., Bar-Yosef 2000: figure 5).

In the context of this issue it is tempting to briefly mention southwest France, a region that provides a different geographic distribution than western Asia. More than one Middle Paleolithic entity was present in southwest France during the Last

Glacial period, and each is represented by numerous sites. The best known among the late Mousterian "paleo-cultures" are the Mousterian of Acheulean Tradition and Quina-type Mousterian (Mellars 1996 and references therein; see Delagnes and Meignen this volume). Such a general contemporaneity reflects the ecological richness of a region where the Atlantic climate was favorable to the survival of animals and humans. Reconstructions of the climatic conditions during Oxygen Isotope Stage (OIS) 3 demonstrate a series of fluctuations on a magnitude of one millennium and a half between colder and warmer phases, with increasingly colder conditions towards OIS 2 (Van Andel 2002, 2003). Under such deteriorating climatic conditions in the northern latitudes of Europe, this region became an attraction for those living on the edge. The flow of migrants into this vast region, maintaining their own traditions of making stone tools, resulted in the observed variability among both operational sequences and the shaping of the retouched forms (e.g., Mellars 1996; Rigaud 2000).

Several scholars would like to see the increase in colder conditions as the main reason for the extinction of the Neandertals (d'Errico and Sánchez Goñi 2003). And while the increasing environmental hazards of colder climates drive populations to extinctions (Gamble et al. 2004) we should note that the Cro-Magnon groups moving into Europe from the east possibly generated an additional pressure on the local Neandertal groups (Bocquet-Appel and Demars 2000a, 2000b). The arrival and colonization by the Cro-Magnons probably had the same aspects of adaptations to the new landscapes as noted in North America (Meltzer 1989, 2002). However, identifying the lithic industries with the invading or local "people" is not easy in the case of the late Middle and earliest Upper Paleoltihic, and one of the best cases of several contradictory opinions is concerning "who produced" the Châtelperronian. For over a century there has been a consensus that this industry marks the onset of the Upper Paleolithic period. Since the discovery of Neandertal remains in St. Cesaire almost 25 years ago it became a common notion that the last Neandertals in the region authored the Châtelperronian. The presence of assemblages rich in blades and Upper Paleolithic tool forms such as the Bachokirian and Bohunician, dated to the same general time span, casts doubts on the equation of the Châtelperronian as the product of Neandertals. Without getting into a detailed description of these various lithic industries and others, there are today several entities that represent Initial Upper Paleolithic (e.g., Kozlowski 2000), and for the writer of these pages, the archaeological expressions of modern humans moving into Europe. In addition, an observation made by Rigaud (1998) is illuminative in the context of the ambiguities related to the Châtelperronian. He stressed the fact that Châtelperronian assemblages are rich in Mousterian elements only when they overlie Mousterian layers. Once we take into account the taphonomy of the lithic objects, recognizing the products of the modern humans as they migrate into Europe becomes an easier task.

In sum, identifying past territories by means of archaeological observations is an achievable goal. It brings us closer to the reality of human groups as biological viable entities, their means of identifying themselves, their values of traditional knapping techniques, and it begs a discussion of past demographies.

MIDDLE PALEOLITHIC POPULATIONS

Both the establishment of territories and the presumed dispersals during the late Middle Paleolithic and early Upper Paleolithic raise the issue of population size, gene flow, or drift, which requires us to estimate hunter-gatherer population densities in different ecological zones. Despite the theoretical hazards involved in employing particular numbers as a basis for calculating ancient population sizes, archaeologists and geneticists (*e.g.*, Hassan 1981; Relethford 2001) find it critical for their work. Hence, numbers are derived from the available literature on foragers. The suggested density ratios range from 0.20 to 0.0073 person per square kilometer (see Binford 2001). In a genetics-oriented study Relethford (2001:168–177) employs the value of 0.03 persons per square kilometer as an approximation of Middle Paleolithic population densities and for evaluating the potential of extinction and recolonization simulations. Briefly, the main components of Relethford's simulation are an effective population size (defined as 250 to 400 people), the ratio of breeding population size to census size, and the size of the global territories inhabited by foragers some 200,000 years ago. The simulation shows the operation of processes of extinction and recolonization, which in general support a replacement model. Harsh climatic conditions during the last two cycles of glaciation possibly imply very low population densities of Neandertals as well as some archaic modern humans in marginal regions such as northern Europe, northern Asia, and various deserts.

An alternative model, which assumes constant gene flow, would obviously support the multiregional model. In this case we should expect constant migration between groups and across populations and therefore should notice the results of exchange and acculturation. For example, the transmission of knapping techniques such as the Levallois methods could have been the most fundamental result of intergroup contacts. Another option would be the adoption of particular tool forms. That such expectations are not borne out is clearly indicated by published reports from the different African and Eurasian regions. Certain commonalties observed in core reduction strategies due to equifinality and limitations imposed by raw material may obliterate the overall picture. Still, it is my contention (as explained above) that we definitely can identify different "paleo-cultures" across the Middle Paleolithic world. The disappearance of several "paleo-cultures" may correspond to lineage extinctions and the abandonment of particular areas, common phenomena during the long Middle Paleolithic time span (*e.g.*, Gamble *et al.* 2004; see Hovers and Belfer-Cohen this volume).

In sum, once territories are defined we may simulate population size, perhaps in more precise ways than was possible until recently. Efforts in this direction are already published and obviously they are easier concerning Upper Paleolithic "paleo-cultures" (Bocquet-Appel and Demars 2000a, 2000b).

That these models may apply also to western Asia is justified by the commonplace notion that both Neandertal and modern human populations were present in the region. However, the morphometric definitions of the available fossils and the distribution of their cranial and post-cranial traits have also a different interpretation (Arensburg and Belfer-Cohen 1998). This controversy, however, does not seriously undermine the general agreement that the Late Mousterian population in the Levant could have marked a migration into a region already occupied by others (Bar-Yosef 1988; Shea 2003 this volume). The fact that both the locals (Skhul-Qafzeh group) and the invaders were using similar Levallois methods, and often similar retouched pieces, made it clear to many that there is no correlation between human morphotypes and the lithic industries (*e.g.*, Hovers 1997). This becomes even clearer when similar technical knowledge and final products were shared and made by archaic modern humans across North Africa, beyond the world of the Neandertals (Trinkaus and Howells 1979; McBrearty and Brooks 2000; White *et al.* 2003).

FROM MIDDLE TO UPPER PALEOLITHIC: THE QUESTION OF CULTURAL TRANSITIONS

In discussing populations and territory I have already expressed the view that the cultural transition from the Middle to the Upper Paleolithic across Europe was the result of several human migration and colonization events. With Africa being the cradle of modern humans according to various genetic studies, the Levantine Corridor is the natural place to look for the evidence of past movements. The possibility that the origin of modern humans could have been in the Levant is not discussed here as a biological issue, although it was once suggested (Stringer 1989). What I would like to illustrate is the intricate relationship between biology and material remains.

The basic assumption is that the operational sequence is a learned behavior and therefore reflects biological continuity. Several lithic analyses suggest that the Early Upper Paleolithic assemblages in the Levant display a continuity from the late Mousterian (Garrod 1955, 1962; Copeland 1975; Marks 1983; Meignen and Bar-Yosef 2002). The primary arguments for this conclusion are related to the change in core reduction strategies. Assemblages of Initial Upper Paleolithic age (*e.g.*, Boker Tachtit level 1, Ksar 'Akil layers XXV–XXI) contain often, but not always, a blade industry and Levallois points with a "Y" scar pattern (Marks 1983, 1993; Volkman 1983). Core refitting demonstrated that this combination resulted from bidirectional detachments, with facetted platforms. Some researchers see this kind of shift as directly emerging from the convergent Levallois method, the dominant method in most late Mousterian assemblages, and interpret the morphological and core reduction attributes associated with this Initial Upper Paleolithic operational sequence as reflecting "cultural" continuity.

Two questions are raised by this scenario:

1. If most biological anthropologists agree that the Late Mousterian industries in the Levant were produced by local Neandertals, how should we interpret the change in the operational sequence, which is briefly described above?

2. Did the Levantine transition from a Levallois method to a new core reduction strategy, which preserved some of the earlier Levalloisian characteristics, occur through diffusion and migration into the Levant following its invention elsewhere?

The answers, as expected, are diverse and incite further research and discussions, while operational sequences of the Initial Upper Paleolithic remain under investigation. The view that lithic continuity is an expression of a learned technical tradition of stone tool manufacturing may reflect, due to the way such knowledge is being passed from one generation to the next, a biological continuity. This would imply that late Levantine Neandertals were responsible for the observable changes of the Initial Upper Paleolithic. Alternatively, Late Mousterian fossils in the region may not have been of Neandertal descent (Arensburg and Belfer-Cohen 1998) but should be viewed as the direct descendents of the Skhul-Qafzeh group, which would imply that modern humans were responsible for the Initial Upper Paleolithic industries.

Another option is that what we call the "Emiran" or "Transitional Industry" was invented elsewhere, perhaps in the Nile Valley or East Africa, possessing a typical Levallois background, and arrived in the Levant with the migrating modern humans. In such a case, the stratigraphic superposition of an indigenous Levallois-dominated Late Mousterian and a foreign Initial Upper Paleolithic assemblage would create the impression that it had emerged locally. Long-distance migrations—as predicted by all published models—would also explain the similarity between the Bohunician in central Europe (where a Levalloiso-Mousterian is entirely absent) and the Levantine Initial Upper Paleolithic (Tostevin 2000; Skrdla 2003). It should be emphasized that in this scenario there are no claims for biological continuity between the earlier Skhul-Qafzeh group and the early Upper Paleolithic.

CONCLUSIONS

Brevity in my closing statement seems justified and I may forego elaborate conclusions in this paper, as the entire text is a "discussion." Perhaps more than reacting to the presentations in the original session and to papers in this volume, I have at times lingered on those questions that trouble me most in an attempt to apply my experience and intuitive interpretations to the most pressing issues pertaining to the archaeology of the Middle Paleolithic period.

I feel that the issue of the differential use of the commonly employed terminology should be resolved by making a detailed glossary available to all students of prehistory. Once in a while it is worthwhile to meet each other and ask "what do you really mean by using this or that term?"

Following the establishment of a chronological framework, we will continue to struggle to reach a resolution in recognizing past populations, their cultural remains, territories, and histories. We generally hope that ancient DNA studies would bring us closer to the living people of the past. We know that the rare samples published to date of mitochondrial DNA fragments extracted from a few European Neandertals (Tchentscher *et al.* 2000), while different from modern, Upper Paleolithic, fossils (Caramelli *et al.* 2003), cannot as yet provide a clear picture. However, the morphometric differences between the two populations had nothing to do with the capacities of the Neandertals for modern behavior as defined by archaeologists (*e.g.*, Zilhão and d'Errico 1999; Wadley 2001; Hovers and Belfer-Cohen this volume).

At the same time, the lack of human skeletal remains in early Aurignacian deposits is disturbing. As is the case in almost all Upper Paleolithic contexts in the Levant, we are not sure whether there was a biological replacement across most of Europe and southwest Asia, which would be interpreted as portraying strong competition between two populations, although the evidence of absence of cultural continuities supports this model. However, we are looking for additional Middle and Upper Paleolithic burials where skeletal remains are well preserved. While a few Neandertal skeletal remains have produced ancient DNA, the lack of early Upper Paleolithic human relics is disturbing.

One potential explanation for the apparent rarity of Upper Paleolithic burials stems perhaps from a behavioral change. Unlike Neandertals in Eurasia who often buried the dead in their sites, it is possible that during the Upper Paleolithic human corpses were more often interred outside the living areas or in specific locations. Perhaps this explains the circumstances of burials such as the triple one in Dolni Vestonice (Moravia) or the (much later) Ohalo II burial (Israel). The karstic cave of Mladec was a special site (Svoboda 2000), yet we have only rare Upper Paleolithic graves within the occupied areas of sites such as in Sungir (Russia), or Nahal Ein Gev I (Israel).

The issue of mortuary practices is one of several cultural attributes that were instrumental in forming the observed archaeological differences between the Upper and Middle Paleolithic. It appears to me that mortuary practices of Upper Paleolithic groups require additional research and perhaps even changes in the excavation strategies by incorporating the "outside" area of the main habitations. Only then we can support or disprove arguments concerning cultural continuity of burial customs.

Along with this "wish list" I should mention that elsewhere (Bar-Yosef 1992, 1998a, 2000, 2002) I followed previously published ideas and interpretations and explained why and how I see the archaeological evidence as suggesting that the Upper Paleolithic revolution is visible archaeologically over most of Eurasia. I see this revolution as both a technological and social one, leading to economic and organizational changes, similar in nature to those that occurred at a much later time during the Neolithic Revolution. However, Eurasia is not the only mega-continent. Given that, the interpretation of the Middle-Later Stone Age transition in sub-Saharan Africa (McBrearty and Brooks 2000) poses a very intriguing question within the context of global cultural evolution, one that will require further discussion in the future.

ACKNOWLEDGEMENTS

I am grateful to Wren Fournier for copy editing this paper, and to my colleagues Anna Belfer-Cohen, Erella Hovers, Steve L. Kuhn and Liliane Meignen for the lively discussions and numerous useful comments on an earlier version of this manuscript. Needless to say I am the sole party responsible for the expressed views.

REFERENCES CITED

Adler D.S. 2003. *Late Middle Paleolithic Patterns of Lithic Reduction, Mobility and Land Use in the Southern Caucasus*. Ph.D. Dissertation, Harvard University

Arensburg B. and A. Belfer-Cohen 1998. Sapiens and Neandertals: rethinking the Levantine Middle Paleolithic hominids. In T. Akazawa, K. Aoki and O. Bar-Yosef (Eds.), *Neandertals and Modern Humans in Western Asia*, pp. 323–332. New York: Plenum Press.

Barkai R., A. Gopher, S.E. Lauritzen and A. Frumkin 2003. The end of the Lower Paleolithic in the Levant: U-series dates from Qesem cave, Israel. *Nature* 423: 977–979.

Bar-Yosef O. 1988. The date of Southwest Asian Neanderthals. In E. Trinkaus (Ed.), *L'Homme de Néandertal: l'Anatomie* (ERAUL 30), pp. 31–38. Liège: Université de Liège.

Bar-Yosef O. 1990–1991. Mousterian adaptations- a global view. *Quaternaria Nova* 1: 575–591.

Bar-Yosef O. 1992. The role of Western Asia in modern human origins. *Philosophical Transactions of the Royal Society of London B* 337:193–200.

Bar-Yosef O. 1998a. The chronology of the Middle Paleolithic of the Levant. In T. Akazawa, K. Aoki and O. Bar-Yosef (Eds.), *Neandertals and Modern Humans in Western Asia*, pp. 39–56. New York: Plenum Press.

Bar-Yosef O. 1998b. Jordan prehistory: a view from the west. In D.O. Henry (Ed.), *The Prehistoric Archaeology of Jordan* (BAR International Series 705), pp. 162–178. Oxford: Archaeopress.

Bar-Yosef O. 2000. The Middle and Early Upper Paleolithic in Southwest Asia and neighboring Regions. In O. Bar-Yosef and D. Pilbeam (Eds.), *The Geography of Neandertals and Modern Humans in Europe and the Greater Mediterranean,* pp. 107–156. Cambridge MA: Peabody Museum, Harvard University.

Bar-Yosef O. 2002. The Upper Paleolithic revolution. *Annual Review of Anthropology* 31: 363–393.

Bar-Yosef O. and L. Meignen 1992. Insights into Levantine Middle Paleolithic cultural variability. In H.L. Dibble and P. Mellars (Eds.), *The Middle Paleolithic: Adaptation, Behavior, and Variability* (University Museum Monographs 78), pp. 163–182. Philadelphia: University of Pennsylvania, The University Museum.

Binford L.R. 2001. *Constructing Frames of Reference*. Berkeley: University of California Press.

Birdsell J.B. 1971. Ecology, spacing mechanisms and adaptive behaviour in aboriginal land tenure. In R. Crocombe (Ed.), *Land Tenure in the Pacific*, pp. 334–36. Melbourne: Oxford University Press.

Boëda E. 1995. Levallois: a volumetric construction, methods, a technique. In H.L. Dibble and O. Bar-Yosef (Eds.), *The Definition and Interpretation of Levallois Technology* (Monographs in World Archaeology 23), pp. 41–68. Madison: Prehistory Press.

Boëda E., J.-M. Geneste and L. Meignen 1990. Identification de chaînes opératoires lithiques du Paléolithique ancien et moyen. *Paléo* 2: 43–80.

Boëda E., C. Griggo and S. Noel-Soriano 2001. Differents modes d'occupation du site d'Umm el Tlel au cours du Paléolithique moyen (El Kowm, Syrie centrale). *Paléorient* 27: 13–28.

Bocquet-Appel J.-P. and P.-Y. Demars 2000a. Neanderthal contraction and modern human colonization of Europe. *Antiquity* 74: 544–552.

Bocquet-Appel J.-P. and P.-Y. Demars 2000b. Population kinetics in the Upper Palaeolithic in Western Europe. *Journal of Archaeological Science* 27: 551–570.

Caramelli D., C. Lalueza-Fox, C. Vernesi, M. Lari, A. Casoli, F. Mallegni, B. Chiarelli, I. Dupanloup, J. Bertanpetit, G. Barbujani and G. Bertorelle 2003. Evidence for a genetic discontinuity between Neandertals and 24,000-year-old anatomically modern Europeans. *Proceedings of the National Academy of Science USA* 100: 6593–6597.

Carbonell E., M. Mosquera, X. Pedro Rodríguez, R. Sala and J. van der Made 1999. Out of Africa: the dispersal of the earliest technical systems reconsidered. *Journal of Anthropological Archaeology* 18: 119–136.

Clark G. 1970. *Aspects of Prehistory*. Berkeley: University of California Press.

Clark G.A., J. Schuldenrein, M.L. Donaldson, H.P. Schwarcz, W.J. Rink and S.K. Fish 1997. Chronostratigraphic contexts of Middle Paleolithic horizons at the 'Ain Difla rockshelter (WHS 634), West-Central Jordan. In H.-G. Gebel, Z. Kafafi and G.O. Rollefson (Eds.), *The Prehistory of Jordan, II. Perspectives from 1997* (Studies in Early Near Eastern Production, Subsistence and Environment 4), pp. 77–100. Berlin: Ex Oriente.

Clark J.D. 1988. The Middle Stone Age of East Africa and the beginnings of regional identity. *Journal of World Prehistory* 2(3): 235–306.

Clark J.D. 1992. Asian and African perspectives on the origins of modern humans. *Philosophical Transactions of the Royal Society of London; series B* 337(1280): 201–216.

Copeland L. 1975. The Middle and Upper Palaeolithic of Lebanon and Syria in the light of recent research. In F. Wendorf and A.E. Marks (Eds.), *Problems in Prehistory: North Africa and the Levant*, pp. 317–350. Dallas: SMU Press.

Copeland L. 1991. The Late Acheulean knapping-floor at C-Spring, Azraq Oasis, Jordan. *Levant* XXIII: 1–6.

Copeland L. 1998. The Lower Paleolithic of Jordan.In D.O. Henry (Ed.), *The Prehistoric Archaeology of Jordan* (BAR International Series 705), pp. 5–22. Oxford: Archaeopress.

Deacon H.J. and J. Deacon 1999. *Human Beginnings in South Africa: Uncovering the Secrets of the Stone Age*. Cape Town and Walnut Creek, CA: D. Phillips and Altamira Press,

d'Errico F. and M.F. Sánchez Goñi 2003. Neandertal extinction and the millennial scale climatic variability of OIS 3. *Quaternary Science Reviews* 22: 769–788.

Farrand W.R. 1979. Chronology and paleoenvironment of Levantine prehistoric sites as seen from sediment studies. *Journal of Archaeological Science* 6: 369–392.

Foley R. and M.M. Lahr 1997. Mode 3 technologies and the evolution of modern humans. *Cambridge Archaeological Journal* 7: 3–36.

Gamble C., W. Davies, P. Pettit, and M. Richards 2004. Climate change and evolving human diversity in Europe during the last glacial. *Philosophical Transactions of the Royal Society of London B* 359: 2243–2254.

Garrod D.A.E. 1955. The Mugharet el Emireh in Lower Galilee: type station of the Emiran Industry. *Journal of the Royal Anthropological Institute* 85: 141–162.

Garrod D. 1962. The Middle Palaeolithic of the Near East and the problem of Mount Carmel. *Journal of the Royal Anthropological Institute* 92: 232–259.

Geneste J.-M. 1985. *Analyse lithique d'industries moustériennes du Périgord: une approche technologique du comportement des groupes humaines au Paléolithique moyen*. Ph.D. Dissertation, Université Bordeaux I.

Gilead I. 1988. Le site moustérien de Fara II (Néguev septentrional, Israël) et le remontage de son industrie. *L'Anthropologie* 92: 797–808.

Golovanova L.V. and V.B. Doronichev 2003. The Middle Paleolithic of the Caucasus. *Journal of World Prehistory* 17: 71–140.

Goren-Inbar N. 1990. *Quneitra: a Mousterian Site on the Golan Heights* (Qedem 31). Jerusalem: Institute of Archaeology, Hebrew University.

Goren-Inbar N. and A. Belfer-Cohen 1998. The technological abilities of the Levantine Mousterians: cultural and mental capacities. In T. Akazawa, K. Aoki and O. Bar-Yosef (Eds.), *Neandertals and Modern Humans in Western Asia*, pp. 205–221. New York: Plenum Press.

Grün R. and C.B. Stringer 1991. Electron spin resonance dating and the evolution of modern humans. *Archaeometry* 33: 153–199.

Grün R., H.P. Schwarcz and C.B. Stringer 1991. ESR dating of teeth from Garrod's Tabun cave collection. *Journal of Human Evolution* 20: 231–248.

Hassan F.A. 1981. *Demographic Archaeology*. New York: Academic Press.

Henry D.O. 1995. *Prehistoric Cultural Ecology and Evolution*. New York: Plenum Press.

Henry D.O. 1998. The Middle Paleolithic of Jordan. In D.O. Henry (Ed.), *The Prehistoric Archaeology of Jordan* (BAR International Series 705), pp. 23–38. Oxford: Archaeopress.

Henry D.O. 2004. *Neanderthals in the Levant: Behavioral Organization and the Beginnings of Human Modernity* (New Approaches to Anthropological Archaeology 1). Continuum International Publishing Group.

Hovers E. 1997. *Variability of Lithic Assemblages and Settlement Patterns in the Levantine Middle Paleolithic: Implications for the Development of Human Behavior.* Ph.D. Dissertation, The Hebrew University.

Hovers E. 1998. The lithic assemblages of Amud Cave: implications for understanding the end of the Mousterian in the Levant. In T. Akazawa, K. Aoki and O. Bar-Yosef (Eds.), *Neandertals and Modern Humans in Western Asia*, pp. 143–163. New York: Plenum Press.

Hovers E. 2001. Territorial behavior in the Middle Paleolithic of the Southern Levant. In N. Conard (Ed.), *Settlement Dynamics of the Middle Paleolithic and Middle Stone Age*, pp. 123–152. Tübingen: Kerns Verlag.

Jelinek A.J. 1977. The Lower Paleolithic: current evidence and interpretations. *Annual Review of Anthropology* 6: 11–32.

Kerry K.W. and D.O. Henry 2000. Conceptual domains, competence, and *Chaîne Opèratoire* in the Levantine Mousterian. In L.E. Stager, J.A. Greene and M.D. Coogan (Eds.), *The Archaeology of Jordan and Beyond: Essays in Honor of James A. Sauer*, pp. 238–254. Winona Lake: Eisenbrauns.

Kozlowski J. K. 2000. The problem of cultural continuity between the Middle and the Upper Paleolithic in Central and Eastern Europe. In O. Bar-Yosef and D. Pilbeam (Eds.), *The Geography of Neandertals and Modern Humans in Europe and the Greater Mediterranean*, pp. 77–105. Cambridge, MA: Peabody Museum, Harvard University.

Kuhn S.L. 1995. *Mousterian Lithic Technology: an Ecological Perspective*. Princeton: Princeton University Press.

Locht J.L. 2002. *Bettencourt-Saint-Ouen (Somme): cinque occupations paléolithiques au début de la dernièr glaciation* (Documents d'Archéologie Française 90). Paris: Éditions de la Maison des science de l'Homme.

Marks A. 1983. The Middle to Upper Paleolithic transition in the Levant. In F. Wendorf and A.E. Close (Eds.), *Advances in World Archaeology*, vol. 2., pp. 51–98. New York: Academic Press.

Marks A. E. 1990. The Middle and Upper Palaeolithic of the Near East and the Nile Valley: the problem of cultural transformations. In P. Mellars (Ed.), *The Emergence of Modern Humans*, pp. 56–80. Ithaca: Cornell University Press.

Marks A. E. 1992. Upper Pleistocene archaeology and the origins of modern man: a view from the Levant and adjacent areas. In T. Akazawa, K. Aoki and T. Kimura (Eds.), *The Evolution and Dispersal of Modern Humans in Asia*, pp. 229–252. Tokyo: Hokusen-Sha.

Marks A. E. 1993. The Early Upper Paleolithic: the view from the Levant. In H. Knecht, A. Pike-Tay and R. White (Eds.), *Before Lascaux: the Complete Record of the Early Upper Paleolithic*, pp. 5–22. Boca Raton: CRC Press.

Marks A. and K. Monigal 1995. Modeling the production of elongated blanks from the Early Levantine Mousterian at Rosh Ein Mor. In H.L. Dibble and O. Bar-Yosef (Eds.), *The Definition and Interpretation of Levallois Technology* (Monographs in World Archaeology 23), pp. 267–278. Madison: Prehistory Press.

McBrearty S. and A.S. Brooks 2000. The revolution that wasn't: a new interpretation of the origin of modern human behavior. *Journal of Human Evolution* 39: 453–563.

McDermott F., R. Grün, C.B. Stringer and C.J. Hawkesworth 1993. Mass spectrometric U-series dates for Israeli Neanderthal/early modern hominid sites. *Nature* 363: 252–255

Meignen L. 1995. Levallois lithic production systems in the Middle Paleolithic of the Near East: The case of the unidirectional method. In H.L. Dibble and O. Bar-Yosef (Eds.), *The Definition and Interpretation of Levallois Technology* (Monographs in World Archaeology 23), pp. 361–380. Madison: Prehistory Press,

Meignen L. 1998a. Le Paléolithique moyen au Levant sud et central: que nous apprennent les données récentes? In M. Otte (Ed.), *Préhistoire d'Anatolie: genèse de deux mondes* (ERAUL 85), pp. 685–708. Liège: Université de Liège.

Meignen L. 1998b. Hayonim Cave lithic assemblages in the context of the Near Eastern Middle Paleolithic: a preliminary report. In T. Akazawa, K. Aoki and O. Bar-Yosef (Eds.), *Neandertals and Modern Humans in Western Asia*, pp. 165–180. New York: Plenum Press.

Meignen L. and O. Bar-Yosef 1988. Variabilité technologique au Proche Orient: l'exemple de Kebara. In M. Otte (Ed.), *L'Homme de Néandertal: La Technique* (ERAUL 31), pp. 81–95. Liège: Université de Liège.

Meignen L. and O. Bar-Yosef 1991. Les outillages lithiques moustériens de Kebara. In O. Bar-Yosef and B. Vandermeersch (Eds.), *Le Squelette moustérien de Kebara 2, Mt. Carmel, Israël*, pp. 49–76. Paris: CNRS.

Meignen L. and O. Bar-Yosef 1992. Middle Paleolithic variability in Kebara Cave, Israel. In T. Akazawa, K. Aoki and T. Kimura (Eds.), *The Evolution and Dispersal of Modern Humans in Asia*, pp. 129–148. Tokyo: Hokusen-sha.

Meignen L. and O. Bar-Yosef 2002. The lithic industries of the Middle and Upper Paleolithic of the Levant: continuity or break? *Archaeology, Ethnology & Anthropology of Eurasia* 3: 12–21.

Meignen L., O. Bar-Yosef, N. Mercier, H. Valladas, P. Goldberg and B. Vandermeerch 2001. Apport des datations au problème de l'origin des hommes modernes au Proche-Orient. In J.-N. Barrandon, P. Guibert and V. Michel (Eds.), *Datation. XXI Reconctres Internationales d'Archéologie et d'Histoire d'Antibes*, pp. 295–313. Antibes: Editions APDCA.

Monigal K. 2002. *The Levanitine Leptolithic: Blade Production from the Lower Paleolithic to the Dawn of the Upper Paleolithic*. Ph.D. Dissertation, Southern Methodist University.

Mellars P. 1996. *The Neanderthal Legacy: An Archaeological Perspective from Western Europe*. Princeton: Princeton University Press.

Meltzer D.J. 1989. Why don't we know when the first people came to North America? *American Antiquity* 54: 471–490.

Meltzer D.J. 2002. What do you do when no one's been there before? thoughts on the exploration and colonization of new lands. *Memoirs of the California Academy of Sciences* 27: 27–58.

Mercier N. 1992. *Apport des méthods radionucléeaires de datation à l'étude de peupllement de l'Europe et du Proche-Orient au cours du Pléistocene moyen et supérieur*. Thése Doctorat, Universite of Bordeaux I

Mercier N., H. Valladas, G. Valladas, J.L. Reyss, A. Jelinek, L. Meignen and J.L. Joron 1995. TL dates of burnt flints from Jelinek's excavations at Tabun and their implications. *Journal of Archaeological Science* 22: 495–510.

Mercier N., H. Valladas, L. Froget, J.L. Joron and A. Ronen 2000. Datation par la thermoluminescence de la base du gisement paléolithique de Tabun (Mont Carmel, Israël). *Compte rendu de l'Academie des Sciences* 330: 731–738.

Minugh-Purvis N. 1993. Reexamination of the immature hominid maxilla from Tangier, Morocco. *American Journal of Physical Anthropology* 92: 449–461.

Olszewski D.I. and H.L. Dibble (Eds.) 1993. *The Paleolithic Prehistory of the Zagros-Taurus*. Philadelphia: University of Pennsylvania, University Museum.

Pigeot N. 1991. Reflexions sur l'histoire technique de l'homme: de l'évolution cognitive a l'évolution culturelle. *Paléo* 3:167–200.

Ploux S. 1991. Technologie, technicité, techniciens: méthode de détermination d'auteurs et comportements techniques individuels. In *25 Ans d'études technologiques en préhistoire. Bilan et perspectives. XI Rencontres Internationales d'Archéologie et d'Histoire d'Antibes*, pp. 201–214. Antibes: APDCA.

Porat N., L.P. Zhou, M. Chazan, T. Noy and L. Kolska Horwitz 1999. Dating the Lower Paleolithic open-air site of Holon, Israel by Luminescence and ESR techniques. *Quaternary Research* 51: 328–341.

Relethford J. 2001. *Genetics and the Search for Modern Human Origins*. New York: Wiley-Liss.

Rigaud J.-P. 1998. A propos de la contemporanéité du Castelperronien et de l'Aurignacien ancien dans le nord-est de l'Aquitaine: une révision des données et ses implications. In J. Zilhão, T. Aubry and A. F. Carvalho (Eds.), *Les prémiers hommes modernes de la péninsule Ibérique: actes du colloque de la commission VIII de l'UISPP*, pp. 61–68. Vila Nova De Foz Côa: Instituto Portugues de Arqueologia.

Rigaud J.-P. 2000. Late Neandertals in the South West of France and the emergence of the Upper Palaeolithic. In C.B. Stringer, R.N.E. Barton and J.C. Finlayson (Eds.), *Neanderthals on the Edge: Papers from a Conference Marking the 150thAnniversary of the Forbes' Quarry Discovery, Gibraltar*, pp. 27–31. Oxford: Oxbow Books.

Rink W.J. 2001. Beyond C14 dating: a user's guide to long-range dating methods in archaeology. In P. Goldberg, V.T. Holliday and C.R. Ferring (Eds.), *Earth Sciences and Archaeology*, pp. 385–417. New York: Kluwer Academic/Plenum.

Rink W.J., H.P. Schwarcz, H.K. Lee, J. Rees-Jones, R. Rabinovich and E. Hovers 2001. Electron spin resonance (ESR) and thermal ionization mass spectrometric (TIMS) Th230 /U234 dating of teeth in Middle Paleolithic layers at Amud Cave, Israel. *Geoarchaeology* 16: 701–717.

Rink W.J., D. Richter, H.P. Schwarcz, A.E. Marks, K. Monigal and D. Kaufman 2003. Age of the Middle Palaeolithic site of Rosh Ein Mor, Central Negev, Israel: implications for the age range of the Early Levantine Mousterian of the Levantine Corridor. *Journal of Archaeological Science* 30: 195–204.

Rink W.J., H.P. Schwarcz, A. Ronen, and A. Tsatskin 2004. Confirmation of near 400 ka age for the Yabrudian industry at Tabun cave, Israel. *Journal of Archaeological Science* 31: 15–20.

Sackett J.R. 1981. From de Mortillet to Bordes: a century of French Palaeolithic research. In G. Daniel (Ed.), *Towards a History of Archaeology*, pp. 85–99. London: Thames and Hudson.

Schlanger N. 1996. Understanding Levallois: lithic technology and cognitive archaeology. *Cambridge Archaeological Journal* 6: 231–254.

Shea J.J. 2003. The Middle Paleolithic of the East Mediterranean Levant. *Journal of World Prehistory* 17: 313–394.

Sellet F. 1995. Levallois or not Levallois: does it really matter? Learning from an African case. In H.L. Dibble and O. Bar-Yosef (Eds.), *The Definition and Interpretation of Levallois Technology* (Monographs in World Archaeology 23), pp. 25–40. Madison: Prehistory Press.

Skrdla P. 2003. Comparison of Boker Tachtit and Stránská Skála MP-UP transitional industries. *Journal of the Israel Prehistoric Society* 33: 37–73.

Stringer C.B. 1989. The origin of early modern humans: a comparison of the European and non-European evidence. In P. Mellars and C.B. Stringer (Eds.), *The Human Revolution: Behavioural and Biological Perspectives in the Origins of Modern Humans*, pp. 232–244. Edinburgh: Edinburgh University Press.

Svoboda J. 2000. The depositional context of the Early Upper Paleolithic human fossils from the Koneprusy (Zlaty kun) and Mladec Caves, Czech Republic. *Journal of Human Evolution* 38(3): 523–536

Tchentscher F., C. Capelli, H. Geisert, H. Krainitzki, R.W. Schmitz and M. Krings, M. (2000). Mitochondrial DNA sequences from the Neandertals. In J. Orschiedt (Ed.), *Neanderthals and Modern Humans—Discussing the Transition: Central and Eastern Europe*, pp. 303–314. Mettmann: Neanderthal Museum.

Tindale N.B. 1974. *Aboriginal Tribes of Australia: Their Terrain, Environmental Controls, Distribution, Limits and Proper Names*. Berkeley: University of California Press.

Tostevin G.B. 2000. *Behavioral Change and Regional Variation Across the Middle to Upper Paleolithic Transition in Central Europe, Eastern Europe, and the Levant*. Ph.D. Dissertation, Harvard University.

Trinkaus E. and W.W. Howells 1979. The Neanderthals. *Scientific American* 241: 118–133.

Valladas H., J.L. Joron, G. Valladas, B. Arensburg, O. Bar-Yosef, A. Belfer-Cohen, P. Goldberg, H. Laville, L. Meignen, Y. Rak, E. Tchernov, A.-M. Tillier and B. Vandermeersch 1987. Thermoluminescence dates for the Neanderthal burial site at Kebara in Israel. *Nature* 330: 159–160.

Valladas H., J.L. Reyss, J.L. Joron, G. Valladas, O. Bar-Yosef and B. Vandermeersch 1988. Thermoluminescence dating of Mousterian 'Proto-Cro-Magnon' remains from Israel and the origin of modern man. *Nature* 331: 614–615.

Valladas H., N. Mercier, E. Hovers, L. Froget, J.-L. Joron, W.H. Kimbel and Y. Rak 1999. TL dates for the Neanderthal Site of the Amud Cave, Israel. *Journal of Archaeological Science* 26: 259–268.

van Andel T.H. 2002. The climate and landscape of the middle part of the Weichselian glaciation in Europe: the Stage 3 Project. *Quaternary Research* 57: 2–8.

van Andel T.H. Ed. 2003. *Neanderthals and Modern Humans in the European Landscape During the Last Glaciation: Archaeological Results of the Stage 3 Project*. Cambridge: McDonald Institute for Archaeological Research.

Van Peer P. 1992. *The Levallois Reduction Strategy* (Monographs in World Archaeology 13). Madison: Prehistory Press.

Van Peer P. 1998. The Nile Corridor and the Out-of-Africa model: an examination of the archaeological record. *Current Anthropology* 39 (Supplement): S115–S140.

Volkman P. 1983. Boker Tachtit: core reconstructions. In A.E. Marks (Ed.), *Prehistory and Paleoenvironments in the Central Negev, Israel, vol. 3: The Avdat/Aqev Area (Part 3)*, pp. 127–190. Dallas: Southern Methodist University Press.

Wadley L. 2001. What is cultural modernity? A general view and a South African perspective from Rose Cottage Cave. *Cambridge Archaeological Journal* 11: 201–221.

Wagner G.A. 1998. *Age Determination of Young Rocks and Artifacts: Physical and Chemical Clocks in Quaternary Geology and Archaeology*. Translated by S. Schiegl. Natural Science in Archaeology. Berlin: Springer Verlag.

White T.D., B. Asfaw, D. DeGusta, H. Gilbert, G.D. Richards, G. Suwa and F.C. Howell 2003. Pleistocene *Homo sapiens* from Middle Awash, Ethiopia. *Nature* 423: 742–747.

Yalçinkaya I., M. Otte, O. Bar-Yosef, J. Kozlowski, J.M. Léotard and H. Taskiran 1993. The excavations at Karain Cave, south-western Turkey: an interim report. In D.I. Olszewski and H.L. Dibble (Eds.), *The Paleolithic Prehistory of the Zagros-Taurus*, pp. 100–106. Philadelphia: The University Museum of the University of Pennsylvania.

Zilhão J. 2001. *Anatomically Archaic, Behaviorally Modern: The Last Neanderthals and Their Destiny*. Drieëntwintigste Kroon-Voordracht. Amsterdam: Stichting Nederland Museum voor Anthropologie en Praehistorie.

Zilhão J. and F. d'Errico 1999. The chronology and taphonomy of the earliest Aurignacian and its implications for the understanding of Neanderthal extinction. *Journal of World Prehistory* 13: 1–68.

.

Index